INTERNATIONAL
ENCYCLOPEDIA
of
and
WOMEN
SPORTS

INTERNATIONAL ENCYCLOPEDIA

of

and

WOMEN

SPORTS

VOLUME I

Edited by

KAREN CHRISTENSEN

ALLEN GUTTMANN

GERTRUD PFISTER

Macmillan Reference USA

an imprint of the Gale Group

New York • Detroit • San Francisco • London • Boston • Woodbridge, CT

Macmillan Reference USA
1633 Broadway
New York, NY 10019

The Gale Group
27500 Drake Rd.
Farmington Hills, MI 48331

ISBN 0-02-864954-0 (set)
ISBN 0-02-864951-6 (vol. 1)
ISBN 0-02-864952-4 (vol. 2)
ISBN 0-02-864953-2 (vol. 3)

Printed in the United States of America

1 2 3 4 5 6 7 8 9 10

Library of Congress Cataloging-in-Publication Data

International encyclopedia of women and sports / edited by Karen Christensen,
   Allen Guttman, Gertrud Pfister.
      p. cm.
   Includes bibliographical references and index.
   1. Sports for women—Encyclopedias. 2. Women athletes—Encyclopedias.
   I. Christensen, Karen, 1957– II. Guttmann, Allen. III. Pfister, Gertrud, 1945–

GV709.I58 2000
796'.082—dc21   00-062518

CONTENTS

PREFACE

The concept of the *International Encyclopedia of Women and Sports* originated with our understanding of the inadequacy of women's sports coverage in scholarly reference works. Even publications specifically related to sports often focus overwhelmingly on men, or limit their scope to sports in North America and Europe. Our goal, therefore, was to acknowledge the importance of women in sports at the global level, both from a historical perspective and in light of rapid developments in the field at the close of the twentieth century. With the growing acceptance of women's participation in contact sports like ice hockey, along with tremendous interest in women's sports events like the Women's World Cup in 1999, and the increasing coverage of women's sports in the media, this publication is particularly timely. However, the rapid changes in women's sports even in the eighteen months it took to complete the project required the encyclopedia's constant evolution. Controversies over gender-verification tests and performance-enhancing drugs, along with political and economic factors such as the Asian economic crisis in 1998, are just a few of the developments impacting women's sports around the world.

While there is broad and growing support for women's sports, they are not growing without opposition or difficulty. Not all nations support women's sports and not all sports are open to women. Women occupy very few sport leadership roles, female athletes make much less money than men, and women continue to have fewer opportunities than men in sports-related fields. Even in the United States, which through the Title IX ruling of 1972 and other initiatives has been a leading promoter of women's sports, American universities continue to challenge Title IX and claim that equity in sports for all will mean less sport for everyone.

WHAT IS WOMEN'S SPORT?

Any complete study of women's sports must examine feminist theory, political and religious beliefs, the commercial world, medical research, and the educational establishment, all of which we have considered in the formation of this first multi-volume, international encyclopedia on the topic. Our first task, however, was to define what is meant by women's sports, in order to decide what to cover in the encyclopedia. This task proved to be fraught with difficulty on several levels. First, women's sports have been largely ignored by academic researchers, making reliable information on the topic hard to find. Second, prejudice in the male-dominated world of sports undermines the importance of women's participation, as well as the study of it; for example, an official of the Association of Sports Historians in Britain told us that he could see no reason to study women's sports and that none of the association's members listed women's sports as an interest. Third, the perception of women's sports as something completely new has resulted in the prevalent ignorance of the very real history of women's involvement in sports which extends back even as far as Ancient Greece. Fourth, many nations lack the means or ability to document the development and achievements of women's sports. For example, we have no article on women's sports in the Philippines because the women's sports organization there closed in 1998 after funding was cut off as a result of political problems and the Asian economic crisis.

Some people thought we should show only positive attitudes towards women's sports, as part of the emerging culture of women's sports in the United States where women's sports are actively promoted and supported. While being positive, we have also deliberately included many extracts that criticize women's sports to demonstrate how much opposition early athletes—and ordinary women who wanted to ride a bike or run—had to face. We also want to make clear that women's sports are not accepted today in all nations. For example, women athletes in some South American nations are dismissed as "lesbians" or "trouble-makers" and even successful programs such as the Brazilian women's soccer team are ignored by the media. Similarly, we have made sure that controversial topics such as lesbianism, gender verification, sexual harassment, and exploitation of female sexuality are fully covered.

In previous sports publications, we defined an activity as a sport if it involved two or more competitors, a goal of winning, clear criteria for determining the winner, and victory determined mainly by the relative physical ability of the competitors. When we began work on the *International Encyclopedia of Women and Sports*, however, we used a broader definition to reflect the diversity of women's sports, including hiking, backpacking, yoga practice, and dance. No scholarly work on women in sports has encompassed such a broad range before, and even some of our editorial board felt that we were being too ambitious. We are pleased, however, to offer readers information on athleticism in modern dance, the role of Girl Scouts in women's outdoor adventure activities in the 1930s, and traditional sports and games around the world along with major articles on women's golf, tennis, and basketball.

COVERAGE

In the end, our efforts at defining the field of women's sport produced a list of over four hundred topics which we classified into seven general categories:

(1) sports and athletic activities

(2) women's sport in society and the culture of women's sport

(3) health issues

(4) organizations

(5) events

(6) national programs

(7) people

The encyclopedia contains nearly 150 articles covering individual sports, groups of related sports, and athletic activities. Each article covers the history of the sport, the history of women's participation, basic rules of play, and the current status of women's participation. In addition to the sport itself, many articles also provide information about women's involvement in the governing bodies of the sport and in support roles such as coaching and training, and data on records and results.

The relationship between women's sports and society is complex, and only became the subject of study in the last decades of the twentieth century. Most scholars agree that societal forces such as male control of public society (what some European scholars call the "hegemony of male patriarchy"), beliefs about female physical limitations, the division of labor by sex which placed women in or near the home, and the association of sports with warfare all contributed to the lack, and in many cases the absence, of women's participation in sports until the late 1800s. Similarly, the rise of new social forces such as women's equality, easy and rapid mass communication and transportation, nationalism, and the commercialization of sports have fueled the development of women's sports around the world since the 1960s.

Altogether, we provide sixty-five articles that cover topics that fall within the rubrics of sport in society and the culture of sports, covering such issues as aggression, media, commercialization, lesbianism and homophobia, values and ethics, and religion. Culture of sports articles which involve non-competitive aspects of sports cover issues such as gender verification, drugs and drug testing, motivation, family involvement, marketing, sexual harassment, and sponsorship.

For most sports fans, sports is about the success of individual athletes. We provide biographies of over 130 women who have been influential in the development of women's sport. Winnowing the list of influential women down was no easy task, but the basic selection criteria we followed was that the woman played a major role in developing women's sports, served as a model for other women, or exemplified some major development in women's sport. Thus, Martha Graham is included because of her athletic innovations in dance, Billie Jean King because of her advocacy for tennis and women's sport in general, Martina Hingis because she is an example of the trend toward younger athletes in tennis, Pirjo Haeggman because she was the first female International Olympic Committee member, Alice Milliat because of her promotion of women's sports in the 1920s, Merlene Ottey because of her longevity in track, and Ghada Shouaa because of her prominence as an Arab athlete. Although coverage is heavier for Western athletes because modern women's sport developed in the West, we have made a conscious effort to include coverage of women from Asia, Africa, and Latin America, as well.

Perhaps the most ambitious component of this project was the decision to provide articles on the history and current status of women's physical education and sports in every nation of the world. We knew from the beginning that this goal was impossible as political and economic realities in many nations and the continuing resistance to women's sports make it difficult to obtain full or trustworthy information. In the end, we were able to produce seventy-five articles covering women's sport in specific nations or in regions such as Africa, the Caribbean, or Islamic nations. While these articles vary widely in the type, amount, and depth of information they provide, they are a crucial first step in beginning to systematically document women's sport around the world.

Women's participation in sports raises many health issues, both for the recreational and professional athlete. With articles written mainly by physicians or other medical professionals, we address twenty-two major health issues in women's sport ranging from the "Female Athlete Triad" (amenorrhea, osteoporosis, eating disorders) to endurance, from puberty to stress management. These articles summarize the current state of medical knowledge about these issues, many of which are currently the subject of intensive research.

Finally, to give full coverage to everything about women's sports, this encyclopedia provides coverage of twelve organizations active in women's sport and eighteen international multi-sport competitions. Both the organizations and the competitions are major forces in the push for the development and spread of women's sports. The competitions, such as the Olympics or the Asian Games, are especially significant as it is often only during these events that women's sports receive major media attention. While this encyclopedia is not meant to be about records and results, we have made sure that the statistics buff will not be disappointed. Many of the sports articles provide results and records as do the biographies of athletes. In addition, four appendices provide a wealth of statistical information.

METHODOLOGY

Two years ago we had no idea how difficult the topic of women's sports would be and how many people and organizations would need to be involved in creating this publication. Women's sports is not a "mature" topic of scholarly and journalistic inquiry. The number of scholars who study women's sports, while increasing, is small and there is only one scholarly journal devoted to the topic. Similarly, women's sports medicine is a rapidly growing field, but is in its infancy compared to other specialities in medicine.

While most of our coverage is on North America and Europe because women's sports are more developed in these regions than anywhere else, the encyclopedia includes a great deal of information on women's sports in Latin America, Africa, and Asia, both in specific country articles and in more general entries. The breadth and depth of coverage depended on the resourcefulness of our international contributors who wrote on such diverse topics as women's sports under the Italian fascists, women in classical mythology, and physical education in Latin America. Articles were written by contributors from thirty-nine nations, with material that was used as the basis for articles supplied by consultants in twelve additional nations. Articles were translated from German, French, Italian, and Japanese. Most important, the articles on women's sports in countries of the world are almost all written by people living in those countries. This unique international perspective is one of the strengths of this work.

The international contributors are responsible for the unprecedented amount of information on women's sports around the world, particularly on topics with no source of information in English or even in the language of the nation. Enn Mainla of the Estonian Sports Museum originally told us that there was no information on women's sports in that country, but then decided to undertake the job of gathering information himself, writing an article on women's sports in Estonia and having it translated into English. Not long before this work went to press, we received a package from Malawi with an article about women's sports and physical education. A German scholar who studied aggression in team sports provided us with a groundbreaking article on the subject. Many contributors did original research from primary sources and also interviewed athletes and administrators to provide the most complete picture of this exciting area of human endeavor.

ILLUSTRATIONS AND SIDEBARS

The photographs and other illustrations in this encyclopedia are a vital part of its coverage, beyond making the work more visually appealing. They range from eighteenth-century engravings of women participating in falconry to women rowers at the 1996 Chinese Water Splashing Festival. Sidebars are another important component of the encyclopedia and are drawn from a wide variety of primary sources, both historical and ethnographic. Our intention is to highlight the variety of physical activities in which women have been involved through the ages, and also to show many views about women's bodies, women's strength (and weakness), and women's beauty—all topics that affect how sports and athletes are viewed and valued. Sport for women did not begin in the twentieth century. Medieval smock races, Victorian prize fights, aristocratic fox hunting, and Indian running are all part of the panorama of women's sports through the ages, and reflect many of the same desires and issues that face women in sport today.

GLOBAL WOMEN'S SPORTS

Most of our final work took place during the Women's World Cup of 1999 and we were lucky enough to attend a double header at Foxboro Stadium in Massachusetts. The thrill of the matches and the huge crowd was compounded when we returned to our hotel at midnight and found the lobby full of players from the U.S., Mexican, and North Korean teams we had watched play earlier

in the evening. Instead of studying women's sports, we were in the midst of it. We watched the players sign soccer balls and pose for photographs with their fans, and we talked to several members and coaches of the three teams. We found it enlightening to mingle among the calm and confident American players, talk to North Korean officials as the team dined on a buffet of American Chinese food, and chat with 16-year-old Monica, the youngest member of the Mexican team. Perhaps most striking was the fact that they were wide awake, happy, excited, and hungry, although it was midnight and they had just played ninety minutes of end-to-end soccer at the height of a heat wave.

It is fitting that this encyclopedia will appear in print soon after the closing of the 2000 Summer Olympics in Sydney, Australia. The Olympics is perhaps the most important showcase for women's sports, with events broadcast around the world and reported daily by the media. Women gold medalists become instant celebrities in their homelands and sometimes around the world. Because of the significance of the Olympics, we considered delaying publication of this encyclopedia to allow us to cover the Year 2000 Games. However, we did not want to see the publication of this much-needed resource delayed a day longer than necessary. This encyclopedia is not intended to be a detailed source of information on current events, even though we have updated articles through June 2000. The *International Encyclopedia of Women and Sports* covers all aspects of the history and culture or women's sports, the sports themselves, and women's sports in the their societal context. Over 400 detailed articles provide context, background information, significant ethnographic and anecdotal information on women's sports to provide a better understanding of the 2000 (and future) Olympic Games.

Karen Christensen and David Levinson
Berkshire Reference Works,
part of Berkshire Publishing Groups LLC
http://www.berkshirepublishing.com
Great Barrington, Massachusetts

INTRODUCTION

While women have probably never been as involved in sports (either as participants or spectators) as men, sports have rarely been a totally male domain. Throughout history, in places and cultures around the globe, women have pursued physical activities from ball games to competitive running, from archery to dancing. The girls of ancient Sparta, for instance, participated in sports just as the boys did, a fact commemorated millenia later by the Impressionist painter Edgar Degas in *Spartan Girls Challenging the Boys* (1860). And while sports have almost always been more important in men's lives than in women's, the rate of participation for girls and young women is now much closer to that for boys and young men than it was in the past. In the United States, for example, during the 1971–72 school year, boys were twelve times as likely to be involved in interscholastic sports as girls were; in the late 1990s, boys continued to be more active, but the ratio was only two to one. Similar trends have been documented in northern and western Europe, and opportunities for women in sport are expanding all over the world.

If blanket statements about the exclusion of women from the world of sports continue to appear in the mass media, in spite of growing coverage of the world of women's sports, historians are partly at fault because they have, until quite recently, failed to adequately document the history of women's sports. It was not until the 1980s that sports historians—many of them represented in this encyclopedia—began to pay close attention to the stellar achievements of female athletes in Europe and North America. One major goal of the *International Encyclopedia of Women and Sports* is to globalize that coverage by reporting international achievements and by indicating areas where more research is needed.

Whether one considers the prowess of Margot of Hainault, who vanquished the male tennis players of medieval Paris, or the exploits of female sumo wrestlers in eighteenth-century Japan, or the spectacular successes of African-American sprinters, one must always take into account the distinctiveness of times and places as well as the complicated ways that gender has interacted with social class. At any given historical moment, some women have indeed been excluded from sports while others have been intensely involved.

Social class has always been an important factor. In the Victorian era, for example, while medical experts debated whether or not strenuous exercise endangered a girl's capacity to conceive and bear children, working-class women were actively competing in six-day bicycle races. Middle-class American women like Margaret Abbott had to wait until 1900 to be admitted into Olympic competition (she won a gold medal in golf), but a Greek peasant known to us only as Melpomone ran from Marathon to Athens in 1896 just to prove how misguided the Olympic organizers were to bar women from the Games.

Religion, too, is a factor. Since the dawn of the Christian era, many Christian denominations—both Roman Catholic and Protestant—have been suspicious of sports, which they saw as closely associated with pagan cults, but twentieth-century theologians have concluded that sports, for women as well as for men, are quite compatible with a Christian life. Fundamentalist Islamic leaders, on the other hand, are adamant about the sinfulness of female athletes who compete before male spectators while dressed (or undressed) in shorts and jerseys.

The stages of the life cycle are another factor determining whether a female will be encouraged to engage in sports or warned that athletic participation is detrimental to her health and her social status. While young girls of most cultures have been granted the freedom to run races and play ball games, the onset of puberty was for centuries taken as a signal for European and American girls to shift their attention from the excitement of sports contests to the rituals of courtship. Today, however, an adolescent girl is just as likely to find her future mate on the tennis court or to attract his (or her) attention when she kicks a soccer goal. If this is, indeed, the happy outcome of her athleticism, her success is akin to that of African girls of the Diola, the Yala, and the Njabi tribes, who traditionally wrestled as part of their ritual initiation into mature womanhood. Although marriages and careers tend, now as in the past, to limit opportunities for sports participation, adult women are somewhat freer than they were to continue as recreational or even as elite athletes.

Age sometimes plays an unexpected role. In modern Japan, women over sixty are an exception to the well-substantiated generalization that men are more likely than women to be active in sports. Thanks in part to the fact that they are on the whole in better health than their husbands, Japanese women outnumber men in gateball (a game similar to croquet) and other sports popular among the elderly.

That the state of a woman's health influences her sports participation is no more surprising than the fact that sports are at the center of the contemporary fitness boom. What needs to be explained, however, is why the example of Spartan eugenic policy had so little impact on European and American beliefs about the female role of wife and mother. Why was it not until after the publication in 1829 of *Kalisthenie* by the Swiss author Phokian Clias that significant numbers of European and American medical experts and physical educators began to urge moderate exercise as a countermeasure to the debility that was widely thought to be endemic among middle-class women? If reproduction was deemed to be a woman's destiny, why did it take so long for the world to notice that physically active women are more likely than their sedentary sisters to survive the ordeal of childbirth and to deliver robust progeny? And, finally, was it accidental that the physical educators of Nazi Germany—who did evoke the Spartan example—coupled their eugenics program with the systematic murder of women whom they judged to be unfit? These hard question are closely related to a number of other questions addressed not only by historians but also by physiologists, social psychologists, sociologists, and economists.

Although the physiological facts about women's bodies have not changed in the course of historical time, more or less objective scientific research on sports and the human body is a recent phenomenon. Accurate information about the relationship of sports to biomechanics and the menstrual cycle, for instance, must still, even at the end of the twentieth century, compete with myths about the anatomical disadvantages of the female athlete.

More controversial still are social-psychological topics like motivation, socialization into sports, and the complex relationship between sports and female sexuality. Lesbianism and the Gay Games, for example, are salient topics about which it is difficult, but not impossible, to speak with light as well as heat. Another set of related topics has occasioned intense debate. Do sports enhance or diminish femininity? Is the fitness boom and the quest for an athletic body good for women because an improved body image enhances self-esteem or is the fitness industry part of a politically retrogressive regime imposed by the mass media, a version of what the feminist author Naomi Wolf called "the beauty trap"?

Sociological and economic questions are equally important. How, for instance, have women's sports been organized, administered, managed, financed? Have women at long last begun to take charge of women's sports in the schools and in national and international sports organizations? Questions of this sort lead inevitably to an analysis of sports sponsorship, commercialization, marketing, and the role of the mass media. While the encyclopedia format requires the separation of entries, it is essential to remember that these are always interrelated matters. The difficulties encountered by the promoters of women's professional basketball, for instance, are closely connected to the reluctance of advertisers to sponsor the women's game. And their reluctance, in turn, is based on the fact that women's sports have, with a few exceptions such as figure skating, attracted fewer spectators than men's sports. If women's professional basketball has finally begun to attract large numbers of spectators, one reason is that the image of the female basketball player has changed, and will continue to change as even more spectators attend games or watch them on television.

Discussions of sports equipment or sportswear may seem at first to involve only technical matters like the design of skis or the invention of synthetic fabrics, but they also raise interesting questions about the female athlete's social role. How exactly did the late-nineteenth-century vogue of the bicycle contribute to women's geographical mobility? Was the early-twentieth- century transition from tennis skirts to tennis shorts motivated by the players' desire for un-hampered movement on court or by their sense of themselves as emancipated women?

In short, the *International Encyclopedia of Women and Sports* is an attempt to provide the reader with the fullest possible account of the history and present state of women's sports in her or his own country and elsewhere around the world.

Allen Guttmann, Gertrud Pfister,
and Karen Christensen

ACKNOWLEDGMENTS

This work would not exist without people on every continent who were excited about our project and aims. The *International Encyclopedia of Women and Sports* is, appropriately, the work of a global team of scholars and sportspeople who, in addition to the usual encyclopedia tasks of writing and reviewing articles, suggested topics, passed on names, sent information, and circulated our requests for information to colleagues around the world. They helped with photographs, sent material for our historical sidebars, and gave us an occasional slap on the back, too, encouraging us to persevere in what sometimes seemed an impossible endurance race. The most important of these people were Karen Christensen's co-editors. At the close of 2000 Allen Guttmann was president-elect of the North American Society for Sport Historians (NASSH) and Gertrud Pfister was the president of the International Society for the History of Physical Education and Sport (ISHPES), the world's leading associations for the study of sport. Not only did they recruit authors and review articles, but they worked tirelessly to ensure that our coverage was broad, accurate, and historically complete. Their general knowledge of sports history enriches many of the articles written by colleagues around the world, and Allen deserves special mention for his generous translation efforts.

The editors were assisted throughout the project by a diverse advisory board of colleagues, some of whom have been involved in the development of women's studies and women's sports since the 1960s. Others come from the growing community of scholars who study women's sports. The board members deserve much credit for their support, advice, and patience with our endless requests for further assistance. Wayne Wilson of the Amateur Athletic Foundation of Los Angeles (AAF) was particularly helpful when we had been unable to locate essential information,

and he also supplied photographs and suggested a number of biographical subjects from regions of the world we were eager to see represented.

Our contributors were a diverse group and brought to this project not only expertise but the fortitude necessary to deal with endless succession of queries from us for more information and help with new topics. Some of them reviewed other articles to ensure that our coverage of related sports was consistent and accurate. Many articles were themselves team efforts, as we paired people or co-authored articles ourselves, in order to provide the broadest coverage possible. We gathered information and sent it to authors or passed on our contacts in countries outside the United States. Some intrepid scholars jumped in to take on topics that they had never written about before, such as the international history of women's participation in rowing, golf, and cross-country running. David Levinson, whose scholarly expertise is in world cultures and sports, edited and also rewrote many articles on women's sports in countries around the world, adding important information on cultural and religious issues. Over the course of many months he reviewed hundreds of articles to check sports coverage and cultural content and provided an essential modern sports perspective to the encyclopedia as a whole.

The following organizations also helped to create this uniquely varied and comprehensive encyclopedia: NAASH, ISHPES, International Olympic Committee (IOC), United States Olympic Committee (USIOC), Islamic Women's Sports Solidarity Council (IWSSC), Women's Sports Foundation (WSF), WomenSport International, and Sport England.

As in the world of sports, there are many people behind the scenes who help to make victory possible. The following list is only partial; we know there were other people who circulated our listserv postings and sent us names and pieces of data and we thank all of them, named and unnamed, and look forward to receiving further information and data on the changing world of women's sports: F.B. Adeyanju, American Horse Shows Association, Gregory Alegi, Patricia Andreucci, Joseph Arbena, Velinda Baker, Robert Banks, Josephina Barzon, Douglas Booth, Trice Cameron, Sheila Cutler, Dana Cummings, Michael DeMarco of the *Journal of Asian Martial Arts,* Julie Dyson, Patricia Eckert, Diana Everett, Floris van der Merwe, Ann Hall, Raymond Hastert, Joan Hult, Mary McConnaughey, Karyn Moore, Cynthia Morrison, Carole Oglesby, Sharon Phillips, Nina Roberts, Kurt Sonderegger, Margaret Talbot, Carlos Vera Guardia, and Larry Weindruch of the National Sporting Goods Association.

This project originated with Berkshire Reference Works and our staff deserves praise for their enthusiasm and fortitude. Three of them, Shana Stalker and Robin O'Sullivan, and Frances Fusco, were college athletes themselves and brought a special level of enthusiasm to the task of creating the first comprehensive international coverage of women's sports.

READER'S GUIDE

COUNTRIES AND REGIONS

Poland
Portugal
Rome, Ancient
Russia and Belarus
Senegal
Serbia and Montenegro—see Yugoslavia
Singapore
Slovakia—see Czechoslovakia; Czech Republic;
    Slovakian Republic
Slovenia—see Yugoslavia
South Africa
South Korea
Spain
Sweden
Syria
Thailand
Turkey
Ukraine
United Kingdom
United States
Venezuela
Yugoslavia
Zambia

EVENTS

African Games
Asian Games
Commonwealth Games
Deaf Olympics
Gay Games
Highland Games
International Women's Games
Islamic Countries' Women's Sports Solidarity
    Council and Games
Latin American Multisport Festivals
Maccabiah Games
Native American Games and Sports
Olympics
Pan-American Games
Paralympics
Senior Games—see Senior Sports
Special Olympics
World University Games

ISSUES

Administration
Advertising
Aggression
Animal Rights

Art
Beauty
Body Image
Brighton Declaration
Burnout
Coaching
Coeducational Sport
Commodification and Commercialization
Community
Competition
Contact Sports
Cooperation
Disability Sport
Drugs and Drug Testing
Environment
Family Involvement
Fashion
Femininity
Feminism
Gender Equity
Gender Verification
Homophobia
Intercollegiate Athletics
Intramural Sports
Law
Lesbianism
Literature
Magazines
Management
Marketing
Media
Mental Conditioning
Military Sports
Motherhood
Motivation
Movies
Mythology
Officiating
Ownership
Personality Traits
Physical Education
Politics
Professionalism
Puberty
Race and Ethnicity
Recruitment
Religion
School Achievement
Self-Defense

Self-Esteem
Senior Sports
Sexual Harassment
Sexuality
Socialization
Spectators
Sponsorship
Sportswear Industry
Technology
Title IX
Unionism
Values and Ethics
Youth Sports

MEDICINE AND HEALTH

Aging
Amenorrhea
Anemia
Athletic Training
Biomechanics
Body Composition
Breast Health
Eating Disorders
Endurance
Immunity
Injury
Medicine
Menstrual Cycle
Nutrition
Osteoporosis
Pain
Performance
Reproduction
Stress and Stress Management

ORGANIZATIONS

Asia Conference on Women and Sports
Association for Intercollegiate Athletics for
    Women (AIAW)
International Association of Physical
    Education and Sport for Girls and Women
    (IAPESGW)
International Council for Health, Physical Edu-
    cation, Recreation, Sport and Dance (ICH-
    PERSD)
International Olympic Committee
International Working Group on Women and
    Sport
Islamic Countries' Women's Sports Solidarity
    Council and Games

National Association for Girls and Women in
    Sport
Sport Association for Arab Women
Windhoek Call for Action
WomenSport International
Women's Sports Foundation

SPORTS

Acrobatics
Aerobics
Aikido
Air Sports
All-American Girls Professional Baseball League
Archery
Arm Wrestling
Auto Racing
Badminton
Ballooning
Baseball
Basketball
Baton Twirling
Biathlon
Billiards
Boating, Ice
Bobsledding
Bodybuilding
Boomerang Throwing
Bowls and Bowling
Boxing
Broomball
Bullfighting
Camogie
Canoeing and Kayaking
Cheerleading
Cockfighting
Cresta Sledding—see Sledding–Skeleton (Cresta
    Run) Tobogganing
Cricket
Croquet
Cross-Country Running
Cross-Country Skiing—see Skiing, Cross-Country
Curling
Cycling
Dance
DanceSport
Darts
Diving
Double Dutch
Duathlon
Extreme Sports

LIST OF ARTICLES

Abbott, Margaret
John E. Findling

Acrobatics
A.B. Frederick

Administration
R. Vivian Acosta

Advertising
Allen Guttmann

Aerobics
Pirkko Markula

Afghanistan
Berkshire Reference Works

Africa
Rabiatou Njoya
Mickey Friedman

African Games
Daniel Bell

Aggression
Gunter A. Pilz

Aging
Patricia Vertinsky

Aikido
Diane Skoss

Ainsworth, Dorothy Sears
Gertrud Pfister

Air Sports
Gregory Alegi

All-American Girls Professional Baseball League
Susan E. Johnson

Amenorrhea
Lorna A. Marshall, M.D.

Anemia
Sally S. Harris, M.D.

Animal Rights
Wesley V. Jamison

Anne, Princess
Bershire Reference Works

Applebee, Constance
Shawn Ladda

Archery
John Lowerson
Urla Hill

Argentina
Mariá Graciela Rodríguez

Arm Wrestling
John Townes

Art
Allen Guttmann

Asia Conference on Women and Sports
Berkshire Reference Works

Asian Games
Hai Ren

Association for Intercollegiate Athletics
   for Women
Ying Wu

LIST OF CONTRIBUTORS

Andrea Abbas
Keele University, Keele, United Kingdom
Heptathlon

Nabilah Ahmed Abdel Rahman
Alexandria University, Alexandria, Egypt
Egypt

R. Vivian Acosta
Brooklyn College, City University of New York, Brooklyn, NY
Administration
Race and Ethnicity

Daryl Adair
University of Canberra, Australia
Long Distance Flying
Markham, Beryl

Mary Louise Adams
Queen's University, Kingston, Ontario, Canada
Skating, Ice Figure

F. B. Adyanju
Nigeria

Marjorie J. Albohm
Orthopaedic Research and Sports Medicine
Athletic Training
Pain

Gregory Alegi
Italian Air Force Academy
Air Sports
Ballooning
Gliding
Hang Gliding
Parachuting

E. John B. Allen
Plymouth State College, Plymouth, NH
Skiing, Alpine

Julia M. K. Alleyne
Sunnybrook & Women's College Health Sciences Centre, Toronto, Ontario, Canada
Breast Health

Todd Allison
Canadian National Development Team
Skiing, Freestyle

Helena Altmann
Brazil

Ellis Amdur
Seattle, WA
Naginata

J. P. Anderson
De Montfort University, Leicester, England
Blair, Bonnie
Durack, Fanny
Goolagong, Evonne
Ostermeyer, Micheline
Pentathlon, Modern
Skating, Ice Speed
Wade, Virginia
Whitbread, Fatima

Nicholas G. Aplin
Nanyang Technological University, Singapore
Indonesia
Singapore

Cem Atabeyoglu
Turkey

Christiane Ayotte
Institut National de la Recherche Scientifique–Sante, Quebec, Canada
Drugs and Drug Testing

John Bale
Keele University, Keele, United Kingdom
Track and Field–Running and Hurdling

Debra Ann Ballinger
Virginia Commonwealth University, Richmond, VA
Collett Vare, Glenna
Decker Slaney, Mary
DeFrantz, Anita
Fishing
Golf
Lopez, Nancy
Professionalism
Smith, Robyn C.

Susan J. Bandy
East Tennessee State University, Johnson City, TN
Lenglen, Suzanne

Becky Beal
University of the Pacific, Stockton, CA
Skateboarding

Dawn Dawson Bean
Santa Ana, CA
Swimming, Synchronized

Edward R. Beauchamp
University of Hawaii, Honolulu, HI
Boxing

Daniel Bell
International Games Archive
African Games
Islamic Countries' Women's Sports Solidarity Council and Games
World University Games

Beryl Bender Birch
New York Road Runners Club, New York, NY
Yoga

Berkshire Reference Works editors
Great Barrington, MA
Afghanistan
Anne, Princess
Asia Conference on Women and Sports
International Working Group on Women and Sport
Jamaica
Liechtenstein
Luge
Ottey, Merlene
Sepaktakraw
Speedball
Sport Association for Arab Women

Gai Ingham Berlage
Iona College
Baseball

Diethelm Blecking
Institut fur Sportgeschichte
Czechoslovakia; Czech Republic; Slovakian Republic
Poland
Sokol Movement
Yugoslavia

Tim Boggan
USA Table Tennis, Colorado Springs, CO
Table Tennis

Anne Bolin
Elon College, NC
Bodybuilding

Gherardo Bonini
Historical Archives of European Communities, Italy
Compagnoni, Deborah
Diving
Dod, Charlotte
Ender, Kornelia
Fikotová, Olga
Greece
Kenya
Lines, Mary
Meyfarth, Ulrike
Mittermaier, Rosi
Moser-Proell, Annemarie
Otto, Kristin

Schneider, Vreni
Szewinska, Irena Kirszenstein

Dale R. Bonsall
Sexual Harrassment

John R. Bowman
University of North Carolina at Pembroke,
Pembroke, NC
Cooperation

Kelly Boyer Sagert
Lorain, OH
Boomerang Throwing
Budd, Zola
Joyner-Kersee, Jackie
Yamaguchi, Kristi Tsuya

Celia Brackenridge
Cheltenham and Gloucester College, United
Kingdom
WomenSport International

Norma Baraldi Briseño
Mexico City, Mexico
Mexico

Michel Brousse
Université de Bordeaux, France
Judo and Jujutsu

Varda Burstyn
Ontario, Canada
Politics

Susan Butt
University of British Columbia, Vancouver,
British Columbia, Canada
Mental Conditioning
Personality Traits

Colette Soto Caballero
Mexico

Linda Carpenter
Brooklyn College, Brooklyn, New York
Race and Ethnicity

Richard Cashman
University of New South Wales, Sydney,
Australia
Cricket

Joan M. Chandler
University of Texas
Media

Patrick Chaplin
Anglia Polytechnic University
Darts

Jefferey Charlston
George Washington University, Washington, D.C.
Skating, Roller
Underwater Sports

H. E. Chehabi
Boston University, Boston, MA
Iran

Garry Chick
Penn State University, University Park, PA
Billiards

Carol L. Christensen
San Jose State University, San Jose, CA
Immunity

Karen Christensen
Berkshire Reference Works, Great Barrington, MA
Breast Health
Yoga

Sarah Chung
Taekwondo

Rebecca A. Clark
Los Angeles, CA
Deaf Olympics
Paralympics
Special Olympics

Annie Clement
Florida State University, Tallahassee, FL
Law

Jay Coakley
University of Colorado, Boulder, CO
Youth Sports

Mary A. Conti
East Brunswick, NJ
Horseback Riding

Pamela Cooper
Runner's World
Marathon and Distance Running
Waitz, Greta
Walking, Fitness

Susan Coopersmith
University of Maine
Cameroon
Zambia

Doris R. Corbett
International Council for Health, Physical
Education, Recreation, Sport and Dance
(ICHPERSD)

Jonathan Cornwell
Sabatini, Gabriela

Scott Crawford
Eastern Illinois University, Charleston, IL
Oakley, Annie
Shooting

Mike Cronin
*International Centre for Sports History and
Culture, Leicester, England*
Bobsledding
Camogie
Football, Gaelic
Ireland

Bart Crum
Uithoorn, The Netherlands
Korfball

Carlos Fernando Ferrera da Cunta Júnior
Brazil

Michaela Czech
*Georg-August-University of Göttingen,
Gottingen, Germany*
Biathlon
Cranz, Christl

Braham Dabscheck
*University of New South Wales, Sydney,
Australia*
Unionism

Joanna Davenport
Auburn University, Auburn, Alabama
Sears, Eleonora
Tennis

Lisa Delpy
George Washington University, Washington, D.C.
Management
Marketing

Karen DePauw
Washington State University, Pullman, WA
Disability Sport

Mary Jane De Souza
New Britain General Hospital, New Britain, CT
Osteoporosis

Bernadette Deville-Danthu
Universite de Lyon, Lyon, France
Senegal

Ro DiBrezzo
Human Performance Lab
Biomechanics

Rosa Diketmueller
Vienna University, Vienna, Austria
Austria

Kristine Drakich
University of Toronto, Toronto, Ontario, Canada
Volleyball, Beach

Jessica Edwards
Roehampton Institute, London, England
Feminism

Heike Egger
Deutsches Sport-und Olympia-Museum, Cologne,
Germany
Fashion

Henning Eichberg
Slagelse, Denmark
Volkssport

George Eisen
Central Connecticut State University, New
Britain, CT
Maccabiah Games

Nour Elhouda Karfoul
Syrian Olympic Committee, Damascus, Syria
Syria

Agnes Elling
Tilberg University, Tilberg, Holland
Netherlands, The

Lynn Embrey
Edith Cowan University, Perth, Australia
Bergman-Österberg, Martina
Joyce, Joan
Schott, Marge
Softball

Diana Everett
National Association for Girls and Women in
Sport, Reuton, VA
National Association for Girls and Women in
Sport

Kari Fasting
Norwegian University of Sport and Physical
Education
Norway

John E. Findling
Indiana University, Southeast
Abbott, Margaret
Bueno, Maria
Mallory, Molla
Wills, Helen

Kay Flatten
Croquet

Susan L. Forbes
University of Western Ontario, Waterloo,
Ontario, Canada
Lacrosse

Inza Fort
Biomechanics

A.B. Frederick
ROOTS Project
Acrobatics
Comaneci, Nadia
Gymnastics
Latynina, Larissa Semyenovna
Retton, Mary Lou
Tourischeva, Ludmilla Ivanova

Gavin Freeman
Australian Institute for Sport, Canberra,
Australia
Skiing, Water

Mickey Friedman
Great Barrington, MA
Africa
Double Dutch
Egypt
Islamic Countries' Women's Sports Solidarity
Council and Games
Nigeria
Women's Sports Foundation

Francesca Garello
Greece, Ancient
Rome, Ancient

J. Nadine Gelberg
Rochester Institute of Technology, Rochester, NY
Technology

Laura Gajardo Ghilardi
Chilean Sports Direction
Chile

Silvana Vilodre Goellnes
Brazil

Teresa González Aja
Universidad Politécnica de Madrid, Madrid, Spain
Spain

Gigliola Gori
University of Urbino, Urbino, Italy
Italy

Ann C. Grandjean
International Center for Sports Nutrition
Nutrition

Jane Granskog
Triathlon

B. Christine Green
Griffith University, Nathan, Australia
Football, Flag

Steve Greenfield
University of Westminster, Westminster, England
Contact Sports

Laurie Gullion
Greenfield Community College, Greenfield, MA
Canoeing and Kayaking

Nese Gundogan
*National Olympic Committee of Turkey, Istanbul,
    Turkey*
Turkey

Sharon R. Guthrie
California State University
Self-Defense

Allen Guttmann
Amherst College, Amherst, MA
Advertising
Art
Blankers-Koen, Fanny
Boulmerka, Hassiba
Colón, Mariá Caridad
Cynisca
Hitomi Kinue
International Women's Games
Kristiansen, Ingrid
Literature
Milliat, Alice
Olympics
Physical Education
Professionalism
Salisbury, The Marchioness of
Spectators
Yegorova, Ljubov

Chung-Hae Hahm
South Korea

Sandra Kimberly Hall
University of Hawaii, Honolulu, HI
Sunn, Rell
Surfing

Nancy Hamilton
University of Northern Iowa, Cedar Falls, IA
Senior Sports

Elizabeth A. Hanley
*Pennsylvania State University, University Park,
    PA*
DanceSport

Jennifer Hargreaves
Roehampton Institute, London, England
Feminism
South Africa

Kimberly G. Harmon
University of Washington, Seattle, WA
Medicine

Sally S. Harris, M.D.
Stanford University, Stanford, CA
Anemia

Ilse Hartmann-Tews
Media

Cynthia A. Hasbrook
University of Wisconsin, Milwaukee, WI
Family Involvement
Socialization

Manuela Hasse
Lisbon's Technical University, Lisbon, Portugal
Mota, Rosa
Portugal

Penny Hastings
Hastings Communications, Austin, Texas
Recruitment

Emily M. Haymes
Florida State University, Tallahassee, FL
Environment

Leslie Heaphy
Kent State University, Kent, OH
Earhart, Amelia
Ederle, Gertrude
Football
Gibson, Althea

Leslie Heywood
State University of New York, Binghamton, NY
Cross-Country Running
Femininity

Urla Hill
San Francisco State University, San Francisco, CA
Archery
Rudolph, Wilma

Marijke den Hollander
Catholic University of Belgium, Louvain, Belgium
Isabelle of the Netherlands
Kerrigan, Nancy

Margery Holman
University of Windsor, Windsor, Ontario, Canada
Volleyball

Fan Hong
De Montfort University, Leicester, England
China
Fu Mingxia
Yang Xiuqiong

Adam R. Hornbuckle
Alexandria, VA
Walsh, Stella

Mary Hricko
Kent State University, Kent, OH
Track and Field–Jumping and Throwing

Jim Hunstein
Manchester, MD
Broomball
Flying Disc
Snowshoe Racing
Surf Lifesaving

Keiko Ikeda
Yamaguchi University, Yamaguchi, Japan
Japan

Flor Isava
International Olympic Committee, Caracas, Venezuela
Venezuela

John J. Jackson
University of Victoria, Victoria, British Columbia, Canada
Badminton

Lorna Jackson
Moray House Institute of Education, Edinburgh, Scotland
Shinty

Wesley V. Jamison
Worcester Polytechnic Institute, Worcester, MA
Animal Rights

Susan E. Johnson
Anchorage, AK
All-American Girls Professional Baseball League

Denise Jones
South Africa

Annemarie Jutel
University of Otago, Dunedin, New Zealand
Body Image
New Zealand

Irene M. Kadammanja
Malawi

K. Kardelis
Lithuanian Institute of Physical Education
Lithuania

Haim Kaufman
Wingate Institute, Tel-Aviv, Israel
Israel

S. Kavalianskas
Lithuania

Joanne Kay
University of Montreal, Montreal, Quebec, Canada
Extreme Sports

Joyce Kay
De Montfort University, Leicester, England
Horse Racing

Eileen Kennedy
United Kingdom

Kendall Kic
Portland, OR
Footbag

Bruce Kidd
University of Toronto, Toronto, Canada
Canada

Deborah Klens-Bigman
New York, NY
Iaido

Darlene A. Kluka
Grambling State University, Grambling, LA
Caslavska, Vera
International Council for Health, Physical
    Education, Recreation, Sport and Dance
    (ICHPERSD)
Lee, Mabel
Lieberman-Cline, Nancy
Navratilova, Martina

Annelies Knoppers
University of Utrecht, Utrecht, Netherlands
Netherlands, The

Wendy M. Kohrt
Washington University, Seattle, WA
Body Composition

M. I. Komoto
International Budo University, Chiba, Japan
Kendo

Arnd Krüger
Georg-August-University, Gottingen, Germany
Mensendieck, Bess M.

Heike Kuhn
German Sports University
Longo-Ciprelli, Jeannie

Shawn Ladda
Manhattan College, Riverdale, NY
Applebee, Constance
Berenson, Senda
Coachman, Alice
Court, Margaret Smith
De Varona, Donna
Lopiano, Donna

Horacio A. Laffaye
Yale University, New Haven, CT
Polo

Leena Laine
Vantaa, Finland
Björkstén, Elli
Finland
Kallio, Elin
Sweden

Terry Lawton
Los Angeles Harbor College, Los Angeles, CA
Officiating

LeCompte, Mary Lou
University of Texas
Rodeo

Helen Jefferson Lenskyj
*Ontario Institute for Studies in Education,
    Toronto, Ontario, Canada*
Homophobia
Lesbianism

Arnold LeUnes
Texas A & M University, College Station, Texas
Cuthbert, Betty
Didrikson Zaharias, Mildred (Babe)

David Levinson
*Berkshire Reference Works, Great Barrington,
    MA*
Africa
Chi Cheng
Graf, Steffi
Griffith-Joyner, Florence
Kenya
Latvia

Liechtenstein
Mutola, Maria
Shouaa, Ghada
Summitt, Pat
Usha, P.T.

Gerd von der Lippe
College of Telemark, Telemark, Norway
Handball, Team
Henie, Sonja
Skiing, Cross-Country
Ski Jumping

Cathy D. Lirgg
University of Arkansas, Little Rock, AR
Coeducational Sport

Arne Ljungqvist
International Olympic Committee
Gender Verification

Cara Joy Lockman Hall
Rockville, MD
Costa Rica
Evans, Janet
Fraser, Dawn
Wakeboarding

Sue Lopez
Southampton, England
Soccer

Donna A. Lopiano
Women's Sports Foundation
Gender Equity
Title IX
Values and Ethics

Nancy L. Lough
Iowa State University, Ames, IA
Commodification and Commercialization
Sponsorship

Kristi Lowenthal
Lincoln, NE
Snowboarding

John Lowerson
University of Sussex, Sussex, England
Archery
Bowls and Bowling
Foxhunting
Rounders and Stoolball

Janet Luehring-Lindquist
Belvidere, IL
Fleming, Peggy
Hamill, Dorothy
Kerrigan, Nancy

Gordon MacDonald
Ontario, Canada
Berlioux, Monique
Haeggman, Pirjo

Charlotte MacNaughton
Alberta Orienteering Association, Edmonton,
Alberta, Canada
Orienteering

Enn Mainla
Eesti Spordimuuseum
Estonia

Bill Mallon
Duke University, Durham, NC
Catherwood, Ethel
Keleti, Ágnes
Laumann, Silken Suzette
Scott, Barbara Ann
Smetanina, Raisa Petrovna

Pirkko Markula
University of Waikato, Hamilton, New Zealand
Aerobics

Aimee E. Marlow
Boston College
Burnout

Lorna A. Marshall, M.D.
Virginia Mason Medical Center, Boston, MA
Amenorrhea
Menstrual Cycle

Peter Mauritsch
Institut fur Alte Geschichte und Altertumskun
Mythology

R. Mazeikiene
Lithuania

Monica McCabe Cardoza
Ridgewood, NJ
Karate

Robin McConnell
Massey University, New Zealand
Rugby

Richard V. McGehee
Southeastern Louisiana University, Hammond,
LA
Latin America Multisport Festivals
Pan American Games

Tamara McKernan
Ringette Alberta
Hockey, In-Line
Ringette

Claudia Meimbresse
Georg-August-University, Gottingen, Germany
Mensendieck, Bess M.

Gordon T. Mellor
De Montfort University, Leicester, England
Falconry

Victor Andrade de Melo
Rio de Janeiro, Brazil
Brazil

Molly Merryman
Kent State University, Kent, OH
Movies

Barbara B. Meyer
University of Wisconsin-Milwaukee, Milwaukee,
WI
School Achievement

Andy Miah
De Montfort University, Leicester, England
Boating, Ice

Astra Mille
Latvia Women's Sports Association
Latvia

Brian E. Miller
New Britain General Hospital, New Britain, CN
Osteoporosis

Dorothy Jane Mills
Naples, FL
Curling

Edeltraud Minar
CSIDUNAH
Honduras

Wilma Miranda
Northern Illinois University, Dekalb, IL
Wilderness Adventure

Karen D. Mittleman
Princeton, NJ
Endurance

Michelle F. Mottola
University of Western Ontario, Waterloo,
Ontario, Canada
Reproduction

Helen Myers
New Mexico State University, Las Cruces, NM
Dance
Graham, Martha

Young-Il Na
Yongin University, Yongin, Kyonggi, South Korea
South Korea

Kezia Nalweya
Sports Department, Zambia
Zambia

John Nauright
University of Queensland, Brisbane, Australia
Netball

Kelly Nelson
Brandeis University, Waltham, MA
Basketball
Miller, Cheryl

Poll, Sylvia
Tabei Junko

R. Renee Newcomer
West Virginia University
Injury

Rabiatou Njoya
Supreme Council for Sports in Africa, Yaoundé,
Cameroon
Africa

Guy Osborn
Contact Sports

Robin O'Sullivan
Berkshire Reference Works, Great Barrington, MA
Ultimate

Mary L. O'Toole
University of Tennessee, Knoxville, TN
Performance

Claire Pagen
U.S. Hang Gliding Association, Colorado Springs,
CO
Hang Gliding

Wendy Painter
Austin, TX
Butcher, Susan
Holm, Eleanor
Korbut, Olga
Krone, Julie
Marble, Alice
Mulhall, Lucille
Witt, Katarina

Vicky Paraschak
University of Windsor, Windsor, Ontario, Canada
Native American Games and Sports

Kirstin Pauka
University of Hawaii, Honolulu, HI
Silat

Katharine Pawelko
Western Illinois University, Macomb, IL
Cycling
Sledding–Skeleton (Cresta Run) Tobogganing

Kirsti Pedersen
Finnmark College, Alta, Norway
Sled Dog Racing

Gertrud Pfister
Freie Universitat Berlin, Berlin, Germany
Ainsworth, Dorothy Sears
Beauty
Beese, Amelie
Bergmann, Gretel
Diem, Liselott
Germany
Henoch, Lilli
Mayer, Helene
Motherhood
Profé, Alice
Puberty
Religion
Streicher, Margarete

Sharon Phillips
Women and Sport Australian Sports Commission,
Belconnen, Australia
Australia

Gunter A. Pilz
Universitat Hannover, Hanover, Germany
Aggression

Sarah Pink
University of Derby, Derby, England
Bullfighting
Cintrón, Conchita

Barbara Pinto Green
Fredericksburg, VA
Cockfighting

Brenda G. Pitts
Florida State University, Tallahassee, FL
Gay Games

Lynda B. Ransdell
University of Kentucky, Lexington, KY
Mountain Biking

Gerald Redmond
University of Alberta, Edmonton, Alberta, Canada
Commonwealth Games
Highland Games

Shirley H. M. Reekie
San Jose State University, San Jose, CA
Sailing

Justine E. Reel
University of North Carolina, Chapel Hill, NC
Cheerleading

Maarten Reilingh
Taekwondo

Hai Ren
Beijing University of Physical Education, Beijing, China
Asian Games
Tai Chi
Tug-of-War
Wushu

Roland Renson
Catholic University, Lourain, Belgium
Belgium

James Riordan
University of Surrey, Guildford, Surrey, England
Russia and Belarus
Ukraine
Worker Sports

Gianna Rivola
Brisighella, Italy
Motorcycle Racing

Janet Robertson
Boulder, CO
Mountaineering

Mariá Graciela Rodríguez
Argentina

M. Karen Ruder
Castleton State College, Castleton, VT
Competition

Charlotte Bradley Rues
Mexico

Bettina Rulofs
Media

Jaime S. Ruud
Nutrition

Supitr Samahito
Kasetsart University, Thailand
Thailand

Gopal Sankaran
West Chester University, West Chester, PA
Sexual Harassment

Kimberly S. Schimmel
Kent State University, Kent, OH
Ownership

Angela Schneider
University of Western Ontario, London, Ontario, Canada
Rowing
Values and Ethics

Eugenia S. Scott
Butler University, Indianapolis, IN
Goalball

Dahn Shaulis
University of Nevada, Reno, NV
Pedestrianism

Christine M. Shelton
Smith College, Northampton, MA
Coaching
Colombia

Teoh Chin Sim
Singapore Sports Council
Singapore

Susie Simcock
World Squash Federation, Hastings, Great Britain
Squash

Mari-Kristin Sisjord
Norwegian University of Sport and Physical Education
Wrestling

Diane Skoss
Berkeley Heights, NJ
Aikido

Shana Stalker
Berkshire Reference Works, Great Barrington, MA
Hamm, Mia

Mary Zeiss Stange
Skidmore College, Saratoga Springs, NY
Hunting

Linda S. Stanley
*University of British Columbia, Vancouver,
British Columbia, Canada*
Hockey, Floor
Innebandy
Swimming, Open-Water

B. James Starr
Howard University, Washington D.C.
Duathlon

Brian Stoddart
*University of New England, New South Wales,
Australia*
Caribbean

Nancy L. Struna
University of Maryland, College Park, Maryland
United States

Mila C. Su
Penn State University, University Park, PA
Hockey, Field
Hockey, Ice

Jorunn Sundgot-Borgen
*The Norwegian University of Sport and Physical
Education*
Eating Disorders

Katalin Szikora
Hungarian University of Physical Education
Hungary

Margaret Talbot
*Leeds Metropolitan University, Leeds, United
Kingdom*
International Association of Physical Education
and Sport for Girls and Women
(IAPESGW)

Angela Teja
Instituto Superiore di Educazione Fisica Stata
Greece, Ancient
Rome, Ancient

Thierry Terret
University of Lyon, Lyon, France
France
Polo, Water
Swimming, Distance
Swimming, Speed

Nancy Theberge
*University of Waterloo, Waterloo, Ontario,
Canada*
Community

Lee Thompson
Osaka Gakuin University
Sumo Wrestling

Jeffrey R. Tishman
U.S. Fencing Coaches Association, New York, NY
Fencing

Jan Todd
University of Texas, Austin, TX
Powerlifting
Roberts, Kate
Weightlifting

John Townes
Pittsfield, MA
Arm Wrestling
Speedboating

Else Trangbaek
University of Copenhagen, Copenhagen, Denmark
Denmark
Ling Gymnastics

Wray Vamplew
De Montfort University, Leicester, England
Horse Racing

Patricia Vertinsky
*University of British Columbia, Vancouver,
British Columbia, Canada*
Aging

Kevin Vicroy
U.S. Olympic Committee
Racquetball

Karin A. E. Volkwein
West Chester University, West Chester, PA
Sexual Harassment

Erik De Vroede
Instituut voor Lichamelijke Opleiding
Sportswear Industry

Barbara T. Waite
Coralville, IA
Self-Esteem
Stress and Stress Management

Wanda Ellen Wakefield
State University of New York, Brockport, NY
Military Sports
Sexuality

Edward J. (Ted) Wallbutton
World Squash Federation, Hastings, Great Britain
Squash

Amanda Weaver
Queensland, Australia
Cricket
Joy, Nancy

Ingomar Weiler
Institut fur Alte Geschichte und Altertumskun
Mythology

Moni Wekesa
Special Olympics, Inc.
Namibia

Belinda Wheaton
Roehampton Institute, London, England
United Kingdom
Windsurfing

Anita White
The Sports Council
Brighton Declaration
Windhoek Call for Action

Valerie J. Ludwig Willman
Valparaiso University, Valparaiso, IN
Baton Twirling
Motivation

Wayne Wilson
Amateur Athletic Foundation
El Moutawakel, Nawal
Magazines

Suzanne Wise
Appalachian State University, Boone, NC
Auto Racing
Guthrie, Janet
Muldowney, Shirley

Mark Wood
Hingis, Martina

Janet Woolum
Arizona State University, Phoenix, AZ
Evert, Chris
King, Billie Jean
Seles, Monica

Alison M. Wrynn
State University of New York, Cortland, NY
Lifeguarding

Ying Wu
Millersville University, Millersville, PA
Association for Intercollegiate Athletics for
    Women
Intercollegiate Athletics
Intramural Sports

Yan Xuening
Fu Mingxia
Yang Xiuqiong

Rita Yerkes
Aurora University, Aurora, IL
Wilderness Adventure

ABBOTT, MARGARET

(1878–1955)

U.S. GOLFER

Although she was not a competitive athlete, Margaret Abbott nonetheless entered and won the women's golf competition in the Paris Olympic Games of 1900, attributing her victory to the fact that she dressed appropriately for the sport.

Abbott was born and raised in the Chicago area and apparently learned to play golf at the Chicago Golf Club in Wheaton, Illinois. In 1899, she went to Paris to study art, accompanied by her mother, Mary Ives Abbott, a novelist and literary editor. The following year, she and her mother both entered the women's golf competition at the Paris Olympic Games. A total of ten women competed in the nine-hole event, played at the Société de Sport de Compiègne, and Abbott's score of forty-seven was good enough to win the event, for which she received a porcelain bowl. Pauline Whittier of the United States was second with a forty-nine, and Daria Pratt, also of the United States, finished third with a fifty-five. Abbott later credited her victory to the fact that she had dressed appropriately, while the French competitors had played in high heels and tight skirts. This was Abbott's only competitive golf experience; as far as can be determined, she never played competitive golf again.

While in Paris, Abbott met the writer and humorist Finley Peter Dunne (1867–1936), whom she married in 1902. They had four children and lived among the literary elite in New York City, spending an occasional winter in Palm Beach. In the early 1930s, they moved to Los Angeles, where a few years later their son Philip (b. 1908) came to pursue a successful career as a Hollywood screenwriter, producer, and director. Abbott died in Greenwich, Connecticut.

John E. Findling

Bibliography

Wallechinsky, David. (1996) *The Complete Book of the Summer Olympics.* New York: Little, Brown.

ACROBATICS

Acrobatics is the practice and sport of performing unusual and difficult physical feats, known as elements, sometimes in a choreographed sequence, either alone or in a group. Acrobats are a select group of highly skilled, agile athletes adept in balancing on their hands and feet and somersaulting in the air and on the ground. Acrobatic performances range from the simple to the "death-defying," a term used today to describe circus acts or some of the emerging activities subsumed under such "extreme sports" as in-line skating, skateboarding, and freestyle skiing. These and other developing sports have acrobatic components, including a variety of aerial rotations. Such gyrations of the body about the hip-to-hip axis, known generally as somersaulting, and rotations around the long axis of the body (twisting) have become defining elements of activities described as acrobatic in nature.

HISTORY

Tumbling is the most ancient form of acrobatics. Varieties of tumbling were associated with the religious rituals of ancient peoples, and drawings found on various media before the written word confirm that ancient peoples knew some elements of acrobatics well and that both men and women performed them. Egyptian hieroglyphics show women performing back bends, cartwheels, and somersaults. The famous dance of Salomé described in the Bible was likely a combination of acrobatics and dance.

The Greeks coined the term *akrobates*, literally, walking on tiptoes, suggesting extremes of human

Chinese acrobat, 1989. (Alison Wright/Corbis)

for foot races in the ancient Olympics. Eventually the course for races became an oval, a rough ancestor of the modern stadium. Races for horses devised by the Greeks were staged in a hippodrome, literally a racecourse for horses. The Roman circus (from the Greek *kirkos,* meaning a "circle" or "ring") emerged as a combination of the stadium and hippodrome and contained enough seats to accommodate thousands. The ring remains an important part of the traveling circus, which has one to three rings under a large tent. Roman structures for such activities were much bigger than the more modest athletic facilities devised by the Greeks. The Circus Maximus included four-horse chariot racing, and spectators wagered on the outcome.

Gnaeus Pompeius Magnus, better known as Pompey, a popular Roman general who led the Roman legions to multiple legendary victories, founded the Circus Maximus around 50 BCE. Pompey financed this forerunner of the modern circus to gain support for his desire to rule Rome. He produced an extravaganza that included a battle among lions, elephants, and condemned criminals who were released into the arena, and resulted in a bloody spectacle. In the modern circus, lions and elephants are still displayed. Pompey's circus also featured acrobatic feats of great daring and dexterity presented to appeal to the masses and to cultivate support for the ambitious general. The circus' advance publicity and parade attracted 150,000 Romans.

When Christianity took hold in Europe, acrobatic activity was discouraged, with some proclaiming it sinful, and it was relegated to migrating troupes of entertainers from the Dark Ages until the Renaissance. During the Renaissance, gymnastics was divided into two distinct schools of thought and practice. One group was medical gymnastics, which included physical exercise for purposes of health. The second was gymnastics for its own sake; an attempt to explore the limits of human movement. Acrobatics and the circus were included in this second group.

During the Enlightenment, the circus reemerged in the form of small wandering troupes of performers. Over the centuries, these groups gradually increased in size and developed a more regular circuit of performances, with The Ringling Brothers and Barnum & Bailey circuses being well-

movement. Some experts believe that death-defying acrobatics were associated with funeral rites. A *salto mortale,* or "death leap," may be derived from such practices. A *salto mortale* is, in modern terms, a somersault. It is performed either backward or forward. The performer leaves the ground from a run, turns 360 degrees in the air, and lands on the feet. Since the performer cannot see the landing on a front somersault, it conforms more to the idea of a "death leap."

The Chinese, Egyptians, and Greeks all left recorded evidence of acrobatic activity. The acrobatics of the bull leaper of Knossos, Crete, is well known and resembles feats of the modern rodeo clown. Some researchers believe one or two of the figures displayed in the Minoan fresco of the bull leaper were women.

The Greek stadium was based on the *stade,* a course of 185 meters (203 yards) in length, laid out

CIRQUE DU SOLEIL

Modern circus companies use acrobats and perhaps the best-known of these is the Cirque du Soleil, which was founded in Quebec in 1984. The company employs over 450 performers including acrobats who climb poles, perform on trampolines, perform in pairs, and do balancing and contortion acts. The Cirque du Soleil is headquartered in Montreal, has a permanent show in Las Vegas, and has performed in 123 cities around the world. Altogether, it is estimated that some 23 million people have seen Cirque du Soleil acrobatic performances.

known examples. One of the latter's most famous stars was Lillian Lietzel (Lillian Alize Pelikan), who could do twenty-seven pull-ups with her right arm followed by seventeen with her left.

RULES AND PLAY

Gymnastic competition, the first of the modern acrobatic sports, initially appeared for an international audience at the Olympic Games in 1896. Organized competition in sport acrobatics has existed since the 1973 founding of the International Federation of Sports Acrobatics (IFSA). Organizers of the IFSA decided very early not to sponsor any events employing apparatus—neither heavy apparatus such as the parallel bars nor hand apparatus such as clubs, wands, and hoops. The one exception has been the use of a variety of tumbling surfaces and a floor or platform similar to that used in artistic gymnastics and rhythmic sport gymnastics. The platform is used for all events but tumbling. Sport acrobatics appeals to men and women of all sizes. In 1999 the IFSA merged with the larger International Gymnastics Federation (FIG). The FIG is now the international governing body for artistic, rhythmic, acrobatic, aerobic, and general gymnastics.

The IFSA sponsors a number of acrobatic disciplines in competition. The first is tumbling for men and women. In this, participants get three passes, or runs, down the 25-meter (27.5-yard) track and must do (1) a somersaulting pass, (2) a twisting pass, and (3) a combined pass that involves both somersaulting and twisting. The second discipline, for men, women, and mixed pairs, consists of routines, set to music, of balancing and throwing of partners. One, called an "understander," involves a "top mounter" who performs a variety of handstands and is thrown, or "pitched," by the larger partner. The third discipline is women's trios, which involves a variety of balancing and pyramids. The fourth is men's fours, a variety of "four highs," constructed with three men supported by a fourth. It is not unusual to see the lightest man performing a one-hand stand on the head of the third man.

Tumbling has been one of the strongest sports in the United States, with U.S. gymnastic and tumbling governing bodies sponsoring more tumbling competitions than any other country for more than 100 years. The one time it was an event in the Olympics (1932), three contenders from the United States won the gold, silver, and bronze medals—Rowland Wolfe, Eddie Gross, and William Herrmann, respectively. American women have also been prominent in tumbling. Judy Wills was the first international champion in both trampolining and tumbling, and won the first five world championships on the trampoline (1964–1968). Barbara Galleher Tonry won an amazing six straight national titles, with a total of nine titles in the 1950s and 1960s.

In the modern circus, acrobats perform all kinds of feats on creative apparatus and on horseback. The well-known Canadian Cirque de Soleil (circus of the sun), founded in 1984, has performed on three continents. The Cirque recruits acrobats from all over the world who are skilled at pole climbing, bungee jumping, teeter board, trampoline work, balancing, contortions, and two-acrobat displays.

CONCLUSION

Over several thousand years, acrobatics has evolved from a ritual practice to a modern sport. The intricate tumbling passes of the modern platform tumbler performing multiple twisting somersaults illustrate the never-ending quest for complexity in sport acrobatics.

A. B. Frederick

See also Gymnastics

Bibliography

Joseph, Ludwig H. (1949) "Gymnastics from the Middle Ages to the 18th Century." *Ciba Symposia* 10 (March–April): 30.

May, Earl Chapin. (1963) *The Circus from Rome to Ringling.* New York: Dover Publications.

Robinson, Rachel Sargent. (1955) "Sources for the History of Greek Athletics." Cincinnati, OH: the author.

Simons, Minot, II. (1995) *Women's Gymnastics: A History.* Carmel, CA: Welwyn Publishing Co.

Touny, Ahmed E. (n.d.) *Sports History with Ancient Egyptians.* The Egyptian Olympic Committee.

ADMINISTRATION

Administration, or management, is about getting things done and in sports involves the management of people, things, places, events, and time. Prior to the passage of Title IX in the United States in 1972, women played a major role in the management of women's sports and women's intercollegiate athletics in the United States but virtually no role in the management of men's sports. Since then, women have continued to play a very limited role in men's sports and international sports administration, and their role in the management of women's sports has decreased.

THE STATUS OF WOMEN AS ATHLETIC LEADERS

With the advent of Title IX and the explosion of opportunities for female athletes, there was an ironic decline in the number of women serving both as coaches and administrators in athletic programs for women. Prior to Title IX, the percentage of women serving as intercollegiate coaches in female athletics programs exceeded 90 percent. Six years later, in 1978, the year of mandatory Title IX compliance, the percentage of

women serving as coaches had dropped to 58.2. In 1998, the percentage was 47.4.

The data on secondary school sport administration mirror those at the intercollegiate level. Prior to Title IX, many female educators were indeed coaching their female students' teams not for the pay but for the love of sport and commitment to their female students. In most instances, the female physical education teachers volunteered their time to give quality sport experiences to the female students who wished to participate in sport beyond their regular physical education classes. Often the efforts of those volunteering their time and expertise went unnoticed by the school administrators and the communities being served.

Before Title IX, few men considered coaching female sports teams. However, Title IX brought an infusion of monetary support and prestige to female sports and more attention to those who served as coaches. The changes in benefits thus enticed more men to enter the female sport arena as coaches.

The same fate, although more devastating, has fallen upon women who serve as athletic administrators. Again, prior to 1972, 90 percent of female programs were administered by women. After the mandated compliance date of 1978, the percentage of head female athletic administrators dropped to 20 percent in 1980 and to 15 percent in 1986.

Although programs for women continue to increase, opportunities for female administrators have continued to decrease. In 1998, only 19.4 percent of women's intercollegiate programs were directed by women. Even more startling, no women at all were involved in any administrative capacity in one out of five programs in the same year. Also in 1998, women held only 38 percent of the administrative positions in women's programs. This figure represents an all-time high since the 1978 mandated compliance with Title IX. In the National Collegiate Athletic Association, it is more likely for a woman to be the head of an athletics program in the smaller colleges of Division III than in the larger Division I schools.

Perceptions about the causes of the decrease in the number of women serving as coaches and administrators differ according to gender. Men and women both agree that women tend to "burn

JUDY LEVERING, FIRST FEMALE PRESIDENT OF THE U.S. TENNIS ASSOCIATION (USTA)

The first female president in the 118-year history of the United States Tennis Association (USTA) was Judy Levering who was elected to the position in January, 1999. In 1997–1998 she had served the association as first vice-president. Never a ranked or professional tennis player, Levering began playing as a young girl in a public park across from her home in Kansas City. After her children were born she became involved in youth tennis and the National Junior Tennis League and then with the regional and the national tennis association. A lifelong player, she draws on her own experience with tennis to promote youth and community tennis as a sport with both physical and mental benefits. Known as the "Velvet Hammer" because of her persistent but polite style, she was instrumental in having the new stadium at the National Tennis Center in Queens, New York, named for African-American tennis star, Arthur Ashe, rather than for a corporate sponsor.

out" and leave the sport profession earlier than men do. However, men believe there are fewer qualified female coaches and administrators, that they fail to apply for jobs, and that they have greater constraints on their time due to family responsibilities. Women, on the other hand, cite the strength of the "old boys" network, the lack of support systems for females, and discrimination in the hiring process. Another reason may be gender-role stereotyping among athletic administrators. The "homologous reproduction" theory may support this stereotyping tendency among those doing the hiring; that is, the tendency for people in dominant positions to employ in subordinate positions those of like sex as well as other similar characteristics. Indeed, the data show that if a female athletic director is doing the hiring, there will be more female coaches in the program.

Regardless of the perceptions of or reasons for the low number of females serving as coaches and athletic administrators, the lack of visibility for women as leaders in the sport world sends negative messages to young women who may seek professional roles in sports. Perhaps even more important may be the small number of women who can serve as role models to both male and female athletes.

RESPONSIBILITIES OF SPORT ADMINISTRATORS

Administration implies being in charge, being the boss, being the one who is expected to deal with all the day-to-day processes of operating a business or, in this case, a sports-related program. In sport, the term *administration* is slowly being replaced by the term *management*. Few administrators/managers make a distinction between the terms, and thus both terms may be used interchangeably.

Administrators can have positive and negative impacts on people and programs. The role of an administrator is diverse, and the work is neverending. Maintaining perspective and a balanced view of the goals to be achieved by the organization should be a personal goal for all administrators. At times administrators feel overwhelmed with tasks, problems, and people and therefore lose sight of the program's goals. Not everyone can be an effective administrator. To be successful an individual must be people-oriented, a good listener, able to deal with difficult situations and make difficult decisions, and have good planning, organizational, and leadership skills. Other traits—such as a sense of humor, common sense, integrity, the ability to deal with stress and long hours, and the willingness to try innovative ideas (methods)—are also needed. Perhaps one of the most important elements in administration is creating an atmosphere of trust between management and staff members. Additionally, successful administrators let their staff members know they are valued and important team members who are capable of making decisions on their own. When all members of an organization can say "we did it together," that organization is more likely to grow strong and become a model for excellence.

Among the responsibilities and tasks that administrators perform are the following:

- Establish program goals and create a plan for achievement.

- Select and put into place the sport activities that will be a part of the program.

- Create job descriptions for each member of the athletics/sport staff.

- Hire needed personnel, such as additional administrative staff, coaches, assistant coaches, team physician(s), athletic trainers, and other staff as needed.

- Create job evaluation tools for all personnel, measure and monitor individual performances, hold formal and individual evaluation conferences in a timely fashion.

- In conjunction with the staff, create and establish policies and procedures for the entire program.

- In conjunction with the staff, create codes of conduct for all members of the staff and athletes.

- Hold and chair sport department meetings on a regular basis.

- Interact with other campus administrators and become involved with campus-wide events.

- Create an efficient, friendly, and responsive front office.

- Prepare and monitor an equitable budget.

- Purchase medical insurance for student athletes or make other arrangements for medical coverage.

- Create an equitable public relations program.

- Adhere to eligibility standards for athletes established by sports governing bodies.

- Purchase all necessary sports-related equipment and office supplies and devise a method to control inventory.

- Plan, prepare, and schedule contests for teams.

- Plan and schedule transportation, accommodations, and meals for "away" contests.

- Schedule practice times and facilities for all teams.

- Schedule facilities and support personnel, and prepare procedures, for home games.

- Schedule necessary security for practices and games.

- Secure game officials for all home games.

- Become professionally involved in league and conference meetings and activities.

- Encourage and/or require coaches and other staff members to join and be contributing members of professional organizations.

The above listing of responsibilities is by no means inclusive. There are countless matters that must be handled on a daily basis. Big and small matters may arise at a moment's notice. The head administrator should not attempt to solve all problems but should recognize the problems that can be delegated to other staff members. If an administrator attempts to deal with everything, she may lose sight of the big picture, and the result will be a program in chaos.

ADMINISTRATIVE STYLES

All administrators have individual leadership styles that fit their personalities. While there are as many styles as there are administrators, most can be classified into four generally accepted categories. An *autocratic* administrator is a nononsense leader who makes all the decisions without input or consultation from other staff members. This type of administrator is dictatorial and rules through fear. Workers do as they are told, creativity is nonexistent, and turnover is great.

The *democratic* administrator seeks inclusiveness and listens to staff members when critical decisions need to be made. All opinions and ideas are discussed in an open forum, and the final decision is made by the group rather than the administrator. The staff will feel that the program is the result of everyone working together; thus energy and creativity will abound and the program will have the ability to progress.

The *laissez-faire* administrator is very relaxed, with an essential philosophy of "live and let live." All individuals in the organization are given the latitude to fulfill their responsibilities in their own ways. There is very little direction and almost no accountability; some employees will flourish while others will flounder. The possibility of the program falling into utter chaos is great.

The *eclectic* leader discards the negative and weak aspects of the various leadership styles while adopting the strong points and using them to advantage.

In addition to using a leadership style that works for the individual and program, the sport administrator must have a working knowledge of many team and individual sports, as well as understanding the personality types of the participants and the coaches. The administrator needs to have the ability to work with and supervise individuals with diverse backgrounds and to balance diplomacy with strength.

To date, nearly all research on leadership and management—both within and outside sports—has focused on men. Little is known about women as managers and if and how they differ from their male counterparts, including possible differences in management style. This is an important topic for future management research.

R. Vivian Acosta

See also Management; Title IX; Unionism

An 1893 Palais de Glace advertisement featuring an anonymous woman, far removed from today's celebrity endorsements. (Historical Picture Archive/Corbis)

ADOLESCENCE *see* Puberty

ADVERTISING

For more than a century, physically attractive men and women have been used in advertisements. As sports became an increasingly important part of people's lives, more and more advertisements associated athletes with goods and services offered for sale. The anonymous athletes featured in early advertisements–such as the smiling female ice-skater in Jules Cheret's 1893 poster for the Palais de Glace (in Paris)–have gradually been replaced by well-known sports heroes and heroines. The heroes earn more for their explicit or implicit endorsements than the heroines do, but the difference in earnings is smaller than it was.

Coca-Cola's first advertisements, in 1905, posed a handsome young man with golf clubs next to a lovely young girl dressed for tennis. In the 1930s and 1940s, famed swimmers like Maureen O'Sullivan and Helen Madison touted Coca-Cola. In 1948, high-jumper Alice Coachman, the first African American woman to win an

Olympic championship, posed with a smile and a Coke.

Track and field star Mildred "Babe" Didrikson jeopardized her amateur status in 1932 when she endorsed Dodge automobiles, but the collapse of the amateur rule in the 1980s brought a flood of endorsements for every imaginable product. It was no surprise when Florence Griffith-Joyner endorsed Mizuno sporting goods, but she also urged her myriad Japanese admirers to use Aga film, Proxy shoes, Mitsubishi appliances, Toshiba copiers, and LNJ toys. Figure skaters like Sonja Henie, Dorothy Hamill, Katarina Witt, Kristi Yamaguchi, and Nancy Kerrigan, who combine athletic talent with sexual attractiveness, have been similarly successful in attracting commercial sponsors in the United States and abroad.

That female athletes are often erotically attractive as well as athletically talented has led some feminists to denounce their appearance in advertisements as degrading and pornographic. In a similar but somewhat less radical vein, Susan Bordo has analyzed a number of advertisements in which the slender bodies of athletic women are depicted and concluded that such idealized images are coercive and contribute to the eating disorders rampant among young women. On the other hand, beach volleyball player Gabrielle Reece has proclaimed her right to market her athletic good looks in any way that she chooses. As long as advertisements featuring physically attractive female athletes continue to sell everything from milk to motorcycles, criticism of the practice is likely to be ineffective.

Allen Guttmann

Bibliography

Bordo, Susan. (1993) *Unbearable Weight.* Berkeley: University of California Press.

Reece, Gabrielle, and Karen Karbo. (1997) *Big Girl in the Middle.* New York: Crown.

AEROBICS

Aerobics is an exercise form that has come to mean a choreographed routine, done to music, that stimulates heart rate and respiration while toning muscles. Aerobics is generally done in a class, although many people also exercise along with videotapes. The name itself is a derivative of *aerobic*, which means "with oxygen." Worldwide in appeal, aerobics is both a popular mass fitness activity and a competitive sport. This diversity grew out of its origins in the United States.

HISTORY

The word *aerobics* first appeared to the fitness world in 1968, when Kenneth Cooper, a doctor in the United States Air Force, published his book *Aerobics.* Cooper was concerned about the increased heart disease rates and decreased physical activity rates of Americans. He developed a training system, called aerobics, that included a variety of exercises that stimulated heart and lung activity for a time period sufficiently long to produce beneficial changes in the body. Millions took up Cooper's "aerobic challenge," which was mostly associated with running. Nevertheless, despite a growing number of these fitness enthusiasts, many women, like Cooper's wife Mildred, did not seem to enjoy running. Aerobic dancing developed as one alternative to running for women interested in improving their physical fitness.

Women around the world have always exercised to music. Asian dance forms, Finnish women's gymnastics, Swedish gymnastics, and different forms of folk dancing have inspired women to move. American women had exercised to music in YMCAs or YWCAs or while watching Jack LaLanne's daily half-hour televised exercise program, but aerobic dance was institutionalized simultaneously but separately by Jacki Sorensen and Judi Sheppard Missett in 1969. These two women were the first to establish nationwide fitness businesses. Both of their programs derived heavily from dance. Sorensen's aerobic dancing used popular ballroom and folk dance steps to apply the principles of Cooper's aerobic exercise programs to music; Sheppard Missett, a former dance teacher, simplified jazz dance movements into nontechnical "jazzercise" classes. These early aerobics classes emphasized the enjoyment of dancing and the playful nature of women's exercise.

After Sorensen and Sheppard Missett had generated considerable interest, different aerobics gurus and fitness specialists popularized their own aerobics workouts. Among the most influential was Richard Simmons's program, which was started in the 1970s. The emphasis in Simmons's exercise programs, however, shifted from dance and fun to the weight-loss benefits of exercise. Consequently, aerobics began to be closely connected with improved appearance.

Aerobics gained popularity steadily among American women in the following years, but it did not take off as a mass movement until the actress Jane Fonda entered the fitness field. Fonda's success was largely based on the premise of aerobics as a "body shaper." She provided a widely distributed image that enabled aerobics to grow into a mass cultural phenomenon. Women all over the world still read the exercise advice in Fonda's *Workout Book* (1981) and follow her exercise videotapes. Her early exercise programs consisted primarily of resistance exercises for differ-

An aerobics class works out using glides. (Ken Redding/Corbis)

ent parts of the body performed in one spot. Therefore, although Fonda encouraged her participants to work hard and discipline themselves to obtain the desired body changes, her programs did not, in the true sense of the word, contain aerobic exercises. Fonda's early workouts were seriously criticized as unsuitable for ordinary exercises. Her later videotapes aimed to avoid harmful, contraindicated movements. However, Fonda created an important new concept for aerobics: celebrity "self-help" exercise books and videos. Today many female celebrities (for example, Cindy Crawford and Elle MacPherson) promote their own exercise programs. These beautiful women employ professional fitness experts to design and demonstrate in their programs, thus further cementing the notion that aerobics is a means to an improved body. When aerobics became a means to the perfect body, it also became increasingly commercialized, professionalized, institutionalized, and specialized.

The commercial nature of aerobics was intensified through high injury rates that plagued the sport in the early 1980s. A study conducted by the American Aerobics Association in 1981 and 1982 showed that 55 percent of the participants and 80 percent of the instructors suffered from injuries, mostly of the legs. Shoe manufacturers responded quickly by creating shoes designed to the specific needs of aerobics. Reebok quickly captured the expanding aerobics market. Nike at one point dismissed the aerobics market but later launched an extensive advertising campaign specifically targeting women and by the 1990s had become one of the leaders in aerobics-wear production. Many other manufacturers compete for a share of the huge aerobics shoe and apparel market.

The high injury rate also drove the leaders of the industry to develop new forms of aerobics. The earliest development was the creation of low-impact aerobics to reduce lower-limb injuries. Unlike high-impact aerobics, which involved jumping, hopping, and running, during the low-impact class one foot was always kept on the ground to eliminate the stress on knees, shins, and ankles. Therefore, low-impact classes meant safer workouts.

This notion of safety underlined the next important development within aerobics. Step aerobics, created by Gin Miller as a rehabilitation program for her own knee injury, became immensely popular. Miller developed her idea in connection with Reebok, which manufactured the platforms (and special shoes) needed for this exercise form. Miller promoted worldwide her format of stepping up and down from the platform with different, choreographed patterns.

Improved instructor training, as well as new types of shoes and exercises, were part of the development toward safer aerobics. In 1982 Kathy and Peter Davis created IDEA (International Dance Exercise Association, now called International Association of Fitness Professionals) to provide fitness professionals easier access to fitness information. Since then, IDEA has grown to 23,000 members in eighty-three countries. In 1986 the three main North American associations for fitness professionals—Aerobic and Fitness Association of America (AFAA), American College of Sports Medicine (ACSM), and IDEA—started designing criteria for national certification for aerobics instructors. Many other certifying programs were subsequently instituted around the world.

Besides instructor training and certification, an important function for fitness organizations is to convene annual fitness conventions that serve as platforms to disseminate new information in the field. The first IDEA convention was held in 1985. Following the example of the United States, fitness professionals in different countries created their own formal organizations to establish training standards for the industry and provide information for their members through professional magazines and conventions. In 1983, Americans Karen and Howard Schwartz founded the National Aerobic Championship and developed aerobics into a competitive sport.

RULES AND PLAY

The first aerobics competitions were held in the United States in 1984. These national aerobics championships led to the staging of the first world aerobics championships, held in 1990 in conjunction with the IDEA international convention. The original judging criteria were based on the Olympic sports of gymnastics and figure skating. The aerobics competition routine lasts two

Step aerobics is a popular workout in health clubs. (Duomo/Corbis)

presentation (artistic excellence), technical merit, and difficulty.

CONCLUSION

As aerobics evolved into a formally organized, commercialized, and professionalized industry, the meaning of the term became increasingly blurred. In the late 1990s, some fitness professionals preferred the term *group exercise* to *aerobics*. This is because instructor-led exercise-to-music classes have diversified to include equipment-based exercise (such as indoor cycling and circuit training with multiple pieces of equipment), water fitness, and body–mind training (such as nonimpact aerobics, yoga, and tai-chi). New group exercise forms include sport movement and sport training techniques.

This development also attracted more men into group exercise. In addition, new, specialized fitness classes catered to the needs of children, pregnant women, and older adults. Group exercise participants work out for varied reasons. Although many still attend classes to slim and tone their bodies, group exercise classes have the potential to emphasize other, more achievable exercise benefits such as better mobility, functionality, fun, and social interaction.

Pirkko Markula

Bibliography

Aerobic Dance-Exercise Instructor Manual. (1987) IDEA Foundation.

Cole, Cheryl L., and Amy Hribar. (1995) "Celebrity Feminism: Nike Style, Sport-Fordism, Transcendence, and Consumer Power." *Sociology of Sport Journal* 12: 269–347.

Cooper, Kenneth H. (1968) *Aerobics.* New York: Simon & Schuster.

Fonda, Jane. (1981) *Jane Fonda's Workout Book.* New York: Simon & Schuster.

Kagan, Elizabeth, and Margaret Morse. (1988) "The Body Electronic: Aerobic Exercise on Video." *The Drama Review* 32: 164–180.

Markula, Pirkko. (1995) "Firm But Shapely, Fit But Sexy, Strong But Thin: The Postmodern Aerobicizing Female Bodies." *Sociology of Sport Journal* 12: 424–453.

Ryan, Patricia. (1997) "Beyond Aerobics." *IDEA Today* (July–August): 60–71.

Sorensen, Jacki. (1979) *Aerobic Dancing.* New York: Rawson, Wade.

minutes and includes compulsory exercises (four consecutive, stationary, and identical repetitions of jumping jacks, alternate high leg kicks, and push-ups), obligatory exercises, and creative exercises. The competitors are judged based on skill (strength, flexibility, execution) and presentation (choreography, showmanship, appearance).

Two organizations, the Association of National Aerobic Championships Worldwide (ANAC) and the International Aerobics Federation (IAF), have held worldwide aerobics competitions. In 1997, the International Gymnastics Federation (FIG) adopted competitive aerobics, now sportaerobics, as a new discipline that was recognized by the International Olympic Committee (IOC). Following this recognition, the judging criteria of sportaerobics changed to resemble Olympic gymnastics: competitors now score for

Tarantin, Elaine. (1992) "Aerobic Competition Yesterday, Today and Tomorrow." *IDEA Today* (July–August): 49–52.

AFGHANISTAN

Afghanistan is located in West Asia at the crossroads of Asia and Europe. Following twenty years of revolution against Soviet control and internal political turmoil, the size of the population is unknown but was estimated at about 23 million in 1999. During the period of British control, which began in 1880, women were discouraged from participating in sports because physical exercise was seen as unladylike and detrimental to good health.

When Afghanistan gained its independence from Great Britain in 1919, the new government strove to modernize the country. Part of this involved developing physical education programs for girls based on the belief that such programs would improve women's health and therefore strengthen the nation. Volleyball and basketball programs were instituted in every girls' high school, and teams from different schools competed regularly. At the university level, intramural team sports were introduced at Kabul University, and physical education was offered as a program at Kabul Polytechnic Institute. In the mid-1970s, the government announced an ambitious agenda to further develop sports for girls and women by building facilities and funding programs for swimming, tennis, table tennis, badminton, and gymnastics. Women who graduated from the sports program at Kabul Polytechnic would supervise the women's programs. However, in 1978, following a bloody coup that overthrew the republic, the nation's political structure began to collapse as factions began fighting for political power. The Soviet Union intervened by sending troops, who remained until 1989. Under these circumstances, programs such as those for women's sports could no longer be supported by the government.

In the post-Soviet struggle for political control, the Taliban, a fundamentalist Muslim movement with social, political, and religious elements, controlled almost the entire nation by 1999. In accord with their Muslim beliefs, they restricted the role of women in Afghan society, and women were no longer permitted to participate in sports in public. As a result, Afghan women have not participated in the two Islamic Solidarity Council Women's Games in Iran. No Afghan woman has ever competed in the Olympics. As long as the Taliban dominates the nation, prospects for women's sports look limited at best.

The Editors

Bibliography

Rahimi, Fahima. (1977) "Women in Afghanistan: A Progress Report." *Kabul Times*. Kabul, Afghanistan.

AFRICA

The opportunity for girls and women to participate in sports in African nations and in regional and international competitions has been increasing since the 1980s. However, in many African nations these opportunities remain limited and, compared to other nations, women's sport in Africa is still in the early stages of development. Girls and women in Africa face many historical, psychological, social, and cultural barriers when it comes to participating fully in sports and fitness activities. Thus, while a young girl is at school, sometimes until she is twenty, she is encouraged and able to participate in sports, but after that, her environment, parents, husband, religion, and other sociocultural barriers will make it very difficult for her to continue.

BARRIERS TO WOMEN'S PARTICIPATION

The many barriers that have limited women's participation in sport can be divided into three chronological categories: traditional barriers that existed before European colonization, new barriers resulting from colonization, and postcolonial barriers.

Prior to colonization, women in many African societies played a variety of roles, with many women heavily involved in the growing and processing of food in addition to caring for the home and children. Women performed as much as 60 to 80 percent of the agricultural work in many African societies. In most societies women worked harder than men, had far less leisure time, and participated less in activities outside the home or family group, such as in government or religion. Not surprisingly, women's participation in sport was also limited, and anthropologists who studied African societies in the early twentieth century say little about women in sports. The only exception is wrestling, as some women in societies in West Africa did wrestle, both against one another in harvest festivals and against their new husbands as part of the marriage ritual. In general, though, women's participation in recreational or competitive physical activity was minimal and was restricted mostly to games such as *allan barka* (a pulling and throwing game), *aku agbe* (hide and seek), and *sue* (a balancing game).

European (British, French, German, Portuguese, Spanish, Belgian, and Italian) colonial control, which influenced African life from the mid-nineteenth century to the early 1960s, did little to change the traditional situation other than to repress men's sports and replace them with European ones, such as soccer and cricket and, later, basketball. Women were defined by colonial officials (despite women's agricultural labor) as weak and therefore were not allowed to participate in these sports. Instead, as in traditional times, they were directed toward games such as short egg and lime races and skipping rope. The one major exception to this was the willingness of British colonial officials in some nations to allow women to compete in track and field events, sports that African women in nations such as Nigeria, Mozambique, and Kenya excelled in following the end of colonial rule.

With the end of colonial rule in the 1960s, many African nations experienced a period of economic and political turmoil, and the development of sports was far less important than issues such as poverty, government stability, and ethnic relations. Nonetheless, the leaders of some nations saw success in international sports as a means to enhance their international reputations.

For example, male distance runners from Ethiopia and Kenya became successful in the international sports world.

Less attention was given to women's sports, and it was not until the 1980s in some nations and the 1990s in others that women began demanding a sport agenda for women. Several factors were involved in the emergence of this interest in women's sport. One was the international feminist movement. Another was the spread of international sport culture to Africa though videos, music, and television. A third was the recognition by some African women that sport can be a means to escape poverty and domination by men. For example, a survey of students at the University of Ife in Nigeria in 1984 showed that 90 percent viewed sports as a means to a better education and 95 percent viewed sports as a means to a better job. They also cited physical fitness as another important reason for participating in sports. Women who saw sports as a means to upward social mobility often ignored traditional sports and opted instead for popular Western sports such as tennis, squash, swimming, equestrian sports, and physical training in health clubs. The same is true for women who competed at the international level in sports such as track and field and basketball, as success often led to living and training in Europe and North America as well as substantial financial rewards.

Despite women's growing interest in sports, many barriers remain to their full participation. Some of these barriers date to traditional times, others to the colonial era, and others are more recent. In addition, they may affect different categories of women (urban/rural, educated/uneducated, upper class/lower class) in different ways. Some of these barriers are cultural definitions of what a woman should look like. For example, the belief in some societies that a thin woman will cause suffering and poverty for her parents and then for her husband hardly encourages young women to engage in physical activities to remain thin. There is also the worry that girls and women can endanger their fertility by developing their muscles through too much exercise or activity. Another obstacle is cultural meanings associated with breast-feeding. In some African societies, the breast-feeding period is often a time of limited physical activity for the

AFRICAN ATHLETES AND TRAINING

Most elite African women athletes who excel in sports such as track, distance running, basketball, soccer, and volleyball train in Europe, Asia, or North America. These locations offer better training facilities, coaches, and support staff as well as the opportunity to participate in major competitions or play for better-paying professional teams. Coaches from Europe and their representatives in Africa routinely scout for potential world-class females athletes in Africa. The All Africa Games are especially important in this regard as they serve as a showcase for the premier athletes on the continent.

mother that may last from one to two years. Also, in many African societies, there is often criticism of women who wear sports outfits and uniforms. People fear that if a women is seen in public in such attire, she will be unable to find a husband. And there is the general concern that sport activities, including practice and competition, will take too much time away from school and family responsibilities.

In some Muslim communities, especially in North Africa, religious beliefs and practices preclude women from participating in sport activities with men and limit the time women can participate in sports among themselves. Even women such as Hassiba Boulmerka of Algeria—the world champion in the 1500-meter distance in 1991 and 1995, and the Olympic champion in 1992—was criticized at home by conservative Muslims for appearing in public with her body partially uncovered. She defended herself by pointing out that her identities as a Muslim and as an athlete required that she dress differently for each. For Muslim women who wish to follow conservative Muslim rules, the Islamic Women's Solidarity Games provide an alternative for international competition.

THE 1990s

The 1990s have been a period of rapid growth for sports in general and for women's sports across much of Africa. Certainly, economic and political problems have stymied or even halted the growth of women's sports in some nations, but on the whole, women's sports have grown more rapidly than ever before at the national, regional, and international levels. At the national level, many nations have taken their first concrete steps to promote women's sports. In twelve nations (Botswana, Gambia, Ghana, Lesotho, Madagascar, Mauritius, Namibia, Seychelles, South Africa, Swaziland, Uganda, and Zimbabwe), either the National Olympic Committee or another national sport organization has endorsed the Brighton Declaration supporting the development of women's sports. Eight nations (Algeria, Chad, Egypt, Ghana, Namibia, Nigeria, Seychelles, South Africa) have formed organizations to deal specifically with women's sport issues at the national level. And several nations, such as Malawi, Zambia, Zimbabwe, Namibia, Swaziland, and Egypt, have instituted policies to ensure that women will be represented in decision-making positions in national sport organizations, although in all African nations (as in nearly all nations), the overwhelming majority of decision-making positions are held by men and coaching opportunities for women remain very limited.

At the regional level, more women participated in the 1995 sixth African Games than ever before, constituting 30 percent of the total contestants. In addition to participating, the world-class women athletes, such as the 800-meter runner Maria Mutola from Mozambique, were used by the Games' organizers to promote the event and attract spectators. Across Africa, track and field, basketball, and soccer are emerging as the major sports for women. At the international level, many African nations have, since independence in the 1960s, been using sports to promote their images in the international community. Promotion of women's sports at this level came later than for men's sports across the continent, but it has been increasing since the 1980s. For example, in 1980 only sixteen African nations sent women to the Olympics, while in 1996 the number had risen to forty-one.

The number of female athletes in the Olympics has increased as well, from 67 in 1984 to 81 in 1988 to 137 in 1992 to 153 in 1996. The nations that sent the largest female delegations in 1996 were South Africa (twenty), Nigeria (fifteen), Angola (fifteen), Zambia (twelve), and Kenya (ten), with most nations sending fewer than five athletes. The majority of African nations send relatively few women to the Olympics, with the teams of over half the nations having 25 percent or fewer female athletes and nine sending no women at all. But, at the same time, of the ten nations in the world whose 1996 Olympic teams were more than 55 percent women, four were in Africa (Angola, Madagascar, Mali, and Zaire). The other six nations were China, Norway, Luxembourg, Albania, Belize, and St. Kitts. Finally, the convening of the second International Conference on Women and Sports in May 1998 at Windhoek, Namibia, was an important real and symbolic statement about the growing interest in women's sport in Africa.

AFRICAN WOMEN IN SPORT ASSOCIATION

The first International Conference on Women and Sports was held in May 1994 in Brighton, England. The conference, entitled "Women, Sport and the Challenge of Change," was attended by 280 delegates from eighty-two countries, representing governmental and nongovernmental organizations, national Olympic committees, international and national sports federations, and educational and research institutions. The conference issued "The Brighton Declaration," which called for active and equal participation for women in all aspects of sports.

One of the international sports organizations at Brighton was the Supreme Council for Sport in Africa, and it was during that conference that a group of African women issued a declaration of intent to create the African Women in Sport Association (AWISA). It was thought that AWISA would be built at the grassroots level and encompass a network of national women's sports associations. It was at the second International Con-

ference on Women and Sports in May 1998 at Windhoek, Namibia, that AWISA was formally launched.

The Supreme Council for Sports in Africa and AWISA are working to overcome the various obstacles discussed earlier and to increase women's participation in the African Games and the Olympics. The African Games, which take place one year before the Olympics, has events for both men and women. AWISA is committed in the years to come to promote equality in all aspects of sports, whether at school, in leisure activities, or at the competitive level, and operates on the belief that "The African woman athlete has no time to spare. . . . She must be ready at any moment . . . to defend her rights against any barrier."

Rabiatou Njoya, David Levinson,
and Mickey Friedman

See also African Games; Cameroon; Egypt; Kenya; Nigeria; South Africa

Bibliography

Adedeji, John A. (1984) "Women's Sport in Developing Countries." *International Council of Sport Science and Physical Education Review* 7: 36–43.

Baker, William J., and James A. Mangan, eds. (1987) *Sport in Africa: Essays in Social History.* New York: Africana.

International Working Group on Women and Sport. (1998) *Women & Sport: From Brighton to Windhoek Facing the Challenge.* London: United Kingdom Sports Council.

Seager, Joni. (1997) *The State of Women in the World Atlas.* 2d ed. London: Penguin Reference.

Wagner, Eric C., ed. (1989) *Sport in Asia and Africa: A Comparative Handbook.* Westport, CT: Greenwood Press.

AFRICAN GAMES

The women of Africa have participated in each edition of the African Games, despite the restrictions of gender expectations, social and economic status, and the influence of Islam. The first African Games in Brazzaville, Congo, in 1965 saw

HOSTING THE AFRICAN GAMES

Nigeria was selected to host the eighth All Africa Games in 2003, thirty years after hosting the 1973 Games. The Games bring much attention to the host nation as they are the premier sporting event for the continent and an important event especially for female athletes. However, hosting the Games is not without controversy; critics note the expense of staging the Games reduces already scarce resources in poor African nations that might be better used to provide basic services to peoples of the nation or to the host city.

women from eighteen countries participate in two sports—athletics and basketball. Men from twenty-nine countries had ten sports to choose from.

As the Games continued, women found more opportunities to participate. In 1973 at the second Games in Lagos, Nigeria, women's swimming was

Hassiba Boulmerka of Algeria. (S. Carmona/Corbis)

added. Egypt's Faten Afifi won four gold medals. In athletics, Ghana's Alice Annum, the 1970 Commonwealth Games winner and sixth-place finisher at the Munich Olympics, won both the 100- and 200-meter events. Volleyball, tennis, and table tennis were included as women's sports in the Games of 1978 in Algiers, Algeria. The star of the Games was swimmer Myriem Mizouni from Tunisia, who won nine gold medals and one bronze in eleven races. Hanna Afriye became the second Ghanaian woman in a row to win both the 100- and 200-meter races on the track. While women participated in a limited number of events, it was rare, but not unheard of, for women to hold coaching and administrative positions in the more progressive African nations. One major exception was the Kenyan Netball Association, which had women in its top six administrative posts, as well as a woman as the national team coach.

Financial difficulties postponed the 1982 games in Nairobi, Kenya, to 1987. Handball was added, giving women seven sports in which to compete. In running events, women from Kenya and Nigeria dominated, taking every gold medal. Nigeria's relay teams broke African records—the 4 × 100 in 43.44.00 and the 4 × 400 in 3:27.08. Susan Sirma won gold for Kenya in the 1500- and 3000-meter events. In 1991 at the Games in Cairo, Egypt, gymnastics was added for women, bringing the total number of sports available for women to eight, still less than half of the seventeen sports by then available for men.

In the early 1990s many women athletes in Africa emerged as international stars in their own right, primarily in track and field. Hassiba Boulmerka (Algeria), Derartu Tulu (Ethiopia), Elena Meyer (South Africa), and Nigeria's 4 × 100-meter relay team all won medals at the 1992 Barcelona Olympic Games. In 1991 Boulmerka became the first woman from Africa to win a world championship in track and field. African Games organizers finally began to advertise the presence of these women champions at the Games in order to draw more spectators.

Women were at the center of controversy at certain points in the 1995 Games in Harare, Zimbabwe. Gender verification became an issue when an Egyptian handball player was accused of being a man. There was an official protest from Egypt that the lace sleeves worn by the South African gymnasts were too sexy. Nonetheless, a positive legacy of the Games in Harare was that programs were begun in Zimbabwe specifically to promote the participation of women and children in sports. The African Games of 1999 were held in Johannesburg, South Africa.

Daniel Bell

Bibliography

Boit, Mike. (1989) "Where Are All the Kenyan Women Runners?" *Olympic Review* (May): 206–210.

Ukah, Matthias. (1990) "Socio-Cultural Forces in Growth of All African Games." *Journal of the International Council for Health, Physical Education and Recreation.* 26, 2:16–20.

AGGRESSION

A study of the literature on aggression can give the impression that aggressive behavior is an innate and unalterable result of sexual differences. Eleanor Maccoby, for instance, calls upon biology to explain the fact that boys are more aggressive than girls. Individualistic, psychological explanations like hers are reductionistic and ignore the social, cultural, and historical causes and conditions of aggressive behavior. Such explanations account neither for the influence of social codes nor for the changes in the balance of power between the sexes. Unlike Maccoby, Norbert Elias pays attention to the codes of gender-specific behavior and to the processes of social change that typically determine not only the relations among

individuals in groups and within social classes but also the inner dynamics of individual personality.

Aggressive expression of the biological variable of "sexuality" is mediated by culture. The fact that men are more aggressive than women says nothing about the ways in which male and female aggression is expressed in various societies, cultures, social classes, and age groups, nor does it begin to explain the varying manifestations of aggression in men's and women's sports. Sex-specific aggression is always conditioned by the historical context and the many different ways that humans have found to live with one another. In short, interpersonal aggression is neither natural nor unalterable. In the final analysis, aggression is determined by power relations within specific social figurations. To the degree that aggression is frequently the result of the inequalities of power between the sexes, less inequality between men and women means less difference in the degree and the forms of the aggressive behavior they exhibit. This is certainly the case in the world of sports.

MODERN UNDERSTANDING OF AGGRESSION IN SPORTS

The problem of aggression in sports can be understood and interpreted only within the context of long-term social trends. In opposition to the common tendency to consider sports as an isolated social phenomenon, Elias considers sports as "manifestations of specific social developments" that will continue to change "in response to future social developments" (1975, 105). According to Elias, the aggression that one sees in today's sports is a more or less socially acceptable and "on the whole moderated incarnation of the impulse to brutal aggression" (1977, 279) that accompanied sports in earlier times. This tendency to mute expressions of physical aggression can be quite clearly discerned in the origin and evolution of the rules and regulations of modern sports. The history of the rules and regulations of any given sport can be seen as the history of the progressive tabooing of physical aggression.

The history of soccer (association football) is a good example. The first written rules date from 1845. They limited "hacking" (kicking an opponent's shins) and expressly banned metal-studded boots. In 1874 stomping, punching, and tripping were banned. In 1884 referees were introduced as agents of external aggression control. In 1909 players who committed serious fouls were sent from the field. The well-known yellow and red cards made their appearance in 1970. The result is a version of soccer that is much less violent than the medieval game from which it evolved. The same sort of evolution resulted in Olympic freestyle wrestling, which is far different from the brutal pancratium of the ancient games.

In comparison with ordinary daily behavior, however, the degree of physical aggression permitted in sports is quite remarkable: the boxer's knockout punch, the ice hockey player's body check, the American football player's tackle—to name but a few examples—are actions that would land an ordinary citizen in jail were he or she to perform them on the street. In sports, aggression is to a certain degree normal. This is, in fact, one of the reasons that sports, especially the more violent sports, were long thought to be unsuitable for women. If aggression is a male trait, it was thought, then females are ipso facto out of place within the "masculine domain."

EXPRESSIVE AND INSTRUMENTAL AGGRESSION

The argument based on the "figurational" sociology of Norbert Elias—that the physical aggression of sports has been muted and controlled—makes sense if we distinguish carefully between expressive and instrumental aggression. The first is quite emotional, tends to be spontaneous, and occurs without the burden of a guilty conscience. Instrumental aggression, on the other hand, has little to do with the emotional—even pleasurable—expression of aggressive impulses. Instrumental aggression is precisely calculated, planned, and rational. It is a conscious transgression of the standards of socially acceptable behavior in order to achieve some "higher" purpose—like winning the game. The ends justify the means.

Blinkert makes this clear when he writes, "To an increasing degree in the course of industrialized modernization, we can observe a very specific type of orientation to social norms" that can be termed "a utilitarian, calculating perspective" (1988, 397). Behind this attitude is the assumption

that human behavior is simply a matter of cost-benefit analysis. Accordingly, unethical behavior is seen not as pathological but rather as a thoroughly rational form of conflict resolution.

The theory of muted aggression refers primarily to expressive aggression. As expressive aggression has become muted in the twentieth century, instrumental aggression has been on the increase. The balance between the two kinds of aggression has shifted toward the latter. Just as the extent of acceptable physical aggression in various sports differs, so does the balance between expressive and instrumental aggression. It is no surprise that sports with a large dose of expressive aggression are especially popular in social and cultural milieus where physical aggression is felt to be a legitimate way to pursue one's interests. In the world of sports as in society generally, the theory of muted aggression has to be revised to acknowledge that a decline in expressive aggression has occurred at the same time that we have seen a rise in the level of instrumental aggression. Fewer soccer players kick their opponents in the shins for the fun of it, but many more commit "tactical" fouls to prevent their opponents from kicking a goal.

CHANGES IN EXPRESSIVE AND INSTRUMENTAL AGGRESSION IN WOMEN'S SPORTS

The history of women's sports—or, more precisely, of women's physical activity—mirrors the place of women in society and the sex-specific differences that are the results of the balance of power between the sexes. This means that the story of aggression in women's sports is full of twists and turns. We are told that the physical exercises and the athletic contests of Spartan women included rough sports such as wrestling and boxing. "The severe laws of Lycurgus laid down not only running exercises, ball and hoop games, but also discus throwing, wrestling and even pugilism for the country girls. With this training women would be capable of managing the family's affairs and sometimes those of public importance, with the necessary firmness during the many occasions when men were away on the battlefield." The emphasis on aggressive sports was consonant with Spartan fertility cults and with the Spartan woman's most important social role, "to be a fertile mother of a robust line" (Durantez 1976, 174). Spartan women were characterized by physical strength and health equal to that of the men and by the same ambition to win glory on the basis of courage. In contrast, Athenian women, once they were married, lived more sheltered and domesticated lives and rarely if ever participated in sports. Roman women were in this respect closer to the Athenian than to the Spartan model.

The principal physical exercises and sports of medieval and Renaissance women consisted mainly of folk dances and occasional games of folk football (which allowed for a good deal of aggression). Footraces occurred not as part of some program of physical education but rather in conjunction with the festivities surrounding a tournament or an archery contest. Many if not most of these footraces were for prostitutes. The physical activities of aristocratic women were less restricted. Hunting and hawking were allowed, and there is some evidence that they participated in archery and in the game of court tennis. For the most part, however, they were sports spectators rather than active participants. At a medieval tournament, men fought and women watched. By the end of the sixteenth century, the tournament had turned into a theatrical performance and women were allowed to play a minor part as damsels in need of rescue or as goddesses accepting the knights' homage. In courtly society, conspicuous consumption was the norm, and the codes of beauty left no place for expressive or instrumental aggression.

With the rise of modern industrial society came shifts in the balance of power between the sexes. With these shifts came an increase in the amount of aggression deemed appropriate for women's sports. With greater freedom of action and a relaxation of traditional codes of femininity, the aggression displayed within women's sports became increasingly physical. This was certainly the case in England, where women of the working class not only watched boxing matches but stripped to their undergarments and fought in the ring.

Early in the nineteenth century, there were efforts in Europe and North America to include a concern for girls' and women's health within educational institutions. European writers like Phokian Clias and Moritz Kloss, along with American spokespersons like Catharine Beecher and Diocletian Lewis, developed theories of physical education for girls and women that stressed traditional feminine characteristics such as lightness, delicacy, grace, and beauty. There was near-unanimity about the inappropriateness of serious sports competition for women. Anything that remotely resembled violent behavior was vehemently rejected. Women's physical education was shaped by a concern for grace and elegance.

Toward the end of the century, however, the newly established women's colleges of Great Britain and the United States began to offer their students a chance to play tennis, cricket, field hockey, lacrosse, and baseball. On the European continent, a number of aggressively athletic upper-class women made names for themselves as fencers. American missionaries and educators in China and Japan were able to introduce modern sports to a small number of upper-class girls and women. Similarly, a few privileged Latin American girls and women were given access to modern sports.

Early in the twentieth century, a vogue for "women's" exercises and sports spread through the European and American middle class. (Women of the working class continued to appear in public as boxers, wrestlers, and weightlifters.) In addition to the sports already popular at women's colleges, golf, swimming, skiing, and ice skating became popular. The codes of behavior and the rules and regulations of these sports were usually modified to make them appropriately "feminine." The rules for women's basketball, which restricted the players to zones and forbade dribbling and close guarding, were typical. It was during the last half of the twentieth century, in the wake of the feminist movement, that the athletic code for women included a tolerance for endurance, strength, competitiveness, and aggression.

If we look at the increase in the number of women participating in various sports in the last few decades, we see that the most rapid increases have occurred in sports that can be categorized as either "ritualized aggressive" or "openly aggressive." Volleyball, basketball (with the same rules as the men's game), soccer, rugby, and the martial

GIRLS AND FOOTBALL

Football, a violent and aggressive sport, is not popular with girls and women. A survey of football participation in U.S. schools in 1998–1999 showed that only 708 girls were on high school teams as compared to 983,000 boys. Girls who play in Pop Warner leagues (for pre-high school youth) do so against younger boys.

arts have all attracted large numbers of female participants. The transformation of women's sports in the direction of a greater tolerance of expressive aggression can be observed in the evolution of the Olympic Games. Until 1972, apart from a restricted number of track and field disciplines, female Olympians competed mostly in sports—like golf, tennis, archery, gymnastics, swimming, and diving—that more or less conformed to traditional codes of femininity. These were sports that allowed little or no opportunity for physical aggression. In 1976 rougher and more strenuous sports were introduced—basketball, team handball, rowing. Four years later, women competed in ice hockey. Soccer followed. Since then, there is hardly an Olympic sport in which women do not compete.

Contrary to the trend in men's sports, in which expressive aggression has been muted, women's sports have shown a marked increase in aggression. A striking example of this can be seen in boxing and wrestling, two combat sports in which self-assured, dedicated, and successful women now compete to become national, European, or world champions. Although the trend is now counter to that in men's sports, we can expect women's sports in the future to become more like men's sports in that instrumental aggression will play a larger role than expressive aggression. We should not assume that women will become increasingly willing to inflict spontaneous physical aggression upon one another, but rather that they will become more expert in tactical fouls and other instrumentally aggressive techniques.

Some observers believe that women's acceptance of rough play, physical aggression, and a win-at-all-costs attitude will be temporary. In the long run, they argue, traditional "feminine" char-acteristics—like sensitivity, communicativeness, solidarity, and concern for others—will come once again to the fore. There seems little evidence of this at the moment. If we look at sports in which women have been competing for some time, we see that their games are contested with the same roughness and toughness as the men's. At the international level, coaches take inculcating these attributes as one of their most important obligations. They feel they must "aid [female] athletes in overcoming their fear of hitting, being hit, and the pain of physical contact and stress—experiences not generally part of female growing-up" (Smith 1972, 106).

A good example of this is the training regimen of the Japanese volleyball team. The players, wrote Michael Smith, "are brutalized to the point that they are relatively impervious to stress and pain during games" (1972, 106). Developments in women's soccer and team handball indicate an increase in toughness, aggressiveness, and both kinds of aggression, expressive as well as instrumental. In other words, the women's game will conform to the standards of the men's game. The differences disappear.

Empirical research into the readiness to commit acts of instrumental aggression shows this. In youth soccer, there is no significant sex-specific difference in the assessment of intentional fouls committed in order to win a game. Boys and girls agree that such fouls are "unfair but tactically clever" (Pilz 1995a). They are equally ready to commit such fouls themselves in actual play. The similarity of male and female attitudes is equally clear when it comes to doping, which is a special form of instrumental aggression. In certain disciplines, women are actually more likely than men to resort to banned substances. Brigitte Berendonk noted as early as 1978 that there are sports in which 90 percent of the world-class female athletes have become dependent on anabolic steroids.

CHANGES IN (AGGRESSIVE) PERSONALITY STRUCTURES

If one accepts the theoretical framework developed by Norbert Elias, it is clear that there is a close relationship between society's institutional structure and the dynamics of personality structure. Changes in the former lead to changes in social codes and in personality structure. When women make their way into institutions that had been wholly or predominantly male, they tend to adapt to men's standards. It is, therefore, no surprise that male and female handball players show no statistically significant differences when asked about the degree to which they themselves are competitive, robust, ambitious, tough, aggressive, and ready to take risks. Empirical studies demonstrate that the most physically aggressive and competitive sports (which are, of course, those whose codes depart most from traditional notions of femininity) are those in which male and female personality structures most resemble one another. As early as 1972, Michael Smith commented, "as sex-roles blur, as sport for women continues to expand—including a move toward greater participation in body contact activities—and as winning assumes greater importance, women's sport seems bound to become more characterized by aggression" (103). John E. Kane came to the similar conclusion that "the general impression remains, however, and it would seem to have a lot of face validity, that success in competitive sport may need certain personality supports and these are more similar than dissimilar for men and women" (1972, 28).

AGGRESSION: NO LONGER A MALE PRIVILEGE

Inevitably, the dominant codes of modern industrial society, which emphasize competitive success, have affected the evolution of women's sports. To be aggressive, competitive, achievement-oriented, and risk-seeking is no longer a purely male privilege. Striking a balance between aggressive competition and peaceful cooperation is less a question of gender than a question of the values and standards of society to which men and women

pay homage. As Pearl Berlin wrote, "One can't compete in sport and be non-competitive; one can't shoot for goals and be non-aggressive; one can't practice for two physically demanding hours a day and be physically weak; one can't put one's skill on the line against an opponent and be too afraid to take risks; one can't come out of the court or field or pool against opponents who have demonstrated their superiority and be wanting in courage; one can't live many hours a week to train for competition and not have self-discipline; one can't accept the results of the contest as proof of who's best for the moment and be unobjective; one can't strive to win, win, win and not be achievement-oriented" (1974, 382). The more sports become professionalized, the more the end—victory—takes precedence over the means. And the greater the material rewards of athletic success, the greater the temptation to sacrifice the rules in order to gain the spoils of victory. This holds true for women's sports as well as men's.

Muting expressive and instrumental aggression in sports is less a question of the dominance of one sex or the other than it is a matter of the social and institutional contexts within which sports occur. Accordingly, an increase in the extent and intensity of women's involvement in sports can accelerate the process of muting expressive aggression even as instrumental aggression remains widespread. The potential for aggression is present in women just as it is in men. The observable differences in the manifestation of this aggressive potential results from differences in socialization and role expectations. Although women are even today less likely than men to employ physical aggression against other people, it is a mistake to describe women as "the peaceful sex" (Rose 1993). After all, we have seen in recent years—as a paradoxical result of emancipatory processes—an increase of interpersonal physical aggression by and among girls and women. The reentry of women into boxing and other combat sports is one example of this trend; the increase in the number of female "football hooligans" is another (Pilz 1995b).

Women as Victims of Aggression

Despite the convergence of male and female behavior, women continue to be the victims of aggression. This is especially true in the world of sports because physical proximity, if not physical contact, is a central element in sports. Empirical studies of aggression against women in sports, long a taboo topic for investigation, show that an alarming (and increasing) number of female athletes have been the victim of sexual aggression, sexual harassment, and sexual abuse. Schoolgirls and grown women who participate in sports are dependent on their coaches, who are mostly male, and close relationships bring with them the risk of unethical behavior. There is an urgent need for research into this problem, which to a lesser degree affects the lives of boys as well as girls.

Gunter A. Pilz

See also Personality Traits; Self-Defense; Sexual Harassment; Socialization

Bibliography

Berendonk, Brigette. (1978) *Doping-Vonder Forschung Zum Betrug.* Reinbek: Rohwolt.

Berlin, Pearl. (1974) "The Woman Athlete." In *The American Woman in Sport,* edited by Ellen W. Gerber. Reading, MA: Addison-Wesley, 283–400.

Blinkert, B. (1988) "Kriminalität als Modernisierungs-risiko." *Soziale Welt* 39: 397–412.

Durantez, C. (1976) "Women at Olympia." *Olympic Review* 101/102: 171–175; 103/104: 296–300.

Elias, Norbert. (1975) "Die Genese des Sports als Soziologisches Problem." In *Texte zur Soziologie des Sports,* edited by Kurt Hammerich and Klaus Heinemann. Schorndorf: Karl Hofmann, 81–109.

———. (1977) *Über den Prozess der Zivilisation.* Frankfurt: Suhrkamp.

Engelfried, C., ed. (1997) *Auszeit: Sexualität, Gewalt und Abhängigkeit im Sport.* Frankfurt: Campus.

Guttmann, Allen. (1984) *Sports Spectators.* New York: Columbia University Press.

———. (1991) *Women's Sports: A History.* New York: Columbia University Press.

Kane, J. E. (1972) "Psychological Aspects of Sport with Special Reference to the Female." In *Women and Sport,* Series 2, edited by Dorothy V. Harris. State College, PA: Pennsylvania State University: Women and Sport: A National Research Conference, 19–34.

Klein, Michael, and Birgit Palzkill. (1966) *Gewalt Gegen Mädchen und Frauen im Sport.* Erfurt: Eigenverlag.

Maccoby, Eleanor E., and C. N. Jacklin, eds. (1974) *The Psychology of Sex Differences.* Stanford, CA: Stanford University Press.

Mathys, F. K. (1958) "Erholung bei Turnen und Spiel." *Olympisches Feuer* 8: 11–13.

Pilz, Gunter A. (1982) *Wandlungen der Gewalt im Sport.* Ahrensburg: Czwalina.

———. (1995a) "Performance in Sport: Education in Fair Play?" *International Review for the Sociology of Sport* 30: 391–418.

———. (1995b) "Weibliche Fan-Gruppen im Sport." In *Fair Play für Mädchen und Frauen im Sport?,* edited by Inge Berndt and Ursula Voigt. Frankfurt: DOG.

Rose, Lotte. (1993) "Jugend und Gewalt." *Olympische Jugend* 1: 4–6.

Smith, Michael D. (1972) "Aggression and the Female Athlete." In *Women and Sport,* edited by Dorothy V. Harris. State College, PA: Pennsylvania State University: Women and Sport: A National Research Conference, 91–114.

AGING

The term *aging* in its broadest sense refers to the physical and psychological changes that occur with the passage of time. Technically, everyone ages at the same rate—one day at a time—but how much and how fast people change with age varies greatly within the population. The old adage "you've reached old age when all you exercise is caution" is no longer true of aging women and their attitude toward sport and exercise.

To be sure, many functional abilities are reduced with aging, but an increasing amount of scientific information is becoming available about the potential performance capacities of the elderly, particularly strength and power. As a result, a new emphasis is being placed on "active" life expectancy as the relevant concept in aging and exercise. Converging evidence across many disciplines suggests that women who pursue and maintain a healthy and physically active lifestyle will, in their later years, remain involved in society in personally satisfying and socially useful ways and are more likely to experience the highest possible functioning and quality of life during those years. In fact, physical activity in daily living, organized exercise, and sport are consistently identified as among the most significant interventions in the life of the elderly female. Whether she has been active all her life or is a recent convert to exercise, the physically active older woman is likely to be physiologically one or two decades younger than her sedentary contemporary, to have greater functional independence, reduced mortality risk, and an overall increased quality of life. Despite evidence of the positive effects of exercise, however, real and perceived barriers to healthful exercise continue to impede the transition to a "fit" aging process.

THE BENEFITS OF EXERCISE FOR OLDER WOMEN

The benefits of exercise for older women have been well established in scientific literature. For some women, physical activity, exercise, and sport carry intrinsic psychological rewards such as feelings of well-being and self-actualization, but the most common motivation to become active seems to be the desire to improve health and personal fitness. In general, women can expect two types of benefits: immediate short-term contributions to enhanced physical, social, and emotional well-being; and long-term contributions to good health, resistance to illness, optimization of self-care and functional independence, reduced mortality risk, and increased longevity and quality of life.

The short-term benefits include significant and same-day improvements in flexibility and joint mobility, elevated alertness and cognitive function, stress reduction, muscle relaxation, positive mood states, and better sleep. Other positive effects include a boost to self-image and feelings of adequacy, a sense of control, and enjoyable shared experiences with others of the same age. Increased confidence and well-being are seen as reasons for older people to get active. Perhaps in part because exercise can promote a new interest in life, it also improves many aspects of cognitive functioning.

The broader health benefits of regular exercise can be realized months or years later. They include increased longevity; an elevated immune response and reduced risk of cancer; lower risk of dying from coronary heart disease because of the side effects of exercise, such as effective weight control, lower blood pressure, increased aerobic fitness, and improved cholesterol levels; and the slowing of osteoporosis, or age-related weakening of the bones. Weight-bearing exercises such as walking, aerobics, running, and weightlifting have been shown to retard bone loss in older women and increase the amount of calcium they absorb. Women who have greater bone mass have a reduced incidence of serious falls, the form of accident that kills more elderly people than any other.

Exercise also plays a role in enhancing body image and improving appearance. It is claimed that thick skin is good skin, and some say that those who have been active throughout their lives ultimately have thicker skin and fewer wrinkles. In addition, preserving a healthy body weight brings its own benefits. These include more control over appetite while allowing a larger food intake, thereby increasing the probability that a person will consume a nutritionally sound diet; reduced symptoms of menopause; and increased muscle strength to carry out activities of daily living and also diminish fatigue.

Increasingly, epidemiologists, exercise scientists, and health professionals agree that physical activity need not be intense for it to improve health. Health benefits appear to be proportional to amount of activity, and significant physiological changes in elderly adults involved in low-intensity activities such as walking and cycling have been documented. With the emphasis on amount rather than intensity of physical activity, elderly women have more options to select from when incorporating exercise into their lives. Walking, however, seems to be the most popular choice, followed by gardening, swimming, and cycling.

Finally, longevity appears to be influenced by the general activity profile of an individual's lifestyle. Landmark longitudinal studies, such as that conducted by Paffenbarger and colleagues with 17,000 Harvard graduates on the relationship of activity to survival, suggest that longevity is influenced by the amount and intensity of habitual physical activity that a person engages in throughout life. This and other studies have shown that, though regular exercise may not extend the maximum life span of humans, holistic health gains and a contribution to the quality of life are real possibilities for elderly women.

EXERCISE AS A VEHICLE FOR SOCIAL INTERACTION

Social support, particularly by one's spouse, and social interaction are thought to be among the most important factors in staying with and enjoying activity programs. This may be because active people influence others to become active or because they merely tend to choose active friends. Whatever the cause, it still seems clear that a supportive milieu is important for starting and continuing activity. Women who have been in the workforce are more likely to have a social support system to depend upon, as well as the self-esteem that plays a role in keeping them physically active. Certainly poor health and institutionalization combine to hinder women's ability to maintain former social networks and to lessen their desire to be active. Group exercise programs, physical activity, sports, and leisure pursuits thus help them to make new social contacts, which they need as their personal social support dwindles through widowhood and loss of friends and siblings.

BARRIERS TO HEALTHFUL PHYSICAL ACTIVITY

The well-documented benefits of exercise for aging women, however, have not led to a parallel increase in activity among this group. Large-scale health and fitness surveys consistently report that women over sixty-five are quite resistant to the idea of increasing their level of physical activity.

Physical activity data from the U.S. Surgeon General's Report shows that one in two women over seventy-four years of age are inactive. The sedentary habit begins in the teenage years or earlier, is reinforced over the life span, and is evidenced repeatedly in the popular media, in educational materials, and by peers and family. There is still a lot of "take it easy" when it comes to attitudes concerning the active elderly.

Beyond the extensive exercise benefits lost to elderly women who are truly inactive are the numerous potential risks and real or perceived obstacles or barriers to actual participation. In general terms, the most probable determinants of sedentary behavior are declining physical power and genuine ill health; activity limitations and physical malaise; social and cultural deterrents to activity, such as lack of friends, lack of resources, and ethnic differences in attitudes toward active elderly women; inexperience or lack of confidence in exercise and sport situations; and fear of injury. Poorly informed ideas about exercise many times go unchallenged, and older women are permitted a level of physical helplessness not unlike that of the disabled.

PHYSICAL DECLINE AND ILL HEALTH

Until recently, older women all too readily accepted the notion that aging inevitably robs them of strength and fitness and prevents them from enjoying physical activity, even though many of them reach their sixties, seventies, and eighties free from specific life-threatening diseases. Physical declines and ill health do generate real barriers to exercise, though it is difficult to distinguish functional limitations from the restrictions imposed by disease and illness. Hypertension and respiratory problems are major deterrents to exercise. Also, aging women are particularly vulnerable to a number of chronic disorders that impede their motivation to move; for example, older women are twice as likely as men to have arthritis and rheumatism that limit their daily activities. In addition to these limitations, those who do attempt to exercise may encounter patronizing or overly cautious leadership in senior sport and fitness programs, or lack of encouragement from their doctors and families, all of which simply serve to reinforce the aging decline process physiologically as well as psychologically.

If one views the study of older adults as a story about survivors, then the superior longevity of women should be considered a success story. In fact, aging for women is in many ways the survival of the unfittest. On average, women live six or seven years longer than men in North America, Europe, and Japan. Yet lifelong limitations placed upon the social and economic status of women lead many to late-life dependency. In the case of the very old (most of whom are women), there is a fine line between frailty and disability, especially for those over eighty-five, up to half of whom reside in institutions or homes for the aged. It is in these settings that the frail elderly perceive a loss of control over their lives and can easily learn to be helpless.

SOCIAL AND CULTURAL DETERRENTS TO PHYSICAL ACTIVITY

Women experience old age differently than men and are more likely to live their later years alone, with lower incomes and more chronic health problems and disabilities compared to men in the same age group. This bitter fruit of their extra years is bound to have an effect on their active life expectancy. Traditionally expected to take responsibility for management of home and family, they have had far less opportunity for personal leisure and sporting opportunities than their male counterparts. Older women, in particular, not only have to overcome ageist views about what is

A middle-aged woman keeps young by playing tennis. (Neal Preston/Corbis)

appropriate physical behavior for late life but also must break through other barriers such as personal lethargy, time demands from an ailing spouse (and sometimes, in the "sandwich generation," returning children and grandchildren), chronic pain, and the inconvenience of incontinence. Further common barriers to exercise are lack of available facilities or transportation to leisure opportunities or supervised programs, as well as limited financial resources.

Feminists argue persuasively that a double standard of aging persists for women—that to be old and female is a sort of double jeopardy and that social and cultural factors perpetuate the progressive discouragement of females from sport and physical activity as they age.

Central to the feminist perspective is the proposition that older women's lack of power and status results from the limited options open to them earlier in their lives. Societal definitions of what women can do and be have traditionally been narrower than they have been for men. Conditioning to these views begins in early childhood. In the case of exercise, girls' early life experience of physical activity and sport with parents as role models appears to be critical to the development of positive attitudes about vigorous physical activity. School programs, however dimly remembered by the time a girl becomes an older woman, function to further emphasize what physical activity is appropriate for which gender. These programs for girls have tended to de-emphasize aggressive competition and sports, as well as activities that require strength, strategy, and power. Attitudes about suitable types of activity for females, time constraints, negative attitudes, and fears concerning the safety of vigorous exertion have until recently discouraged and deterred many elderly women from remaining active.

An important contributing factor to negative attitudes about exercise is the fear of wearing out the body—a fear encouraged by the late-nineteenth-century orthodox medical analogy that likened the body to a machine, and continued with Pearl's rate-of-living theory and Selye's stress hypothesis. According to these theories, the greater the rate of energy expenditure and oxygen utilization, the shorter the life span, or the more vigorous the exercise, the greater the stress and accompanying long-term harmful effects. Though abundant studies show that, contrary to machines, bodies do not wear out in proportion to their use, old fears linger that joints will wear out, bones will break, and the heart may stop.

RISKS OF INJURY

The occurrence of accidental injuries to the bones and soft tissues of the elderly body through direct sport or activity participation is not well documented. Sudden death while exercising is rare, though the risk is higher for those with cardiovascular disease or those who are on particular medications. Bone fractures are common in postmenopausal women, and though weight-bearing exercise is known to contribute to the maintenance of bone mass, women are often afraid that they might damage themselves during such vigorous activity. Furthermore, they often overesti-

mate their own daily level of exertion through exercise, believing that they are far more active than they really are. Compared to falls of old people in their own homes, on icy streets, and in cars and hospitals, injury from sport and exercise participation is insignificant. Musculoskeletal fatigue, soreness, joint stiffness, and delayed recovery from physical activity are all particular risks for those who are unaccustomed to exercise and who do not initiate activity at a low intensity. Indeed, the first experience with an exercise program for an elderly woman can turn out to be a very painful encounter and one that may provide a negative incentive for the future.

MENOPAUSE AND THE AGING FEMALE BODY

Strategies to promote physical activity among menopausal women are a focus of special concern, since throughout history women have been thought to be old after menopause. Menopause remains to this day a relatively unstudied area, tied as it has been in Western society to loss of attractiveness, fertility, and function—what commentators in the past have termed "the death of the woman in the woman." But, in fact, menopause is incredibly varied, and most women possess little accurate information about it because stereotyped menopausal images and biased information about "the change of life" are a widespread and persistent part of Western culture. Some current efforts focus on persuading peri-menopausal women—those who are approaching an age when they might expect signs of menopause—that they should all embark upon a lifelong regimen of hormone-replacement therapy. This trend underlines the extreme way in which menopause has come to be considered a medical problem in the twentieth century. It also illustrates the ways in which drug prescriptions, which are tied to a theory of deficit and loss, have predominated over lifestyle changes, such as vigorous physical activity, which may be equally beneficial and are almost certainly more likely to be benign. Many women are beginning to find that joining self-help groups, seeking natural remedies, and getting more exercise can be potent health measures at this time of life. Certainly, one thing that is urgently needed is greater clarity about the role of exercise in menopausal

CANADA'S SPORTIEST SENIOR LADIES

Ivy Granston of Vancouver is a world record holder in the seventy-plus category who runs everything from the 100- to 10,000-meter. Now over eighty and legally blind, she epitomizes the possibilities of the aging body in action. Her achievements demonstrate much of what is known about gender, aging, and physical activity: that gender differences can blur over the life course; that motivation for sport matters as much as age; and that individual variability from day to day means that older athletes do better to measure themselves not against others but against their own standards. The goal of elderly athletes is to be the best possible without letting age be a barrier. There is no definitive finish line to lifelong fitness.

Betty Jean McHugh, the fastest grandmother in the West, celebrated her seventieth birthday recently by running the Honolulu marathon with her son. McHugh recently set the Canadian record in her age group for the 400- and 800-meter at the British Columbia Summer Games, and she holds the Canadian record for the 5,000-meter. A mother of four and grandmother of four, McHugh ran her first race—the women's 10K—at fifty-two. Two years later she ran her first marathon, and she has never looked back. She would have started earlier, she says, had she known how much she would love it—and had it been more acceptable. "It wasn't supposed to be a woman's thing. When I first started running I used to sneak out after dark." Indeed, there was no such thing as an Olympic women's marathon until Los Angeles in 1984, and the women's 5,000- and 10,000-meter were not established until 1988. Now it isn't at all unusual for women to come to running late in life.

women, who can expect to live for thirty years or more after menopause.

ELDERLY WOMEN AS ROLE MODELS: MASTER'S ATHLETES

For women beyond menopause, it is now evident that those in their eighth and ninth decades can achieve significant health and strength benefits from exercise. Very elderly women, in their seventies and beyond, are running marathons, winning championships in such sports as swimming, climbing mountains, and demonstrating remarkable strength, ability, and determination in physical pursuits. They present role models that can chip away at deleterious stereotypes of aging women—and their numbers are growing. Older adults, such as Master's athletes, who consider exercise and physical competition to be a high priority in their lives report that they experience a high quality of life. Master's athletes are physically elite seniors who keep training and competing well into their later years and exhibit fitness comparable to individuals who are thirty to fifty years younger. Trained women over eighty, for example, are achieving performance times in the mile run that approximate those of the average teenage girl. In Master's championships and senior games competitions at all levels, senior women athletes (although still far fewer than men) are now demonstrating that they do not need to accept a major decline of aerobic power and muscle strength as inevitable features of aging and that they are prepared to condition their bodies through rigorous training regimens, not for health alone but rather for the pleasure of developing skilled performance. They are a testament to the remarkable resilience of the human body when it is properly maintained and to the role of sport in successful aging.

TOWARD SUCCESSFUL AGING AND NEW SPORTING IDEALS FOR WOMEN

Impelled by the realization that by the year 2025, 20 percent of the population in North America and parts of Europe will be over fifty-five years of age, exercise advocates increasingly focus on the complex dynamics of successful aging and the need to separate the ideas of aging and inactivity. The year 1999 was declared by the United Nations as the International Year of Older Persons. This provided a unique opportunity for gender matters to figure more prominently in social policies designed to encourage healthful and pleasurable exercise and provide accessible opportunities for participation. Contrary to historical stereotype and popular opinion, most older women are fit enough to enjoy full lives, and many manage well despite handicaps. National and international initiatives in health promotion and population health are reflecting more fully the realization that the factors that influence the lifestyle practices of the elderly, including exercise and sport, are multiple and interactive, deeply embedded within particular social, economic, and physical environments. Researchers have begun to listen more closely to the expressed experiences of the elderly themselves, the "natives" of that time of life, who can best describe what activities they enjoy, what barriers are placed in their way, and how they are affected by negative stereotypes of the aging female. As more and more elderly women challenge the limiting stereotypes of the aging female body and seek new paths to active living, they are disrupting the cultural story line of loss and decline that has constrained them in the past. Aging is, after all, an individual affair, and while the first truth about aging is that everybody does it, the second truth is that everybody does it differently.

Patricia Vertinsky

See also Osteoporosis; Senior Sports

Bibliography

Aird, Elizabeth. (1998) "Fastest Grandma in the West." *The Vancouver Sun.* 23 July.

Allmer, Henning, et al. (1996) *Bewegung, Spiel und Sport im Alter: I.* Cologne: Bundes Institut für Sportwissenschaft.

Blair, Steven, Harold Kohl, Neil Gordon, and Ralph Paffenbarger. (1992) "How Much Physical Activity Is Good for Your Health?" *Annual Review of Public Health* 13: 99–126.

Brown, David R. (1992) "Physical Activity, Aging and Psychological Well-Being: An Overview of the Research." *Canadian Journal of Sport Science* 17, 3: 185–193.

Chodzo-Zajko, Wojtek J. (1991) "Physical Fitness, Cognitive Performance and Aging." *Medicine and Science in Sports and Exercise* 23, 7: 868–872.

Denk, Heinz, and Dieter Pache. (1996) *Bewegung, Spiel und Sport im Alter II.* Cologne: Bundes Institut für Sportwissenschaft.

Dishman, Rod K. (1990) "Determinants of Participation in Physical Activity." In *Exercise, Fitness and Health: A Consensus of Current Knowledge,* edited by C. Bouchard, R. J. Shephard, T. Stephens, J. R. Sutton, and B. D. McPherson. Champaign, IL: Human Kinetics, 75–101.

Kinsella, Kevin. (1992) "Changes in Life Expectancy." *American Journal of Clinical Nutrition* 55: 11965–12025.

Lupton, Deborah. (1996) "Constructing the Menopausal Body: The Discourses on Hormone Replacement Therapy." *Body and Society* 2, 1: 91–97.

Minkler, Meredith, and Carol Estes, eds. (1991) *Critical Perspectives on Aging: The Political Economy of Growing Old.* New York: Baywood.

O'Brien, Sandra J., and Patricia A. Vertinsky. (1990) "Elderly Women, Exercise and Healthy Aging." *Journal of Women and Aging* 2, 3: 41–65.

———. (1991) "Unfit Survivors: Exercise as a Resource for Aging Women." *The Gerontologist* 31, 3: 347–357.

Paffenbarger, Ralph, Robert Hyde, Alvin Wing, et al. (1986) "Physical Activity, All Causes Mortality and Longevity of College Alumni." *New England Journal of Medicine* 314, 10: 604–613.

Shephard, Roy J. (1994) "Determinants of Exercise in People Aged 65 and Older." In *Advances in Exercise Adherence,* edited by Rod K. Dishman. Champaign, IL: Human Kinetics, 343–360.

———. (1997) *Aging, Physical Activity and Health.* Champaign, IL: Human Kinetics.

Spirduso, Waneen W. (1995) *Physical Dimensions of Aging.* Champaign, IL: Human Kinetics.

Stains, Lawrence Roy. (1998) "Super Immunity." *Prevention* 50, 3: 101–105, 178–184.

U.S. Department of Health and Human Services. (1996) *Physical Activity and Health: A Report of the Surgeon General.* Atlanta, GA: U.S. Department of Health and Human Services, Centers for Disease Control and Prevention, National Center for Chronic Disease, Prevention and Health Promotion.

Verbrugge, Lois M. (1994) "Disability in Late Life." In *Aging and Quality of Life,* edited by R. P. Abeles, H. G. Gift, and M. G. Ory. New York: Springer, 79–98.

Vertinsky, Patricia A. (1991) "Old Age, Gender and Physical Activity: The Biomedicalization of Aging." *Journal of Sport History* 18, 1: 64–80.

———. (1994) *The Eternally Wounded Woman: Women, Exercise and Doctors.* Chicago: University of Illinois Press.

———. (1995) "Stereotypes of Aging Women and Exercise: A Historical Perspective." *Journal of Aging and Physical Activity* 3: 223–237.

AIKIDO

Aikido is a traditional martial art that consists primarily of grabs, balance-breaking, throws, and pins. It does not teach punching, kicking, or grappling. The sport form of aikido was developed by Tomiki Kenji between about 1950 and 1970 at Waseda University in Tokyo, Japan. Tomiki aikido, as it is now called, derives from two modern Japanese martial arts, aikido and judo, which in turn were derived from older systems of unarmed combat and self-defense. Women were involved in aikido from its early development in Japan, although their participation in competition was limited until 1987. Elsewhere, women have competed since the 1960s.

HISTORY

Kano Jigoro (1860–1938), founder of judo, modernized jujutsu throwing and grappling techniques to create a system of physical education that includes competition. Aikido founder Ueshiba Morihei (1883–1969) combined the techniques of Daito-ryu aikijujutsu with a complex spiritual philosophy to create a "peaceful" martial art focused on avoiding conflict by blending with an opponent's energy to neutralize aggression. Tomiki studied directly under both these men, uniting Ueshiba's aikido techniques with Kano's philosophy of physical education to create his own distinctive form of competitive aikido.

Tomiki aikido is now administered by the Japan Aikido Association (JAA), founded in 1974; international issues are overseen by the Tomiki Aikido International Network, established in 1993. National organizations also exist in Europe, Australia, the United States, Brazil, and Russia.

Tomiki Kenji started training in judo when he was ten years old and began to train with Ueshiba in 1926. In 1936 he was sent to Japanese-occupied Manchuria to teach martial arts at Daido Gakuin and Kenkoku University, and he began to develop a logical curriculum for aikido that differed significantly from the traditional "watch the master demonstrate, then try it" style he had experienced under Ueshiba. Tomiki returned Japan in 1948

and took a position at his alma mater, Waseda University, becoming a founding member of the physical education department faculty in 1954. There he worked with members of the university judo club, teaching them aikido basics to supplement their judo training. A group of these students formally became the Waseda University Aikido Club in 1958. Contingent upon the club's official status was the development of a system whereby students from different universities could compete with one another.

MAKING AIKIDO SAFE

The first difficulty Tomiki faced was ensuring the safety of the participants. Kano had not incorporated aikijujutsu-style joint-locks and pins into judo precisely because they were too dangerous. During the 1950s Tomiki and his students worked to synthesize and organize a series of seventeen techniques that were suitable for free practice. This set of techniques, or *kata*, still forms the basis of Tomiki aikido as the *randori no kata* (set of techniques for free practice; also known as the *junana-hon no kata*, or set of seventeen techniques).

Once this group of safe techniques had been identified and codified in a sequence for teaching purposes, Tomiki began to experiment with different forms of competition. He tried empty-handed defenses against a variety of attacks, including punches, kicks, and leg sweeps, as well as attacks with various weapons. By 1961 he had developed *toshu randori*, or empty-handed free practice, a form quite similar to judo, with both competitors using both offense and defense to execute aikido techniques to score.

This format was not entirely successful, however, because aikido techniques require a committed attack from a mid-range distance, and there was no incentive to attack. Tomiki's solution to this dilemma was to arm one of the competitors with a rubber "scoring implement" intended to represent a knife (*tanto* in Japanese). *Tanto randori* (free practice with a knife) was introduced in 1965, and the first university tournament was held in Japan in 1969.

While the Waseda University students were developing *randori*, Tomiki was also working with his two adult assistants, Ohba Hideo and Miyake Tsunako, to develop the *koryu no kata*, based more directly on Ueshiba's teachings. These sets of techniques are performed in pairs, with a designated attacker (*uke*) and defender (*tori*). The six *koryu no kata*, together with the *randori no kata*, provide the basis for the other main form of Tomiki aikido competition, *kata embu*, a prepared technical demonstration of selected techniques performed in front of a panel of judges, who evaluate each pair and award points for technical mastery. The *kata* were designed to refine the practitioners' understandings of the subtleties of distancing, timing, trajectories, and initiative, and to provide an enjoyable form of practice for those who might be less interested in the rough-and-tumble of *randori* matches.

Miyake, who was among the first women to practice judo at the Kodokan in the early 1940s, recruited several young women *judoka* to join her at early morning practices at the Aoyama Wrestling Hall during the 1960s, where they continued to refine the *kata*. Two of these, Sakai Kinuyo and Yamagata Mitsue, are still active as instructors and judges in Japan, and at sixth *dan* are the most highly ranked Japanese women in the JAA.

WOMEN AND COMPETITION

Until 1987, *kata embu* was the only form of competition open to women in Japan. In the rest of the world, however, women have taken active competitive roles from the very beginning. Tomiki aikido was first practiced regularly outside of Japan in 1960, when Yamada Senta introduced it to judo students in the London area. Lee Ah Loi, in 1999 the highest-ranked woman in the JAA, began her training in 1961 with Yamada. She has since been a major force in the organization and growth of Tomiki aikido in Europe, as well as a founding member of the European Aikido Association (EAA). The author of the most comprehensive guide to Tomiki aikido in English, she owns and instructs at the Yawara Centre, home of the Jugokan Aikido Club, in Wandsworth, London.

RULES AND PLAY

Learning how to fall safely is as important as learning how to perform an effective technique. Training occurs in pairs, beginning just outside of attacking distance; one person performs the technique while the other is thrown or controlled, and the *dojo* (training hall) usually has some form of matting on the floor to help absorb the shock of the falls. Techniques, sometimes practiced in choreographed sequences known as *kata*, may be against either unarmed or armed opponents. Practitioners wear judo- or karate-style white training uniforms, held closed by a cloth belt wrapped around the waist. The color of the belt usually denotes skill level; the most common colors are white (beginner), brown (advanced beginner), and black (a serious student of the art, awarded at *shodan*, or first-degree black belt), but particularly outside of Japan, a variety of colors may be seen. A *hakama* (long pleated culottes-like garment) is sometimes worn over the uniform pants, though in Tomiki aikido, this is generally reserved for *kata embu*, or demonstration, competition.

Today *tanto randori* is the centerpiece of competitive aikido. Generally, matches consist of two halves of one-and-a-half or two minutes each. The competitors take turns as defender (*toshu*) and attacker (*tanto*), exchanging the rubber knife at the half. Points are scored when the defender executes an aikido technique (limited to those in the *randori no kata*) or when the attacker succeeds with one of five permitted *kaeshiwaza*, or countertechniques. The attacker may also score with a straight thrust of the *tanto* within the target area—above the belt to the armpit on the front, back, or sides of the torso.

Various prohibited actions, such as grabbing the opponent's uniform or punching with the *tanto*, are penalized by awarding points to the opponent. Tournaments commonly include men's and women's individual events as well as men's team competition. Mixed teams comprised of two men and one woman have proved popular, and new formats continue to be developed. Competition takes place on a matted surface with a marked boundary of 9.1 square meters (30 square feet); matches are judged by three referees.

Tomiki aikido was introduced to Australia by Leoni Heap (later Gay), who had received six months of special teacher's training in England before arriving in Melbourne to begin instruction at Frank Dando's judo club. Tomiki aikido clubs are now active in Melbourne, Sydney, Brisbane, Perth, and Adelaide. Perth's Keishinkan Aikido Club is run by fourth *dan* Katie Noad, who spent four years training and competing in Japan before her return to Australia in 1989.

The development of Tomiki aikido in the United States during the 1960s and 1970s was slow and sporadic, occurring in small isolated groups started primarily by servicemen who had met and trained with Tomiki, Ohba, and Miyake while stationed in Japan. Bob Dziubla was the first American to spend any significant amount of time training in Japan; beginning in the later half of the 1980s, he was instrumental in bringing together most of the U.S. groups. The first U.S. national tournament took place in 1990, and today Tomiki aikido clubs are found throughout the country, under the administration of the JAA (USA), a not-for-profit group organized that same year.

Another American, Diane Bauerle (now Skoss), moved to Tokyo as a first *dan* in 1987. An active *kata* competitor, she was tied for fourth in the *dai-san kata* division—the highest placing of any non-Japanese in *kata*—at the First International Sports Aikido Open Tournament in 1989. She was also a member of the first official Japanese team sent to the 1991 British Aikido Association Silver Jubilee Tournament in Cardiff, Wales, where she and her partner, Horie Hiroko, placed second in their division. These two women were also the Kanto-area *kata* champions in 1990 and 1992.

CONCLUSION

International tournaments have been held regularly since 1989, beginning with the First International Sports Aikido Open Tournament in Tenri, Japan. The second "official" international tournament was held in 1993 at Katsuura in Chiba, Japan. International events are now held every other year; the United States hosted a tournament in 1995, and Imabari, Japan, was the location for the 1997 event. The First International Tomiki Aikido Festival took place in Brisbane, Australia, in August 1999, and Osaka became the venue in 2001. Women have been taking part and will continue to take part in these competitions.

Diane Skoss

Bibliography

Lee, Ah Loi. (1996) *Tomiki Aikido*. New York: Talman Company.

Pranin, Stanley A. (1991) *The Aiki News Encyclopedia of Aikido*. Tokyo: Aiki News.

———., ed. (1993) *Aikido Masters: Prewar Students of Morihei Ueshiba*. Tokyo: Aiki News.

Shishida, Fumiaki. (1989) "The Life of Kenji Tomiki." *Aiki News* 81.

———, and Tetsuro Nariyama. (1985) *Aikido Kyoshitsu* (Aikido Course). Tokyo: Taishukan Shoten.

Tomiki Kenji. (1970) *Judo and Aikido*. Tokyo: Japan Travel Bureau.

———. (1992) "Competition Aikido: A System of Practice for the Striking Techniques and Joint Techniques." *The JAA (USA) Aikido Times* 4: 2–4.

Ueshiba, Morihei. (1991) *Budo: Teachings of the Founder of Aikido.* Tokyo: Kodansha International.

———. (1993) *The Essence of Aikido: Spiritual Teachings of Morihei Ueshiba.* Tokyo: Kodansha International.

———. (1997) *Budo Training in Aikido.* Tokyo: Sugawara Martial Arts Institute/Japan Publications.

Waseda, Aikidobu. (1988) *Waseda Daigaku Aikidobu Sobu 30 Shunen Kinenshi* (Commemorating the thirtieth anniversary of Waseda University Aikido Club's founding). Tokyo: Tomon Aikidokai.

AINSWORTH, DOROTHY SEARS

(1894–1976)

U.S. PHYSICAL EDUCATOR AND WOMEN'S SPORT ADVOCATE

The women in charge of physical education at girls' schools and women's colleges in the United States in the early twentieth century developed their own particular concept of physical culture. It was characterized not only by freedom and variety but also by a lack of orientation toward competition and contest, as Dorothy Ainsworth was able to demonstrate in her *History of Physical Education in Colleges for Women*, published in 1930.

Dorothy Sears Ainsworth was born in 1894 and from an early age began to take an enthusiastic interest in sport, especially basketball. She became a gymnastics teacher and from 1926 to 1960 was director of the physical education department of Smith College in Northampton, Massachusetts. She became a leader of the women's physical education movement, earning a doctorate in 1930 and being elected president of the National Association for Physical Education of College Women in 1937; after World War II she was appointed president of the American Association of Health, Physical Education and Recreation. In 1949, as a result of her initiative, the first International Congress on Female Physical Education and Women's Sport took place in Copenhagen. At the next meeting in Paris in 1953, the International Association of Physical Education and Sport for Girls and Women (IAPESGW) was founded and Ainsworth was elected its first president. In 1961 she handed over her office to Marie Thérèse Eyquem, who was succeeded in 1965 by Liselott Diem.

In 1930 Ainsworth set down the principles of physical education for women's colleges. Her aims were to improve the physical condition and health of the students; to take into account their individual needs in view of the different motives, abilities, and skills they brought with them; and to motivate and enable them to practice sport after leaving college. Great importance was attached to the possibility the students had of developing and realizing their own ideas in the sports they practiced. It was not a question of enhancing the colleges' fame by offering sports to a small number of talented athletes, but of reaching as many of the young women as possible and integrating them into college sports. The prefeminist motto was: "A girl for every sport and a sport for every girl."

As an alternative to sports contests, the colleges organized "play days," at which fun, recreation, cooperation, and togetherness took the place of competition and record breaking. The female physical educators held the view that the sexes were different and that because of this it was necessary for them to have their separate domains and a different form of education. They believed in the existence of specifically female qualities, which, as Ainsworth demanded at the congress in Copenhagen mentioned above, ought to be reflected in women's sports. The views and activities of women's sports organizations in the United States, including the Women's Division of the National Amateur Athletic Federation, were wholly at variance with the aims and initiatives of women's sports organizations elsewhere, for example, the Fédération Sportive Féminine Internationale (FSFI). While the American women's motto was "play for play's sake," the FSFI took up the fight for women's admission to the athletic events of the Olympic Games.

For her outstanding achievements, Dorothy Ainsworth received numerous honors and awards. Among others, she was awarded the degree of Doctor of Science *honoris causa* from Smith College, the Per Henrik Ling medal from the Swedish Gymnastics Society, the highest award in the field of physical education and sport in France, and awards from the emperor of Japan and the United States government.

Gertrud Pfister

Bibliography

Betts, Edith, and Hazel Peterson. (1985) "Dorothy Sears Ainsworth." *Journal of Physical Education, Recreation and Dance* 56: 63–67.

Davenport, L. (1985) "Pioneer Leaders in Physical Education and Sport." *Journal of Physical Education, Recreation and Dance* 58, 5: 46–50.

Guttmann, Allen. (1991) *Women's Sports: A History.* New York: Columbia University Press.

Peterson, Hazel. (1968) "Dorothy S. Ainsworth: Her Life, Professional Career, and Contributions to Physical Education." Unpublished doctoral dissertation, Ohio State University, Columbus.

AIR SPORTS

Those whose lives involve constant travel by air may forget the fascination of flight and its recreational side. Flying for recreation and competition remains very popular. For example, in Britain in the 1990s it was second only to soccer (association football) in popularity, as measured in number of spectators. Women have always been involved in the production end of the aircraft industry, but when they first sought to become pilots, they faced public opinion that saw flying as unsuitable for women. Today fewer girls and women than men fly for recreation, but many barriers to access have been removed and opportunities for the professional involvement of women have increased, making women a distinct presence in sport flying.

HISTORY

In the Greek myth of Daedulus and Icarus, the father and son were not flying for recreation as they sought to escape from the island of Crete. Their story nevertheless reminds us that flight has long been a goal of humans. That myth also slowed achievement of that dream, emphasizing as it did the belief that people would only fly like birds, with flapping wings. For humans to duplicate birds' flight is a physiological impossibility, given humans' lower weight/muscle ratio. In 1783 some aspiring fliers were able to shift their thinking to another model; the Montgolfier brothers developed the hot-air balloon in France. In 1784 Marie-Elisabeth Thible became the first woman to fly as a passenger, but fifteen years would pass before Jeanne Labrosse would fly solo. By then ballooning, often in conjunction with parachuting, had turned into an exhibition for fairs and rich private parties, with some women entering the field professionally.

George Cayley (1773–1857) identified the main elements of heavier-than-air flight, including drag, thrust, the advantages of cambered, or slightly curved, aerofoils to produce lift, and the need for a tail. This allowed him to build the first glider that could carry a person. Like other pioneers, including Otto Lilienthal (1848–1896), Cayley saw gliding as a stepping stone to powered, sustained, and controlled flight. Wilbur and Orville Wright achieved this dream on 17 December 1903, when they combined a gradual experimental approach with sound mechanical skills.

Despite their initial limitations, airplanes were always cheaper and more practical than balloons, which made it easier for women to participate. On 8 July 1908, during an air display in Turin, Thérèse Peltier was a passenger in a 150-meter (490-foot) flight in the Voisin biplane piloted by Léon Delagrange and thus became the first woman to leave the ground in an airplane. The world's first licensed woman pilot was Elise Deroche, a former dancer also known as "Baroness de Laroche" (1886–1919), who soloed on 22 October 1909 and earned French license number 36 on 8 March 1910. In 1913 she was awarded the cup that the magazine *Femina* established in 1910 to promote women's flying. Belgian Hélène Dutrieu had won the first two; her sporting successes included winning the 1911 King of Italy cup in Florence against a field of fourteen men.

The journalist Harriet Quimby (1884–1912) was the first American woman to obtain a pilot's license (number 37, issued 2 August 1911). On 12 April 1912 Quimby became the first woman, and only the fifth person, to fly the English Channel. She foresaw the potential of commercial aviation and of

Harriet Quimby in a monoplane, 1912. (Bettmann/Corbis)

women's role in it, but sadly, her career was cut short by a fatal accident in Boston. Her vision would soon begin to materialize through such pioneers as Katharine Stinson and her sister Marjorie, both of the United States, who set up a flying school in San Antonio, Texas, and trained British and Canadian students during World War I. At least five women sport pilots flew operationally with the Imperial Russian Air Service during World War I.

During the years between the wars, the so-called golden age of aviation, flying was perhaps the sport that most strongly embodied the Olympic motto *Citius, altius, fortius* (Swifter, higher, stronger), as aviators seemed to set a new record daily. Women both starred in this frenzy and watched it. Sometimes, their feats were pure showmanship: Laura Ingalls, like many other early American pilots a nurse by training, at one time held world records for both men and women for consecutive loops (980, for each of which she was paid a dollar) and barrel rolls (714). Several American women starred in marathon flights aimed solely at staying aloft as long as possible: in January 1931 Bobbie Trout and Edna May Cooper flew for 122 hours, while in August 1932 Louise Thaden and Frances Marsalis overflew New York for eight days. On both occasions the aircraft were refueled in flight from another airplane.

The most famous American aviatrixes were Amelia Earhart (1897–1937) and Jacqueline Coch-

ran (c. 1910–1980). Raised in extreme poverty by foster parents, Cochran went, in her own words, from "dustbowl to stardust" and made her fortune in the cosmetics industry. She earned her license in 1932 after three weeks of training and went on to become the most successful woman sport pilot of all time. In 1938 Cochran won the Bendix Trophy against all-male competition. Twenty years later, she would become Fédération Aéronautique International (FAI) president, in charge of air sports across the world. She remains the only woman to have held that position. With the largest contingent of women pilots by far, the United States was also the first to develop a dedicated air race, the 1929 "Women's Air Derby." Dubbed the "Powder Puff Derby" by the press, this was a straightforward two-category speed race from Santa Monica, California, to Cleveland, Ohio, that coincided with the National Air Races (organized by the National Aeronautics Administration). An attempt by Hollywood to enroll starlets with male "co-pilots" was thwarted, so entrants were legitimate women pilots like Florence "Pancho" Barnes, Blanche Noyes, Ruth Elders, and of course, Earhart. Thea Rasche, from Germany, and Chubbie Miller, from England, made the event international. Louise Thaden and Phoebe Omlie placed first in the two categories, which were based on engine size.

While speed and endurance appealed to Americans, the French, Germans, and British were fascinated by long-distance flights, which combined the exotic with colonialism and an intuitive feeling of a shrinking world. Between 1930 and 1937, France's Maryse Hilsz (1901–1946) improved three times on her Paris–Saigon record, as well as performing other notable flights to Madagascar and Tokyo. German pilots Marga von Etzdorf (1907–1933) and Elly Beinhorn performed similar sensational long-distance flights. Great Britain produced a group of sport pilots too numerous to list that included the Duchess of Bedford (1866–1937), Sophie Elliott Lynn (later Lady Heath), Amy Johnson (1904–1941; she briefly formed a team with her husband, Jim Mollison, but they soon divorced), and Beryl Markham. In 1933 Jean Batten performed the first flight from England to New Zealand in a mere 11 days and 45 minutes.

These flights remained individual accomplishments everywhere except the United States,

HOW LADY HEATH
SAW THE OLYMPIC GAMES (1928)

Lady Heath, the famous British airwoman, utilized her ability as a pilot in a novel way to secure admission to the Olympic Stadium at Amsterdam.

When the British women athletes decided to stay away from the Olympiad, Lady Heath's name was erased from the register of officials, but she did not intend to miss the Olympiad, and finding there were no tickets, she set out in her aeroplane, and circled above the Stadium.

Then she dropped a note to this effect: "I shall continue circling around until tickets of admission are left at the front office. When these arrangements are made, place coats in the shape of a cross in the centre of the Stadium and I will immediately make a landing and come along."

The request was complied with. Lady Heath returned to the Stadium by car, and has since acted in an official capacity.

From African World, *11 August 1928, 119.*

---

where the Powder Puff Derby led to the forming of "The Ninety-Nines" under Earhart's presidency. The organization listed as its purpose "good fellowship, jobs, and a central office and files on women in aviation" and was named after the number of charter members (99 out of the 117 American licensed women pilots). In 1979 membership stood at more than 5,000, with 154 chapters in the United States and 25 in other nations. The European equivalent, the Fédération Européenne des Femmes Pilotes, was formed in 1950 and had about 1,000 members in 1993. In addition to programs such as "air marking" American towns to aid navigation (painting names of locations on the ground to make them easily recognizable from the air, hence aiding sport pilots during cross-country flights), the Ninety-Nines sponsored two unique speed events: the All Women's Trans American Race (AWTAR, again known as the Powder Puff Derby; the name was resurrected for publicity purposes) and its sister international race (AWIAR, or the Angel Derby). Both were open to all-women crews only, with aircraft handicapped according to their speed and a 300-horsepower engine limit. AWTAR, which started in 1947 with two airplanes and three crews, had grown to more than 200 members by its thirtieth anniversary.

Even when the novelty wore off, women pilots continued to perform remarkable feats: in 1966 Sheila Scott (1927–1988) made a solo round-the-world flight in a single-engine Piper Comanche. Five years later, Scott became the first person to fly solo over the North Pole.

OVERCOMING DISCRIMINATION

Since the inception of flight, women flew over the objections of men and often of society in general. In Germany in 1911, student pilot Melli Beese (1886–1925) found that male colleagues had sabotaged her aircraft. Minorities fared even worse: Bessie Coleman (1892–1926) had to immigrate to France to earn her license, because no flying school in the United States would accept an African American woman as a student. She passed her exam on 15 June 1921, becoming the first licensed African American pilot of either sex. Returning to America, "Queen Bess" (as she was known) performed at air shows wearing a pseudo-military flight suit of her own design. Before Coleman could realize her goal of establishing a flying school for African Americans, she fell to her death during a display for which she had inexplicably neglected to wear a parachute.

More than by individual exploits, the suitability of women as pilots was confirmed by the United States Women's Airforce Service Pilots (WASP) program, a large and statistically meaningful sample during World War II; it was run in

Bessie Coleman, the first licensed African American pilot of either sex. (Underwood & Underwood/Corbis)

conjunction with the military, although the women were not part of armed services. According to training director Cochran, 58.7 percent of the 1,830 students graduated, with a 32.9 percent elimination rate (lower than among male cadet pilots) and 8 percent resignations. Fatality and accident rates were comparable to those for male pilots, as were levels of operational fatigue. Although the WASP aimed to be representative of "the country as a whole," no African American applicants were accepted, nor were they allowed to join the 1938 Civilian Pilot Training Program (CPTP) or other wartime schemes.

The cost of technology was a more objective barrier, particularly in the pursuit of absolute records requiring state-of-the-art aircraft. Cost was not as much a consideration for men, who could draw on state support via the military and often had considerable personal fortunes. A major exception was Lady Lucy Houston (1857–1936), the eccentric former dancer who, having inherited a

vast fortune from her third husband, in 1931 sponsored with £100,000 the British team that secured the Schneider Trophy seaplane speed race.

Given the capital-intensive nature of aviation, it is no accident that women were offered some of the most significant opportunities to fly by nations with government-controlled economies. Although the success of Hanna Reitsch (1912–1979) under the Nazi regime is perhaps the best-known example, her case was by no means unique. With similar support from the Fascist regime, the marquise Carina Negrone (1911–1991) of Italy set many records, including the women's world altitude record (12,043 meters, or 39,741 feet, on 24 June 1935). Unlike Reitsch, however, Negrone did not overtly associate with Fascism; postwar, this allowed her to return to competitions, setting a world distance record for amphibious craft in 1954 and serving as president of the Aero Club di Genova between 1956 and 1963.

Although the regimes exploited these women's positive propaganda value, their achievements nevertheless ran contrary to the governments' basic policy, which confined women to traditional roles. Other governments encouraged women to fly to show their commitment to progress and change. In Turkey, President Kemal Ataturk's modernization drive included sending his adopted daughter Sabiha Gökçen to civil and military flying schools. Before becoming a flying instructor, Gökçen even flew combat missions against Kurdish rebels. For decades the Soviet Union had the largest women's flying program; during World War II this enabled them to field three women's air regiments coordinated by former record holder Marina Raskova. Until the 1991 collapse of the Soviet bloc, massive state support in terms of jobs, aircraft, and training facilities allowed Eastern European teams to dominate women's aerobatic championships, with some opposition from the French, who placed second in the 1978 world championships.

MODERN AIR SPORTS

The FAI remains the governing body for air sports. Founded in 1905 and comprising the national aeronautics clubs or their equivalents, it issues sporting licenses, sets rules, and certifies all international records. For this purpose, air sports are divided into five main categories: balloons, airships, powered aircraft, unpowered aircraft, and rotorcraft, with further subdivisions according to weight, configuration, and other variables. Each holds its own world and regional championships; in addition, in part to redress the persisting exclusion of air sports from the Olympics, the FAI has launched the World Air Games (WAG), the first of which were held in 1997 in Antalya, Turkey.

Prompted by the availability of surplus fighters, speed races continued for some years after World War II: in 1947 American Marge Hurlburt set a 337-miles-per-hour (mph) (542 kilometers-per-hour [kph]) record in a clipped-wing Corsair in Florida, and in 1948 Lettice Curtis briefly raced a Spitfire in England setting a 313.208 mph (504 kph) women's British national record for speed over a closed circuit. But for all practical purposes the war ended the age of achievement and marked the start of the emphasis on safety and reliability. Soon pure speed racing became extinct outside the United States. Also, the advent of the jet age put world records beyond the reach of all but government-sponsored pilots: it was only as the daughter-in-law of the French president that Jacqueline Auriol (1917–) gained access to the jet fighters in which she broke the women's speed record five times between 1951 and 1963. To become the first woman to fly at the speed of sound (18 May 1953) and over twice as fast (11 May 1963), Jacqueline Cochran borrowed jet fighters from the manufacturers.

A major, if exceptional, extension of the age of achievement was the nonstop, unrefueled, round-the-world flight made 14–23 December 1986 by the *Voyager*, crewed by Dick Rutan and Jeana Yeager, who lived airborne for nine days in a space two feet wide. The entire program cost $2 million, all raised by donations and sponsorship. Another significant first flight, albeit more scientific than sporting, was made by Janice Brown on 7 August 1980 in the *Gossamer Penguin*, the world's first solar-powered aircraft. Brown was selected because her weight, a mere 45 kilograms (99 pounds), would not overly tax the weak engine. About the only reasonably achievable records are now for point-to-point flights: an extreme case is represented by Cochran, who on 22 April 1962 broke or established twenty-nine new records flying between New Orleans and Bonn.

These factors explain why the air rally has become the most common type of race for powered aircraft, allowing pilots to compete on skill rather than resources. Participants are awarded points or penalties based on their ability to navigate accurately and keep calculated times, leading to two-person (pilot plus navigator) crews. Precision landing events are also often included, while any speed runs are made on a handicap basis. Women represent a minority of participants, often as navigators in husband/wife teams such as that of Luciano and Giuliana Nustrini, five-time winners of the Italian national championship who died together in February 1999 while flying in New Zealand. Rallies also help young pilots build up the confidence and experience needed to enter the field professionally; such was the course followed by, among others, Fiorenza De Bernardi (1926–), who in 1967 became the first Italian woman airline pilot. But many others competed for sport's sake, like Mutz Tremse, winner of the 1970 German rally championship and of the 1967 and 1973 women's rallies.

In aerobatics, judges assess a pilot's ability to perform maneuvers according to a set of rules (the Aresti code) and within a prescribed area (the box). Each entrant must fly a combination of maneuvers, which she and the judges select, that balance creativity and ability to follow a program. Because performance depends on key technical features (that is, wing loading, specific excess power, strength), aerobatic pilots fly special aircraft suited to little else. The first woman known to have participated in an aerobatic maneuver is Trehawke Davis at Hendon, England in September 1913, while German Liesel Bach (1905–1992) was the star prewar woman aerobatic pilot, although by no means the only one.

The popularity of ultralights, paragliding, and other inexpensive forms of recreational flying has expanded the opportunities for women's participation in air sports. In many cases, achievements in these fields follow upon the patterns of sixty years before.

THE AVIATION INDUSTRY

Women have always played significant roles in the aviation industry, which in the days of early fabric-covered airplanes valued their skill as seamstresses. Already in 1912 Beese had set up a flying school, but because she married a French citizen this was requisitioned in 1914. In Italy, beginning in 1927, Giuseppina Agusta built up the small family aviation business into a leading helicopter manufacturer. Olive Ann Beech founded Beech Aircraft in 1931 with her husband Walter, became president following his death in 1950, and ran the company—one of the two largest general aviation manufacturers in the world—for thirty years. During World War II, women's presence in aviation boomed; by late 1943 the American aircraft industry alone employed more than 478,000 women. Popularly known as "Rosie the Riveter," these women also served as flight engineers, instructors, and ferry and test pilots. After the war, some would remain in the field, although many years would pass before women airline pilots became commonplace. In 1964 Maria Luisa Protto became chairman of Siai Marchetti, a historic company that had fallen in decline after World War II, and reestablished it as a builder of complete aircraft, including the successful SF.260 sportplane. No account of women in aviation would be complete without mention of Timina Guasti (1902–1991), who in 1929—together with her husband, aviation industrialist Gianni Caproni—founded the Caproni Museum, today one of the world's finest private historic aviation collections. Her daughter Maria Fede Caproni (1933–) carries on Guasti's work.

CONCLUSION

Through the efforts and sacrifices of many women, today the role of women in aviation in any capacity is no longer a curiosity but an integral part of one of the most important aspects of modern society. Indeed, at present the factor that most limits women's presence in air sports is the general loss of interest in speed and record-breaking brought about by the general acceptance of flying as a tool and commodity.

Gregory Alegi

See also Ballooning; Earhart, Amelia; Hang Gliding; Long Distance Flying; Markham, Beryl; Parachuting; Soaring

Bibliography

Bragg, Janet Harmon (with Marjorie M. Kriz). (1996) *Soaring Above Setbacks*. Washington, DC: Smithsonian Institution Press.

Cochran, Jacqueline (with Floyd Odlum). (1954) *The Stars at Noon*. Boston: Little Brown.

Curtis, Lettice. (1985) *Forty Years On: A Spitfire Flies Again*. Olney: Nelson & Saunders.

De Bernardi, Fiorenza, ed. (1984) *Pink Line: A Gallery of European Women Pilots*. Rome: Aeritalia.

Gunston, Bill, ed. (1992) *Chronicle of Aviation*. London: Chronicle.

History of the Ninety-Nines, Inc. (1979) Oklahoma City: The Ninety-Nines, Inc.

Jablonski, Edward. (1968) *Ladybirds: Women in Aviation*. New York: Hawthorn Books.

Jackson, Bernard. (1981) "Lady Houston: One of the Few." *Aeroplane Monthly* 9, 8 (August): 451–454.

Mason, Francis K., and Martin Windrow, eds. (1970) *Air Facts and Feats: A Record of Aerospace Achievement*. New York: Doubleday.

The Ninety-Nines, Inc. <http://www.ninety-nines.org>. 1999.

Plehiger, Russell. (1989) *Marathon Flyers*. Detroit: Harlo.

Rado, Gheorghe. (1993) *Prioritati si Recorduri Mondiale de Aviatie*. Bucharest: Tehnoprod.

Robène, Luc. (1998) *L'Homme à la Conquête de l'Air*. Paris: L'Harmattan.

ALL-AMERICAN GIRLS PROFESSIONAL BASEBALL LEAGUE

The All-American Girls Professional Baseball League (AAGPBL) fielded highly competitive teams of more than 500 women hardball players from 1943 to 1954. The twelve years of the League is the longest period any women's professional team sport has existed in the United States. At its height, in 1948, the league consisted of ten fabulously named teams and entertained more than a million spectators in such middle-sized midwestern cities as Rockford, Illinois (the Peaches), Racine,

Wisconsin (the Belles), Fort Wayne, Indiana (the Daisies), and Grand Rapids, Michigan (the Chicks).

The AAGPBL was started by Philip Wrigley, owner of the Chicago Cubs, who feared that World War II might force cancellation of the 1943 men's major league season (it didn't), causing fans to forget baseball. His solution—at once economic and patriotic—was to field women's teams, for during the war years women were encouraged to do all the things normally reserved for men: work in factories, join the armed services, and, in the case of sports, play baseball. Scouts recruited the girls (some were still teenagers) from softball leagues throughout the United States, Canada, and Cuba. In an era when the average salary was about $40 per week, the players were paid between $55 and $150 per week for a 125-game season. They played nearly every day, with doubleheaders on many weekends, traveling from city to city by bus.

At first the women played softball, but swiftly the base paths and distance from mound to plate were lengthened and the pitchers hurled overhand a ball that had shrunk to the regulation hardball size of 9 to 9¼ inches. For the first time in the history of sports in the United States, women were professionals playing baseball in a league of their own.

The caliber of play was excellent and exciting. Max Carey, a Pittsburgh Pirates Hall of Famer, who managed a team and was league president for six years, called the final game of the 1946 championship series, a fourteen-inning contest between the Peaches and the Belles the greatest game he had ever seen, male or female. Peach Carolyn Morris pitched a no-hitter for nine innings and was not removed until the twelfth. Belles pitcher Joanne Winter allowed thirteen hits, but the Peaches couldn't put them together to produce a run. The scoreless game went into extra innings. Then, in the bottom of the fourteenth, Sophie Kurys of the Belles got a hit, stole second, and, in the midst of stealing third, saw her teammate Betty Trezza hit the ball to right field. Kurys slid home to win the game. That same year Kurys, the "Flint [Michigan] Flash," stole 201 bases. Her career record of 1,114 stolen bases was surpassed by male major leaguer Rickey Henderson in the late 1990s.

Perhaps the best all-around player was Dottie Kamenshek. When she retired at the beginning of

the 1952 season, the Peaches' first baseman had led the league for one or more seasons in at-bats, runs scored, hits, singles, fewest strike outs, and batting average—.316 in 1946, .306 in 1947. (The best batting average for an AAGPBL player was that of Joanne Weaver, .429 in 1954, the last professional ballplayer in history to hit over .400.) In 1950 Dottie was offered a chance to play professional minor-league baseball with men, but she declined, saying, "I want to finish out my career with the Peaches." Wally Pip, himself a great defensive first baseman for the 1920s New York Yankees, called Dottie "the fanciest fielding first baseman I've ever seen—man or woman." Dottie Schroeder, a shortstop and the only woman to play all twelve seasons with the league, was another fielding standout. Cubs manager Charlie Grimm, watching her work out one day said, "If she was a boy, I'd give $50,000 for her."

Dorothy "Dottie" Schroeder of the Ft. Wayne Daisies in the All-American Girls Baseball League. Schroeder was the only player to play in every season of the league's existence. (Northern Indiana Center for History)

ALL AMERICAN GIRLS' VICTORY SONG

Batter up—hear that call.
The time has come for one and all
To play ball.

For we're the members of the All American
    League.
We come from cities near and far.
We've got Canadians, Irishmen, and Swedes.
We're all for one,
We're one for all,
We're All American.

Each girl stands,
Her head so proudly high,
Her motto DO or DIE.
She's not the one to use
Or need an alibi.
Our chaperones are not too soft;
They're not too tough.
Our managers are on the ball.
We've got a President, who really knows his stuff.
We're all for one
We're one for all
We're ALL Americans.

The fact that the All-Americans were not boys, however, was of major interest to promoters of the league. They believed, "The more feminine the appearance of the performer, the more dramatic her performance." The explicit admonition to the women was that they should "look like girls and play like men." To this end the tomboys and working-class and farm girls who made up the vast majority of players were made to wear skirts when they played ball and were subjected to "charm schools" during spring training. There they were taught the basics of makeup, hair styling, carriage, and deportment. Dottie Schroeder evaluated the experience: "We learned how to walk and how to talk. They were deadly earnest about this. Well, being brought up as I was, I didn't outwardly scoff at it, but inwardly I did, because I thought, 'They're going to teach me how to be graceful? I learned how to be graceful by playing ball out in the pasture, side-steppin' all the cowpies!'"

The fans may have first come to the ballpark to see "an amazing spectacle," but they came back to watch the players hit the ball hard, pitch well, make some good plays, and, with any luck, win. It was important for fans, especially little girls, to see women doing something physical and difficult and fun together. It was important for the players, who got the rare chance to play this sport they

loved. And it was important for the owners, managers, and fans to see that—given the opportunity—women excel at hardball.

The league folded after the 1954 season, a casualty of both economic and social factors. Increasingly erratic ownership and promotion, combined with that constant threat to live entertainment, the television, caused attendance to decline. In addition, social propaganda strongly suggested that—World War II and the Korean War being over—women should leave the factories, offices, and ballparks to the men.

For forty years little mention was made of the league. But in the late 1970s, with the rise of the second wave of feminism, interest was rekindled in women's history, and the All-Americans were rediscovered. A first reunion was held in 1982, and by the end of the century the women had an active Player's Association, a newsletter, and reunions every few years; they are part of a permanent exhibit at the National Baseball Hall of Fame in Cooperstown, New York, honoring the achievements of women in baseball.

In 1994 a major motion picture, *A League of Their Own*, introduced the nation and then the world to the achievements of the All-Americans. As the credits roll at the end of this film, two teams of old ladies are shown playing ball with great enthusiasm. They are, of course, the All-Americans themselves, ironically seen in their old age by vastly more people than ever saw them play in person in their youth.

Dottie Collins, a former Fort Wayne pitcher and in 1999 president of the Player's Association, said in an interview what many players feel: "At the time, you know, we were just kids having fun. Not until it was all over did we look back and realize we had been pioneers."

Susan E. Johnson

See also Baseball; Softball

Bibliography

Browne, Lois (1992). *Girls of Summer.* Toronto, Canada: HarperCollins.

Gregorich, Barbara (1993). *Women at Play.* New York: Harcourt Brace.

Johnson, Susan E. (1994) *When Women Played Hardball.* Seattle, WA: Seal Press.

Macy, Sue (1993). *A Whole New Ball Game.* New York: Henry Holt.

AMATEURISM *see* Professionalism

AMENORRHEA

Amenorrhea, or absence of menstrual bleeding, is relatively common, occurring in 2–5 percent of the female population in the world and in as many as 8.5 percent of adolescents (ages twelve to eighteen). Since the 1970s, it has been recognized that amenorrhea may be more common in certain groups of athletes, particularly ballet dancers and long-distance runners. Studies show that gymnasts, cyclists, rowers, swimmers, recreational weightlifters, and competitive bodybuilders may also be at increased risk. The number of female athletes with amenorrhea has been difficult to determine accurately, but various studies have estimated that more than one-half of some groups of athletes are amenorrheic.

PATTERNS OF AMENORRHEA

Certain characteristics of an athlete seem to predispose her to having "exercise-associated" or "athletic" amenorrhea. She is likely to weigh less, have a lower percentage of body fat, and have lost more weight after she began vigorous physical activity than her counterparts with normal menstrual cycles. She is more likely to be a vegetarian or to consume low amounts of dietary protein. Eating disorders such as anorexia and bulimia are common, especially in adolescent and highly competitive athletes. An amenorrheic athlete is more likely to have a history of irregular menstrual periods before she starts training. She is likely to exercise intensely and to associate a higher level of stress with training than does an athlete with a normal menstrual cycle.

Initially, amenorrhea was viewed as a result of strenuous exercise. Gradually, amenorrhea in some athletes was found to be associated with disordered eating and bone loss, giving rise to the concept of the "female athlete triad"—disordered eating, amenorrhea, and osteoporosis. Amenorrhea is the element of the triad that will bring a female athlete to the attention of medical professionals. Sport medicine personnel may also then investigate the possibilities of disordered eating and osteoporosis.

DEFINITIONS

Amenorrhea usually refers to the absence of menstrual bleeding for six months or for a length of time equal to the sum of three previous menstrual cycles. To standardize future reports, the International Olympic Committee (IOC) has defined exercise-associated amenorrhea as one period or fewer in a year. In medical terms, young women who have not had any menstrual bleeding by sixteen years of age, or by fourteen years of age in the absence of breast or sexual hair development, are considered to have *primary amenorrhea. Secondary amenorrhea* refers to those women who have had at least one menstrual period before developing amenorrhea.

CAUSES OF EXERCISE-ASSOCIATED AMENORRHEA

Exercise-associated amenorrhea is generally considered to be part of "hypothalamic amenorrhea." Except for pregnancy, hypothalamic amenorrhea is the most common cause of secondary amenorrhea. A hormone, gonadotropin-releasing hormone (GnRH), is absent or is released abnormally by the hypothalamus (part of the brain). The pituitary gland and, in turn, the ovaries do not receive the signals to function appropriately. Eggs do not mature properly, so inadequate estrogen is produced by the ovary. Low estrogen levels are present in women with this disorder, resulting in thinning of the wall of the vagina and, eventually, bone loss.

Whether exercise alone can cause amenorrhea remains unclear. In fact, the recognition of the female athlete triad has fueled this controversy. Weight loss and psychological stresses are known to cause hypothalamic amenorrhea. The strong association of eating disorders with amenorrhea in the athlete suggests that weight loss or extreme changes in weight may explain many cases of amenorrhea.

Most likely, exercise-associated amenorrhea is the result of the varied contributions of weight loss, lowered body fat, and emotional and physical stress in individual athletes. That not all thin athletes become amenorrheic suggests individual variations in the reproductive system.

Most experts agree that high levels of exercise may result in malfunctioning of the hypothalamus. It is possible that athletes who become amenorrheic do not consume enough calories to meet their levels of energy use. Somehow, the hypothalamus senses this energy drain, and amenorrhea results. In order to survive, the body stops its reproductive potential, which prevents a woman with inadequate energy stores from undergoing the additional stress of pregnancy.

MEDICAL EVALUATION
OF THE AMENORRHEIC ATHLETE

Experts advise that any athlete who has the symptom of amenorrhea should see a physician or other health care provider for a thorough evaluation. It is not safe to immediately assume that the lack of menstrual periods is exercise-associated or athletic amenorrhea.

Amenorrhea has many other causes besides exercise. The most common of these is pregnancy, which *must* be considered first, in athletes and nonathletes. It is considered even in sexually active women with longstanding amenorrhea; the first

ovulation can occur before the first menses. Delayed appropriate prenatal care or delayed decision to terminate a pregnancy can have serious health consequences for an athlete. Other causes of amenorrhea include small tumors of the pituitary gland, early menopause, and developmental abnormalities of the uterus. Certain medications, such as anabolic steroids, can also cause amenorrhea.

The diagnosis of exercise-associated amenorrhea is considered to be a diagnosis of exclusion. Since no single test confirms the diagnosis, physicians consider that an athlete carries this diagnosis only when all other potential causes for amenorrhea have been excluded through a complete evaluation.

A medical evaluation for amenorrhea includes a thorough medical and nutritional history, a general physical and pelvic examination, and some blood tests. Blood tests usually include a pregnancy test, measurement of thyroid hormones, and measurement of pituitary hormones that control the menstrual cycle. Sometimes a test to measure the density of bone is also used to determine whether any bone loss has already occurred.

TREATMENT OF EXERCISE-ASSOCIATED
AMENORRHEA

Recommendations for treatment of the athlete are based on the recognized short- and long-term consequences of amenorrhea. Many athletes find the absence of menstrual bleeding desirable in the short term because menstrual periods may create practical problems in training and competition, and athletes may resist recommendations for treatment that might result in the return of menstrual bleeding.

Amenorrheic athletes do not seem to experience performance disadvantages or advantages because of their menstrual function. Musculoskeletal injuries such as stress fractures, however, are increased in athletes with menstrual irregularities, in part because of bone loss. In the short term, any associated eating disorder poses the greatest threat to the amenorrheic athlete; 10–18 percent of women with untreated eating disorders may die because of the disorder.

The long-term consequences of untreated exercise-associated amenorrhea are not completely understood. Concern has centered on bone loss as a result of low estrogen levels. In

WHEN MENSTRUATION STOPS

Amenorrhea, the absence of menstruation, along with disordered eating and osteoporosis, form the female athlete disorder triad. Of the three, amenorrhea is particularly important because it is the one most likely to come first to the attention of medical personnel and thus may also make the physician aware of related medical problems, including disordered eating and osteoporosis. While female athletes may not notice the early stages of osteoporosis and may hide their disordered eating, the cessation of menstruation may indicate pregnancy and, therefore, leads the athlete to seek medical attention.

spite of lifestyle changes that eventually restore menstrual periods, previously amenorrheic athletes usually cannot regain bone density that equals the values in women with normal menstrual cycles. Intensive exercise directed at specific locations usually does not completely prevent bone loss at that site. It has been suggested that the extremes of impact loading in gymnastics might prevent bone loss even in the amenorrheic athlete.

TREATING THE DISORDER

Recommendations for treatment usually involve eliminating behaviors that may have contributed to the development of amenorrhea. Eating disorders are identified and treated. Caloric intake is adjusted so that it approximately equals calorie use. Important emotional stress factors, such as a need to overachieve, are identified and addressed. A decrease in exercise intensity, a 2–3 percent increase in weight, or both may be encouraged, especially for adolescents who might continue training for many years. However, even with these changes, normal menses may not be restored for months or even years.

Other treatment recommendations are intended to prevent bone loss and to restore as much as possible of the bone already lost because of low estrogen levels. All amenorrheic athletes are directed to supplement their food consumption to reach a calcium intake of 1200–1500 mg/day and vitamin D intake of 400–600 IU/day. Estrogen replacement has been shown to be necessary to protect against bone loss in the amenorrheic athlete. Whether or not the athlete is sexually active, oral contraceptive pills are recommended as a source of estrogen, although this option is not available to all women for religious, cultural, or personal reasons.

When there is no other underlying menstrual abnormality, exercise-associated amenorrhea seems to be reversible. The ability to conceive a child is usually established with the onset of normal menstrual cycles.

Finally, prevention is the best approach to exercise-associated amenorrhea. Experts argue that athletes, coaches, athletic trainers, and parents should be counseled about the possible consequences of overtraining and poor nutritional habits and that they should be educated to recognize and discourage disordered eating. In addition, athletes should learn to develop healthy attitudes toward nutrition and weight, while still realizing their athletic potential.

Lorna A. Marshall

See also Eating Disorders; Menstrual Cycle; Osteoporosis; Reproduction

Bibliography

Marshall, L. A. (1994) "Clinical Evaluation of Amenorrhea in Active and Athletic Women." *Clinical Sports Medicine* 13: 371–387.

Schwartz, B., D. C. Cumming, R. D. Riordan, et al. (1981) "Exercise-Associated Amenorrhea: A Distinct Entity?" *American Journal of Obstetrics and Gynecology* 141: 662–670.

Yeager, K. K., R. Agostini, A. Nattiv, and B. Drinkwater. (1993) "The Female Athlete Triad: Disordered Eating, Amenorrhea, Osteoporosis" (commentary). *Medical Science Sports Exercise* 25: 775–777.

ANEMIA

Anemia is one of the most common medical conditions affecting female athletes. When unrecognized and untreated, anemia can impair athletic performance and general well-being. Anemia is easily diagnosed and treated and is usually preventable. Iron-deficiency anemia is the most common type of anemia seen among female athletes. However, two other types of exercise-related anemia, dilutional pseudoanemia and exercise-induced hemolysis, are also issues for female athletes.

DEFINITIONS

Anemia is a condition in which the number of red blood cells circulating through the body is lower than normal. Red blood cells are necessary to carry oxygen from the lungs to the muscles. When this capacity is diminished, muscles tire more easily and endurance is impaired. Symptoms in athletes may include tiredness, becoming easily fatigued during exercise, the feeling of muscle burning, shortness of breath, nausea, and pale appearance. Anemia is diagnosed by a simple blood test that measures hemoglobin and hematocrit, the components of red blood cells responsible for carrying oxygen. Blood tests show that anemia is present when hemoglobin or hematocrit values fall below the normal range. Normal ranges for adolescent and adult females are hemoglobin between 12 and 16 g/dl and hematocrit between 36% and 46%. Values for hemoglobin are normally 0.5 g/dl lower in blacks, and hematocrit is 4% higher for each 1999-meter (3280-foot) increase in altitude. On an individual basis, significant overlap exists between normal and abnormal values, so the diagnosis of anemia must be made relative to an individual's baseline normal range. For example, a hemoglobin value of 13 g/dl, although within the normal range, may represent anemia for a woman whose normal baseline hemoglobin level is 13.5 g/dl. Alternatively, a hemoglobin value of 11.5 g/dl, although below the normal range, may not represent anemia for a woman for whom this is her normal baseline level.

Physicians know that iron stores in the body are depleted before clinically recognized anemia (characterized by hemoglobin and hematocrit below the normal range) occurs. Therefore, they often find it necessary to look beyond hemoglobin and hematocrit when screening for the early stages of iron-deficiency anemia and differentiating iron-deficiency anemia from other forms of anemia.

SPORT ANEMIA

In active women, low hemoglobin and hematocrit values may not represent true anemia, but may instead be due to "sport anemia," also referred to as dilutional pseudoanemia. In this condition, hemoglobin is altered as a result of increased blood plasma volume, which is caused by endurance exercise training, resulting in artificially low values of hemoglobin and hematocrit. Endurance training causes an increase in blood plasma volume proportional to the amount and intensity of endurance exercise. For example, a 5 percent increase in plasma volume can result from a moderate jogging program, while the training of an elite distance runner can induce a 20 percent increase. Although hemoglobin concentration decreases due to this dilutional effect, red blood cell mass remains normal or is often increased; therefore, oxygen-carrying capacity in the blood is not impaired (hence the term "pseudoanemia" or "false anemia").

Physicians most commonly observe this condition in elite endurance athletes, in previously sedentary individuals initiating an exercise program, and among athletes who are increasing their training intensity. This type of anemia can be distinguished from iron-deficiency anemia because microscopic appearance of the red blood cells and measures of iron stores (such as ferritin) are normal, it does not respond to iron supplementation, and it is unlikely to result in severe anemia—that is, levels will not become extremely low.

Not all female athletes are equally at risk for anemia. Among high risk factors are: (1) disadvantaged socioeconomic background; (2) dietary restriction such as vegetarian diet, weight-loss diets, or fad diets; (3) intense or prolonged endurance training; (4) personal or family history of anemia, bleeding disorders, or chronic disease;

(5) excessive menstrual flow; (6) use of anti-inflammatory medications; (7) recent volunteer blood donation; and (8) recent childbirth.

EXERCISE-INDUCED HEMOLYTIC ANEMIA

Exercise-induced hemolytic anemia is caused by the hemolysis (destruction of red blood cells) that can occur due to the physical stress that exercise places on red blood cells. Hemolysis can occur in both high- and low-impact sports. In high-impact sports such as running, it is thought that the physical trauma of repetitive hard foot strikes leads to the destruction of red blood cells. For this reason the term "foot strike hemolysis" has been used to describe this condition. However, red blood cell destruction has also been documented among competitive swimmers and other athletes not participating in running activities. Red blood cells may be damaged by injury due to muscular contraction, lactic acid buildup (which occurs with intense or prolonged exercise), or increased body temperature.

The condition is most commonly observed in middle-aged distance runners, particularly those who are overweight, run on hard surfaces, wear poorly cushioned shoes, and run with a heavy gait. Prevention and treatment focus on encouraging runners to have lean body composition, run on soft surfaces, run lightly on their feet, and wear well-cushioned shoes and insoles. For most athletes, exercise-induced hemolysis is of little consequence, since it is rarely severe enough to cause appreciable iron loss. However, there is the potential that small differences in red blood cell numbers may result in a competitive disadvantage for world-class athletes.

IRON-DEFICIENCY ANEMIA

Prevalence of iron deficiency anemia ranges up to 20 percent in studies of adolescent female athletes and is particularly high in cross-country runners. An additional 20–60 percent of female athletes are iron-deficient but not yet anemic (low ferritin, normal hemoglobin). Development of iron deficiency during training was found to occur in 20 percent of female runners in the United States and was found to be preventable by iron supplementation. Adolescent girls may be particularly susceptible because of increased iron needs to meet the demands of growth and to counteract the blood loss caused by the onset of menses, as well as erratic dietary practices.

CAUSES

Although athletes may experience iron loss through sweat, urine, gastrointestinal sources, or hemolysis, these losses are usually negligble and not significant enough to cause appreciable iron deficiency. Excessive use of nonsteroidal anti-inflammatory medication (aspirin, ibuprofen) may increase gastrointestinal losses due to gastrointestinal bleeding. The most common cause of iron deficiency in female athletes and nonathletes alike is inadequate dietary intake of iron to compensate for menstrual losses.

Inadequate dietary intake of iron is the primary cause of iron deficiency in female athletes. In the United States, the Recommended Daily Allowance (RDA) for iron to meet basic daily needs for females is 15 mg/day. The average diet in the United States contains 5–7 mg of iron per 1,000 calories. Therefore, women need approximately 3,000 calories per day to get at least the RDA of 15 mg of iron. However, many female athletes consume less than 2,000 calories daily, particularly female athletes participating in sports that emphasize lean body physique, such as gymnastics. In addition, many female athletes, in an attempt to eat healthfully and reduce fat intake, eat little red meat, the primary food source of iron. Vegetarian diets pose an increased risk of anemia due to lower bioavailability and quantities of iron in nonmeat foods.

EFFECTS ON PERFORMANCE

Anemia clearly impairs physical performance and is linked to diminished maximum oxygen consumption, decreased physical work capacity, lower endurance, increased lactic acidosis (a by-product of anaerobic metabolism), and increased fatigue. It is unclear whether iron deficiency in the absence of anemia (nonanemic iron deficiency) impairs performance, although it is likely to represent a preanemic state.

Studies of the effects of iron supplementation on the performance of nonanemic iron-deficient athletes have produced conflicting results. Some studies in female runners following iron supplementation have shown improvements in measures of endurance, such as treadmill times, run times, and lower blood lactate levels during submaximal exercise (exercise that is intense but in which the participant does not reach the point of total exhaustion and inability to continue). In many instances, iron supplementation also led to improvements in hemoglobin levels, suggesting that the beneficial effects were seen because of correction of a mild anemia. These studies illustrate the important point that it is clinically difficult to distinguish mild anemia from nonanemic iron deficiency and that although a hemoglobin value may technically fall within the normal range, it may nevertheless represent mild anemia that will respond to iron supplementation. However, other studies have failed to show beneficial effects on performance of iron supplementation of nonanemic iron-deficient athletes. They suggest that when hemoglobin levels are not improved, iron supplementation does not improve performance, despite an increase in ferritin levels.

PREVENTION

Preventive efforts should emphasize adequate dietary intake of iron over supplements because of the greater bioavailability of iron in food sources—that is, the body better absorbs iron that comes from food. Strategies to increase dietary intake of iron are: (1) eat iron-rich foods such as lean red meat, dark meat of poultry, fish, cereals, pasta and bread enriched with iron, dried fruits, beans, tofu, and spinach; (2) recognize that meat sources of iron are absorbed better than nonmeat sources of iron; (3) enhance iron absorption from foods by concurrently eating foods containing vitamin C, such as fruit juices; (4) avoid inhibitors of iron absorption such as tea, wheat bran, milk, and antacids; (5) cook in iron skillets; and (6) if unable to meet daily iron needs through diet, take a supplement containing the RDA for iron (18 mg), such as a multivitamin with iron. Vegetarians can be advised of a number of nonmeat sources of dietary iron (eggs, dried fruit, kidney beans, cream of wheat, and fortified cereal). Iron supplementation is the mainstay of treatment of iron deficiency, as it is usually not feasible to increase dietary intake of iron enough to reverse iron deficiency.

Sally S. Harris

See also Menstrual Cycle; Nutrition

Bibliography

Clement, D. B., and R. C. Asmundson. (1984) "Iron Status and Sports Performance." *Sports Medicine* 1: 65–74.

Fogelholm, M., L. Jaakkola, and T. Lampisjavi. (1992) "Effects of Iron Supplementation in Female Athletes with Low Serum Ferritin Concentration." *International Journal of Sports Medicine* 13: 158–162.

Harris, S. S. (1995) "Helping Active Women Avoid Anemia." *Physician and Sports Medicine* 23, 5: 35–48.

Haymes, E. M. (1993) "Dietary Iron Needs in Exercising Women: A Rational Plan to Follow in Evaluating Iron Status." *Medicine, Exercise, Nutrition & Health* 2: 203–212.

Haymes, E. M., and D. M. Spillman. (1989) "Iron Status of Women Distance Runners, Sprinters, and Control Women." *International Journal of Sports Medicine* 10: 430–433.

Lamanca, J., and E. Haymes. (1989) "Effects of Dietary Iron Supplementation on Endurance." *Medicine and Science in Sports & Exercise* 21: S77.

Newhouse, I. J., D. B. Clement, J. E. Taunton, and D. C. McKenzie. (1989) "The Effect of Prelatent/Latent Iron Deficiency on Physical Work Capacity." *Medicine and Science in Sports & Exercise* 21: 263–268.

Nickerson, H. J., M. Holubets, and B. R. Weiler. (1989) "Causes of Iron Deficiency in Adolescent Athletes." *Journal of Pediatrics* 114: 657–659.

Plowman, S. A., and P. C. McSwegin. (1981) "The Effects of Iron Supplementation on Female Cross Country Runners." *Journal of Sports Medicine and Physical Fitness* 21, 4: 407–416.

Risser, W. L., E. J. Lee, H. B. Poindexter, M. S. West, J. M. Pivarnik, J. M. H. Risser, and J. F. Hickson. (1988) "Iron Deficiency in Female Athletes: Its Prevalence and Impact on Performance." *Medicine and Science in Sports & Exercise* 20: 116–121.

Rowland, T. W., S. A. Black, and J. F. Kelleher. (1987) "Iron Deficiency in Adolescent Endurance Athletes." *Journal of Adolescent Health Care* 8, 4: 322–326.

Rowland, T. W., M. B. Deisroth, G. M. Green, and J. F. Kelleher. (1988) "The Effect of Iron Therapy on the Exercise Capacity of Nonanemic Iron-Deficient Adolescent Runners." *American Journal of Diseases of Children* 142: 165–169.

Rowland, T. W., and J. F. Kelleher. (1989) "Iron Deficiency in Athletes: Insights from High School Swimmers." *American Journal of Diseases of Children* 143: 197–200.

Selby, G. B., and E. R. Eichner. (1986) "Endurance Swimming, Intravascular Hemolysis, Anemia, and Iron Depletion: New Perspective on Athlete's Anemia." *American Journal of Medicine* 81: 791–794.

Yoshida, T., M. Udo, and M. Chida. (1990) "Dietary Iron Supplement During Severe Physical Training in Competitive Female Distance Runners." *Sports Training and Medical Rehabilitation* 1: 279–285.

ANIMAL RIGHTS

Animal rights is the broad term used to describe a movement that opposes the use for human pleasure or profit of an animal in ways that might interfere with its well being or life, or its quality of existence. The animal rights movement strikes directly at the heart of animal-based sports. Whether the activity is hunting, chasing, showing, riding, or viewing animals in sport, animal rights proponents question whether humans have the right to use animals for either pleasure or sustenance.

HISTORY

The contemporary animal rights movement is descended from the nineteenth-century antivivisection movement. Historians argue that this earlier movement came from people's deep-seated reactions to the changes of industrialization and modernization. Many people believed that the social upheaval caused by these shifts resulted in the moral decay of their society. In Victorian times, then, antivivisectionists saw animal abuse as evidence of this decay. Society had become more barbarous, and animals paid the price.

At this same time, as the theory of biological evolution became more prominent, some people—including notable philosophers—began to see the similarities among different species. They reasoned that if the species are similar, then animals should have the same rights as humans. This presented a real dilemma for sports enthu-siasts. From their own experience, they saw that animals are indeed similar to humans, a view generally confirmed by emerging scientific and philosophical theories.

In the nineteenth century, many women backed the animal rights movement, as they do now. The movement was also largely middle class. Some historians believe that women's interest in animal rights grew from their own oppressed position in society. They too sought equal rights, and in supporting animal rights, they spoke for those who could not speak for themselves. The antivivisectionist movement was limited in its objectives; blood sports were the chief target.

THE MODERN ANIMAL RIGHTS MOVEMENT

By the end of the twentieth century, the modern animal rights movement went far beyond the single issue of blood sports and questioned virtually all forms of animal use. Animal rights activists also made full use of modern media technology to publicize their cause. They described animal rights in moral terms and spread this ideology widely. As in the Victorian era, modern animal rights leaders discovered that people fear social upheaval and respond to fundamentalist calls for a return to a simpler time of what have become known as "family values." They noted a widespread discontent with the complexity and lack of morality in modern life. The modern movement, however, found a broader range of people accepting of their ideas, at least in their more moderate forms.

PHILOSOPHIES

Behind the day-to-day decisions that people make about how they use animals and animal products lie several philosophies that also extend back into the nineteenth century: utilitarianism and moral rights. The philosophy of utilitarianism is based on the notion that any ethical decision—a decision that involves a question of right and wrong—should provide the greatest possible pleasure and the least possible pain. Its creed is "The greatest good, for the greatest number, for the longest time." Activists argue that since animals and people both feel pain and pleasure, anyone who makes an ethical decision should consider animals and people as equal. Peter Singer's *Animal Liberation,* published in 1975, popularized for the first time the notion that animal's interests and people's interests are equivalent, and that they should be treated in equivalent ways.

The second philosophical argument, moral rights, emphasizes the inherent value of higher mammals. Tom Regan's *The Case for Animal Rights,* published in 1985, argued that since animals have consciousness, expectations, and desires, they have inherent value. Because they have inherent value, they likewise have personal autonomy—the right to decide themselves what to do. Hence, Regan advocated protecting animals' right of autonomy by extending them inalienable rights, or rights that could not be taken away. Regan's argument helped link the notion of rights to the cause of protecting animals.

FEMINISM AND ANIMAL RIGHTS

A large number of animal rights activists are women. Various explanations have been put forth to explain why this is so. One theory, known as the sociobiological hypothesis, holds that women are born as nurturers, are naturally emotive and intuitive, and thus open to mothering instincts. Hence, women involved in the animal rights movement are supplementing their inherent mothering, nurturing, and protective instincts for human babies with the symbolic protection of animals. Studies have shown that most female activists are unmarried and childless. In this context, so the argument goes, women are responding to biological urges to behave in a nurturing fashion. This view has an appeal that reflects fundamentalist and essentialist calls for a return to traditional family and social roles for women.

Another theory, known as the philosophical-ideological hypothesis, argues that women are more receptive to the cause of animal rights because of their oppressed position in society. Women are themselves victims of systematic discrimination and oppression brought about by a women-hating patriarchal society, and therefore consciously identify with the oppression of animals. As a result, women can experience, vicariously, the oppression of animals, as well as their liberation through animal rights activism. In this view, animal rights activism becomes a political outlet, and although women may be powerless to help themselves, they can nevertheless help animals to escape their oppression.

Neither opinion sufficiently explains the participation of women in the movement. Both opinions overlook the participation of men in the movement, and neither view explains why most women in the United States are not animal rights activists. The philosophical-ideological view holds a circular charm in that evidence against it is used as proof of its validity. That most women are not animal rights activists only proves that society is oppressive.

THE ANIMAL RIGHTS MOVEMENT

The movement consists of groups that can be subdivided into three categories. In the 1992 book *The Animal Rights Crusade,* these groups are called the "welfarists," the "pragmatists," and the "fundamentalists." Welfarists are the least extreme. They believe that animals deserve compassion and protection, but that there are some boundaries between species. They advocate minimizing animal cruelty and animal populations. Strategies include legislation, education, funding animal shelters, and cooperation with existing agencies. The pragmatists take things a step further. They believe that animals deserve moral and legal consideration in balance with human interests, but that there is also some hierarchy of animals. They seek to eliminate animal suffering by reducing and replacing existing uses of animals. Their strategies include protests coupled to practical ways of cooperating, negotiating, and accepting short-term compromises. The most extreme group, the fundamentalists, argues that animals, regardless of species, have absolute moral and legal rights to autonomy and self-determination. They seek immediate abolition of all animal exploitation. Their strategy is to condemn those who—as they view it—exploit animals, and they practice civil disobedience and direct actions to end animal use. Data indicate that all activists share similar demographic features: they tend to be highly educated, middle-aged, middle-class white females from urban areas with the inclination and the political will to affect change. Furthermore, like their Victorian counterparts, activists are motivated by moralistic concerns rather

A demonstration of the League Against Cruel Sports, an animal rights organization. (Hulton-Deutsch Collection/Corbis)

than scientific, economic, or leisure-use justifications for animal exploitation.

Several factors explain why this message appeals to a broad audience. Modern society has become rapidly urbanized, and people feel a sentimental longing to return to an idealized rural life, one in which they live close to nature and animals. Pet ownership, which has grown explosively, is one manifestation of this desire. Scholars suggest that many people are essentially making family members of pets, generally vesting them with all the rights and privileges (and sometimes more) of other members of the household. Like the Victorian movement, the modern movement drew inspiration from scientific research, specifically the evidence that primates and marine mammals have the ability to think, live in complex social groups, and communicate through language; and evolutionary theories that

humans and animals were biologically related. In effect, scientists argued that animals were much more similar to humans than previously thought or imagined. These findings tantalized city dwellers who experienced animals as pets and through other highly anthropomorphized images.

For all these reasons, philosophical arguments for animal rights found public acceptance. Indeed, if pets deserve protection and nurturing, if ferrets and collies are actual family members, and if scientists like Jane Goodall confirm this belief, then how can society allow trapping mink and hunting foxes? Hence, following in the footsteps of the civil rights and women's movement, which a generation earlier helped to sensitize the public to the ideals of equality, the animal rights movement seeks only to further extend the ethical circle to include animals.

IMPLICATIONS OF THE MOVEMENT

Activists do not claim that animals have the right to vote. However, they do claim that animals have the right to life, liberty, and the pursuit of their happiness. As philosopher Bernard Rollin states, "a deer has a right to its 'deerness,'" independent of human-caused pain and suffering. Simply stated, animals should be allowed the same existential self-actualization as their human peers. The implications of this philosophy for sports cannot be overstated.

While it is sometimes argued that animal rights activists, although highly visible, have had little actual success, in the United States, animal sporting events as diverse as rodeos and greyhound races have had to justify their existence in the face of animal rights publicity. To impose their philosophy, activists used a variety of methods—from protests and disruptions to lawsuits intended to block events. A striking example of the potential success of the animal rights movement came in the fall of 1996, when animal rights initiatives passed in eight of ten states. Furthermore, U.S. activists planned a continued wave of legislation to ban animal-based sports over the objections of sporting enthusiasts. Their political strategy involved targeting individual sporting practices comprised of smaller constituent groups. By simple majority politics, activists knew that sports such as rodeos, trophy fishing, and deer hunting would eventually garner little support from a population that neither participates in nor understands them.

In response, the sporting community has increased efforts at public education intended to justify its existence, and sporting groups now actively recruit women in efforts to proselytize for their sport. A case in point is the "Becoming an Outdoorswoman" program. This program emphasizes recruiting women into a variety of outdoor activities, with the effect of increased participation in such blood sports as deer hunting. Emphasizing the aesthetic qualities of the outdoor experience and fostering a noncompetitive, socializing environment among other like-minded women, this and other programs have met with qualified success. Nevertheless, although women comprise the fastest growing percentage of new hunters, the total number of women in blood sports has not grown substantially.

What are the implications of animal rights for people who interact with animals? The contemporary American animal rights movement advocates the radical extension of egalitarianism, thus granting inalienable rights to all animals. The question before sport in general, and women in sports in particular are, "How can the exploitation of animals be justified for human pleasure?" One wonders, as well, if women will increasingly identify vicariously with the oppression and plight of the animals they ride, kill, or groom—and perhaps abandon these sports altogether.

Wesley V. Jamison

Bibliography

Adams, Carol, and Josephine Donovan. (1995) *Animals and Women: Feminist Theoretical Explorations.* London: Duke University Press.

Dizard, Jan. (1994) *Going Wild: Hunting, Animal Rights, and the Contested Meaning of Nature.* Amherst, MA: The University of Massachusetts Press.

French, Richard. (1975) *Antivivisection and Medical Science in Victorian England.* Princeton, UK: Princeton University Press.

Jasper, James, and Dorothy Nelkin. (1992) *The Animal Rights Crusade: The Growth of a Moral Protest.* New York: The Free Press.

Nash, Roderick. (1989) *The Rights of Nature: A History of Environmental Ethics.* Madison, WI: The University of Wisconsin Press.

Regan, Tom. (1985) *The Case for Animal Rights.* Berkeley, CA: The University of California Press.

Singer, Peter. (1975) *Animal Liberation: A New Ethics for our Treatment of Animals.* New York: Avon Books.

Sperling, Susan. (1988) *Animal Liberators: Research and Morality.* Berkeley, CA: The University of California Press.

Strange, Mary. (1997) *Woman the Hunter.* Boston, MA: Beacon Press.

ANIMAL SPORTS *see* Cockfighting, Horseback Riding, Horse Racing, Sled Dog Racing

ANNE, PRINCESS

(1950–)

BRITISH EQUESTRIENNE

Princess Anne Elizabeth Alice Louise Windsor, daughter of Queen Elizabeth II and Prince Philip of Great Britain, was born on 15 August 1950. Shielded, at her parents' wish, from the public eye to a considerable degree, she became known nonetheless as an independent and strong-willed princess, an active tomboy who loved sports and hated the unnatural behavior expected of royalty. Anne preferred outrunning and outriding her older brother, Prince Charles, to making prim public appearances. She especially loved sailing with her father on the days that her parents took leave from their royal duties to spend time with their children. Princess Anne's love of equestrian sports and her participation in world-level competitions in the 1970s are key features of her public identity.

Anne's mother was an accomplished rider, and although Anne did not begin training for major competitive events until she was about eighteen, riding was part of her life from the time she was a small child. When she began competing, she rose quickly to the top of her chosen sport, eventing. She was attracted to eventing, a three-day equestrian event that combines dressage, show jumping, and cross-country riding into one grueling competition. Anne said she liked eventing because it offered her the chance to succeed or fail based on her own abilities, regardless of her royal status. After riding seriously for only three years, she took first place in the 1971 European championships, one of the most prestigious competitions in her sport. She instantly became one of the sport's stars. She was named "Sports Personality of the Year" by the BBC and "Sportswoman of the Year" by the Sports Writers Association, the *Daily Express* newspaper, and *World Sport* magazine. She continued making headlines over the following years. In 1975 her all-female European championship team took the silver medal, disproving the belief that women lack the stamina or strength to compete in eventing. Anne

Princess Anne, riding Columbus, the Queen's horse, jumps an obstacle on the cross-country course at the 1972 Windsor Horse Trials. (Hulton-Deutsch Collection/Corbis)

also took the individual silver that year and was named to the Olympic team for the 1976 Games in Montreal. Her performance at the Olympics was disappointing but she continued riding, telling reporters time and time again that she was having too much fun to quit.

After the 1976 Olympics and the birth of her first child the following year, Anne attracted little attention as a sportswoman. Now officially known as the Princess Royal, she has continued to be an active horsewoman but is best known today for her involvement in a number of social causes, notably her work for the Save the Children Fund. Her first marriage, in 1973, was to a fellow equestrian, British naval officer Mark Phillips. They had two children—Peter, born in 1977, and Zara, born in 1981. After divorcing Phillips in 1992, Anne married Captain Timothy Laurence in December of the same year.

The Editors

Bibliography

Cathcart, Helen. (1973) *Anne and the Princesses Royal.* London: W. H. Allen & Co.

Courtney, Nicholas. (1986) *Princess Anne: A Biography.* Anstey, Leicestershire: F. A. Thorpe (Publishing).

Parker, John. (1989) *The Princess Royal.* London: Hamish Hamilton.

APPLEBEE, CONSTANCE

(1873–1981)

U.S. EDUCATOR AND PIONEER IN FIELD HOCKEY

Constance Applebee is considered to be the pioneer of field hockey in the United States. Throughout her life, she tirelessly coached, promoted, and organized the game, and helped expand the opportunities for American women to participate in the sport.

Growing up as a frail girl in her native England, she had reason to feel that physical education and health were important. She became a physical education teacher after attending the British College of Physical Education. Her special passion among sports was field hockey, which she believed to be ideal for promoting physical and mental health in young women.

In 1901 Applebee attended the Harvard Summer School of Physical Education, then under the direction of Dr. Dudley Sargent, a renowned leader in the field. At Sargent's suggestion, she provided a field hockey demonstration in Cambridge, Massachusetts. While at Harvard, Applebee met Harriet Ballantine, the director of physical education at Vassar College. Through this association, Applebee introduced the game at Vassar and Bryn Mawr. She later went on to coach at Bryn Mawr for sixty years. In addition to teaching, Applebee was instrumental in the organization of the sport. In 1922 she attended the inaugural meeting in Philadelphia of the United States Field Hockey Association, the organizational leader of the game responsible for standardizing the rules in the United States.

Applebee also worked to expand the opportunities for girls to play field hockey. She ran a field hockey camp in the Pocono Mountains in Pennsylvania to train the next generation in the intricacies of the game. She was also the editor and publisher of *The Sportswoman*, the first American sports magazine designed especially for women. Applebee and her colleagues lobbied the International Olympic Committee to have field hockey accepted as an event in the 1920 Olympic Games, but field hockey did not become an Olympic sport until 1980.

Applebee's historic contributions to field hockey in the United States gained her many honors. She was inducted into the United States Field Hockey Association Hall of Fame and the International Women's Sports Hall of Fame and received the Award of Merit from the Association for Intercollegiate Athletics for Women. A woman of amazing stamina, she coached until she was 95 years old and died at the age of 107.

Shawn Ladda

Bibliography

Gerber, Ellen W., Jan Felshin, Pearl Berlin, and Waneen Wynick. (1974) *The American Woman in Sport.* Reading, MA: Addison-Wesley.

Layden, Joe. (1997) *Women in Sports.* Los Angeles: General Publishing Group.

ARCHERY

The most readily identifiable branch of archery as a sport for women, target shooting, is a relatively modern offshoot of an activity originally both functional and violent. Perhaps it is competitive field archery, with its simulated use of wilderness hunting, that has the closest link to the sport's ori-

ARCHERY IN ELIZABETHAN ENGLAND

(1558–1603)

In order to keep the practice of archery from declining, most parishes were provided with butts and marks which were erected at public expense and located in a convenient open place. While interest in this sport was fed by concern about foreign invasion, public-spirited citizens often contributed valuable prizes to winners in contests. Along with such displays of skill went pageants and festive celebrations. Queen Elizabeth encouraged this sport by becoming a fair marksman with the bow and arrow as she hunted deer, and caused the ladies to try to match their skill with hers. Though she must of necessity be surpassed by no one, still she tried to keep the love of the game high, even after she was convinced that archery was to be replaced by firearms and that there was much evasion of the archery laws.

Lu Emily Pearson
(1957) Elizabethans at Home. Stanford, CA: Stanford University Press.

gins; it is far more popular in the United States, where it has uneasy links with survivalism, than in Europe.

Shooting arrows from a wooden bow emerged almost worldwide in prehistoric times as a means of hunting for food as well as for tribal defense and aggression. By the time civilizations emerged in Mesopotamia, the Mediterranean, Central America, and ancient China, archery was well developed as a symbol of male prowess. Paradoxically, in the Artemis/Diana myths of classical Greece and Rome, it was a divine female archer who symbolized both hunting and sudden death for women. She was also linked with the mythological bringers of death to men, the Amazons, who were said to have cut off their right breasts to facilitate drawing bowstrings. Modern feminist thinking tends to deny their existence, as well as their self-mutilation, as a misreading of Greek linguistics, but the ascription has remained fairly powerful as a general term of opprobrium for sporting women.

It was well into the later Middle Ages before European women, for the most part of aristocratic classes, began to appear in archery records. It was hunting for pleasure that attracted them, often using light but accurate crossbows rather than the masculine longbow against carefully driven game, particularly deer, in private parks. Members of various European royal families were prominent in this occasional shooting, as also were England's Ann Boleyn, who apparently used her archery skill as one of numerous devices to seduce Henry VIII, and her daughter Queen Elizabeth I, for whom it was another instrument in propping up her Gloriana legend.

DEVELOPMENT IN ENGLAND

Such archery was hardly necessary for survival. The real growth in the sport came when use of the bow for procuring food or victory had become effectively obsolete. Eighteenth-century target archery grew because it fitted some of the leisure and courtship requirements of a landed aristocracy, particularly in Britain, and because it slotted into the neo-medievalism of the Romantic movement. A number of genteel British societies were formed for shooting modified longbows, most notably the Royal Toxophilite Society in 1781 ("Royal" after 1847), and women entered play through these. Although shooting was male-dominated, there seem to have been few barriers to women's participation. Indeed, they were given a symbolic function that still remains. Each tournament was shot under the auspices of a Lady Paramount, based on the role of noblewomen at tournaments in the courtly chivalry of the Middle Ages. But this reinvention was also practical—the holder of the post had a specific role as arbitrator, which assumed a clear knowledge of the sport and its precedents.

Victorian women archers in William Powell Frith's painting *The Fair Toxophilites*. (The Royal Albert Museum)

When archery grew in the United States after the 1870s, similar appointments were made but with the essential difference that the holder had an active role as captain of the women's team.

Tournaments became increasingly common amongst the gentry and their grander urban imitators. Most archery was practiced in extensive private grounds and was often subsumed into wider opportunities for social intercourse and courtship; rarely was it followed only for its own sake and exercise—it was a respectable arena in which the sexes could meet. One of the best descriptions of this occurs in Anthony Trollope's novel *Barchester Towers* (1857), where the sport is incidental to a country house fete during which several romantic entanglements are made more complicated.

The Victorians brought a new seriousness of purpose and increasing organization and regulation to tournaments that adapted well to the mobility of the railway age; national competition became possible, even though the numbers of participants did not increase enormously. When tournaments were organized into "rounds," women could still shoot on near-equal terms with men, but provision was also made for perceived differences in stamina and physique. The Grand National Archery Society came into being at a meeting at Leamington Spa in 1841 and was reorganized in the 1860s, becoming the governing body for the English sport. For "ladies" it standardized the National Round as forty-eight arrows shot at 60 yards and twenty-four at 50 yards, rather than the longer York Round for men. An increasing number of sports manufacturers recognized women's role by providing bows with a lesser draw strength (usually 22 to 32 pounds weight) and shorter arrows than those provided for men. Since the 1940s bows, originally wooden, have been made of steel and composites, and arrows are often made of alloys. The size of the round target, mounted on a stand, is the same for both sexes—some 4 feet in diameter, with a backing made of straw to absorb and protect the arrows and a cloth face divided into rings; white (1 point), black (3), blue (5), and red (7), with a gold center (9).

The later nineteenth century saw a continued limited growth despite the alternatives offered by croquet and lawn tennis, which demanded less space. Local private groups and societies were increasingly organized into county federations, and women competed nationally in almost every year after their first National Tournament in York in 1844. Archery was said to be an ideal pursuit for isolated dwellers in country houses and also to offer "a gentle and elegant amusement for young ladies, and most suitable to the matron who feels it undignified to take part in some outdoor games and yet is quite young enough to enjoy them." That claim came from Alice B. Legh, by far the best late-nineteenth-century woman archer, who had won the national championship seven times in the 1880s, after her mother had won it four times. She went on to praise its relatively low cost and the fact that, apart from minor alterations in tailoring to allow for greater freedom of movement, it required little specialized clothing.

In the words of Colonel H. Warlord, a leading late Victorian commentator, "There is no pastime more graceful than archery, or in which if properly done, the female figure shows to more advantage." For many younger women, men remained a primary target. It is worth comparing the colonel's patronizing remarks and the ease with which women were accepted into the limited social world of archery with the contemporary vituperation poured out by many middle-class male golfers, who claimed that admiring women's figures would destroy concentration on their game. Archery also seems to have been exempt from the fears of giving women masculine characteristics blamed on so many other sports.

DEVELOPMENT IN THE UNITED STATES

Archery first became popular in the United States in the late nineteenth century. James Maurice Thompson and his brother, William H. Thompson, popularized the sport after serving in the Civil War and then played an instrumental role in the founding of the National Archery Association of the United States in Crawfordsville, Indiana, in 1879. In addition to being the organization's first president, James Thompson wrote many articles in periodicals and magazines. His "The Witchery of Archery," "with its detailed and enthusiastic explanations," is credited with leading many participants to archery and inspiring the formation of twenty clubs within a year and a national tournament in White Stocking Park in Chicago. Will Thompson, his brother, won the first national men's title and four more titles through 1908.

In women's competition, Mrs. M. C. Howell, of Cincinnati, Ohio, was considered to be one of the finest archers over a twenty-year period: she captured national titles seventeen times between 1883 and 1907. Miss Cynthia M. Wesson, of Springfield and Cotuit, Massachusetts, was a three-time winner at the national level, winning titles in 1915, 1916, and 1920. Howell and Weston also competed on men's teams. Dorothy Smith Cummings won her first national championship at age sixteen and went on to capture seven national titles from 1919 through 1931. She was, according to Robert Rhode, the "last champion to win the N.A.A. title and establish world records, without having the benefit of sights, or artificial point-of-aim." Rhode also credits Louis C. Smith, Cummings's father, with encouraging women to participate. Archery also blossomed at the collegiate level in physical education courses. In 1920 the University of Wisconsin's Mary A. Brownell wrote: "Since it was undesirable to have archery

Women practicing archery in fur coats at the Archery Butts, St. Mellons Country Club, near Cardiff, Wales. (Hulton-Deutsch Collection/Corbis)

known as the weaklings' sport, the University of Wisconsin's Women's Athletic Association gave it equal place with all other sports." In "Archery for Women," Brownell discussed how archery provided "a picturesque and fascinating out-door sport which interests all types of girls."

> Archery as a sport in the University of Wisconsin was introduced rather in the nature of an experiment. It was felt that a certain type of girl, who, on account of various health defects, was unable to take part in the more vigorous games such as hockey, field and track, baseball and tennis, was much in need of home out-door recreation. Since archery requires nothing more vigorous in the way of exercise than walking, even the more serious heart cases would thus be enabled to enjoy an out-door sport which would otherwise have been denied them.

Brownell's article shows that the demise of the sport at the Olympic level did not have an impact on the sport at the collegiate level. She wrote: "While archery is not likely ever to become as popular a sport as hockey, for instance, still its devotees are as enthusiastic about it as any sport I know. It has been increasing in popularity for the last ten years."

Archery was named "an emerging sport" by the National Collegiate Athletic Association (NCAA) in 1994. Other "emerging sports" named that year included badminton, bowling, crew, ice hockey, squash, synchronized swimming, team handball, and water polo. Of those nine sports, only crew was an NCAA championship-level sport as of 1999. In that same year, although there were many colleges and universities with club-level teams, Virginia's James Madison University and New York's Columbia University were the only institutions with registered NCAA archery teams in the United States. (Forty schools must be registered within the NCAA during a two-year period before the sport can take on a competitive status.) American collegiate clubs had been formed at Arizona State University, the University of California at San Diego, Case Western Reserve University, Rensselaer Polytechnical Institute, Texas A&M, the University of Texas, the University of Washington, and the University of Virginia, among others. In the United Kingdom there were university clubs at Southampton, Sheffield, Cambridge, Exeter, Liverpool, and Oxford. In Canada, the University of Toronto also had a club.

OLYMPIC COMPETITION

When the Olympic movement emerged in the 1890s, archery played a minor role and women first shot in 1904. Unlike many other Olympic sports, archery was an activity that welcomed women. It was perceived as "acceptable" because it was a sport in which women could compete while wearing a dress. At the 1904 Games held in St. Louis, Missouri, Americans Lida Howell, Emma Cook, and Jessie Pollack captured the gold, silver, and bronze medals, respectively. The Cincinnati Archers of the United States won the team competition. Archery was first properly organized as representing nations rather than individuals during the London Games of 1908, where twenty-five British women shot alongside fifteen men as the national team, the only one that fielded both sexes.

The sport was dropped from the Olympic Games in 1920 because a set of international rules had not been developed by that time. As a result, participants often found it rather difficult to compete, as host countries were forced to use their own rules and format. With the founding of an international governing body, the Fédération Internationale de Tir a l'Arc (FITA), in 1931, however, standardized rules for competition were instituted. The first world championship was held that same year. According to George Helwig, the vice president of FITA from 1972 to 1976, coaches from the United States used to travel to other countries in order to gain support for the sport's return to the Olympic Games. After several countries adopted FITA's rules, archery was reinstated in the Olympic Games in 1972.

MODERN NATIONAL AND INTERNATIONAL COMPETITION

Despite the elimination of the sport from the Olympic Games, competition—unbroken except for a wartime interlude from 1942 to 1945—remained strong for women at the national and international levels. Perhaps the finest international competitor of all time was Poland's Janina Kurkowska. Kurkowska had a remarkable career, winning seven titles in international competition from 1931 to 1950 and world titles in 1933, 1934, 1936, and 1939. Although she suffered from poor health after spending several years in concentration camps during World War II, Kurkowska captured her fifth world title in 1947. Also worthy of note is the fact that Kurkowska placed second and third in the world target championships in 1931 and 1932; during those years, the men and women's competition were combined.

Jean Lee, of Springfield, Massachusetts, won four consecutive national titles from 1948 to 1951, and she was also the first American woman to capture world titles, in 1950 and 1952. Mrs. Ann Weber Corby won five national titles (in 1940, 1946, 1947, 1952, and 1953), and Carol Meinhart won four (1956–1959). After Lee captured the women's world title in 1950, Sweden's Hans Deutgen remarked that it was the first time he had ever been beaten by a woman and it would be the last. Deutgen, who placed first in the men's competition, finished with an aggregate score of 3,141. Lee finished at 3,254. In 1952, she also beat out Sweden's men's champion, Stellen Anderson. Lee scored 3,185, and Anderson scored 3,151. When archery was reintroduced in Olympic competition in 1972, Doreen Wilber of the United States captured the gold medal. American Luann Ryon, of Riverside, California, was the gold medalist at the 1976 Olympic Games in Montreal, Canada, and also captured four national titles (in 1976, 1977, 1978, and 1982).

Perhaps the most successful team of the 1970s and early 1980s was that of the Soviet Union. Emma Gaptchenko took the bronze in 1972 in Munich; Valentina Kovpan and Zebiniso Rustamova collected the silver and bronze medals in Montreal in 1976; Keto Losaberidze and Natalya Butuzova were the gold and silver medal winners, respectively, in 1980 in Moscow.

The South Korean women have dominated Olympic archery since 1984, capturing eight of twelve medals, including four gold. Seo Hyang-soon (gold) and Kim Jin-ho (bronze) were winners in Los Angeles in 1984; Kim Soo-nyung (gold), Wang Hee-kyung (silver), and Yun Young-sook (bronze) in Seoul, Korea, in 1988; and Cho Youn Jeong (gold) and Kim Soo Nyung (silver) in Barcelona, Spain, in 1992. In Atlanta, Georgia, in 1996, Korean archer Kim Kyung-Wook took the gold. The Korean archers were expected to continue their dominance.

From the 1970s through the 1990s, the scoring format of the sport has also changed in Olympic competition. During the 1970s and 1980s, archers shot thirty-six arrows from 30, 50, 60, and 70 meters in what was known as the FITA "round." In the Olympic round, which began in the 1992 Games, the range is 70 meters. Throughout the preliminary rounds, archers shoot seventy-two arrows in twelve "ends" of six arrows each. The top eight archers proceed to the semi-finals and shoot twelve arrows. The final four contestants shoot twelve arrows to determine the gold, silver, and bronze medal winners.

CONCLUSION

Although women were initially allowed to participate because archery was viewed as gentle and refined, in reality it takes tremendous strength and acumen to participate in this sport with bloody roots, and the women who engage in this sport are certainly not weaklings. What is unique about archery, compared to other sports, is that, in the modern era, women take an equal role, both in competition and in governance.

John Lowerson and Urla Hill

Bibliography

Brownell, Mary A. (1920) "Archery for Women." *American Physical Education Review* 25: 124–126.

Burke, Edmund. (1957) *The History of Archery.* New York: William Morrow.

Guttmann, Allen. (1991) *Women's Sports: A History.* New York: Columbia University Press.

Hickok, Ralph. "Hickok Sports History." http://www.hickoksports.com/history/archery.shtml.

Kramarae, Cheris, and Paula A. Trachler. (1992) *Amazons, Bluestockings and Crones: A Feminist Dictionary.* London: Pandora.

Lowerson, John. (1993) *Sport and the English Middle Classes, 1870–1914.* Manchester, England: Manchester University Press.

McCrone, K. E. (1988) *Sport and the Emancipation of English Women, 1870–1914.* London: Routledge.

Menke, Frank G. (1953) *The Encyclopedia of Sports.* New York: A.S. Barnes.

Rhode, Robert. (1960) *Archery Champions.* Minneapolis, MN.

U.S. Olympic Committee. (1996) *A Basic Guide to Archery.* Glendale, CA: Griffin.

Wiseman, Howard, and Fred Brundle. (1958) *Archery from A–Z.* London: Faber.

Additional information provided by Shirley Comes-Jeffrey (National Collegiate Athletic Association), George Helwig, Bill Kellick (National Archery Association), Robert Rhode, and M. J. Rogers (Arco Olympic Training Center).

ARGENTINA

Argentina is located in the southern half of South America and has a population of about 35 million. Colonized by Spain, after a complex history of wars and political battles for the territory, Argentina gained independence in 1816. The Argentinean government actively encouraged emigration from Europe, and Argentina had become a multiethnic society by the early twentieth century, with sizable populations from Italy and Spain. The European, multiethnic nature of Argentinean society has influenced both the nature and level of participation in sports, including that of women.

EARLY HISTORY

When industrial development and the British railways arrived in Argentina in the middle of the nineteenth century, so, too, did sports, and the first soccer (association football) clubs were founded. Between 1880 and 1920, in tandem with a flood of immigrants primarily from Italy and Spain, significant political, cultural, and economic changes took place in Argentina, including industrial expansion, the regulation of the educational system, and the implementation of the universal vote. There was also a successful effort to develop a strong sense of Argentinean nationalism that led to, among other things, the adoption of sports in general and of soccer as the national sport in particular.

During this period women were largely barred from sports. However, European educational philosophy of the late nineteenth century that supported physical education for women influenced the Common Education Law approved in 1884, which included gymnastics in the required curriculum. Similarly, the National System of Physical Education, created by Enrique Romero Brest in 1905, treated both sexes equally. However, in Argentina, sports and physical education were not considered to be the same, and sports activities offered by clubs and associations were for men only until the second half of the twentieth century.

Except for a few women from the upper class, like Miryam Stefford (1905–1931) or Carola Lorenzini (1899–1941), who were dedicated to aviation, the average woman did not have the opportunity to participate in sports. The major exception was Blanca Torterolo (1912–1989), who set the South American track and field record in the 100-meter dash with a time of 12.7 seconds in 1931. Her sister, Clotilde, participated in rowing, field hockey, track and field, and basketball at a time when sports were an unconventional pursuit for women.

In the 1930s and 1940s, discrimination against female athletes began to abate. This was due, in large part, to the outstanding performance of Jeanette Campbell, who won the silver medal in the 100-meter freestyle swim at the 1936 Berlin Olympic Games (a record that stood in Argentina for twenty-six years). Born in Bayona, France, Campbell became a citizen of Argentina in 1935, after successfully competing in the 1932 Los Angeles Olympic Games. There she set the South American freestyle record, as well as the Argentinean record in the backstroke. Campbell's performance was remarkable, considering not only that women were not allowed to compete in the South American championships until 1935 in Rio de Janeiro, but also that she was able to train only in the summer at a club that discouraged swimming but supported rugby, tennis, and cricket. Even with these limitations, she placed second in Berlin, winning the silver medal. When the Olympic Games of Tokyo were canceled because of World War II, Campbell retired, but the family swimming tradition continued with her daughter, Susana Peper, who won the 1960 South American championship in the 100-meter breaststroke.

THE MODERN ERA

Between 1945 and 1955, the political and cultural landscape of Argentina was transformed. Under the leadership of Juan Perón, the industrial sector was developed and more attention was given to the needs of the poor, the peasants, and the workers. Their rights were expanded, and women were given the right to vote and other civil and economic liberties which greatly increased their participation in civil life.

These new civil liberties also had an influence on women's participation in sports. First, sports were encouraged in general, and second, programs were started to specifically promote women's sports participation. As part of these initiatives, the *Campeonatos Infantiles Evita* (children's championships of Evita) and the *Torneos Juveniles Hombre Nuevo* (youth tournaments of the new man) were established, as was the girls' division of the *Union de Estudiantes Secundarios,* (high school students' union), which organized sports competitions for teenage girls. An outstanding sportswoman of this era was Noemi Simonetto, winner of the silver medal in the long jump in the London Olympic Games of 1948. She also won several South American championships and set many Argentinean records, including one for the high jump that stood for twenty-four years. Simonetto is one of three Argentinean women to have won an Olympic medal, with Campbell and, later, Gabriela Sabatini being the other two.

During the Perón era, women also became active in sports administration. One of the first women to work in sports administration was Elsa Irigoyen, who, in addition to achieving success in track and field and fencing, was president of the *Ateneo Deportivo Evita* (sport cultural club Evita). Another noteworthy pioneer was Mary Teran de Weiss (1918–1984), who excelled in tennis, a sport considered the domain of the Argentinean upper class. Ranked first for seven years and the Pan-American champion at the Buenos Aires Games in 1951, she was appointed by Juan Perón to serve as chief of the municipal sports fields. From this position she tried to popularize tennis. With the fall of the Perón government in 1955, and having alienated upper-class supporters of tennis through her popularization efforts, Weiss went into exile in Spain.

The 1970s, along with seeing women attain leadership roles, produced two outstanding athletes in different sports. Marina Lezcano, a horse-woman of exceptional ability, achieved success in a domain traditionally dominated by men. The pinnacle of her career was in 1978, when, at the age of twenty, she won the four most important races on the annual turf racing schedule, earning her the quadruple crown. The other leading woman athlete was Beatriz Alloco, who competed in track and field. At age twenty-two, she became the fastest female athlete in South America and, although she did not win any Olympic medals, she set twenty-seven Argentinean records and won three gold medals in the 1980 South American Championship in Bucamaranga, Colombia, in the 100-meter, 200-meter, and 4×100-meter relay.

In the late 1970s and the 1980s, women began to excel in other sports. By the close of the decade, roller skating had become a highly visible sport for women, and some of Argentina's top female athletes were roller skaters. The most successful was Nora Vega (1961–), who won her first of four gold medals at the 1979 Pan-American Games in Puerto Rico and in that same year also won the world championship in Italy. She took the world championship again in Italy in 1988 and in New Zealand in 1989. Other noteworthy roller skaters were Claudia Rodriguez and Roxana Sastre.

In the 1980s into the 1990s, field hockey emerged as a major sport for women and one in which they competed at the international level. The national team won gold medals at the Pan-American Games at Indianapolis in 1987, Havana in 1991, and Mar del Plata, Argentina, in 1995. Although they have been less successful outside of the Americas, their efforts are noteworthy because they are amateur athletes who successfully competed against professional international teams. The best-known female athlete produced by Argentina is the tennis player Gabriela Sabatini (1970–), who in the 1980s and 1990s won fourteen professional tournaments, including the U.S. Open in 1990, and became the third Argentinean woman to win an Olympic medal when she finished second in women's singles at the Seoul Olympics in 1988. The heiress of an important tradition of tennis players in Argentina and pampered by the international press, at fifteen years old she was the youngest semifinalist at the French Open. She retired in 1997, reaping the benefits of having performed in a globalized and media-driven culture, which gave her, perhaps, more fame than any other female Argentinean athlete.

María Graciela Rodríguez

Bibliography

Aisenstein, Angela. (1998) "La Educacion Fisica en el Nuevo Contexto Educativo: en Busca del Eslabon Perdido." In *Deporte y Sociedad*. Buenos Aires: Eudeba.

Arbena, Jose. (1996) "In Search of the Latin American Female Athlete: A Bibliographical Odyssey." Paper presented at the annual meeting of the North American Society for Sport History, Auburn, AL, 24–27 May.

Frydenberg, Julio. (1991) "La Fundacion de los Clubes de Futbol: ¿Fenomeno de la Cultura Popular?" Paper presented at the Simposio de Cultura y Politica, 3ras. Jornadas de Historia, Buenos Aires: Facultad de Filosofia y Letras. U.B.A., September.

Morelli, Li liana. (1990) *Mujeres Deportistas*. Buenos Aires: El Planeta.

Ramirez, Pablo. (1995) "Las Deportistas." In *Todo es Historia* 335. Buenos Aires: Junio.

Rodríguez, María Graciela. (1996) "Pan, Circo y Algo Mas." In *Cuestion de Pelotas. Futbol. Deporte. Sociedad,* edited by P. Alabarces and M. G. Rodriguez. Buenos Aires: Cultura.

ARM WRESTLING

Arm wrestling is a specific form of wrestling focused on exertion of the hands, wrists, arms, and upper body. Although the traditional stereotypes associated with arm wrestling are those of masculine contests of strength, numerous women are active in the sport as competitors, promoters, and officials.

HISTORY

Armsports have existed in most cultures throughout history, often on an informal basis. Modern armsports include organized competitions, leagues, and circuits, and they are conducted on both an amateur and professional basis. The sports are popular in many countries, including the United States, India, Britain, and Russia.

A movement to organize armsports as a legitimate athletic pursuit emerged in the United States in the 1950s and 1960s, with early tournaments in Scranton, Pennsylvania, and Petaloma, California, as well as other locales. Proponents sought to popularize the sports and establish an organized framework for tournaments. Rules that govern such factors as how the contestants position themselves and the ways other parts of the body may not be used were also developed.

This development led to the formation of such organizations as the American Arm Wrestling Association (AAA) and the United States Wristwrestling/Armwrestling Association (USWA/USAA), as well as many other regional associations. The movement took hold throughout the world, and the World Armsport Federation (WAF) became an international sanctioning body for the sports. By 1999 more than seventy nations were represented in the WAF. As the sports continued to gain popularity, efforts were launched to have armsports included as an official Olympic event.

Women became increasingly active in armsports in the 1970s. Many of the women who originally participated in armsports had the encouragement of male arm wrestling relatives. Prominent early female competitors included Karyn Jubinville (who entered the sport in 1971 at age twelve), Cindy Baker, Kari Tremblay, and Dot Jones. In 1985 Jeanette Davis received the first annual Female Armwrestler of the Year award from the AAA. Grace Ann Swift earned four world titles between 1987 and 1994. Chris Baliko held the world title four times between 1993 and 1997. Karen Brisson Curavoo gained recognition when she proved that the sport is also suited to older athletes. She began arm wrestling at age fifteen in 1978 and earned three world titles in the late 1970s and early 1980s. She retired to raise a family and then, in the 1990s, she returned to active competition.

RULES AND PLAY

In basic arm wrestling, two opponents face each other across a table and grip each other's hands with arms bent at the elbow. When the match (or pull) begins, each contestant presses her hand and arm in an arc toward the table. Each contest-

Although known traditionally as a male-dominated sport, arm wrestling has a number of active female participants. (Philip Gould/Corbis)

ant is pulling in an opposing direction, with the goal of forcing the opponent's hand and forearm flat against the table for a pin, while also resisting her opponent's effort to do the same. The term *armsports* has been coined to encompass arm wrestling and variations such as wristwrestling (which has somewhat different body positions).

Armsports require a combination of wrist, arm, and upper-body strength and overall endurance. While size and strength are important, the sports' characteristics are also suited to people with smaller builds. Psychological and physical strategies are as important as sheer strength, because the sports are also mental contests of willpower and concentration.

Organized armsports include men's and women's divisions, and events are held in differing weight classes. They are also categorized by right-handed or left-handed events. Women also compete with men in certain events. In 1998, for example, Barb Zalepa, a Canadian champion who had won six world titles, gained recognition when she defeated several prominent males to win a tournament in Huntsville, Ontario.

Women have also been active in the organizational and promotional aspects of the sports. Sue Patton, a member of a prominent arm wrestling family, was very influential in the establishment of organized armsports. Numerous other women have been both prominent competitors and promoters of the sport, including Mary McConnaughy, Colleen Corbett, and Denise Wattles. Karen Bean became one of the top referees in the world.

John Townes

Bibliography

ArmBender Magazine. Scranton, PA: American Arm wrestling Association Inc.

ArmSports Newsletter. Billings, MT: Denise Wattles, publisher.

USWA/USAA Web site: <http://www.arm wrestling.com>.

WAF and AAA Web site: <http://www.usit.com/armsport>.

ART

Among the earliest images of women engaged in sports is an Egyptian relief carved into the walls of the Temple of Karnak (c. 1480 BCE). It shows Queen Hatshepsut engaged in a ceremonial run demonstrating her fitness to rule the kingdom. A Minoan fresco from about the same time, discovered by Sir Arthur Evans in the Palace of Minos in Crete, depicts a girl who is boldly gripping the horns of a bull as she prepares to leap over it. Like Hatshepsut's run, this leap was probably part of a religious ritual.

Antiquity's most famous female athlete was the mythic princess Atalanta. Ancient vase paintings often depicted Atalanta as a wrestler. Artists of the Renaissance, such as Peter Paul Rubens and Guido Reni, were drawn to her exploits as a huntress and a runner. Reni's 1620 version of the myth portrays a voluptuous Atalanta about to lose a race (and her virginity) as she pauses greedily to gather the golden apples tossed in her path by her outpaced suitor. That Greek girls actually ran races we know not only from literary sources but also from an archaic bronze figure and from Roman copies of a Hellenistic marble statue. Both represent running girls wearing short tunics, with their right breasts bare. These girls were almost certainly engaged in sports with religious significance, perhaps the games celebrated at Olympia in honor of the goddess Hera.

The aura of the sacred is wholly absent from the most famous Roman illustration of female athletes. The work known as the "Bikini Mosaic" from the Piazza Armerina in Sicily (fourth century CE) presents ten young women whose attire prompted the mosaic's name. They most probably represent a javelin thrower, a discus thrower, a jumper, two runners, two ballplayers, and three unspecified athletes holding their prizes. Terra-cotta statuettes and the figures on a stele in Halicarnassus in Asia Minor indicate that a few women, probably slaves, competed as gladiators.

In Renaissance art, aristocratic women occasionally appear playing ball or as hunters. A 1435 fresco by Antonio Pisano shows an elegantly dressed young woman playing a game that resembles shuttlecock. (Women playing a very similar game appear on Japanese screen paintings of approximately the same period.) Pol de Limbourg illustrated a Renaissance breviary with a mounted group of female falconers, and Francesco Primaticcio portrayed Diane de Poitiers, mistress of Henri II of France, in the guise of her namesake, the huntress-goddess Diana. From Primaticcio's time to the present, Diana has remained popular with painters and sculptors. She appears in works by Jean Goujon, Titian (Tiziano Vecellio), Peter Paul Rubens, Jean-Alexandre-Joseph Falguière, and Augustus St. Gaudens (who placed her on top of Madison Square Garden). The twentieth-century sculptor Paul Manship cast a bronze Atalanta as well as a beautifully executed Diana.

Mortal huntresses figure frequently in English sporting art. John Wooton's *Lady Henrietta Harley Hunting with Harriers* (c. 1740) and John Collett's *Ladies Shooting Poney* (1780) are typical of the genre. Target archery was another sport deemed appropriate for respectable women. Robert Smirke and John Emes produced a 1794 aquatint entitled *A Meeting of the Society of Royal British Archers*. The ladies shoot while the gentlemen gallantly assist and admire. A fine 1872 painting by William Powell Frith depicts his three gorgeously (and expensively) dressed daughters as a trio of archers.

By the late nineteenth century, the list of acceptable sports for decent women had lengthened to include croquet, tennis, ice skating, cycling, and golf. In *Croquet* (c. 1878) by James Tissot, an attractive young woman uses her mallet to pin back her crooked arms and make her pose a bit more provocative. No fewer than five oils by Winslow Homer (1836–1910) also show women at croquet. The French Impressionist Edouard Manet (1832–1883) and some minor artists were also attracted by colorfully dressed women engaged in croquet.

Female tennis players appear in the work of artists as different in their styles as the British academic Sir John Lavery, the German Impressionist Max Liebermann, the Belgian Symbolist Ferdinand Khnopff, the French specialist in art deco Marcel Gromaire, the Italian Surrealist Carlo Carrà, and the American Pop Art painter Mike Francis. The mood of these pictures varies from the pastoral of Lavery's *The Tennis Party* (1885) to the grotesqueness of *Advantage, Mrs. Cunningham* (1976), by Francis, in which one of the players, caught in the reflection of the main figure's sunglasses, bends gracelessly and exposes her naked buttocks.

Skaters have figured in the work of countless artists. Perhaps their attraction lies in the contrast of the colors of their clothes and the swiftness of their motion with the icy stillness of a winter landscape, which is certainly the case in Vassily Kandinsky's *Ice-Skating* (1906). The subject became locally popular in the sixteenth century with such Dutch and Flemish painters as Hendrik Avercamp and Lucas van Valckenborgh. Their work often depicts female skaters who have fallen—as in Valckenborgh's *Antwerp and the Frozen Schelde* (1590). As late as 1914, George Bellows was more interested in the women's bright clothing than in their exploits on the ice. By 1925, however, when the German Expressionist Ernst Ludwig Kirchner painted *The Skaters*, the focus was again on skating, as women match the men glide for glide.

The female cyclist figured in nineteenth-century literature as a symbol of female emancipation, and as such she also inspired many visual artists. French girls competed in races as early as 1868, but few painters noticed. Leisurely touring rather than strenuous racing drew their attention. At the turn of the century, Jean Béraud painted an idyllic scene in which a group of bloomer-clad cyclists pause at an outdoor café in a Parisian park. Fernand Léger and the contemporary Canadian painter Alex Colville continued the genre. In the former's 1949 *Hommage to Louis David*, cyclists are a colorful image of *joie de vivre*. In the latter's 1981 *Cyclist and Raven*, the *joie* has become distinctly erotic. The emphasis is on the curves of the cyclist's body. She stares at the bird; the viewer stares at her.

Although golf has been popular since the late nineteenth century among upper-class women, the sport has seldom excited the artistic imagination. Nineteenth-century artists were more interested in female wrestlers than in golfers. Some painters, such as Eugène Delacroix and Edgar Degas, were obviously attracted by the erotic appeal of muscular female bodies. Both of them depicted Spartan girls as wrestlers. Other artists, such as Amadée-Charles-Henri Cham, were repelled by muscular women. In his 1868 caricature, a pair of tubby women pull and tug at each other before a crowd of leering men. In the twentieth century, the tradition of positive treatment was most notably represented by Aristide Maillol's sculpture *The Wrestlers* (1900).

The wrestler's motto—no holds barred—might serve as a rubric for the twentieth-century treatment of female athletes. Women have made their way into a vast number of sports domains from which they were once excluded, and artists have followed them. Fritz Köthe's *Mobile* (1986), for instance, features a female automobile racer.

Artists have not neglected the traditionally feminine sports. *Beach Scene, New London*, a brightly Impressionistic canvas done by William Glackens in 1919, reminds the viewer that swimmers have, for centuries, attracted artists fascinated by the human body. The gentle game of shuttlecock caught the eye of Maurice Denis in 1900 as it had an even greater French artist, Jean-Baptiste-Siméon Chardin, in 1741. Chardin's indoor scene portrays a little girl holding her racquet and her shuttlecock. Denis preferred a game in progress; he set it in a peaceful forest glade and emphasized his Arcadian motif with pastel shades of green and yellow. David Inshaw achieved a similar effect with a similar game; his *Badminton* was done in 1973.

Like cycling, rowing occurs in both leisurely and strenuously competitive forms. In Max Liebermann's *On the Alster in Hamburg* (1910), women do row their boats, but their fluffy dresses and floppy hats signify membership in a social world far different from that of Marcel Gromaire's *Banks of the Marne* (1925) and Alex Colville's *Laser* (1976), two depictions of taut bodies capable of meeting the physical demands of competitive rowing and sailing.

Two of the century's most famous artists—Willi Baumeister and Pablo Picasso—were among the relatively few artists to portray female runners. The German artist's boyishly slender runner, painted in 1927, is nude except for a blue headband. She seems to dance rather than to run. In contrast, the runners depicted in *The Race* (1922) have the massive bodies typical of Picasso's classical period. Their tunics and exposed left breasts are probably an allusion to the garb of ancient Spartan runners.

The twentieth-century Polish artist Tamara de Lempicka may have been the only woman to produce a number of works devoted to female athletes. Among them were self-portraits as a skier (1929) and an automobile driver (1925). Her work, like Willi Baumeister's in the 1920s, was in the art deco style popular then. Fritz Köthe's portrait of a female automobile racer, mentioned above, was done as a kind of collage. *Mobile,* painted in garishly bright colors, is an exercise in visual confusion. The helmeted driver's foregrounded portrait appears to be ripped through the middle, revealing the right half of a racing car parked behind the plane of the portrait.

Since California is the symbolic if not the actual birthplace of skateboarding, rollerblading, and other activities that the French refer to as *les sports californiens,* it may be appropriate to conclude with two California artists. *The Meeting, or Have a Nice Day, Mr. Hockney* (1981), by Peter Blake, is a clever allusion to Gustave Courbet's *Bonjour, Monsieur Courbet* (1854). In Blake's picture, an acrobatic young woman, crouching on roller skates, whizzes past three stiffly erect foregrounded male figures. A mural by Richard Cronk, *Venus on the Half Shell* (1981), alludes to Sandro Botticelli's famous portrait of the goddess. In Cronk's modern version, Venus wears running shorts and is roller-skating her way between a group of tennis players and an elderly man with a walker. Botticelli's seashell hovers surrealistically just behind her.

Allen Guttmann

Bibliography

Guttmann, Allen. (1991) *Women's Sports: A History.* New York: Columbia University Press.

Kühnst, Peter. (1996) *Sports: A Cultural History in the Mirror of Art.* Dresden: Verlag der Kunst.

Musée des Beaux-Arts de Mons. (1984) *Art et Sport.* Mons, Belgium: Musée des Beaux-Arts.

ASIA CONFERENCE ON WOMEN AND SPORTS

The first conference on women's sport across Asia took place in Manila, the Philippines, on 5–10 March 1996. The conference was sponsored by the International Council for Health, Physical Education, Recreation, Sports and Dance (ICHPERSD) and was attended by some 150 women and men from more than a dozen Asian nations. The purpose of the conference was to share information about women's sports, discuss current issues, and promote women's sports across Asia. Sessions covered a wide range of topics, including the history of women's sports, performance, disabilities, the environment, nutrition, breast cancer, aging, coaching, physical fitness and exercise, and status reports on women's sports in ten Asian nations. A highlight of the conference was a 5-kilometer run on the second day, which drew 1,000 women who then participated in mass aerobic exercises after reaching Manila's Rizal Memorial Stadium.

An important goal of the conference was to create unity among women and sportswomen to promote women's sports across Asia. Formal progress toward this goal began with the signing of a Sport Covenant for Women and the promulgation of the Manila Declaration on Women and Sport. Those who signed the covenant agreed "to live an active, healthy, and productive life through sport; and to provide equal access to an opportunity for all women to participate in year-round physical fitness, sport, and recreation activities." They also pledged to support, promote, and implement the "Sports for All" movement and resolutions adopted at the conference.

The Manila Declaration is based to some extent on the Brighton Declaration of 1994, which supported the development of women's sports around the world. The Manila Declaration is meant for thirty-six Asian nations and in its foreword sets forth the following agenda:

It is in the interest of equality, development and peace that a commitment be made by governmental, nongovernmental and all those institutions involved in sport to apply the Principles set out in this Declaration, by developing appropriate policies, structures and mechanisms which:

ensure that women and girls have the opportunity to participate in sport in a safe and supportive environment which preserves the rights and dignity of and respect for the individual;

increase the involvement of women in sport at all levels and in all functions and roles;

ensure that the knowledge, experience and values of women contribute to the development of sport;

and promote the recognition by women of the intrinsic values of sport and its contribution to personal development and health lifestyle.

Since the conference, only limited progress has been made toward implementing the Manila Declaration and promoting women's sports in a general sense across Asia. Obstacles to progress include the considerable linguistic, cultural, religious, and political variation across Asia; political unrest and conflict in some regions and nations; and the economic crisis that began in 1998 that has reduced or eliminated resources for women's sports. When progress has been made it has more often been in specific nations through the efforts of small groups of women.

The Editors

See also Afghanistan; Asian Games; Australia; China; Indonesia; International Council for Health, Physical Education, Recreation, Sports and Dance; Iran; Islamic Countries' Women's Sports Solidarity Council and Games; Israel; Japan; Singapore; South Korea; Syria; Thailand; Turkey.

Information provided by Darlene Kluka and Josefina Bauzon.

ASIAN GAMES

The Asian Games are the largest regional sports competition in the world. Since their inception in 1951, they have grown from eleven nations and six sports to forty-one nations and thirty-five sports in 1998. Similarly, women's participation has grown from 31 athletes in 1951 to 2,138 in 1998.

HISTORY

The Games' origin can be traced back to the Far East Games, which existed in the early twentieth century. In September 1911 E. S. Brown, F. K. L. Crone, and W. Tuthry, the directors of the YMCA in the Philippines, Japan, and China, respectively, proposed to set up an Asian sport organization to meet the demands of sport development of the region. After a series of discussions among physical educators and sports administrators in these countries, the Far East Sport Association was established in 1912. Organized by this group, the Far East Olympic Games were held in Manila the following year. Later the name was changed to the Far East Games at the request of the International Olympic Committee (IOC).

In the first eight Games, only the three founding nations took part, joined later by India, Indonesia, and Vietnam. In 1920 the IOC officially recognized the Far East Sport Association as a regional organization, the first that the IOC so acknowledged. The Games were held ten times from 1913 to 1934. Women's volleyball and tennis were introduced as the demonstration events in the sixth Games in 1923, and women's track and field and swimming events were added to the program of the ninth Games. The Games were terminated in 1934 as serious political conflicts developed among the Asian nations, the result of the rise of militarism in Japan.

The current Asian Games may also contain some elements of the West Asian Games, another regional event in Asia. These Games, however, were held only once, in 1934, with India, Afghanistan, Pakistan, and Ceylon (Sri Lanka) taking part.

After World War II significant social change, both broad and deep, spread across Asia. With Asian countries becoming independent and their economies and cultures developing, Asian peoples increasingly sought to become less isolated from one another and to strengthen their interactions to help heal the wounds left by wars and other societal disasters. Recognizing these

Athletes from Taiwan and Japan at the 13th Asian Games in Bangkok in 1998. (Stephen Shaver/Corbis)

social needs, in 1947 the Indian prime minister, Jawahalal Nehru, proposed the creation of Asian sports games at a conference on relations among Asian countries. During the Olympic Games held in London in 1948, Dr. Guru Dutt Sondhi from India suggested to thirteen sport delegations from Asia the idea of discussing Asian Games. India received little support initially, and only ten people from six countries attended the discussion. Nevertheless, representatives at this meeting decided to set up an Asian athletic federation and hold the first Asian athletic championships in New Delhi, India, in 1949. To transform this goal into reality, a planning committee was set up to draft the charter for the Asian Amateur Athletic Federation. On 13 February 1949, the Asian Amateur Athletic Federation was formally established, although its name was soon changed to the Asian Games Federation (AGF). It was decided to hold the first Asian

Games in 1950 in New Delhi, but they were in fact delayed until March 1951. Since then, the Asian Games have been held regularly once every four years, at the middle of the four-year cycle of the Olympic Games.

In December 1982 the Olympic Council of Asia (OCA) was established. As one of the pan-regional governing bodies of all sports and an affiliate of the IOC, the OCA replaced the Asian Games Federation and took over the responsibility for the Asian Games. As a permanent sport administrative agency in Asia, the OCA has carried out its functions more efficiently than the AGF, and the Games developed rapidly after 1982. As of 1999, OCA had forty-four member nations eligible to send their sports teams to the Asian Games. These nations are grouped into four regions: East Asia, Southeast Asia, South Central Asia, and West Asia.

ORGANIZATION AND EVENTS

As with the Olympic Games, the majority of sports events in the Asian Games originated in the West, but some traditional Asian sports are also included, endowing the Games with unique characteristics. There are many sports included in the Games, with the number of sports and events depending on the host country and organizing committee. The traditional Asian sports are briefly described here.

Judo is combat between two contestants. The participants compete within a 9-meter-square (30-foot-square) ring, situated on a site approximately 15 meters (49 feet) square covered with tatami mats. The combatants use various throwing and immobilizing tricks. The competition time is 5 minutes for men, 4 minutes for women.

Kabaddi is a male team sport that originated in India. In kabaddi competition two teams, with seven players on each side, compete with each other for higher scores by touching or capturing the players of the opposing team.

Karate do includes kumite matches and kata competition. The former is a match of two players fighting with each other, mainly using their hands and legs. The latter is an individual performance, based on the kata (form) routine of offense, defense, and counterattack against an imaginary enemy.

Sepaktakraw is a team ball-kicking match that originated in Southeast Asia. The ball used in the game is woven of rattan stems or made of plastic. The game was introduced for the first time in the 1990 Asian Games held in Beijing, China, and was played again in 1994 at Hiroshima, Japan. The 1998 Bangkok Asian Games included men and women's sepaktakraw events.

Taekwondo originated in Korea. It resembles wrestling; two competitors, wearing protective equipment, hit and kick each other with their hands and legs.

Wushu encompasses the traditional Chinese martial arts. Wushu in the Asian Games has three events: taijiquan tai chi quan, nan quan, and chang quan.

ASIAN SOLIDARITY

Beyond their function as a sporting event, the Asian Games are also intended to be a forum for cultural exchange, and the official program of the Games includes exhibitions of architecture, painting, and sculpture as well as performances of music and other traditional arts. These activities and displays are intended to foster mutual respect among Asian peoples, with the mutual goal of striving together to build an attractive, dynamic Asia. The slogan "Asian Harmony" referred to this goal in the twelfth Asian Games.

In conjunction with the Games, organizers also sponsor a sport scientific congress. At the 1998 Bangkok Games, the scientific conference had the theme "Modern Way of Sports." Sport scientists, most of them from Asia, discussed the interrelationships between sports and the modern lifestyle of Asian peoples.

To obtain financial assistance from the private sector, the organizers of the Games routinely look for commercial partners. For exam-

Naoko Takahashi cries as she waves the Japanese flag after winning the women's marathon and the first gold medal of the 13th Asian Games in Bangkok in 1998. (Torsten Blackwood/Corbis)

ple, the organizing committee of the 1998 Bangkok Games had the following companies as official partners: Samsung (electronics), Otsuka (sports drinks), Carlsberg (beverages), Toyota (automobiles), Thai Airways International, Samart (telecommunications), Caltex (petroleum), Acer (computer), Fuji Xerox (copiers and other equipment), Laem Thong Bank, and Football Thai Factory.

WOMEN'S PARTICIPATION

Women's participation in the Asian Games was initially very modest, a trend that, to a degree,

THE LARGEST ASIAN GAMES OF THE TWENTIETH CENTURY

The 13th Asian Games, held from 6 December to 20 December 1998 in Bangkok, were the largest Games since the event's inception. Nearly 10,000 athletes and officials from forty-one Asian nations participated, with 1,226 medals awarded. About 20% of the athletes (2,138) were women, with China, South Korea, and Japan taking most of the medals. Unlike some earlier games, the Bangkok Games went off smoothly with minimal political disruption.

reflected the limited social status of Asian women at that time. The inaugural Games did have women participants, but this did not signify genuine and complete participation by women. Rather, it was essentially symbolic; the Games offered few events for women, and few women took part in them. Women could take part in only nine events, all of which belonged to the single sport of track and field. Only thirty-one female athletes from four Asian countries took part: fifteen from India, eight from Japan, six from Indonesia, and two from Singapore. The number of women athletes was so small that they represented only about 0.6 percent of the total number of the athletes participating in the Games.

In the Games that followed, however, both the number of female athletes and events for women have increased slowly and steadily, and a significant improvement can be observed since the late 1980s (see Table 1). The obvious gap remains, though, between male and female participation rates. Asian women still have a long way to go before they will be on equal terms with their male counterparts in the high-performance sports.

Game organizers have noted the imbalance in the participation rates of the two genders and have made some efforts to improve the situation. In one symbolic gesture, a male–female pair of mascots was designed for the 1994 twelfth Asian Games held in Hiroshima, Japan. These two charming doves, named PoPPo (male) and CuCCu (female), hand in hand, seemed to call for fair and harmonious sports in Asia without any sex discrimination.

Hai Ren

See also Judo and Jujutsu; Karate; Sepaktakraw; Taekwondo; Wushu

Bibliography

Gu, Shiquan. (1989) *Sport History in China*. Beijing: Beijing University of Physical Education Press.

He, Qijun, and Hu Xiao Fen, eds. (1989) *History of Modern Sport in China*. Beijing: Beijing University of Physical Education Press.

Hu, Xinming. (1990) *Highlights in Asian Games*. Beijing: Olympic Press.

Liu, Xiang Fu. (1990) *A Complete Book of Asian Games*. Beijing: People's University Press.

Liu, Xiuwu. (1990) *Asian Sports*. Beijing: People's Sport Press.

Table 1. Comparison of Male and Female Participation in Asian Games

City	Date	Number of NOCs	Number of Sports for Males	Number of Sports for Females	Number of Total Athletes	Number of Female Athletes
New Delhi	1951	11	6	1	489	31
Manila	1954	18	8	3	970	98
Tokyo	1958	20	13	5	1422	121
Jakarta	1962	17	13	7	1545	203
Bangkok	1966	18	14	7	1945	376
Bangkok	1970	18	13	5	1752	259
Tehran	1974	25	16	10	2363	443
Bangkok	1978	25	19	12	2879	557
New Delhi	1982	33	21	11	3345	600
Seoul	1986	27	25	16	3420	755
Beijing	1990	37	26	23	6117	1462
Hiroshima	1994	42	33	26	6828	1017
Bangkok	1998	41	35	29	6832	2138

ASSOCIATION FOR INTERCOLLEGIATE ATHLETICS FOR WOMEN

The Association for Intercollegiate Athletics for Women (AIAW) is the first national governing body of women's intercollegiate athletics to be organized on the basis of institutional memberships. The association was created in late 1971 as a structure within the Division for Girls and Women's Sports (DGWS) of the American Association for Health, Physical Education and Recreation (AAHPER). On 1 June 1972 the AIAW began its official operation.

The AIAW's immediate predecessor was the Commission on Intercollegiate Athletics for Women (CIAW). This organization was formed by the DGWS in 1966 in response to the growing numbers of competitive opportunities for women in intercollegiate athletics. This growth brought with it a need for leadership and control. The CIAW established standards and controlled competitions by sanctioning regional tournaments; promoting the formation and growth of governing bodies of women physical educators at local, state, and regional levels; and holding national championships in seven sports—badminton, basketball, golf, gymnastics, swimming and diving, track and field, and volleyball.

The commission, however, had limited power and lacked the resources necessary to deal with the expanding needs and problems of collegiate athletics. The female physical education leaders therefore formed an association of institutional memberships, the AIAW. In June 1972, the AIAW replaced the CIAW.

The mission of the AIAW was to provide governance and leadership to assure that women's intercollegiate athletics had high standards and were educationally sound. As a governing body, one of AIAW's major purposes was to hold national intercollegiate championships for women. The AIAW began with 278 charter members in 1971–1972. A decade later, it had a membership of more than 960 institutions and had become the largest membership organization in the history of collegiate athletics. By 1980–1981, the AIAW had established three competitive divisions with a total of forty-one national championships.

Almost from its inception, the AIAW was faced with legal challenges to its sex-separate policies. Only weeks after the association began operating. Congress passed Title IX of the Education Amendments of 1972, prohibiting sex discrimination in all educational activities, including intercollegiate athletics. Seven months later, the AIAW was sued in a sex-discrimination case (*Kellmeyer, et al. v. NEA, et al.*) by eleven female student athletes and their coaches at two Florida colleges. The women challenged AIAW's scholarship policy, which disqualified recipients of athletic scholarships from participating in AIAW championships. They believed that if men were given scholarships based on their athletic talents, so should women. Foreseeing inevitable defeat in the court and, consequently, loss of its institutional members, the DGWS/AIAW revised its scholarship policy by removing its discriminatory aspects. The *Kellmeyer* case essentially ruined the integrity of AIAW's philosophical commitment to the "educational model" of college athletics. The change of its scholarship policy, nevertheless, greatly contributed to the rapid growth of the women's organization. By 1975, the AIAW had gained publicity through the nationally televised AIAW championships.

Commercial sponsorship soon followed. Eastman Kodak Company became the first major commercial backer of AIAW championships. With its potential of financial success and desire for organizational autonomy, the AIAW became an independent legal entity in June 1979 by separating itself from the AAHPER. At the peak of its commercial success in 1979–1980, the AIAW signed a four-year, million-dollar contract with the television network NBC for the rights to broadcast AIAW championships. The AIAW, however, was not able to collect all the NBC money when the network, in 1981, refused to honor the contract. NBC claimed that the AIAW could no longer stage the quality championships on which the contract was based, after which, in the same year, the National Collegiate Athletic Association (NCAA) began to offer championships for women.

Traditionally a men's organization, the NCAA had shown its muted but "vital" interest in women's athletics since the early 1960s as part of its strategy to expand its influence in U.S. amateur sports. In 1973, shortly after the passage of Title IX, the NCAA rescinded its rule prohibiting women from participating in NCAA events. The NCAA's intention to move into the separate sphere of women's athletics met strong resistance from the women in the AIAW. Throughout the rest of the 1970s, the NCAA fought on three fronts: in Congress, in an attempt to exempt men's college athletics from compliance with Title IX regulations; in the federal courts, challenging the government's authority to extend Title IX to intercollegiate athletic programs; and within its own membership, to legitimize the NCAA as an organization governing intercollegiate athletics for both men and women. All three attempts failed in the 1970s.

While the NCAA failed to seize control of women's intercollegiate athletics in the 1970s, it ultimately succeeded in the 1980s. The NCAA's attempt to govern women's athletics was aided by a conflict within the AIAW. Dissatisfied with the AIAW as a governing body, a group of women within the AIAW formed the Council of Collegiate Women Athletic Administrators (CCWAA) in 1979 to lead women into the NCAA structure. Shortly after, the NCAA successfully implemented its own program for women, first in Divisions II and III (1980), and then in Division I (1981). To satisfy the women, the NCAA not only guaranteed minimum representation of women in NCAA decision-making organs but also offered the same championship travel reimbursement for male and female participants.

The impact of the NCAA's entry into women's athletics on the AIWA was immediate and substantial. Before the end of 1981, the AIAW had lost a considerable number of member institutions and their membership dues, championship participants, television revenues, and commercial sponsors. Anticipating that the situation would worsen, the AIAW leadership decided to disband the association. On 30 June 1982, the AIAW officially ceased business except for channeling all of its energies and resources into the antitrust lawsuit against the NCAA. Eight months later, the AIAW lost its lawsuit in the U.S. district court. Finally, in May 1984, the U.S. court of appeals in the District of Columbia rejected the AIAW's appeal, a loss that ended the decade-long existence of the AIAW.

Ying Wu

Bibliography

Hult, Joan S. (1991) "The Legacy of AIAW." In *A Century of Women's Basketball: From Frailty to Final Four,* edited by Joan S. Hult and Marianna Trekell. Reston, VA: American Alliance for Health, Physical Education, Recreation and Dance, 281–307.

———. (1994) "The Story of Women's Athletics: Manipulating a Dream 1890–1985." In *Women and Sport: Interdisciplinary Perspectives,* edited by Margaret D. Costa and Sharon R. Guthrie. Champaign, IL: Human Kinetics, 83–106.

Hunt, Virginia. (1976) "Governance of Women's Intercollegiate Athletics: An Historical Perspective." Unpublished doctoral dissertation, University of North Carolina, Greensboro.

Wu, Ying. (1997) "The Demise of the AIAW and Women's Control of Intercollegiate Athletics for Women: The Sex-Separate Policy in the Reality of the NCAA, Cold War, and Title IX." Unpublished doctoral dissertation, Pennsylvania State University, State College.

ATHLETICS *see* Track and Field

ATHLETIC TRAINING

Athletic training is the process that all athletes, male and female, go through to prepare to compete in their sports. Training consists of work on the sport itself and its components, as well as exercises that build the strength, endurance, and flexibility that athletes need to achieve their potential. Athletic training also serves as a means to prevent injury.

WOMEN AND TRAINING

During the early years of women's participation in organized sport, little emphasis was placed on strength training and conditioning, both of which are primary factors in injury prevention and mechanically correct performance. Sports by their very nature invite injury. Female athletes are exposed to the same injury risks as their male counterparts and, therefore, deserve the same considerations regarding injury prevention and management.

Many myths and misconceptions, however, surrounded females' participation in these activities. Skepticism and apprehension prevailed based on anticipated risks to women's reproductive capabilities and musculoskeletal systems. These concerns arose from perceived differences in anatomical and physiological strength between the genders. Through much research and concentrated efforts that used scientific data to dispel these myths, strength and conditioning programs gradually became accepted and implemented for female athletes at all levels of competition.

Acceptance did not guarantee access. Male athletes had previously been the sole occupants of weight rooms and conditioning areas. Facility availability became an immediate deterrent to this newfound interest and to the conditioning goals of women athletes. Through Title IX legislation, these hurdles were gradually overcome, and facilities were either added for women or made co-educational.

Resolution of these questions—was training appropriate? where could women train?—did not settle the matter. Social issues then came to the fore, and many young women were prevented from reaching their performance potential because of the somewhat negative perception of the stereotypical athletic female physique. Over time, these issues also were resolved and became less influential. Today, strength and conditioning are accepted and embraced as valued and necessary prerequisites for participation in sports for both genders.

TRAINING AND INJURY

The role of physical training in the prevention of injury is well documented and cannot be over-emphasized. Once women were encouraged to participate in strength and conditioning programs, and their levels of participation increased and became equal to those of men, the injury patterns and rates between male and female athletes became quite similar. Generally speaking, the same injuries seen in men's sports are seen in comparable women's sports, and the management of these injuries by certified athletic trainers is also similar. Strength and conditioning programs for female athletes are now included at all levels of participation in sports. Females can now benefit from the positive effects of strength and

DON'T FEAR YOUR MUSCLES!

A Nineteenth-Century Woman Recruits Female Bowlers

And, ladies, when some jealous and false prophet arises to decry your noble efforts by drawing a forbidding picture of your great-great-grandchildren as huge, muscular amazons divested of sweet womanly charms by too steady encroachment on the field where men alone are fitted to excel, believe him not! By some happy provision of kind Nature, no matter if the woman's biceps grow as firm as steel, the member remains as softly rounded, as tenderly curved, as though no greater strain than the weight of jeweled ornaments had been laid upon them. This is a comforting assurance, and one that may induce many hitherto prudent ladies to lay aside old fashioned prejudice and join the growing host of womankind in the bowling alley.

MARGARET BISLAND
(1890) "Bowling for Women" Outing. 16 April.

An athlete trains by running sprints up stadium steps. (Robert Trubia/Corbis)

conditioning programs, essential components of athletic participation. The female athlete is finally being afforded the opportunity to reach her performance potential.

THE ATHLETIC TRAINER

The certified athletic trainer is an allied health care professional who provides health and injury care to physically active people of all ages. In cooperation with physicians and other health care professionals, the certified athletic trainer functions as an integral part of the health care team, providing skills in the prevention, recognition, immediate care, treatment, and rehabilitation of musculoskeletal injuries. The four-year degree program consists of a national written examination and an oral practical examination, offered at

more than 100 institutions throughout the United States. Through a combination of classroom education and clinical experience, the athletic trainer is prepared to apply a wide variety of specific health care skills and knowledge within varied settings.

HISTORY

The field of athletic training was recognized by the American Medical Association in 1990 as an allied health profession. Its history, however, can be traced back to the early 1900s, when athletic trainers were responsible for providing health and injury care for individuals participating in organized athletics such as the Olympic Games. When football became a national sport, it was obvious that someone was needed to care for the players' inevitable injuries. The profession of athletic training developed from that need.

The professional association for certified athletic trainers, the National Athletic Trainers' Association (NATA), was founded in 1950. It is a worldwide association that now has more than 23,000 members, primarily from Canada, Japan, and the United States. The mission of NATA and goal of the certified athletic trainer is to provide health and injury care to physically active people of all ages through the prevention, treatment, and rehabilitation of acute and chronic activity-related injury and illness. The National Athletic Trainers' Association Board of Certification (NATABOC), incorporated in 1989, provides a certification program for entry-level athletic trainers and continuing education standards for certified athletic trainers.

Studies of the outcome of athletic training have shown that the methods that trainers use are effective in treating musculoskeletal injuries at all body locations and that certified athletic trainers produce excellent results in returning individuals quickly to their pre-injury status. These techniques are used extensively outside athletics as well. Studies have also demonstrated that athletic training methods are extremely effective in improving work-related disorders and that rehabilitation provided by certified athletic trainers significantly improves the functional status of patients following reconstructive surgery of major joints.

Precisely what athletic trainers do—known as their scope of practice—is defined by specific competencies. These competencies, referred to as Athletic Training Competencies for Health Care for the Physically Active, define the areas of expertise of the entry-level athletic trainer. They are based on, but not limited to, the following educational areas:

Risk management

Assessment/evaluation

Acute care

General medical and disabilities

Pathology of injury and illness

Pharmacological aspects of injury and illness

Nutritional aspects of injury and illness

Illness

Therapeutic exercise

Therapeutic modalities

Health care administration

Professional development and responsibilities

Psychosocial intervention and referral

In earlier decades, athletic trainers practiced primarily in academics, professional, and amateur athletic settings. Since about 1980, there has been a significant increase in the number of certified athletic trainers working in sport medicine clinics, hospitals, and industrial settings. NATA reports that more than 15,000 nationally certified athletic trainers work in the following settings: 23 percent in clinical settings, 7.9 percent in professional sports settings, 16.7 percent in colleges or universities, 5.2 percent in hospitals, 14.8 percent coach high school teams, 1.6 percent in two-year colleges, 13.4 percent in high schools/clinics (training rooms), and 0.7 percent in industrial settings. The other 17.33% are certified but not practicing in a field related to athletic training.

WOMEN AS ATHLETIC TRAINERS

Once an exclusively male-dominated profession, the field of athletic training has changed dramatically in relation to the inclusion of women. The increase in participation by girls and women in sport and physical activity, encouraged and enhanced by Title IX, created a need for health and injury care for these emerging athletic populations. As a result, women began pursuing careers as athletic trainers. Initially serving only female sports participants, women athletic trainers now provide health and injury care to participants of both genders across all age ranges.

NATA has clearly demonstrated its commitment and attentiveness to the specific needs and concerns of the female population. Since the early 1970s, certified female athletic trainers have played a significant role in the development of NATA and the profession of athletic training, and they have provided health and injury care for physically active individuals of all ages. At the turn of the century, more than 50 percent of the membership of NATA was female. Women are represented on all major NATA committees, chair several of those committees, and are represented on NATA's board of directors. Women have served as both the executive director of NATA and as the president of its research and education foundation. This foundation has specifically awarded grants to female scientists serving as principal investigators of studies of issues of critical importance to physically active females, such as anterior cruciate ligament injuries and eating disorders.

Marjorie J. Albohm

See also Endurance; Injury

Bibliography

National Athletic Trainers' Association Web site: <http://www.nata.org>.

Information for this article was provided by the National Athletic Trainers' Association, Dallas TX; NATA Research and Education Foundation, Dallas, TX; and NATA Board of Certification, Omaha, NE.

AUSTRALIA

Australia is a large island nation in the South Pacific with a population of 18 million. Its history is rich in sport, and women have contributed significantly to that history. The many champion women of Australian sports have largely triumphed over a system that worked strenuously against them.

Australia was founded with a pioneering spirit that encouraged a masculine culture, while social etiquette supposedly restricted women to parlor games. The reality, however, was that the physical demands of pioneering life meant colonial women became proficient shooters, rowers, archers, swimmers, and equestrians.

Around the time of Australia's federation, at the start of the twentieth century, sport became a means for an emerging nation to establish itself on the world scene. This early lust for international success outweighed sexual prejudice, and even today men—and women—who succeed on international sports fields become national icons. Men who succeed domestically are also lionized by the media and the public. This acceptance and adulation does not extend to women on the domestic level.

EARLY HISTORY

The largely unsung efforts of Australian sportswomen have a strong and long history. Many of the early sports established in Australia were popular in England, among them cricket, croquet, tennis, and cycling. What is believed to be the world's first bicycle race for women was held over a 3.2-kilometer (2-mile) course at Ashfield, New South Wales, in 1888. The first Australian championship in golf (male or female) was the Australian Ladies' Championship, played in Geelong, Victoria, in August 1894, yet it would be more than three decades before an independent, autonomous women's amateur golf-controlling body would be formed. Even then, women could only become "associate members," having access to the course only on special days, mainly during the week. This practice persisted until the 1970s—and then it required equal opportunity legislation to correct it.

The development of a formal education system for girls in the 1870s had a huge impact on the growth of sport and recreation. Private schools promoted a culture of strenuous physical activity. From these schools sprang a group the press labeled "the new women" who would eventually return to the school system after university to perpetuate sporting traditions. Government schools were somewhat slower to adopt physical culture curricula or activities. Swimming was one of the few sports government schools promoted, largely because of the safety factor involved in learn-to-swim and life-saving classes.

Although the number of women wanting to take swimming lessons swelled as a result, access to municipal swimming pools was restricted to "ladies hour." This hampered the growth of competitive swimming for women. Women were further bound by the fashion of the day, which stipulated neck-to-knee woolen costumes. Swimming champion Annette Kellerman (1888–1975) had a huge impact on the evolution of bathing costumes after being arrested on a Boston beach in 1907 for wearing a one-piece, skirtless bathing suit. Swimming for women had another boost in 1912 when Sydney's Sarah (Fanny) Durack (1889–1956) and Mina (Wilhelmina) Wylie (1891–1984) took the 100-meter freestyle gold and silver medals at the Stockholm Olympics, the first swimming event open to women at the Games.

TWENTIETH CENTURY

Women enjoyed a growing range of sports in the first two decades of the new century. Swimming's popularity saw the formation of female surf clubs, although the all-male Surf Life Saving Association banned women from gaining the bronze medallion to qualify them as life-savers. Traditional male sports like rugby league and Australian rules football had also opened up to women, but the grounds were only available on Sundays and women drew the ire of clergy across the country for playing on "God's day." Around this time a sports academy in Adelaide, South Australia, found netball had become so popular that it had to offer extended playing hours between 6:00 and 11:00 PM. The idea of women playing "after hours" was a real social change.

In the 1930s women and sport lobby groups began to spring up around the country. High on their agenda was the need for more women's sports grounds. Fanned by a new wave of confident and empowered women, fresh from universities where they had enjoyed the spoils of the suffrage movement, women's sports began a new era—played, administered, and promoted by women for women. Sportswomen began writing for the press, with writers like Ruth Preddy and Lois Quarrell doing much to lead the way. In Melbourne, Victoria, in the mid-1930s, *The Sportswoman*, a monthly newspaper devoted entirely to women's sport, was published. World War II signaled the end of many of these dedicated publications and columns. Women did not truly re-enter sports journalism in any numbers until the 1980s, ushered in by antidiscrimination legislation.

World War II brought most international and national competition to a halt, but local competitions thrived. Factories organized interfactory competitions, and sports clubs continued to grow, feeding on support for morale-building activities. After the war the popular press turned women's attention to more domestic matters. Athletes who succeeded during the next decade received media attention that often focused on their personal lives. Shirley Strickland (track and field) was often described as a housewife and mother despite the fact that she had a Ph.D. in nuclear physics and later went on to become a key administrator and coach.

Strickland's is among many women's names associated with the 1956 Melbourne Olympics. Australia's 44 women athletes won seven gold, two silver, and three bronze medals, while the men's team, 243 strong, won six gold, six silver, and eleven bronze medals. In total, women have comprised 23 percent of Australian Olympic teams from 1948 to 1996 but have won 38 percent of the medals.

The major growth sports for women between 1950 and 1970 were tennis, golf, and squash—all generally regarded as "ladylike." This was the era that saw the rise of innovative administrators like Nell Hopman (tennis) and Gertrude McLeod (golf) and sports champions like squash player Heather McKay (nee Blundell, 1941–) and tennis players Margaret Court (nee Smith, 1942–) and Evonne Goolagong (1951–). Goolagong, an indigenous Australian, was removed from her

One of Australia's premier athletes, Cathy Freeman, explodes from the starting blocks in the 1996 Atlanta Olympic Games. (Wally McNamee)

home and grew up in a white family, gaining access to facilities and opportunities her indigenous cousins did not have. Her formative years saw the passing of legislation that freed indigenous Australians from social restrictions and allowed them to join sporting clubs. Only a handful of indigenous women have made their mark representing Australia. One of the most recognized is 400-meter world champion Cathy Freeman (track and field). Today, many aboriginal women play in their own community competitions as well as entering teams in mainstream sporting competitions.

1970–1990

In the two decades between 1970 and 1990, women took up a broader range of sports and the popularity of team sports increased. The 1976 Olympic Games proved a low point for Australian sport. The Australian team of 184 competitors came away with just one silver and four bronze medals. The 35 women on the team did not contribute to the final tally. Efforts to bolster Australia's across-the-board sporting performance failed to concentrate on the historical source of medal victories—women. The athletic union nominated no women athletes for Olympic track and field scholarships in 1977. Women had to wait

VIGORO

Vigoro, an Australian women's sport like cricket, was invented in about 1900 and became organized in 1919 with the formation of the Vigoro Association. In the 1990s, the sport remained confined to Australia where it is played in leagues in New South Wales, Tasmania, and Queensland. There are teams and test matches for various age categories, beginning with girls under the age of 13 up through seniors. Vigoro remains an exclusively female sport, although it was invented by a man (John George Grant) and men played the major role in its administration for several decades after its founding.

An amateur sport, vigoro is different from cricket in that it fields twelve players with the extra player being a second bowler. There are also differences in how the ball is bowled and how the game is scored, making vigoro a lower scoring but much faster sport than cricket. The governing body is the Australian Women's Vigoro Association, with the greatest popularity in Queensland where the Queensland Ladies Vigoro Association has some 1,500 members.

until the Australian Institute of Sport opened in 1981 before receiving financial support and encouragement. Financial support for women in professional sports was virtually nonexistent. Women began lobbying for more prize money as stories filtered through of gross inequities. In 1984 a triathlon held in Geelong, Victoria, offered prizes to both female and male competitors. The first woman home received a bicycle, and the first male to finish received two round-trip air tickets to Hawaii.

In the late 1980s, government moves helped open the door for more women to participate. In 1984 the Commonwealth Sex Discrimination Act was passed, followed by several state equal opportunity acts. These made it unlawful to discriminate against a person on the grounds of sex, marital status, or pregnancy. Sporting clubs were forced to offer full membership to women.

Throughout the mid-1980s, a series of surveys revealed that schoolgirls were disadvantaged, that they had few role models in sport, and that those who did not play sports were low achievers. In 1984, the Australian government launched a program to increase girls' self-esteem through physical education, the Girls in Physical Education Project. A major initiative came the following year with the establishment of the federal government working group on women in sport. Its report in 1985, *Women, Sport and the Media*, proposed the establishment of the Women's Sport Unit attached to the Australian Sports Commis-

sion. The unit came into being in 1988 and developed the national Active Girls campaign, which promoted sport to girls. By being attached to the Australian Sports Commission, the women and sport unit gained direct input into policy development.

1990s

In the 1990s, the Women's Sport Unit worked with national nongovernment groups such as Womensport Australia as well as other government agencies, including the Australian Coaching Council, to address issues as diverse as harassment in sports, sports groups' amalgamations, poor media coverage, mentoring, improving access to facilities and resources, and low numbers of women in leadership positions. The unit also coordinated women's policy development and contributed to women's involvement in a new national physical activity push, Active Australia.

Despite these efforts, in 1998 less than 15 percent of national sporting organizations had women as presidents. Less than 25 percent had female executive directors or general managers. Around 11 percent of accredited high-performance coaches were women. A survey of sports coverage in Australian media revealed further problems. During the Atlanta Olympics, up to 41 percent of the sports coverage of metropolitan papers was devoted to women's sports, largely because of the outstanding performances of Australian women. In the corresponding two weeks in the following non-Olympic year, women's sports received less than 10 percent of sports coverage. Coverage of women's sports on television was even worse, involving less than 2 percent of total sportscasting time.

This coverage was disproportionate in comparison with statistics showing that more than 3.5 million of the country's 9 million women and girls participate in sport and physical activity. From this pool have come world or Olympic champions in a range of sports. Sportswomen like Dawn Fraser (swimming), Karrie Webb and Jan Stephenson (golf), and Michelle Timms (basketball) are globally recognized. Others like Kay Cottee (solo sailing), Louise Sauvage (wheelchair athletics), and Zali Steggall (slalom skiing) have pushed both their personal boundaries as well as barriers to women's participation generally.

Sharon Phillips

Bibliography

Cashman, Richard. (1997) *Australian Sport Through Time: The History of Sport in Australia.* Sydney: Random House Pty Ltd.

Daly, John A. (1982) *Ours Were the Hearts to Dare.* Adelaide: Gillingham Printers Pty Ltd.

———. (1994) *Feminae Ludens.* Adelaide: Openbook Publishers.

Gordon, Harry. (1994) *Australia and the Olympic Games.* Brisbane: University of Queensland Press.

Griffin, Rhonda, Sharon McLeod, and Toni O'Malley. (1996) *Outstanding Australian Sportswomen.* Canberra: Australian Sports Commission.

Mikosza, Janine. (1997) *Inching Forward: Newspaper Coverage and Portrayal of Women's Sport in Australia.* Canberra: Womensport Australia.

Participation in Sport and Physical Activities 1996/1997. Australian Bureau of Statistics Catalogue 4177.0.

Participation in Sport and Physical Activities 1997/1998. Australian Bureau of Statistics Catalogue 4177.0.

Phillips, Dennis H. (1996) *Australian Women at the Olympic Games 1912–92.* Sydney: Kangaroo Press Pty Ltd.

Phillips, Murray. (1997) *An Illusory Image: A Report on the Media Coverage and Portrayal of Women's Sport in Australia 1996.* Canberra: Australian Sports Commission.

Stell, Marion K. (1991) *Half the Race: A History of Australian Women in Sport.* Sydney: Angus and Robertson Pty Ltd.

AUSTRIA

Austria is a small, landlocked nation with a population of about 8 million located in Western Europe. One-third of Austria's surface is dominated by the Alps, with peaks as high as 3,800 meters (12,500 feet) and some covered with snow all year. Austria's climate is cold and icy during winter, warm and sometimes rainy during summer. This terrain and climate have made winter sports especially popular and have limited participation in summer sports by both women and men.

HISTORY

Women's participation in physical education and sport dates to the early nineteenth century, a time when Austrian women, like other women in Europe, had limited political and economic rights and limited opportunity for achievement in education and employment. In addition, Austrian morality restricted women's participation in public events and required that they wear heavy and restrictive clothing that further limited their participation in sports. Physical activity and education were opened to women only after physicians suggested that physical activity would make girls and young women healthier and more physically attractive, two attributes considered desirable by Austrian men. Accordingly, the first (private) *Turnanstalt* (gym organization) was founded in Vienna in 1839 by Albert von Stephani. At the same time, courses in gymnastics and physical movement were developed explicitly for girls.

The movement toward physical education for girls seemed to move forward in 1869 when new education rules stipulated that all Austrian students must participate in physical education. However, there were few female teachers, so programs for girls were much slower to develop than those for boys. In 1883 the education law was amended, and physical education—especially for girls—was no longer required, largely because of new societal standards of sexual morality that again restricted the physical activity and dress of women. In 1912 physical education was again

With its mountainous terrain, Austria has produced many world-class alpine skiers including Renate Goetschl, shown here, on her way to taking first place in the World Alpine Championships in Vail, Colorado, in 1999. (Corbis)

OUTSIDE THE SCHOOLS

Although Austrians widely accepted the value of physical education for girls at the beginning of the twentieth century, women's sports activities outside the educational system were not so readily embraced. The acceptance of women's sports in Austria was to some extent the result of the changing social circumstances of women in general. Rosa Mayreder (1858–1938), the women's rights activist and author, pointed out that the bicycle (used in Austria since 1889) had a greater role in women's emancipation than all the activities of the women's liberation movement put together.

The history of women's participation in biking is typical of many other women's sports at the recreational level: (1) struggles against restrictions placed by men and women, (2) negative media coverage, (3) acceptance (mostly because of health benefits), (4) emergence as a recreational activity, (5) virtually no participation by women at the highest level of the sport and no coverage in the media. In the 1990s, the average Austrian woman was free to take part in just about any kind of sport she chose. However, they were only rarely able to do so as freely and as easily as men because of old prejudices about the appropriateness of women's participation in sports. Thus, many women did not continue to participate beyond school, although there were also many women who chose to participate despite the societal obstacles.

WOMEN IN INTERNATIONAL SPORT

Austria is inseparably connected with winter sports, especially with Alpine skiing. There is a long list of Austrian female winners of world championships or Olympic gold medals in skiing: Gerda Paumgarten (1936), Trude Jochum-Beiser (1950, 1952), Trude Klecker (1954), Christl Haas (1962, 1964), Marianne Jahn (1962), Olga Pall (1962), Annemarie Moser-Pröll (1972, 1980), Petra Kronberger (1988, 1992), Anita Wachter (1988), Sigrid Wolf (1988), Ulli Maier (1989, 1991), and Renate Goetschl (1997). Austrian women have also been champions in figure skating: Herma Szabo (1924), Helene Engelmann (1914, 1922, 1924), Lilly Scholz (1929), Eva Pawlik (1948), Sissi Schwarz (1956), and Trixi Schuba (1968, 1972); in speed

made mandatory in the schools. At that time, largely through the efforts of educator Margarete Streicher (1891–1985), physical education for girls and boys became an important component of education in Austrian schools. In the 1990s, girls spent between two and four hours per week in physical education classes. Girls and boys took physical education together from ages seven to ten and then were segregated, a practice at odds with that of most other Western European nations. This segregation was once criticized as too conservative but became accepted because it allowed for the development of women's sports, provided jobs for female physical education teachers and coaches, and helped prevent women's sports from being totally enveloped by men's sports. The importance of girls' physical education in Austria was reflected in the election of Julika Ullmann (1941–) as vice president of the International Association of Physical Education and Sports for Girls and Women (IAPESGW) and as the president of the International Committee of Sports-Pedagogy.

"THE QUEEN OF THE CHASE" —THE EMPRESS ELIZABETH OF AUSTRIA (1837–1898)

"Sisi," a Bavarian princess, married the Emperor of Austria, Franz Josef, in 1854. After the birth of their four children who were removed for separate formal upbringing, she became increasingly discontented with the "golden fetters" of one of the most rigid royal courts in Europe and suffered often from depression. A keen horserider since childhood, she spent much time away from Austria in search of freedom and excitement, often using a pseudonym to reduce formality. She was already a grandmother when she first encountered foxhunting in England in 1874. Two years later she moved to the British Isles for the hunting season and returned for several years. She hunted both in the English Midlands and in Ireland.

A bold, almost reckless rider, she was led through the fields by a pilot, Captain Bay Middleton, a handsome, enthusiastic cavalry officer ten years her junior. The empress found foxhunting a liberating experience after the rigid Vienna court life. Whatever the rumours about her relationship with male admirers away from the hunt, her position in one of the grandest European royal families protected her from ostracism. Instead, she became a model for other aristocratic and socially ambitious women. The press published engravings of her hunting exploits, and she enjoyed being painted on horseback.

Her hunting career lasted less than a decade, however, as family crises, ill health, and depression reduced her mobility. On 10 September 1898 she was assassinated in Geneva, Switzerland, by an Italian anarchist, Luigi Lu-cheni, who stabbed her to death with a home-made dagger. "Sisi" has remained a foxhunting legend and histories of the sport frequently reprint an anonymous piece of doggerel written after an Irish hunt:

The Queen of the Chase!
The Queen! Yes, the Empress!
Look, look, how she flies,
With a hand that never fails
And a pluck that never dies.
The best man in England can't lead her—he's down!
"Bay" Middleton's back is done beautifully brown.

Hark horn and hark halloa!
Come on for a place!
He must ride who would follow
The Queen of the Chase!

skating: Emesey Hunnyadi (1994); and in tobogganing: Doris Neuner (1992).

Although less numerous, Austrian women have also performed well at the international level in track and field: Herma Bauma (1934), Ilona Gusenbauer (1971, 1972), Eva Janko (1968), Liese Prokop (1967, 1968, 1969), Sigrid Kirchmann (1993, 1994), and Theresia Kiesl (1996); in fencing: Ellen Müller-Preis (1932, 1936, 1948); in table tennis: Trude Pritzi (1938, 1939, 1947); in judo: Gerda Winkelbauer (1980) and Edith Horvath (1980); in canoeing: Uschi Profanter (1996); and in the Special Olympics: Andrea Scherney (1996). Handball is the only team sport in which Austrian women are internationally ranked near the top of the sport.

WOMEN'S SPORT IN THE 1990s

Although Austrian girls and young women participated in school sports and there were many successful female athletes, women's sport participation was not yet equal to that of men. The situation in the 1990s can be summarized as follows. First, while many engaged in sports, almost no women held leadership positions, and the higher the position, the fewer the women. Second, men received greater financial support from the government and the private sector and got greater rewards for their successful performances. Third, media coverage of women's sports was significantly less than men's and was dominated by stereotypical (and sometimes subtly discriminating) descriptions of women athletes. In addition, there were no female sports journalists in Austria. Fourth, women were underrepresented in the world of sports research, with fewer women than men in sport science departments and no women holding the position of full professor. In an effort to change this situation, supporters of women's sports set forth the "Women in Sports" platform in early 1997 as a means of starting the process of changing men's and women's perceptions about sports and sport administration.

Rosa Diketmueller

Bibliography

Adam, Norbert. (1986) *Österreichs Sportidole*. Vienna: Bohmann.

Bachmann, Andrea. (1998) " 'Wie eine Katze schmiegt sie sich an, an die Hochsprunglatte'—Geschlechterdifferenz in der Sportberichterstattung." Salzburg, Austria.

Diketmueller, Rosa. (1998) "Vormarsch der Frauen (-forschung) in den Sportwissenschaften?—Entwicklungslinien mit Seitenblicken auf Österreich." In *Spectrum der Sportwissenschaften* (Nr. 2).

———, and Julika Ullmann. (1999) "Von der Frauenbewegung zur Frauenforschung: Stand und Potentiale Feministischer Frauenforschung in den Sportwissenschaften." In *BMWF (Hrsg.), Frauenforschung, Feministische Forschung, Gender Studies: Entwicklungen und Perspektiven (Materialienband zur Förderung von Frauen in der Wissenschaft; Bd. 8).* Vienna: ÖSD-Verlag.

Grössing, Stefan, ed. (1991) *Margarete Streicher—Ein Leben für die Leibeserziehung.* (Schriftenreihe des Streicher-Archivs, Bd. 1). Salzburg, Austria.

Hargreaves, Jennifer. (1994) *Sporting Females: Critical Issues in the History and Sociology of Women's Sports.* New York: Routledge.

Pfister, Gertrud. (1998) "Die Anfänge des Frauenturnens und Frauensports in Österreich." In *Bruckmüller, Ernst & Strohmeyer, Hannes (Hrsg.).* Turnen und Sport in der Geschichte Österreichs. Vienna: ÖBV, 86–104.

Spachinger, Maria-Susanne, and Sylvia Titze. (1991) "Sport und Emanzipation." In *Sport, Sinn und Wahn.* Steirische Landesausstellung in Mürzzuschlag. Graz, Austria.

AUTO RACING

Automobile racing comes in many varieties but always has essentially the same goal: whatever the endpoint of the race, the driver who gets there in the shortest time wins. Women have raced and continue to race automobiles, but they have done so in the face of considerable opposition by male drivers and by sponsors who are reluctant to back a woman.

HISTORY

The gasoline-engine-powered automobile made its debut on 9 April 1865 in Vienna, Austria. Afterward Siegfried Marcus, its inventor, abandoned his "explosive wheelbarrow" and moved on to electric lighting. Others developed the idea, however, and the first automobile trip was a drive of about 80 kilometers (50 miles) by Frau Berta Benz from Mannheim to Pforzheim in 1888. By 1894 a group of Frenchmen had organized a Paris-to-Rouen *Course de Voitures sans Chevaux* (a race of the horseless carriages), a distance of 127 kilometers (79 miles).

From the beginning, auto racing was dominated by male competitors and spectators, but a few women were sufficiently adventurous to flout convention and take up the new sport, although hampered by strict fashion codes that dictated long, full skirts and large picture hats protected by linen dusters and veils tied under the chin. Perhaps the first woman to race competitively was Madame Laumaille, who in 1898 led her class at the half-way point of the two-day Marseilles–Nice race and finished fourth, two places ahead of her husband. Madame Labrousse of Paris competed in the Tour de France in 1899. Camille du Gast (?–1942) was legendary for her driving prowess and set a high standard for later women competitors. In 1901 she drove in the Paris–Berlin race against 170 men, starting 122nd and finishing 33rd. The only female entrant in the 1903 Paris–Madrid race, she sacrificed a high finish to aid a driver seriously injured in one of the many crashes that marred the race. In 1904 she was asked to drive for the Benz team, but race organizers protested and the offer was withdrawn. Another highly successful woman racer in the early years of the century was Dorothy Levitt, the first Englishwoman to compete in public auto races. In 1904 she entered the Heresford 1609-kilometer (1000-mile) trial, the only woman in a field of top drivers. Her driving was so competent that the men accepted her fully. In the 1907 Herkomer Trophy Race in Germany, Levitt easily defeated all other women entrants and finished fourth in a field of 172 men and women, even though her car had less power than many others. She also participated in many hill-climbs and wrote a book, *The Woman and the Car.*

Between the wars a number of European women raced competitively. Madame Jennky (French) became the first woman to win a major European hill-climb, capturing the event at Gaillon in 1927. Elisabeth Junek (Czech, 1900–?) finished second overall (and first in the ladies' competition) in the 1926 Swiss Grand Prix and in the top five in the 1927 and 1928 Targa Florio road race.

It was 1930 before women were first allowed to compete in the Le Mans endurance race, which lasted twenty-four hours. Among the eighteen teams entered that year were Madame Mareuse and Madame Odette Siko, driving a Bugatti. They also competed in 1931. Two women's teams entered in 1932, and in 1935 a team of three M.G.s were entered with female drivers. Women have regularly competed since and have a number of wins to their credit.

In 1933 the (English) Royal Automobile Club granted women permission to compete in open meetings at Brookland racetrack on equal terms with male drivers. Among those who took advantage of the opportunity was Kay Petre, "the Idol of Brooklands," whose skill and professionalism were admired by many male competitors. Petre raced at Le Mans several times in the mid-1930s and drove in the 1936 South African Grand Prix, finishing eleventh even though the special fuel she had ordered for the car never arrived. Following a serious accident in 1937, she joined the Austin works team as a design consultant. Gwenda Glubb Janson Stewart Hawkes (three marriages) drove everything from ambulances in World War I Russia to dog sleds in Canada. A rival of Petre, she participated in auto racing with an eye to breaking records; at one time she held seventy-six of them. She was the "queen of the track" in France and held the record at Montlhery

for the fastest lap ever by a man or a woman. Other World War II–era drivers of note included Elsie "Bill" Wisdom, who regularly competed in the Monte Carlo Rally with an all-female crew, Dorothy Stanley Turner, Margaret Allan, and Maria Antonietta Avanzo.

A number of excellent women racers emerged following the war. Claudine Trautmann (1931–), one of the most successful women rally competitors, won the French Ladies' Championship nine times and was a works driver for Citroën. Pat Moss Carlsson (1935?–), sister of Formula One driver Stirling Moss, had a very successful racing career against men and women, as did Sheila Van Damm (1922–1987), Betty Skelton (1926–), Anne Hall, and Pamela Murphy. Denise McCluggage (1927–) did more than race. She founded the auto-racing weekly *Competition Press,* which later merged with *Autoweek.* In the 1960s the Macmillan Ring-Free Oil Company of the United States sponsored the Motor Maids, a team of women drivers who raced and did promotional appearances for their sponsor. The original team members were Smokey Drolet, Suzy Dietrich, Donna Mae Mims, and Janet Guthrie.

While women competed regularly in sports car events, trials, and hill-climbs, they were conspicuously absent in other types of racing. Formula One racing offers a handful of drivers the chance to race about fifteen weekends a year, and few women have succeeded in getting rides on the Grand Prix circuit. Gilberte Thirion finished fifth in the 1952 German Grand Prix. Lella Lombardi, "The Tigress of Turin" (1943–1992), competed in twelve Grand Prix races in 1975–1976 and is the only woman ever to win a championship point, garnering half a point for finishing sixth in the 1975 Spanish Grand Prix in Barcelona. She was considered by many the best woman driver in the world. Maria Teresa Deflilippis competed in three Grand Prix races for Maserati in 1958 and was the leading Italian driver at Monza that year before engine trouble forced her to retire. The spectators were torn between wanting to cheer for an Italian and jeer a woman driver.

Among the female pioneers in American closed-track racing were Louise Smith (1916–), Sara Christian, and Ethel Flock, who drove on the dirt tracks of stock car racing. National Association of Stock Car Automobile Racing (NASCAR)

RACING'S FASTEST WOMEN

Although Shirley Muldowney and Janet Guthrie have drawn the most attention as female participants in the male-dominated auto sports, they are not the only women to participate successfully. Others include Jessica Willard, the "Queen of Diamonds" in drag racing; Lyn St. James, Rookie of the Year at the Indianapolis 500 in 1972; Patty Moise, who races in NASCAR's Busch Grand National events; Sarah Fisher, who became the first female regular Indy racing league driver in 1999; Angelle Seeling, who drag races motorcycles in the National Hot Rod Association; and Tammy Jo Kirk, who races in NASCAR truck events.

founder Bill France, Sr., wanted a few women racers as a publicity ploy, but they proved to be more than he bargained for, frequently beating their male competition. In 1949 "Stock-Car Sara" Christian won six of seventeen races. Smith, who raced from 1946 to 1956, was known for a proclivity to crash, but her hell-bent-for-leather driving style also netted thirty-eight victories, including the 1952 race in Buffalo, New York, where she was forced to start last because she was a woman. Wilbur Shaw, president of the Indianapolis Motor Speedway, told reporters that Smith could probably pass the rookie test required for Indy 500 aspirants. However, speedway rules prohibited women from driving at the Brickyard.

THE MODERN ERA

"In company with the first lady ever to qualify at Indianapolis, gentlemen, start your engines." Those historic words at the beginning of the 1977 Indianapolis 500 chronicled a significant moment in the history of women in auto racing as Janet Guthrie (1938–) joined a field of thirty-two male drivers, the first woman to compete in the Memorial Day weekend classic. Her car was beset with mechanical problems and she was forced to retire, finishing twenty-ninth. Her second start at Indianapolis, in 1978, proved more successful: she started fifteenth and finished ninth. Guthrie was followed by Lyn St. James (1947–), who in 1992 became the second woman to qualify for the Indianapolis 500 and at forty-five its oldest rookie. Driving a Dick Simon car, she started twenty-seventh and finished eleventh and was subsequently named rookie of the year. She competed at Indianapolis regularly. In 2000, St. James and Sarah Fischer became the first two women to

drive in the same Indianapolis 500. Unfortunately they failed to finish when they had a minor accident on the 64th lap.

Women have been most successful in drag racing. The trail blazer was Shirley "Cha Cha" Muldowney (1940–), the first woman licensed to drive Top Fuel dragsters, whose 5,000-horsepower engines allow them to go faster than any other car over a quarter-mile course. By 1982 she had won three National Hot Rod Association (NHRA) Top Fuel World Championships. At the time, she was the only driver to have won it more than once. Another pioneer in drag racing was Agnes E. M. B. "Aggi" Hendricks of Canada, who in 1979 began competing in the all-male driving class of jet aircraft–engine drag cars. She was named the International Hot Rod Association (IHRA) Showman of the Year three times and in 1982 was its Jet Car Nationals champion.

TOP RACERS OF THE 1990s

In the footsteps of these groundbreakers have followed a number of women, and there are some bright stars on the horizon. Shelley Anderson (1964–) of the United States has had a successful career in NHRA Top Fuel competition; Viveca Averstedt of Sweden has been a drag-racing star in Europe; Patty Moise (pronounced Mow-ees, 1960–), also of the United States, has driven partial seasons in NASCAR Winston Cup and Busch Grand National Series for a number of years; Shawna Robinson competed in NASCAR events during the late 1980s and early 1990s, driving in the Busch Grand National Series in 1991 through 1995; Angie Wilson had competed in the NASCAR Goody's Dash Series; and Tammy Jo Kirk had driven in the NASCAR Craftsman Truck

Series. Kirk's sponsorship by Lovable, a lingerie manufacturer, was by itself an interesting statement about auto racing and femininity.

CULTURAL AND ECONOMIC ASPECTS

While women participated in European racing without much comment, North America was another matter. In the 1941 film *The Blonde Comet*, a female auto racer is leading the Indianapolis 500 but quits the race so that the man she loves, who has crashed his car, can borrow her's and win. With the exception of the Sports Car Club of America (SCCA) and the International Motor Sports Association (IMSA), where women have long been involved in all aspects of racing, the pervasive attitude was that racing was for men only. The combination of breathtaking speed and raw power epitomizes the macho image, and the fact that auto racing is a sport in which women and men can compete directly is seen by many as a challenge to male virility. Italian Formula One racer Lella Lombardi noted that "only in the United States have I recently encountered real prejudice. So many American race drivers behave like male chauvinists instead of men who practice a sport!" (Holder 1997: 26).

Symbolic of American attitudes is the trophy queen, an attractive, skimpily clad woman who presents trophies and kisses to male winners. Would-be female drivers, crew members, and journalists seeking to enter the old boys' club have encountered formidable resistance, both legal and attitudinal. Some tracks have barred women from driving, or restricted them to ladies' classes, and many have had a "no women in the pits" policy. The male racing fraternity justified the prohibition with excuses that they couldn't swear with women around or that fragile females might get hurt or be distracting or that they would just be in the way. A NASCAR official in the early 1970s explained that women in the pits would be "an insurance problem" and would cause inappropriate sexual encounters. The rules of most racing organizations did not mention women at all, but some noted specifically that women were not allowed in the pits or that each car was allowed a certain number of *men*. The United States Auto Club (USAC) sprint car rulebook referred to "pitmen" and provided two passes for each competitor to ensure a female presence in the stands. Sanctioning organizations still

Eleanor Allards of the British Women's Team is greeted by gendarmes at Boulogne with a bouquet of flowers during the 1950 Monte Carlo Rally. (Hulton-Deutsch Collection/Corbis)

require that drivers have a competition license as proof of sufficient experience and skills in order to race without danger to other drivers, and licenses can be denied for amorphous reasons. Female drag racers were denied professional driving credentials for a number of years. And while women drivers were never specifically prohibited from competing by NASCAR, it became increasingly difficult for them to get their cars past inspection in the Grand National Series. Women in racing also came under attack from other women: some drivers' wives and girlfriends complained that female racers' only interest in the sport was the chance to get close to the male drivers. From the variety of suspect reasons, one must conclude that women were not welcome in American racing.

Legal prohibitions against women are a thing of the past. The pit gate is open, and a number of women are passing through it, not only as drivers and crew, but as car owners, journalists, photographers, racing association officials, and public relations personnel. Subtle discrimination is still common, however; NASCAR has a "no shorts" rule in the pit and garage area, and female media representatives tend to be given more trouble than their male colleagues. When women do

AUTOMOBILE RACING FIRSTS

1898 Mme. Laumaille, the first woman automobile racer, finishes fourth in the Marseilles to Nice race; her husband finishes sixth.

1899 Genevra Mudge is the first American woman to drive a race car.

1909 Joan Newton Cuneo is the first woman to win an auto race in the United States, defeating Walter Donnelly for the National Amateur Championship in New Orleans, Louisiana.

1958 Maria-Teresa de Filippis is the first woman to start a World Championship Formula One race, finishing tenth in the Belgian Grand Prix.

1963 Donna Mae Mims is the first woman to win a SCCA Class Championship, taking the Class H Production crown against thirty-one men in a points race.

1968 Patsy Burt is the first and only woman to win the standing start kilometer event at the Brighton (England) Speed Trials.

1973 Shirley Muldowney is the first woman to hold a Top Fuel dragster racing license.

1975 Lella Lombardi, the "Tiger of Turin," is the first and only woman to race the entire Formula One season and to win a championship point.

1975 Karren Stead, eleven, of Morrisville, Pennsylvania, is the first female to win the National Soapbox Derby.

1976 Arlene Hiss is the first woman to race in a USAC Indy car event, competing in the Phoenix 150.

1976 Janet Guthrie is the first woman to drive in a NASCAR superspeedway event, finishing fifteenth in the World 600 in Charlotte, North Carolina.

1976 Shirley Muldowney is the first woman to win a professional drag racing event, taking the Top Fuel class at the Spring Nationals in Columbus, Ohio.

1977 Janet Guthrie is the first woman to start in the Indianapolis 500. She is forced to retire due to mechanical difficulties after twenty-seven laps.

1977 Shirley Muldowney is the first woman to win the NHRA Top Fuel drag racing championship. In 1982 she is the first driver, male or female, to win three NHRA Top Fuel championships.

1982 Diane Teel is the first woman to compete in the NASCAR Busch Grand National Series race, starting at Martinsville, Virginia.

1982 Verta Henell is the first woman to win a NASCAR track championship, taking the Ascot Park, California, Limited Stock Car Division.

1985 Lyn St. James is the first woman to win an IMSA GTO race, at Elkhart Lake, Michigan.

1985 Lyn St. James is the first woman to win a professional road race driving solo, at Watkins Glen, New York.

1986 Patty Moise is the first woman to win an IMSA Kelly American Challenge race, at Portland, Oregon.

1987 Patty Moise is the first woman to win a NASCAR Busch Grand National Series event, the Winn-Dixie Challenge Qualifying Race at the Charlotte (NC) Motor Speedway.

1988 Shawna Robinson is the first woman to win a NASCAR feature race, a Dash Series event at the Asheville (NC) Speedway.

1990 Shirley Muldowney is the first and only woman to be inducted into the Motorsports Hall of Fame of America.

1991 Tammy Jo Kirk is the first woman to compete in the NASCAR Slim Jim Pro Series, finishing nineteenth in the point standings.

1992 Lyn St. James, forty-five, is the oldest rookie ever to qualify for the Indianapolis 500.

1995 Tammy Jo Kirk is the first woman to win the prestigious Snowball Derby stock car race.

1996 Danielle Del Ferraro is the first three-time winner in the All-American Soap Box Derby, winning the Kit Car championship in 1993, the Masters championship in 1994, and the Masters Division Rally Car championship in 1996.

1996 Shelly Anderson records the fastest speed ever in a Top Fuel drag race, going 508.814 kmh (316.23 mph) at the Chief Auto Parts Nationals in Ennis, Texas.

1999 Louise Smith is the first woman to be inducted into the International Motorsports Hall of Fame.

breach the barrier, the media attention they receive emphasizes their physical appearance. Female drivers are cute blondes with trim figures and million-dollar smiles who like to garden and cook, while males are shown in the context of the racing world and their physical attributes are rarely mentioned. The clear implication is that the female driver is a woman who happens to race rather than a racer who happens to be a woman. Some male drivers will go to great lengths to discourage women racers. In a 1994 NASCAR Grand National race, driver Mike Wallace, who had earlier threatened to put pole-sitter Shawna Robinson out of the race, apparently intentionally caused her to crash. Jennifer Cobb, who races in Kansas, has had several wins, but notes, "There should have been more. I've had guys put me out on the last lap. It's hard to say if they did it because I was a woman or not, but when a total stranger takes you out and they are in a slower car, then something must be up. Most of my competitors respect me and the female thing is not an issue. But every once in a while you run into some immature driver. Guys who think like that are inevitably losers, because they are concentrating so hard on seeing to it that the girl doesn't win, that they lose any chance to win themselves" (Benson 1997: 54).

Fortunately, this misperception is slowly changing. A male mechanic for Tammy Jo Kirk commented, "This is no lady; this is a racer" (NASCAR Special 1998). Tom Jenson, executive director of NASCAR's *Winston Cup Scene* magazine, thinks that a markedly successful woman driver would do much to alter perceptions. "The bottom line is racers respect results. I think they would get past gender and color and the other things that society has a problem getting by if that driver demonstrated they are capable. I don't know if you need a female Jeff Gordon, but you need at least someone who runs in the top 10" (Hill 1998: A4).

There is still a widely held belief that women are not strong enough to withstand the physical stress of piloting a balky race car at high speeds for hours at a time. Male drivers find it harder to trust their female counterparts on the track. Men involved in racing accidents provoke little comment, but a wreck involving a woman is quickly pointed out. The implication is that she is incapable of handling the car and is a danger to herself and others.

However, a NASA-funded study on the physiology of race car drivers found that racing is more mentally than physically stressful. What is required is a high level of concentration for hours on end and the ability to withstand heat. Janet Guthrie agrees that mental strength is of primary importance in racing: "I drive the car, I don't carry it." She says, "I guarantee you 100 percent there is no difference whatsoever on the race track. The main part of racing is not so much physical as mental. The physical demands are there, for sure, but determination, concentration, emotional detachment, and desire are the most important qualities. A racing driver is a racing driver" (Dowling 1978: 63). Before puberty, there is virtually no difference in the strength between boys and girls; a nine-year-old girl may in fact be stronger than her male counterpart, but her lack of practice makes her less skillful. Most girls don't learn the hand–eye coordination needed for racing. Boys spend years throwing balls and driving go-carts, developing needed motor skills. By the time a girl becomes interested in racing, she may be in her late teens and lag behind in the quick movements needed to succeed. As coed competition becomes commonplace, girls will develop skills at the same time and pace as boys. Women tend to fare well in endurance races such as Le Mans because mental stamina replaces physical strength as the primary factor. These races also benefit from teamwork, an area in which women tend to excel. Some women drivers disagree, however. They believe that in smaller stock cars a woman can hold her own with a man but that in very powerful vehicles lack of physical strength puts many women at a disadvantage. Improving upper-body strength is crucial for a woman to compete successfully in these classes.

Women racers are divided on the questions of ladies' classes versus open racing. Many support the concept of "powder puff" races in order to attract more women into the sport, suggesting that once women gain skill and experience they have the option of competing in open races. Others note that auto racing offers a level playing field and prefer open racing as a true test of ability.

Auto racing is all about money. The greatest challenge for women racers is attracting the level of sponsorship essential to pay for the team, facilities, and equipment needed to field a competitive car. Men—and most corporate marketing decision makers are men—who choose to spend thousands of dollars on publicity for their products are loathe to bankroll a female racer. Women racers are caught in a "*Catch-22* situation": track time is imperative to build skills but impossible to obtain without a sponsor, and sponsors aren't willing to invest before they have seen good performances on the track. A few women, such as Janet Guthrie, Shirley Muldowney, and Lyn St. James, have overcome the obstacles placed in women's path, but most have not. Even successful women drivers have to scrounge for sponsors. Throughout her exemplary career, Muldowney struggled financially. As successful as she was, sponsorship was difficult to find. Guthrie notes that when she was racing, several good teams, including McLaren and Bignotti, approached her, but she had to bring the sponsorship with her, and nobody was interested. She remarks sardonically that the same people who wonder why there aren't more women in racing "are still puzzling over the question of why there are no black managers in baseball" (Dodds 1994: 234). While 40 percent of NASCAR fans are women, sponsors shy away from backing female drivers. It is especially interesting that companies with products like coffee, laundry detergent, and pantyhose are sponsoring male drivers. Guthrie asserts that if generating publicity were the bottom line, a successful woman driver would be much more lucrative for the company than a man. The real barrier is the "good old boy network." Some men still sound suspiciously like the baseball owners of the 1930s, who were unable to locate African American talent: "I said twenty years ago that if we see a woman with all the right stuff and her own fortune, we'll see a woman in victory lane."

Female anguish over athletic success against male competitors is gradually disappearing. Auto racing is becoming accepted at the grassroots level as a sport for females, and they are getting involved at an earlier age. While boys still dominate in numbers, more and more girls are competing and winning in the All-American Soap Box Derby, the NHRA Junior Dragster races, quarter midget races, and other competitions for children. Chances are the top three performers in a division will include at least one girl.

Increasingly women are also filling nondriving roles. Top Automobile Racing Club of America (ARCA) racer Bill Venturini's all-female racing team included his wife Cathy as crew chief. The CEO of the Melbourne Grand Prix Corporation in the mid-1990s was Judith Griggs, a commercial lawyer who had been involved in Formula One racing for about ten years. Many local tracks are owned and operated by women, and racing organizations often have female public relations officers. Perhaps symbolic of changing cultural attitudes is the presence of a new NASCAR racing team, Washington Erving Motorsports, a minority-led group with a woman, Kathy Thompson, as president.

Handicapped by inadequate financial support, subtle and blatant resistance, and having to be better than the average male driver to win the respect of their colleagues, women have often been competitive but rarely victorious. The only woman racer who has indisputably reached the top of her chosen sport is Shirley Muldowney, who in the late 1970s and early 1980s was the best drag racer in the world, male or female. One disgruntled loser noted that "she drives like a man." Replied Muldowney, "Do you think maybe one day, when be beats me, they'll say 'He drives like a woman?'" (Dowling 1978: 37).

Suzanne Wise

Bibliography

Benson, Michael. (1997) *Women in Racing.* Philadelphia: Chelsea House Publishers.

Bledsoe, Jerry. (1975) "No Women Need Apply (Except with Big Tits)." In *The World's Number One, Flat-Out, All-Time Great, Stock Car Racing Book,* edited by Jerry Bledsoe. Garden City, NY: Doubleday.

Collins, Vincent P. (1966) *Physiologic Observations on Race Car Drivers.* Washington, DC: National Aeronautics and Space Administration.

Davis, S. C. H. (1950) *Atalanta: Women as Racing Drivers.* London: G. T. Foulis.

Dodds, Tracy. (1994) "Why Aren't Women Racing at Indy? Janet Guthrie Knows." In *A Kind of Grace: A Treasury of Sportswriting by Women,* edited by Ron Rapoport. Berkeley, CA: Zenobia Press.

Dowling, Claudia. (1978) "Women Who Race." *WomenSports* 5, 1: 34–37, 63.

Hill, Jemele. (1998) "Breaking the Gender Barrier." *The News & Observer* (Raleigh, North Carolina), 14 February 1998, A1, A4 (final edition).

Holder, William. (1997) "New Racing Women." *Stock Car Racing* 12 (4): 26.

McCart, Joyce. (1976) "Goodbye to the Powder Puffs: Women Stake Their Claim in Stock Car Racing." *Branching Out* 3, 2: 11–13.

Mull, Evelyn. (1958) *Women in Sports Car Competition.* New York: Sports Car Press.

"NASCAR Special." (1998) Special edition of "North Carolina Now." 30 min. North Carolina Public Television, first aired February 10.

"Racey Women." (1977) *Stock Car Racing* 12, 4: 22–31, 69, 76, 81.

Standridge, Joyce. (1992) "Making It in Racing: How Women Are Getting Jobs in Auto Racing." *Stock Car Racing* 27, 2: 59–66.

"Women in Racing." (1972) *Stock Car Racing* 7, 10: 19–32.

Zobel, Judith E. (1972) "Femininity and Achievement in Sports." In *Women and Sport: A National Research Conference*, edited by Dorothy V. Harris. University Park, PA: Pennsylvania State University.

B

BADMINTON

Badminton is one of the world's fastest racket sports, requiring quick reflexes and superb conditioning. In a badminton smash, the shuttlecock has been timed at speeds over 322 kilometers per hour (200 miles per hour) in top international competition. The game is played worldwide by more than 1 billion people. In the 1990s, the top amateur and professional players came from China, East Asia, and Northern Europe. The 1992 Olympic badminton competition was seen on television by more than 1.1 billion viewers. According to a 1993 study, in the United States some 1.2 million people play badminton at least 25 times a year, 760,000 people call badminton their favorite sport, and more than 11.2 million people play the game at least once during the year. Throughout the long history of badminton and its ancient precursors, women have been full participants.

HISTORY

Badminton was adapted from an earlier pastime with roots in the magical ritual of divination. One rite for divining the future was hitting an object with the hand or a bat into the air as often as possible. The number of hits achieved without a miss supposedly indicated the length of one's life; a maximum high score was considered a happy omen for longevity. The game of battledore and shuttlecock originated from the secularization of this rite. Its purpose, if played solo, was to hit the shuttle with a racket into the air as many times as possible, without letting it drop to the ground. With two players, the shuttle was hit backward and forward between them, with a point being scored for each miss on the part of the opponent.

Various versions of this pastime became popular as long as 2,000 years ago in China, Thailand, India, and ancient Greece. It was played by all social classes, by adults, and equally enthusiastically by girls and boys. At first, the palm of the hand was used and then a small bat, originally made of wood, then skin, and finally catgut strings stretched over a frame. The name "battledore" derives from the bat used in washing laundry. The shuttle was originally a rounded piece of cork, with feathers stuck around its flattened top. Probably the early use of cocks' feathers gave it its name; in early days, the feathers were not uniform in size or weight. The first recorded reference to the game in England was in the fourteenth century, and a plate shows a girl and a boy playing the game then referred to as the "toy." It became so popular that, in Leicester, England, Shrove Tuesday was called "shuttlecock day." The streets were crowded with players of all ages. Rhymes chanted as an accompaniment to the play give further evidence of its roots in the ancient practice of divination. A gender-neutral one was:

> Shuttlecock, shuttlecock, tell me true
> How many years have I to go through?
> One, two, three . . .

A girls' rhyme was:

> Grandmother, grandmother
> Tell me no lie
> How many children
> Before I die?
> One, two, three . . .

ORIGIN OF THE NAME

In the 1860s, a group of British army officers on leave from India were attending a house party at Badminton House, the duke of Beaufort's country estate in Gloucestershire. Due to rainy weather, they decided to play indoors the game then called "poona." As word of the game spread among the English gentry, they called it "badminton" after its place of origin. The sport became popular at English seaside resorts and then in the London suburbs. Early photographs of women badminton players wearing long dresses demonstrate their

An illustration of two women playing badminton, formerly called "shuttlecock," from *The Book of Games*, 1812. (Bettmann/Corbis)

clubs founded the Badminton Association of England and wrote the laws that have changed very little since then. By coincidence, Gloucestershire became the base for the International Badminton Federation (IBF). Founded in 1934 with nine members—Canada, Denmark, England, France, Ireland, the Netherlands, New Zealand, Scotland, and Wales—the IBF grew steadily, expanding rapidly after badminton's Olympic debut in 1992 at Barcelona. By 1999, the federation had 138 members worldwide.

RULES AND PLAY

Badminton is played on a rectangular court—13.40 meters long and 6.10 meters wide (44 by 20 feet), divided into equal halves by a 1.524 meter- (5-feet) high net—by two players (or four players in doubles). A rally is won if the shuttle is hit over the net and onto the floor of the opposing side's court. A rally is lost if the shuttle is hit into the net or over the net but outside the opposing side's court. It is also lost if the shuttle touches the receiver or the receiver's clothing, or if the receiver hits it before it crosses the net.

A match is the best of three games. Fifteen points wins a men's game. However, if the score reaches 14–14, the side first reaching 14 can choose either to play to 15 or to set the game to 17 points. The final score will reflect the sum of the points won before setting plus the points gained in setting. Scoring in women's singles is slightly different. Eleven points wins a game, with the option to set the game to 13 points at 10–10.

The players use very light rackets to hit the shuttlecock ("shuttle") with great speed or skillful deception. Top players make few unforced errors, so a contest is mentally stimulating and emo-

continuing involvement with the sport from its earliest, less formalized structure.

The first laws of badminton were printed in India in 1877. Sixteen years later, in Southsea, England, representatives of fourteen badminton

CHINESE DOMINATION OF BADMINTON

According to the International Badminton Federation, at the end of 1999 the top five ranked women players were all from China, with Ye Zhaoying ranked first. In the second five were two women from Denmark and one each from China, Korea, and Japan. In women's doubles, five of the top ten teams were from China, two from Denmark, and one each from Korea, Great Britain, and Indonesia.

Four women play indoor badminton, 1950s. (Bettmann/Corbis)

tionally intense; keen judgment is essential in order to win under pressure. The contrast between the abilities of modern women players with those of earlier players can be seen in the following account from 1911: "It was towards the close of a severe contest that the lady was forced by her antagonist to run across the court at every stroke. She ran so well that she must have covered nearly 50 yards before she failed to return the shuttlecock. The effort was so great she was quite exhausted" (Suffolk and Berkshire, 1911).

Women have always been included and accepted in the sport from the casual recreational level up to the major international competitions. In mixed doubles, women participate equally with men, thanks in part to badminton's obligatory underhand serve, which must have the shut-

tle hit upward to get it over the net. Another contributing factor is the considerable amount of social interaction in the sport, particularly at the recreational level.

COMPETITIONS

The first unofficial all-England championships for men were held in 1899 and for women in 1900. They became "official" in 1904, as badminton gained popularity in Europe, North America, Australia, Asia, and South Africa.

The first international men's team championship, the Thomas Cup, was contested in 1948–1949. The idea for a similar women's competition was first broached in 1950 and was finally established in 1956–1957 when Betty Uber of England donated the first Uber Cup (held every even year). That first final was won by the United States, captained by Margaret Varner, when it defeated Denmark 6–1 in England. It was not until 1989 in Indonesia that the first world mixed-team championship for the Sudirman Cup took place; it was subsequently held in every odd year in conjunction with the world championships. The World Cup competitions took place between 1981 and 1996 to enable top players to earn increased prize money. It was superseded by the World Grand Prix series—a singles and doubles competition open to all players who were members of an IBF-affiliated association. Players earned points toward their world rankings in tournaments nominated by the IBF to participate in the World Grand Prix series. There were "one-star" ($30,000) through "six-star" ($250,000) tournaments, with the Grand Prix finals purse of $350,000; these tournaments included all five events: men's singles, women's singles, men's doubles, women's doubles, and mixed doubles. The men's-singles winner received 6.5 percent of the total prize money while the women's-singles winner got 5.0 percent. There were similar differences in the other events, with the men/women difference rationalized by the fact that there were more contestants in the men's competitions. The differences were fairly slight and the players did not earn the huge sums found in some professional sports. For example, the actual prize money for the 1999 World Grand Prix was: men's singles, $18,600; women's singles, $15,300; men's doubles, $19,500; women's doubles, $17,700; and mixed doubles, $17,700. The Badminton Players' Federation promoted and helped safeguard the interests of top international players and was represented on the IBF Council.

In 1999, the top-ranked women's-singles player was Camilla Martin of Denmark, with Ye Zhaoying and Zhou Mi, both of China, in second and third places. Of the top ten, one was from Europe, six from China, two from Indonesia, and one from Japan. The highest-ranked English woman was placed fourteenth and the top U.S. player, ninety-eighth. In women's doubles, Marlene Thomsen and Rikke Olsen, both from Denmark, were at the top, with the next three spots filled by women from China. Olsen was also the top-ranked mixed-doubles woman player, with

England's Joanne Goode second and Denmark's Ann Jorgensen third. Other women's champions and teams in the later 1990s were Bang Soo Hyun of Korea (Olympic gold, Atlanta, 1996), Ye Zhaoying of China (world championship, Glasgow, 1997), and Susi Susanti of Indonesia (World Grand Prix, Bali, 1996). Indonesia beat China in the 1996 Uber Cup; and China beat Korea in the 1997 Sudirman Cup, with Denmark third, Canada fourteenth, and the United States twenty-fourth.

In 1999, the IBF was governed by a general meeting of delegates from its 138 member associations, with a council appointed to carry on the federation's work during the year. The presidency was a four-year term of office with a maximum of two terms. Seven vice presidents were elected for three years, five continental representatives and twelve other members for two years—all being eligible for reelection. Policy was handled by sixteen different committees, with the day-to-day work carried out by eleven full-time and four part-time staff of the IBF Secretariat. The president was a woman, Lu Shengrong of China.

CONCLUSION

Badminton is a sport to which women have contributed hugely throughout its history—not least at the recreational level, with millions of participants worldwide. Although men have sometimes received more attention than women, the difference has been less marked than in many other sports. Badminton is a democratic and inclusive sport for people of all ages and abilities (and some disabilities).

John J. Jackson

Bibliography

Arlott, John, ed. (1975) *The Oxford Companion to Sports and Games.* New York: Oxford University Press.

Brash, R. (1970) *How Did Sports Begin?* New York: David Mckay.

Cox, J. Charles. (1903) *The Sports and Pastimes of the People of England.* London: Methuen.

International Badminton Federation. *Statutes 1998/99.* Cheltenham, U.K.: Author.

———. Web site at <http://www.IntBadFed.org>.

———. *World Badminton Magazine* (quarterly).

Suffolk and Berkshire, The Earl of, ed. (1911) *The Encyclopedia of Sport and Games.* London: Heinemann.

BALLOONING

Ballooning is a recreational and a competitive sport—recreational if the balloonist wants only to enjoy the sensation of flight, competitive if she wants to arrive at a particular destination first or faster than others. It is a sport for adventurers, who seem unlikely to run out of records to break or new worlds to conquer. Since its inception, women have been among those flying for both pleasure and victory, but their participation has been less than that of men.

HISTORY

Humankind's dream of flight was first achieved in balloons, which derive their lifting power by being filled with a gas less dense than air—hence the "lighter-than-air" (LTA) appelation. The principle was discovered in France by the Montgolfier brothers, whose observation of rising smoke led them to invent the hot-air balloon that took the first man aloft in 1783. On 20 May 1784, four French ladies of the court of Louis XVI became the first women to lift off the ground, albeit in a tethered balloon. Two weeks later, Marie-Elisabeth Thible was the first woman to experience free flight, in a balloon piloted by the painter Fleurant.

When ballooning caught on as a popular attraction, it spawned aeronauts who would perform in public for money. In 1799, Jeanne Labrosse, wife of the leading French pilot André-Jacques Garnerin, became the first woman to solo in any kind of flying machine. She had made her first flight the previous year and would enjoy a long career as a balloonist-parachutist. Her niece Elise Garnerin would follow in her footsteps with an act that consisted of lifting off the ground in a basket connected to a parachute attached to a balloon, pulling a release cable, and gently floating to the ground.

The most famous woman balloonist of the era was Madeleine-Sophie Blanchard, who learned to fly from her husband, Jean-Pierre, the first man to fly in a balloon across the English Channel, and who introduced ballooning to the United States. When he died in 1809, she took up the profession with such success that the following year she was named "Aéronaute officiel de l'Empire." Remarkably, after Napoleon's death, Blanchard's position was confirmed by Louis XVIII, but unfortunately, on 7 July 1819, she became the first woman to die in a flying accident.

Ballooning also marked the beginning of discrimination against women flyers when the Paris police banned flights by two-person mixed-sex crews on account of "the fragility of the female organs, which might be endangered by the low air pressure." The order is thought to have arisen from the confusion between the words "aerostatic" and "ecstatic" in the announcement of an upcoming flight, thereby creating concerns about morality. It was rescinded after the protests of the prospective passenger, Ernestine Henry, who eventually flew with Garnerin on 10 July 1798. Similarly, although the idea of forming an association for flyers was put forward in England by Vera Butler in 1901, for many years the Royal Aeronautic Club (RAC) did not accept women as members. Butler was, however, invited to fly in a balloon with her father (automobile pioneer Charles Rolls) to unfurl the new group's pennant.

Although lighter-than-air craft were largely superseded by the more practical airplane, some women were issued formal balloon licenses. The RAC issued at least one Aeronaut Certificate to a woman, Mrs. Assheton Harbord in 1906—a belated recognition of proficiency because she had already crossed the English Channel several times in her balloon and had won the Krabbe Cup by covering 322.8 kilometers (199.5 miles) in 11 hours and 40 minutes. The Società Aeronautica Italiana issued another such certificate to Giulia Strada, the wife of ballooning pioneer Celestino Usuelli, in recognition of her fifteen ascents between 1908 and 1913. An all-women ballooning club, the "Stella," was formed in Paris in 1909, its activities including members' competitions. By 1912, the club counted some 200 members and was authorized to issue official balloon-pilot licenses.

During World War I, as in the American Civil War and earlier conflicts, balloons were used as aerial observation posts but proved so vulnerable and cumbersome that they were set aside shortly after the armistice. The few exceptions comprised high-altitude research flights, which were the

Illustration of women in a hot air balloon. (Lake County Museum/Corbis)

preserve of men. Thus, women's ballooning was extremely limited; for instance, no women participated in the world's leading ballooning event, the Gordon Bennett Cup. Similarly, although the Fédération Aéronautique Internationale (FAI) recognizes ballooning records, few have been recorded in decades. Since the mid-1980s, there have been several attempts to fly around the world in a balloon, invariably with male crews and funding. Some women have participated in recreational ballooning or in the growing advertising use of shaped balloons.

Despite this unhappy situation, women have occasionally left their mark in modern ballooning. In 1963, Nini Boesman of the Netherlands won the Harmon Trophy for a solo balloon crossing of the Swiss Alps, which took her above the 3974-

meter (13,114-feet) Eiger Peak. On 2–3 March 1983, Hélène Dorigny made the first crossing of the Mediterranean, setting women's world records for both endurance and distance.

RULES AND PLAY

In competitive ballooning, the objective is to travel a greater distance through the air or a greater distance in a shorter time than others who previously made the same journey. Success depends on the skill of the balloonist, the quality of the equipment, and weather conditions, which can slow the journey, blow the balloon off course, or even end the trip. In the 1990s, international politics was a major consideration, with balloonists having to get permission to fly across many nations. Without such permission, the balloonist risks being shot from the air or forced to land. Ballooning is costly, historically attracting only a small following of wealthy participants, although spectacular flights draw the attention of a much wider range of people.

Early balloons were made of silk, rendered airtight by a rubberizing process or by an internal layer of china paper. The exterior was richly decorated in bright colors; the crew sat in a wicker basket, suspended by ropes. Lift was supplied by hot air from a small stove burning straw or similar material, or by hydrogen, which is highly flammable. Modern balloons differ little in concept. Although silk has been replaced by synthetic materials, hot air from an easily controlled gas burner is the preferred form of lift. Hydrogen has been replaced by helium, which is safer but very expensive—hence its use only in long-distance machines. Wicker baskets are still used for recreational flying, but balloonists on endurance flights or seeking records prefer enclosed gondolas with life-support and communications equipment. Colors are still flamboyant.

Airships, or dirigibles, were developed in the late nineteenth century to overcome the impossibility of directing a balloon's flight. An airship is an oblong-shaped balloon with rudders and an engine. Because of their cost and complexity, airships were only used by the military and the nascent airline business. Neither of these sought women pilots, explaining in part why there are very few known women airship pilots. On 29 June 1903, Cuban-born Aida da Acosta soloed in

"Baladeuse," a single-seat dirigible owned by the Brazilian aviation pioneer Alberto Santos-Dumont. The flight started in Neuilly-Saint-James, France, and ended at the Bagatelle polo grounds, disrupting a France–United States game underway. On 21 June 1908, English balloonist and women's-suffrage campaigner Muriel Matters flew as passenger in a small airship to drop "Votes for Women" leaflets over the British Parliament. On 21 November 1919, French actress Gaby Morlay, a veteran of sixty-two flights, was awarded the first women's airship-pilot license in France.

Ballooning remains a recreational and competitive activity, attracting people who participate for the pleasure of floating through the air as well as those who participate to set new speed and distance records. On 20 March 1999, the first nonstop journey around the world, using high-technology equipment, was completed by the team of Bertrand Piccard of Switzerland and Brian Jones of Great Britain. Their balloon took 19 days, 1 hour, and 49 minutes to travel the 42,810 kilometers (29,055 miles) east from Switzerland to the finishing line in Mauritania, North Africa. The challenge now is for this kind of record to be equaled or surpassed by an all-women team.

Gregory Alegi

Bibliography

De Bernardi, Fiorenza, ed. (1984) *Pink Line. A Gallery of European Women Pilots.* Rome: Aeritalia.

Gunston, Bill, ed. (1992) *Chronicle of Aviation.* London: Chronicle.

Jablonski, Edward. (1968) *Ladybirds: Women in Aviation.* New York: Hawthorn Books.

Rado, Gheorghe. (1993) *Prioritati si Recorduri Mondiale de Aviatie.* Bucharest: Tehnoprod.

Robène, Luc. (1998) *L'Homme à la Conquête de l'Air.* Paris: L'Harmattan.

BASEBALL

Baseball is a uniquely American game that developed from the English game of rounders. It has become, if not the national pastime, certainly an important one and a part of American culture. Baseball is considered an American sport, but it is also popular in Japan, Taiwan, Korea, and Latin America. Baseball in the United States has traditionally been considered a male domain. From the sandlot to major league baseball, girls and women have largely been excluded. However, throughout the sport's history, a few determined women have managed to overcome barriers against their playing. Today there is a rich history of women's participation in baseball as players, umpires, and owners, although there is little prospect of a professional league.

HISTORY

Although myth has it that Colonel Abner Doubleday invented baseball in Cooperstown, New York, the game actually originated with the Knickerbocker Base Ball Club of New York, started by Alexander J. Cartwright and several other prominent New York businessmen. On 3 September 1845, Cartwright established the first set of official rules for the game. At first the rules referred to the "New York game" to distinguish it from the earlier "Massachusetts game," which was played primarily in the New England states. One major rule change of the New York game was that players had to be tagged out rather than having the ball thrown at them. Over time the New York rules were accepted as the rules for baseball by the majority of clubs.

By 1854, New York City had four clubs and Brooklyn (at that time a separate city) had another four, with new clubs being formed rapidly. In 1858 the National Association of Base Ball Players was created to organize the various groups and to devise a standard set of rules based on the New York rules. Baseball was also played at elite men's colleges. In 1859 the first official college game was played between Williams College and Amherst College using "Massachusetts game" rules, although eventually the National Association of Base Ball Players succeeded in making the New York rules the basis for today's baseball.

During the Civil War, soldiers from all over the country were introduced to the game, and they continued to play after the war. By the late 1800s little boys grew up playing baseball, and every town had at least one amateur team. Baseball had come to typify all that was good about America. To be American was to love baseball.

Maja Mikulier, 13, of Mostar, Bosnia-Herzegovina, catches the ball during Little League practice at a local Mostar park, 1999. Despite the country's political turmoil, the Mostar team was practicing for the Little League Championships held in Pennsylvania. (AP Photos)

Many believed that baseball taught children (especially those of immigrants) traditional American values. Community residents were proud of belonging to local baseball clubs. Baseball was seen as the great assimilator of the people. It captured the spirit of the nation and was considered the national sport. Baseball along with apple pie and motherhood came to epitomize the American way of life.

The 1871 formation of the National Association of Professional Base Ball Players was the start of professional baseball. In 1876 the organization's name was changed to the National League of Professional Clubs. The rival American League was formed in 1899. Since 1903, the winning teams of each league have played each other in a postseason championship called the Major League World Series. The National and American Leagues have teams in the United States and Canada.

In Japan, baseball was first played in the 1870s. Matsutara Shoriki is credited with starting professional baseball in Japan. Initially, Shoriki helped to sponsor a seventeen-game series between Japanese college all-stars and American major leaguers such as Babe Ruth. The games were so popular that Shoriki founded the first Japanese professional team, the Great Tokyo Base-

ball Club, in 1934. The next year their name was changed to the Tokyo Giants. In 1936 the Japan Pro-Baseball league (JPBL) was formed. Today the JPBL consists of two leagues, the Central and Pacific leagues, which play in the Japan World Series. The Japanese brought baseball to Taiwan during their fifty-year occupation of the island, which began in 1895. The Chinese Taipei Professional League was formed in 1991. A missionary from the United States, P. L. Gillet, introduced baseball to Korea in 1905. Since 1982, Korea has had a six-team professional league.

By the late 1800s, many Latin American and Caribbean countries had been introduced to baseball. Cuba established its first professional baseball team, the Havana Baseball Club, in 1872. In 1878 three Cuban teams formed the first professional league on the island. Today baseball is played in many Latin American and Caribbean countries and is especially popular in Cuba, Puerto Rico, Venezuela, Panama, Nicaragua, Mexico, the Dominican Republic, and the Virgin Islands. Since 1947, there has been a yearly Latin American World Series.

WOMEN'S BASEBALL

Women at the elite eastern women's colleges—Smith, Wellesley, Vassar, Mount Holyoke, Radcliffe, Bryn Mawr, and Barnard—were among the first to embrace the game. The intent of the physical educators at these schools—founded to provide equal educational opportunities for women—was to develop a program of calisthenics that would promote health and physical fitness. The students, however, quickly embraced the game of baseball. In 1866 Vassar had teams of eight players, and by 1876 teams of nine players. Women began to play at Smith College in 1879, at Mount Holyoke in 1891. These women typified the "new woman"—educated, independent, and athletic. They stood in sharp contrast to the Victorian ideal of the "true woman"—weak, passive, frail, and dependent. Other women's colleges also had teams. Wells College in Aurora, New York, had teams in the 1870s; Mills College in Oakland, California, had teams in 1872; Wheaton College in Norton, Massachusetts, had teams in 1900; Pembroke College, the women's college of Brown University in Providence, Rhode Island, had teams in 1905; Agnes Scott Institute in Decatur, Georgia,

AMERICAN WOMEN BALL PLAYERS IN JAPAN

In 1925 the Philadelphia Bobbies toured Japan playing exhibition games against men's B club teams from Japan University, Tedai Club Tokyo Dental University, Medical Toteshu Shiyochiku Kinema, and several other teams. They were scheduled to play fifteen games for $800 a game. The touring team of girls ranged in age from thirteen to twenty-three and were mostly from the Pennsylvania area. Two former major leaguers, Earl Hamilton, a Pirates pitcher, and Eddie Ainsmith, a Washington catcher, accompanied the team and sometimes made up the battery (pitcher/catcher). Initially, the Americans were greeted by large Japanese crowds, but when their play did not live up to expectations, interest waned. At the end of the tour, their sponsors reneged on paying their fare back to the United States. Fortunately, a Japanese hotel owner took pity on them and financed their passage back to Seattle. Edith Houghton, the Bobbies' shortstop, went on to become the first major league baseball scout. The Philadelphia Phillies hired her in 1946.

In 1994 Jodi Haller became the first woman to play organized baseball in Japan as a member of a Japanese team. Playing for Tokyo's Meiji University team, she pitched one and two-thirds innings in Meiji University's win against Tokyo University. Previously, she had pitched for St. Vincent's College in Latrobe, Pennsylvania. In 1996 she attended the Colorado Bullets spring training camp, but did not make the regular team roster.

---

had teams in 1905, one year before the school became a degree-granting college; Skidmore College in Saratoga Springs, New York, had teams in 1916; Hollins College in Hollins, Virginia, had teams in 1917; Goucher College in Baltimore, Maryland, had teams around 1920; Rockford College in Rockford, Illinois, had teams around 1923; and Randolph–Macon Women's College in Lynchburg, Virginia, had teams in the 1920s.

EARLY PROFESSIONAL TEAMS

Promoters as early as the 1860s realized the financial potential of the novelty of having women's teams play men's teams. The first all-female teams were organized purely as publicity stunts. The sensationalism of having pretty, feminine young ladies playing against powerful, muscular men was considered enough to draw crowds regardless of the women's skills.

The earliest record of a women's professional baseball team comes from 1867, when an African American women's team, the Dolly Vardens, formed in Philadelphia. The date of the earliest white women's professional baseball team is difficult to establish. The Blondes and the Brunettes were the first of the women's professional barnstorming teams to gain widespread publicity.

They played their first game on 11 September 1875, in Springfield, Massachusetts. It was promoted as "the first game of baseball ever played in public for gate money between feminine ball-tossers."

By the 1890s women's exhibition games had lost their novelty. The public wanted to see serious baseball. The 1890s heralded a new age in women's baseball, with professional teams springing up across the country. A team known as W. S. Franklin's Young Ladies Baseball Club Number 1 played multiple games against men's teams in 1890–1891. They even played an exhibition game against the New York Giants. They were highly competitive—although their competitive edge may have come from having a few male ringers dressed as women.

At about the same time, Bloomer Girls teams began to appear throughout the country. The name "Bloomer Girls" was generic and used by promoters of traveling teams (New England Bloomer Girls, Chicago Bloomer Girls, Texas Bloomer Girls, etc.). These were serious women's teams that barnstormed across the country playing men's amateur and semiprofessional teams for a percentage of the gate. Although by the 1920s most of the women's teams had disappeared and the number of men's amateur and semiprofessional teams had declined, the New York Bloomer Girls team continued to play until 1935.

WOMEN ON MEN'S TEAMS

By the 1900s women were also being recruited to play on men's teams. Elizabeth Stride or Stroud, whose professional name was Lizzie Arlington, was the first of the female phenoms. She played one game for the Philadelphia Reserves in 1898 and then was hired by Ed Barrow, president of the Atlantic League, to pitch in minor league exhibition games. When she failed to draw crowds, her career ended. Three other women, however, had fairly long semiprofessional careers as players. Alta Weiss played baseball for sixteen years, from 1907 to 1922, Lizzie Murphy for eighteen years, from 1918 to 1935, and Josie Caruso for three years, from 1929 to 1931.

The early 1900s brought other baseball firsts for women. Amanda Clement became the first woman professional umpire in 1904. She umpired semiprofessional games in the Dakotas, Nebraska, Minnesota, and Iowa until about 1911. Helene Britton became the first woman owner of a major league team, the St. Louis Cardinals, in 1911. In 1917 she sold the team.

During the Great Depression of the 1930s, baseball owners searched for gimmicks to attract spectators. Two women athletes, Virne Beatrice "Jackie" Mitchell and Mildred "Babe" Didrikson, were recruited to play in major league exhibition games. In 1931 Joe Engel, owner, promoter, and president of the Chattanooga Lookouts, a class-AA minor league team, signed seventeen-year-old Jackie Mitchell to a contract. He then announced that the young woman was going to pitch in an exhibition game against the New York Yankees—an announcement that made national headlines. On 2 April 1931, Jackie Mitchell struck out Babe Ruth and Lou Gehrig. Pictures of Mitchell striking out these two top players appeared in newspapers and magazines across the country, and moviegoers flocked to see the newsreel that Universal Studios put out. Unfortunately, Mitchell's official professional career was to be short-lived. Baseball Commissioner Kenesaw Mountain Landis announced that women were banned from competing in baseball and that her contract was null and void.

Babe Didrikson gained international fame after winning two gold medals in track and field at the 1932 Olympics in Los Angeles, and she followed her Olympic wins with various promotional events. In 1934, as a publicity gimmick, some major league baseball teams hired her to pitch in spring training games in Florida. She pitched for the St. Louis Cardinals against the Philadelphia Athletics and for the Athletics against the Brooklyn Dodgers.

Two other women played minor league baseball. Frances "Sonny" Dunlop played for the Fayettesville Bears against the Cassville Blues in a class-D minor league game in the Arkansas–Missouri League on 7 September 1936. Apparently, that was her first and only game. In 1948 Betty Evans pitched an exhibition session in Portland Park, Oregon, for the class-AAA Pacific Coast Baseball League. She lived up to her softball nickname, "Bullet Evans," striking out six of nine players.

A LEAGUE OF THEIR OWN

World War II provided another opportunity for women to play baseball. Philip K. Wrigley, the chewing gum magnate and owner of the Chicago Cubs, fearing that major league baseball might have to suspend operations during the war, founded the first and only women's professional baseball league. This league, the All-American Girls' Baseball League (AAGBL), was active in the Midwest from 1943 through 1954. At the peak of its popularity in the 1948 season, nearly a million fans came out to see games. The league folded in 1954, a casualty of the times. Attendance at AAGBL games was affected by competing forms of entertainment—including television—as were minor and major league men's teams. The 1950s also brought major changes in the social definition of women's roles. As in Victorian times, the ideal female role became that of full-time housewife and mother.

Still, women's baseball continued. At the end of the 1954 AAGBL season, Bill Allington, one of the league's most successful coach/managers, put together a barnstorming team of players. For the next three years, the team, called Allington's All-Americans, played exhibition games against men's clubs throughout the United States and Canada. The games were billed as "the battle of the sexes."

EFFA MANLEY—NEGRO LEAGUE EXECUTIVE

Effa Manley was one of the most respected executives in sports during the mid-twentieth century. The wife of Abe Manley, owner of the Newark (New Jersey) Eagles, one of the teams in the Negro League, Effa Manley ran the team and was considered by other team and league officials and the Eagle players as probably the most efficient executive in the league. Unlike the experience of other teams, her players were paid and paid on time, the ball field was in good shape, and the team bus could get the team to its games. She also worked hard to promote the city of Newark, to support the black community, and to make the Negro League successful. When the major leagues were integrated, she went so far as to demand compensation for players from her team who had moved on to the major league teams. Effa Manley wrote *Negro Baseball Before Integration* with Leon Herbert Hardwick and is the subject of James Overmyer's biography, *Queen of the Negro Leagues: Effa Manley and the Newark Eagles.*

WOMEN IN THE NEGRO LEAGUES

The signing of Jackie Robinson by the Brooklyn Dodgers' Montreal farm team in 1945 was a victory against racism, but for the owners of the Negro League teams, it was a financial disaster. By 1953 the Negro National League had disbanded and only four teams were left in the Negro American League. In an attempt to attract people to the games, three African American women were recruited to play on men's teams. Marcenia "Tony" Stone signed with the Indianapolis Clowns in 1953 and then was traded to the Kansas City Monarchs the following year. After trading Stone, the Clowns hired two women to replace her. Mamie "Peanuts" Johnson played second base, and Connie Morgan signed on to pitch. Stone, Johnson, and Morgan were released at the end of the 1954 season for mainly economic reasons. The women were not enough of a novelty to increase gate receipts.

Effa Manley was an important force in Negro League baseball. With her husband, Abe Manley, she was co-owner of the Newark Eagles, a Negro League team, from 1935 to 1948. She was in charge of the day-to-day operation of the team, so that Abe could concentrate on player recruitment. Under her management, the Newark Eagles won the Negro World Series in 1946.

ATTEMPTS THAT FAILED

In 1952 Eleanor Engle, a twenty-four-year-old stenographer, signed a contract to play shortstop for the Harrisburg Senators of the class-B Interstate League. Ford Frick, national baseball commissioner, immediately ruled women ineligible to play.

In 1984 Bob Hope, former vice president of the Atlanta Braves, tried to establish an all-female team in Daytona Beach, Florida, called the Florida Sun Sox. However, the team could not qualify for a franchise, which was instead awarded to a men's minor league team.

ORGANIZED YOUTH BASEBALL

In 1939 Carl Stotz founded Little League Baseball in Williamsport, Pennsylvania, for boys aged eight to twelve. Stotz intended the program to develop qualities of citizenship, sportsmanship, and manhood. Until 1974 girls were excluded from playing. After a lengthy court battle in New Jersey, Little League Baseball, Inc., agreed to admit girls. The U.S. Congress then passed a bill to change the federal Little League charter to read "young people" in place of "boys." President Gerald Ford signed the bill on 26 December 1974.

In 1974 Bunny Taylor, age eleven, became the first girl to pitch a no-hitter in a Little League

College-level women's baseball championship in Los Angeles. (Underwood & Underwood/Corbis)

game. In 1989 Betty Speziale became the first woman to umpire a Little League World Series game and Victoria Brucker, age twelve, became the first American girl to play in the Little League World Series. In 1984 Victoria Roche, a Korean orphan adopted by British parents, became the first girl to play in the Little League World Series. She was a player on the all-star team of Brussels, Belgium, the European championship team. Since then five other girls have played in the world series: Victoria Brucker in 1989 for San Pedro, California; Kelly Craig in 1990 for the Trail, British Columbia, All-Stars; Krissy Wendell in 1994 for the Brooklyn Center American Little League All-Stars; Giselle Hardy in 1991 for the Dhahran Arabian-American Little League; and Sayakara Tsushima in 1998 for Kashima, Japan.

Although no girls played Little League Baseball before 1974, one girl did manage to play American Legion Junior Baseball in 1928. Fourteen-year-old Margaret Gisolo played for Blanford, Indiana, on a team coached by her brother. Margaret's playing went unnoticed until Blanford defeated the Clinton, Indiana, team in the county championships. The coach of the Clinton team immediately filed a protest. He said that Blanford should have to forfeit the game because girls were ineligible to play. The question finally landed with Kenesaw Mountain Landis, the commissioner of major league baseball. He ruled her eligible. Blanford lost in the interstate regional baseball tournament in Chicago. The following year, Margaret Gisolo was informed by the American Legion that girls were no longer eligible.

WOMEN'S BASEBALL IN THE 1990s

In 1993, Bob Hope, by then the head of the events marketing division of Whittle Communications, again tried to start an all-women's baseball team. His effort was spurred not by any public clamor for women's professional baseball but by the release of a movie, *A League of Their Own*. The film about the All-American Girls Baseball League, released by Columbia Pictures on 1 July 1992, was an instant success. On 10 December 1993, Whittle Communications and Coors Brewing Company announced the formation of the Colorado Silver Bullets, an all-women professional baseball team, named for Coors's light beer. Unlike the AAGBL, whose teams played against one another, the Silver Bullets played only against men's teams. For four seasons, 1994–1997, Coors spent about $2.6 million annually to support the Bullets. When Coors didn't renew their sponsorship for the 1998 season, the team disbanded. Fortunately, the idea of a woman's team playing against men's teams in the battle of the sexes was an archaic concept in the 1990s. Women athletes are now accepted in their own right and do not have to prove themselves against men.

WOMEN PLAYERS IN MEN'S MAJOR AND MINOR LEAGUE BASEBALL

In June 1993, Carey Schueler, a left-handed pitcher, was selected in the forty-third round by the Chicago White Sox. She became the first woman to be selected in the major league draft. Her father, Ron Schueler, senior vice president of the White Sox, no doubt influenced the decision. Eighteen-year-old Schueler had last played baseball as a sophomore at Campolindo High School in Moraga, California, where she pitched for the boys' junior varsity team.

In May 1994 Kendra Hanes was signed by the Kentucky Rifles, an independent team in the Frontier League, a nonaffiliated class-A minor league. Her signing was a gimmick to increase gate receipts. The Colorado Silver Bullets had cut her in spring training.

In June 1996, Pamela Davis, a twenty-one-year-old pitcher with the Colorado Silver Bullets, pitched in an exhibition game for the class-AA Jacksonville Suns against the Australian Olympic team. With a scoreless fifth inning, she was credited with a 7–2 victory. Ila Borders grabbed headlines 10 July 1998 when she became the first woman pitcher to start in a minor league baseball game, pitching for the Duluth Superior Dukes against the Sioux Falls Canaries in an 8–3 loss. Borders had been signed by the Northern League's St. Paul Saints following a successful college baseball career at Whittier College in Whittier, California, and had been traded mid-season to the Dukes.

THE FUTURE

The prognosis for women's baseball emerging as a college or professional sport is not good. In the United States, softball is still culturally associated with girls and baseball with boys. Although the Supreme Court in 1974 required Little League baseball to admit girls, most girls play Little League softball. At the high school and college level, baseball is still defined as a men's sport and softball as a women's. Softball is also a women's sport at the Olympics. In 1997 the Women's Professional Fastpitch Softball league (WPF) began play. Unless the opportunity structure for women to play baseball changes, it is unlikely that a woman will play in the major leagues in the near future or that there will be a successful professional women's baseball league.

Gai Ingham Berlage

See also All-American Girls Professional Baseball League

Bibliography
Berlage, Gai Ingham. (1994) *Women in Baseball: The Forgotten History*. Westport, CT: Praeger.

Browne, Lois. (1992) *Girls of Summer: In Their Own League*. Toronto, Canada: HarperCollins.

Gregorich, Barbara. (1993) *Women at Play: The Story of Women in Baseball*. New York: Harcourt Brace.

Johnson, Susan E. (1994) *When Women Played Hardball*. Seattle, WA: Seal Press.

Kindred, Dave. (1995) *The Colorado Silver Bullets: For the Love of the Game*. Atlanta, GA: Longstreet Press.

Seymore, Harold. (1990) *Baseball: The People's Game*. New York: Oxford University Press.

BASKETBALL

Basketball was invented in 1891 by James Naismith (1861–1939), an instructor at the Young Men's Christian Association (YMCA) in Springfield, Massachusetts. He developed the game for

Two University of Kansas women compete for a jump ball, watched by basketball's inventor, James Naismith, in 1926. (Underwood & Underwood/Corbis)

men, but women started playing basketball mere weeks after its invention. It started as a pick-up game. A group of female schoolteachers were eating lunch at the Springfield YMCA, watching a game as they ate. After several lunches as spectators, the women asked if they could play. Naismith agreed. Wearing their street shoes and long dresses with billowy sleeves, they threw a soccer (association football) ball (the first basketball wasn't made until 1894) toward peach baskets nailed down at each end of the court. As time passed, other women joined in—teachers, stenographers, and wives of YMCA instructors. One of these first players, Maude Sherman, later married Naismith. In the spring of 1892, two women's teams competed on the court where the game was born.

Today women play basketball in every corner of the world. Women are dribbling, passing, and shooting from Iraq to Iceland, from Malaysia to Morocco. Basketball is one of the most popular women's team sports in the world.

UNITED STATES

Senda Berenson (1868–1954), known as the "mother of women's basketball," introduced the game to her students at Smith College in 1892. That year, the first women's college basketball game took place between freshmen and sophomores, with all players wearing blouses, bloomers, and dark stockings. Other Smith students decorated the gym with colorful flags and bows. Cheering was considered unladylike, so the young women sang songs during the game. The college president was the only man allowed to watch. This freshman/sophomore basketball game quickly became a major social event on the Smith campus. Soon, similar interclass games were played at such other eastern women's colleges as Bryn Mawr, Vassar, Wellesley, and Mount Holyoke.

The first game between colleges on the West Coast took place when women from the University of California at Berkeley challenged Stanford University. Seven hundred women gathered at San Francisco's Armory Hall to watch the game on 4 April 1896. Men were not allowed to attend. Stanford won, 2–1. The next day's newspaper referred to the players as "muscular maidens" and applauded their lack of roughness.

GIRLS' RULES

As women's basketball spread around the country, there were almost as many sets of rules as teams playing the game. Some girls' teams used the same YMCA rules the boys used, while many teams played a modified version of the game. Many physical educators considered the game too rough and strenuous for women. The fear that women would harm their reproductive and emotional health and become unfeminine playing a "man's game" led to the creation of female versions of basketball. The most distinctive change made to the women's game was to divide the court into sections. While the men's rules allowed all players to run the length of the court, the various women's rules assigned each player to a cer-

WINNERS OF WOMEN'S COLLEGE BASKETBALL TOURNAMENTS

Year	NCAA Division I Finals	NCAA Division II Finals	NCAA Division III Finals	NAIA Finals
1981				Kentucky St.
1982	Louisiana Tech	Cal Poly Pomona	Elizabethtown State	SW Oklahoma
1983	USC	Virginia Union	North Central State	SW Oklahoma
1984	USC	Central Missouri State	Rust College, MS	NC–Asheville
1985	Old Dominion	Cal Poly Pomona	Scranton College	SW Oklahoma
1986	Texas	Cal Poly Pomona	Salem State	Francis Marion, SC
1987	Tennessee	New Haven	Wisconsin-Stevens Pt.	SW Oklahoma
1988	Louisiana Tech	Hampton Institute	Concordia College	Oklahoma City
1989	Tennessee	Delta State	Elizabethtown State	So. Nazarene, OK
1990	Stanford	Delta State	Hope College	SW Oklahoma
1991	Tennessee	North Dakota State	St. Thomas College	Ft. Hays St., KS
1992	Stanford	Delta State	Alma College	I–Arkansas Tech II–Northern St., SD
1993	Texas Tech	North Dakota State	Central Iowa	I–Arkansas Tech II–No. Montana
1994	North Carolina	North Dakota State	Capital College	I–So. Nazarene II–Northern St., SD
1995	Connecticut	North Dakota State	Capital College	I–So. Nazarene II–Western Oregon
1996	Tennessee	North Dakota State	Wisconsin-Oshkosh	I–So. Nazarene II–Western Oregon
1997	Tennessee	North Dakota State	New York University	I–So. Nazarene II–NW Nazarene
1998	Tennessee	North Dakota State	Washington University, MO	I–Union, TN II–Walsh, OH

tain section of the court. Dividing the court was intended to avoid overexertion, emphasize teamwork, and eliminate physical contact.

One such variation was created by Clara Gregory Baer (1863–1938), who is credited with bringing women's basketball to the South. As the physical education director at Sophie Newcomb College in New Orleans, Baer divided the court into seven to eleven sections with one player from each team in each section (thus putting a total of fourteen to twenty-two players on the court). Two-handed shooting and passing were disallowed for fear they would flatten chests. To maintain ladylike decorum, players were forbid-

den to yell or talk loudly on the court. Baer called the game "basquette."

In 1901 the first set of "girls' rules" was published in a book called *Line Basket Ball for Women*. The rules, devised by Smith's Berenson and three other female physical educators, divided the court into three equal regions: front, center, and back. The two forwards in the front section played offense and tried to score. The two centers merely passed the ball from one section to the other, while the backs played defense and guarded the basket. Each team could have anywhere from five to ten players on the court. Players could dribble only three times. Holding the ball for longer than three seconds was a foul, and no physical contact was allowed. When the ball went out of bounds, whichever team got to the ball first got to keep it.

Every one to three years, a Women's Basketball Committee revised the rules. Dribbling, for instance, went from three bounces, to none, to one, to two, then back to three until 1966, when continuous dribbling was allowed. The reason for limiting dribbling was to avoid ball hogs and star players. For decades, coaches were not allowed to talk to their players during the game. And in the years before time-outs were instituted in 1918, coaches could only talk to their players during half time. In fact, until 1916, players were not even allowed to talk to each other on the court.

In 1938 a major rule change occurred. A two-court, six-player style of play was officially adopted. This version of the game was already being used by some teams, especially in cases where the court was too small to reasonably divide in thirds. The two-court game basically created two half-court, three-on-three games. Each team had three guards who played only defense and three forwards who played only offense. No longer were there centers who passed the ball from one end to the other. The three-court game disappeared, and this two-court game with six players became the standard for women's basketball for the next thirty years.

Although having standardized rules facilitated interschool competition, many female physical educators, including Berenson, campaigned against varsity basketball programs for women. They feared competitive basketball would damage young women physically and morally. They advocated a "Play Day" style of intramural basketball in which everyone could play, scores were not important, and females supervised the games. They also sought to avoid the publicity and popularity of men's sports. They encouraged women's athletics but within certain constraints. As a 1937 guidebook noted, "Occasionally it is stimulating to play against a very superior opponent, but it is not wise to play such competition often."

Berenson and her colleagues were influential. Many colleges curtailed interschool competition for years, playing intramural and social games instead. Nevertheless, competitive women's basketball was still played at small-town high schools, at black colleges, and in industrial leagues. In Iowa, annual state high school tournaments started in the early 1920s and almost immediately became a major sporting event, with the girls' tournament routinely outdrawing the boys' tournament. One Iowa state championship team was featured in a *Life* magazine photo essay in the 1940s; and starting in the 1950s, the tournament was broadcast locally on television. Oklahoma and Texas also held state tournaments for high school girls. Byng High School in Ada, Oklahoma, claimed eight state titles under coach Bertha Teague (1906–1991), who compiled a 1,152–115 record from 1927 to 1969. Black colleges encouraged interscholastic, competitive basketball across the segregated South. Tuskegee Institute, Alabama State Teachers College, and South Carolina Agricultural and Mechanical College hosted girls' basketball tournaments for black high schools in the 1920s, 1930s, and 1940s. Industrial leagues flourished from the 1920s through the 1960s. Single working women—most of whom never went to college—played on thousands of teams across the country sponsored by factories, small businesses, newspapers, civic groups, and business schools.

RISE OF NATIONAL COMPETITION

Beginning in 1926, the best of the industrial league women's basketball teams competed in national tournaments sponsored by the Amateur Athletic Union (AAU). Players on these teams wore brightly colored satin shorts and shirts, a sharp contrast to the earlier uniform of knee-length bloomers, loose blouses, and stockings. These competitive tournaments—the earliest ones used the men's rules—also included the crowning of a beauty queen chosen from among the players. One of the earliest AAU basketball stars was sports legend Mildred "Babe" Didrikson (1911–1956), who led her team, the Golden Cyclones of Dallas, to a national basketball title in 1931.

Over the years, the AAU tournament had several dynastic teams. The Hanes Hosiery team of Winston-Salem, North Carolina, clinched three straight AAU championships from 1951 to 1953 during their 102-game winning streak. The Flying Queens of Wayland Baptist College in Plainview, Texas, were the reigning champs from 1954 to 1957. Rita Alexander starred on this team during its four-year undefeated run. Nashville Business

College ended Wayland's 131-game winning streak, going on to claim ten AAU titles of their own. Nera White (1935–) starred on all ten of Nashville's AAU champion teams, being named tournament MVP ten times. The Raytown Piperettes of Missouri, in the late 1960s and early 1970s, were the last AAU dynasty.

African American teams were barred from AAU tournaments until the mid-1950s. Legendary black teams of the 1930s and 1940s, such as the Philadelphia Tribune Girls with star center and tennis ace Ora Washington (1898–1971), never had a chance to compete for these titles.

During this time some women made money playing basketball on barnstorming teams, such as the All-American Red Heads (1936–1971) and the Arkansas Travelers (1949–1966). These teams traveled around the country playing entertaining exhibition games against men's teams.

INTERNATIONAL COMPETITION BEGINS

When the U.S. women started competing internationally in the 1950s, the teams were filled with AAU star players and led by AAU champion coaches—John Head (Nashville Business College), Harley Redin (Wayland Baptist College), and Alberta Cox (Raytown Piperettes). The United States took the gold in the first two world championships in 1953 and 1957 and in Pan-American competition in 1955, 1959, and 1963. Nashville's Joan Crawford played on three of these gold-medal teams and was named to the AAU all-American team each of the thirteen years she played. Hanes Hosiery's Lurlyne Greer Mealhouse set a Pan-American scoring record in 1955 that stood for more than forty years.

At the 1953 World Championship in Santiago, Chile, an estimated 30,000 people watched the final game between the United States and Chile. The U.S. team, which averaged 41 points a game, beat Chile 49–36 for the gold. The championship trophy was so large the team could not bring it back on the plane with them. At the 1957 World Championship in Rio de Janeiro, U.S. and Soviet women played for the first time, initiating a fierce rivalry that would last thirty years. This time the United States secured the gold with a 51–48 win over the Soviet Union. It would be twenty-nine years before the United States would again defeat the Soviets for the world title.

Soviet and American players jostle for the ball during the 1990 Goodwill Games in Seattle, Washington. (Kevin R. Morris/Corbis)

In international competition, the teams played full-court basketball, not the divided court game fostered in the United States. During the 1960s, several rule changes made U.S. women's basketball faster, more exciting, and closer to the full-court game. In 1962, the girls' game officially accepted two roving players. These rovers could cover the whole court, playing both offense and defense. Two players remained as stationary guards and the other two as stationary forwards. Starting in 1966, players could dribble as many times as they wanted. And in 1969, on an experimental basis only, some women's college teams played five-player, full-court basketball.

MODERN ERA

The 1970s was a decade of milestones in women's basketball history. In the United States, the Title IX legislation of 1972 opened the door for more athletic opportunities for girls and women. In 1971 an estimated 100,000 girls played high school hoops. Nine years later, the number had grown to half a million. Title IX also paved the way for the first generation of scholarship athletes, starting in the late 1970s.

Not only were more girls playing basketball, they were no longer playing by girls' rules. Full-court, five-player rules were adopted nationwide in 1971. (The six-player, divided-court game vanished everywhere except Iowa, where high schools played girls' rules exclusively until 1985. Even after 1985 many schools opted to continue playing the divided-court game.) Some opposed the change to full-court play. They argued that fewer girls would be able to play since slower players could no longer specialize as defensive players. There was also some concern that interest in girls' basketball would decline when the distinctive divided-court game was dropped. These fears never came to pass as more and more girls and women learned to play a faster, more athletic style of full-court basketball and gradually more and more people started watching.

During the 1970s, women's college basketball started gaining attention. Women's college teams played in Madison Square Garden and on national television for the first time in 1975. A top-twenty poll of women's college teams started appearing in newspapers in 1976, pioneered by sports writer Mel Greenberg at the *Philadelphia Inquirer*. College stars, not industrial league stars, made up the U.S. teams that competed internationally.

The first national college tournament was held in 1969. Sixteen teams were invited to play at West Chester State College in Pennsylvania. The host team won the tournament, beating Western Carolina in the championship game. The following year, sixteen teams again met and Cal State–Fullerton won the title over West Chester State. In 1971, the first college tournament using five-player, full-court rules was held, with Mississippi College for Women winning the title over West Chester State.

Starting in 1972, the Association for Intercollegiate Athletics for Women (AIAW) sponsored national college championships that aimed to include teams from every region of the country. A small girls' school, Immaculata College of Pennsylvania, won the three-day tournament, cheered on by the school's nuns, who had traveled to Illinois to support the team. West Chester State, in its fourth straight final, finished second. Immaculata, coached by Cathy Rush, won the next two tournaments as well. Ultimately, they played in front of some 3,000 spectators, who, in the beginning, paid nothing to watch the tournament. Teams at these early tournaments showed up wearing anything from polyester shorts to one-piece gym suits to the skirted uniforms worn in the fall by the field hockey team.

Delta State University of Mississippi, led by coach Margaret Wade (1912–1995) and center Lusia Harris-Stewart (1955–), dethroned Immaculata by winning three straight national titles of their own from 1975 to 1977. During that time, the team lost only four games. The Wade Trophy, given annually since 1978 to the top female college player, honors coach Wade, who amassed a career record of 610–112 during her twenty-one years as a high school girls' basketball coach and her six years at Delta State.

In 1978, the women's college tournament followed the final-four format for the first time, with four regional winners meeting for a final showdown. The nationally broadcast championship game showed UCLA, led by Denise Curry and Ann Meyers, beating the University of Maryland for the title. UCLA's win marked the end of smaller colleges, such as Immaculata and Delta State, dominating college play. The following year, Old Dominion University of Norfolk, Virginia, won the national title, earning coach Marianne Crawford Stanley the distinction of being the first woman to win national titles as both a player (at Immaculata) and as a coach. Also in 1979, undefeated South Carolina State won the recently started AIAW tournament for small colleges, marking the first national win by a black college.

Women's basketball made its first appearance in the Olympics in 1976. Six teams competed: Japan, Canada, Bulgaria, the United States, the Soviet Union, and Czechoslovakia. Billie Jean Moore, the coach at Cal State–Fullerton, coached the U.S. team led by high scorer Harris-Stewart of Delta State. With losses to Japan and an unstoppable Soviet team, the United States claimed the silver medal.

Two years later, the first women's professional basketball league was formed, eighty years after the formation of the first men's professional league. Aptly named the Women's Professional Basketball League (WBL), it showcased 1976 Olympians Ann Meyers (1955–) and Nancy

Lieberman-Cline (1958–) and college stars such as Montclair State's Carol Blazejowski (1956–). Salaries generally ranged between $6,000 and $10,000. The first year, nearly 6,000 fans watched as the Houston Angels defeated the Iowa Cornets for the league's first title. After two more seasons, the league folded in 1981 due to a lack of money, media coverage, and steady fan support. Without a professional league at home, some college graduates started going overseas in the 1980s to play for pay in professional leagues in Europe and Asia.

THE 1980s

Control over women's college basketball changed hands in the 1980s. The National Collegiate Athletic Association (NCAA), which governed only men's sports, started showing an interest in women's sports. A battle ensued between supporters of the AIAW, who advocated women's control over women's athletics, and those who wanted to join men's and women's college athletics under the same governing body.

The AIAW sponsored national tournaments in 1980, won by Old Dominion with 6-foot 8-inch Anne Donovan (1961–), and in 1981, when Louisiana Tech won the title. Then in 1982, both the AIAW and the NCAA held national tournaments. Schools had to choose between tournaments. The AIAW tournament, won by Rutgers University, attracted a small crowd, had no national television coverage, and lost money. The NCAA tournament, won by Louisiana Tech, was played before a national television audience and a live audience of nearly 10,000. The NCAA had more resources than the AIAW and won the battle, continuing to sponsor women's national collegiate basketball tournaments. The AIAW disbanded after an unsuccessful antitrust lawsuit. Although there were fewer coaching and leadership positions for women under the NCAA, the players won increasing opportunities to play and to be recognized as sportswomen.

In 1983 and 1984, Cheryl Miller (1964–) led the University of Southern California to back-to-back NCAA national titles and contributed to the visibility of women's basketball with her appearance on the cover of *Sports Illustrated*. Old Dominion was the national champ in 1985, and the Lady Longhorns of the University of Texas at Austin went 34–0 and claimed the national title in

1986 under coach by Judy Conradt (1941–), the first women's college basketball coach to win 600 games. In 1987, when Tennessee won its first of many national titles, the women's final-four tournament sold out for the first time. Runner-up Louisiana Tech finished on top in 1988, and Tennessee reclaimed the title in 1989.

During this decade, the game underwent two changes. In 1984 colleges and then high schools changed to a smaller ball. The new ball, 1 inch less around and 2 ounces lighter than the previous one, was thought to lead to better ball handling and a faster game. A few years later, in 1987, the women's college game adopted the 3-point shot, adding excitement and greater comeback possibilities to the game.

In 1985, the first female Harlem Globetrotter took to the court. Lynette Woodard (1959–), who scored 3,649 points during her career at the University of Kansas, played with the Globetrotters for two years.

It was a gold-medal decade for the national team as the U.S. women won back-to-back golds in the 1984 and 1988 Olympics. (The United States had boycotted the 1980 Olympics.) In 1984, the University of Southern California's Cheryl Miller led the team in scoring, rebounding, steals, and assists. Coach Patricia Head Summitt (1952–) became the first woman to win Olympic medals as a player (in 1976) and as a coach. In 1988 the U.S. team, coached by Kay Yow, finally got to meet and beat the Soviet Union to win the Olympic gold. And for the first time since 1957, the United States beat the Soviet Union to clinch the gold in the 1986 World Championship.

Despite the success of the national teams, American women basketball players hoping to play professionally were forced to look beyond their own borders for spots on foreign teams. Club teams existed in nearly two dozen countries, including Italy, Spain, France, Japan, Brazil, and Israel with salaries varying from team to team. A valued American player could earn $300,000 on a Japanese team or $7,000 on an Austrian one. Some players' contracts included an apartment, language lessons, and a plane ticket home for Christmas.

THE 1990s

Women's college hoops reached new heights in the 1990s. Scoring records were shattered in 1991 when Virginia beat North Carolina State 123–120 after three overtimes. That year also marked the first television package deal to broadcast several regular season games as well as the championship. And for the first time, more people attended the women's final-four tournament than the men's when more than 20,000 people watched Stanford, led by Jennifer Azzi (1969–), beat Auburn for the 1990 title. Starting in 1993, the women's NCAA final-four tournament has been played before sell-out crowds. That year, Sheryl Swoopes (1971–) led her Texas Tech team to the national title, scoring 31 points in the semifinal and a record 47 points in the championship game. Two years later, Swoopes became the first female basketball player to have a sneaker named after her—Nike's "Air Swoopes." Also in the final-four tournament in 1993 was the University of Iowa, coached by Vivian Stringer (1948–), who became the first women's coach to lead two different teams (Cheyney State in 1982) to the NCAA Final Four. In 1995 the University of Connecticut's 35–0 championship season, led by Rebecca Lobo (1973–), garnered unprecedented attention: more people turned on their televisions to watch the women's final than had watched the Super Bowl that year. And the three straight national titles (1996–1998) won by Patricia Head Summitt's University of Tennessee team with star player Chamique Holdsclaw made women's college basketball front-page news.

The growing interest in women's college basketball carried over into support for the 1996 national team. After a disappointing third-place finish in the 1992 Olympics, the 1996 women's national team, coached by Stanford's Tara VanDerveer (1953–), spent one year training and playing teams around the country and around the

world. At the Atlanta Olympics, more than 33,000 spectators watched the U.S. women beat Brazil for the gold medal. Lisa Leslie (1972–) led the scoring and Teresa Edwards (1964–) collected her third gold medal in her fourth Olympic competition.

The success of the 1996 U.S. Olympic gold-medal team helped launch two women's professional leagues. The American Basketball League (ABL) started in the fall of 1996 with eight teams, a forty-game winter season, and an average player salary of $70,000. Players, such as 1996 Olympians Jennifer Azzi and Teresa Edwards, were involved in the start-up of this league. ABL games averaged around 3,500 spectators, although the league attendance leader, the New England Blizzard, drew as many as 11,800. The Columbus (Ohio) Quest won the league's first championship with Olympian and University of Tennessee graduate Nikki McCray (1972–) named league MVP.

In the summer of 1997, a second league started, immediately prompting speculation about the survival of two women's leagues. The Women's National Basketball Association (WNBA), owned by the men's National Basketball Association (NBA), fielded eight teams to play a twenty-eight-game summer season using a distinctive orange and white ball. The players, earning an average salary of $35,000 a season, played in NBA arenas wearing V-neck, sleeveless jerseys and shorts made of lightweight fabric and mesh. An average of 9,000 people came out to watch the games, which were also broadcast by three television networks. The Houston Comets, led by the league's lead scorer and MVP Cynthia Cooper (1963–), won the first championship.

In its second season, the ABL fielded nine teams and again the Columbus Quest won the

UNIVERSITY OF TENNESSEE v. UNIVERSITY OF CONNECTICUT

The hottest rivalry in women's U.S. collegiate basketball is between the University of Tennessee and the University of Connecticut. The rivalry began in 1995 when No. 2 ranked Connecticut, a newcomer to the top rank of women's basketball, upset No. 1 ranked Tennessee. At the end of the season, Connecticut defeated Tennessee for the national title, and in 1997 Tennessee defeated No. 1 Connecticut and ended its undefeated season in the national tournament. The teams meet at least once each year during the regular season in a nationally-televised game.

championship. The WNBA expanded to ten teams in 1998, and the Houston Comets repeated as league victors. The ABL began its third season with new teams in Chicago and Nashville. Fans worried that a sketchy television contract and a poor showing in the college draft would hobble the league. It was bankruptcy, however, that was written on the league's death certificate when it folded on 22 December 1998. As many people had projected, the WNBA, with the NBA's marketing might and name recognition, outlasted the ABL. In 1999, former ABL players began playing in the WNBA, although only fifty were allowed to enter the league that year, so as to not threaten the positions held by current WNBA players. For the 2000 season the WNBA expanded to 16 teams with eight in the Eastern Conference (Charlotte, Cleveland, Detroit, Indiana, Miami, New York, Orlando, and Washington) and eight Western Conference (Houston, Los Angeles, Minnesota, Phoenix, Portland, Sacramento, Seattle, and Utah). The league played a 32-game schedule followed by the playoffs with many games televised on ESPN, NBC, and Lifetime.

As women's basketball entered the twenty-first century, the game had higher attendance and more press and television coverage than ever before. Female basketball players were starting to become household names. Also, the style of play increasingly emphasized speed, jumping, and athleticism along with a solid passing and defensive game. The visibility of the WNBA and the newfound star status of several female players was a boost for women's sports in general.

EUROPE

Basketball arrived in Europe shortly after the game was invented and in some places, such as England, it was a girls' sport for years before boys started playing it. In the 1920s, while American female physical educators were arguing against interschool competition in favor of noncompetitive Play Days, European sportswomen were fighting a different battle. Led by French sports reformer and rower Alice Milliat (1884–1957), sportswomen challenged the International Olympic Committee's (IOC) stance on female competitors. No women competed in the first modern Olympics in 1896 and over the next three decades, women's Olympic participation was limited to a few individual sports: tennis, archery, swimming, and ice skating.

Milliat and others formed the International Federation of Women's Sports (FSFI) in 1921 and held the first Women's Olympic Games in Paris in 1922 with eleven sport events. England claimed the basketball title with an 8–7 win over France. It

THE NAISMITH MEMORIAL BASKETBALL HALL OF FAME INDUCTEES

1984
Senda Berenson
Bertha Teague
Margaret Wade

1992
Lusia Harris-Stewart
Nera White

1993
Ann Meyers
Iulyana Semenova

1994
Carol Blazejowski

1995
Anne Donovan
Cheryl Miller

1996
Nancy Lieberman-Cline

1997
Joan Crawford
Denise Curry

1998
Jody Conradt

1999
Billie Moore

would be, however, another fifty-four years before women's basketball became an Olympic event.

Europe was the first continent to hold women's basketball championships. The first such tournament took place in Rome in 1938. Five countries participated and Italy won. World War II postponed the second European championship until 1950. By then, Soviet women had entered European and international basketball competitions, which they dominated for decades. Soviet teams refused to lose in international competition, capturing six gold medals during their 52–0 winning streak at the world championships from 1959 to 1983. They completely dominated the first two Olympics, averaging more than 100 points per game and outscoring their opponents by more than 30 points. Iulyana Semenova (1952–), the first international female player inducted into the Naismith Memorial Basketball Hall of Fame, scored 32 points in 23 minutes in the Soviet Union's gold-medal win over the United States in the 1976 Olympics. Semenova won thirty-one gold medals during her eighteen-year career. This seven-foot center was voted the most popular athlete in her native Latvia twelve times between 1970 and 1985.

Bulgaria and Yugoslavia have the distinction of being the only countries to beat the Soviet Union during their 147–3 romp through the European championships from 1950 to 1991. They are also the only other European countries with Olympic medals in women's basketball.

Today hundreds of women are paid to play basketball in elite-level club competition in Europe. Italy, Spain, France, Germany, and Greece have particularly strong leagues. Top players from Eastern Europe and the United States vie for spots on these professional teams.

CANADA

Women's basketball history in Canada has an eastern version and a western version. In the eastern provinces, many female physical educators adopted the Play Day attitude that women's sports should be safe, fun, and inclusive. Thus many eastern Canadian schools offered women's basketball only on an intramural basis. (Some schools offered interschool competition but only in individual "ladylike" sports such as tennis, badminton, and swimming.) Where basketball was played, it was a six-player game on a divided court.

These attitudes and women's rules had little influence in western Canada. There, men coached women's teams that played by men's rules and played to win. The most successful team was the Edmonton Commercial Grads, who registered a 502–20 record playing provincial, national, and international competitions between 1915 and 1940. Not only did this team win games, it also scored points for women's athletics as the players showed that women can indeed play competitive, full-court basketball. Basketball inventor James Naismith congratulated the team in a 1936 letter: "My admiration and respect go to you because you have remained unspoiled by your successes, and have retained the womanly graces, notwithstanding your participation in a strenuous game."

The Grads disbanded in 1940, and Vancouver became the women's basketball capital. Various business-sponsored teams from that city won twenty-one out of twenty-six Canadian national titles from 1942 to 1967. By the late 1960s, women across the country were playing full-court, college programs were growing, and a centralized national team was competing internationally. Two high points in Canada's international play are a fourth-place finish in the 1984 Olympics and a trio of bronzes in 1979 at the world championship, the Pan-American Games, and the World University Games.

LATIN AMERICA

South America was the second continent, after Europe, to hold regional women's basketball tournaments. The first South American championship was held in Santiago, Chile, in 1946. Six games were played over the course of twelve days. Chile won. Santiago was also the site of the first women's basketball world championship in 1953. Seven of the ten teams in that first tournament were from Latin America. Chile took the silver, with the United States and France winning the gold and the bronze.

Brazil is a major contender in women's international basketball competitions. They were the world champions in 1994 and finished second at the 1996 Olympics. Two legendary Brazilian players are Hortência Marcari Oliva and Maria Paula da Silva. Also playing on these medal-winning teams was Janeth Arcain (1969–), the first Brazilian to play in the WNBA in the United States. Brazil also has its own professional league.

Cuba is the other Latin American team that can hold its own in the international arena. Cubans played in three of the first six Olympic basketball competitions and won a bronze at the 1990 world championship. Cuba and Brazil are the only countries to have beaten the United States in Pan-American play as of 1999.

ASIA

Basketball arrived in Asia in the 1890s via YMCA missionaries, some of whom played on Naismith's first teams in Springfield, Massachusetts. Girls were initially taught the game by female missionaries and schoolteachers. Girls in the Philippines were playing basketball by the early 1900s. Five teams competed at an athletic carnival in Manila in 1911. Soon afterward, basketball competition for girls was dropped because American educators in the U.S.-occupied Philippines thought the competition was too rough. Girls continued to play basketball recreationally.

In China, women were competing in national basketball tournaments as early as 1924. Women's athletic participation did not meet with the same resistance in China as in the West. Physical activity was encouraged for women on the premise that healthy, strong women bear healthy, strong babies. Women and sports competitions were not seen as a mismatch, particularly for working-class women who did hard physical work. Today women throughout Asia play basketball, from Sri Lanka to Singapore, from Laos to Indonesia.

In 1965 Asian championships for women's basketball began. By 1999, South Korea held the most titles, followed by China. Though Japan was the first Asian country to play women's basketball in the Olympics, South Korea and China won the first medals, with silver- and bronze-medal performances in 1984. South Korea also collected world championship silver medals in 1967 and 1979. China won silver medals at the 1992 Olympics and the 1994 world championship, where Haixia Zheng (1967–), a 6-foot 8-inch center from the Henan Province, was named tournament MVP.

THE PACIFIC

YMCA clubs introduced basketball to Australia around the turn of the century. At first, basketball remained in the shadow of such earlier British imports as cricket and rugby. An additional barrier to the growth of women's basketball was the prevalence of netball. Played only by girls, netball is a derivation of basketball played with five, seven, or nine players on a side. Netball was often called "basket ball" while basketball was designated as "international rules." In the 1970s, this confusion was cleared up when the name "netball" was officially adopted and the word "basketball" came to refer only to the game known internationally as basketball.

The Opals, as the women's national team is called, won Australia's first international basketball medal with their third-place finish at the 1996 Atlanta Olympics. Two years later, the Opals won another bronze at the world championship, edging out defending champion Brazil. Australia's Women's National Basketball League (WNBL), started in 1981, is one of the longest-running women's professional basketball leagues in the world.

WNBL stars and Opals veterans include Robyn Maher (1959–) and Jennifer Cheesman (1957–). Michelle Timms (1965–), the high scorer on the Olympic bronze-medal team, has become an international star. She was the first Australian basketball player, male or female, to play abroad professionally. She has played in Germany, Italy, and the United States, where she was the first foreign-born player to sign with the WNBA.

New Zealand has fielded teams for the 1994 world championship and, since 1974, for the Oceania Championships, where they are perennial runners-up to Australia. New Caledonia entered this regional contest in 1997. World War II and Korean War soldiers brought basketball to many of the Pacific Islands in the 1940s and 1950s, and organized women's club play now takes place in Nauru, Tahiti, Kiribati, and the Cook and Solomon Islands.

AFRICA

Women in some two dozen African countries play basketball in club competition. Teams from nineteen countries have competed in the African championship for women held every two to four years since 1966. Senegal has won the most medals. Teams from Senegal, Zaire, Kenya, and Madagascar have competed in world championships, while teams from Zaire, Angola, and Nigeria have participated in Olympic qualifying tournaments.

In 1996 Zaire became the first African nation to compete in the Olympics in women's basketball. One of the players on that team, Mwadi Mabika (1976–), was hired to play in the WNBA the following year.

THE MIDDLE EAST

The Middle East is the most underrepresented region in women's international competition. No Middle Eastern team competed in the Olympics or in a world championship through the 1990s. However, teams from Iran, Turkey, Lebanon, and Israel have taken part in the World University Games, a competition held every other year for college students and recent graduates.

On a local level, Iraq, Jordan, Kuwait, Turkey, Lebanon, Syria, and Israel have women's basketball clubs. The game is particularly popular in Israel, where the Basketball Association of Israel sponsors around 200 teams for women and girls. National women's basketball tournaments started there in 1958, only ten years after Israel gained statehood. Two teams—Elizur Tel Aviv and Maccabi Tel Aviv—have dominated both the national and state cup competitions.

Certain Muslim practices in Islamic countries do not facilitate female sports participation. Head-to-toe body coverings and religious fasting interfere with athletic endeavors. Still, women in these countries are playing sports. The first two Islamic Women's Games were held in Iran in 1993 and 1997. Athletes from twenty-six countries competed in thirteen different sports, including basketball. Reminiscent of early women's basketball games in the United States, men were not allowed to watch the games.

CONCLUSION

The history of women's basketball is not solely the history of state, national, and international competition. Countless girls and women have played basketball on playgrounds and public courts and in gym classes and community leagues. Basketball is also played by women with disabilities. Wheelchair basketball is played with the same size court and hoop height as regular basketball. Men's and women's teams play by the same rules and sometimes play each other. Women from sixteen countries have competed internationally in wheelchair basketball since 1968.

Wherever and however it is played, women's basketball carries some piece of the spirit breathed into it by those curious, eager schoolteachers in Massachusetts who played the game first.

Kelly Nelson

Bibliography

Beran, Janice. (1993) *From Six-on-Six to Full Court Press: A Century of Iowa Girls' Basketball.* Ames: Iowa State University.

Blais, Madeline. (1995) *In These Girls, Hope Is a Muscle.* New York: Atlantic Monthly Press.

Cahn, Susan. (1994) *Coming On Strong: Gender and Sexuality in Twentieth-Century Women's Sport.* Cambridge, MA: Harvard University Press.

Corbett, Sara. (1997) *Venus to the Hoop: A Gold-Medal Year in Women's Basketball.* New York: Doubleday.

Hult, Joan, and Marianna Trekell, eds. (1991) *A Century of Women's Basketball: From Frailty to Final Four.* Reston, VA: American Alliance for Health, Physical Education, Recreation and Dance.

Kessler, Lauren. (1997) *Full Court Press: A Season in the Life of a Winning Basketball Team and the Women Who Made It Happen.* New York: E. P. Dutton.

Nagy, Boti. (1990) *High Flyers: Women's Basketball in Australia.* Melbourne: Sun Books.

Naismith, James. (1996 [1941]) *Basketball: Its Origin and Development.* Lincoln: University of Nebraska Press.

Neal, Patsy. (1991) *At the Rim: A Celebration of Women's Collegiate Basketball.* Charlottesville, VA: Eastman Kodak Company.

Redin, Harley. (1958) *The Queens Fly High.* Plainview, TX: Wayland College.

BATON TWIRLING

Baton twirling is the practice of manipulating metal rods to create choreographed routines incorporating diverse patterns of movement. Routines typically include jumps, lunges, twists, and other body movements, in combination with shaft movement such as spins, tosses, flips, and slides. Baton twirlers perform alone, in pairs, and in larger groups. Although this recreational and competitive sport includes events for men, the vast majority of its participants are women.

Baton twirling developed as a sport in the United States, with its most rapid growth in the 1950s and 1960s. Although the sport is considered "American," it was influenced by both European and Asian practices. The word "bâton" is French for "stick."

HISTORY

Formalized waving of sticks, swords, and torches has been practiced in various countries and cultures for several centuries. In Europe, twirling originated with military drum directors called "drum majors." They used elongated drumsticks (known as batons) to make their directions more visible for guiding soldiers' marching maneuvers and changing music to which they marched. From the 1600s, there are records of a commanding "master drummer" leading marching soldiers for England's King Edward VI (1547–1553) and accounts of "drummer majors." The "twirling drum majors" who led the British Army's Janissary Band were influenced by Roman jugglers and Turkish marching troops.

Asia and the Pacific Rim have probably also influenced twirling. Samoan sword and knife twirlers spun their weapons in mock duels as well as during religious and military ceremonies. Natives of the Hawaiian Islands twirled flaming torches as they danced to drumbeats. Chinese performing artists incorporated stick twirling into elaborate dances. European travelers who observed these practices may well have adapted them to their own cultures.

Early baton twirling was dominated by men, who were able to handle the heavy drum-major batons. The metamorphosis of the baton from band direction to performance and competition may be related to flag signaling in Switzerland, used to communicate from one Swiss mountaintop to the next. Flag swinging evolved into parade performances, incorporating such twirling maneuvers as circles, flashes, and high pitches to accompany marching. Festivals eventually sponsored flag events in which swingers performed competitively. Swiss and German immigrants brought the tradition to Pennsylvania, most likely influencing modern baton twirling.

Baton twirling as we know it today originated in the United States. The term "majorettes" was probably coined by Major Reuben Webster Mill-

Drum majorettes from Indianapolis, Indiana, performing at the American Legion National Convention in 1947. (Bettmann/Corbis)

saps, founder of Millsaps College in Mississippi after the Civil War, who used this name for his female athletes. By the early 1930s, the term had been adopted by female baton twirlers, whose presence provided a unique addition of color and grace to military, civic, and school marching units. Because the original majorette role was based on traditionally feminine attributes, baton twirling was not commonly practiced by males. At the time, this was one of the few sports viewed as acceptable for women, contributing to its growth and popularity. Even as more sports opened to women, twirling remained female-dominated. Participation increased through the 1950s. Baton twirlers commonly marched in parades, performed with college bands, and participated in community recreation programs.

More recently, the sport has expanded internationally. In the 1950s and 1960s, the Starline Boat Company sponsored the International Twirling Teachers Institute (ITTI) throughout the United States and Europe. This effort to promote baton twirling led to the formation of the World Baton Twirling Federation (WBTF) in 1977. International recognition of baton twirling as a sport came in the World Games in the Netherlands, where it was included as a "promotional sport," and in the United States with its inclusion in the 1999 Junior Olympic Games, sponsored by the Amateur Athletic Union (AAU). Baton twirling was an exhibition sport at the World Games held in Cleveland, Ohio, in August 1999.

RULES AND PLAY

Originally baton twirling included such basics as vertical and horizontal patterns spiced with slides, swings, finger twirls, rolls, and tosses. As the sport evolved, the movements became more complex, with lunges, leaps, twists, and spins in combination with strenuous twirling maneuvers. In 1956, as twirling became more popular, Don Sartell of Janesville, Wisconsin, started the first baton-twirling organization, the National Baton Twirling Association (NBTA). In 1958, the United States Twirling Association (USTA) was established as a democratic, not-for-profit enterprise. Founders of the USTA included John Kirkendale, Bobbie Mae, Nick Michalares, Fred Miller, and George Walbridge. A member of the AAU and the National Council of Youth Sports (NCYS), USTA fosters development of the sport throughout the world. It also represents the United States in the WBTF, whose mission is to standardize and develop the sport internationally.

Since its inception, the NBTA has offered an organized twirling competition with a combination of pageant and baton called "Miss Majorette of America." Contestants are judged on twirling, strutting (marching with intricate baton maneuvers), interviews, and modeling. The pageant has age divisions allowing participation through the college level. The NBTA also holds local, state, and national competitions, allowing participation through age twenty-one. Events include women's and men's solo, two-baton, super-x strut, flag, hoop, show baton, duet, trio-twirling, twirling team, dance team, and corps. America's Youth on Parade (AYOP), the NBTA's national competition, is held annually in July at Notre Dame University in Indiana. Qualifying competitions for the NBTA-sponsored world championships, which began in the Netherlands in 1990, are held every three years at AYOP. In 1993 and 1996, the championships were held in France and Italy, respectively. Most participants were from Europe or North America.

At national and regional conventions, the USTA presents seminars and clinics on baton twirling, sports medicine, dance, sport psychology, and related topics for coaches, judges, athletes, and parents. The USTA National Baton Twirling Championships and Festival of the Future (a national open competition for developing athletes) are held annually at different locations. Events are similar to those of the NBTA. At the nationals, a qualifying competition for the annual WBTF-sponsored world championships is held.

The WBTF designed specialized regulations for baton-twirling routines. Beginning in the 1980 world championships, in Seattle, Washington, these new rules revolutionized the sport. The WBTF's guidelines—including mandatory exclusive use of one baton, performance of compulsory movement sequences, and selection of optional music for freestyle performance—represented dramatic shifts in twirling competition. Coaches and athletes began to incorporate innovative, artistic movement in addition to intricate, dynamic twirling maneuvers into their routines. Team and duet competitions (added in 1981 and 1993, respectively) were also influenced by these guidelines. The WBTF hosts the world championships each summer in alternating member countries. Its members include Australia, Belgium, Canada, England, France, Germany, Ireland, Italy, Japan, the Netherlands, Norway, Scotland, Spain, Switzerland, and the United States. As more nations participated, the United State's competitive domination lessened. From 1980 through 1988, the United States captured the World Cup award for overall performance. From 1989 through 1999, Japan won the award every year except for 1990 and 1991, when Canada captured the titles.

THE FUTURE

Several social changes have diminished female interest in baton twirling. The U.S. 1972 Title IX legislation that mandated equal opportunity for women in sports opened new doors for females in sports, paradoxically drawing women away from twirling into other sports. At the same time, twirling was excluded from the increasingly popular indoor-drill competitions, which decreased band-related opportunities for twirlers. Also, as more women worked full time, there was less interest in earning the modest income to be made from teaching twirling. Another inhibiting factor for teachers and athletes alike was the increased liability insurance required for practice facilities. And perhaps the biggest reason that fewer girls were interested in twirling was inaccurate media portrayal of twirling as an exhibitionistic circus act.

Nevertheless, baton twirling persists. Amateur competitions, recreation programs, and schools continue to provide opportunities. Professional involvement exists via coaching, judging, and administration. New developments are encouraging, including the potential to earn the Presidential Sports Award in baton twirling. In Canada and several other countries, twirling is an officially recognized, government-subsidized sport. Some schools in Japan include twirling in the curriculum. The inclusion of baton twirling in the Junior Olympics is a positive step toward establishing the legitimacy of the sport. As the sport evolves internationally, it may eventually be included in the Olympic Games. Educational and scholarship opportunities may also evolve as the sport becomes more prominent.

Valerie J. (Ludwig) Willman

Bibliography

Atwater, Constance. (1964) *Baton Twirling; The Fundamentals of an Art and a Skill.* Rutland, VT: Charles E. Tuttle.

Miller, Fred J., Gloria Smith, and Perri Ardman. (1978) *The Complete Book of Baton Twirling.* New York: Doubleday.

Robinson, Nancy L. (1980) *Baton Twirling.* New York: Harvey House.

Smith, Susan Rogerson. (1985) *Cheerleader–Baton Twirler: Try Out & Win.* Tom Doherty Associates.

Wheelus, Doris. (1975) *Baton Twirling; A Complete Illustrated Guide.* New York: Sayre Publishing.

Additional information was provided by Kathy Forsythe (executive director of the USTA since 1983); the USTA, Seattle, Washington; the NBTA, Janesville, Wisconsin; and the WBTF, Ontario, Canada.

BEAUTY

The human body is not only the basis of one's physical existence but also a site of social control and a product of social construction and cultural transformation. The body is the interface of the individual with society, the means to present oneself and interact with one's environment. Body management—what we eat, what we interpret as beautiful, the daily rituals of body and beauty care—is determined by prevailing social structures and cultural patterns. Seen from this point of view, it is clear that ethics and techniques related to the body as well as beauty ideals related to the body are neither authentic nor natural, but influenced by culture and society. The bodies of men and women are connected to patterns of interpretation and to social norms that reflect dichotomous and hierarchical gender relations.

On the one hand, social gender relationships are impressed upon the bodies of men and women—the human body becomes gendered and the gender becomes embodied; yet on the other hand, male and female bodies are an important issue in the discourse of gender hierarchy in terms of body function, real and putative performance and characteristics, and weaknesses and strengths. This is especially true in consideration of the legitimization of male dominance and female subordination. Female beauty plays a central role in gender arrangements and their staging in society.

THE REVIVAL OF THE BODY—TRENDS

The revival of the body in the 1970s signals a crisis of the modern industrial society. Increasing society-wide demands for identify, authenticity, and social distinction have led to a revaluation and even a fetishization of the body. Fitness and health, thinness, youthfulness, and sexual attractiveness became the credo of modern society and the leading values of everyday culture. The new body ideal demanded toughness, health, and youth—no traces of work, illness, age, birth, or life in general. The demand continuously expanded for various physical activities from traditional sport to relaxation techniques or body therapies.

A basic assumption of this cult of body, beauty, and health is the conviction that bodies can be manipulated without any restriction and that the body is not dependent on destiny, but rather each person is responsible for his or her body. Form and function of the body are looked upon as products of individual work in which

"THE PURSUIT OF BEAUTY" (1832)

I saw an aged, aged man
One morning near the Row,
Who sat, dejected and forlorn,
Till it was time to go.
It made me quite depressed and bad
To see a man so wholly sad—
I went and told him so.
I asked him why he sat and stared
At all the passers-by,
And why on ladies young and fair
He turned his watery eye.
He looked at me without a word,
And then—it really was absurd—
The man began to cry.
But when his rugged sobs were stayed—
It made my heart rejoice—
He said that of the young and fair
He sought to make a choice.
He was an artist, it appeared—
I might have guessed it by his beard,
Or by his gurgling voice.
His aim in life was to procure
A model fit to paint
As "Beauty on a Pedestal,"
Or "Figure of a Saint,"
But every woman seemed to be

As crooked as a willow tree—
His metaphors were quaint.
"And have you not observed," he asked
"That all the girls you meet
Have either 'Hockey elbows' or
Ungainly 'Cycling feet'?
Their backs are bent, their faces red,
From 'Cricket stoop,' or 'Football head'."
He spoke to me with heat.
"But have you never found," I said,
"Some girl without a fault?
Are all the women in the world
Misshapen, lame or halt?"
He gazed at me with eyes aglow,
And, though the tears had ceased to flow.
His beard was fringed with salt.

"There was a day, I mind it well,
A lady passed me by
In whose physique my searching glance
no blemish could descry.
I followed her at headlong pace,
But when I saw her, face to face,
She had the 'Billiard eye'!"

—*From* Mr. Punch's Book of Sports *(1832)*

money, time, and strength have to be invested in order to create a work of art independent from time and material. Health and beauty are goods that have, therefore, attained an incredibly high value in the modern economy and generated an entire industry sector—fitness and health.

THE FEMALE BODY AND THE BEAUTY IDEAL

The female body is restricted by social norms and social control to a much higher degree than the male body. Whereas society tends to evaluate the male body primarily according to its functions, society regards the bodies of women primarily as a medium for social and sexual attractiveness. Any functional view of women has long been lim-

ited to human reproduction. Because girls and women are defined and judged by their appearance, an aesthetic styling of the body is of great importance for many women. This is shown by the large amount of money spent for slenderness, cosmetics, and plastic surgery. Beauty ideals are continuously reproduced and modified by the mass media, especially by advertisements. But these ideals are often out of reach for "normal" women, especially because the ideals are constantly changing. The discrepancy between ideal and reality frequently leads to the feeling the body and appearance are deficient and to conflicts that demand continuous activities and a strict regime for and management of the body. Therefore, the arrangement and the presentation of the body, from makeup to body styling and exercises, are an important part of the everyday life of women. Women seem not only to use stricter methods for the disciplining of the body, but also to apply a higher standard to the female body than men do. For example, in a survey women tended to judge thinner women more beautiful than men did. Psychologists have found that men are more likely than women to have a positive self-image and that men are also more likely to judge women as more attractive than the women judge themselves to be.

Especially after puberty, deviations from the standards of beauty and thinness, as well as unfeminine behavior, are connected with negative sanctions.

> In society today, out-of-role or tomboy behavior is less acceptable postmenarche when the adolescent girl is encouraged to conform to the female role model. This loss of freedom can feel like a punishment for being a woman, suddenly having to refrain from previously accepted pastimes, with no alternative and positive role being offered. (Ussher 1989; 25)

To be attractive requires not only a well-formed body but also feminine movement. Gracious, soft, and harmonious movements, as well as the connected movement cultures of ballet, other dance, and gymnastics, are regarded as feminine. Women who resist these expectations and ideals risk being confronted with identity conflicts, as Birgit Palzkill, among others, has shown in a study based on interviews with top-level athletes.

For these reasons, women develop a different and in many ways more ambivalent relationship to their bodies than men. Adult women more often than men report not being satisfied with their health and their appearance, but even at an early age, when there are no differences in abilities and performances, girls tend to evaluate their sporting achievements and their competencies more negatively than boys do theirs. This ambivalent and problematic relationship to the body can contribute to the development of eating disorders (anorexia or bulimia) and misuse of drugs, especially of psychophysiological drugs. But it should not be forgotten that women are not the weaker sex where health is concerned. In many

ways—for example, average life duration—men are disadvantaged.

BEAUTY, BODY, PHYSICAL ACTIVITY

The described "ecology of the female body" is connected with specific needs and activities with regard to physical education and sport. Surveys that asked for motives for engaging in sports showed decisive differences between women and men. In a German study, for example, four times more women than men wanted to be active in sports in order to "do something for the figure." Men reported more often than women that they wanted to improve their condition (Opaschwoski 1987). Girls and women tend to choose physical activities that fit their bodies and their beauty ideals, that do not seriously challenge their imagined performance abilities, and that do not provoke conflicts with their identity. Therefore, women focus largely on those sporting activities that allow an aesthetically pleasing presentation and styling of the body according to ruling ideals or that are connected with well-being.

But it is a problem that all these activities are only focusing on some aspects of the movement culture. Studies have shown conclusively that sports and noncompetitive activities such as dance, aerobics, and gymnastics, which appeal to the taste of the majority of women, can have various benefits, for instance, a positive body concept and an increase in well-being. But they can also be connected with negative consequences, since it is often impossible, or at least very difficult, to achieve the promised changes to the body. Many women become frustrated and quit, as evidenced by the fluctuating attendance rate in fitness studios. In addition, the typical feminine sports convey one-sided body and movement experiences. They produce a specific way of dealing with the body that is closely connected with the female role and its restrictions and exclusions.

Even today, few women are active in those types of sports that use the body as a means of confrontation with others or with the environment. The appropriation of the environment and the conquest of new dimensions, the experiences of border lines, the joy of risks and experiments are typically elements of physical activities in which women make up only a small minority, if they participate at all. Thus men are still much

A WOMAN'S PRISON

Mary Wollstonecraft Decries Women's Slavery to Beauty

To preserve personal beauty, woman's glory! the limbs and faculties are cramped with worse than Chinese bands, and the sedentary life which they are condemned to live, whilst boys frolic in the open air, weakens the muscles and relaxes the nerves. . . . Nor can it be expected that a woman will resolutely endeavor to strengthen her constitution and abstain from enervating indulgences, if artificial notions of beauty, and false descriptions of sensibility, have been early entangled with her motives of action. . . . Genteel women are, literally speaking, slaves to their bodies, and glory in their subjection. . . . Taught from their infancy that beauty is woman's scepter, the mind shapes itself to the body, and, roaming round its gilt cage, only seeks to adorn its prison.

MARY WOLLSTONECRAFT
(1792) A Vindication of the Rights of Woman. *London: J. Johnson.*

more likely than women to engage in football and ice hockey, ocean sailing and parachuting, long-distance running and mountain climbing.

But it should also be emphasized that the ways in which boys and men deal with their bodies are also beset with problems. The demand that young males excel at sports can be as oppressive and as destructive to self-esteem as the demand that young women conform to the regnant ideal of female attractiveness. The ritualized image of hard masculinity that is typical of some subcultures as well as the high demand for risk-taking are symptomatic of the difficulties men have with their masculinity.

THE FUTURE?

Here, functions, effects, and causes of the "beauty trap" can be mentioned only briefly: Beauty ideals are used for the continuation of gender arrangements and the gender hierarchy. In a special issue of the German edition of *Psychology Today* (1993) it was suggested that the cult of beauty is the "last means against the emancipation of women." The mass media play a central role in the production and reproduction of beauty ideals. The sports news also contributes to the propagation of the idea of the beautiful sex. On the one hand, women are marginalized in sports reports. On the other hand, as many studies in different countries have shown, female athletes are often defined by their looks and are sometimes even presented primarily as sexual objects.

In the 1990s—from football to boxing, from ski jumping to ice hockey—women participated in sports that broke with the traditional myths of femininity. As women entered the new century, many anticipated that ideals of beauty would change and that perhaps even the pressure to be beautiful would vanish.

Gertrud Pfister

See also Advertising; Gender Equity; Media; Sexuality

Bibliography

Bordo, Susan R. (1989) "The Body and the Reproduction of Femininity: A Feminist Appropriation of Foucault." In *Gender–Body—Knowledge: Feminist Reconstructions of Being and Knowing,* edited by Alison M. Jaggar and Susan R. Bordo. New Brunswick, NJ: Rutgers University Press, 13–34.

———. (1993) *Unbearable Weight: Feminism, Western Culture, and the Body.* Berkely: University of California Press.

Brownmiller, Susan. (1984) *Femininity.* New York: Simon & Schuster.

Cash, Thomas F., and Thomas Pruzinsky, eds. (1990) *Body Images.* New York: Guilford Press.

Drolshagen, Ebba D. (1995) *Des Körpers neue Kleider: Die Herstellung weiblicher Schönheit.* Frankfurt: Fischer.

Falk, Pasi. (1994) *The Consuming Body*. London: Routledge.

Featherstone, Mike, Mike Hepworth, and Bryan S. Turner, eds. (1991) *The Body: Social Process and Cultural Theory*. London: Routledge.

Freedman, Rita. (1986) *Beauty Bound*. Lexington, KY: Lexington Books.

Guttmann, Allen. (1996) *The Erotic in Sports*. New York: Columbia University Press.

Lakoff, Robin Tolmach, and Raquel L. Scherr. (1984) *Face Value: The Politics of Beauty*. Boston: Routledge & Kegan Paul.

Nuber, Ursula, ed. (1995) *Spieglein, Spieglein an der Wand: Der Schönheitskult und die Frauen*. Munich: Heyne.

Opaschowski, Horst W. (1987) *Sport in der Freizeit, Mehr Lust als Leistung: Auf dem Weg zu einem neuen Sportverständnis*. Hamburg: BAT.

Palzkill, Birgit. (1990) *Zwischen Turnschuh und Stöckelschuh: Die Entwicklung lesbischer Identität im Sport*. Bielefeld, Germany: AJZ.

Pfister, Gertrud, ed. (1996) *Frauen in Bewegung: Fit und gesund mit Sport*. Berlin: Orlanda.

Rodin, Judith. (1993) "Die Körper-Falle." *Psychologie Heute* 20:20–23.

Ussher, Jane M. (1989) *The Psychology of the Female Body*. New York: Routledge.

Wolf, Naomi. (1992) *The Beauty Myth*. New York: William Morrow.

BEESE, AMELIE

(1886–1925)

GERMAN AVIATOR

Born in Dresden, Germany, in 1886, Amelie Beese transcended male prejudices to become Germany's first female pilot. She also set two world flight records for women flyers, operated her own flying school, and designed aircraft. Unable to resume a career that had been interrupted by World War I, a disappointed Beese took her own life in 1925.

From her father, an architect, Amelie Hedwig Beese learned to love arts and crafts. From 1906 to 1909 she studied at Stockholm's Royal Academy of Applied Art. There she developed a passion for sailing. Then, despite her considerable ability as a sculptor, she devoted more and more of her time to the rapidly developing world of flying. To satisfy these new desires, she attended classes in mathematics, ship design, aviation, and mechanics at the Technische Hochschule Dresden (a university specializing in technical and scientific

AMELIE BEESE ON FLYING

The day came at last! Naturally I was longing impatiently for the moment when I'd be alone and free, responsible only to myself, when I'd be allowed at long last to soar through my conquered realm. I felt absolutely confident. I had to laugh when I observed Hirth's unease and concern in the minutes before the take-off. I had repeatedly to cut the motor because he recalled some word of caution he had forgotten. It was touching to see him so worried when I was absolutely calm. Thank God! he was finally done with his instructions. The motor was allowed to climb to the necessary RPM, and then I dropped my hand to signal for my first solo take-off.

Everything went as planned. I climbed to about 100 meters—which was actually twice as high as I was supposed to fly. And I flew my two rounds. And now for the landing! I fly lower to test gliding speed, flew once more around the field, and then let the plane descend. . . . With very little power I landed, smoothly and lightly, and rolled to a stop without the bumps that come with a poor touchdown.

From Barbara Spitzer, Melli Beese. *Berlin: Heimatmuseum Treptow, 1992. Translated by Allen Guttmann.*

disciplines such as engineering, architecture, and mathematics).

In 1910, a year after Orville Wright came to Berlin to demonstrate his heavier-than-air flying machine, Beese was able to realize her own dream of flying. She took lessons at the newly built Johannisthal Airport (near Berlin). Despite the subtle discrimination and nasty tricks of her teachers and fellow students, she persevered and became Germany's first female pilot. She received her license in 1911, on her twenty-fifth birthday. That same year she participated successfully in flying competitions and set two world's records for female flyers—the records for long-distance flight and for altitude with a passenger.

In 1912, she founded her own flying school. At the same time, she began to design aircraft, including a "flying boat." In 1913 she married the French pilot Charles Boutard. During World War I, she was considered an enemy alien. She and her husband had their property confiscated, and they were forced to leave Berlin.

After the war, she attempted to resume her career. She planned to fly around the world and to film the exploit for commercial release. Unfortunately, she failed to secure the necessary financial backing. In 1925, she tried unsuccessfully to renew her pilot's license but failed to do so when she crashed while attempting to land. Without flying, life had no meaning for her. Depressed and ill, she shot herself in December 1925.

Gertrud Pfister

Bibliography

Pfister, Gertrud. (1989) *Fliegen—Ihr Leben. Die ersten Pilotinnen.* Berlin: Orlanda.

Spitzer, Barabara. (1992) *Melli Beese.* Berlin: Heimatmuseum Treptow.

BELARUS *see* Russia and Belarus

BELGIUM

Belgium, with a population of about 10 million, is situated at the cultural crossroads of Europe. The frontier between Germanic and Latin languages divides the country into Flanders, the Flemish-speaking north (58 percent of the population), and Wallonia, the French-speaking south. There is also a small German-speaking enclave. At the core lies Brussels, the bilingual capital, which is also the seat of the European Community and NATO headquarters. Having served as both buffer state and battlefield between France and Germany, Belgium also borders the Netherlands to the north and Luxembourg to the east. Moreover, Great Britain is only 50 sea-miles away from its northwestern shore.

Under the reign of the Spanish Hapsburgs, the Low Countries split up in 1585 into the southern Catholic part (later to become Belgium) and the northern Protestant part (later to become the Netherlands). The Low Countries were reunited again briefly from 1815, after Napoleon's defeat at Waterloo (located south of Brussels), to 1830, when Belgium broke away as an independent state.

Belgium's sport history, including the role of women in it, reflects the nation's social and cultural development. In the 1990s, it still enjoyed a rich variety of folk games, which were a product of strong regional identity and civic pride, especially in Bruges, Ghent, Antwerp, and Louvain in Flanders, and Brussels, Mons, Charleroi, and Liège in Wallonia. Yet women have played only a minor role in these games, which are linked with the local pubs, traditional male preserves.

Gymnastics, in the form of German *Turnen*, was introduced as early as 1839 into the port of Antwerp. Female participation, however, was hampered by bourgeois conservatism and Catholic prudery. The State University of Ghent, where, in 1908, the first university institute of physical education (with licentiate and doctoral degrees) in Europe was established, appointed Irène Van der Bracht as the first female university professor in Belgium's history in 1925. The rationale was that female physical education students should be taught by a female instructor. Female gymnastics was organized in similar fashion to the Girl Guides, operating parallel to but independently from the Boy Scouts. For example, in 1932 the Flemish nationalist "gymnasiarch" Maurits Verdonck (1879–1968) was banned from the Catholic Gymnastics Federation, because in his

MARY OF BURGUNDY (1457–1482)—A SHORT LIVED LIFE AND SPORTING DEATH

Mary of Burgundy, the only daughter of the duke of Burgundy Charles the Bold, was born in 1457 in Brussels (Duchy of Brabant). Her mother Isabelle of Bourbon died in 1465. Mary grew up in the Flemish city of Ghent and was one of the most desirable brides on the European matrimonial market. Her official titles ranged from duchess of Burgundy, Brabant, Limburg, and Luxemburg to countess of Flanders, Artois, Holland, Zealand, Hainaut, and Namur. Her first fiancé, Nicolas of Calabria, duke of Lorraine, died in 1473 and her marriage to her second fiancé, Maximillian of Austria, had to be postponed because of the death of her father on the battlefield near Nancy in 1477. They were officially married on 21 April 1477. Her husband arrived four months later in Ghent on 18 August and immediately took power. His political and military agenda consisted mainly of defending the Low Countries against the insatiable territorial appetite of the French king Louis XVI. Mary had three children: the later duke of Burgundy, Philip le Beau (b. 1478), Margaret (b. 1480), and Francis (b. 1481), who died before reaching the age of one.

'Mary the rich,' as she was nicknamed in Flanders, was very keen on physical exercises and falconry was one of her favorite pastimes. In 1482, while hawking in the woods of Wijnendale near Bruges, riding sidesaddled, her horse jumped over a fallen tree, the saddle girths broke, and Mary was thrown off and found unconscious. She refused to have her deep wound properly treated. Some sources say it was because she did not want to alarm her husband, others say it was because of prudery. Her situation deteriorated and she was in a state of constant fever. On 27 March—three weeks after her sporting accident—she died at the age of 25.

Mary of Burgundy was buried in the church of Our Lady in Bruges, where her son Philip le Beau had a monumental gravestone erected. Archeological searches in 1979 revealed a skull which perfectly matched the face of the bronze monument. This suggests that the artist must have used her death mask to accomplish her likeness.

Ganda club in Ghent he trained and coached both male and female members. This "heresy" led to the creation of a separate Catholic Ladies Gymnastics Federation.

The participation of women in modern Belgian sports originated in the leisure class. One of the first breakthroughs occurred in 1897 when Madeleine Habets was allow to enter the Belgian tennis championships. She was followed by others, notably Marie-Rose de Laveleye, who became a three-time national women's tennis champion. Nicknamed "Aunt Mariette," she won her first championship in 1898 at the age of forty-two. Another Belgian tennis star was Anne de Borman, who won the world championship mixed doubles in 1912 with Max Decugis of France. Nelly Adamson from Bruges excelled in the 1930s. After becoming a French citizen through marriage, she won the finals at Roland Garros stadium in Paris in 1948 as Nelly Landry. It was almost fifty years later before a new breed of young women such as Sabine Appelmans and Dominique Van Roost-Monami would represent Belgium on the international tennis circuit.

Count Henri de Baillet-Latour (1876–1942), the Belgian successor to Baron Pierre de Coubertin as president of the Olympic movement from 1925 onward, was as patriarchal as his predecessor regarding women's involvement in sport. At the 1920 Olympics in Antwerp, which were "improvised" under Baillet-Latour's leadership, only seventy-seven women participated. Nevertheless, three stars shone brightly: the French tennis ace Suzanne Lenglen, the U.S. swimming champion

Ethelda Bleibtrey (gold-medal winner in the 100- and 300-meter freestyle races and the 4 × 100-meter relay), and Bleibtrey's fourteen-year-old compatriot Aileen Riggin, who won gold in springboard diving. The water polo display by two Dutch women's teams and the participation of Dutch women in a demonstration of the coed game of korfball also emphasized the presence of women in the Olympics in a country where women would obtain equal voting rights only after World War II, in 1948.

Although the Belgian climate is not conducive to outdoor swimming, Claire Guttenstein (daughter of a future Belgian finance minister) became world champion in the 100-meter freestyle event in 1910. And in 1938 and 1940, respectively, Fernande Caroen, from Ostend, set the world record in the 1000-yard and 500-meter freestyle events. However, she placed a disappointing fourth during the 400-meter freestyle race at the 1948 Olympics in London. Ingrid Lempéreur, who won a bronze medal in the Los Angeles Olympics 200-meter breaststroke in 1984, is the only Belgian female *olympionike* in swimming.

During the 1984 Winter Games at St. Moritz, Switzerland, Belgium's Micheline Lannoy won the gold medal for pairs skating with her partner Pierre Baugniet. On roller skates, some Belgian women have reached world-class status, including Elvire Collin, who, with Fernand Leemans, won the world championships for pairs in 1947 in Washington, D.C. In speed skating, Annie Lambrechts won twenty world championships between 1964 and 1981, as well as two gold medals at the Santa Clara, California, world roller skating championships. Annelies Bredael won a silver medal in the Barcelona 1992 skiff finals. Several Belgian women have excelled in the Paralympics.

Belgium, especially Flanders, won world renown in sport through a pantheon of male cyclists, including Cyriel Van Hauwaert, winner of the Paris-Roubaix in 1908, and Eddy Merckx, a five-time winner of the Tour de France. But the nation also had its "queen of the road," Yvonne Reynders, who won seven world championships between 1959 and 1967, a record equaled only by Beryl Burton of the United Kingdom.

Among the 2,798 sport figures selected in the *Dictionnaire des sports et des sportifs belges* (Encyclopedia of Belgian Sports, 1982), only 13 percent were women. Among these, the most numerous were in track and field (79), and swimming and diving (78), followed by tennis (22), basketball (19), soccer (18), cycling (17), and field hockey (16). An exceptional success story is that of female judo, in which Ingrid Berghmans won the gold all-around medal at the first world championships for women, in New York in 1980. She also won a gold medal in judo demonstration at the Seoul Olympics in 1988. Since then, Heidi Rakels, Ulla Werbrouck, Gella Vandecaveye, and Marie-Isabelle Lomba have also been successful in judo at the international level.

Despite these gains, Belgian sportswomen have not had an easy path toward emancipation. During the generally rebellious 1960s, however, the walls of the male sporting preserves started to crumble. And since then participation of women in sports has gradually increased, penetrating most of men's sporting subcultures. In 1969, according to a Belgian national survey, only 25 percent of adult women responded that they had ever practiced any kind of sport, and only 9 percent after the age of thirty. Ten years later, the rates were 45 percent and 38 percent; and in 1989, they were 56 percent and 46 percent. Women were thus still trailing men (who in 1989 had rates of 72 percent and 55 percent, respectively), but—over a period of twenty years—they had made significant gains.

In the 1990s, however, problems remained. The increase in the number of female sport participants was not paralleled by an increase of women coaches or sports executives. According to a follow-up study in 1989, teenage girls dropped out of sports at an earlier age than ten years earlier. Furthermore, other results showed that twelve to seventeen-year-old Flemish girls had significantly lower physical fitness levels in 1997, compared with similar fitness profiles in 1990. It was perceived that, perhaps for the first time in history, even as adults became more involved in all kinds of physical activities, the younger generation was moving in the opposite direction.

Roland Renson

Bibliography

De Genst, Henri. (1949) *Histoire de l'éducation physique*, vol. 2. Brussels: De Boeck.

D'hoker, Mark, Roland Renson, and Jan Tolleneer, eds. (1994) *Voor lichaam en geest*. Louvain: Universitaire Pers Leuven.

Mathy, Théo, and Christiane Mathy. (1982) *Dictionnaire des sports et des sportifs belges.* Brussels: Legrain.

Renson, Roland. (1996) *The Games Reborn: The Seventh Olympiad Antwerp 1920.* Antwerp: Pandora.

———. (1998) "Sport and the Flemish Movement: Resistance and Accommodation 1868–1914." In *Nationalism in Belgium: Shifting Identities, 1780–1995,* edited by Kas Deprez and Louis Vos. London: Macmillan, 119–126.

Renson, Roland, Eddy De Cramer, and Erik De Vroede. (1997) "Local Heroes." *International Review Sociology of Sport* 32, 1:59–68.

Taks, Marijke, Roland Renson, and Bart Vanreusel. (1991) *Hoe Sportief Is de Vlaming? 1969–1989.* Louvain: K.U. Leuven.

BERENSON, SENDA

(1868–1954)

U.S. EDUCATOR

A Russian immigrant, more interested in music than in sport, Senda Berenson became a pioneer in women's basketball and introduced the game to American women in 1892.

Senda Berenson was born Senda Valvrojenski on 19 March 1868 in Russia. Her family changed its name when it immigrated to the United States. Her father believed in ethnic assimilation and sought to shed the family's Russian Jewish heritage. Although she had little formal education, she spoke several languages and learned a great deal from her older brother Bernard, the art historian.

Berenson had musical aspirations and attended the Boston Conservatory of Music until her poor health forced her to leave at the age of twenty-two. Soon afterward, she entered the Boston Normal School of Gymnastics to help improve her health. The school, under the direction of Mary Homans, inspired Berenson to make a career of physical education upon her graduation in 1892.

In 1892, Berenson accepted a teaching position at Smith College. Soon afterward, reading that James Naismith had invented a game called "basket-ball" (at the nearby Springfield YMCA), she modified the rules to make them acceptable for women and introduced the game to her students. She was instrumental in publishing the first documented rules of women's basketball (in 1901). At the turn of the century, medical experts thought it was important for women to exercise for their health, but there was much concern that this exercise not be too vigorous. Berenson's modified rules, which divided the court into zones and prohibited dribbling and aggressive guarding, made the game much less strenuous. It was not until at least sixty years later that women's basketball was played with the same rules as men's basketball.

Berenson spent her career dedicated to improving the health of all students. She took pride in building the physical education program at Smith College by adding and expanding staff and activities. She worked at Smith College for nineteen years, from 1892 to 1911. She died on 16 February 1954.

In 1985, Senda Berenson was the first woman to be inducted into the Naismith Memorial Basketball Hall of Fame. She was subsequently inducted into the International Women's Sports Hall of Fame.

Shawn Ladda

Bibliography

Hult, Joan S., and Marianna Trekell. (1991) *A Century of Women's Basketball: From Frailty to Final Four.* Reston, VA: American Alliance for Health, Physical Education, Recreation & Dance.

Naismith Memorial Basketball Hall of Fame. Senda Berenson exhibit. Springfield, MA.

BERGMANN, GRETEL

(1914–)

GERMAN HIGH JUMPER

Gretel Bergmann, the daughter of a Jewish factory owner, was born on 12 April 1914 in a small town in southern Germany. Although her family was not religiously observant, she attended a Jewish elementary school. From early childhood, she was fascinated by a number of different sports, including running, skiing, and tennis. Later, as a pupil in a mostly male high school, she learned to play team handball and soccer.

After becoming a member of a sports club in the city of Ulm, she began to train systematically for track and field events and to enter competitions. She quickly established a reputation as one of Germany's elite athletes in her favorite discipline, the high jump.

Her dream was to participate in the 1936 Olympic Games, which were to take place in Berlin. After Adolf Hitler and his National Socialist (Nazi) party came to power in January of 1933, the lives of German Jews changed rapidly and radically. As a Jew, Bergmann was caught up in the catastrophe. She was barred from studying sports at the Deutsche Hochschule für Leibesübungen (German College of Physical Education) and was expelled from her sports club. Her educational plans and professional ambitions were destroyed.

Using her father's business connections, Bergmann was able to continue her education at London Polytechnic. In 1934 she represented her school in intercollegiate competition and won the British national championship in the high jump.

In the meantime, Hitler, who was initially hostile to the idea of the Olympic movement, was persuaded that the games were an ideal propaganda vehicle for his envisioned Third Reich. His declaration of willingness to host the games raised questions on the International Olympic Committee (IOC) about the compatibility of Hitler's racial policies and the IOC charter. Nazi assurances were met with skepticism and there were threats to boycott the Games, notably from several members of the American Olympic Committee. Nazi sport leaders promised to allow German Jews to try out for the national team—if they attained the required performance level.

Bergmann was asked to return to Germany in order to train for the Olympics. Realizing that refusal would endanger her family, she complied with the Nazi request. She joined a Jewish sports club and prepared for the Olympic tryouts. Given the extremely hostile environment in which they had to train, very few Jewish athletes were able to perform at their best, but Bergmann was an exception. As she later recalled, Nazi discrimination

steeled her determination to excel and to disprove racist ideology. In spite of the poor training conditions, she equaled the national record of 1.6 meters.

Although she assumed that this mark qualified her to make the team, she was horrified to hear, shortly before the Games, that her performance was "inadequate." Important as medals were to the Nazi sport bureaucrats, they did not want to see a Jewish athlete on the victor's stand. In the end, although a single athlete with a Jewish father was allowed to compete for the German team in the Summer Games (fencer Helene Mayer), no "full Jew" represented Germany. (Ironically, a Hungarian Jew, Ibolya Czak, won the high jump at 1.6 meters, the exact height that Bergmann had reached.)

Bergmann left Germany in May 1937 with the promise "never to set foot on German soil again." She married Bruno Lambert and created a new life for herself in the United States, settling in New York City.

Gertrud Pfister

Bibliography

Pfister, Gertrud, and Toni Niewerth. (1999) "Jewish Women in Gymnastics and Sport in Germany Until 1938." *Journal of Sport History* 17: (in press).

BERGMAN-ÖSTERBERG, MARTINA

(1849–1915)

ENGLISH EDUCATOR

By any standards, Martina Bergman-Österberg was an outstanding, visionary, and unconventional leader in the physical education of girls and the establishment of teaching as a specialist profession for middle- and upper-class women. Her influence spread well beyond her adopted country, England.

Born on 7 October 1849 in Skane, Sweden, in a period when feminism flourished, Martina Bergman was encouraged by her family to pursue her academic studies. As an independent woman, she traveled throughout Europe in her quest for knowledge. She worked in a variety of positions, including governess and private teacher. While employed as a librarian, she came under the influence of Thuse Brandt, the originator of gynecological massage, and Edvin Per Vilhelm Österberg, who encouraged her to pursue a teaching career. Their combined influence led her, at the age of thirty, to enroll at Stockholm's Royal Central Gymnastic Institute (CGI), where she studied the system of sequential whole-body exercise developed by Per Henrik Ling. Two years later, armed with a certificate to teach Swedish gymnastics, she was recruited to replace another CGI graduate, Froken Concordia Lofving, at the London School Board (LSB). As the Lady Superintendent of Physical Education, Bergman exhibited an enormous capacity for work. She visited schools by day and in the evenings instructed teachers and organized public displays of Swedish gymnastics that attracted large and prestigious audiences, including royalty.

Between 1882 and 1887, she trained more than 1,000 mistresses of physical training for girls in Swedish gymnastics. While still with the LSB, Bergman opened her own teacher-training college at Hampstead in 1885. When the school's facilities were outgrown, a full-time residential college was established at Dartford in 1895. The curriculum, which focused on the scientific basis of physical education, included anatomy, physiology, massage, remedial gymnastics, and games. Bergman herself had come of age too soon to be an exponent of competitive games, but she grasped the significance of the tradition in the British public schools for boys and implemented similar activities at Dartford. The school was well equipped, with access to indoor and outdoor gymnasia, athletic and cycling tracks, fields for lacrosse and field hockey, netball and tennis courts, and a swimming pool. Bergman particularly approved of netball because it seemed consistent with Ling's principles of equal development of both sides of the body. (Netball grew out of basketball, which she had seen during a visit to the United States.) She also required her students to wear relatively simple sports clothing to facilitate movement. In an effort to enforce this requirement, Bergman and her coworker, Margaret Tait, created the gym slip, which became the standard dress in physical education and sport in many English-speaking countries. Students rounded off their professional preparation with teaching practice in local schools and with schoolchildren who came to the college for instruction. Volunteer work with the lower classes was also expected.

Free from the constraints of bureaucracy, Bergman proved also to be an entrepreneur. To ensure the college's viability, students were required to pay substantial fees for their two years of full-time study and private classes were offered in gymnastics, medical gymnastics, and massage. Bergman charged high tuition to attract students from wealthier families and thus challenged the English class system, which had hitherto deemed Swedish gymnastics suitable only for the children of the poor. She believed middle- and upper-class women also needed her exercise system for the perfection of the individual and the "race." Discipline at her college was so strict that students nicknamed her "Napoleon," but students who completed the demanding two-year course knew that they would find employment at a very good salary of £100 (negotiated by Bergman to be commensurate with her students' efforts and achievements). Some graduates were employed by her at Dartford to maintain the rigorous standards. Rhoda Anstey was the first of her former students to establish a physical education college and, true to her character, Bergman was not pleased about having a rival college set up in 1897. Although it is no longer a functioning college, Anstey College celebrated its centennial in 1997. Others also ventured forth to establish their own colleges, such as Bedford, founded by Margaret Stansfeld in 1903. Some pursued careers in massage and clinical work, while others played major roles in the establishment of national sporting associations for lacrosse, field hockey, and netball. Bergman maintained contact with her graduates through newsletters and reunions.

Bergman did not always approve of those who became her competitors. In January 1899, some former students formed the Swedish Physical Educationlists, which later became the Ling Association. They tactfully asked Bergman to be its president, but since she had not played a central role in its foundation, she dissociated herself from it and instead founded the Bergman Union of Trained Gymnastic Teachers.

Under Bergman's leadership, British women physical educators were well in advance of their male counterparts, who toyed with the Swedish system in schools without success. However, Britain's military realized the merits of Swedish gymnastics from the displays mounted by her college students, and the system was adopted by the Royal Navy. When several naval personnel retired and pursued teaching careers in schools such as Eton, Bergman's influence reached middle- and upper-class boys.

Perhaps the most unconventional aspect of Bergman's life was her marriage in 1886 to Edvin Per Vilhelm Österberg. They pursued their separate careers, she in England and he as a school principal in Sweden.

Toward the end of her life, Bergman attempted to transfer her private college to the Board of Education, but the British cabinet declined the radical offer. Instead, a board of trustees was appointed just shortly before her death on 29 July 1915.

In retrospect, Bergman achievements continue to be applauded, but they have been subjected to analysis. Swedish gymnastics, derived from anatomical and physiological principles, provided a scientific basis for healthy exercise, but, when carried out in large classes, the system lacked flexibility and sometimes degenerated into military drill.

However, physical training following the scientific method of Per Henrik Ling was not her primary aim. Her objective was female emancipation and social, economic, and spiritual freedom. In addition to the scientifically based curriculum, courses were provided in music and dancing, literature, art, drama, and current events. Bergman's girls went out as pioneers to change the world for women.

Lynn Embrey

Bibliography

Fletcher, Sheila. (1984) *Women First: The Female Tradition in English Physical Education 1880–1980.* London: Althone Press.

Guttmann, Allen. (1991) *Women's Sports: A History.* New York: Columbia University Press.

Hargreaves, Jennifer. (1994) *Sporting Females: Critical Issues in the History and Sociology of Women's Sports.* London: Routledge.

May, Jonathon. (1969) *Madame Bergman Österberg.* London: Harrap.

McCrone, Kathleen. (1988) *Playing the Game: Sport and the Physical Emancipation of English Women, 1870–1914.* Lexington: University Press of Kentucky.

McIntosh, Peter C. (1968) *Physical Education in England Since 1800,* 2d. ed. London: G. Bell & Sons.

Additional information provided by Sheila Cutler of the Madame Bergman Österberg Union.

BERLIOUX, MONIQUE

(1925–)

FRENCH OLYMPIC ADMINISTRATOR

At a time when women were virtually nonexistent in the administration of sport internationally, Monique Berlioux became the central figure in the day-to-day operations of the International Olympic Committee (IOC), one of the most influential sport organizations in the world.

Born in Metz, France, on 22 December 1925, Berlioux was a courier for the French Resistance during World War II, a national champion in swimming who competed in the 1948 Olympics, and later a sport journalist. She joined the IOC during the late 1960s when it was expanding its secretariat and administrative offices in Lausanne, Switzerland. In 1969, she was appointed to the position of director of press and public relations. Because of the transitions taking place in the secretariat at the time, she became responsible for much of the daily administration of IOC affairs. She won the confidence of the IOC president,

Avery Brundage, and shortly took over the position of IOC director.

Berlioux was noted for her authoritarian nature, which caused some friction with other staff members. Early in her tenure as director, there was a notable turnover of staff at the IOC headquarters. When Lord Killanin was elected to the presidency of the IOC in 1972, he had reservations about Berlioux's style, but he later noted that he came to appreciate her efficiency and loyalty to the IOC. During Killanin's presidency (1972–1980), Berlioux was responsible for conducting much of the IOC's most important business between its annual sessions. These responsibilities included overseeing organizational details surrounding the annual sessions of the IOC, as well as its meetings with the other sport organizations involved in the Olympics, the national Olympic committees, and international sports federations. Killanin also trusted Berlioux to play a major role in the negotiation of television rights and other financial contracts for the IOC. Prior to the 1980 Moscow Olympics, when a boycott was imminent, Killanin chose Berlioux rather than IOC members to accompany him when he visited U.S. President Jimmy Carter and Soviet leader Leonid Brezhnev in an attempt to ensure full participation in the Games. Thus, by the latter years of the 1970s, Berlioux wielded a huge amount of influence over the daily operations of the IOC. This was to cause problems for her under a new IOC president.

Unlike his predecessors, Juan Antonio Samaranch, who was elected president in 1980, took a more direct interest in the daily operations of the IOC. He became the first president since Pierre de Coubertin actually to live in Lausanne and work at IOC headquarters on a daily basis. After several years it became apparent that Berlioux could not work with Samaranch in the way that she had with his predecessors. In 1985 she resigned from her position, ending more than a decade and a half of service to—and leadership of—the IOC and the Olympic movement. The details of her resignation have still not been revealed in their entirety, and it is widely believed that she left the IOC under duress.

Berlioux was an anomaly in the world of sport administration. When the IOC elected its first women members in 1981, Berlioux had already

Monique Berlioux and Juan Antonio Samaranch during a press conference, 1980. (Bettmann/Corbis)

been intimately involved in its affairs for more than a decade. In fact, she had attained a position of influence and authority within the Olympic movement that was greater than that of some IOC members. Although she had numerous detractors both within and outside the IOC, she held her position firmly until she came into conflict with Samaranch. Her career at the IOC proved beyond any doubt that women could be involved successfully at the highest levels of international sport administration.

After her resignation, Berlioux moved to Paris, where she was appointed to the position of deputy mayor. Educated at the Sorbonne, she has also written several volumes on historical aspects of the Olympics.

Gordon MacDonald

Bibliography

International Olympic Committee. (1996) *The International Olympic Committee—One Hundred Years: The Idea—the Presidents—the Achievements*, Vol. 2.

Lausanne, Switzerland: International Olympic Committee.

Killanin, Lord. (1983) *My Olympic Years*. London: Secker and Warburg.

Levesque, Paul. (1993) "A Case Study of the Rise and Demise of Power: Monique Berlioux, IOC Director, 1969–1985." Unpublished paper, faculty of kinesiology, University of Western Ontario, London, Canada.

Lucas, John. (1994) "A Reflection: Madame Monique Berlioux Revisited." *OLYMPIKA: The International Journal of Olympic Studies* 3: 153–55.

BIATHLON

Biathlon is a professional, not a recreational, sport that combines cross-country skiing and target shooting. It began as an all-male sport—with women excluded from international and Olympic participation for more than twenty years—but women now participate, although with slight differences in the events.

HISTORY

Sport historians link modern biathlon with two traditional practices. Prehistoric hunters were the first to combine skiing and shooting in their quest for food. The oldest rock paintings found date back to the Neolithic Age, more than 8,000 years ago, and show hunters with bows and arrows moving by sliding on strips of timber. Hunting on skis was common in Northern Europe as well as in Northern Asia and North America and in the late Middle Ages; shooting while on skis became a military activity as well. Later, ski divisions played a major role in the Great Northern War of 1700–1721 between Sweden and Russia. Soldiers have skied in Scandinavia, Russia, Germany, Austria, and Switzerland. In 1767 the first recorded biathlon competition took place at the Swedish–Norwegian border. The first Winter Olympic Games in 1924 in Chamonix, France, included a military ski patrol race—an early form of biathlon—as a demonstration event. At the forty-third session of the International Olympic Committee in Rome in 1949, Sweden proposed adding biathlon as an all-male individual competition, open also to civilian competitors.

At about this time, the name "biathlon" came into use. In 1958 the first world championships were held in Saalfelden, Austria. The first men's regular Olympic event was held in 1960 in Squaw Valley, California. Since 1957 the Union Internationale du Pentathlon Moderne (UIPM) has been responsible for organizing annual world championships. In 1968 the UIPM became the Union Internationale de Pentathlon Moderne et Biathlon (UIPMB). In 1993 the International Biathlon Union (IBU) emerged from the UIPMB to become the major worldwide biathlon organization. Participation increased from 9 nations and 30 athletes in Squaw Valley, to 32 nations and 200 athletes (105 men and 95 women), in Nagano, Japan, in 1998.

RULES AND PLAY

The only difference between women's and men's biathlon races is the length of the course. Women have two individual competitions of different distances—the 15-kilometer (9.3-mile) and the 7.5-kilometer (4.7-mile) sprint, as well as a 4×7.5-kilometer relay, team competition, and the pursuit competition. The pursuit competition was added to the IBU competitions in 1996. The start is based on the finish times of a previous sprint, the winner starting first, with other competitors starting at time intervals determined by the amount of time by which they finished behind the winner in the sprint race. The first athlete to cross the finish line is the winner.

In all events, rifles must weigh at least 3.5 kilograms (7.7 pounds) but may be heavier. In 1977 the regulations changed, and competitors were required to use small-bore (.22 caliber) rifles rather than army rifle calibers. Athletes harness the rifles to their backs during the race. Technology modified the target system and the skating step increased the speed of the race. The skating step ("free technique") was first used in 1982. On a track 4 meters (13 feet) wide, the athletes glide like an ice skater, in a V-step. Special skis, boots, and poles are needed. Today, shooting facilities and the material of the skis are important and decisive for ranking. The skis used are now grip-waxless, meaning that the bottom surface of the skis is designed so that they grip the snow without a coating of wax. (Early cross-country skis required wax, which was applied by the skier, with different waxes used for different snow and temperature conditions.) Before each race, the athletes are allowed to practice shots at paper targets on the range in order to adjust their rifle sights according to sun and wind conditions.

The sprint race is about 7.5 kilometers (4.7 miles), with competitors starting in intervals of 30 seconds. Athletes shoot from a prone position at a 4.5-centimeter (1.8-inch) target, then stand to shoot at a 11.5-centimeter (4.5-inch) target. Every missed target results in a penalty of skiing an additional 150-meter penalty loop in the sprint and relay events, which takes 20–25 seconds. Until 1988, women had to run only 5 kilometers (3.1 miles) in the sprint event.

In the 15-kilometer (9.3-mile) event the athletes shoot four times from different positions, beginning with the prone position. Until 1988 the women's course was about 10 kilometers (6.2 miles), with three shooting ranges. Targets of the same size are used for every position. Each competitor is allowed five shots at the five black metal targets. The targets are about 50 meters (54.7 yards) away from the competitors. One minute is added to a competitor's time on the 15-kilometer (9.3-mile) course for each miss. The biathlete with the lowest elapsed time is the winner of the race.

For the relay competition, all participants start at the same time. The course is 7.5 kilometers (4.7 miles) long. Competitors have eight bullets to hit the five targets, from the prone as well as standing positions. For each miss, the competitor must make an extra loop. The teammate running next is waiting in a tag zone, and the arriving member must touch her before she can run out on the course. The team first crossing the finish line wins the race. Until 1992 the number of female athletes was relatively small, so that the women's relay had only three athletes on each team. This later increased to four.

The team event was officially accepted as a fourth biathlon discipline in 1986. During 1993–1994, the format was shortened to sprint distances. A team of four athletes shoot in pairs, and only the two shooters ski the 150-meter (164-yard) penalty, while the other two team members are waiting in a special waiting zone. Every miss is followed by an extra penalty round of about 150 meters (164 yards). The whole team must cross the finish within 15 seconds of one another; if they fail, they have an additional minute tacked to their time.

The World Cup started in 1987, when the technical committee of the IBU recommended starting a five-competition World Cup series with three individual and three sprints counting for the season's total. The number of competitions changed during the following seasons. A nine-competition series was organized for the 1998–1999 series. World Cup points are awarded to the top twenty-five athletes. Since 1988–1989, women have competed on the same World Cup circuit as men.

WOMEN'S PARTICIPATION

The Eastern European countries held competitions for women long before international rules had been agreed upon. Women's competitions were also held in Scandinavian countries and in individual cases in North America. The year 1967 was probably the start of formal women's national championships, first organized in Czechoslovakia. They used .22-caliber rifles and shot only in the prone position. The skiing distance was 5 kilometers (3.1 miles). By 1969 the field of participants had grown to fifty-six athletes from eleven teams. The rules were then based mostly on men's rules.

The first Canadian female competitor was Sonja Nehr, who competed in the men's class in the 1978 Canadian championships. Holly Beattie was the first female biathlete in the United States, in the 1978–1979 season. In 1978 Finland and Czechoslovakia requested inclusion of women in UIPMB competitions. Until 1978 sport officials had not considered the possibility that women might participate in international biathlon competitions. Then, during a session of the technical committee of the UIPMB in 1978, a group was assigned the task of modifying rules and designing a program for women's world championships. The male officials took two more years to work out the official rules, after which they were presented on the UIPMB Congress 1980 in Sarajevo. The first event under UIPMB auspices was held in January 1981 in Jachymov, Czechoslovakia.

The women from Poland, Norway, Sweden, and Czechoslovakia competed in a 10-kilometer (6.2-mile) individual event with three shooting

Biathlon is a rigorous winter sport which requires the biathlete to be in peak physical condition. To qualify for the United States Biathlon Association junior development camp, young women between the ages of 13 and 17 must be able to do at least 6 pull-ups, 50 sit-ups in a minute, 28 box jumps in 30 seconds, 40 dips in a minute and run 800 meters in three minutes and 100 meters in 15.5 seconds. The requirements are slightly more rigorous for boys.

rounds, prone–standing–prone, and in a 5-kilometer sprint (3.1-mile) with two shooting rounds. In 1981 a congress decision was made to include women in UIPMB cup competitions, starting with three competitions in the 1983–1984 season. Around 1987 the proposal of several nations to increase women's skiing distances was accepted. Single events were raised to 15 and 7.5 kilometers (9.3 and 4.7 miles), and the relay competition was increased to 3 × 7.5 kilometers (4.7 miles). Also, the number of shooting rounds in the individual races increased to four. By 1988 the junior women's distances were set at 10, 7.5, and 3 × 7.5 kilometers (6.2, 4.7, and 3 × 4.7 miles).

The first women's World Cup took place in 1984 in Chamonix, France, with races of 5 and 10 kilometers (3.1 and 6.2 miles). Thirty-seven women from twelve nations took part. Russian Venera Tchernychova won both races. Because women's participation had declined in the early 1980s, the UIPMB decided to support the 1987 world championships in Falun, Sweden, with travel subsidies. Assistance continued over the next two years, and participation peaked at twenty-eight nations in the 1994 Olympics in Lillehammer, Norway. Until 1988 world championships for women were organized with the junior championships. In 1987–1988, female and male biathletes held their first World Cup circuit together with the same point-scoring system. In 1989 female junior athletes (eighteen to twenty years old) had their first world championship, in Voss, Norway.

Many years of lobbying efforts have been necessary. Gail Niinimaa was an important advocate for the development of women's biathlon sport. At the International Coaching Symposium in Calgary in 1986, she presented a paper, "Women in Biathlon," and in the same year forced the UIPMB executive board and technical committee to accelerate considerations for women. In 1988 at the ninety-fourth session of the International Olympic Committee (IOC) in Seoul, Korea, the officials decided to integrate biathlon into the women's Olympic program of 1992.

Today only a few countries have all-male national biathlon teams. Some nations have a larger female than male team. Biathletes have two different trainers, one for running and one for shooting. Around twenty women, mostly from Canada and Finland, have currently received their International Referee Licence. Since 1993 several women have been elected and appointed to the IBU. These include Dr. Tjasa Andree-Prosenc of Slovenia, who is a member of the legal committee; American Mary Moran, M.D., who is a member of the medical committee; Susi Mittermeier of Germany, a member of the information committee; and Denise Pittuck of Canada, a member of the marketing committee. Media interest in women's biathlon has increased rapidly and is at least equal to, and often higher than, interest in men's competitions. This growing media interest is one important reason why women's competitions no longer follow the men's race.

By 1997 twenty-four nations with eighty-one female athletes were involved in the sport. This figure has been affected by the political changes that have resulted in there being more smaller independent countries with their own national teams. Female biathletes are well known in their countries. Myriam Bedard, for example, was Canada's Sportswoman of the Year after she won her double Olympic gold medal in the sprint and 15-kilometer race in 1994 in Lillehammer. She was the most successful individual female Olympic biathlete. Most of the women who became biathletes began as cross-country skiers. One very successful example was the Swedish athlete Magdalena Forsberg. As of 1999, she was two-time world championship winner and also winner of the 1997 World Cup.

The most successful female biathlete of all time was Petra Schaff Behle. In 1989 she received a certificate from IBU that commended her as "being the most successful female biathlete in the history of our sport." Schaff, born 5 January 1969 in Offenbach, Germany, started her career as a cross-country skier and changed to biathlon in 1986. Her outstanding career began when she won the world championship title in the sprint event of 1988 in Chamonix, France. In following years she won three world championship titles in single events and three world championship titles in the relay and team events. In the Olympics she twice won the silver medal in the relay and won the gold in the relay in 1998 in Nagano, Japan. Her active career ended with the World Cup season 1997–1998.

CONCLUSION

The history of biathlon is marked by an increased number of events and athletes. Though skiing distances have generally decreased, women's skiing distances have increased. The shooting penalties have also decreased. There has been a rapid growth in women's participation. Television has played an important role in bringing about these changes. The introduction of the mass start used in the relay and in some sprint competitions was strongly influenced by the media, because it makes the competition easier for viewers to follow. Environmental considerations are becoming more important in biathlon, and technical changes are expected. Examples of alternate forms of biathlon—such as archery biathlon, snowshoe biathlon, orienteering biathlon, and even roller skiing biathlon—are indicators of the attractiveness of this sport.

Michaela Czech

Bibliography

Heimann, Fritz. (1997) *Kurze geschichtliche Darstellung des Biathlonsports.* International Biathlon Union Calendar 1997/98.

International Biathlon Union Web site. <http://www.ibu.at/ibu-at/>. 1999.

Niinimaa, Veli M. J. (1998) *Double Contest: Biathlon History and Development.* Calgary: Biathlon Alberta, c. 1998.

Petra Behle provided additional information to the author.

BIKING *see* Cycling, Mountain Biking

BILLIARDS

Billiards is a generic term for games played on a rectangular table with a set of balls. It has two basic forms: carom and pocket. In the former, players score points by driving the white cue ball into the object balls—one red and the other white but distinguished by two or three red or black spots—thus scoring a carom. The first player to reach a predetermined number of caroms, or points, wins the game. In some versions, the shooter's cue ball must contact the cushion (the padded wall around the playing surface that prevents balls from falling off the table) one or more times during a successful carom. Three-cushion is the better-known form of carom billiards; in it the cue ball must first strike one of the object balls and at least three cushions before hitting the second object ball.

Pocket billiards is played on tables with six pockets, one in each corner and one in the middle of each of the longer sides of the table, generally with a white cue ball and colored and numbered object balls. In its many different forms, the game is determined principally by players pocketing either a predetermined number of balls or a ball with a specific number, such as the 8- or the 9-ball. Some games, such as English Billiards, combined characteristics of the carom and the pocket games, while snooker, a type of pocket game, involves six numbered balls as well as fifteen red unnumbered balls.

HISTORY

Billiards most likely developed from late-fourteenth- or early-fifteenth-century lawn games similar to croquet that were played in Northern

Europe. The game was then moved indoors and played on a table covered with green cloth, perhaps to simulate grass. The lawn game was probably played on a sunken plot that kept the balls within the playing area. Indoors, "banks" were constructed around the table's edge to prevent the balls from falling off. Though the banks were originally unpadded, shots that involved bouncing a ball off one or more of them were called "bank shots."

The earliest versions of billiards were played on a table with six pockets and a hoop, or "port," similar to a croquet wicket, and a "king," used as a target like a croquet pin. The port and king were discarded during the eighteenth century. Until the end of that century, balls were pushed with a device known as a "mace," rather than struck, as they are now, with a cue stick. Maces varied in form but looked somewhat like a golf wood. However, rather than being flat on the side, the mace was square-fronted, with a shaft 1.2 to 1.5 meters (4 to 5 feet) in length in early versions. Players placed the flat-bottomed head on the table with the handle held at shoulder height and pushed the ball in a similar fashion to shuffleboard. The heads of later maces were curved to be concave so the players could turn them on their sides and sweep the cue ball along the table. Finally, players discovered that they could use the shaft end of the mace for shooting balls lying along the side, or rail, of the table that were difficult to reach or control with the head of the mace. The French word for tail, *queue,* referred to the shaft of the mace and is the etymological root of the modern term "cue."

Exactly how and when billiards came to America from Europe is not certain. It was probably brought by Dutch and English settlers. By the early 1700s American cabinetmakers were producing billiard tables. William Byrd II, a colonial legislator from Westover, Virginia, referred to billiards in his diary on 20 July 1710, and George Washington reportedly won a match in 1748. The game spread through public houses along the Atlantic seaboard, where "in due course it became associated with drinking, gambling, womanizing and dissolute behavior in general" (Grissim 1979, 37). Apparently, Thomas Jefferson would have had a table at Monticello, had there not been a law passed prohibiting the game in Virginia.

RULES AND PLAY

Today, billiard tables typically have a sturdy wood frame and a thick slate playing surface, pro-

BILLIARDS OR POOL?

In 1921, the Brunswick-Balke-Collender Company, then the largest manufacturer of billiards equipment, attempted to sanitize the game by changing the name from pool to pocket billiards. But in the 1920s and 1930s, a poolroom was still a place where a man could dress sloppily, drink, curse, gamble, spit, smoke and otherwise let off steam. Sociologist Ned Polsky, in his classic 1967 study of American poolroom culture *Hustlers, Beats, and Others,* argued that the poolroom of this period functioned as a last bastion of a heterosexual, all-male subculture.

In an effort to distance themselves from the poolroom stigma, professional female players named their group the Women's Professional *Billiard* Alliance (later Association), not the Women's Professional *Pool* Alliance. However, WPBA tournaments and championships have never involved billiards (carom games). Indeed, nine-ball, the current choice for tournament play, is a favorite gambling game for the same reasons it is a favorite for TV coverage: games tend to be brief, fast-paced, and reward skillful players. Because of its reputation as a game specifically designed for gambling, nine-ball play was often prohibited in taverns and pool parlors where authorities sought to suppress wagering. Fortunately, television coverage of WPBA tournaments and the ever increasing numbers of women playing pool in public facilities have improved the image of pool, in general, and nine-ball, in particular.

viding a warp-free solid base that allows balls to travel true. The playing surface and table cushions are covered with cloth. This permits the balls to roll smoothly and provides friction so that shooters can better control their shots by imparting spin to the balls. Tables are twice as long as wide, ranging between 1.8 and 3 meters (6 and 10 feet) in length. Originally made of clay, wood, or ivory, balls are now made of phenolic resin. They range between 5.24 and 6.2 centimeters (2.06 and 2.42 inches) in diameter, depending on the game. Smaller balls are used in snooker, larger ones in carom games. In most pocket games the balls are 5.7 centimeters (2.25 inches) in diameter. Players move the balls by striking them with a cue stick, a long, tapered rod, usually made of wood. The cue is tipped by a pad, usually of leather or a synthetic material similar to leather. A right-handed player holds the thicker end of the cue near its end with the right hand and forms a "bridge" with the left hand, which is placed on the table to cradle the cue. The cue ball is then struck with the tipped end of the cue and propelled toward the object ball. Cues are typically about 1.4 meters (57 inches) long and weigh between 397 and 624 grams (14 to 24 ounces).

Though billiards is a generic term, many people consider only carom games as billiards and call pocket games "pool." The term comes from a collective wager, or ante. Off-track horse-race gambling parlors were once called "poolrooms." For patron entertainment between races, many poolrooms installed billiard tables. Hence, the unsavory connection in the public mind between billiards and gambling.

WOMEN AND BILLIARDS

Billiards was traditionally a men's game, primarily because of its association with taverns, gambling, coarse behavior, and lower social classes. Yet it was also a diversion for members of the upper classes, who were expected to play well, but not too well; skillful play signified a well-rounded education, but too much skill meant a misspent youth. Despite its rough and lower-class associations, billiards has been played by women since it "was brought up from the ground in the fifteenth century" (Shamos 1995, 5). Some of the earliest references to billiards involve women. In Shakespeare's *Anthony and Cleopatra* (circa 1609),

Two English women play snooker in 1940. (Hulton-Deutsch Collection/Corbis)

Cleopatra suggests to Charmian, her handmaiden, "Let us to billiards" (Act II, scene v). While billiards did not exist in Cleopatra's Egypt, it was apparently an acceptable diversion for Englishwomen during Shakespeare's time. Billiards's most gruesome story also involves a woman, Mary Stuart, Queen of Scotland. In 1577, before she was executed for plotting to assassinate her cousin, Queen Elizabeth of England, Mary's captors removed her billiard table during her imprisonment, evidently as part of her punishment. After she was beheaded, her corpse was supposedly covered with cloth torn from her billiard table. In France some 200 years later, Marie Antoinette was also a billiard enthusiast and regularly defeated her husband, Louis XVI, before meeting the same fate as Mary Stuart.

Despite its low repute among the middle classes in colonial America, billiards was often embraced by members of the upper class, who could afford to have their own tables, as well as by lower-class men in taverns and other establishments. Until the second half of the nineteenth century, the few women players typically used a mace, rather than a cue stick, although the cue was quickly replacing the mace among male players, allegedly because of the fear that female players would accidentally tear the table cloth with a

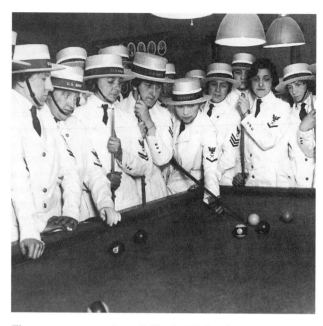

The unsavory reputation of billiards failed to deter many women from playing, including these female members of the U.S. Naval Reserve in 1916. (Corbis)

cue. A more plausible explanation is that some shots require players to lean far over the table, and for women, this meant possibly assuming an "unladylike" posture or even exposing part of their legs or ankles. By using a mace, a player stood upright and thus would avoid the exposure required by the cue stick.

The heyday of billiards in the United States was in the late nineteenth and early twentieth centuries. Among the few female professional players then were May Kaarlus, a turn-of-the-century trick-shot artist, and Ruth McGinnis, who toured with Willie Mosconi, one of the all-time great players, during the 1930s. McGinnis could beat most of the top male players of her day. The Billiards Congress of America (BCA) organized the first national tournament for women in the United States in 1967, which was won by Dorothy Wise. She went on to win the next four titles and became the first female inductee into the BCA Hall of Fame. Jean Balukas won her first U.S. open championship in 1972 and took the next six as well. Between 1977 and 1983, she also won six women's world open championships. In 1985, she became the second female to be inducted into the BCA Hall of Fame.

Women's billiards came into its own after 1976, when the Women's Professional Billiard As-

sociation (WPBA) was formed. The association governs female professional billiards, including game rules, rules of conduct, ethics, equipment specifications, media relations, and the organization and sanctioning of tournaments. It also recognizes hundreds of regional tournaments and tour-qualifying events throughout the United States. In 1993, the WPBA inaugurated the Classic Billiard Tour. This culminates with the WPBA National 9-Ball Championships, which are televised on ESPN and ESPN2. The first Women's Tournament of Champions was held in December 1998 at the same time as the WPBA National 9-Ball Championships and featured the four WPBA 1998 tournament winners in a sudden-death, $25,000, winner-take-all event.

In the 1990s, the WPBA had become a very successful organization. Because male players were divided among several organizations, their marketing and promotion was less effective than the women's, and in the later 1990s, women professionals outearned the top men. In 1995, for example, Loree Jon Jones received close to $100,000 in prize money, more than for a member of the men's tour, and in 1996 Vivian Villarreal earned more than $120,000. Allison Fisher, the top-ranked female billiards player in 1998, had dominated the WPBA tour since late 1995, winning $77,000 in 1996. In 1996 and 1997, she was Player of the Year and winner of the World 9-Ball Championship. In 1998, she played a former top male professional, Grady Mathews, in a limited thirty-one-city tour, 9-ball challenge series. Dubbed "The Beauty and the Beast Tour," this event recalled the male–female challenge tennis matches of the 1970s between Bobby Riggs and Billie Jean King, generating great excitement for fans. Through the end of March 1998, Mathews held an 11–8 match edge over Fisher.

There are also championships for carom and pocket games. Initially, women's championships were contested in straight-pool (also called "14.1"), 8-ball, and, outside the United States, snooker. Dorothy Wise and Jean Balukas won U.S. and world titles in 14.1 and the first two WPBA national championships, in 1978 and 1979, were also 14.1 matches. In 1980, 9-ball became the WPBA championship game. Nine-ball is played with the cue ball and the object balls numbered 1 through 9 on a pocket billiards table. Nine-ball became a tournament favorite because it required strength as well as skill on the break (possibly the only area of billiards where men have a slight advantage over women), fine shot-making ability, and strategic play. Nine-ball games tend to be brief and fast-paced, and often to require spectacular shots, which makes them highly suitable for television coverage.

All billiards games involve physical skill and strategy. However, excepting possibly for the initial break of the object balls—more important in some games than others—physical size and strength are not especially important in billiards. Thus, there is no inherent property of the game itself that prohibits women from equaling men in ability. Furthermore, the excellent screen presence of female professionals in televised matches and the outstanding organizational skills exhibited by the WPBA boded well for the future of the professional game for women in the 1990s.

Today, women are estimated to comprise between one-fourth and one-third of all players; possibly a majority of all new players are women. They are now accepted in pool halls and as members of tavern league teams, a situation that was uncommon as recently as twenty-five years ago. Women's acceptance of billiards and men's acceptance of women players were among the principal reasons for the game's growing popularity with players and spectators, especially on television.

Garry Chick

Bibliography

Billiard Congress of America. (1995) *Billiards: The Official Rules & Records Book.* Iowa City, IA: Billiard Congress of America.

Billiards Digest (April 1998): 20, 5. Chicago: Luby Publishing Inc. Online at <http://www.billiardsdigest.com/>.

Byrne, Robert. (1996) *Byrne's Wonderful World of Pool and Billiards: A Cornucopia of Instruction, Strategy, Anecdote, and Colorful Characters.* New York: Harcourt Brace & Company.

Grissim, John. (1979) *Billiards: Hustlers & Heroes, Legends & Lies and the Search for Higher Truth on the Green Felt.* New York: St. Martin's Press.

Hendricks, William. (1974) *William Hendricks' History of Billiards.* Roxana, IL: William Hendricks.

Shamos, Mike. (1995) "A Brief History of the Noble Game of Billiards." In *Billiards: The Official Rules & Records Book.* Iowa City, IA: Billiard Congress of America, 1–5.

Women's Professional Billiard Association. Web site: <http://www.wpba.com/>.1997.

BIOMECHANICS

In all complex animals, range and speed of movement are governed by muscles. To power movement, muscles must exert forces to support, forces to accelerate or decelerate, and forces to overcome the resistance of the air or water through which movement occurs. Mechanics is that branch of physics that includes the action of forces. Biomechanics is that science as applied to living things, male and female.

Biomechanics is a relatively new subdiscipline of kinesiology. For some, the terms "biomechanics" and "kinesiology" are used interchangeably. However, kinesiology means "the study of motion," which has a very broad focus. In contrast, according to the American Society of Biomechanics, biomechanics refers much more narrowly to the "application of the principles of mechanics to the study of biological systems." In the field of biomechanics, the human body is viewed as a machine—a mechanical system subject to the restrictions of the laws of physics. The body is divided into a collection of body segments connected to one another and pivoting at the joints, moved by muscular and/or externally applied forces.

Biomechanics has grown rapidly and steadily since about 1980 due, in large part, to the improvements in instrumentation in general and to high-speed computers in particular. Pennsylvania State University and Indiana University were perhaps the first two universities to design a laboratory for biomechanics in the 1960s. Today, biomechanics is a part of every curriculum, and almost all departments of kinesiology have biomechanics laboratories.

Although biomechanics is a relatively new discipline, the first "biomechanic" was probably Leonardo da Vinci, who lived from 1452 to 1519. Leonardo's descriptions of the mechanics of movement demonstrated his interest in and knowledge of the musculoskeletal system. In the nineteenth century, the photographer Edward Muybridge used a system of multiple cameras to document the movement of racehorses. In the 1990s, high-speed cinematography was a cornerstone of data collection and analysis of many athletic activities.

Since the study of biomechanics incorporates many other disciplines (physics, engineering, biology, computer science, zoology, and physical and occupational therapy), it is considered by most to be a diversified subdiscipline. Human biomechanics alone can be divided into many areas of study. For example, there are those interested in the elderly and mobility impairments. Others are interested in the growth and development patterns of children. Clinical biomechanics might study gait among individuals with cerebral palsy or daily living activities for individuals with disabilities, whereas occupational biomechanics focuses on work-related injuries and the prevention of those injuries and is particularly interested in safety factors in the workplace.

BIOMECHANICS IN SPORT

In sport, biomechanics is especially concerned with how the human body applies forces to itself and to other bodies with which it comes into contact and, in turn, how the body is affected by external forces. A sound knowledge of biomechanics equips the physical educator, the coach, and the athlete to choose appropriate training techniques and to detect and understand faults that may arise in their use. Joseph Hamill described the major categories of interest and research for the sport biomechanics as improvement of health and physical fitness, injury prevention, equipment design, and improvement of athletic performance.

In recent years, the number of girls and women participating in competitive sports, fitness activities, and recreational activities has grown rapidly and dramatically. Public demand for more information about new performance techniques and exercise regimens, accompanied by a willingness to spend money on scientifically designed running shoes, tennis rackets, exercise equipment, or health-promoting foods and diets, has brought even more support to sports research. Once con-

sidered the weaker sex, women are playing with speed, precision, explosiveness, and power.

Because of women's increased involvement in sports, the traditional reliance on the male body as a medical norm or yardstick of athletic performance is beginning to change. Biomechanical and physiological factors relative to women should be a primary concern for those who teach, coach, and participate in exercise and sport activities. Although much is said about the female athlete, very little research has addressed her performance. General concepts in biomechanics particularly relevant for women include many variables.

Center of Gravity

Perhaps the single most important concept in biomechanics is that of "equilibrium" or "stability," terms that are often used synonymously. "Equilibrium" is defined as that point around which the body freely rotates in any direction with all the opposing forces equal. "Stability," however, is defined as the resistance to the disruption of equilibrium. "Balance" is the ability to control movements. Many different factors affect stability and balance. For example, when the line of gravity is nearer to the base of support, the body is more stable. Because of a slightly wider pelvic girdle and narrower shoulders, women have a lower center of gravity than men and are, therefore, more stable. In balance-related activities, women have an advantage because of their lower center of gravity.

Overuse Injuries

Injuries that are a result of repetitive stress and/or microtrauma fall into a category of overuse injuries, which can occur because of both intrinsic and extrinsic factors. Intrinsic factors are those biomechanical aspects specific to each individual athlete and include bone structure, muscle imbalance and/or weakness, and lack of flexibility. Extrinsic factors are usually sport-specific, including faulty equipment, incorrect shoes, changes in running surfaces, and improper training. Overuse injuries usually begin as mild or moderate nagging soft-tissue injuries and advance into more severe problems if the person does not receive proper care. Some of the more common overuse injuries particular to women who exercise and participate in athletics are Achilles tendonitis, chondromalacia, illiotibial band syndrome, stress fractures, carpal tunnel syndrome, and plantar fascitis. Stress fractures are reported to be the most common type of injury for women in sports and occur most frequently with an increase in training. In addition, incidents of stress fractures are associated with girls or women who have very irregular or no menstrual cycles because of heavy exercise routines.

Pregnancy

Every pregnancy is unique, but all pregnant women have in common significant and multiple physiological and biomechanical changes that affect the body. Some of these changes start as early as conception, but most of the biomechanical adaptations occur during the third trimester. In particular, musculoskeletal changes occur as a result of the hormone relaxin. This causes a progressive relaxation of the joints, which include the ligaments that hold the sacroiliac joint and the symphysis pubis. Women often experience lower back pain as a result of an increase in lordosis (spinal curvature) and upper spine extension. These changes occur to accommodate for the enlarged abdomen as the fetus grows. To compensate for this exaggerated lumbar curve, the center of gravity shifts. The woman must, in essence, lean backward to maintain a sense of stability. During the third trimester, most women will need to modify some of their movement patterns. There is usually an outward rotation (toeing out) of the feet and almost a shuffle gait.

The Knee

The knee is the single largest and most vulnerable joint in the body. According to several studies, females athletes experience knee injuries at twice the rate of their male counterparts. This seems particularly true in such sports as basketball, soccer, and volleyball, all of which require constant pivoting. As with overuse injuries, the predisposition to a knee injury may fall under either intrinsic or extrinsic factors. Intrinsic factors include ligament size and intercondylar notch width, joint laxity, and the quadricep angle (Q-angle), which is the angle made by the tendons of the quadriceps femoris and the ligamentum patella with the center of the patella. Extrinsic factors include motor skill, level of conditioning, muscular strength and coordination, and individual mechanics. Knee injuries that are most common for women are patella femoral pain syndrome, chondromalacia (abnormal softening of cartilage), patella tendonitis, maniacal or cartilage injuries, and ligament injuries. In particular, there seem to be a disproportionate number of anterior cruciate ligament (ACL) injuries in women's athletics—these occur when anterior cruciate ligaments (providing stability to the knee, particularly forward/backward movement) are damaged. The greater incidence of ACL injuries stems from interrelated factors, including hamstring–quadriceps strength imbalances, wider Q-angle, and joint laxity. All these factors do not need to be present to cause the problem—ham–quad strength imbalances alone may add to joint instability.

PUBERTY AND SPORTS INJURIES IN GIRLS

Before puberty, girls and boys are quite similar in the muscular strength they exert in the same activities. But at puberty physiological differences develop which contribute to the types of injuries athletes experience. These differences include greater hamstring strength in males, a wider hip-to-knee ratio in females, longer legs and shorter torsos in females, and less muscle mass and lower bone density in females. In addition, after puberty males and females often use diffeent muscles for the same task, they walk, jump, and land differently. All of these and other differences lead medical experts to recommend that sports programs for girls and women be designed for females and not simply follow the male model.

KNEE INJURIES

Associated with the increased focus on fitness and sport program offerings for girls and women has been a significant increase in injuries. Each year the National Collegiate Athletic Association (NCAA) surveys member institutions regarding injuries and the data show that women gymnasts, soccer, and basketball players have a significantly greater number of knee injuries than their male counterparts. This is especially true of injuries to the anterior cruciate ligament (ACL). The ACL is a dynamic structure whose main function is to provide primary restraint to anterior tibial subluxation (joint moving beyond its maximum range). The majority of ACL injuries occur during non-contact movements such as planting and cutting, pivoting and suddenly decelerating, and straight knee landing. Although the exact reason for gender differences in injuries is not understood, some factors are conditioning, strength training, structure, and hormones. Anatomical differences, especially the quadriceps angle (Q angle), has been cited quite frequently as a cause for ACL tears. The Q angle is the angle formed from a line drawn from the middle of the patella to the anterior superior iliac spine and from the tibial tubercle to the center of the patella. This measure gives an indication of the alignment of the patellofemoral joint, or the amount of lateral pull on the patella. Differences in Q angle between men and women are attributed to a shorter femur and a wider pelvic girdle in women. Q angles exceeding 15 degrees in men and 20 degrees in women are generally considered abnormal. Although several researchers have attempted to show a relationship between increased Q angle and injury, there is no clear evidence for support. However, Q angle describes one aspect of lower limb design, and design of any machinery determines function and degree of performance. The question remains if this limits or enhances sport performance.

Another intrinsic factor attributed to women's knee injuries that is currently receiving attention is the effect of hormones on ligamentous tissue. Female athletes tend to have greater ligament laxity compared to their male counterparts. Relaxin is a hormone found in pregnant women which causes ligament relaxation. Under the influence of relaxin, the articulation between the joints widens and becomes more moveable. A number of variables may effect knee mechanics for women athletes, but more research is needed before knowing which variables are significantly important.

ATHLETIC EQUIPMENT DESIGN AND APPAREL

For many years now, women and girls participating in sports and fitness activities have had to use equipment designed for men by men. Recently, however, some companies have responded to the enormous numbers of women who are now physically active. Shoe companies, as well as sporting goods and athletic wear companies, are making functional design adaptations to meet the needs of the female consumer. In addition, more businesses owned and operated by women are making design changes for the woman athlete. Compared to men, the average woman is shorter and has longer legs, shorter arms, and a shorter torso. Women also have smaller hands and feet, narrower shoulders, and wider hips. Women have a higher percentage of body fat and less lean muscle mass.

There are also biomechanical differences that apply to athletic shoes for women. While most men's athletic shoes are designed on a standard athletic last or mold, many women's shoes are designed on a special mold. Lasts come in two shapes: a straight-lasted shoe is filled in under the medial arch, while the curved-lasted shoe is flared medially at the ball of the foot. Also, women's shoes usually have narrower heels. Although there are a number of sport-specific athletic shoe designs, biomechanical factors such as heel counters, midsoles, and lateral forefoot support are included in all designs.

In summary, biomechanical factors are critical in analyzing and improving the way women execute particular movement skills. Some factors may also cause an increased predisposition to specific injuries. Therefore, it is important to understand the principles of physics as they relate to care and prevention of injuries and to the enhancement of motor performance of individuals.

Ro DiBrezzo
Inza Fort

See also Athletic Training; Injury

Bibliography

Adrian, Marlene, and John Cooper. (1995) *Biomechanics of Human Movement,* 2d ed. Madison, WI: WCB Brown and Benchmark.

Hall, Susan. (1995) *Basic Biomechanics,* 2d ed. St. Louis, MO: Mosby-Year Book.

Hamill, Joseph, and Kathleen Knutzen. (1995) *Biomechanical Basis of Human Movement.* Baltimore: Williams and Wilkins.

Hatze, Harrel. (1974) "The Meaning of the Term 'Biomechanics.' " *Journal of Biomechanics* 7: 189.

Hay, James. (1993) *The Biomechanics of Sports Techniques,* 4th ed. Englewood Cliffs, NJ: Prentice Hall.

Wade, Michael, and John Baker. (1995) *Introduction of Kinesiology.* Madison, WI: WCB Brown and Benchmark.

BJÖRKSTÉN, ELLI

(1870–1947)

FINNISH EDUCATOR AND GYMNASTICS THEORIST

Elisabeth (Elli) Björkstén is the best-known female gymnastics teacher and theorist of the Nordic countries. Her major contribution was the development of a special gymnastic method for women.

She was born into a medical family and received a schooling appropriate for her social class. She completed the course for female gymnastics teachers in a private gymnastic institute in Helsinki (1889–1890), which, at the time, was the only institute educating female gymnastic teachers, followed by a degree at the Royal Gymnastic Central Institute in Stockholm, Sweden (1893–1895). From 1891 to 1913 she worked as a gymnastics teacher at a secondary school in Helsinki. From 1913 to 1938 she worked at the Gymnastic Institute of the University of Helsinki, first as a gymnastics teacher and later as the senior teacher of pedagogical gymnastics. In 1902 and 1910 she made journeys to Germany, Switzerland, France, and Italy, where she came to know some of the most prominent gymnastics and dance schools of the time, such as the Jaques-Dalcroze Institute.

Björkstén found her calling when she joined the Women's Gymnastics Association in Helsinki and became deeply inspired by its leader, Elin Kallio. While training and teaching with this group and at the university, Björkstén was able to develop and examine her method. Between 1906 and 1914 she made several visits to other Nordic countries to present her new gymnastics system. Her international breakthrough came in 1912, when she led her elite group of twelve young women in gray Greek-style gymnastic suits in a demonstration performance at the Olympic Games in Stockholm.

In 1917 Björkstén became the chairperson of the Swedish-language women's gymnastics organization of Finland. In 1922 she was a cofounder of the Nordic Women's Gymnastics Association, and she served as its president until 1938. In these years she also led the association's famous summer courses, attended by many teachers from both inside and outside the Nordic countries.

Elli Björkstén disseminated her method by writing articles, giving lectures, and coauthoring a girls' gymnastics book in 1911. She put her system into its final formulation in her method book, *Kvinnogymnastik I-II* (1918, 1924), which was later translated into six other languages (in English: *Principles of Gymnastics for Girls and Women*). In the 1920s and 1930s she was invited to many European countries to demonstrate her system.

Björkstén reformed the Swedish gymnastic system in favor of women. She abandoned the rigidity and military impression so typical of men's gymnastics and created a freer and more lively form, designed for women's special psychology and physiology. The movements were to be flexible and fluent: Björkstén stressed the grace arising from a fully harmonious movement, from a mental and physical balance, and from an interaction of the mind and body. She developed a rhythmic way of commanding. According to her, women reflected their emotional states in their movements; therefore, the movements were developed specifically for women. She maintained that it was important to build up physical strength only to the extent that was required for a faultless performance. Björkstén never approved of women's participation in competitive sports.

Leena Laine

Bibliography

Björkstén, Elli. (1932) *Principles of Gymnastics for Girls and Women, Part I*, translated from the second Swedish edition by Agnes Dawson and E. M. Wilkie. London: J. & A. Churchill.

————. (1934) *Principles of Gymnastics for Girls and Women, Part II*, translated from the second Swedish edition by S. Kreuger and J. H. Wicksteed. London: J. & A. Churchill.

Laine, Leena. (1989) "In Search of Physical Culture for Women: Elli Björkstén and Women's Gymnastics." *Scandinavian Journal of Sports Sciences* 11, 1: 15–20.

Lewis, Madalynne S. (1970) "A Philosophy of Finnish Women's Physical Education as Represented in Selected Writings of Elin Kallio, Elli Björkstén and Hilma Jalkanen." Unpublished doctoral dissertation, University of Southern California.

Wichmann, Gertrud (1965). *Elli Björkstén*. Helsinki: Nordiskt Förbund för Kvinnogymnastik and Finlands Svenska Gymnastikförbund.

Bonnie Blair celebrating her gold medal victory in the 1992 Olympics in Albertville, France. (AP/Wide World Photos)

BLAIR, BONNIE

(1964–)

U.S. SPEED SKATER

Bonnie Blair's five gold medals and one bronze in the three consecutive Winter Olympics from 1988 to 1994 made her America's most successful female winter sports athlete. Blair was born in Champaign, Illinois, on 18 March 1962, the youngest of six children. All her brothers and sisters were avid skaters, and Blair joined the family trips to various American cities where they could race. She began skating at age two and consistently won her races as a small child.

Until she was sixteen, Blair competed in pack-style races, more commonly known as short-track speed skating. In December 1979, she was per-suaded to try the long track, which at that time was the only recognized form of speed skating at the Olympic level. Despite having to skate last in the U.S. Olympic trials (when the ice is softer and slower), with no head-to-head competition (her partner had scratched), she qualified for the 1980 Olympics in Lake Placid.

Blair's first Olympic success came eight years later in Calgary, where she captured gold and a world record in the 500-meter race, as well as a bronze in the 1000-meter. She was also fourth in the 1500-meter. In the Albertville Olympics in 1992, Blair took gold in both of the sprint events. She repeated this feat in Lillehammer at the 1994 Olympics. She also won the World Sprint Championships in 1989, 1994, and 1995 and held the world record in the 500-meter four times. Blair's fame and success promoted speed skating as a sport throughout the United States and increased its popularity. A sign of her celebrity status was that she was the only female speed skater ever to grace the cover of *Sports Illustrated.* Blair retired from competitive racing after the World Sprint Championships in 1995 but remained active in the sport by coaching, conducting clinics, and encouraging others to participate.

J. P. Anderson

Bibliography

Brownlee, Shannon. (1988) "Yanks on the Move." *Sports Illustrated* (27 January): 236–244.

Chronicle of the Olympics. (1998) London: Dorling Kindersley.

Looney, Douglas S. (1989) "Bring Back Bonnie." *Sports Illustrated* (6 March): 32–33.

Reilly, Rick. (1988) "The Mettle to Medal." *Sports Illustrated* (7 March): 50–57.

Wallechinsky, David. (1992) *The Complete Book of the Olympics.* London: Aurum Press.

BLANKERS-KOEN, FANNY

(1918–)

DUTCH TRACK AND FIELD ATHLETE

The Dutch track and field phenomenon Francina "Fanny" Blankers-Koen was described in 1956 by an Olympic historian as the most famous woman in the history of female athletics. Known as "the Flying Housewife," she won her Olympic gold medals and world championships while conducting a busy domestic life.

Fanny Koen was born in Amsterdam in 1918. As an eighteen-year-old, she competed in the 1936 Berlin Olympics, where she tied for sixth place in the high jump. She also ran on the Netherlands' fifth-place 4 × 100-meter relay team. Four years later, she married her coach, Jan Blankers. During World War II, she set world records in the 80-meter hurdles (1942), the high jump (1943), and the long jump (1943). The high-jump record was set a scant two months after the birth of her first child.

Fanny Blankers-Koen running away from the field in the 80-meter hurdles at the 1948 London Olympics. (Bettmann/Corbis)

A month before the 1948 Olympics, she tied the world record for 100 meters (11.5 seconds) and lowered her own world record for the 80-meter hurdles to 11.0 seconds. Over the protests of her husband, she went to London's Wembley Stadium to compete in the first postwar Olympics. She won gold medals in the 100-meter and 200-meter sprints and in the 80-meter hurdles. She ran the anchor leg of the 4 × 100-meter relay and overtook Australia's Joyce King to earn a fourth gold medal. She was unquestionably the most impressive woman at the games. Had Olympic rules not limited her to three individual events, she might have won the high jump and the long jump as well. In neither event did the Olympic victor reach Blankers-Koen's 1943 marks.

At the time of this extraordinary performance, she was in the early months of her third pregnancy. The expectant mother was given a heroine's welcome when she returned home. She received her accolades while riding through Amsterdam in a carriage pulled by four white horses. A new variety of rose was named for her, and a statue was erected in her honor. She is said to have marveled modestly at her fame, "All I did was win some foot races."

Two years later, at the European championships in Brussels, she repeated her victories in the 100-meter and 200-meter sprints and in the 80-meter hurdles. In Helsinki in 1952, she participated in her third Olympics, but with less success. In the final of the 80-meter hurdles, her foot struck the hurdles and she stumbled and dropped out of the race. She continued to compete in the Netherlands, however, and had accumulated fifty-five Dutch titles by the time she finally retired in 1955.

Avery Brundage, president of the International Olympic Committee from 1952 to 1972, is considered by many to have been an opponent of women's sports, but he was dazzled by Blankers-Koen's 1948 performance. Describing her in his unpublished autobiography, he was uncharacteristically lyrical: "A new type of woman [was] appearing—lithe, supple, physically disciplined, strong, slender and efficient, like the Goddesses of ancient Greece" (Guttmann 1992, 82). Others present at the 1948 Olympics were more ambivalent about women who excelled in "unfeminine" endeavors. The London *Daily Graphic* reassured its readers that all was well: "Fastest Woman in the World is an Expert Cook" (Guttmann 1991, 200).

She, too, may have had moments of ambivalence. Her nickname, "the Flying Housewife," was derived from the answer she gave when asked why she had nearly missed the starting time for the Olympic 4 ×100-meter relay race. She replied that she had been shopping for bath towels: "I am, after all, a Dutch housewife."

Allen Guttmann

Bibliography

Guttmann, Allen. (1991) *Women's Sports.* New York: Columbia University Press.

———. (1992) *The Olympics.* Urbana: University of Illinois Press.

Lawson, Gerald. (1997) *World Record Breakers in Track and Field Athletics.* Champaign, IL: Human Kinetics.

Mezö, Ferenc. (1956) *Les Jeux Olympiques Modernes.* Budapest: Pannonia.

BOATING, ICE

Ice boating is practiced with one of three types of sail to propel a craft across snow or ice, using only the wind for power. Women began participating only when it became a form of recreation, rather than transport. Today they are involved at all levels, although most serve as crew members, not captains.

HISTORY

Some literature suggests that ice boats constructed from bones were used around 4,000 years ago. Contemporary versions of ice boating began around the seventeenth century in the Netherlands, where such boats were used to transport goods over ice. As was typical of the time, women had little involvement with the captaining of such vehicles. Ice boating spread to the United States around the mid-1800s, where it was enjoyed as a sport for wealthy sailors, and it still has a tremendous following in North America. At the end of the 1990s, ice boating was one of the fastest-growing sports in Northern Europe and the former Soviet Union.

RULES AND PLAY

Basic ice and snow sailing rigs fall into three classes: ice surfers (mono- or multi-ski with windsurfing sail), skimbats (hand-held foils that resemble hang gliders—cloth mounted on metal tubing), and kites (the boat is pulled along by a large kite controlled by a hand-held pressure bar). Restricted to ice-covered lakes, the sport is most popular within the Ice Belt, an area approximately 150 (241 kilometers) miles wide, circling the globe near the forty-fifth parallel.

There are various classes of ice boating. One of the earliest competition boats was the Skeeter, a lightweight front-steering boat capable of high speeds, the first of which was built in the early 1930s. However, the most popular ice boats is the DN (Detroit News) class, named after the newspaper that invested in the design of the first DN boat back in 1936. The DN rider is cradled by the boat and lies on her back, steering with a tiller held between the knees. Ice boating is the fastest way to sail, with the top speeds as of 1999 exceeding 150 miles (241 kilometers) per hour.

WOMEN IN COMPETITION IN THE 1990s

Female participation is low, which is somewhat surprising because ice boating is a sport in which both sexes can compete on equal terms. Although no competitions are organized strictly for women, they are able to participate freely in a sport that is dominated by men. The organization of the sport tends to consist of crews, of which only one member can be the helmsperson. While most crews seem to have a man at the helm, the involvement of women as part of the crew is significant. One longtime female competitor and helmsperson is Jane Pegel, who began DN-class competition in 1956. Pegel had a successful career in the sport; she won the North American DN-class championship twice and was ranked very high in the competition on numerous occasions. Pegel was still participating in this high-velocity sport at age sixty-five, racing mainly in conditions when a keen sense of sailing is more important than its physical requirements.

Andy Miah

Gunnar Johnston and her braker at the 1927 Spetzli Boblet Challenge. (Hulton-Deutsch Collection/Corbis)

Bibliography

Andresen, J. (1974) *Sailing on Ice.* London: Yoseloff.

Bladerunner Ice Boat Company. "Bladerunner." <http://www.iceboats.com>. 1999.

Robberson, K. (1988) "The Thrill of Sailing on Ice." *Women's Sports and Fitness* (January): 82.

Zacharias, Pat. "Rearview Mirror: Sailing on Lake St. Clair's Icy Winter Winds." <http://www.detnews.com/history/>. n.d.

BOBSLEDDING

Bobsledding is a competitive sport in which participants guide a fast-moving sled as it shoots down an icy track created for that purpose. In its early days, it was a model of emancipation, with women competing as equals alongside men. This changed in the 1920s and 1930s, when women were systematically shut out. At the beginning of the twenty-first century, bobsled, one of the most exciting and popular of winter sports, still excludes women from the Olympic Games.

HISTORY

The sport of bobsled emerged in nineteenth-century Switzerland. According to the standard version, it was invented in the 1870s by vacationing English tourists at St. Moritz in the Swiss Alps. The aim of the first sleds was to carry two or more people as quickly as possible down a snow-covered road between St. Moritz and Celerina. The new sport grew quickly in popularity, and the first identifiable modern bobsled appeared in 1886. It was made by Wilson Smith, an Englishman, with the help of Christian Mathias, a St. Moritz blacksmith. The sport caught on so quickly that the first run designed specifically for bobsledding was built in 1903 in St. Moritz.

The first formally organized races were for bobsleds carrying five or six people. The early informal rules required all competing sleds to contain at least one woman team member. In 1897, the St. Moritz Bobsled Club was founded and codified that provision. At that time, the number of people on a bobsled varied from race to race. Unlike now, when women race only in two-person bobsleds, in the late nineteenth and early twentieth century they took part in a wide selection of bobsled combinations. The rules of the St. Moritz club, which

WOMEN'S BOBSLED AND THE RAF

To run a bobsled team is hugely expensive; without substantial sustained investment, it is impossible to keep a team going. Women's bobsled in the 1980s had difficulties in attracting funding or competitors because there were no international events in the sport. The successful advent of organized women's competitions in the 1990s was in large part due to efforts by the British Royal Air Force (RAF).

The RAF has always been a key player in British men's bobsled and has always had close links with the British Bobsleigh Association, the national federation of the FIBT. With so much of the RAF based in Germany and elsewhere in Europe, members of the armed services have always had easy access to bobsled runs. Building on this accessibility, and using bobsled as a way of encouraging physical fitness, team spirit, and elite sport, the RAF has always been keen to encourage its service people to take part in the sport.

In the 1980s the RAF encouraged its service women to participate in bobsledding and began building an active team. By the late 1990s, the Great Britain women's team routinely traveled around the world with the RAF men's team. It included driver Michelle Coy, a technical supply specialist at ARF Bruggen, and braker Cheryl Done, a physical training instructor at RAF Wittering. The RAF was one of the prime movers behind the organization of the Women's Bobsled World Cup, playing a key role in convincing the FIBT to recognize the sport. It has also campaigned relentlessly for the inclusion of women's bobsled at the Olympics.

---

became standard for the sport, stipulated at least one woman on a three-person bobsled or two women on a five-person team. The high profile and formalized role of women in the sport's first thirty years reflected its social status as a winter pastime that was exclusive to the leisured class. As with early lawn tennis, bobsled was considered to be an acceptable and respectable sport for women. It required virtually no training or application, only social connection and wealth.

RULES AND PLAY

In women's races, bobsled teams consist of two people: a brake and a pilot. Their aim is to drive their bobsled down a 1600-meter (1750-yard) course as quickly as possible. The course is built of compacted ice and includes a series of steep turns to be navigated. At the start of the track the bobsledders push their sled for 50 meters (55 yards) to build up as much speed as possible. After this initial sprint, the brake and driver must get into the sled as it moves down the track. On the descent, the bobsled reaches speeds approaching 130 kilometers (80.6 miles) per hour. The time is taken at the bottom of the run, and the team with the lowest aggregate time from four separate runs over two days is the winner.

WOMEN'S PARTICIPATION

Although women competed in its earliest days, they were completely excluded from bobsled by the 1930s. This reflected its change from a pastime of the idle-rich to a professional sport, formalized with the founding of the Fédération Internationale de Bobsleigh et de Tobogganing (FIBT) in 1923, which was instrumental in having bobsled accepted as a sport for the first Winter Olympics in the following year.

Prior to the inauguration of the Games at Chamonix, FIBT banned women from competing in bobsled. No longer just an enjoyable winter sport for both genders, bobsled was viewed as an elite sport for men that was too dangerous for women. After Chamonix, women were slowly but surely excluded from all European bobsled events, although they continued, for a time, to compete in the less socially exclusive atmosphere of North America. However, in 1938, after Katherine Dewey had driven her way to victory in the U.S. national championships, they were banned from subsequent bobsled championships by the U.S. Amateur Athletic

Union (AAU). In AAU's view, Dewey's win was improper: bobsled was "a man's sport."

For nearly sixty years, women were excluded from organized bobsled racing, denied recognition by FIBT and the Olympic Games' organizers. They only began competing again on an organized basis in bobsled events during the 1990s. In 1995 women's bobsled was finally recognized by the FIBT, which, with the support of different national bodies, began to campaign for women's bobsled to be included in the Winter Olympics. On 2 October 1999, the International Olympic Committee announced that women's bobsledding had been accepted as an Olympic sport for the 2002 Winter Olympics in Salt Lake City, Utah.

THE COST OF PARTICIPATION

In the 1995–1996 and 1996–1997 seasons, sixteen crews from ten different nations took part in the FIBT six-race World Cup series. The races are held at venues across North America and Europe. The 1997–1998 season extended the series to ten races at five venues: Calgary, Canada; Salt Lake City, United States; Igls, Austria; La Plange, France; and Winterberg, Germany.

Bobsledding is expensive. Without the lure of Olympic competition, it has been difficult for many aspiring women's teams to gain the necessary sponsorship to get a bobsled up and running. The bobsled itself costs nearly $30,000 and must be replaced annually to compete at the elite level. To take part in major events, teams must practice on a quality track, of which, in 1999, only twenty-two were FIBT-recognized. To practice costs a team $8,000 or more each year in addition to travel costs. Transportation of bobsleds and their teams throughout Europe and North America requires an annual budget of $15,000 or more. Clothing, including race suits, helmets, and the necessary specialized running shoes, amounts to $1,500 for each team member. The combination of the high cost of bobsledding and the discrimination that has kept women bobsledders out of the Olympics has resulted in a sport with few women competitors that survive only through the intervention of state bodies. In Britain, for example, the women's bobsled team is run under the auspices of the Royal Air Force and has charitable status. The women on the team are all serving members of the Air Force, without whose help

and organization the team would probably not survive.

CONCLUSION

In many ways, the history of women's bobsled has turned full circle. It began as a winter pastime of the social elite. Within such an elite, women were allowed to take part; indeed, they were encouraged. Once bobsled was caught up in the machinery of modern sporting organization, women were, as was so often the case across all sports, excluded. The late 1990s saw the reintroduction of organized women's bobsled, but the prohibitive costs make it once more socially exclusive or charity-dependent. Although it is an immensely popular television spectacle during the Winter Olympics, bobsled is most unlikely to become a mass-participation sport. Within such a rarefied and elite context, women will have to continue the fight for equal rights of competition. It is hoped that the first Winter Olympiads of the twenty-first century will make it possible for women bobsledders to compete equally with men, as they did in the late nineteenth century.

Mike Cronin

Bibliography

"Bobsleigh and Olympism." (1984) *Olympic Review* 206 (December): 1003–1030.

Kotter, K. (1984) "Le bobsleigh et la fédération internationale de bobsleigh et de toboganning." *Message-Olympique* (June): 59–66.

Mallon, Bill. (1992) "On Two Blades and a Few Prayers." *Olympian* 18, 6: 54–55.

O'Brien, A., and M. O'Bryan, (1976) *Bobsled and Luge.* Canada: Colban.

Wallenchinsky, David. (1998) *The Complete Book of the Winter Olympics.* New York: Overlook Press.

BODYBUILDING

Bodybuilding is defined as exercising with weights to reshape the physique by adding muscle mass and by separating and defining the various muscle groups. Whether practiced by men or women, bodybuilding is a performance sport. Women bodybuilders display their physiques on stage in a series of mandatory poses and carry out a routine of poses choreographed to music. Modern bodybuilding competitions for women began in 1975 as a derivative of men's bodybuilding. (The first contest for men was in 1901.) The physique exhibitions of the music halls of an earlier era, however, are part of the ancestry of competitive women's bodybuilding.

HISTORY

Health reform in the mid-nineteenth century combined with early feminism to promote the novel idea that exercise was healthy for women and that women's muscles could be beautiful. This was contrary to the dominant white middle-class notion of femininity as fragile and ethereal, the embodiment of which was enhanced by the custom of tightly laced corsets that continued through the turn of the century. Health reform and feminism made some inroads, but women remained hesitant to exercise for fear of losing their "natural" curves (created by tight lacing) and developing muscular bodies. Then, in the late nineteenth century and early twentieth century, beauty standards evolved to include the athletic aesthetic of the "Gibson Girl."

In the late 1800s, strongmen and muscular display provided the roots for the physical culture movement that branched out into various sports. This variety notwithstanding, the movement maintained some continuity through the late 1930s, when men's physique contests started to become their own distinctive form of athletic contest.

It was in this milieu in the first part of the twentieth century that Eugene Sandow, well established in a successful career as a Prussian strongman and entrepreneur, began to try to bring women into his physical culture enterprises. Sandow challenged prevailing views of the passive and frail woman, and he was extremely critical of corsets. He promoted the idea of a femininity that included strength and exercise for all women in order to bring them good health and cure illness. Similarly, Bernarr MacFadden, an American who also promoted men's physical culture, saw an opportunity to include women in his enterprises. In 1889 MacFadden began to publish the periodical *Physical Culture* in the United States, and his second issue contained his first articles on women's health and exercise.

MacFadden was a strong advocate of the benefits of exercise for women. He founded the first women's magazine, *Women's Physical Development,* in 1900, and changed the name in 1903 to *Beauty and Health: Women's Physical Development.* In addition, MacFadden may have been the first to sponsor a women's physique competition, a precursor of modern women's bodybuilding competitions: from 1903 to 1905 he held local and regional physique competitions that finished with a grand competition, in which the "best and most perfectly formed woman" won a prize.

MacFadden fell prey to his own success. His cultivation of women's physique competitions inadvertently stopped the sport until the 1970s. In 1905, shortly before his Madison Square Garden Mammoth Physical Culture Exhibition, which included the finale of the women's competition, MacFadden's office was raided by Anthony Comstock of the Society for the Suppression of Vice. Comstock accused MacFadden of pandering pornography. Included among the alleged pornographic materials that Comstock acquired in his raid were posters of the finalists of the women's physique competition, who were dressed in white, form-fitting, leotard-like exercise wear.

Publicity about MacFadden's subsequent arrest and the court ruling that he was indeed dealing in pornography was an advertisement that attracted even more spectators. The Mammoth Physical Culture Exhibition had an audience of 20,000 and turned away 5,000 more. That was, however, the end of his enterprise. MacFadden stopped publishing materials and promoting women's physiques just at the time when he was starting to have an effect on women's physique development. This seriously impeded the development of women's participation in physical culture exhibitions and competitions.

Music halls and circuses of the late nineteenth century and early twentieth century were also venues for displays of women's physiques, although their strength was displayed along with their development. One muscular diva was Sandwina, who performed with the Barnum and Bailey Circus in 1910. Standing 6 feet 1 inch tall and weighing 209 pounds, she could jerk 280 pounds over her head and was able to carry her husband over her head using one arm. Although Vulcana (Katie Roberts) performed through the 1940s, no real audience for strongwomen developed until the final two decades of the nineteenth century and first two of the twentieth century. Although women's strength performances embodied some elements of modern bodybuilding in that their well-developed physiques were part of their acts, the related weight-training sports of Olympic Weightlifting and Powerlifting may just as easily claim them as antecedents. Women's bodybuilding may be contrasted with various resistance training approaches whose goal is not to develop larger muscles, but to tone the muscles and enhance bone density.

BODYBUILDING AS A SUBCULTURE

Women bodybuilders differ from women who do resistance training by the subcultural context of their experience, which includes competition as the salient and self-identifying feature. In the majority of cases, women who identify themselves as bodybuilders are active competitors, have aspirations to compete, or have competed in the past. Robert Duff and Lawrence Hong, in a study of 205 women bodybuilders registered with the International Federation of Bodybuilders (one of several bodybuilding organizations), found that 74 percent were active competitors, while many of the others were either anticipating their first competition or were temporarily sidelined due to injury.

Women's bodybuilding as a performance sport is derived from men's bodybuilding, although it started much later, in 1975. Bodybuilding competitions for men and women may look fairly similar in format, but the process, the competition, and the milieu represent different things culturally in Western society. Men's bodybuilding is a sport that reproduces and amplifies Western beliefs about the differences between men and women. Muscles signify masculinity in Western culture, and they testify that these differences are primarily based on biology.

Women's bodybuilding represents a different cultural agenda. The female bodybuilder is in a position to do just the opposite—to challenge these views that place biology at the center of male–female differences, that in fact reduce these differences to biology. The woman competitor's body is a statement of rebellion against this view, a way of contributing to the wider redefinition of womanhood and femininity underway in society. This redefinition challenges this facing-off of men

Kay Wick of South Carolina trains for a bodybuilding contest. (Bettmann/Corbis)

against women, in which muscularity embodies power and privilege as the natural purview of men and hence masculinity. Women bodybuilders challenge the Western view of women as the weaker sex; instead they live and embody a femininity that includes strength and muscularity.

Two major influences in the development of women's bodybuilding were the reintroduction of resistance training for women athletes in the 1950s and the feminist movement of the 1960s. Resistance training for women in general gained a large following in the 1970s, as the fitness industry exploded. Health clubs and spas enticed women by offering aerobics classes, selling fashionable athletic attire, and providing color-coordinated locker rooms with amenities such as blow dryers and curling irons. These gyms became part of the history of bodybuilding as the sport moved into the scientific and contemporary pavilions of nutrition and training. By the 1980s, women bodybuilders preferred the hard-core gyms where men trained.

As Tom Platz, Mr. Universe 1978, reminisces, "Prior to 1983, the gym was a man's sanctuary . . . [t]here was also just a handful of girls who trained in those days." Today lifting weights and doing resistance training are integral to the modern fitness industry for women.

DEVELOPMENT OF COMPETITIONS

Since its inception in the late 1970s, the sport of women's bodybuilding has been transformed from one in which the competitors wore high heels and rarely performed muscular poses, such as a front double biceps, which were discouraged anyway. These bodybuilding contests were accused of being nothing more than beauty pageants. The seeds of early women's bodybuilding lie in the occasional beauty body contest held during men's bodybuilding events. For example, a Ms. Body Beautiful competition was held during the 1973 World Bodybuilding Guild Mr. America Championships, and a Miss America competition was held during the Mr. Olympia contest at the Brooklyn Academy of Music. It was not until the 1980s that women's bodybuilding contests were legitimized as competitions in their own right, not just as auxiliaries for male competitions. The first Miss (now Ms.) Olympia contest was held in 1980 and set the standard for women's international and professional titles that continues today.

Through the 1980s and 1990s bodybuilding continued to grow as a big business. The women competitors have, over time, achieved degrees of muscularity, symmetry, and definition believed impossible for women. Nevertheless, since its beginnings, women bodybuilders have debated the issue of muscularity versus femininity.

ORGANIZATIONS

The organizations for women's competitive bodybuilding are entrenched in men's bodybuilding organizations. The various organizations have women's representatives within them to deal with specific issues of interest to women at the local and national levels. No separate women's organizations exist, although in the early 1980s, Doris Barrilleaux founded and was president of the now-defunct American Federation of Women Bodybuilders. Barrilleaux may be credited as the parent of women's bodybuilding. At the age of forty-seven she began competing in what purported to be women's physique contests but were in reality beauty pageants. Her dislike of these contests and her vision of women's bodybuilding, which featured muscular development, led her to establish the Superior Physique Association and to begin publishing the *SPA News*, a newsletter for women bodybuilders, in 1979. As Barrilleaux continued her involvement in women's bodybuilding, she brought to the sport her excellent skills as a physique photographer, her history as a competitor and organizer, and also her concern for natural drug-free bodybuilding. As early as 1983, Barrilleaux lobbied the International Federation of Bodybuilders to test the women competitors for illicit performance-enhancing drugs.

Bodybuilding is organized formally at both the amateur and professional levels through a number of associations, each with a bureaucracy, bylaws, agendas, membership fees, contests, and promotions, as well as personnel consisting of judges, promoters, competitors, and fans. Prominent among these are International Federation of Bodybuilders (IFBB) and the National Physique Committee (NPC), founded by Ben and Joe Weider. The Amateur Athletic Union (AAU) was involved early on in bodybuilding, holding its first Mr. America contest in 1939 (running as the Mr. and Mrs. America contests as of 1999).

The 1990s also brought the establishment of organizations targeted to drug-free athletes, as well as the promotion of drug-free shows by existing organizations, such as the AAU, NPC (amateur), and IFBB (international and professional), from the local to the international level. Organizations that test for illicit drugs typically use lie detector tests as well as urinalysis to disqualify users of a variety of banned substances, including steroids, growth hormone, insulin, diuretics, and other prescription drugs. The burgeoning of drug-testing organizations since the late 1980s has occurred in part because the public has become more aware of anabolic steroid use among athletes in general. Drug-testing organizations include, among others, the AAU; the World Natural

Bodybuilding Federation (WNBF), which sponsors professional and some amateur bodybuilding; and the National Gym Association (NGA), a WNBF-affiliated amateur organization. The NPC also offers some competitions that require drug tests.

The drug-testing organizations and competitions are international in scope. The WNBF, for example, includes a number of country affiliates. Although bodybuilding is not yet an Olympic event, the World Games of Bodybuilding (sponsored by the IFBB), inaugurated in 1981 and held every four years, is an Olympics of bodybuilding. All competitors are tested for drugs in their home countries and in the host country of the competition. The 1997 World Games of Bodybuilding were held in Lahti, Finland, with thirty-eight competitors from seventeen countries.

MUSCULARITY/FEMININITY DEBATE

The debate over masculinity and femininity continues in women's bodybuilding. The basic question is: How muscular can a woman be and still be feminine? From the beginning of women's bodybuilding in the late 1970s, the women athletes were confronted with this dilemma. They wanted to be taken seriously as athletes, and despite their muscularity, they wanted to maintain their femininity. Because muscles stand for masculinity, women involved in bodybuilding have warded off the dreaded threat of being called unfeminine by attempting to redefine notions of femininity to include strength and muscularity. In 1979, after winning the first major women's bodybuilding competition, Lisa Lyon stated, "Women can be strong, muscular, and at the same time feminine." And women bodybuilders today still echo this concern. Kim Chizevsky, the 1998 Ms. Olympia, declared that "people need to start changing their views about women bodybuilders. We're strong muscular women, but we're beautiful feminine women too."

Although the debate over femininity and muscularity was inflamed by anabolic steroid use among women competitors, this debate actually existed prior to the reported use of steroids by competitors. Time has shown that virtually any activity that threatens gender norms will call into question the gender authenticity of its participants. This debate surfaced in the infancy of women's bodybuilding, when Gloria Miller Fudge kicked off her high heels. It arose again when Cammie Lusko, in the 1980 Miss Olympia, presented a hard-core muscular routine, using poses associated with men's bodybuilding and displaying her muscularity: she drove the audience wild but didn't even place in the competition.

That women bodybuilders at elite levels have been becoming more muscular has been attributed to the increasing use of anabolic steroid. In the early days, however, although women did not commonly use steroids, the debate over muscles and femininity was already under way. For example, Charles Gaines and George Butler, in discussing Cammie Lusko and Auby Paulick in the 1980 Miss Olympia, stated: "They tensed for all they were worth, clenching their fists and showing . . . real female muscle—not just curvy humps of hard flesh, but rippled, delineated, vein-splayed muscle, in their thighs, their shoulders, their stomachs, and their chests, all historically soft and comforting areas of a woman," (1974).

Between 1980 and 1989, the sport of bodybuilding as epitomized in the Ms. Olympia contest deferred to society's view of femininity. The judges selected athletic, slim, and graceful women, such as Rachel McLish and Cory Everson, as opposed to the more muscular competitors such as Bev Francis. The debate over the direction the sport would take was resolved with the retirement from competition of Cory Everson in 1989. Everson, six-time Ms. Olympia champion, was not known for having a great deal of muscle mass but was said to embody the perfect combination of symmetry, muscularity, and femininity.

In 1990 Lenda Murray won the Ms. Olympia over Bev Francis, known as a woman whose muscle mass had been way ahead of its time. Francis, who had the year before trimmed her physique down to be competitive with Everson, lost to the heavily muscled Murray because she was not muscular enough. The following year Francis muscled up again but again came in second to Murray, this time because the judges felt she was too muscular. Francis subsequently retired, and the 1992 Olympia became the stage on which the debate was resolved in favor of muscularity. Lenda Murray won yet again and remained undefeated until the even more muscular but also ultra-ripped (lean) and hard Kim Chizevsky claimed the title in 1996 and continued to hold it through 1998.

This trend for increasing muscle mass is illustrated in the increasing body weights of the competitors; in 1983 the average weight of the Ms. Olympia contenders was 121 pounds, while in 1997 it was 155 pounds.

Although steroids do play a role in enhanced muscularity, other factors have accelerated progress, in both men and women: the competitors have been training over a longer period of time, their muscles have matured, and the sport has enjoyed an explosion in scientific research on training techniques and nutrition.

Also caught in the muscularity/femininity debate are judging standards, known in the bodybuilding community to be unstable: even as the emphasis on muscularity seemed to be predominant, the woman bodybuilder was often required to maintain a seemingly ineffable quality of femininity that was never defined or clearly articulated in the judging criteria. In different years and at different professional contests (which often set the standards for the amateur competitions), judges might sometimes emphasize muscularity over symmetry (which is often equated with femininity in the debates) and at other times the reverse. Yet, over time, the women continue to push the limits of muscularity.

BODYBUILDING AND THE WESTERN VIEW OF GENDER

Women's bodybuilding as a sport rebels against traditional notions of femininity by going against the belief that femininity equals weakness. Women bodybuilders pursue the male imperative to lift weights, become strong, and display their strength through their dense muscularity. In doing so, they are contributing to a broader, ongoing redefinition of femininity and womanhood. Bodybuilding as a sport symbolically sustains traditional images of masculinity as associated with strength and power, embodied in the ideal of the male bodybuilder. Images of this body type signify youth, health, sexual virility, and power. Arnold Schwarzenegger illustrated this in his dialogue in the movie *Pumping Iron*, where he directly links pumping up the muscles to male sexual arousal and orgasm. Competitive women's bodybuilding blurs gender differences. This oc-

curs not only through the muscularity of the competitive women bodybuilder but also in the subculture of bodybuilding itself, where gender is enacted in the gym. In these less public spheres, serious athletes are serious athletes regardless of gender.

RULES AND PLAY

Women are judged by the same criteria as men, although femininity does become an issue in the judging process. Judges rely on three primary criteria. These include the depth and development of muscularity; symmetry, or the proportions of the body parts/muscle groups in relation to one another (for example, shoulder width and muscularity in relationship to waist and thighs); and definition, generally defined as the degree of visibility of muscle striations, leanness, and general hardness of the body. Related to this is the visibility of veins and the thinness or transparency of the skin, called vascularity.

The bodybuilder strives to achieve muscular size and density as well as make her body more symmetrical through development of various muscle groups. To do so, she follows a rigorous training plan and a strategy for continual improvement. Competitors' preparation for contests includes disciplined dieting and attention to nutrition, posing practice, and the preparation of a choreographed posing routine.

In the subculture of bodybuilding, muscular development and definition are not regarded as qualities that belong exclusively to men or women. The difference between the two genders is one of degree, not kind. Thus, bodybuilders do not consider muscles a physical symbol of masculinity, but rather a generic quality available to humans. This goes against society's notions of biological characteristics. Despite bodybuilding's history as a bastion of masculinity, in the hard-core gyms gender is not the most important factor. Being serious and training hard are the badges of those who are members of the subculture.

At the local, state, and national levels, competitions consist of two segments. In the morning portion, the majority of the judging decisions are made. The judges rank the competitors in each class, and the winners of each class are decided. Usually placements are from first to fifth. The overall winners are selected in evening shows (bodybuilding contests are also referred to as shows because of their performance aspect) as the winner of each class competes for the overall title. The trophies are given during the evening show. National and international competitions, both professional and amateur, may have different agendas. For example, professionals in the IFBB are typically judged in three rounds based on symmetry, muscularity, and posing ability as displayed in the choreographed posing routine. The latter is not usually a factor in the amateur contests, although it is significant in posing competitions for couples.

Competitors are usually placed in weight categories, although some organizations, such as the AAU, also include height categories. Master's categories for women (and men) are also included at various shows. The age requirements vary among organizations; some begin the master's category at age thirty and others at thirty-five years of age. The general trend has been for the competitions to offer more age categories for master's men than for women, with some competitions offering master's categories only only for men. Some organizations and promoters have recently begun to offer more age categories for women at the local and regional levels. Several organizations, among them the NPC and the AAU, have national master's competitions. At the international level, the IFBB's Mr. Olympia contest includes the men's master's Olympia, although the Ms. Olympia does not have a women's master's Olympia.

Since 1994, with the increasing popularity of Ms. Fitness competitions (a competition that combines elements of beauty pageants with those of an aerobics competition), various bodybuilding writers have pronounced the death knell of bodybuilding. Marion Roach, in a 1998 *New York Times* article, wrote, "Fitness competition, a slenderized version of women's bodybuilding, has eclipsed some of the bulked up muscle shows in participant and audience popularity," (1998). Roach cites NPC statistics on registration for the National Bodybuilding and Fitness Championships for 1997, in which fitness competitors outnumbered bodybuilding women for the first time since fitness entered the venue.

What might be the case, however, is that the rise of natural bodybuilding organizations and those that test for drug use has splintered the competitors among these different organizations, thereby affecting the number of women competitors in any one show. The 1997 Women's World Amateur Bodybuilding and Fitness Championships attracted fifty-seven bodybuilding competitors from thirty-four countries, compared to its first championships, in 1983, which attracted thirty-seven competitors from twenty-two countries. Ben Weider, who along with Joe Weider founded IFFB, finally succeeded after fifty-two years of effort in gaining International Olympic Committee acceptance of bodybuilding as a demonstration sport for the 2000 Sydney Games. This bodes well for the sport of women's bodybuilding.

CONCLUSION

Women's natural competitive bodybuilding is a sport that spans all age groups, from teen to master's. Bodybuilding for women requires no special skills except determination. Although a woman who is genetically predisposed to have a symmetrical form and muscle groups that can be built up readily may begin with a competitive edge, those not so endowed can compensate and successfully compete through knowledge and scientific training techniques, good nutrition, and management of the development of muscle groups. All in all, women's competitive bodybuilding is a most democratic sport. For example, Marjorie Newlin, who began weightlifting in 1992, accumulated twenty-five bodybuilding trophies in six years. In 1999, at age seventy-eight, she was still competing.

Anne Bolin

See also Beauty; Drugs and Drug Testing; Sexuality

Bibliography

Banner, Lois. (1983) *American Beauty*. Chicago: University of Chicago Press.

Boff, Vic. (1990) "The President's Message." *Iron Game History* 1, 1:12–13.

Bolin, Anne. (1992) "Vandalized Vanity: Feminine Physiques Betrayed and Portrayed." In *Tattoo, Torture, Mutilation and Adornment: The Denaturalization of the Body in Culture and Text*, edited by F. Mascia-Lees. Albany: State University of New York Press, 79–90.

———. (1997) "Flex Appeal, Food and Fat: Competitive Bodybuilding, Gender and Diet." In *Building Bodies*, edited by Pamela L. Moore. New Brunswick, NJ: Rutgers University Press, 184–208.

———. (1998) "Debating the Athletic Aesthetic." Paper presented at the annual meeting of the North American Association for the Study of Sport Sociology. Las Vegas, Nevada, November 4–7.

Chapman, David L. (1994) *Sandow the Magnificent: Eugene Sandow and the Beginnings of Bodybuilding.* Urbana: University of Illinois Press.

Cohn, Nik. (1981) *Women of Iron.* New York: Wideview Books.

Del Rey, Pat. (1977) "Apologetics and Androgyny: The Past and the Future." *Frontiers* 3: 8–10.

———. (1978) "The Apologetic and Women in Sport." In *Women and Sport: From Myth to Reality,* edited by C. A. Oglesby. Philadelphia: Lea and Febiger, 107–111.

Duff, Robert W., and Lawrence K. Hong. (1984) "Self-images of Women Bodybuilders." *Sociology of Sport Journal* 1: 374–380.

Duguin, Mary E. (1982) "The Importance of Sport in Building Women's Potential." *Journal of Physical Education, Recreation, and Dance* 53: 18–20, 36.

Gaines, Charles, and George Butler. (1974) *Pumping Iron.* New York: Simon and Schuster.

———. (1983) "Iron Sisters." *Psychology Today* 17: 65–69.

———. (1984) *Pumping Iron II: The Unprecedented Women.* New York: Simon and Schuster.

Guttmann, Allen. (1991) *Women's Sports: A History.* New York: Columbia University Press.

Hilsen, Herbert. (1991) "Letter to the Editor." *Iron Game History* 1, 415: 19–20.

Holloway, Jean Barrett, Denise Gater, Meg Ritchie, et al. (1994) "Strength Training for Female Athletes: A Position Paper: Part I." *National Strength and Conditioning Association Journal* 11, 4:43–55.

Klein, Alan. (1986) "Pumping Irony: Crisis and Contradiction in Bodybuilding." *Sociology of Sport Journal* 3, 2: 112–133.

———. (1993) *Little Big Men: Gender Construction and Bodybuilding Subculture.* Albany: State University of New York Press.

McLish, Rachel. (1984) *Flex Appeal.* New York: Warner Books.

Messner, Michael A. (1993) "Theorizing Gendered Bodies: Beyond the Subject/Object Dichotomy." In *Exercising Power: The Making and Remarking of the Body,* edited by Cheryl Cole, John Loy, and Michael Messner. Albany: State University of New York Press.

Mishkind, Marc E., Judith Rodin, Lisa Silberstein, and Ruth Striegel-Moore. (1987) "The Embodiment of Masculinity: Cultural, Psychological and Behavioral Dimensions." In *Changing Men: New Directions in Research on Men and Masculinity,* edited by Michael S. Kimmel. Newbury Park, CA: Sage Publications, 37–52.

Rader, Benjamin G. (1990) *American Sports: From the Age of Folk Games to the Age of Televised Sports.* Englewood Cliffs, NJ: Prentice Hall.

Roach, Marion. (1998) "Female Bodybuilders Discover Curves." *New York Times* (10 November): 9.

Sabo, Don. (1985) "Sport, Patriarchy, and Male Identity: New Questions About Men and Sport." *Arena Review* 9, 2: 1–30.

Schwarzenegger, Arnold. (1985) *Encyclopedia of Modern Bodybuilding.* New York: Simon and Schuster.

Snyder, E., and S. Kivlin. (1975) "Women Athletes and Aspects of Psychological Well-Being and Body Imagery." *Research Quarterly* 46: 191–199.

Todd, Jan. (1991) "Bernarr MacFadden: Reformer of Feminine Form." *Iron Game History* 1 (4/5):3–8.

Todd, Terry. (1995) "Mac and Jan." *Iron Game History* 3, 6: 17–19.

Vertinsky, Patricia. (1990) *The Eternally Wounded Woman: Women, Doctors, and Exercise in the Late Nineteenth Century.* Manchester, UK: Manchester University Press.

Weider, Betty, and Joe Weider. (1981) *The Weider Book of Bodybuilding for Women.* Chicago: Contemporary Books.

BODY COMPOSITION

Body composition is an important determinant of performance in many sports. In activities that require lifting the body, such as gymnastics, or moving the body long distances, such as marathon running, excess body fat can have a negative effect on performance. A high lean-to-fat ratio is obviously desirable for athletes who participate in these types of sports. Reducing body fat can improve performance in some athletes. But in others, who are already sufficiently lean, it can have an adverse effect not only on performance but also on health. In recent years, as the number of girls and women participating in athletics has grown, health professionals have become increasingly concerned about the negative effects of reduced body fat in already lean athletes. Their concern has grown as they became aware of a condition referred to as the "female athlete triad," which consists of disordered eating, amenorrhea (absence of menstrual periods), and premature osteoporosis (bone loss).

Exercise is known to be important for preventing osteoporosis, but even vigorous activity may not be sufficient to prevent the early onset of the disease in some young amenorrheic female athletes, whose risk for osteoporosis can be similar to that of a seventy-year-old woman because of low estrogen levels. Because the triad is more prevalent among female athletes who participate in sports in which successful performance is dependent on a low body-fat content, coaches and athletes must be careful in determining the ideal body weight for performance. They must consider the effect of weight loss on performance in light of its potential effect on the athlete's health.

BODY COMPOSITION AND ATHLETIC PERFORMANCE

Across sports, body composition is an important factor of successful athletic performance. Fat levels as a percentage of body weight tend to be lower among athletes participating in individual rather than team sports, and lowest in sports that require moving or lifting the body mass (that is, running, jumping, gymnastics, and the like). Within a sport, elite sportswomen tend to have lower relative body-fat levels than nonelite competitors, and athletes tend to have less fat than nonathletes, regardless of the activity.

That elite athletes tend to have lower body-fat levels than nonelite athletes in a sport raises the question of whether body composition can be manipulated to enhance performance. Can competitive female runners who have a relatively low body-fat content of 17–21 percent of their body weight become elite runners if they reduce their fat content to the level that is characteristic of elite runners, 12–14 percent? The answer to this question is not known. Rapid weight loss (that is, to make a weight requirement for competition, such as wrestling) does not appear to improve performance; in fact, it may adversely affect it. Little is known about the effects of gradual weight loss on performance in athletes who are already relatively lean. Dieting usually results in a loss of both fat and lean tissue. In overweight people, performing regular exercise while dieting can help to maintain lean body mass during weight loss. When athletes who are relatively lean, however, try to lose weight by dieting, about one-fourth to one-half of what they lose is muscle mass. The loss of muscle mass may counteract any potential benefit that decreasing body fat might have on performance. Although athletes in such sports as running and gymnastics are often encouraged by coaches and/or parents to attain very low body-fat levels, there is little or no scientific evidence that weight reduction will enhance performance in already lean athletes.

BODY COMPOSITION AND HEALTH

Being overweight increases the risk for many diseases, including coronary artery disease, diabetes

---

SPORTS SLOW AGING PROCESS

A normal feature of aging is a decline in muscle mass and an accompanying increase in body fat which leads to a decline in the lean-to-fat ratio, one marker of physical fitness. Older athletes, even those who train with the same frequency, intensity, and duration as younger athletes, will naturally have more body fat and less muscle mass. However, fat increase and muscle mass reduction can be controlled at all ages by cardiovascular and resistance training, and older athletes often have a healthier lean-to-fat ratio than do younger non-athletes.

mellitus, and hypertension (high blood pressure). Weight loss is generally associated with improved health. Being markedly underweight can also be unhealthy, and weight loss in an already lean individual may result in adverse changes in health. Although athletes are generally very healthy, it is now recognized that increasing numbers of young female athletes are at risk for developing premature osteoporosis.

Low body weight is a risk factor for osteoporosis and being overweight provides a degree of protection against this disorder. In fact, total body weight seems to be a more important determinant of bone strength than either fat or lean mass. Nevertheless, women and men who have a large muscle mass generally also have a large bone mass. It would seem, therefore, that athletes' relatively high levels of lean body mass would be protective against osteoporosis, even when body fat levels are low. Amenorrheic athletes generally have lower bone mineral density (that is, increased risk for osteoporosis) than athletes with normal menses matched for body composition. This suggests that estrogen insufficiency, rather than body composition, is the important determinant of the premature osteoporosis that is characteristic of the female athlete triad.

An important question about body composition and the female athlete is whether reducing fat mass below a certain level leads to amenorrhea and increased risk for osteoporosis. It was once proposed that maintenance of normal menstrual function required a body-fat content of at least 22 percent of body weight. This notion has been effectively dispelled, as many athletes with normal menses have been shown to have body-fat levels less than 22 percent of body weight. However, this does not rule out the possibility that amenorrhea occurs as a result of changes in body composition. It is possible that a certain level of body fat is necessary for normal menstrual function, but that it varies widely among individuals. Careful monitoring of changes in body composition and changes in menstrual function in individual athletes is necessary to determine whether such thresholds exist.

ASSESSMENT OF BODY COMPOSITION TO ESTABLISH WEIGHT GOALS

There are numerous methods for evaluating body composition, ranging from simple, inex-

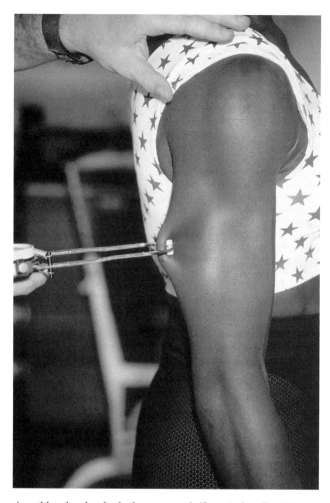

An athlete has her body fat measured. (Sean Aidan; Eye Ubiquitous/Corbis)

pensive techniques (calipers to measure skinfold thickness) to very expensive sophisticated measures (magnetic resonance imaging). All the different methods can yield highly variable results for a given individual. Given this variation, the judiciousness of using such information to establish body-weight goals for the purpose of optimizing athletic performance becomes highly questionable. It is not difficult to imagine how an overestimation of fatness could lead an athlete—possibly influenced by their coaches or parents—to set unrealistic goals for weight loss and to change their behavior in ways that could have adverse effects on their physical or psychological health. Researchers have suggested that an acceptable range of values, rather than a specific body-fat level, be recommended for athletes in a particular sport. However, given that some of the common methods of assessing body composition yield estimates of fatness that vary within an individual by 20 percent of body weight or more, the range of values would indeed have to be generous to encompass this degree of variability.

CONCLUSION

Because body composition is an important determinant of sports performance, acceptable ranges of body-fat levels need to be established within given sports, and the ranges must be specific to the method of measurement. There must also be an ongoing effort to evaluate the appropriateness of such guidelines, with the focus being the overall health of the athlete. At a minimum, it is recommended that athletes, under the guidance of their parents or coaches, maintain records of body weight, menstrual function, and training level to assist in finding the ideal body weight for health and performance.

Wendy M. Kohrt

See also Amenorrhea; Eating Disorders; Nutrition; Osteoporosis; Performance

Bibliography

Ballor, D. L., and E. T. Poehlman. (1994) "Exercise-Training Enhances Fat-Free Mass Preservation During Diet-Induced Weight Loss: A Meta-Analytical Finding." *International Journal of Obesity and Related Metabolic Disorders* 18: 35–40.

Brownell, Kelly D., S. Nelson Steen, and Jack H. Wilmore. (1987) "Weight Regulation Practices in Athletes: Analysis of Metabolic and Health Effects." *Medicine and Science in Sports and Exercise* 19: 546–556.

Fogelholm, M. (1994) "Effects of Body Weight Reduction on Sports Performance." *Sports Medicine* 18: 249–267.

Frisch, Rose E., and J. W. McArthur. (1974) "Menstrual Cycles: Fatness as a Determinant for Minimum Weight or Height Necessary for Their Maintenance or Onset." *Science* 185: 949–951.

Inger, F., and J. Sundgot-Borgen. (1991) "Influence of Body Weight Regulation on Maximal Oxygen Uptake in Female Elite Athletes." *Scandinavian Journal of Medicine and Science in Sports* 1: 141–146.

Koutedakis, Yiannis, P. J. Pacy, R. M. Quevedo, D. J. Millward, R. Hesp, Colin Boreham, and N. C. Craig Sharp. (1994) "The Effects of Two Different Periods of Weight-Reduction on Selected Performance Parameters in Elite Lightweight Oarswomen." *International Journal of Sports Medicine* 15: 472–477.

Pacy, P. J., M. Quevedo, N. R. Gibson, M. Cox, Yiannis Koutedakis, and J. Millward. (1995) "Body Composition Measurement in Elite Heavyweight Oarswomen: A Comparison of Five Methods." *Journal of Sports Medicine and Physical Fitness* 35: 67–74.

Snow-Harter, Christine, and Robert Marcus. (1991) "Exercise, Bone Mineral Density, and Osteoporosis." In *Exercise and Sport Sciences Reviews,* edited by John O. Holloszy. Baltimore: Williams & Wilkins, 351–388.

Yeager, K. K., Rosemary Agostini, A. Nattiv, and Barbara Drinkwater. (1993) "The Female Athlete Triad: Disordered Eating, Amenorrhea, Osteoporosis." *Medicine and Science in Sports and Exercise* 25: 775–777.

BODY IMAGE

Visual images of the body are critical to self-perception. When people reflect on who they are, or who they believe they should be, they tend to think in terms of how they look. When people describe other people, they refer to their appearance, rarely to their smell, feel, or sound. Sight seems to represent truth in a way that other forms of perception cannot. People put more trust in vision than in their other senses, especially with respect to their own identities. People often visualize goals for themselves. When people think of getting fit, they visualize the new fit body. When they think of a new job, they often picture themselves in the imagined unfamiliar environment. People like to "see" results and be "shown" the truth. After all, we'll only believe it when we see it!

An individual's identity hinges upon his or her body image. When a young child sees herself in the mirror and recognizes, for the first time, that the image moves when she moves her body, she starts to acknowledge her individual identity. She can understand that she fits into a world of people that she has observed from the outside. She becomes a member of society, aware of what visually "constitutes" a person and aware of categories of people (children, women, redheads) within this community.

SWIMMING CRAFTS A BEAUTIFUL FIGURE

A New York Times *Review of Annette Kellerman's Books on Swimming and Beauty*

How to Swim. By Annette Kellermann. Illustrated. New York: George H. Doran Company. $2.

Physical Beauty: How to Keep It. By Annette Kellermann. Illustrated. New York: George H. Doran Company. $2.

These two books by Miss Kellermann, known in many parts of the world as one of the most skillful, daring, and successful of women swimmers, fit together admirably and supplement each other in every respect. . . . The greater part of this volume, however, is devoted to practical instruction for the would-be swimmer. Miss Kellerman is most enthusiastic about the benefits in health, strength, and beauty women can gain from swimming, and over and over again she stresses this point. She thinks "swimming is the best sport in the world for women," that it is, pre-eminently, "the women's sport," because women can swim more gracefully than men and can make a better showing in it than they can in most other sports. And the more a woman swims and the more proficient she becomes, the more beautiful and graceful and better proportioned it makes her figure.... In the volume on "Physical Beauty" Miss Kellermann makes it quite plain throughout the pages that the only beauty she thinks it worth while to consider for a moment is the beauty that comes from being well, strong, and fit, from a body well proportioned and muscular rather than fat, and from the poise and carriage gained by trained muscles, controlled nerves, properly functioning organs and pure blood bounding through the arteries. All these things she is firmly convinced it is quite within the power of most women to have, if they want to take the trouble necessary to compass them. . . . All the descriptions of exercises are full, careful, and lucid, and throughout Miss Kellermann sets forth her convictions and the reasons for them with vigor and cogency. As in the other volume, many full-page plates show the author's graceful and beautiful figure going through the exercises described in the text.

New York Times Book Review (1918) 9 June: 269, 274.

Self-identity is not as simple as recognizing the form contained in an envelope of skin. Psychological and sociohistorical factors are as important as anatomy in the picture we create of ourselves for ourselves. We base the construction of our own body-image on three things: what we believe bodies in general should look like and how they should function, what we have experienced perceptually in our own lives, and how we feel emotionally about our lives and our bodies.

BODY IMAGE AND SOCIETY

Societal norms and variations over time and geography explain and generate many of the emotions, perceptions, and conceptions that women commonly hold about their body images. The ideal image of the Western female body has changed many times, altering with the social values of the times. As testimony to this, consider the elegant Greek maiden, the Roman matron, the menaced medieval damsel, the languishing Victorian lady, and, now, the lanky and taut fitness enthusiast.

The existence of a physical ideal opens the door to many forms of social control regulation—to be seen or not to be seen is among the fundamental choices we make. From the initial visual image that helps the child to identify herself as part of the human species to the images of the frail Victorian or of the exceptionally tall and slender supermodel created by institutions such as the

THE BODY STEREOTYPES ASSOCIATED WITH CHEERLEADING

The idea that Western society supports different ideal body images for women and men is supported by research on weight and body type among female and male cheerleaders conducted by Justine Reel and Diane Gill of the University of North Carolina at Greensboro. Female cheerleaders are expected to be short, shapely, blond, and feminine. Males are expected to be tall and muscular. These expectations sometimes lead female cheerleaders to engage in disordered eating behaviors to lose or control their weight and males to use steroids to build body mass.

medical fraternity or the media—all contribute to producing an ideal image. This ideal constitutes a kind of measuring tool that people use when they look at themselves and at other people and that they then use to manage their own actions as well as to judge those of others. Deviation from the standard leads to social sanctions and marginalization of individual behaviors, practices, and body types. As a result, the body image serves to regulate how people look and what people do. Laziness or dullness is associated with people who are heavy, for no other reason than their distance from our standard of an ideal physique. "She should do something about her weight!"—as if to suggest that she is derelict in her responsibilities. And if we tend to be overweight, we are likely to regulate, or control, our lifestyle to avoid these negative judgments. We might diet or, alternatively, dress to conceal our weight.

An example of how people construct standards of body image through existing social and cultural beliefs is visible in recent history. In the mid-to late nineteenth century, predominantly male medical professionals restricted the activities and behaviors of middle-class women. Because they believed that menstrual bleeding depleted a limited store of energy that could not be recovered, they mandated that young girls and women curtail their physical activity significantly so as not to further weaken their waning strength. Since women were seen as frail and vulnerable beings, femininity became associated, at least in the privileged classes, with an image of daintiness and fragility. This image was further reinforced by fashion trends, such as tightly laced corsets that created a delicate profile. At the same time, working-class woman were expected to be robust—as they were expected to be in all historical periods. We can view an even earlier example to understand how society and reigning beliefs, not biology, define what constitutes the ideal female body. In medieval Europe, many women and clerics believed that feeding the mortal body starved the immortal soul. As a result, restrictive eating and fasting became a characteristic of female spirituality in the Middle Ages, and physical wasting was associated with saintliness.

Control through image and gaze is also evident in other social relations. Parents have expectations of how children should or ought to look, and these expectations typically follow gender lines. Girls learn how to present their bodies in pleasing ways: from the earliest days, parents often tie a ribbon around the head of a bald-headed infant girl. As she gets older, they might admonish her to take care of herself and her clothes, and to keep her hair out of her face, in order to maintain certain standards of decorum. Even the most progressive parents, however, may reward the rough-and-tumble behavior of a boy, despite dirt, torn clothing, and dishevelment. Such conduct demonstrates strength and drive, which are positive features for a boy. Girls must be prepared to be seen at all times as objects to be gazed upon by others and also by themselves.

Self-scrutiny of body image is another form of control that persists in contemporary culture. There is less need for medical men or Greek patriarchs to control the image of women, because women have internalized that control. Social expectations and beauty advice direct women to gaze upon their bodies and to continually evaluate every movement, blemish, and deviation from the standardized norm. In *The Lady's Realm* magazine in 1904, in a column devoted to women's beauty concerns, "Narcissa" wrote, "I would advise every woman over twenty-five to sit before a good mirror in the very strongest light and mercilessly criticize herself." Women were thus taught how to "watch themselves," and they still continue to receive messages reinforcing this need for self-scrutiny, self-control, and, frequently, self-condemnation.

As surveyors of their own body image, women are encouraged to take responsibility for how they look. "New Year, new body!" heralds an advertisement for an all-women's gym. "Make your New Year's resolution happen!"—as if completely changing the look of the body were merely a question of resolve and discipline. The visual aesthetics of health include standards of weight, age, skin, color, and muscle definition that are always prescriptive and often elusive. Media images would suggest that a tanned, but Caucasian, lean, but not scrawny, large-breasted, thin-hipped woman with sparkling white teeth, full lips, pert nose, and no wrinkles or gray hair is someone who has taken total charge of herself. Those who fail to achieve this image must improve their resolve, or, as another gym suggests, in an illustrated brochure featuring a muscular female buttock, be "some-body!" Although numerous studies have shown that women who are active in sports or in exercise programs have a more positive body image than their less active counterparts, the ideals promulgated by the mass media can be physically and psychologically destructive. Promised a beautiful body by the gym industry, a magazine, or a television advertisement, today's women are situated as were their great-grandmothers, who read Narcissa's words a century ago. The struggling exerciser who cannot see that her anatomy deviates from the ideal image and that no amount of self-cultivation will allow her to achieve this image is engaging in the same critical self-scrutiny recommended to women of the Victorian period. Too often, the result is self-incrimination and poor self-esteem, which lead to problems among women in adhering to meaningful and fulfilling exercise programs.

CONCLUSION

Body image is an important component of our individuality, but it is not the only source of infor-
mation about who we are. When we walk under a low tree branch, for example, we do not use a mirror to judge how much space there is and whether or not we need to stoop. We rely on other information: our visual perception of the branch as opposed to that of our body, the input we receive from proprioception, the touch of the twigs as they brush through our hair, and the height of our hand as we hold on to the branch under which we are ducking. Physical activity and sports are not static visual states of tight, lean, sculpted, and attractive bodies but rather a dynamic state of movement—fluid, changing and active. Relying on body image to describe who we are, or to underline who we should be, locks us into a static aesthetic that is neither practical nor real. Though a heavy historical legacy of ideas about how women should look, should watch themselves and be watched, burdens us today, our identity need not be constructed through a purely visual image of our body. We actively experience our lives from the inside. We have thoughts, emotions, and urges. We smell, taste, hear, and feel. We are far more than just passive occupants or vigilant guardians of a physical form.

Annemarie Jutel

See also Eating Disorders; Nutrition; Sexuality

Bibliography

Bermudez, Jose Luis, Anthony Marcel, and Naomi Eilan. (1995) *The Body and the Self.* Cambridge, MA: MIT Press.

Bordo, Susan. (1993) *Unbearable Weight: Feminism, Western Culture, and the Body.* Berkeley: University of California Press.

Brumberg, Joan J. (1989) *Fasting Girls: The Surprising History of Anorexia Nervosa.* New York: NAL/Dutton.

Cash, Thomas F., and Thomas Pruzinsky, eds. (1990) *Body Images.* New York: Guilford.

Fraser, Laura. (1997) *Losing It: America's Obsession with Weight and the Industry That Feeds It.* New York: Penguin.

Grosz, Elizabeth. (1994) *Volatile Bodies: Toward a Corporeal Feminism.* Bloomington: University of Indiana Press.

Honer, Anne. (1985) "Beschreibung einer Lebens-Welt." *Zeitschrift für Soziologie* 14, 2: 131–39.

Klein, Richard. (1996) *Eat Fat.* New York: Vintage Books.

Radley, Alan. (1991) *The Body and Social Psychology.* New York: Springer-Verlag.

Schilder, Paul. (1978) *The Image and Appearance of the Human Body: Studies in the Constructive Energies of the Psyche.* New York: International Universities Press.

Spitzack, Carole. (1990) *Confessing Excess: Women and the Politics of Body Reduction.* Albany: State University of New York Press.

Synnott, Anthony. (1993) *The Body Social: Symbolism, Self and Society.* New York: Routledge.

Ussher, Jane. (1989) *The Psychology of the Female Body.* New York: Routledge.

BOOMERANG THROWING

Boomerang throwing is a recreational and competitive sport in which participants try to achieve specified effects in their throws: distance, tricks, extended time aloft, and the like. The winner is the person (or team) most successful at accomplishing these feats. Although usually linked with Australian culture, boomerang throwing as a competitive sport actually originated in the United States. It is primarily a male sport, but some women have participated at the international level since the competitive sport began in 1981.

HISTORY

Long believed to be of Australian origin, boomerangs from other parts of the world may predate those depicted in the 15,000-year-old cave paintings of the Australian Aborigines. In 1987, a 23,000-year-old throw stick (different from a boomerang, which returns, a throw stick generally travels in a straight line) made from a mammoth's tusk was discovered in Poland. A replica of this implement reportedly returned when thrown. Boomerangs and throw sticks were found in King Tutankhamen's tomb (1350 BCE) in Egypt, where they were perhaps used as early as 2000 BCE. Boomerangs were used as a hunting

decoy for birds. Ducks might see a boomerang and believe it to be an eagle. They would huddle under the "eagle," making them an easy target for a hunter with a net. The throw sticks were used for hunting ground game.

A 1968 *Scientific American* article on boomerangs stimulated interest in them in the United States. Yearly workshops by the Smithsonian Institution on making and throwing boomerangs fueled this interest, and in 1981 the United States Boomerang Association (USBA) was formed. That same year, a U.S. boomerang team challenged and beat an Australian team in the first international competition. Its success sparked today's multinational tournaments.

WOMEN IN BOOMERANG THROWING

The 1981 U.S. team consisted of all men, yet it was coached by a U.S. woman boomerang thrower, Ali Fujino. Another U.S. woman, Betsylew Miale-Gix, competes directly against men. The only woman worldwide to place first in a boomerang tournament, she accomplished this feat twice, as a member of the international women's team in the world championships in New Zealand in 1996 and as member of the U.S. team in the world championships in 1998. She also serves the sport administratively, as Fujino once did. Each was president of the USBA, and Miale-Gix was the association's secretary in 1998–1999. She is also the originator of Toss Across America, wherein throwers coordinate teaching events across the country on a single day. May 1999 marked the tenth annual Toss Across America.

RULES AND PLAY

The United States and Australia have basically defined the sport of competitive boomerang throwing in the handbooks of the USBA and of the Boomerang Association of Australia. However, most nations follow the European standard for competition, at least for scoring and ranking.

In a boomerang competition, six events are standard, with juggling and long-distance throwing optional. In Australian round, the competitor throws the boomerang and then tries to catch it in the bull's-eye, which is the center of a circle 100 meters (109 yards) in diameter outlined on a grass field. Within this circle are five concentric circles,

NOT A HUNTING WEAPON

In 1770, explorer Captain Cook arrived in Botany Bay, Australia, where he observed natives wielding curved sticks. Aborigines described these sticks in lyrical terms, using names such as nanjal, baranganj, kali, wilgi, barngeet, and tootgundy. When Cook asked about a particular stick, natives called it a boomerang.

Fascinated, Cook brought the boomerang home to England, intriguing people. In February 1838, a writer in the *Dublin University Magazine* explained, "Of all the advantages we have derived from our Australian settlements, none seems to have given more universal satisfaction than the introduction of some crooked pieces of wood shaped like the crescent moon, and called boomerang or kilee. Ever since their structure has been fully understood, carpenters appear to have ceased from all other work; the windows of toy shops exhibit little else; walking sticks and umbrellas have gone out of fashion; and even in this rainy season, no man carries anything but a boomerang; nor does this species of madness appear to be abating."

Cook, however, misunderstood one vital fact. Aborigines hunted with non-returning sticks called kylies. They also tossed returning sticks, but these were decoys, not weapons; returners were also used for entertainment and ceremonial purposes.

When Cook lumped the returning stick with the hunting stick, he started the myth that boomerangs were weapons, a common misconception even today. Cartoons and action films often portray boomerangs incorrectly. One notable exception was the movie *The Bagdad Cafe*. In it, boomerang thrower Alan Scott Craig played the part of a thrower, with rave reviews in the *San Francisco Chronicle* and *Newsweek*.

Because of Cook's discovery, people also believed that boomerangs were invented in Australia. This may or may not be true, but the oldest throwing stick uncovered so far has been discovered in the Oblazowa Rock in southern Poland, a Mammoth tusk stick estimated to be 20,300 years old.

Boomerangs actually existed throughout the ancient world, with sticks of gold-tipped ivory and gilded ebony placed in King Tutankhamen's pyramid. While these were not discovered until the twentieth century, American author Mark Twain was already aware of the myriad of possibilities of the boomerang's origin. "Either someone with a boomerang arrived in Australia in the days of antiquity," Twain wrote, "or the Australian aborigines re-invented it. It will take some time to find out which of these two propositions is the fact. But there is no hurry."

laid out in the same fashion as an archery target. A boomerang landing in the bull's-eye is worth 10 points. Subsequent larger circles award points on a declining scale of 8, 6, 4, and 2, respectively. The accuracy event includes hitting the bull's-eye as well as distance and catching ability. In fast catch, the thrower makes five throws and catches with the same boomerang as rapidly as possible. In maximum time aloft, the competitor tries to keep the boomerang in the air for the longest time possible. Trick catching requires making difficult catches—one-handed, behind the back, under the leg, and with the feet—in the attempt to accumulate points.

The last two competition events require special boomerangs. In doubling, two boomerangs are thrown and then caught upon return at the same time. In juggling, which is optional, the objective is to keep two identical boomerangs alternating in the air for as many throws as possible without dropping either.

When space allows, a separate event, long-distance throwing, may be held not for competition, but for fun. The current world record is 149 meters (163 yards), which lends credence to the possibility that Australian Aborigines may, indeed, have thrown their boomerangs distances once thought impossible.

CULTURAL VARIATIONS

Cultural attitudes toward the boomerang vary. The Australians favor preserving the original materials and shape of the boomerang and maintaining the nature of the tournaments as they stand now. The French seek world-record performances and hold competitions intended to achieve new records; they prefer more technologically advanced boomerang design over traditional shapes and colors. The Germans hold craftsmanship and successful performance in high regard. German and Swedish engineers create boomerangs with intricate inlaid patterns and use high-tech materials (fiberglass, Kevlar) in their crafting. In the United States, the favored boomerang is one that will win a tournament versus one that is aesthetically pleasing or designed to break world records. The use of innovative materials coupled with radical designs has given U.S. competitors success in international competition.

Boomerang throwing, which still retains its amateur status, becomes a demonstration sport in the 2000 Olympics, and Miale-Gix hopes this will serve as a catalyst to get women to join the still-emerging sport. "Women have just as much potential to do well," she says, "in both recreational and competitive throwing as men, given arm strength and enough enthusiasm to stick with the sport."

Kelly Boyer Sagert

Bibliography

Mason, Bernard Sterling. (1974) *Boomerangs: How to Make and Throw Them.* New York: Dover Publications.

Ruhe, Benjamin. (1977) *Many Happy Returns: The Art and Sport of Boomeranging.* New York: Viking Press.

———. (1985) *Boomerang: How to Throw It, Catch It, and Make It Your Own.* New York: Workman.

Sagert, Kelly Boyer. (1996) *About Boomerangs: America's Silent Sport.* North Ridgeville, OH: Plant-Speak Publications.

Additional information was provided by Tony Brazelton (Many Happy Returns, Champaign, IL) and Ted Bailey (Boomerang News, Ann Arbor, MI).

BOSNIA AND HERZEGOVINA

see Yugoslavia

BOULMERKA, HASSIBA

(1968–)

ALGERIAN MIDDLE-DISTANCE RUNNER

Hassiba Boulmerka was the first African woman to win a world championship in track and field, and the first Algerian to win an Olympic gold medal. Although she often ran poorly against mediocre opponents whom she should have beaten easily, she demonstrated an uncanny ability to surpass herself when the eyes of the entire world were upon her.

Boulmerka was born in Constantine, Algeria, on 10 July 1968 and grew up in the Atlas Mountains region of the interior. A somewhat indifferent student, she enjoyed running over the mountainous terrain, and her family supported her interest and training program. She won the 800- and 1500-meter African championships in 1988 and 1989, but in her first try for an Olympic medal, in Seoul in 1988, she was eliminated in the heats. Three years later, she won the first of two world championships in the 1500-meter race. Her time of 4:02:21 was, however, nearly 10 seconds slower than the world record of the Soviet Union's Tatyana Kazankina's (set in 1980). In the 1992 Olympics in Barcelona, Boulmerka lowered her own 1500-meter time to 3:55:30 and won the race. In 1995, she won a second world championship.

At the 1996 Olympics in Atlanta, she was among the favorites to win the 1500-meter race, but in the semifinals she collided with another runner, losing her balance and staggering out of her lane. She remained on her feet but lost so much time that she finished a distant last in 4:23:86, nearly 10 seconds behind Russia's Ludmilla Rogachova. Boulmerka's coach protested, but it was unclear who had run into whom, and Boulmerka was not allowed to advance to the finals, which were won by Austria's Theresia Kiesl

Hassiba Boulmerka competes in the 1500-meter event at the 1996 Olympic Games in Atlanta. (Mike King)

in 4:09:44, a time slower than Boulmerka's time in Barcelona. In 1996 Boulmerka was one of the seven athletes elected by the Atlanta Olympic athletes to serve on the IOC Athletes' Commission. In 2000, she also serves on the Algerian NOC Athletes' Commission and on the IOC's Women and Sport Working Group.

Boulmerka's career was politically as well as athletically dramatic. In the 1990s, Algeria was violently torn between Islamic fundamentalists seeking to create a Muslim nation and a government that prevented them from coming to power. The fundamentalists considered a female runner's exposed arms and legs to be blasphemous to Islam and repeatedly threatened Boulmerka with death. She answered that her actions as a runner and as a Muslim were separate and that she could be both. Nonetheless, given the

threats and the thousands of killings by the Algerian fundamentalists, she left Algeria.

Allen Guttmann

BOWLS AND BOWLING

Bowls and bowling include a group of activities that involve rolling or throwing balls at targets with the intent of hitting or knocking them over. "Bowls" generally refers to variants of the game played in Europe and the United Kingdom, while "bowling" is the Americanized version of the sport played in the United States. The full participation of women in bowls and bowling is fairly recent.

HISTORY

Bowls and bowling claim their origins in antiquity. Rolling or throwing small balls at various targets is said to be portrayed in carvings from ancient Mediterranean civilizations, but there are very long gaps in the evidence. Bocce has claims to have been played in Italy since the days of classical Rome, with distinctive regional variations. Bocce (literally, "bowls") and *pétanque/boules*, played in Italy and France, respectively, are traditional peasant games that were long played exclusively by men.

PEASANT RECREATIONS: BOCCE AND PÉTANQUE/BOULES

In the Mediterranean countries of Italy and France, these broadly similar games emerged primarily as agents for male bonding. Men took over the sandy or gravel spaces of village squares for play, which was often associated with drinking during the warmer months from April to October. The games have common elements: the small and relatively heavy balls are tossed from a fixed line toward a target. Both have been codified only recently, as they have been adapted to wider usage and urban play.

Bowls, as with many medieval and Renaissance European folk customs, is quite difficult to reconstruct in terms of whether both men and women took part. Only as the games began to be played with formal rules in the late nineteenth century has the role of women been given an occasionally controversial prominence.

Significant differences remain between women's playing as part of family recreation in these sports so deeply rooted in European masculine peasant cultures and their part in those games that have been developed in the wider contexts of the white-dominated sections of the former British Empire and North America. That women are confined to amateur status is also an issue; this is perhaps a remnant of the social and religious purity they have long been supposed to represent.

Since the 1980s, however, urbanization has started to break down bocce's traditional maleness. This has been even more the case in the United States, the country to which it has been most successfully exported along with other aspects of Italian immigrant culture. Here it has developed increasingly as a means of family bonding in suburbia; women tend to play within extended domestic teams rather than in separate organizations, but the situation remains very fluid.

Pétanque/boules is broadly similar in history, although its spread outside the former French colonial empire owes more to tourists taking the game home to Britain than to ethnic migration. It has been codified since about 1910, having emerged from older games played in southern France.

Bowls, rolling a heavy wooden ball biased with a metal weight toward a small jack, has been played in Britain since at least the Middle Ages, and little-changed versions are still played by exclusively male clubs in a few places, including Lewes and Southampton. A limited amount of evidence shows occasional female participation in more domestic versions during the Tudor and Stuart periods—the great diarist Samuel Pepys played with his wife in the 1660s. But it was with the reemergence and popularization of the masculine game at the end of the nineteenth century that women appeared as both serious and segregated contenders.

BOCCE AND PÉTANQUE: RULES AND PLAY

Bocce uses an "alley" or "rink" 18.3 meters (60 feet) long by 2.4 meters (8 feet) wide. As it has become more popular in cities, more indoor facilities have

A bowler competes in the 1952 Ladies' Open Bowls Tournament in Southend, England. (Hulton-Deutsch Collection/Corbis)

been constructed, which often house several such pitches. Each player tosses a bowl to get as close as possible to a smaller target bowl, the *pallino*, which has already been thrown to lie at least 1.4 meters (5 feet) beyond a central regulator peg. The player usually walks up to do this within a separate area.

Competitors may play either as singles with two shots each or in teams of up to six people with four shots each. It is organized into various regional and national federations but, until recently, had no organized international competition because it was played largely in Italy.

The name pétanque comes from the Provençal *pé* (foot) and *tanque* (stake). This refers to the position from which the metal boule ("bowl") is thrown at the small wooden target, the *cochonnet*, which has been tossed some 6 to 10 meters (19.7 to 32.8 feet) into a space roughly 12 by 1.3 meters (39.4 by 4.3 feet). Scoring depends on the player's skill in getting a bowl closer to the target than the opponent's bowl. In the 1980s, indoor urban

"THE HAT AND BLAZER BRIGADE"
BRITISH BOWLING DRESS

The dress code adopted since the 1920s by women playing bowls has not been without controversy. Whereas women participating in bocce/pentanque or bowling have opted largely for the practical informality of trousers and similar leisurewear, bowls players have a very limited and regulated choice. The emphasis is on a uniform which seems to be a mixture derived from the lawn tennis wear of the early 1920s and male cricketing dress. It is best suited for the fine weather of the summer months. Jewelry, such as earrings and brooches, has long been forbidden; wedding rings and watches are acceptable. A white, cream, or gray skirt with a hem well below the knees and a white/cream blouse are compulsory, as are formal stockings, usually brown; the bare legs made fashionable by Princess Diana in other circumstances are respectably covered on the lawns. Flat-heeled brown, white, or gray leather shoes, soft-soled to protect the green, are mandatory; there is no market for the ambitious and fashion-changing sports manufacturers here. Cream or navy blue blazers may be worn, and soft white or cream rainwear made of artificial fabrics has slowly crept in. By far the most distinctive, and much-ridiculed, item is the hat. Although a few now play bare-headed, the norm is still a white soft-brimmed hat which is a mixture of the male Panama and solid women's styles of the early 1920s. A colored band may indicate the player's team allegiance, but that is the only adornment. The visors or colored baseball hats beloved by women golfers have no place in women's bowls. Not surprisingly, there has been a number of attempts to throw off the staid and conservative image the uniform suggests, which some critics have likened to the older uniforms of the Salvation Army. These moves have largely failed. Divided skirts (culottes) were eventually allowed after much debate, but Australian attempts in the early 1990s to introduce brightly striped colored garb, bringing the game "out of the Dark Ages," were soon squashed at a local level. The uniform remains, only slightly modified. As such, it is usually worn with great pride by players of all ages, a central sign of another "unchanging" tradition which the British have exported so successfully. Its survival is seen as another sign of just how serious ("fanatic," according to some observers) women are about the game and about its perceived purity and order.

arenas extended the playing season to year-round. Codification led in 1945 to the organization of a national body, the Federation Française de Pétanque et Jeu Provençal, and eventually to world championships as visitors from neighboring countries, as well as those in the former French Empire, took up the game.

One major factor in opening play up to women came with the formation of a British Pétanque Association, in 1975, at a time when they were being admitted more readily, in southern England at least, to pubs. While some women play independently in league games, their partners are drawn largely from their families and both sexes, reflecting the domestication of a previously singularly masculine preserve. This domestication is even more pronounced when it is remembered that most games are recreational and played on family space in gardens or at vacation sites.

BOWLS: RULES AND PLAY

There are two main versions of the modern game, both played seasonally out of doors and with broad similarities. The "lawn" version is played on level grass greens. These are squares of between 31 and 41 meters (102 and 134.5 feet) that are usually divided into rinks of up to 5.5 meters (18 feet) wide, to allow several matches to be played side by side. The green is surrounded by a shallow ditch and a bank at least 23 centimeters (9 inches) high.

The second version, called the "crown" version, may be played on either a square or a rectangular area, but it must be a minimum of 25 meters (82 feet) wide. It usually rises to a central crown up to 35 centimeters (13.8 inches) high. Both games use "woods," now usually made of artificial materials, which are "biased," weighted to one side, so that a direct line is virtually impossible. These are bowled at a smaller "jack" up to 6.4 centimeters (2.5 inches) in diameter. Players, grouped in various combinations, usually play with up to four bowls each, the winner being the player whose wood comes closest to the jack.

WOMEN'S PARTICIPATION IN BOWLS

Bowls has frequently and inaccurately been portrayed as a semisedentary game for the middle-aged. At the beginning of the twentieth century, male clubs were recognized, in a semipublic and partly humorous way, as a refuge from both over-domestication and feminine domination.

At that time, however, a case was advanced that play would benefit women in two ways. It would improve the health of women who were excluded from more active pursuits by age and convention, and it would also extend the women's role from the more traditional one of making tea for visiting teams—the "ladies" became "women" players. Playing was also promoted as an additional means of inculcating graceful movement. Such pressures led the London authorities to make limited separate playing facilities in public parks available for women in 1906.

Most developments since then have seen an uneasy coexistence with men's clubs in both private and public spaces. Women have progressed more rapidly in the "lawn" game, with its flat greens in the predominantly southern and middle-class areas, than in the "crown" game, with its uneven greens and semiprofessionalism in more northern and working-class towns. The first specifically female club was probably founded in 1910 in Kingston Canbury, near London. The great boom came in the decade after the end of World War I when bowls became a somewhat unlikely tool in the growth of women's independence.

Although British women moved steadily toward greater playing organization, this was one area in which the country's power did not automatically cause it to lead in imperial developments. The slightly freer culture of white

groups in some of the colonies had already led South Africa and Australia to form women's bowls associations, and England's leading women lawn bowls players followed suit, opting for the purposeful-sounding English Women's Bowling Association, or EWBA (a rival "Ladies' Association" was very short-lived).

The EWBA was founded in 1931, with the support of many male players, and grew rapidly thereafter, pulling many existing county associations together and prompting the formation of new ones. Eventually it grew to have almost 2,000 affiliated clubs. It was matched, on a smaller scale, by the emergence of the English Women's Bowling Federation for the crown green game. The two bodies' regional influence has closely matched the distribution and the social cachet of their parallel sports. Their most significant role has been in organizing ladders of championships up to the international level. Perhaps the peak of recognition for the lawn game came with its inclusion in the Commonwealth Games in 1982.

WOMEN CHAMPIONS

Over the decades, various key women players have emerged, but few could match the doyenne of the lawn game, Mavis Steele (1928–1998), widely regarded as the absolute epitome of the restrained English sense of female play that her followers have tried so hard to emulate. Solidly middle class, apparently reserved and normally very dignified, and with a passion for minutiae that showed in her impeccable appearance, she began to play (against men) in the 1940s. She soon moved into serious women's competition play, first appearing in England in 1959. She made 129 appearances for her country in the last ten days before she died.

The winner of many championships and honored by the queen, Steele was a formidable figure, very difficult for aspiring bowlers to equal but a major model for women's independent sporting role. She did much to dispel the notion that the game is suitable only for older women with no paid employment. The full age range is now well represented, and the playing of matches has had to adapt to the sharply changing women's employment patterns of Britain since the 1960s. Weekday play still favors those who are retired.

Although there are honorific prizes in the women-only lawn tournaments—culminating in the annual championships held for years in the Sussex seaside resort of Worthing—any hint of professionalism has been firmly resisted in women's lawn bowls. By comparison, the crown variant has developed a women's version of the male semi- and fully professional sponsored tournaments firmly located in the north of England. Early competition prizes in the 1930s consisted largely of useful domestic goods.

After World War II, financial incentives began to appear, although at a level much below the male equivalents. With sponsorship, the top champions could win thousands of pounds by the 1980s, although they were still a long way from the more obviously glamorous women's sports, even when their matches were televised. The key change came with the organization in 1977 of a women's annual Waterloo Championship, named after the long-established male one. Several thousand women now take part in this circuit, but few are fully professional.

INDOOR VARIANTS

Women players have also found a new outlet in the late twentieth-century development of a previously eccentric minority version of the sport, indoor bowls, usually played on special carpets up to 46 meters long in shared multipurpose halls. More than 250 clubs for playing this winter game have emerged in England, often with membership drawn largely from those who play the seasonally restricted outdoor game. It has its own hierarchy of tournaments, largely under the auspices of the National Indoor Bowls Council formed in 1964, but a great deal of the play is between older husbands and wives, another extension of domestic bonding.

INTERNATIONAL PLAY

As with a number of other quintessentially British sports, women's bowls has spread among Anglophiles in the United States as well as throughout the former British Empire. Like cricket, its following in the United States is limited and strongest in the eastern seaboard states, where women are among the approximately 7,000 players affiliated with the American Lawn Bowls Association, formed in 1915. But it is deeply rooted in the dominant white suburban cultures of South Africa, New Zealand, and Australia.

In Australia, in particular, it is often an arena for sharp clashes between women themselves over issues such as dress and apparent cultural dependency on Britain's former power. It is also a major target of semiaffectionate male criticism because of Australia's uneasy history of macho male cultural dominance. The formidable dedication of many female bowlers is often portrayed as a threat more to male power than to the more traditional restrictions expected from domesticity.

BOWLING IN NORTH AMERICA

The various games that involve bowling at skittles or pins grew largely as an Americanization of European men's play linked with taverns and pubs. As such, they had a distinctly working-class following tied to a culture formed around recreational alcohol consumption. In this setting, views on the role of women in these games have been ambivalent. It was with the popularization in the United States of tenpin bowling (and its Canadian variations) that women emerged more signifi-

BOWLING'S ONLY TRIPLE-CROWN WINNER

The only professional ten-pin bowler (woman or man) to win the triple crown of bowling twice (for women the U.S. Open, WIBC Queens, and Sam's Town Invitational) is Aleta Sill of the United States. Sill, a professional for 19 years, was also the leading career money winner on the women's tour, with $998,892 as of September, 1999. One more victory would make her the first woman to earn more than one million dollars in her career.

cantly, although some historians have pointed out that the greatest female following is blue-collar in its origins. When bowling became a respectable family activity in the 1950s, women usually entered it as wives or daughters playing alongside their menfolk in friendly games—it had become another wholesome prop to suburban lifestyles, an image it has largely retained. That move had accompanied its mechanization and the shift to larger, specialist premises that attracted larger groups. As a way of meeting high investment costs, promoters set out to popularize bowling among women.

Women have gradually emerged as independent players, and it is no accident that a number of the standard rule manuals are written by women. When local leagues emerged, women were quick to organize. The overall rules were standardized by the American Bowling Congress, founded in 1895, and the Women's International Bowling Congress, a women's organization that emerged in 1916, well before the game assumed its mantle of suburban respectability—although it is said that women's presence led to a rapid cleanup of the alleys. The 1950s brought an increasing professionalism with commercial sponsorship. The Women's Professional Bowling Association (WPBA) (later changed to "Tour") was formed in 1959, a year after its male equivalent.

At this level of the sport, women's participation is relatively small and sparsely funded by male standards, although play is vibrant and important as one aspect of career development in sport and as a source of models for playing performance. The four major events on the women's tour are the Bowling Proprietors' Association of America (BPAA) U.S. Open, the Women's International Bowling Congress (WIBC) Queens, Sam's Town Invitational, and the WPBA National Championship. The leading women bowlers earn only about 60 percent of that earned by the leading men. For example, in 1997 the earnings of the top ten men ranged from $75,000 to $166,000, while for women the figure fell to between $44,000 and $117,000. On 4 January 2000, the WIBC and the WPBA joined forces to promote women's bowling in the United States. The WIBC began a series of promotions and commercial sponsorships during telecasts of WPBA tournaments on the ESPN2 network. In turn, the WPBA

agreed to help promote WIBC programs and membership, in addition to providing speakers for WIBC events. The various alley games have largely involved women at local amateur and domestic recreational levels, particularly when exported overseas to such places as Britain.

CONCLUSION

For women, bowling offers various advantages that make its continued growth likely, on both professional and recreational levels. Many communities have bowling alleys, and casual play requires no serious investment of time or money. Provided prize money keeps pace with interest, more women may take up professional bowling. Whether the North American form of bowling will spread further remains an open question.

John Lowerson

Bibliography

Collins, M. F., and C. S. Logue. (1976) *Indoor Bowls.* London: Sports Council.

Dunstan, Keith. (1987) *The Bowls Dictionary.* Netwon Abbot, UK: David and Charles.

Freeman, Garth. (1987) *Pentanque: The French Game of Bowls.* Leatherhead, UK: Carreau Press.

Harrison, Joyce M., and Ron Maxey. (1987) *Bowling.* Glenview, IL: Scott, Freeman.

Marchiano, Armando. (1980) *Bocce, che passione!* Padua, Italy: Casa Editrice MEB.

Martin, Loan L., Ruth E. Tandy, and Charlene Agne-Traub. (1994) *Bowling.* Madison, WI: William C. Brown and Benchmark.

Newby, Donald. (1991) *Bowls Year Book.* London: Pan Books.

Philips, Keith, ed. (1990) *The New BBC Book of Bowls.* London: BBC.

Pognani, Mario. (1995) *The Joy of Bocce.* Indianapolis: Masters Press.

BOXING

The sport of boxing is essentially a fistfight with rules and equipment. Like street brawls, barroom fights, and war, it was for a long time almost exclusively a male activity. Physicians, who have witnessed the injuries and permanent brain damage that occur, decry boxing. It has become so intensely commercialized at its highest levels that millions of dollars ride on matches that end almost as soon as they begin. It has also become one of the latest arenas for equal opportunity: boxing for women, once treated as a kind of freak show, has now become a legitimate and popular sport.

Ever since Christy Martin and Deidre Gogarty stole the show on the 16 March 1996 Mike Tyson–Frank Bruno heavyweight championship card in Las Vegas, more and more fans, male and female, have been attracted to women's boxing as a hot new sport. Only a few years earlier women's boxing was widely viewed as a sideshow or sexual exploitation at its worst. The Martin–Gogarty fight, however, proved to the 1.1 million people watching on pay-per-view television (the second most watched card on pay-per-view up to that time) that women could actually fight with skill, bleed, "get rocked," come back for more, and continue to until the final bell. Martin became the first woman athlete to appear on the cover of *Sports Illustrated,* which depicted her, bloodied, in the heat of battle. This fight, and the subsequent publicity, may have been the turning point that moved women's boxing from the fringes of sexploitation into the mainstream. Although women's boxing faces strong, emotional opposition from many male traditionalists, it has supporters, too: a USA Network poll reported that more than 80 percent of fans wanted to see more women's boxing on television.

A strange irony has emerged from this rise in fan interest. Women have never received the kind of money that top-ranked male boxers enjoy. Now, however, because of the relative lack of women available, the law of supply and demand allows many neophyte women to earn more than male boxers of the same level of skill and experience ($200 per round).

HISTORY

The roots of boxing are found in ancient Greece and Rome, but with the decline and fall of the latter it disappeared for about a thousand years, then reemerged in Great Britain in the seventeenth century. Historians generally fix the birth of modern boxing to 1719 with James Figg, the "Father of Boxing," acclaimed as Britain's first national champion. One of the greatest problems in documenting the early history of women's boxing is that it was viewed as a form of entertainment (as opposed to a serious sport), and very few records are extant. It was basically an underground activity that was usually viewed as disreputable and dangerous. Certainly it was not an activity condoned outside of a working-class context. The social prohibition against female boxing (still powerful today) can probably be attributed primarily to the idea of woman as childbearer.

Despite this widespread prohibition, however, bare-knuckles matches between women, using the same rules as the men, were not uncommon in early eighteenth-century England and, to a slightly lesser extent, in France. These activities appear to have been more spectacle than sport, but they were regularly reported in the *Times* of London. Allen Guttmann recounts a 1710 bout in which a European traveler was impressed that two women "had both fought stoutly and drawn blood." One of the earliest English women boxers was Elizabeth Wilkinson, of London, who fought as early as 1722. The *London Journal*, possibly describing one of her matches, concluded that the women pugilists "maintained the Battle with great Valour for a long Time, to the no small Satisfaction of the Spectators." A few years later, in 1728, Wilkinson defeated Ann Field at Putney Heath, London, to become the British and European female champion. The general attitude of the public toward women's boxing was not supportive. Indeed, it was almost exclusively an activity of a few women, trapped in the lower classes and ranked no better than a step above prostitution.

Nevertheless, a good number of women's matches took place during the nineteenth century, one of which saw the two combatants with "their faces entirely covered with blood." In 1807 the *Times* of London described a fight between Mary Mahoney and Betty Dyson, commenting that, at the end of forty minutes, both "Amazons" were "hideously disfigured by hard blows."

The participation of women in combat sports is not an entirely new phenomenon. Women have for many years been active participants in the martial arts, wrestling, kick boxing, tough-women competitions, "foxy" boxing (scantily clad women with no boxing skill, wearing huge gloves and flailing away in front of a predominantly male au-

SETTLING SCORES IN EIGHTEENTH-CENTURY BRITAIN (1722)

The columns of the newspapers were perpetually studded with challenges from both amateur and professional boxers and prize-fighters, male as well as female. The following are samples of them selected from the 'London Journal' for June 1722:

> I, Elizabeth Wilkinson, of Clerkenwell, having had some words with Hannah Highfield and requiring satisfaction, do invite her to meet me on the stage and box with me for three guineas, each woman holding half-a-crown in each hand, and the first woman that drops her money to lose the battle.

Mrs. Highfield signified her acceptance of this challenge in the following terms: –

> I, Hannah Highfield, of Newgate Market, hearing of the resolution of Elizabeth, will not fail to give her more blows than words, desiring home blows and from her no favour.

And it is satisfactory to learn, on the unimpeachable testimony of the press, that these two Amazons 'maintained the battle with great valour for a long time.' The following advertisement, which is very similar in character, is extracted from the issue of the 'Daily Post' for October 7, 1728:

> At Mr. Stokes's Amphitheatre in Islington Road, this present Monday, being the 7th of October, will be a complete boxing match by the two following championesses: 'Whereas I, Ann Field, of Stoke Newington, ass driver, well-known for my abilities in boxing in my own defence wherever it happened in my way, having been affronted by Mrs. Stokes, styled the European championess, do fairly invite her to a trial of her best skill in boxing for ten pounds, fair rise and fall; and question not but to give her such proofs of my judgment that shall oblige her to acknowledge me championess of the stage, to the satisfaction of all my friends.'

Answer to the foregoing: –

> I, Elizabeth Stokes, of the City of London, have not fought in this way since I fought the famous boxing woman of Billingsgate 9 minutes, and gained a complete victory, which is six years ago; but as the famous Stoke Newington ass woman dares me to fight her for ten pounds, I do assure her I will not fail meeting her for the said sum, and doubt not that the blows which I shall present her with will be more difficult for her to digest than any she ever gave her asses.

WILLIAM CONNOR SYDNEY
(1891) England and the English in the Eighteenth Century: Chapters in the Social History of the Times. *London: Ward and Downey.*

dience), and the like, as well as boxing as such. This "boxing" has a prurient element; many women in England stepped into the ring stripped to the waist. In France, although women did not strip, female boxers wore very skimpy outfits designed to show off their feminine endowments, and matches were usually held in music halls and cabarets.

Women's participation in boxing in Australia was frowned on and, indeed, illegal in most states. Nevertheless, there is evidence that it did occur. In 1847, for example, "Annie the Nailer" and "Lizzie the Bullock" settled their differences in a Wooloomooloo prize ring, and a century later a Miss Cathie Thomas fought another woman known as Sam Smiling at a Fairfield promotion.

Until quite recently, the only other Australian matches took place in various strip clubs.

One of the first recorded boxing matches between women in the United States took place on 16 March 1876. Held at Harry Hill's Theater, a popular New York theatrical venue, the match saw Nell Saunders outpunch Rose Hartland, to the delight of the mostly male crowd. It is ironic that for her winning effort, Miss Saunders was awarded a silver butter dish. Although both women trained hard for this match and had well-known male professionals working in their corners, the fight was seen more as an exhibition than anything else. About 1880 there were serious attempts by self-styled morals groups and some crusading newspapers to put a stop to male boxing, which was still illegal in most states. These efforts resulted in a number of "shameful" stories dealing with female matches. These matches took place in all parts of the country, and histories of San Francisco recount a number of instances in which Barbary Coast dance-hall girls fought many a bloody match. Indeed, the *Chicago Tribune* commented that as "beastly" as prizefights were between males, "there is an unutterable loathsomeness in the worse brutality of abandoned, wretched women beating each other almost to nudity, for the amusement of a group of blackguards, even lower in the scale of humanity than the women themselves." This approbation did not put an end to women's boxing; indeed, in 1884 a Miss Hattie Stewart of Norfolk, Virginia, was recognized as the world's female champion.

During the 1890s women's boxing was a popular form of entertainment in saloons and on the vaudeville circuit. Among the leading practitioners around the turn of the century were Hattie Leslie and Alice Leary, who fought a memorable 1888 match in Buffalo, New York. Both women were reportedly undefeated, with Leslie having knocked out forty-seven of fifty-two opponents and Leary, twenty-nine of thirty-four. Accounts of the fight detail seven bloody rounds culminating in a knockout of Leslie. Other women who plied their trade prior to World War I were Crystal Bennett, Jean LeMarr, and, arguably the best woman boxer of her era, Polly Burns.

Polly Burns was indeed widely acknowledged as women's champion in 1900. Born in Ireland in 1881, the young Burns began boxing in the wild and woolly world of carnivals and side shows at age sixteen. She laced up the gloves in fairground fights, mostly against male opponents, and more than held her own. She won her "title" in Paris in 1900 when her opponent, Mamie Donovan of Texas, failed to show up on the day of the scheduled match.

THE TWENTIETH CENTURY

Although hard evidence has not been found, several sources suggest that women's boxing was a display event at the third Olympic Games in St. Louis in 1904. The archives of the International Olympic Committee (IOC) do contain a photograph of two women boxing at St. Louis. The caption reads: "Women's boxing events held in conjunction with the World Fair gave a sideshow air to the [1904] St. Louis games."

Women's boxing also enjoyed a brief vogue in the Germany of the 1920s and 1930s. Up until 1919, it remained underground because of a police prohibition on all boxing, but with the forming, in December 1920, of the German Reich Association for Amateur Boxing, women were attracted as a way to express a stronger, more aggressive self. Many, however, feared that a

SHE BOXED, BUT PROBABLY DIDN'T WRITE

Belle Gordon, the most famous turn-of-the-century vaudeville athlete who did an act demonstrating boxing and punching techniques, was supposedly the author of *Physical Culture for Women* (New York: Police Gazette Publishing Company, 1913). Scholars, however, doubt that she actually wrote the book.

woman would become manly and coarsened through sport in general, but especially through boxing. Despite this attitude, women did engage in boxing in Weimar Germany; the German College for Physical Education included boxing in its course of instruction for female candidates. Also, many celebrities, including the legendary singer and actress Marlene Dietrich, incorporated various boxing drills into their exercise routines.

Although there are no known records of boxing matches between men and women in Weimar Germany, it clearly was a concern, since the Federation of German Fist Fighters passed a resolution banning such matches completely in 1925. Hitler's confidante Ernst "Putzi" Hanfstaengel includes an incident involving Hitler in his 1957 memoirs. It seems that in 1923 the two men attended a female boxing evening, and Hitler insisted on staying for a number of matches.

In the United States during the 1930s, women's boxing continued as a variety act. Mickey Walker, a former world-champion middleweight, trained a group of women who toured the country showing off their pugilistic skills in nightclubs, theaters, and other nonsporting venues. This informal—that is, nonsanctioned—boxing may have been made more acceptable in society's eyes because the postwar period had seen athletes such as Babe Didrickson Zaharias helping to legitimize female participation in athletics. Indeed, Didrickson actually sparred with Jack Dempsey as a publicity stunt.

The very idea of women participating in boxing was anathema for many, and especially for men. In November 1933 Pope Pius XI condemned women who so much as attended a boxing match as not helping to preserve "the dignity and grace peculiar to women."

For fifteen years in the 1940s and 1950s, the best-known female boxer was a young English girl from Yorkshire, Barbara Buttrick, who, at 4 feet 11 inches, weighed in at about 100 pounds. Buttrick competed in both Europe and North America and is estimated to have fought more than 500 "exhibition" matches against men, while compiling an enviable 31–1 record against the best women fighters of her time. Her only loss was a unanimous eight-round decision at the hands of American JoAnn Hagen, who was seven inches taller and thirty pounds heavier. Buttrick,

Mrs. Bobby Burns, photographed in 1929, applied to the Maryland Boxing Commission for permission to fight all comers in the featherweight class. (Underwood and Underwood/Corbis)

founder of the Women's International Boxing Association (WIBF), has served as its president and a roving ambassador of goodwill.

The 1970s saw the beginnings of serious and sustained challenges to the dictates of state boxing commissions that had long been controlled by white males. Caroline Svendsen became the first woman to receive a boxing license in the United States (Nevada), and Pat Pineda won a legal challenge against the reluctant state of California to secure her boxing license. Jackie Tonawanda also filed suit against the New York State Athletic Commission to secure her right to box. At around the same time, a young fighter, Marion Bermudez, was also making history. Bermudez, a veteran martial artist, challenged the Amateur Athletic Union (AAU) by demanding that she be allowed to participate in a Golden Gloves tournament.

The courts supported Bermudez's challenge, and her ability was legitimized when she easily defeated her male opponent, Anthony Suarez, in the tournament's opening round of competition. Although Bermudez lost her second-round match, she proved that a serious, well-trained woman could compete in the toughest of individual sports. Another breakthrough on the American scene occurred when northern California native Shirley "Zebra Girl" Tucker, with the support of the American Civil Liberties Union, forced the California State Boxing Commission to change its regulations and allow female boxers to fight more than the four rounds. Also in 1975, Jackie Tonawanda fought Larry Rodiana in Madison Square Garden. This bout was not only a male-versus-female event, but it also pitted a boxer (Towanonda) against a kick boxer (Rodiana). Tonawanda won by a second-round knockout and finished her career with a record of 36–1.

It should be noted that it is impossible to make any generalizations on the basis of a handful of mixed-gender matches (except that women can be competitive), and it should also be pointed out that when Lucia Riyker, arguably the best female fighter of modern times, fought Thai kick boxer Adam Jaidee, she was knocked out in the only defeat of her career. Another talented boxer, Marian "Tyger" Trimar, possessed great talent but was never able to develop it because of lack of competition in her weight class (Trimar was a 148-pound welterweight).

The apparent potential star of the 1970s was an athlete from New Orleans who had grown tired of fencing and was attracted to boxing. Five feet ten inches tall with green eyes and blonde hair, the striking Cathy "Cat" Davis quickly became the most recognizable boxer of her time and was even profiled by PBS in an hour-long documentary. She easily defeated a series of inferior opponents to build an impressive ring record. Davis became the first female to be featured on the cover of a major boxing magazine and played an important role in pushing women's boxing into society's consciousness. Unfortunately her limited boxing ability was exposed in a devastating knockout loss to Ernestine Jones on 7 June 1978.

While Davis was essentially a U.S. east coast phenomenon, broader participation by women was taking place in California. One of the best of these women, Graciella Casillas, a truly excellent fighter with devastating punching power, knocked out Deborah Wright with one punch, from which she did not revive for 10 minutes.

WOMEN OFFICIALS

As early as 2 May 1940, Belle Martell became the first women to referee a boxing match in the United States by officiating an eight-match card in San Bernardino, California. It was not until 1974, however, that Carol Polis became the first woman licensed by the New York State Athletic Commission to serve as a boxing judge.

The growing popularity of women's boxing began to diminish in the 1980s and essentially appeared to have died off, replaced by so-called foxy boxing, born in singles' bars in southern California. This activity had little to do with boxing as a sport and everything to do with the exploitation of scantily clad young women whose goal was less "boxing" than amusing the customers. On the other hand, so-called "tough-women" contests also began to appear. These were usually unskilled brawls between lower-class, financially needy women willing to do virtually anything to support themselves. It should be noted, however, that this is how Christy Martin got started.

Despite this decline, several important legal developments occurred in the 1980s and helped to lay the groundwork for a revival in the next decade. One of the most important of these was instituted by nineteen-year-old Jill Lafler, a community college student who was denied an opportunity to compete in the Lansing, Michigan, Golden Gloves tournament. She turned to the courts for relief but was denied on the grounds that she had failed to prove that she was irreparably harmed by not being allowed to fight. Significantly, however, the court said that there was no objection to a separate women's tournament, thus setting a precedent for women's amateur boxing.

On the East Coast, in April 1992, a Massachusetts Superior Court ruled that Gail Grandchamp was illegally discriminated against in being barred from boxing solely on the grounds of gender. A few years earlier, in 1986, probably the most famous boxing gym in North America, the fabled Gleason's Gym in Brooklyn, opened its doors to women who wanted to train in an au-

FIRST WOMAN HEAD OF THE INTERNATIONAL BOXING FEDERATION

In June 2000 the International Boxing Federation (I.B.F.) elected Hiawatha G. Knight, a former Michigan boxing official from Detroit, as its president. The first woman to head a boxing sanctioning organization, she replaced Robert W. Lee who resigned after being indicted by the U.S. government on racketeering charges. Knight had been vice-president of the I.B.F.

thentic environment. Most of the women who entered Gleason's had no desire to compete and wanted only to get in shape and tone their bodies. Nevertheless, this acceptance did much to encourage those few who did want to compete.

In 1991, Dallas Malloy of Bellingham, Washington, sued USA Boxing for the right to participate in its amateur tournament, and, after several legal setbacks, a federal judge ruled in her favor. This resulted in the changing of the USA Boxing's board of governors rules and the first female bout held in the state. Malloy won a decision over both USA Boxing and her boxing opponent. The following year the Amateur International Boxing Association (AIBA) officially recognized women's boxing. At the close of the century, there was a serious attempt underway to make women's boxing part of the 2004 Olympics.

WHY WOMEN BOX

At a time when men's boxing is in serious decline, marked by the proliferation of meaningless titles from questionable organizations, bizarre behavior both within and outside the ring, the machinations of shady promoters, and the like, women are entering boxing in unprecedented numbers. This prompts a question: Why? One of the initial impulses for many women is the great workout boxing training provides, as well as the sense of empowerment it gives them in a crime-ridden society. After participating in "boxercise" classes, many women found that they wanted more, and some began to drift toward competing and eventually turning professional.

One of the long-term developments has been the emergence of several women's boxing clubs on university campuses, such as Notre Dame and the University of Michigan. Most of the current crop of top female fighters, however, have emerged from the world of martial arts and kick boxing, which have traditionally been much more female-friendly than boxing. From these backgrounds have come Lucia Riyker, Regina Halmich, Bonnie Canino, Kathy Long, and others.

Whether this early momentum will be maintained is not at all clear. Since the Martin–Gogarty fight brought women boxers into the public eye, a number of serious problems have been identified. Most of them will probably be solved in time, but the often spotty and inconsistent quality of women boxers has resulted into embarrassing mismatches. This is caused by promoters who want to meet the public's interest and sometimes put a totally unqualified woman in the ring in order to draw paying customers. The managers of top women fighters may go along with this in order to pad their fighter's record and to cash in on an easy victory. A more fundamental problem, however, is the small pool of qualified boxers, few of whom have had much experience. It is not uncommon to see a young woman with a handful of fights against so-called tomato cans fighting for a championship. "Tomato cans" is an old boxing expression describing a series of weak, overmatched opponents who have little or no chance of winning. It is a common method of padding one's record.

The women who are the standouts today, particularly those with an extensive martial arts or kick boxing background, possess experience and a skill level seldom matched by the other women. The great boxing writer A. J. Liebling was undoubtedly correct when he referred to boxing as "the red light district of the sport's world." This situation can improve with time as more women start boxing earlier and attain a solid amateur experience before moving into the professional

Laila Ali, daughter of former heavyweight boxing champion Muhammad Ali, is one of several female boxers who followed their champion fathers into the ring in the late 1990s. (AP/Wide World Photos)

ranks. The interesting question is whether the female side of the boxing world will be a mirror image of the men's or be able to be substantially different. Some commentators believe that early indications (the involvement of boxing promoters like Don King and Bob Arum; the often unprofessional behavior of late-1990s icon Christy Martin, and other factors) are not promising. A more positive possibility, however, is that as women gain the kind of extensive amateur experience that male professionals commonly have, the level of competition will increase dramatically. With the burgeoning of state and national amateur tournaments, this appears to be starting.

The development in women's boxing which drew the most media attention in the late twentieth and early twenty-first centuries was the emergence of former male heavyweight champions' daughters as professional boxers. The first was Laila Ali, the daughter of Muhammad Ali,

followed by Jacqueline Frazier, daughter of Joe Frazier; Freeda Foreman, daughter of George Foreman; and Maria Johansson, daughter of Swedish boxer Ingemar Johansson. The Ali, Frazier, and Foreman daughters all won their first matches, while Johansson lost hers. All three suggested that their ultimate goal was to fight each other.

RULES AND PLAY

Although boxing is boxing, several significant differences separate men's and women's boxing. Breast protectors are mandatory for women, but groin protectors are optional; waivers must be signed guaranteeing that a participant is not pregnant; rounds in women's fights are 2 rather than 3 minutes long; and women officials must be in charge of pre-fight weigh-ins.

These rule differences generally reflect an ingrained male attitude about what women can and cannot do. For many years it was thought that getting hit in the breast could cause cancer in a woman, a belief since proved false. Yet the breasts are sensitive areas, so often-uncomfortable breast protectors are required. Much of the same attitude, entirely justified in this instance, prevents pregnant women from fighting. Indeed, in a recent important match in New York, the fight was canceled because one of the participants was found to be pregnant.

Boxing purists often argue that women's matches should mirror the 3-minute rounds of male bouts. But perhaps the 2-minute round is responsible for the virtual nonstop action of women's fights because the participants have less need to conserve their energy and can go nonstop. Whether true or not, there is a widespread perception that a typical women's match is more likely to be characterized by nonstop action.

The requirement for women to conduct weigh-ins for female fighters is understandable but is not always honored in practice, perhaps because of the paucity of women boxing officials. Another significant difference, not codified in the rules but perhaps inherent in the minds of many male referees, is their propensity to intervene and halt a fight between women long before they would take the same action in a male bout. Certainly nobody wants to see a fighter injured, but early stoppages often appear to be based more on the fighter's gender than on damage or punishment received.

ISSUES FOR THE FUTURE

For those supporters of women's boxing concerned about its future, positive legal decisions and women's subsequent participation in amateur boxing, plus the establishment of the women's national championships in the summer of 1997, argue well for the sport. It is in tournaments of this kind that young female boxers will get the amateur experience that will allow the shallow talent pool of good fighters to expand and deepen and end the frequent mismatches plaguing women's boxing at the end of the century.

Boxing for younger girls has been a controversial issue in England, and it was not until 17 March 1998 that English authorities bowed to a court order and allowed fourteen-year-old Emma Brammer to step into the ring against Andrea Prime before a crowd of 300 spectators in Leicester. During the same period, an aspiring professional with very good skills, Jane Couch, was fighting the British boxing authorities for her right to earn a living in the ring. Her sex-discrimination case eventually prevailed and the "Fleetwood Assassin" took her place in the sport.

Two of the stars of women's boxing in the 1990s were Kathy Collins, the only woman ever to have won three world championships, and Lea Mehlinger, a young woman who, in 1998, took one of Collin's belts away with a split-decision win in Atlantic City. For every Collins or Mehlinger, however, there were many fighters who were poorly trained and had limited talent.

When they are thrown in with a skilled boxer, the results are not only not pretty, but dangerous as well. If women's boxing can get through this period with a handful of top fighters but an abundance of lesser talents, the sport may soar when the talent pool expands and deepens. Until that day, however, opponents of women's boxing who contend that it is an unsafe sport point to the 13 December 1996 bout in St. Joseph, Missouri, in which Katherine Dallam was knocked out by Sumya Anani (an emerging potential superstar). She collapsed in her dressing room after the fight, then underwent extensive surgery and hospitalization for a broken nose and a broken blood vessel in her head. Fortunately, Dallam survived.

Despite its mixed history, women's boxing is unquestionably legal, and the courts have consistently affirmed this right. The establishment of amateur boxing organizations for women is a positive step forward. Boxing for women was still illegal in Australia in 1999, and frowned upon in many other countries, but several European countries have thriving amateur programs for women, and the amateur sport is beginning to grow in North America. International competitions are beginning to emerge in several places. The sport is also a victim of the political correctness police (often other women), who maintain that women should not box. What they do not seem to realize is that should a woman freely choose to box, it is not only her right to do so, but it can be an empowering experience. Women's boxing also has to fight a continuous battle against male opponents who maintain not only that it is unnatural for women to box but that women fighters also reduce opportunities for more deserving male boxers. The obstacles to the sport reaching its full potential are many, but the prospects for that to happen seem reasonably good.

Edward R. Beauchamp

Bibliography

Cahn, Susan K. (1994) *Coming on Strong: Gender and Sexuality in Twentieth-Century Women's Sports.* Cambridge, MA: Harvard University Press.

Cayleff, Susan E. (1995) *Babe: The Life and Legend of Babe Didrikson Zaharias.* Urbana: University of Illinois Press.

Denfeld, Rene. (1997) *Kill the Body, the Head Will Fall: A Closer Look at Women, Violence, and Aggression.* New York: Warner Books.

Guttmann, Allen. (1991) *The Erotic in Sport.* New York: Columbia University Press.

———. (1996) *Women's Sports: A History.* New York: Columbia University Press.

Kroeger, Brooke. (1994) *Nellie Bly: Daredevil, Reporter, Feminist.* New York: Times Books.

Nelson, Mariah Burton. (1991) *Are We Winning Yet? How Women Are Changing Sports.* New York: Random House.

———. (1994) *The Stronger Women Get, the More Men Love Football: Sexism and the American Culture of Sports.* New York: Harcourt Brace.

Oglesby, Carole A., ed. (1978) *Women and Sport: From Myth to Reality.* Philadelphia: Lea and Febiger.

Salmonson, Jessica Amanda. (1991) *The Encyclopedia of Amazons: Women Warriors from Antiquity to the Modern Era.* New York: Paragon House.

Williamson, Nancy P., and William O. Johnson. (1979) *"Whatta Gal!" The Babe Didrikson Story.* Boston: Little, Brown.

BRAZIL

Brazil is located in northeastern South America and has a population of about 140 million. Discovered by Portuguese explorers, it is the only country in South America that uses Portuguese as its official language. Brazil gained independence from Portugal in 1822. In addition to wrestling, running, and other sports of the indigenous peoples of Brazil, such premodern sports as horseback riding were common in the eighteenth and nineteenth centuries. Modern sports emerged around 1830, introduced by European immigrants or by Brazilian admirers of European—especially British—sports.

EARLY HISTORY

Until the second half of the nineteenth century, the extremely conservative structure of Brazilian society limited women's participation in sports. Girls were brought up to become wives and mothers, and physical activity was not viewed as necessary preparation. From the middle of the nineteenth century on, however, this gradually began to change. Shortly after gaining its independence from Portugal, Brazil sought recognition from the great nations of the world and, aware of European technological progress and cultural dominance, fostered the consumption of imported goods and the adoption of foreign customs. For middle- and upper-class Brazilian women, these European innovations included an increased concern with health and physical appearance, and they became a more prominent presence in the cities.

In this context, sport became increasingly possible as an avenue of social participation. It was already acceptable as an aristocratic pursuit and was considered healthful and family-oriented. At horse races and rowing events (the first sports developed in Brazil), women were present as spectators. Accompanying their husbands, they paraded in dresses of the latest fashion. Women moved relatively quickly from being spectators to being participants. By the end of the nineteenth century, some upper- and middle-class women were actively taking part in sports as jockeys in horse racing, cyclists, and track and field athletes.

THE TWENTIETH CENTURY

As Brazil entered the twentieth century, it experienced significant changes in its political, economic, and cultural life. This was the period of industrial expansion, investment in education for the elite, and an emphasis on health and hygiene. Sports acquired greater importance in this period. Increasingly, they were identified as an instrument of national identity in the international community and as an means for maintaining and improving the physical condition of the population. Recreational clubs proliferated, as did sports teams, federations, championships, regattas, competitions, athletic demonstrations, gymnastic clubs, parks, and stadiums in the cities.

The increased importance of sports was paralleled by more opportunity for female athletes. Horse racing, rowing, swimming, pole vaulting, fencing, tennis, track and field, volleyball, basketball, gymnastics, archery, and cycling brought together women from different ethnic groups, social classes, and religious backgrounds. In the 1930s, Maria Lenk (1915–) became the first female to gain real distinction in Brazilian sports. Lenk, a swimmer, set world records and was the first South American woman to participate in the Olympic Games. At Los Angeles in 1932, she competed in the breaststroke, freestyle, and backstroke events, finishing in eighth place in the 200-meter breaststroke. In 1936 at the Berlin Olympics, she competed as one of the first women in the butterfly, and in 1939 she broke two world records (in the 200- and 400-meter breaststroke events). In 1936 five other female athletes were part of the Brazilian team: the fencer Hilda von Puttkammer and the swimmers Siglinda Lenk, Piedade Coutinho, Helena Salles, and Scylla Venâncio. The best result was fifth place in the 400-meter free-

The Brazilian women's beach volleyball team in competition at the 1996 Olympic Games in Atlanta. (TempSport)

style event by Piedade Coutinho. It is worth noting that three of these six pioneering women had German ancestry. At the end of the 1950s and beginning of the 1960s, another Brazilian woman rose to international sporting fame. The tennis player Maria Esther Bueno gained a place in sports history by winning the Wimbledon singles championship in 1959, 1960, and 1965. In 1958, 1960, 1963, 1965, and 1966, she was a winner in the doubles events as well.

The second half of the twentieth century also brought increased government involvement in and promotion of sports. Industrial growth, urbanization, and the development of media determined the rapid growth of sports as a cultural phenomenon. From the 1960s through the 1970s, under military dictatorship, the government offered many incentives to develop sports activities, resulting in more female participation. Volleyball, basketball, swimming, tennis, and track and field became increasingly popular.

REGIONAL AND INTERNATIONAL COMPETITION

Since the 1970s, women have also been more involved in competition outside Brazil, including the South American, Pan-American, and Olympic Games and world championships in various sports. The women's volleyball team won both the Pan-American and world championships; the basketball team won the world championship in 1971 and has often been ranked as one of the top six teams in the world.

The number of Brazilian women on the Brazilian Olympic team has continued to increase (from fifteen in 1980 to thirty-three in 1988 to fifty in 1992 to sixty-five in 1996), and in 1996 Brazil sent more women to the Olympics than any other nation in the Americas other than Canada and the United States. Although more and more Brazilian women have taken part in the Olympic Games, it was not until the 1996 Atlanta Games that a woman won a medal: Jaqueline Silva and Sandra

BRAZIL'S FIRST OLYMPIC MEDALS

Brazilian women won their first Olympic medals at the 1996 Olympics in Barcelona when Jaqueline Silva and Sandra Pires won the gold and Monica Rodriques and Adriana Ramos Samuel won the silver in beach volleyball.

Pires won the gold medal in the first-ever beach volleyball doubles event, and Mônica Rodrigues and Adriana Ramos Samuel won the silver in the same event.

PROGRESS AND BARRIERS

Brazilian women's sports made great progress over the course of the twentieth century, but this does not mean that men and women have the same opportunities as athletes or that prejudice concerning female participation does not exist. Many women take part in sports, but the number of female participants remains far fewer than the number of male participants. This difference is visible across the spectrum of sports, from the Olympic Games to sports clubs, school activities, professional sports, and media coverage of sports. Furthermore, women play only a small role in the leadership and management of sports organizations and federations.

The growing participation of Brazilian women in sports is indeed the result of the social movement toward female equality. It is also due, however, to the discovery of women as a "potential slice of the market." Similarly, the female body is regarded as an excellent commercial vehicle for both the production and the consumption of material goods. Female athletes buy sporting goods, and winning athletes are recruited to endorse products.

Soccer—Brazil's most popular sport—is a good example of the current position of women in sports in general. Many Brazilian women now play soccer in clubs and in recreational groups, the number of the regional and national championship events open to women is increasing, and the national team is one of the best in the world. Women's soccer also serves as an excellent source of profit for the sporting goods industry, and at-tractive female soccer players are used in advertising for soccer-associated products. Nonetheless, there are almost no women on soccer commissions or in administrative positions. In addition, considerable bias and negative stereotyping are still attached to women's participation in soccer. For example, female soccer players are often suspected of homosexuality, and medical experts can still be found who warn of the dangers of the impact of the ball on a woman's reproductive health.

Despite these obstacles, the 1980s and 1990s were notable for the entrance of women into sports previously considered too violent for female participation; by the end of the century, women were competing in judo, water polo, and handball in addition to soccer, basketball, volleyball, beach volleyball, tennis, swimming, and other sports previously open to women. These new and expanding opportunities were due largely to the efforts of female athletes and advocates of women's sports who had overcome the cultural barriers mentioned above to make sports more widely available to women in Brazil.

Silvana Vilodre Goellner, Victor Andrade de Melo, Carlos Fernando Ferreira da Cunha Júnior, and Helena Altmann

BREAST HEALTH

The breast is an organ that produces milk for infants but is also a sexual ornament and a powerful symbol for both men and women. Artists as well as writers have used the breast over the centuries to represent alternatively power and submission, motherhood and sexuality. Images of breasts have had a wide variety of meanings in different cultures and different eras, affecting how contemporary women view and care for their breasts today.

There is debate over the relevance of breasts to women's sports. Some people believe that even to discuss breasts and sports is to stigmatize women unfairly as less able than men to compete in sports because of their physical attributes. Others take the pragmatic view that for many women, especially those who are not professional or elite athletes, breasts are a genuine issue and, for some women, a practical problem in sports and physical activity.

There are many ways in which the breast influences women's participation in sport. Bouncing breasts may attract the attention of spectators, and distract the woman running or playing volleyball. Many women, including professional athletes who want lucrative sponsorship deals, want to appear sexy, like the TV stars and models who are both muscular and curvaceous. Some athletes who feel that their breasts put them at a competitive disadvantage have breast reduction surgery. A high percentage of women need some breast support during exercise and sport, and women who participate in contact sports may need to wear breast protection.

Nonathletes who are overweight or who simply have large breasts may hesitate to be physically active because of the difficulty, and expense, of dealing with their breasts. In addition, the simple fact that women are expected to keep their breasts covered in public means that they must, in athletic competition, wear more clothing than men. Research shows that athletic and physically active women are less likely to develop breast and other forms of cancer, yet another connection between breasts and sports.

There are sports—skating, gymnastics, rhythmic gymnastics—where small body size, including breast size, are favorable for competition. Women with large breasts may have difficulty with balance and coordination in these sports. Sports with weight requirements also appear to work against athletes with larger breasts. Weight is a composition of muscle, fat, water, and solid structures (bones and organs). As breasts are made of fatty tissue and fat weighs less than muscle, a woman with large breasts may well have less muscle than a male athlete or a smaller-breasted female who weighs the same as she does.

HISTORY

Before the fourteenth century, women wore loose tuniclike clothing, and felt no particular need to "support" their breasts. Thereafter, women wore anything from metallic, armorlike hinged garments, to wooden and boned support stays. As recently as the early twentieth century, women still wore tightly laced corsets to support their figures. Even little girls wore stiff "waists" to "support the body healthfully," as one advertiser put it. Victorian medical practices treated the woman like a fragile object in need of support and protection. The fact that the breast was symbolic of womanhood would explain why such attention was placed on supporting and caring for the breast, an attitude that persists in contemporary fashion and beauty culture. Still, the use of bras as undergarments is not universal; in many countries around the world, the bra is used for neither support nor fashion.

The idea that breasts interfere with women's strength and physical competence goes back to the story of the Amazons, who are said to have removed a breast in order to be good archers. Women golfers have been told that their breasts make them less able than men, and an argument against women bullfighters early in the twentieth century was that the risk of having a breast gored was too dangerous because doctors were not trained to deal with wounds to the female anatomy.

Interestingly, despite some fears of damage to the breast arising from vigorous exercise, from the beginning of the twentieth century women were encouraged to use mild exercise to enhance their bust, both for reduction and augmentation purposes. One popular arm and chest exercise was accompanied by the chant of "we must, we must, we must increase our bust." Exercise may contribute to increased chest muscle tone and to body fat reduction, but will not change the size of the breast itself.

In fact, it is difficult to damage the breasts while exercising, unless one receives a direct and powerful blow to the chest. Contrary to popular

Two women, dressed for skating, model a utility bra. (Hulton-Deutsch Collection/Corbis)

belief, sport will not lead to saggy breasts or an inability to breast-feed. Sagging is due to hormonal and tissue changes.

SUPPORT

The need for breast support depends on the type of sport or physical activity in which a woman participates. Any sport with regular up and down movement means that breasts will bounce. A runner, therefore, needs more support than someone doing karate or riding a bicycle. Some women exercise without wearing any kind of support garment or bra, and report no feelings of discomfort. Many women, however, and especially those with large breasts, find it difficult to achieve both support and comfort.

The first sportsbra was the Jogbra, invented in the United States in 1978 by Hinda Miller and Lisa Lindahl. Their original creation was developed from two jockstraps (athletic supporters) being sewn together in order to better hold their breasts while they ran, and the original name for

the bra was the Jock Bra. Sportsbras work by either compressing and thus immobilizing the breasts against the chest wall or by enclosing each breast in a fabric cup made of supportive or heavy-duty material. Sportsbras come in a wide variety of styles and are designed for many different athletes, such as runners and boxers, as well as for women who have undergone breast surgery. Styles range from polar fleece versions to tank-tops that allow women to wear their bras in public.

Despite the efforts of sportsbra manufacturers, breasts still bounce. Sportsbras reduce bouncing by only 55 percent versus 38 percent by the everyday bra. Support is determined both by design, and by the fabric used in making the top. To decrease the vertical movement of the breasts (the up-and-down bobbing), the material used must have minimal vertical elasticity. To further prevent the bobbing, the breasts must also be drawn closer to the center of gravity by a top that has a flattening effect. This distributes the breast mass across the chest, and encourages them to move *with* the body, instead of in opposition, as occurs when there is bobbing. Large-breasted women may not be able to wear a flattening bandeau shape, but can choose a sportsbra that has individual cups, each one of which has a flattening effect. The degree to which the top is anchored, both above and below the breasts, also determines support; sportsbras are usually much wider than a traditional bra and come higher up on the chest. There is neither plunging neckline nor exposed cleavage in an effective sportsbra.

COMFORT

Smaller-breasted women often report more discomfort from their bras than from the bobbing that the bras intend to prevent. Other women may experience mild discomfort due to bobbing or chafing from garments. Occasionally, women may develop a rash in the areas of moisture build-up. Properly fitting and well-designed sport garments can go a long way toward alleviating these problems.

In addition to support, other features can enhance comfort. Highly supportive fabrics do not breathe well, so vented panel insets are welcome. The bra straps come in a variety of styles—crossed, traditional, or racerback—and may enhance or detract from a woman's comfort. The straps must not allow vertical movement, nor should they have abrasive seams or lace. All of the seams should be flat and smooth. A large-breasted woman may find that the weight of her breasts causes the straps to dig into her shoulders. The racerback style may alleviate this problem. Some women wear two tops—a lighter exercise top under the more supportive bra, or vice versa, or a swimsuit over a sportsbra.

Seams across the mid-cup are irritating to the nipple during exercise. Perspiration-drenched fabric can be irritating on its own. Sometimes, for a long-duration event such as a marathon, a bandage over the nipple, or a barrier cream may be helpful. Barrier cream can be used at other spots of friction—notably at seam lines. Hooks and eyes, as well as any metal closures should be avoided for the same reason. One can sometimes benefit by wearing the bra inside out, so that the finished side of the seam is against the skin rather than the more ragged inside seam.

BREAST REDUCTION AND AUGMENTATION

Breast reduction surgery is still used for two purposes—cosmetics or persistent thoracic back pain that does not respond to conservative treatment. Breast reduction is done less frequently than before, however, because it does not always resolve back pain and it is major surgery. As more and more body types are accepted and less rigid body types are stereotyped into specific sport there is less need. Also, the development of sportsbras for larger cups and postural exercises have made a great difference.

Women who have breast implants may face problems when they participate in sports, both because of larger breast size and because there have been incidences of silicone implant ruptures in contact sports. This is a major risk as the silicone can be toxic to adjacent tissues, causing chronic pain and immune system stress.

BREAST PROTECTION

Although the use of chest or breast protectors by women is advocated, little is known of their efficacy and potentially positive or negative effects on athletic performance. Female participation in high-contact sports such as rugby, hockey, and

martial arts has increased dramatically since the 1980s, raising concern regarding the injury to the female breast and the need for protective equipment. Some experts believe that breast protection is not used often enough, and then usually only after breast contusion injury has occurred.

In contact sports, sportsbras need to be padded with a protective shell in order to reduce the impact of direct blows to the chest causing breast and chest hematomas, contusions, and lacerations. Special safety equipment now available for women includes a broad breast piece used in fencing and a single breast protector used in archery. The fit of protective gear is important to avoid abrasions or interference with the athlete's range of movement.

BREASTFEEDING

The biological function of the breast is to nourish infants. Many women's breasts increase in size during pregnancy, and women who never needed a sportsbra before find that they need to wear one during pregnancy and breastfeeding. Motherhood, however, need not interfere with sports participation. Breastfeeding is an excellent way for sporting women to feed their infants when they return to training and even when competing. The time and money savings are significant—no bottles to wash, no formulas to prepare. It is the healthiest method of child feeding, for both mother and baby. Maternal milk is the most perfectly adapted food for the infant, and the hormonal advantages of lactation permit a more rapid return to health for the nursing mother. The uterus responds to prolactin, a hormone stimulated by breastfeeding, by returning to prepregnancy size more quickly.

Breastfeeding will not wear down the nursing mother. Often, the fatigue of pregnancy, delivery, and being a new mother is attributed to breastfeeding. But, if she gets enough rest, eats well, and reintroduces training gradually, breastfeeding will not be tiring. Many women have trained, competed, and even set personal records while lactating.

Mothers are advised to exercise immediately after feeding baby (because this seems to reduce the chance of engorgement), to wear a comfortable and supportive bra, and to keep the nipple area dry. Nursing pads may be helpful in case of

RACE FOR THE CURE

The Susan G. Komen Breast Cancer Foundation Race for the Cure is a national series of 5K runs to raise money for research, screening, treatment, and education about breast cancer. In 1999 runs were held in 78 cities with about 700,000 participants. The runs also provide support to those who have fought breast cancer and acknowledges their struggle. Over 50% of the funds go to support local programs, and 25% goes to national research and programs.

leakage. While nursing, the active mother should make sure her fluid intake is adequate.

BREAST CANCER

Breast cancer is a common disease, affecting women of all ages. Athletic women, though not immune, seem to have a lower incidence of breast cancer than the general population. Women who exercise regularly appear to have a 25 percent lower risk of breast cancer than women who are physically inactive. Women under fifty years and who are of normal weight appear to benefit the most. Girls who are competitive athletes in high school and college have a lower risk of breast cancer throughout most of their adult lives. The exact causes of these statistics are not known. One theory is that exercising women have lower estrogen levels and less obesity, which both may reduce breast cancer risk.

Treatment of breast cancer may involve surgery, chemotherapy, radiation, or a combination of these approaches. Whether or not a woman can continue to exercise during treatment depends on the individual woman, her treatment protocol, and how she responds to it. Some treatment modalities and some complications may make it impossible for a woman to exercise at all. Most women will choose to reduce their exercise patterns significantly, and may find that just taking a walk is enough. Intensity should be reduced during chemotherapy and radiation if fatigue is present, and repetitive motion of the arm on the side of surgery may need to be curtailed if swelling develops.

On the other hand, exercise may be an important component in coping and in emotional recovery during treatment. Even if hospitalized, some gentle range of movement exercises, stationary cycling, or walking in the corridor may help a woman with breast cancer to cope. A return to training after treatment must be gradual and gentle. In any case, it must be adapted to each person's individual needs and capabilities.

CONCLUSION

Breast health is a concern for all women, but active women and athletes face special issues, which are being addressed through education and new products that support and protect breasts during sports participation. Women's breasts need not restrict their participation in sports, and in many ways an active lifestyle that includes sports also enhances breast health.

Julia M. K. Alleyne
Karen Christensen

Bibliography

Fontanel, Beatrice. (1997) *Support and Seduction: A History of Corsets and Bras*. Trans. by Willard Wood. New York: Harry N. Abrams.

Gehlsen, Gale, and Marjorie Albohm. (1980) "Evaluation of Sport Bras." *The Physician and Sportsmedicine* 8, 10: 89–96.

Jutel, Annemarie. (1995) *The New Zealand Woman's Guide to Running*. Dunedin, New Zealand: Longacre Press.

Lorentzen, Deana, and LaJean Lawson. (1987) "Selected Sports Bras; A Biomechanical Analysis of Breast." *The Physician and Sportsmedicine* 15, 5: 128–137.

McTiernan, Anne. (1997) "Exercise and Breast Cancer: Time to Get Moving?" *The New England Journal of Medicine* 18 (1 May): 336.

Yalom, Marilyn. (1997) *A History of the Breast*. New York: Alfred A. Knopf.

BRIGHTON DECLARATION

The first World Conference on Women and Sport was held 5–8 May 1994 in Brighton, England. The conference, entitled "Women, Sport and the Challenge of Change," was attended by 280 delegates from eighty-two countries, representing governmental and nongovernmental organizations, national Olympic committees, international and national sports federations, and educational and research institutions.

The participants came together to confront the obstacles facing women's involvement and participation in sports activities and to help propel and increase that involvement in sports at all levels and in all roles: athletes, managers, coaches, referees, trainers, and administrators. The primary purpose and result was the writing and publication of the Brighton Declaration on women's participation in sports. Other outcomes of the conference were an International Strategy for Women and Sport and an International Working Group.

One reason for producing a declaration was to have a widely accepted statement of principles about women and sport which related to worldwide human and women's rights agendas. Conference organizers believed that such a statement could be used as a lever with governmental and non-governmental organizations to raise awareness and affirm the status of women and sport. The hope was that if key organizations signed up to the Declaration, they would demonstrate a commitment as a platform for future action.

EARLY DRAFTS

An initial drafting team consisted of Julia Bracewell, a member of the British Sports Council; Pendukeni Ivula-Ithana, the Namibian Minister for Youth and Sport; Sue Baker-Finch of the Australian Sports Commission; and John Scott of the International Affairs Unit of the Sports Council. In her initial remarks at the conference, Julia Bracewell, a successful fencer as well as a lawyer, pro-

vided a framework for implementing change. She noted that change will not come the same way in all organizations and nations and that change may come at the local, national, or regional level. In addition, multiple and changing strategies will be needed to effect change. She also pointed out that change takes place in social, political, and economic contexts and that those contexts will influence the resources and structures that can hinder or assist change efforts. In some contexts, legislation will be needed to legitimize efforts to effect change. In addition, how fast change takes place will also vary, with change coming quickly in some nations and organizations and much more slowly in others. Regardless of the context, she pointed out that the Brighton Declaration will help and closed her remarks by emphasizing important themes: "But whatever stage you are at, the Declaration should help you. . . . I am sure that all of you respect the differences between you and respect each other's different approach to ensure change happens. At the end of the day, the most important thing is to give all women opportunities to be involved in all aspects of sport and to change sport's culture."

PRELIMINARY WORKSHOPS

In addition to discussing issues and developing consensus for the Brighton Declaration, conference participants simultaneously took part in a variety of workshops, covering issues such as physical education, sports science, sports administration, coaching, and elite performance. Workshop leaders and participants discussed the central issues and problems and opportunities that underlie the provisions of The Brighton Declaration.

The "Physical Education and Sports Science" workshop addressed the issues of sports research, how to develop gender equality in physical education and sports science programs, how to increase the number of women and influence of women in higher education and research in physical education and sports science, and how research could be applied to the critical health problems of female athletes: eating disorders, amenorrhea, and osteoporosis. The group recommended various actions and strategies. They included encouraging more women to become researchers in order to bring a female perspective to

TEXT OF THE BRIGHTON DECLARATION

Scope and Aims of the Declaration

1. Scope

This Declaration is addressed to all those governments, public authorities, organisations, businesses, educational and research establishments, women's organisations and individuals who are responsible for, or who directly or indirectly influence, the conduct, development, or promotion of sport or who are in any way involved in the employment, education, management, training, development, or care of women in sport. This Declaration is meant to complement all sporting, local, national and international charters, laws, schools, codes, rules, and regulations relating to women.

2. Aims

The overriding aim is to develop a sporting culture that enables and values the full involvement of women in every aspect of sport.

It is in the interests of equality, development and peace that a commitment be made by governmental, non-governmental organisations and all those institutions involved in sport to apply the Principles set out in this Declaration by developing appropriate policies, structures and mechanisms which:

- ensure that all women and girls have the opportunity to participate in sport in a safe and supportive environment which preserves the rights, dignity, and respect of the individual;
- increase the involvement of women in sport at all levels and in all functions and roles;
- ensure that the knowledge, experiences, and values of women contribute to the development of sport;
- promote the recognition of women's involvement in sport as a contribution to public life, community development, and in building a healthy nation;
- promote the recognition by women of the intrinsic value of sport and its contribution to personal development and healthy lifestyle.

The Principles

1. Equity and Equality in Society and Sport
   A. Every effort should be made by state and government machineries to ensure that in-

stitutions and organisations responsible for sport comply with the equality provisions of the Charter of the United Nations, the Universal Declaration of Human Rights and the UN Convention on the Elimination of All Forms of Discrimination against Women.
   B. Equal opportunity to participate and be involved in sport whether for the purpose of leisure and recreation, health promotion, or high performance, is the right of every woman, regardless of race, color, language, religion, creed, sexual orientation, age, marital status, disability, political belief or affiliation, national or social origin.
   C. Resources, power, and responsibility should be allocated fairly and without discrimination on the basis of sex, but such allocation should redress any inequitable balance in the benefits available to women and men.

2. Facilities

Women's participation in sport is influenced by the extent, variety, and accessibility of facilities. The planning, design, and management of these should appropriately and equitably meet the particular needs of women in the community, with special attention given to the need for child care provision and safety.

3. School and Junior Sport

Research demonstrates that girls and boys approach sport from markedly different perspectives. Those responsible for sport, education, recreation, and physical education of young people should ensure that an equitable range of opportunities and learning experience, which accommodate the values, attitudes, and aspirations of girls, is incorporated in programmes to develop physical fitness and basic sport skills of young people.

4. Developing Participation

Women's participation in sport is influenced by the range of activities available. Those responsible for delivering sporting opportunities and programmes should provide and promote activities which meet women's needs and aspirations.

(continues)

5. High Performance Sport
   A. Governments and sports organisations should provide equal opportunities to women to reach their sports performance potential by ensuring that all activities and programmes relating to performance improvements take account of the specific needs of female athletes.
   B. Those supporting elite and/or professional athletes should ensure that competition opportunities, rewards, incentives, recognition, sponsorship, promotion, and other forms of support are provided fairly and equitably to both women and men.

6. Leadership in Sport
Women are under-represented in the leadership and decision making of all sport and sport-related organisations. Those responsible for these areas should develop policies and programmes and design structures which increase the number of women coaches, advisors, decision makers, officials, administrators, and sports personnel at all levels with special attention given to recruitment, development, and retention.

7. Education, Training, and Development
Those responsible for the education, training, and development of coaches and other sports personnel should ensure that education processes and experiences address issues relating to gender equity and the needs of female athletes, equitably reflect women's role in sport, and take account of women's leadership experiences, values, and attitudes.

8. Sports Information and Research
Those responsible for research and providing information on sport should develop policies and programmes to increase knowledge and understanding about women and sport and ensure that research norms and standards are based on research on women and men.

9. Resources
Those responsible for the allocation of resources should ensure that support is available for sportswomen, women's programmes, and special measures to advance this Declaration of Principles.

10. Domestic and International Cooperation
Government and non-government organisations should incorporate the promotion of issues of gender equity and the sharing of examples of good practice in women and sport policies and programmes in their associations with other organisations, within both domestic and international arenas.

research; undertaking further research on what girls and women think and feel about themselves, sport, and their relationship with sport; and using targeted recruitment to increase the number of women in all higher education institutions at all levels. They also agreed that gender-equity training should form part of all physical education and sports science courses in higher education institutions and that experts in nutrition, medicine, psychology, sociology, biomechanics, and other key areas should be involved as advisers to athletic departments and sports teams.

The "National and International Sports Administration" workshop looked at the barriers to change in sports and the different ways change had taken place in a variety of organizations. Participants talked about the multiple problems that women face: an imbalance of time, facilities, and finances in favor of male athletes; organizations with fewer resources, organizational infrastructures, female role models, and familiarity with the politics of sports; and the attitudes of men and other women and a lack of understanding of women's needs. They discussed, too, the additional responsibilities that women have within society, including balancing family and career, which are often complicated by cultural beliefs.

The workshop recommended that the conference organizers and participants publicize the Brighton Declaration and use it to lobby political leaders and those in positions of power in their national sports organizations. In addition, they recommended that women's sports advocates link the year 2000 with the "Coming of Age" of women in sports.

The "Coaching and Elite Performance" workshop focused on three areas: women as coaches; girls and women as athletes; and equity in competitive opportunities. Participants noted the various obstacles that impede women's participation in coaching and suggested a series of steps to overcome those obstacles. They suggested that child care be made available at training courses; that schedules recognize women's typical family commitments; that support courses be offered to help women gain self-confidence; and that courses better reflect women's values and aspirations.

POOLING IDEAS

A plenary session began with reports from the workshop sessions. Then Celia Brackenridge of Great Britain spoke about the need to develop international networks for women in sports for mutual support and to provide a forum for the exchange of ideas, skills, advice, information, and resources. The interrelated components of the network are women and government, women and nongovernmental groups (mainly voluntary or not-for-profit organizations), and women and sports. Brackenridge stated that women lack resources and influence and so often have a weak relationship to government, but that they tend to have a stronger relationship to, and greater success with, nongovernmental organizations. Additionally, she noted women's ambivalent relationship with sports. Many women have been exposed to sport only through physical education programs in school, with very mixed results. Brackenridge suggested that progress would most likely come because of the action of nongovernmental groups, much as the civil rights, peace, women's, and environmental movements helped promote social change. Brackenridge declared: "For us to challenge rather than simply participate in sport there needs to be a concerted effort to articulate what I call the transformative values of sport. By this I mean we must be prepared to stand up and be counted on the issues, to expose the causes of crisis, and to put into place alternative systems and approaches which will, ultimately, make sport a more humane activity for both men *and* women. We have heard examples this week of some of the more shocking aspects of sports and physical activity for women: pressure on gymnasts and dancers to submit to extreme diets and training regimes which cause premature bone loss and skeletal decline; expectations from male coaches of sexual favors from their female athletes in return for team selection; ostracism and humiliation of lesbians in sport; degradation of women by male com-

mittee members. . . . These practices must be stopped and positive changes brought about which will enhance the dignity of women and men and emphasize all the good things which we know physical activity and sport have to offer us."

THE DECLARATION IN PROCESS

Discussion of the declaration began with acknowledgments of the substantial input the draft committee received during debates, from written submissions of many individual participants and from groups working together. A final draft was submitted to the conference and was approved. The Brighton Declaration called for governments and all agencies concerned with sports to create policies and initiatives to the following purposes:

1) ensure that all women and girls have the opportunity to participate in sport in a safe and supportive environment which preserves the rights, dignity, and respect of the individual;
2) increase the involvement of women in sport at all levels and in all functions and roles;
3) ensure that the knowledge, experiences, and values of women contribute to the development of sport;
4) promote the recognition of women's involvement in sport as a contribution to public life, community development, and in building a healthy nation;
5) promote the recognition by women of the intrinsic value of sport and its contribution to personal development and healthy lifestyle.

The declaration was endorsed by delegates from many nations, large and small, including St. Vincent and the Grenadines, Russia, Bahrain, the United Kingdom, Mexico, the Philippines, Ghana, Australia, the United States, Guyana, Lesotho, and Hungary. Conference organizers and participants pledged to develop an international effort to extend the work of the conference in the coming years and to promote a more equitable approach to sports throughout the world.

FURTHER EFFORTS

This effort, coordinated by the International Working Group on Women and Sport, continued during the fourth World Conference on Women held in Beijing in 1995, where important principles from the Brighton Declaration were incorporated into the Beijing conference's own platform for action. This latter document included calls for access to recreational and sports facilities for women; gender-sensitive programs; and support for the advancement of women in physical education, coaching, training, and administrative programs.

Over the next few years, the Brighton Declaration was adopted or endorsed by more than 200 national and international organizations, including the Caribbean and Commonwealth Head of Government, the European Ministers of Sport, the Supreme Council for Sport in Africa, the International Olympic and Paralympic Committees, and the Commonwealth Games Federation. It has been translated into French, Spanish, Portuguese, Lithuanian, Arabic, and German, and concrete action was taken on many fronts.

National and local initiatives included the U.S. Girl Scouts program promoting sports for girls ranging in ages from five to seventeen called "Sports and Girls Equals a Winning Team." In Europe, the "Tri for Life" initiative encourages girls and women to participate in triathlon events.

On 19–22 May 1998, 400 delegates from seventy-four countries attended the second World Conference on Women and Sport in Windhoek, Namibia, to celebrate the success of Brighton and coordinate future activities to continue to promote and enhance and encourage participation by women.

Anita White

Bibliography

The Sports Council. (1994) *Women, Sport and the Challenge of Change.* London: Author.

BROOMBALL

Broomball has been around for about a century. It resembles field hockey more than ice hockey, although it is played on a rink. Players hit a ball, not a puck, and wear shoes, not skates. Since there is no need to be able to skate, anyone can play broomball. Broomball offers men's, women's, junior, and coed teams. Competition ranges from highly competitive leagues to recreational leagues and informal pick-up games.

HISTORY

Little is known about the early beginnings of broomball. Just about the only thing historians agree on is that it started in Canada in the late 1890s or early 1900s. The conventional story is that it began among athletes, especially women, who wanted to play ice hockey but either couldn't skate or weren't quite up to the rough play of the men at that time. For women, broomball was a viable and logical option, since men controlled hockey. One other version of the history has it first played by Russian streetcar drivers using a small ball and a broom on the winter ice on their lunch breaks. Another claims that small boys were swatting a ball with their toy brooms and this intrigued a group of soccer (association football) players. Yet another story has the game first played by the Native Americans of eastern Canada using a ball and stick and tree stumps for goals. That game was called stickball and is considered a precursor to field hockey. This is probably the closest to the actual origin of broomball, since it is most like field hockey but played on ice.

The first recorded broomball games were played in Saskatchewan in 1909 and in Ontario in 1911. The game continued to spread throughout Canada until it eventually achieved national status with the formation of the Canadian Broomball Federation, the sport's governing body. It continued to spread to many countries thanks in large part to expatriate Canadians teaching enthusiastic locals. The first world broomball championship was held in 1991 in British Columbia and featured teams from all over the world.

Broomball started in the United States in Minnesota as early as 1954 but did not gain real popularity until 1961, when teams were formed and leagues organized. By 1964 rapid growth actually hurt the sport because of a lack of facilities in the face of the growing number of leagues. In 1994 the United States Broomball Association was formed. Broomball has been proposed as a demonstration sport in the 2002 Olympics.

An informal version of broomball is played late at night when ice time is available on a regular rink with hockey-size goals. This is how the popularity of the sport continues to grow—largely by word of mouth from fanatics to recruits in these social settings.

RULES AND PLAY

Broomball is played on a regular ice hockey rink and the intention is the same: score more goals than the other team. There are six players per team on the ice at a time, including a goalie, two defenders, and three attackers; most teams include up to fourteen players. A game consists of two 20-minute periods and checking is usually prohibited at all but the elite men's and women's levels. Two referees control the action by calling many of the same penalties as in hockey.

Play is very similar to hockey, and it starts with a face-off. Players move the ball around the ice with their sticks, typically pushing it in front of them as they run. They shoot with the same type of shots as used in hockey. One difference in broomball is that the red line (center line) is used to establish off-side and the blue lines are used only as a guide to determine offensive and defensive zones. The broomball goals are 7 feet (2.1 meters) wide and 5 feet (1.5 meters) high.

As the name implies, the game was originally played with wood-handled straw brooms. They were dipped in water and then frozen for stiffness so as to better control and shoot the ball. This has evolved over the years to paddle-shaped sticks with hard rubber or plastic blades and aluminum or wood shafts.

Helmets are mandatory for play to protect the head and temple from injury should the player fall. Most players wear a hockey helmet with a face cage or shield. Knee and elbow pads are recommended, and most players prefer the hard vinyl hockey-style pads rather than the hard plastic pads used for in-line skating or soft pads like volleyball knee pads. Some players, particularly in advanced leagues, like padding around the hips and rear. Goalies often use padded chest protectors, hockey goalie pads, and a blocker. They are not permitted to use a glove as hockey goalies are. Protective gloves are also essential to shield fingers, hands, and wrists from close-in stick work. Hockey or lacrosse gloves work best, since those players have the same protection needs. Special broomball shoes, which have about an inch (2.5 centimeters) of soft rubber for traction, a hard toe cap, and padded ankles, are used by serious competitors, but many recreational players wear sneakers or lightweight hiking boots. Shin guards, genital protection, and mouth guards are all recommended for men and women.

The ball used in broomball is generally about 5 inches (12.5 centimeters) in diameter. The material and finish vary depending on the league. The rougher the surface, the better control the players have. Most balls are made of special rubber or plastic, since they must withstand hard hits at low temperatures. Some leagues use a leather ball with built-in panels similar to a soccer ball, but these are not sanctioned by any major organizations for competition.

Moscow-style, or Russian-style, broomball is a specialized version of the sport. Instead of a standard stick, players use a shortened stick with a hook on the end similar to that used in field hockey. This version is played on a shortened rink (or sideways on a regular rink) or even on iced-over tennis courts. The rules are similar, but players may not kick the ball or touch it with their hands.

Jim Hunstein

Bibliography

Alberta Broomball Association. Web site: <http://www.cadvision.com/broomball>. 1998.

Broomball World. <http://www.ozemail.com.au>. 1998.

BUDD, ZOLA

(1966–)

SOUTH AFRICAN RUNNER

The running career of Zola Budd was haunted by controversy. While this barefoot athlete set more than one world record, she is best remembered as the woman who tripped U.S. runner Mary Decker during the 3000-meter run in the 1984 Olympics.

Subsequently exonerated from any wrongdoing, Budd claimed that she had been running at a medal pace but that she slowed down after hearing boos from the crowd and thus finished in seventh place.

Zola Budd is the daughter of Frank, a printer and Englishman by birth, and Tossie, an Afrikaner caterer. Budd's sister Jenny died when the runner was just fourteen. "The loss of Jenny had a major effect on my running career," Budd said. "By escaping from death, I ran into world class."

In 1982, a year after Jenny's death, Budd won the South African national women's championships in both the 3000- and the 1500-meter events. Two years later, she shattered the 5000-meter world record, ironically held by Decker, by more than 6 seconds. Unfortunately, because of South Africa's exile status (due to its position on apartheid), her world-record run was never officially recorded.

Budd's family and coach sought a way to circumvent the worldwide sporting ban on South Africa. In 1984, she flew to England under the assumed name of Hamilton. In less than a fortnight, she was awarded British citizenship and allowed to compete for Great Britain in the 1984 Olympics, but her reputation was tainted when London's *Daily Mail* allegedly paid more than $100,000 for exclusive rights to her Olympic story.

When the media approached Budd, she refused to take a public stand on apartheid. Eyes downcast, she said that she was "just a runner, not a politician." Much later, she commented that, as a Christian, she found apartheid intolerable, but those words arrived too late to satisfy anti-apartheid groups. Budd's stress over the Decker incident and the apartheid controversies have been blamed for her health problems and even for her parents' divorce.

Budd came back to win the 1985 world cross-country championship and to set a world record for the 5000-meter race in London. In 1986, she repeated her feat as the world's cross-country champion and set a world record in the 3000-meter indoor event. After she attended a track event in South Africa, however, officials threatened to ban her from the 1988 Olympics, so she withdrew from consideration.

Beset by poor health and family problems, including the murder of her estranged father, Budd

Zola Budd practicing for the 1984 Olympics. (Hulton-Deutsch Collection/Corbis)

had difficulty getting her career back on track. In 1992, as a member of the South African Olympic track team, she was eliminated in a qualifying heat. In the mid-1990s, with apartheid ended, South Africa was again admitted to international events, but Budd's running career had ended. Now the mother of a young daughter, Budd was asked if she'd like the child to become a runner. "If she wants to run, I would encourage her," she replied, "but I'd rather she did something else—like play the cello."

Kelly Boyer Sagert

Bibliography

Brand, David. (1988) "I Can't Take It Anymore: A Depressed Zola Budd Turns Her Back on Her Running Career." *Time* (23 May): 70.

Johnson, William Oscar. (1991) "When I Began Running Again." *Sports Illustrated* (24 June): 70.

MacKay, Duncan. (1997) "Zola Budd Races On with New Perspective." *London Observer* (30 March): 27C.

Neff, Craig. (1988) "A Runner Runs Home." *Sports Illustrated* (23 May): 26.

"Olympic Heroes Then & Now: Zola Budd Pieter: She's No Longer Barefoot, But Still on the Run—From Her Past." (1996) *People* (15 July): 113ff.

Wilson, Neil. (1988) "Zola Back and Running, with a New Alias." *The Independent Archive* (18 September): 37.

BUENO, MARIA

(1939–)

BRAZILIAN TENNIS PLAYER

Maria Esther Audion Bueno is the most successful female tennis player ever to come from Latin America. Born on 11 October 1939 in São Paulo, Brazil, the daughter of a veterinary surgeon, she began playing tennis at age five. Self-taught, she developed a style of play similar to that of the men with whom she often practiced. She won the Brazilian women's championship in 1954 and, as Brazil's representative, she won the women's title at the 1955 Pan-American Games. In the meantime, she earned a teaching certificate at the Colegio Santa Ines and taught elementary school in São Paulo.

In 1958, Bueno won the women's doubles at Wimbledon, with Althea Gibson of the United States as her partner; they were finalists at the U.S. National tournament. The following year, she won the first of her Wimbledon singles championships, beating Darlene Hard of Great Britain in straight sets. After winning nineteen of thirty-five tournaments in 1959, she was ranked the top female tennis player in the world and named the Associated Press Female Athlete of the Year. In 1960, she repeated her Wimbledon triumph by beating Sandra Reynolds of the United States, but she lost to Hard in the final match of the U.S. National tournament. Out of competition because of hepatitis from June 1961 until April 1962, she did not regain championship form until September 1963, when she won the U.S. National title over

Maria Bueno (foreground) serves to Nancy Richey during their national tennis tournament match in 1960. (Bettmann/Corbis)

Margaret Smith of Australia. After victories at Wimbledon and in the U.S. Nationals in 1964, she again was ranked the top female tennis player.

In 1965, Bueno defaulted in the finals of the Australian National tournament because of a knee injury. She failed to win either Wimbledon or the U.S. Nationals and had knee surgery in the fall of that year. She returned to competition at the French National tournament in the spring of 1966 but did not reach top form until the Wimbledon finals, where she lost to Billie Jean King of the United States. Later that year, she won the U.S. National title for the fourth time before being sidelined by injury once again. A comeback try at Wimbledon in 1968 was unsuccessful. By the end of the decade, she was back in Brazil, coaching children. A full-time resident of Brazil, Bueno has represented a Brazilian textile firm in Europe and done public relations work for other companies.

She was elected to the International Tennis Hall of Fame in 1975.

John E. Findling

Bibliography

Davidson, Owe, and Clarence Medlycott Jones. (1971) *Great Women Tennis Players.* London: Pelham Books.

BULLFIGHTING

Although some writers refer to bullfighting as a blood sport, most anthropologists of the bullfight would argue that definition is incorrect since it is not rooted in bullfight culture. The Spanish bullfight, *et toreo*, is an international event performed in the bullrings of Spain, Portugal, France, and Latin America. It has been a male-dominated sport historically and traditionally, but in the 1990s the Spanish bullfight was transformed by the entry of women performers to its professional league tables as *matadores de toros* for the first time. The presence of women performers in the *toreo* remains an issue with some aficionados, but more and more are coming to accept them as the equals of their male counterparts.

HISTORY

Its myths of origin all depict early versions of bullfighting as a male activity. The present rules and structure of the bullfight were undoubtedly developed in Spain, but its ancient origins are a disputed topic. Some believe it evolved from North African bull worship, while others seek its origin in the initiation rituals of the Roman legionnaires of the Mithraic cult. Although bull-related festivities reportedly took place in Spain in the eleventh and twelfth centuries, it was not until the sixteenth century that bullfighting became an important public celebration. The bullfight of this period, performed by noblemen on horseback, was linked to ideals of tournament and military prestige. Noblewomen participated as spectators, and the only "women" performers were men disguised as women for comic effect. Distinct male and female roles were maintained in the eighteenth century when professional nonaristocratic foot performers became the protagonists in the performance. The horseback performance, not totally abandoned, developed as today's *rejoneo* (horseback bullfighting), while the triumphant male *torero* figure (performing on foot) became the dominant image of bullfighting culture. During this period the bullfight became increasingly regulated and organized: bullrings were constructed; rule books were produced; and by the mid-nineteenth century bullfighting was a legislated, professional, and still largely male activity.

However, seventeenth- to nineteenth-century journals, travelers' accounts, and artistic representations show evidence of women's participation even this early. Goya's (late eighteenth-century) print, *La Pajuelera* (c. 1750–1760), depicts a woman on horseback killing a bull. Other tales of women who performed disguised as men abound throughout the history of women's bullfighting. Performance reports and advertising posters indicate that during this period several women performers were popular; Teresa Alonso (b. late eighteenth century) and Martina Garcia (b. 1814) were prominent in the early nineteenth century. Women began to have an increasingly high profile in bullfighting during the late nineteenth and early twentieth centuries, until women's performances were temporarily prohibited in 1908 by the minister Juan de la Cierva because it was seen as morally and culturally inappropriate for women to perform as bullfighters. The now almost legendary names of this period of the history of women's bullfighting are La Fragosa (b. 1866); Teresa Bolsi (b. mid-nineteenth century), who is famous for Doré's nineteenth century depiction of her standing triumphantly over a dead bull wearing a crinoline dress; and the still controversial La Reverte (b. 1878). Although these women achieved some acclaim for their performances, neither the public nor the critics treated them as if they belonged in the same category as male bullfighters. Women's bullfighting was considered a different activity, using smaller and less dangerous bulls and often performed alongside comic performances, including dwarf bullfighters. The distinction was also reflected in the Spanish language: women were not called *toreros* but *toreras*—the feminine version.

Conchita Cintrón, female horseback bullfighter, 1941. (Hulton-Deutsch Collection/Corbis)

The arguments made by traditionalist bullfighting enthusiasts (*aficionados*) against women's bullfighting include an astonishing variety of claims ranging from the everyday to the outlandish. For example, some advance the unsurprising case that women are not physically strong or agile enough to be bullfighters. Some women performers lent support to this argument by imposing limitations on themselves, like the 1930s bullfighter Mary Gomez, who never killed a bull because she believed women's arms were too weak to accomplish this.

Others claim that women are not sufficiently brave to be bullfighters and that those who try only do so because they do not have a complete understanding of the real danger that bullfighting presents. One of the most derogatory theories is that women simply do not have the intelligence or artistic talent to bullfight. A slightly different approach is advanced by those who state that it is morally wrong for women to be bullfighters. Others merely assume that women and men have different roles to play in society and that women's role does not include performing with bulls in a public arena.

Nevertheless, the skill of some women bullfighters did make an enduring impression. The most respected woman performer of the early twentieth century was Juanita Cruz (b. 1917), of whom ex-bullfighter Domingo Ortega declared, "She was the pure bullfighter represented in the body of a woman." Cruz's debut public performance was in 1932, and her career was at its peak when in 1934 the Franco dictatorship prohibited women from performing on foot in public. His action cut short the ambition of a whole generation of women bullfighters. Unable to continue her career in Spain, Cruz went to Latin America, where she graduated to professional status.

Juanita Cruz was not the only woman performer to have her career in Spain halted by Franco's ban, although some, like Cruz, managed to continue elsewhere. Under his rule women were allowed to participate only in the *rejoneo*. During this period the *rejoneadora* Conchita Cintrón, born in Chile in 1922, developed an outstanding career in Latin America, and later Spain, as a horseback performer. However, in Spain women did not legally perform again in public on foot until 1974, when a campaign led by the woman bullfighter Angela Hernandez (b. 1946) ended the ban.

Nevertheless, the ban's effects were far-reaching and profoundly altered the history of women in bullfighting. Between the 1930s and 1970s the bullfight underwent key transformations through the innovative styles of leading male bullfighters Belmonte (1892–1962) and Manolete (1917–1947). It thus developed as an exclusively male activity, performed by men and supported by the traditionalist ideology of Franco's politics that relegated women to the kitchen.

How bullfighting might have developed over that forty-year period had women been allowed to participate will remain an unanswered question. However, since the reentry of women such as Angela Hernandez (b. 1946) and Maribel Atienza (b. 1959) into bullfighting in the 1970s, the number of women taking part has gradually increased in what is now a media-dominated and very structured and regulated amateur and professional bullfighting league. The women performers of the 1970s and 1980s participated at the amateur *novillero* stage, but they were never referred to by the masculine title of *novillero* or *torero*; they were instead called *novilleras*. Like their predecessors, they faced fierce criticism, and their careers were usually short-lived. Only in the

1990s did women foot performers become fully established as bullfighters.

The stunning career of Cristina Sanchez has come to symbolize a new status for women in bullfighting. Sanchez, born near Madrid in 1971, graduated as the top student from the Madrid bullfighting school in 1989. She continued on to become one of the most successful young *novilleros* of her time. Sanchez maintained her place at the top of the *novillero* leagues until 1996, when she became the first woman to take the *alternativa*, graduating to professional *torero* status in Nimes, France, one of the bullrings included in the Spanish circuit. Unlike her predecessors, Sanchez insists on being called a *torero*, rather than the feminized *torera*. Although she rejects the label of feminist, she argues that, as performers, men and women should be treated as equals. Her success during the early 1990s was followed by that of several other hopeful young women performers, such as the *novilleros* Yolanda Caravajal (b. 1968), Laura Valencia (b. 1971), and the successful Mari Paz Vega (b. 1974), who was granted professional *torero* status in 1997.

TRAINING

Many boys and young men aspire to be a *matador de toros*, but very few succeed in making it even into the *novillero* ranks. For women it is much more difficult. The young performer passes through three amateur stages, fighting first yearling bulls as a *beccerista*, then two-year-old bulls as a *novillero* without *picadors*, and finally fighting three-year-old animals as a *novillero* with the *picador* stage. The next step is to professional *torero* status: as *matador de toros* (literally, a "killer of bulls"). This is achieved through taking the *alternativa*, a graduation performance in which the bullfighter performs with full-grown four-year-old bulls for the first time and is recognized as *torero* by his or her co-performers.

RULES AND PLAY

Male and female bullfighters follow the same career structure and are subject to set performance rules. Although there are national variations of the performance, the professional and amateur international league tables are compiled according to the established rules of the standard Spanish bullfight.

The contemporary standard performance usually takes place in the late afternoon. Three bullfighters, supported by their *cuadrillas* (teams of assistants), kill a total of six bulls. Each bullfighter is allowed 20 minutes to perform with each of the two bulls allocated to him or her. The performance is divided into three stages. In the first, the mounted *picadors* enter the ring on sturdy horses protected by padding. They move their horses to attract the bull, and as it charges, they lance its neck muscles with a strong spear. Second, the bullfighter's foot assistants (*banderilleros*) each take two *banderillas*—short, decorated, spiked sticks with hooked ends. They run toward the bull, leaping to place these in its neck muscle until a total of six are lodged. During the first two stages, simultaneously with the actions of the assistants, the *matador de toros*, the main performer, uses the pink cape to perform with the bull, then finally takes the *muleta*, the red cape, and completes the performance with a series of sophisticated cape passes and ultimately the kill, the most demanding and dangerous movements of the whole performance. Not all performances are successful (i.e., the bullfighter kills the bull cleanly and survives uninjured); although bullfighters are rarely killed, they are often injured. Most performances follow this format, although during the initial stages of a performer's career, when he or she fights smaller bulls, the *picador* stage is excluded.

WOMEN MOVING AHEAD

Women performers now appear to be well established, but they are not universally accepted in the social world of bullfighting. Many (male and female) traditionalist members of the bullfighting public still believe that the performance should be a strictly male preserve. Some opponents refer to the origin myths of bullfighting to support the idea that women never had been bullfighters—and never should be! Others try to justify women's exclusion by referring to biological or cultural differences between men and women, arguing that the shape, strength, or even intelligence of women is not appropriate for bullfighting. Some male bullfighters, like the leading performer Jesulin de Ubrique (b. 1974), share such sexist sentiments and have refused to perform in the same arena as Cristina Sanchez. However, such opposition appears to have done little to damage the careers of the women bullfighters of the 1990s. They performed in a contemporary Spanish context that, since Franco's death in the 1970s, was transformed into a society where women were expected to take prominent roles in public life. Moreover, they became popular bull-fighters in an age of "media bullfighting"—the era of the televised bullfight, in which many bull-fight fans kept in touch with the bullfighting world through television and specialist maga-zines rather that by attending live performances. Women bullfighters received extensive and sym-pathetic media coverage. In fact, like their male counterparts, they became media stars in their own right. Through the media, an increasing number of bullfight enthusiasts were able to form their own opinions about women performers, and a surprising number were ready to concede that those viewed were as good as men.

Even those who oppose women bullfighters admit that women should play a part in the bull-fight. Some agree that the supportive role of women in bullfighting may extend to anything but performance, while the most traditional com-mentators would only allow women to attend the performance as ornamental, pretty spectators. However, the strength of their resistance to the presence of women in bullfighting seems to be failing. In addition to invading the male sphere of performance, women are stepping out of their tra-ditional beautiful-spectator role to become in-creasingly active in all aspects of bullfighting cul-ture. In the 1990s women played amateur and professional roles in the bullfighting world, such as event and career management, running bull-breeding ranches, and bullfight photography and journalism. In short, in late twentieth-century Spain, where women participated as leaders in public arenas such as politics and business, they also began to play key roles in breaking the tradi-tional masculine hold on bullfighting.

Sarah Pink

Bibliography

Boada, Emilia, and Fermin Cebolla. (1976) *Las Senori-tas Toreras: Historia, erotica y politica del toreo fem-inino.* Madrid: Ediciones Felmar.

Feiner, Muriel. (1995) *La Mujer en el Mundo del Toro.* Madrid: Alianza Editorial, S.A.

Marvin, Garry. (1988) *Bullfight.* Oxford: Blackwell.

Mitchell, Timothy. (1991) *Blood Sport.* Philadelphia: University of Pennsylvania Press.

Pink, Sarah. (1997) *Women and Bullfighting: Gender, Sex, and the Consumption of Tradition.* Oxford: Berg.

BURNOUT

Since the early 1980s the phenomenon of burnout in sports has been a buzzword. This recognition along with the negative outcomes associated with it has led to numerous research projects con-ducted on the subject. Burnout occurs when ath-letes find themselves wanting to leave athletics behind, because the passion they once felt for their sport is gone. Burnout is a common phe-nomenon encountered by many athletes at some point in their athletic careers, but it is most nota-bly associated with athletes of championship cal-iber who drop out of competition, often at the be-ginning of their careers, despite immense investments made by coaches, parents, partners, and the athletes themselves, as well as the prom-ise of future excellence.

DEFINITIONS

Burnout is a phenomenon that has many facets, yet even with the increased attention it has re-ceived, there is still a great deal to be understood about it. More than simple disengagement, lazi-ness, or boredom, burnout is a complete loss of desire to compete, to challenge the self, to feel the highs and lows associated with sport, to deal with recurring injuries or constant fatigue. It could be an indication that an athlete wants to try new ac-tivities, or wants to leave sport altogether, or finds that the time and commitment demands of the sport outweigh the rewards. Burnout duration time is variable, and perhaps this is the most frus-trating point of all for athletes, coaches, and train-ers alike. Some need only weeks to reengage, while others will leave for a lifetime.

Thomas Raedeke (1997) explains that "most discussion of athlete burnout stems from a stress perspective, which highlights that burnout is a response to chronic stress" (397). Focusing only on stress in relation to burnout leads to simple, reductionistic thinking, excluding other possible causes from the investigation process. Heeding the warning, several researchers have employed other perspectives that allow for other variables to enter the burnout equation. Raedeke's work on burnout in male and female swimmers revealed that athletes who felt "entrapped" by their sport, "or locked in to the role of being an athlete are likely to burn out. This occurs when individuals do not really *want* to participate but feel they *have* to maintain their involvement" (emphasis in original, 410).

Raedeke's sport "commitment framework" is only one alternative used in the study of burnout. Jay Coakley (1992) maintains that burnout should not be studied as a strictly psychological phenomenon, but as a social problem. "The roots of burnout," he contends, "are grounded in the social organization of high performance sport" (271). The organization of athletics in North America sets up a system "making young athletes completely dependent on coaches and parent-sponsors" (283). Because of this, these athletes feel that they have very little control over their lives and that their options are limited. Chances for these athletes to develop "desired alternative identities" are constrained (282). Only by changing the very structures that support the world of athletics will athletes be empowered and some forms of burnout ended.

BURNOUT AND WOMEN ATHLETES

For women, burnout takes on a special significance; women are encountering not only the physical pressures of sport but also societal pressures that constantly demand them to defend themselves as athletes. Women are fighting a long history in which women's participation in sport has been defined as deviant. Perhaps more than anything else in many societies, the arena of sport is defined and controlled by masculine ideals. As a result, physicality in women is always suspect and, more often than not, there are very real consequences for participation in sport. These consequences come in a variety of forms, from unequal access to facilities, equipment, and staffing, to the limited variety of organized sports available to women, to psychological abuse from parents, peers, and coaches.

Most people grow up in societies that place very different values on male and female athletic competition. For men, athletic competition is akin to a rite of passage into manhood. This is especially true in the United States, where masculinity is asserted through sport participation. It is, as sociologist Donald Sabo calls, "the way manhood has been defined".

For women, the experience can be quite the opposite. The more women participate, the more their "femininity" is supposedly defied, leading to resistance and alienation. This is especially true for younger athletes. Experts note that it is little wonder that so many young women leave athletics early on, given the tremendous pressures they are facing at a crucial time in their development.

The societal pressures women face may lead to a questioning of self and the true value of athletics in their lives. They may ask themselves if femininity and sport can go together and how they can strike a balance between the two. Some may believe that striving for this goal is inappropriate, for it (weds all to very strict masculine/feminine dichotomy) places one in an either–or position. Sport researcher and theorist Ann Hall insists that a reliance on "dichotomy forces a polarization and ignores overlaps" (1996, 14). It denies people the chance to explore the many differences and similarities that exist in our athletic experiences based on race, ethnicity, class, and sexuality lines.

There is no doubt that burnout is a complicated phenomenon and that many issues must be taken into account to understand it. For women, burnout is intricate. The societal pressures encountered throughout their lives that discourage them from athletic participation alone are enough to lead a person to burnout. A harder task ahead will be to conceptualize ways in which burnout can be deterred. It is true that not all people suffering burnout can be convinced to stay with their sport. In some cases, in fact, burnout can be seen as a positive vehicle for athletes who feel overwhelmed and need to disengage, or who want to try something new.

This aside, there are still steps that could be taken to prevent burnout from claiming women athletes with promising careers ahead of them. Responsibility must fall on the backs of parents, coaches, partners, and friends of athletes who may be able to intervene and come to the aid of an athlete who appears to be floundering. This step is especially important in preventing burnout in younger athletes. In these younger years, placing less importance on winning and strict competition may also be helpful.

More than anything else, however, athletic participation needs to be encouraged and framed as a positive thing for men and women alike. Women, in particular, need to break away from traps that question sexuality and femininity as well as their relation to athletics, for these only obscure the vision of what athletic participation is really about.

Aimee E. Marlow

See also Stress and Stress Management

Bibliography

Coakley, Jay. (1992) "Burnout Among Adolescent Athletes: A Personal Failure or Social Problem?" *Sociology of Sport Journal* 9:271–285.

Hall, M. Ann. (1996) *Feminism and Sporting Bodies: Essays on Theory and Practice.* Champaign, IL: Human Kinetics.

Raedeke, Thomas D. (1997) "Is Athletic Burnout More Than Just Stress? A Sport Commitment Perspective." *Journal of Sport and Exercise Psychology* 19:396–471.

Sabo, Donald. (1998) "Pigskin, Patriarchy and Pain." In *Race, Class and Gender in the United States: An Integrated Study,* 4th ed., edited by Paula S. Rothenberg. New York: St. Martin's Press.

BUTCHER, SUSAN

(1954–)

U.S. SLED DOG RACER

Four-time winner of the Iditarod Trail Sled Dog Race, Susan Butcher has demonstrated talent, courage, perseverance, and physical strength in an event that had been dominated by male competitors.

Susan Butcher Monson was born 26 December 1954 in Cambridge, Massachusetts. Her

Susan Butcher. (Walker and Company)

parents expected her to become a veterinarian because she was always so good with animals. She got her first dog at the age of four and before long was walking an entire pack of neighborhood dogs every day after school. By studying the dogs' interactions, she became attuned to understanding dogs' moods and methods of communication.

Even as a child, Butcher preferred the wilderness to the city, and at the age of eight, she wrote a paper titled "I Hate the City." Butcher was diagnosed with mild dyslexia in junior high school. Her difficulties at school were compounded by her dislike of staying inside and sitting still. She preferred doing more physical things and learning through experience.

Butcher's parents did not constrain their daughter to the gender roles prevalent at the time. Butcher played sports year-round and researched sled dog racing (also called "mushing") while she was in high school. By the time she was sixteen, she had also studied boating and carpentry. She applied to a boat-building school, but her application was rejected because she was female.

In 1973, she read about the 1157-mile Iditarod Trail Sled Dog Race and decided that she wanted to win it someday. This race is a grueling undertaking for its mushers, who face blizzards, wild animals, roaring winds, thin ice, and sleep deprivation during the ten to thirteen days they travel the trail with their dogs.

Butcher entered her first Iditarod in 1978 and finished in nineteenth place. A year later, she reached ninth place. In 1980 and 1981, she came in fifth. When she finished second in 1982, people really began to take notice. During these races Butcher had faced some terrifying problems. In 1982, her sled skidded into a tree; she and fifteen of her dogs were injured. In 1984, her team fell through thin ice while crossing a frozen river. Her worst experience, however, was in 1985. Butcher was competing with a strong team of dogs and was in very good position in the race when she came across a pregnant moose. The moose attacked Butcher's team, killing two of her dogs and injuring thirteen others. Butcher was forced to withdraw from the race and watch as Libby Riddles became the first woman to win the Iditarod.

In 1986, Butcher won her first Iditarod, finally achieving the goal she had set for herself thirteen years earlier. She repeated her victory in 1987, 1988, and 1990. She continued to place in the top five through 1994, when she retired from the race to concentrate on the kennel that she and her husband, Dave Monson, ran in Eureka, Alaska. Butcher never acknowledged that gender rivalry was an aspect of the Iditarod. While the mass media emphasized the fact that she was female, she commented in a 1997 interview in *Women's Sports and Fitness* magazine that it was never her goal to be the best woman musher or the first woman to win the Iditarod—her goal was simply to be the top Iditarod racer.

Butcher's persistent presence in the sport of mushing has made her a legend among mushers, sled dog breeders and trainers, and racing enthusiasts. Butcher was respected not because she was the first woman to race or to win the Iditarod, but because of the devotion and care she gave to her team, her skill in breeding and training dogs, the love she had for her sport, and her perseverance in the face of overwhelming obstacles.

Wendy Painter

Bibliography

American Academy of Achievement. "Susan Butcher Interview." <http://www.achievement.org/autodoc/page/but0int-1>. 1991.

Dolan, Ellen M. (1993) *Susan Butcher and the Iditarod Trail.* New York: Walker Publishing Company.

Hood, Mary H. (1996) *A Fan's Guide to the Iditarod.* Loveland, CO: Alpine Blue Ribbon Books.

Johnson, Anne Janette. (1996) *Great Women in Sports.* Detroit: Visible Ink Press.

Sherwonit, Bill. (1991) *Iditarod: The Great Race to Nome.* Anchorage, AK: Alaska Northwest Books.

C

CAMEROON

The Republic of Cameroon is located in West Africa and has a population of about 13 million. The country has a long tradition of informal athletics for girls, but women are permitted to participate in competitive sports only in a very limited fashion.

Throughout what is now Cameroon, nineteenth-century travelers observed women and girls competing in foot races, stilt walking, treading (a hopping game), and playing hopscotch/catch and a dancing game. In the past, adult men and women also wrestled for sport and to settle kin and intervillage disputes. In southern Cameroon, wrestling was an ancestor ritual accompanied by drums, while in the Cameroon forest it was institutionalized as a sport with rigid rules and exacting judges. Although adults no longer wrestle, matches remain competitive play for boys and girls. Among young women, running is now the most popular form of sport and competition. Soccer is the only other village sport, probably because it requires minimal equipment.

In primary schools, physical education is limited to preparation for the physical component of the primary school degree examination (CEPE). Throughout the country, secondary schools require female students to perform 2 hours of athletics and 1 hour of manual labor each week. In towns, secondary schools introduce young women to gymnastics, track and field, basketball, handball, and volleyball. Women at city schools also have facilities for swimming, lawn tennis, squash, field hockey, and golf.

Most women, however, do not continue sports beyond primary school. Burdensome farm work, family responsibilities, and frequent pregnancies define their lives, and they are rarely involved in sports after childhood. In the northern provinces, Muslim law further constrains women's participation in sports.

Recently, however, women have participated in the track and field events at the annual Cameroon Scholar and University Sports Organization's (CSUSO) Games for students. Top amateur athletes, governed by the Association des Comités Nationaux Olympiques d'Afrique, move up to compete internationally. As a university student, Leonie Mani qualified in the 200- and 400-meter events for the Eighteenth Universiade (1995) in Fukuoka, Japan, but did not compete. At the 1996 African Athletic Competition in Yaoundé, Cameroon, Georgette Nkoma in the 100-meter sprint and the 400-meter relay team won Cameroon's first gold medals in women's international games. The relay team was less successful as Cameroon's first female Olympic competitors in the 1996 Summer Olympics. They did not finish the race.

While Cameroon's female professional athletes in other sports must pursue their goals abroad, soccer players can aspire to earn positions with the national women's professional club, Les Liones. The club failed to qualify for the Fédération Internationale de Football Association's 1991, 1995, and 1999 Women's World Cup tournaments but will continue to vie for a slot in that contest.

Susan Coopersmith

Bibliography

Adedeji, J. A. (1982) "Social Change and Women in African Sport." *International Social Science Journal* 34:210–218.

Cohen, Greta L. (1993) "Sport in the Global Community." In *Women in Sport: Issues and Controversies,* edited by Greta L. Cohen. Newbury Park, CA: Sage, 305–319.

Deville-Danthu, Bernadette. (1997) *Le Sport en Noir et Blanc.* Paris: Harmattan.

Mazrui, Ali A. (1987) "Africa's Triple Heritage of Play: Reflections on the Gender Gap." In *Sport in Africa: Essays in Social History,* edited by W. J. Baker and J.A. Mangan. New York: Africana, 217–228.

Paul, Sigrid. (1987) "The Wrestling Tradition and Its Social Functions." In *Sport in Africa: Essays in Social History,* edited by W. J. Baker and J. A, Managan. New York: Africana, 23–46.

Tessmann, Günter. (1913) *Die Pangwe: Völkerkundliche Monographie eines west-afrikanischen Negerstammes,* Vol 2. Berlin: Ernst Wasmuth.

CAMOGIE

Camogie is a game of Irish origin and remains predominantly a game of Ireland. It is quite clearly a women's derivative of hurling, the national sport of Ireland, a fast and forcefully played ball-and-stick game played by two teams of fifteen players each. As a distinct sport, hurling has origins that stretch back nearly 2,000 years. It became widely played across Ireland in its modern form after the leaders of the Gaelic Athletic Association (GAA) drew up the rules in 1884. Camogie is played elsewhere across the globe by members of the Irish Diaspora, those Irish men and women who live outside their native land.

CAMOGIE AND IRISH NATIONALISM

Camogie is a sport born of Irish women's nationalist sentiments. The GAA had strong links with the nationalist movements that formed the backbone of the Irish revolution that began in the late 1890s against British rule in Ireland. The revolution would culminate in the War of Independence fought between the British and the Irish Republican Army (IRA) and the division of Ireland between the independent South, and the British North.

Women played a key role in the revolutionary period as soldiers, organizers, fund-raisers, and ideologues. Because the GAA played such a key role in revolutionary activity, it was natural that nationalist-minded women would turn their attention to the Gaelic sports. These sports, Gaelic football and hurling, were viewed as representative of good Irish values, such as morality and strength, and had ancient Irish origins. They were also a complete counterbalance to what the Irish saw as the "corrupt" sports of the British imperialists, such as soccer (association football) and cricket, both closely associated with the British Army.

That camogie was, indeed, a political statement as well as a game became clear in 1917. The strong links between the GAA and the activities of political nationalists were demonstrated that year at the funeral of Thomas Ashe. Arrested by the British for inciting the civil population, Ashe had gone on a hunger strike in prison in an attempt to secure political status for nationalist prisoners. He died as a result of force-feeding, and his funeral became a showcase for the aspirations of nationalist politics. Because Ashe had been a leading member of the GAA, a large number of GAA members attended his funeral. At the core of this group were scores of women in full mourning dress carrying their camogie sticks (*camog*).

HISTORY

Hurling was a game that was deemed too violent and masculine for women in the context of the early twentieth century, and thus women evolved their own game. The first games of what can be identified as camogie were apparently played in 1902 by members of the Gaelic League, a radical Irish language and cultural organization. In these early days the game was heavily based on the rules and spirit of hurling. In 1904 the first formal rules of camogie were drawn up. The term "camogie" was dreamed up by the Cork language scholar Tadhg O Donnchadha. As with many other Irish terms that originated in the late nineteenth and early twentieth century, "camogie" was a word for a game whose invented traditions were representative of Irish characteristics but that had no actual roots in Irish folklore or history—and thus had no traditional name. The first game was organized in Craobh a' Chéitinnigh, the Keating branch of the Gaelic League, and was played on 17 July 1904 in Navan, near Dublin, between two Dublin-based clubs; Craobh a' Chéitinnigh defeated Cúchulaoinns 1–0.

Cumann Camógaíochta, the Camogie Association of Ireland (CAA), was founded on 25 February 1905 by women who played the sport. By the start of the World War I, camogie was being played in seventeen of Ireland's thirty-two counties. By then it had also spread to London and New York, each of which had some six teams. Although a distinct body responsible for the administration of camogie, the CAA works in conjunction with the GAA. The women's association is organized in the same way as the GAA, and its tournaments are run on a similar basis.

The 1997 All-Ireland Final between Galway and Cork was viewed by many commentators on Gaelic games as a classic match and served as an excellent advertisement for camogie, especially as it was one of the first women's All-Ireland finals to be shown live on RTE, the Irish state television network. Cork won the O'Duffy cup awarded to the winning All-Ireland squad, their third senior camogie title in five years. The game was hard fought, and the fortunes of two key characters extol the virtue of the game. Sharon Glyn, leading Galway scorer in their semi-final game, should have posed the biggest threat to Cork. In the days before the game, however, she had been rushed to the hospital with lung and chest complaints after collapsing at training. Despite the injury scare, Glyn took to the field, and all Cork supporters hoped for that fairytale ending of victory over adversity. Glyn's efforts nearly brought about such an ending. She played well and got in front of goal regularly, only to see the majority of her shots saved. In the saving of Glyn's shots on goal was the true hero of the day, Cork goalie Cora Keohane.

The local parish is the base for all Gaelic games. It is here that teams are organized on the local and at the widest participation level. The parish teams play in league tournaments, and over the course of the season (March to September) the best players are selected to play at the county level. The thirty-two counties play knockout matches in four separate groupings based on the four provinces of Ireland (Ulster, Connaught, Leinster, and Munster). The county winners of the four provincial titles play off in semifinals for the privilege of playing in the All-Ireland final at the GAA's headquarters, Croke Park. The first official intercounty games were played on 12 July 1912 between Dublin and Louth at Croke Park, the Dubliners winning 2–1.

Camogie has been fortunate in that, since its early years, it is has attracted committed and long-serving administrators who have done much to promote the game, including such legendary figures as Una Bean Úi Phuirséach and Shelia McNulty, who both served as president and general secretary of the association. Men have also been centrally important in the promotion of the game. Unlike other sports and cultures in which men appear to hold back and discourage the growth of women's sport, the committee men and promoters of Gaelic games have worked well with the women who organized camogie. Camogie is seen as part of the cultural and nationalistic crusade to promote an independent sense of Irishness that is the ultimate function of Gaelic games. As such, men have been keen advocates of camogie and view it as an equally valid and important expression of Irish sporting and nationalistic culture as either hurling or Gaelic football. These men included Séan O'Duffy, who worked for seventy-five years promoting camogie, and Pádraig Puirséal, the legendary Gaelic games correspondent of *The Irish Press*, who did his utmost to promote the game in his columns.

RULES AND PLAY

Camogie is played by two teams, each with twelve women. The field is similar to the pitch used for Gaelic football and hurling, although slightly smaller. The standard measurements are 110 meters (361 feet) long and 68 meters (223 feet) wide. The stick (*camog*) is based on the hurley (*caman*) of the men's game, although it usually made to a lighterweight specification. The stick is used to advance the ball, pass to a teammate, shoot at the goal, or take the ball from the other team. At either end of the pitch are H-shaped goal posts in the same style as the posts used in Rugby Union. The bottom sections of the posts are netted, as in soccer. To score, a player must hit the ball (*sliothar*) over the top section of the uprights for 1 point, or else hit the ball into the bottom net for 3 points. The winner of the game is the team with the highest total score. Players wear footwear, shorts, and shirts bearing the colors of their team or county, and some players will choose to wear headguards to protect them from injuries caused by the ball or stick.

Given the GAA's dominant role in the new Irish state that was formed in 1922, Gaelic games became the officially sanctioned sports in Ireland and were encouraged at the school level. As the foremost women's game, camogie was positioned as the main game for girls in schools, a tradition that continues to the present. As the main school sport for girls, camogie has a huge pool of players, supporters, and organizers for its adult competitions. It currently has 78,000 playing members: 14,000 at the under-thirteen age level, 40,000 between ages thirteen and eighteen, 20,000 between ages nineteen and thirty-five, and 4,000 players in the over-thirty-five category. Until the 1990s, camogie was unchallenged as the most popular sport for women in Ireland. It now faces serious challenges from the growth in support for women's Gaelic football.

FURTHER AFIELD

All the Gaelic games have been taken overseas by those millions of Irish men and women who have left Ireland's shores over the centuries. Other aspects of Irish culture, such as music, have survived transplantation to another nation better than have the games, but pockets of activity remain. Irish emigrants apparently prefer sporting assimilation to sporting separation and have thus more readily adapted to sports such as baseball and Australian Rules football, rather than continuing Gaelic games in foreign fields. Nevertheless, the GAA is an international organization, and GAA clubs can be found across the globe in nations such as the United States, Canada, China, South Africa, Argentina, Australia, and the United Kingdom. Camogie is usually found in all those clubs. It may not be as buoyant as Gaelic football or hurling, but it has its core of women adherents who play camogie in the same way, with the same rules, and with the same enthusiasm as they do on the playing fields of Clare or Roscommon.

Mike Cronin

Bibliography

Camogie Association of Ireland. (1984) *Scéal na Camógaíochta* [History of camogie]. Dublin: Camogie Association.

———. (1990) *Playing Rules and Constitution.* Dublin: Camogie Association.

———. (1996) *Control of Matches and Playing Rules.* Dublin: Camogie Association.

Cronin, Mike. (1999) *Sport and Nationalism in Ireland: Gaelic Games, Soccer and Transformations in Irish National Identity Since 1884.* Dublin: Four Courts Press.

Cumann Lúthchleas Gael. (1984) *A Century of Service, 1884–1984.* Dublin: Cumann Lúthchleas Gael.

De Búrca, Marcus. (1980) *The GAA: A History of the Gaelic Athletic Association.* Dublin: Cumann Lúthchleas Gael.

Hughes, Anthony. (1997) "The Irish Community." In *Sporting Immigrants,* edited by Philip A. Mosely, Richard Cashman, John O'Hara, and Hilary Weatherburn. Crow's Nest, New South Wales, Australia: Walla Walla Press.

Mandle, W. F. (1987) *The Gaelic Athletic Association and Irish Nationalist Politics 1884–1924.* London: Christopher Helm.

CANADA

Canada is the northernmost country of North America, with an area of 3.8 million square miles and a population of approximately 30 million people. The range of terrain is as broad as the country, and opportunity for sports abounds. Women have long been involved in sports in Canada, and today women are sometimes disproportionately represented in elite sports competition, with slightly more women than men having represented Canada at the 1996 Olympic Games in Atlanta.

THE FIRST WAVE

English-speaking, middle- and upper-class women in feminist organizations, urban social clubs, and the newly coeducational universities were the first to make systematic efforts to create athletic opportunities for girls and women in Canada in the last half of the nineteenth century. Sport was considered a masculine pursuit, and these women had to contend with countless attempts at discouragement, fanned by ridicule, condescension, and "moral physiology." But they persisted, aided by the successful battle for dress reform, the fashion of the athletic Gibson girl, and the growing advocacy of physical activity for women by progressive physical educators.

As early as 1883 a national tennis championship was held in Toronto. In the 1890s, the mass manufacture of the "safety bicycle" gave many women the chance to pursue unsupervised physical activity for the first time. After the turn of the century, university women and university-educated high school teachers led a growing number of women into basketball and ice hockey, while younger girls played softball in the public playgrounds created by such organizations as the National Council of Women. In the Finnish and Swedish immigrant clubs, girls and women were actively involved in gymnastics festivals and picnic games.

The 1920s were a period of such rapid growth, accomplishment, and visibility that some historians have called it "the Golden Age" of women's sports. Buoyed by the victory of suffrage and the confident assumption of so many traditionally masculine tasks during World War I, Canadian women attempted every sport there was. They excelled at track and field, swimming, basketball, ice hockey, and softball. Familiar faces in the mass media included Fanny "Bobbie" Rosenfeld (1905–1969), Ethel Catherwood (1908–1987), and Myrtle Cook (1902–1989), who led the Canadian track team to top honors at the 1928 Olympics in Amsterdam; the Edmonton Grads, who won seventeen consecutive North American and four Olympic basketball tournaments (organized by le Fédération Sportive Féminine Internationale); and the Preston (Ontario) Rivulettes, who lost only two of more than 300 games in ice hockey. These women attracted record crowds wherever they competed, often outdrawing their male counterparts. A number of sportswomen, notably Rosenfeld, Cook, Alexandrine Gibb (1891–1958), and Phyllis Griffiths (1905–1978) wrote daily newspaper columns, actively contributing to the popularity of their sister athletes. It was the only period in Canadian history when women's own voices about sports were regularly heard.

At the same time, stimulated by first-wave, "separate-sphere" feminism, these women athletes sought to ensure "girls' sports run by girls." In 1924, perennial golf champion Ada Mackenzie (1891–1973) opened the Ladies Golf and Tennis

A Canadian basketball player drives against a defender during the 1990 Goodwill Games in Seattle, Washington. (Kevin R. Morris)

Club just north of Toronto, with prime tee times reserved exclusively for women. In 1926, Gibb, Mabel Ray (1882–1961), and others formed the Women's Amateur Athletic Federation (WAAF) to promote increased sport participation and better health. The WAAF initiated Canadian women's participation in the Olympic Games and the Women's World Games, established uniform standards for the seven sports it governed, began leadership development courses, and created the first national sports award for women, the Velma Springstead Trophy, named after the gifted Hamilton high school jumper who died tragically of pneumonia in 1926 at the age of twenty. The first winner was Saskatoon swimmer Phyllis Dewar (1916–1961). The federation also attempted to link the isolated pockets of activity across the country and to link leaders in high schools, universities, and the community organizations where working-class girls and women took part in athletics.

Two members of the Canadian ice hockey team surround two U.S. players during the final game at the 1998 Winter Olympics. (Wally McNamee)

Public enthusiasm for women's sports waned during the Depression for several reasons. One was the ideological accompaniment to the ever more desperate competition for jobs. Another was the escalating masculinization of the sports–media complex, as entrepreneurs realized that sports attracted male listeners and readers for advertisers better than any other form of programming. As women were pushed to the margins of the public landscape of sports, it became much harder to attract and retain female sports leaders and raise funds for women's activities. These pressures were intensified by postwar reconstruction, which focused on consumption by women in the home. The most celebrated athlete of the period, demure and "feminine" Olympic figure-skating champion Barbara Ann Scott (1928–), seemed to embody these values and, ironically, the turn away from vigorous sports. During the 1950s, teams and

leagues disappeared, newspapers abandoned regular coverage of women's sports, and the WAAF ceased operations. A few strong champions captured the public imagination—marathon swimmer Marilyn Bell (1937–), shot-putter Jacqueline MacDonald (1932–), gymnast Ernestine Russell (1938–), and downhill skier Lucille Wheeler (1935–)—but most would-be athletes faced obstacles at every turn. In hockey, manufacturers stopped making skates for women. When it was discovered that a nine-year-old Toronto all-star, Ab Hoffman, was really Abigail, a girl, public incredulity and indignation forced her from the team.

THE SECOND WAVE

The revival of women's sports began in the 1960s with second-wave feminism, the counterculture's glorification of pleasure for its own sake, the opening of physical activity to women, and a broad yearning for a more just society. In high schools and universities burgeoning with the baby-boom generation, girls and young women sought out sports programs in increasing numbers and many administrators obliged by providing them. They were inspired by irreverent feminists such as Abby Hoffman (1947–), who left her hockey disappointment behind to become a four-time Olympian in track and field, and aggressive competitors such as swimmer Elaine "Mighty Mouse" Tanner (1951–) and downhill skier Nancy "Tiger" Greene (1943–).

State support for the Olympic sports, begun with the enactment of the Fitness and Amateur Sport Act in 1961 and accelerated after 1970 with the creation of Sport Canada and similar programs in the provinces, contributed significantly. Such support provided a stage for women to shine, financial support, and television coverage, especially important at the time of the inter-national events hosted by Canada, such as the 1967 Pan-American Games, the 1976 Olympics, the 1978 and 1994 Commonwealth Games, and the 1988 Winter Olympics. In Quebec, the Quiet Revolution and the secularization of education brought French-speaking girls and women into sports for the first time, and they, too, lost little time in making their presence known.

Today Canadian female athletes actually have more representation on the national teams that participate in international events such as the Olympic Games than do the men. Although the Olympic program continues to provide more events for men, Canadian women win as many places as men on Canadian teams, and win as many medals. In fact, slightly more women than men represented Canada at the 1996 Games in Atlanta. At the 1998 Winter Olympics in Nagano, the women's hockey team was just as popular as the men's team, which included well-known players from the National Hockey League.

THE CANADIAN CHARTER OF RIGHTS AND FREEDOMS

During the 1990s, Canadian efforts to provide girls and women with sporting opportunities shifted focus from equality to equity. Whereas "equality" means treating persons the same, "equity" means treating persons in ways which are fair, recognizing that they may well have different needs and interests. Put in terms of a familiar sporting metaphor, if "equality" means providing everyone the same starting line, "equity" means helping everyone reach the most appropriate finish line. The focus on "equity" grew out of a series of Supreme Court interpretations of the Canadian Charter of Rights and Freedoms, which were passed by the Canadian Parliament in 1982 and went into effect in 1985. Sections 15 and 28 of the Charter provide for equality between males and females, allow for programs of affirmative action, and prohibit discrimination on an open-ended list of grounds. Pressed by Women's Legal Education and Action Fund (LEAF), the Court has gradually come to accept that fairness requires recognition of women's different experiences and needs.

Thus, in sports, girls and women have full access to the social resources available, even if it means allocating them in different ways (e.g. providing funds to a greater number of sports and teams). This broad interpretation has now been taken up by a number of public and voluntary institutions.

Canadian feminists have also used the Charter and human rights legislation to advance women's interests in other ways. In a series of mid-1980s test cases, Justine Blaney drew upon the Charter to overturn a provision in the Ontario Human Rights Code exempting sports from its provisions and then used the revised Code to win the right to play in the all-male Ontario Hockey Association, where opportunities were superior. In 1990, Ann Peel used the Canadian Human Rights Code and Court rulings on the Charter to pressure Sport Canada to continue her national team financial stipends during pregnancy. (Previously, national team athletes who became pregnant were cut off financial support, although injured athletes continued to receive funding.)

But while girls and women won new opportunities to play, women who aspired to leadership lost ground. With second-wave feminism's rejection of separate spheres, many of the once-separate women's programs that had long existed in schools and universities were brought under male leadership. Men got most of the jobs created by the expansion in female participation. While a few have won influential positions, women are woefully underrepresented in sports leadership overall. Women who have occupied these higher slots include Abby Hoffman as director-general of Sport Canada between 1981 and 1993, Carol Anne Letheren as chief executive officer of the Canadian Olympic Association and member of the International Olympic Committee, and Judy Kent as president of the Commonwealth Games Association of Canada.

Nevertheless, Canadian sportswomen have succeeded in persuading the major sports organizations in the public and Olympic sectors to accept gender equity in all aspects of sports as a fundamental policy objective. The chief vehicle for these efforts has been the Canadian Association for the Advancement of Women and Sport (CAAWS), formed in 1981 by a coalition of academics and sport and women's movement activists. The CAAWS has pressured governments, sports bodies, games organizing committees, and professional associations to commit to and realize gender equity. The organization has also undertaken program and research initiatives (such as "On the Move" to increase the participation of girls and women in municipal recreation); challenged the mass media to improve its coverage of women; affirmed outstanding athletes and organizers through annual awards; and publicly fought against homophobia. A more recent initiative was the development of sexual harassment policies and procedures for the Canadian sports community. During the 1990s, traditional authorities seemed discredited by the report of the Royal Commission into the Use of Drugs and Banned Practices Intended to Increase Athletic Performance (the Dubin Inquiry), and then by highly publicized revelations about sexual abuse in hockey and other sports. The CAAWS leaders, however, such as Marion Lay and Marg McGregor, emerged as respected spokespersons for the Pan-Canadian system as a whole.

CAAWS and Sport Canada was designated the 2002 hosts (in Ottawa) of the third International Conference on Women and Sport, organized by the International Working Group on Women and Sport (the first two were held in Brighton, England, and Windhoek, Namibia, respectively). Both organizations continue to work to strengthen the place of women in the leadership of Canadian sport and to set the agenda for another century of advancement. And holding the third international conference in Ottawa is a fitting tribute to the activism so long associated with women's sports in Canada.

Bruce Kidd

Bibliography

Canadian Association for the Advancement of Women and Sport and Physical Activity. (1993) *Towards Gender Equity for Women in Sport: A Handbook for National Sports Organizations.* Ottawa: Author.

——. (1994) *On the Move.* Ottawa: Author.

——. (1994) *Harassment in Sport: A Guide to Policies, Procedures and Resources.* Ottawa: Author.

Cochrane, Jean, and Abby Hoffman. (1977) *Women in Canadian Sports.* Toronto: Fitzhenry and Whiteside.

Etue, Elizabeth, and Megan Williams. (1996) *On the Edge: Women Making Hockey History.* Toronto: Second Story Press.

Gurney, Helen. (1982) *Girls' Sports: A Century of Progress.* Toronto: Ontario Federation of School Athletic Associations.

Hall, Ann, and Dorothy Richardson. (1982) *Fair Ball: Towards Sex Equality in Canadian Sport.* Ottawa: Canadian Advisory Council on the Status of Women.

Kidd, Bruce. (1996) *The Struggle for Canadian Sport.* Toronto: University of Toronto Press.

Lenskyj, Helen. (1986) *Out of Bounds: Women, Sport and Sexuality.* Toronto: Women's Press.

Long, Wendy. (1995) *Celebrating Excellence: Canadian Women Athletes.* Vancouver: Polestar.

Rosack, Sherene. (1991) *Canadian Feminism and the Law: The Women's Legal Education and Action Fund and the Pursuit of Equality.* Toronto: Second Story Press.

Vail, Susan, and Phyllis Berck. (1995) *Walking the Talk: A Handbook for Ontario Sport Leaders About Full and Fair Access for Women and Girls.* Toronto: Ontario Ministry of Culture, Tourism and Recreation.

CANOEING AND KAYAKING

Canoeing and kayaking are both paddle sports whose chief difference is the type of craft used, with the variations in handling prompted by that difference. Canoes are open; kayaks are closed except for an opening for the paddler. The paddle of a canoe has a single blade; a kayak paddle has a blade on each end of the shaft. Women and men practice both for recreation and competition.

Both sports have become extremely popular, perhaps because they can be practiced in so many different ways and styles. More women may be taking up the sport and manufacturers are now producing more responsive equipment made of lighter materials. This enables women to participate more easily and successfully.

Paddle sports appeal to a wide audience—from risk-taking women who seek the excitement of mountain streams, professionals escaping job stress by exploring newly cleaned urban rivers, to women with physical limitations who find freedom and reward through the mobility afforded by their boats. Reminders in contemporary craft of the traditional lines of a Greenland Inuit kayak or umiak, a Maori dugout, or a Native American birch-bark canoe bring a sense of tradition to paddle sports, appreciated by many modern paddlers.

HISTORY

Before the Europeans who colonized North America adopted paddling as a mode of transportation and recreation, the peoples of earlier indigenous cultures of North America, Greenland, and the former Soviet Union used canoes and kayaks. Builders stretched the skins of seal, walrus, or caribou around wooden frames and fastened them with sinew, baleen, bones, or antlers. Later, the presence of metal tools and toggles in North American boat construction signaled contact with European explorers. Ingenious craftsmen, the Inuit peoples used local materials to develop a variety of functional designs for different conditions, each of which could handle very different types of water and activities.

Kayaks were traditionally used to hunt sea animals, including large mammals such as walruses and whales. The kayaks themselves were relatively small, ranging from 12 to 16 feet, which made them highly maneuverable for chasing prey. Because only the men hunted in these societies, the kayak has been associated primarily with men.

The umiak or canoe was a large, undecked skin boat of 25 to 40 feet used to carry large groups of people and heavy loads of cargo. Sometimes used for hunting, it could be paddled, rowed, or sailed long distances. In Greenland the umiak came to be defined as the women's boat because women used these huge boats when they handled the transport of communities of people to new settlements. Umiaks are believed to be the oldest working boats. Petroglyphs in Norway from 3000 BCE show illustrations of what some archaeologists believe to be open skin boats. These seaworthy craft are also believed to have aided Asian peoples in their migration to the New World.

When European explorers arrived in the New World in the 1600s, the original dugout or hollowed-out log of native peoples had given way to the birch-bark canoe used by woodland Indians. These lighter, more versatile craft enabled explorers to navigate the thousands of miles of inland lakes and rivers, portaging over land divides to reach new watersheds. As early as the 1700s, traders or voyageurs penetrated the Canadian wilderness by canoe to send furs back out for shipment to Europe.

The earliest recreational canoeing was probably native races, but the development of canoeing as a more formal activity began around 1850 in the Peterborough region of Ontario, Canada. Craftsmen began to develop plank-style canoes, that, by the end of the century, led to an explosion in building boats at more affordable prices—a development welcomed by the general public. English barrister John MacGregor brought an oak canoe to Europe. It was propelled by sail and with a double-bladed paddle similar to the one that kayakers use today. MacGregor recorded

The sport of kayaking became popular in the 1980s. (Amos Nachoum)

his exploits in 1866 in the popular *A Thousand Miles in the Rob Roy Canoe on the Rivers and Lakes of Europe,* which fueled an amazing rise in canoe travel for pleasure on both continents.

The popularity of canoeing as an egalitarian activity in the late 1800s came at a time when the public interest in recreation in general, including bicycling, was rising. Increasingly industrialized nations could produce sporting goods more cheaply, and Victorian attitudes that treated recreation as a frivolous activity were changing. The canoe became a popular vehicle for cruising, camping, and courting, and in North America and Europe, it was considered an acceptable activity for women.

A delightful 1897 book called *Manners for Women* provided advice on suitable river costumes, which could be less "rigorously tailor-cut." The author, described only as Mrs. Humphrey, allowed that lace-trimmed white petticoats and black patent shoes were very out of place in a boat. Women's colleges in the United States, such as Smith and Wellesley, added canoeing as a healthful activity for young women, and women's periodicals such as *Cosmopolitan* began to laud the health-enhancing virtues of canoeing. The United States American Canoe Association (ACA) formed in 1880, however, allowed women to join only as associate or nonvoting members, despite three honorary memberships awarded to important non-American men such as John Mac-

Gregor and Worrington Baden-Powell, the brother of the Boy Scouts' founder. The establishment of local canoe clubs in North America and Europe continued to promote canoeing after the turn of the century, but despite the popularity of races and regattas, no women appear in ACA race results from that period. It was not until 1944 that women became full voting members of the association.

Canoe regattas and races are generally believed to have predated recorded history, and they have figured prominently in the rituals of ancient cultures. Canoeing and kayaking as Olympic sports for men began as demonstration sports in 1924 in Paris and became full medal events in 1936 in Berlin. In 1972 white-water-slalom racing entered the Munich Olympics, but it made only its third appearance during the 1996 Olympics in Atlanta.

The International Canoe Federation has governed Olympic racing since World War II. Olympic racing includes world championships, the Pan-American Games, and other international events in off-Olympic years. National governing bodies within each country develop training and racing opportunities for athletes, often in conjunction with local clubs and private schools that have traditionally supported the development of canoe and kayak racing.

The Sydney 2000 Games have inspired the construction of a $3.5-million (Australian dollars) slalom course. This major sport and recreation facility is expected to enhance the training of canoeists and kayakers in the surrounding countries and make them a more dominant force in competition. Australia's Danielle Woodward won a silver medal in slalom at the Barcelona Olympics, which helped prompt the nation to include the sport.

STYLES OF CRAFT

The functional designs of earlier years are still apparent in today's crafts, which have different names around the world. The traditional open canoe, which originated from the dugout tree of native Americans, is called a canoe in North America, but the British call it a "Canadian canoe" or a "Canadian." What North Americans call a kayak, a boat with a top deck, has been called a "canoe" in Britain. The Britons and the

MANLESS CANOEING

During the early years of the twentieth century advertisements from canoeing manufacturers and travel organizations featured women in the bow (front) of canoes being steered along by men. The July 1903 issue of *Sail and Sweep* magazine included the following ditty beneath a picture of a woman being paddled in a canoe:

A sweet little maid with hair like night,
And eyes of the self-same hue
Reclining at ease, with charming grace,
'Gainst the thwart of my canoe.

The idea of "manless canoeing" was still a novel idea in some quarters, and fears about the nature of woman's involvement began to surface. The January 1905 edition of *Sail and Sweep* profiled singer Jessie Barlett Davis as an ardent outdoorswoman who paddled, fished, and hunted for partridge and deer while wearing men's breeches. The author, Edgar Guest, expressed admiration cloaked in surprise that she "handled the frail (canoe) with the skill of an Indian," negotiating a rapid "as if she had spent all her life on water." Guest felt compelled to note that "with it all there is nothing of the Tom Boy or hoyden about her . . . no member of the party ever forgets that Mrs. Davis is a woman."

Germans are united here, for the German word "Kanu" refers to that same decked boat known in the United States as a kayak. The word "kayak," apparently originated with the Inuit word "qayaq."

In the United States, almost 25 million people paddled a canoe, kayaked, or rafted in 1995, a figure that represents approximately 12.5 percent of the total population. A closer look at the overall numbers reveals that 14 million people canoe, 2.6 million kayak, and 15.2 million paddle inflatables such as rafts. Of the 14 million who canoe, 5.34 million are women, which is about 2.7 percent of the American population. More than 880,000 women kayak, and 6.8 million paddle inflatables.

Women worldwide are taking to these sports for similar reasons. While canoeing used to appeal to people who also participated in hiking and backpacking, the activity has a much broader appeal today, and women often see it as a way to start to gain outdoor skills. In Europe and mountainous countries such as New Zealand, kayaking was once the province of competitors and hardcore adventurers who could handle the rigors of steep, alpine rivers. But more recreational paddlers are discovering the joys of learning to negotiate this abundance of white water. River kayaks are shorter, highly maneuverable boats, and would-be paddlers require instruction to paddle them safely in swift water. Women have been traditionally amenable to instruction, can now afford to pay for it, and are valued customers at paddling schools worldwide.

Sea kayaking is experiencing a surge in growth internationally as a result of a general growing interest in adventure travel. These longer, sleeker boats are extremely easy to paddle and very stable, so they offer women a secure introduction to an outdoor experience. They also allow them to explore such beautiful and exotic locations as sea caves in Thailand, the rocky shores and surf around Great Britain and Norway, the dolphin-filled bays and straits of New Zealand, and the island chains within the United States' Great Lakes.

Anyone who fears being enclosed in a kayak can try newer sit-on-top kayaks, which seem like modified surfboards and actually have their origins in surfing cultures along the Pacific Ocean. These boats look like the bottom half of a kayak with a seat and foot supports that allow paddlers to control the boat.

Canoes are a sensible option for women with families, because they are larger than kayaks and can carry more people and gear. Their larger size also allows a greater opportunity for wilderness travel for extended periods of time. Exciting vari-

Elisabeth Micheler-Jones of Germany kayaks through raging rapids as she competes in the slalom event at the 1996 Olympic Games. (TempSport)

ations on canoeing have evolved with women participating in white-water rodeos (trick competitions) and freestyle (a type of water ballet set to music). Women with backgrounds in gymnastics and dance perform especially well in these disciplines.

In Olympic competition, the European designation still dominates; canoe racing is used as an overall, inclusive category, but the results are divided into the areas of canoeing and kayaking. Kayaking results fall under the title "canoe racing."

RULES AND PLAY

In flat-water sprint racing, the athletes compete head to head on calm bodies of water in 500- and 1,000-meter distances. The events require speed, strength, and endurance to be successful and are exciting to watch. In the Olympics, women's events were added at London in 1948. However, women compete only in kayaking, not canoeing, in single, double, and four-women kayaks in 500-meter races. The four-woman kayak event was added in 1984.

Sprint contests begin with qualifying heats, and the eight fastest qualifiers advance directly to the semifinals. The rest compete in a second-chance round known as a *repechage* (French for "fishing again"), and the four fastest boats ad-

vance to the semifinals. The top six semifinalists take part in the final, while the other six take part in a *petit*-final to determine seventh through twelfth places. Soviet and German women dominated in the early years, while more recently a variety of nations have been represented at the winner's podium.

Development of a slalom site can be a difficult and expensive process for a host country when a natural white-water site is unavailable. Single kayakers negotiate a 25-gate course suspended over stretches of white-water rapids 300–600 meters long. The athlete attempts to negotiate as quickly as possible a series of hanging poles called gates in designated upstream or downstream facing positions. The kayakers try to complete the course without accruing penalties from touching poles (two seconds) or missing gates (fifty seconds). The challenge is to be fast and clean through the gates in frothy white water. Paddlers take two runs down the course, and both runs are added together for the final score. Women paddle the same white-water stretch as men, although the gates may be placed differently.

Most competition occurs in non-Olympic events, which draw a larger segment of the paddling population. Marathon canoe racing offers a lively mix of events and distances, from 5 miles to "ultra" distances of 250 miles. A common distance of 7 to 15 miles takes two to three hours. While marathons are usually geared toward canoeing, many offer a division for kayakers as well.

Women and girls can enter a variety of classes, including juniors, masters (forty years and older), women, families, and plus classes that specialize in the skills needed to use aluminum and plastic craft. They can also choose from solo or tandem (two-person) categories. The diversity of opportunity lets women select a level of competition tailored to their desires, which is why marathon canoeing is so popular. The emphasis is straight-ahead speed in long, narrow boats that are designed to track well. The water is usually calm, and the race might require one or more *portages* (carries around dams).

White-water downriver races are a variation on canoe marathons and can be nearly as long. Racers need to descend rapids and avoid obstacles in the turbulent waters, so a higher degree

LONG DISTANCE PADDLING

Mina Hubbard, a 35-year-old widow who canoed across the uncharted Labrador peninsula from east to west in 1905, was the first white traveler to complete such an arduous traverse. A deeper and darker story exists behind her remarkable journey, because she succeeded in this goal where her husband had died of starvation two years earlier. In *A Woman's Way Through Unknown Labrador*, Mrs. Hubbard fiercely recounts how she vindicated her husband's reputation by completing his dream, yet she devotes few words to the immensity of her undertaking in a cold and inhospitable land.

United in spirit with Mrs. Hubbard was a modern-day traveler from Hawaii. When Audrey Sutherland finished paddling alone from Ketchikan to Juneau, Alaska, in 1993, she had completed a 7,000-mile trip in her inflatable kayak. Though over 60, Sutherland considered anything under 300 miles to be a short trip.

of skill is needed. Canoes are often started individually, about a minute or so apart, to avoid congestion in the difficult sections. These competitions are as much about a paddler's strategy on white water as they are about conditioning. A type of downriver racing for kayakers is called wild water, in which paddlers race for time down a five-mile stretch of highly technical white water. Kayakers use extremely sleek, tippy boats to negotiate about twenty minutes of crashing water, which makes the sport a more aerobic activity than slalom.

Freestyle canoeing is a new style of competition that requires a series of choreographed moves on flat water set to music; it is paddling's version of figure skating, and some liken it to a dance on water. Competitors are judged on the artistic merit of their program as well as the technical difficulty of their moves. Dramatic boat leans combined with slow-motion maneuvers test the paddler's balance and precision, and as the sport evolves, women are introducing more dynamic elements such as gymnastic stunts into their routines. Events for women include solo and tandem competition, and they are particularly popular in regions with ponds and flat water rivers, and among people who don't crave the thrill of white water.

White-water rodeo is another emerging spectator sport, in which competitors execute a series of difficult moves in a river play spot characterized by waves and holes, which are depressions below rocks or ledges where the river rolls back on itself. The hole enables a competitor to perform stunts without getting washed away downstream; getting flushed out is considered poor form. Spectators delight in seeing competitors spin around on waves, cartwheel end over end, and perform paddle tricks; the wilder the ride, the better.

Canoe polo, which is really performed in kayaks, was conceived in England in the late 1970s to improve the boat-handling skills of racers. A variation on horse polo and hockey, it asks teams of five paddlers to pass a ball into a goal at the end of a playing court, such as a pool. The ball can be thrown, carried on the kayak cockpit, or smacked with the paddle. Short boats that turn quickly are best, and contact with other kayakers' boats is legal. Getting checked by another player in this sport means that a competitor had better be comfortable flipping over. Canoe polo is very popular in Europe, where women and children participate on club teams, and the International Canoe Federation governs the fast-growing sport.

THE BUSINESS OF PADDLE SPORTS

The United States is particularly representative of women's dominance in the business of paddle sports, where by the late 1990s many owned and managed manufacturing and service businesses. Bunny Johns, president of the Nantahala Outdoor Center and former racer, was working with the nation's largest paddling school to set the standards for excellent professional instruction. Dana

Chladek, an American kayaker who won a bronze medal at the Barcelona Olympics, owned a women's paddle clothing business called Rapidstyle, and Kay Henry started Mad River Canoe Company in Vermont and became one of the leading developers of canoes in the United States. Judy Harrison, author of a book on canoeing with kids, was co-owner and publisher of *Canoe & Kayak* magazine, while Janet Zeller, a U.S. Forest Service administrator dealing with issues of access to facilities, was in 1999 president of the American Canoe Association.

CONCLUSION

The versatility of canoeing and kayaking makes these sports very attractive to women and girls, who can find a paddling style tailored to their needs. Women who enjoy recreational paddling often express an appreciation for the outdoor environment through which they are traveling, and they enjoy paddling as a social activity with other people. Women who enjoy competitive paddling often appreciate how it allows them to combine their strength with efficient technique in order to make good tactical decisions in competition. Gliding smoothly across water has lured women to paddle sports since Victorian times.

Laurie Gullion

Bibliography

Arina, E. Y. (1987) *Inuit Kayaks in Canada. A Review of Historical Records and Construction.* Ottawa: National Museums of Canada.

Endicott, William T. (1980) *To Win the Worlds: A Textbook for Elite Slalomists and Their Coaches.* Baltimore, MD: Reese Press.

Ford, Kent. (1995) *Kayaking.* Champaign, IL: Human Kinetics Publishers.

Gullion, Laurie. (1994) *Canoeing.* Champaign, IL: Human Kinetics Publishers.

Heed, Peter, and Dick Mansfield. (1992) *Canoe Racing.* Syracuse, NY: Acorn Publishing.

Hubbard, Mina. (1908) *A Woman's Way Through Unknown Labrador.* London: McClure Co.

Humphrey, Mrs. ([1897] 1993) *Manners for Women.* Reprint, Kent, England: Pryor Publications.

"Legends of Paddling." (1994) *Canoe & Kayak* (October): 60–61.

Snaith, Skip. (1997) *Umiak: An Illustrated Guide.* Eastsound, WA: Walrose & Hyde.

CARIBBEAN

The term "Caribbean" encompasses a variety of cultures and historical landscapes of the island nations of the Caribbean Sea. Thus, women's sports experiences there inevitably reflect many conflicting characteristics. A starting point for much of the region is its heritage of slavery. In areas dominated by the French and the English, for example, the evolution of sports and/or games for women was stunted, in some respects irrevocably. The slave experience had both an immediate and a more abiding impact.

In Barbados, one of the colonial possessions held longest by the English (1625–1966), organized sports among women of any social class took a very long time to develop. The colonial masters allowed their women access to sports, but almost exclusively as a social rather than a competitive activity. Post-slavery circumstances saw nonwhite males entering sports, but they took on much of the "sport as a male bastion," making nonwhite women doubly marginalized.

The history of cricket (the most notable Caribbean sport transplanted from England) is instructive here. Organized formally from the late nineteenth century onward, it incorporated women of all colors as spectators rather than players. Reports from the 1880s onward, when referring to white women, always presented them as an adornment of the game. As nonwhite women became involved, they often appeared in reports either as spectators (women are still among the most perceptive of Caribbean cricket watchers) or, more important, as purveyors of food, an extension of their important role as traders of agricultural goods.

It took Barbadian women, and those in other English-speaking Caribbean sites, a long time to become players. Ironically, as male West Indies cricketers became all-conquering in the 1980s, their women counterparts were among the weakest players in the world as a result of the social barriers they faced in entering the game.

But women played a significant role in getting the males to cricket parity. Throughout the Caribbean cricket clubs, women frequently played important organizational and support roles. West Indies women were among the first in the world to become regular media commentators on cricket, because they were respected for their knowledge and insight. The importance of these institutional roles was borne out in some analyses of the late-1990s collapse of Caribbean male cricket power—one argument was that young males were not taking to the game as before because young women had lost interest in cricket as a social venue and force.

An important question about the definition of "sport" arises from considerations about these institutional roles. Civic activity of all kinds played a significant part in sustaining the liberation movement under colonial rule. Song and dance were key elements in maintaining the struggle, and women were leaders in those activities. Carnival was an important resistance vehicle throughout the region. So were churches and their music, calypso, street theater, and many preserved as well as invented traditions. Women were central to these social practices, many of which were carried over into sports sites throughout the region during the twentieth century. Crowd behavior patterns, dances, and songs at these sites are often supported and/or orchestrated by women. In that sense, the direct playing role might not have been the most significant one socially.

THE ENGLISH-SPEAKING CARIBBEAN

In the English-speaking Caribbean, women did take part in some sports. In colonial days white women played tennis and golf and took part in swimming and sailing and all other sports activities that occurred in the "club" atmosphere—the "club" being a center for white social activity.

After independence, particularly, other Caribbean women gradually worked their way into sports. Netball was a key game. Played throughout the post-British world, netball was dominated in the 1990s by Australia, New Zealand, and, increasingly, Caribbean teams. Those from Trinidad and Tobago and from Jamaica, especially, have become renowned. The combined Caribbean team has been very prominent, and in the 1990s other world teams expected from the Caribbean ones a vigorous, physical, fast, and skilled performance.

Basketball also became a rapidly growing sport in the Caribbean. Part of the attraction, un-

doubtedly, was that it is a world game compared to the geographically and culturally restricted netball; in addition, U.S. basketball games could be watched on television. Like their male counterparts, Caribbean women have seen basketball as a potential social escape via American college sports into a professional sports career.

Track and field was one of the most persistent vehicles of athletic achievement for Caribbean women in the 1980s and 1990s. Jamaica's Merlene Ottey was one of the most prolific world medal sprint winners during this period. Among the most recognized of world athletes, she has been a principal ambassador for Jamaica and the Caribbean. She was joined by fellow Jamaicans Grace Jackson, Jacqueline Pusey, Juliet Cuthbert, Merlene Frazer, and Marilyn Neufville, who have all run world-class times. A distinguished addition to that Jamaican list was Dione Hemmings, the 1996 Olympic champion and record holder in the 400-meter hurdles.

THE SPANISH- AND FRENCH-SPEAKING CARIBBEAN

In the non-English-speaking Caribbean, some of those patterns are replicated but others are quite different, very often because of differences in ideology and political control. In Cuba, for example, especially during the Castro era, women moved into sports quite significantly as part of deliberate social reconstruction. Volleyball, for example, became a world-class activity in Cuba. The Cuban women won their first world title in 1978, and by the 1990s they were dominant in that competition as well as in the Olympics. While less successful, women in other Caribbean locations have also taken to volleyball with enthusiasm, finding in it an expression of both power and solidarity. At a later point, the market-driven, sexual image–oriented version of beach volleyball also became a major vehicle for international promotion and success for Caribbean women.

Cuban women have been successful in many other sports. They were very prominent in judo at the 1992 Olympics, for example, winning one gold (Odalis Reve Jiminez in the middleweight division), a silver, and two bronze medals. On a population-rated basis, this was an outstanding achievement, but it has not been an isolated one—

Merlene Frazier (right) of Jamaica runs in the women's 400-meter race at the 1996 Olympic Games. (Wally McNamee)

sport has given Cuban women a voice in many areas.

BEYOND THE CARIBBEAN

There has been another major involvement of Caribbean women in sports—they have become wage laborers in sports-associated manufacturing. By the 1990s, for example, all baseballs used in the American major leagues were being manufactured in Costa Rica, where the Rawlings company had located its plant. As early as 1964 Rawlings had shifted from St. Louis to Puerto Rico, then went to Haiti in 1969 before moving to Costa Rica in 1990. The moves were dictated by labor costs, and women were always the major force because they could be paid less than men. Caribbean women, then, have played an important but curious part in American baseball.

There has been a similarly indirect and influential impact by Caribbean women upon sports throughout the world. Relocated women and their offspring have become prominent in international-level events while appearing for their "new" countries, a trend that is evident at events such as the Olympic Games, the Commonwealth Games, and world championships. The 1984 Olympic women's javelin champion, for example, was Tessa Sanderson. She competed for Great Britain, but she was born in Jamaica and remained there until sent for by her parents when they had established themselves in the new country. She be-

came a great athlete for her new country, while being acutely aware of not being fully accepted in all social quarters because of her color.

There are many similar stories to be found throughout the sports world, leading to the inescapable conclusion that Caribbean women have been major contributors to the developing sports culture in several quite different but significant ways.

Brian Stoddart

See also Jamaica; Netball

Bibliography

Beckles, Hilary McDonald, and Brian Stoddart, eds. (1995) *Liberation Cricket: West Indies Cricket Culture.* Manchester, UK: Manchester University Press.

Sage, George. (1994) "Deindustrialization and the American Sporting Goods Industry." In *Sport in the Global Village,* edited by Ralph C. Wilcox. Morgantown, WV: Fitness Information Technology.

Sanderson, Tessa, with Leon Hickman. (1986) *Tessa: My Life in Athletics.* London: Willow Books.

CASLAVSKA, VERA

(1942–)

CZECHOSLOVAKIAN GYMNAST, GYMNASTICS JUDGE, AND GYMNASTICS COACH

Two-time Olympic gymnastics champion Vera Caslavska was a national hero who emerged in her sport at the same time that her nation emerged into independence. Perhaps being born in the midst of World War II in Prague on 3 May 1942 provided Caslavska with the will to survive, to be focused, to be dedicated to a cause, and to be determined to rise above obstacles and prosper. An avid painter, Caslavska has attempted to depict the emotions that have prevailed throughout her life: passion, joy, sorrow, diligence, determination to complete what is started, competitiveness, and a drive to be the best. In her career coaching career. She has been the driving force behind Klub Sparta, one of the largest gymnastics clubs in Prague. The club's members include seasoned and novice gymnasts who have been some of the prominent and upcoming gymnasts in the Olympic movement. Additionally, she was president of the Czech Olympic Committee throughout the 1990s. In 1993, under her leadership, the Czech Olympic Committee was officially acknowledged by the International Olympic Committee (IOC). She was awarded the International Prize of Baron de Coubertin in 1989 and has been honored with the IOC's Silver Olympic Order in 1991 and the IOC Fair Play Award in 1995.

In early 1990, Caslavska was appointed as an adviser to Czech President Vaclav Havel in the areas of health services, youth sport, and education.

Darlene A. Kluka

Bibliography

Czechoslovak Gymnastic Federation Handbook (1992) Prague: Czechoslovak Gymnastic Federation.

Kluka, Darlene, P. Jansa, and P. Rehor. (1997) "The Sokol Movement: Nation Building in the Czech Republic, the United States, and Canada." *ICHPERSD Journal* 36, 1: 47–51.

"Nenapadne jubileum." (April 1995). *Revue Ceskeho Olympijskeho vyboru*. Prague: Tiskarna Flora.

Vera Caslavaska displays her three gold and one silver medal at the 1968 Olympics. (AP Photos)

as a gymnast, a judge, and a coach, Caslavska utilized many of the qualities she had so eloquently characterized on canvas.

She began participating in Sokol (the Pan-Slavic movement) gymnastics seriously at age fifteen. By the time she was thirty, she had amassed 140 medals, 22 of them in European, world, and Olympic competition: 97 gold, 32 silver, and 11 bronze. She was voted one of the ten greatest female summer Olympians of the twentieth century by a six-member panel of experts assembled by the Associated Press. One of the most photographed gymnasts of all time, she served as a model for millions of young girls and boys.

Caslavska had a passionate pride in her native Czech land. That sense of nationalism was severely tested in 1968 when Soviet tanks moved into Prague, the land was remapped, and the nation became a Soviet satellite. Caslavska was persecuted for her views on the invasion and faced reprisals that restricted her freedom to compete internationally. In 1968, after the Olympics in Mexico City, Caslavska married the middle-distance runner Josef Odlozil. They had two children, Martin and Radka, but divorced after several years.

After retiring from competition, Caslavska officiated at two Olympic Games and began a

CATHERWOOD, ETHEL

(1910–1987)

CANADIAN FIELD ATHLETE

Ethel Catherwood became the first Canadian woman to win an Olympic gold medal when she won the high jump at the 1928 Olympic Games in Amsterdam. Catherwood was born on 2 May 1910, in Toronto, Ontario. She first became known in Canada in July 1926 when she cleared what was then a national record of 4 feet 11 inches at a meet in her native Saskatoon. In September 1926, at the Saskatchewan championships in Regina, Catherwood cleared 5 feet 2⁷/₁₆ inches to claim her first world high jump record. In 1927 Catherwood competed in her first Canadian Amateur Athletic Union (AAU) championship. There she won the high jump with a mark of 5 feet 2 inches and also won the javelin throw. In 1928 she repeated her Canadian titles in both events, held in Halifax, Nova Scotia. Her javelin mark of 118 feet 8 inches at Halifax set a new Canadian record and her winning high jump of 5 feet 3 inches produced her second world record.

Prior to the Amsterdam Olympics in 1928, Catherwood lost her world record to Carolina Gisolf of the Netherlands, and the two jumpers were co-favorites to win the Olympic high jump. Gisolf was the crowd favorite, competing in her native country, but Catherwood was the media darling. Because of her beauty, they christened her "The Saskatoon Lily," and she was the most photographed female athlete in Amsterdam. Pushed by both Gisolf and America's Mildred Wiley, Catherwood did not win easily. But when the bar was raised to 5 feet 2 inches, only Catherwood could clear it, and she won the gold medal. In 1928 the javelin throw was not yet contested at the Olympic Games, denying her the opportunity to compete in two field events.

After the Olympics, Catherwood briefly toured Europe before returning to a tumultuous parade in Canada.

Ethel Catherwood continued to compete in track and field athletics after the 1928 Olympics. She did not compete at the 1929 Canadian AAU championships, but her high-jump mark of 5 feet 2 inches in Saskatoon in July 1929 topped the Canadian list for the year. In 1930 she again won the Canadian title in both the high jump and javelin throw. In 1931 Catherwood repeated her javelin title at the Canadian championships held in Wetaskiwin, Alberta. But she finished third in the high jump in Wetaskiwin, hampered by a series of injuries, and then retired from athletics.

In 1929 Catherwood had secretly married James McLaren. The marriage did not last, and they divorced in Reno, Nevada, in July 1932. She moved to San Francisco, where she married Byron Mitchell a few months after her divorce. Catherwood died on 18 September 1987.

Bill Mallon

Bibliography

Cosentino, Frank, and Glynn Leyshon. (1975) *Olympic Gold: Canada's Winner in the Summer Games.* Toronto: Holt, Rinehart and Winston.

Wise, S. F., and Douglas Fisher. (1974) *Canada's Sporting Heroes.* Don Mills, Ontario: General Publishing Company.

CHEERLEADING

Cheerleading is a sport that combines stunting, tumbling, dancing, cheering, and crowd psychology. It is practiced in tandem with other sports, as cheerleaders continue to perform at athletic events and also alone in competition, often in televised events. Cheerleading has flourished in the United States for just over a century, although women have participated only since the 1920s. The sport did not spread beyond the United States until the 1980s.

HISTORY

Cheerleading started with a male "yell leader," who single-handedly roused the crowd to motivate the team. Johnny Campbell of the University of Minnesota, in 1898, has been credited as the first cheerleader. In the 1840s, prior to the creation of cheerleaders, organized cheering was part of military tradition in the U.S. Army and Navy. The first documented cheering at a sporting event occurred at the 1869 Rutgers–Princeton football game in which "Siss, boom, ahhh!" was heard from the college cheering sections. Initially, cheers were led by substitute or injured players on the bench, who would seek fan support at critical points of the game. By the late 1890s, yell leaders who were captains of baseball, track, and other sports teams were designated as cheerleaders. In the early 1900s, the position of yell leader at one's school was nearly as prestigious as that of quarterback of the football team. After nearly three decades of having captains as yell leaders, noncaptain lettermen began to join the ranks of cheerleading, as captains opted to spend their Saturday afternoons in the stands.

Over the years, cheerleading squads of four or more members replaced individual yell leaders.

Women became cheerleaders in the 1920s, although in a limited way and with some opposition. Men continued to dominate the practice. Gamma Sigma, a national honorary cheerleading fraternity, was formed before World War II and annually selected eleven men for an All-American cheerleading squad. Champion squad members were evaluated by sportswriters and sportscasters according to the following criteria: cheering-section reaction; ability to select the most appropriate psychological moment for a cheer; and gymnastics or acrobatic talents. The winners each year were rewarded with the All-American insignia, which consisted of a shield with two crossed megaphones.

Cheerleading innovations have dazzled crowds throughout the sport's history. One of the best known was the card trick, which consisted of having various cheering sections hold up designated cards to form colored images. Although both the University of Southern California and Stanford University have claimed authorship, a similar card trick was most likely used at the Yale Bowl on Dedication Day in 1914. At a football game in Utah in 1954, Denver (the visiting team) used another innovation to surprise its opponent. The Denver team, in effect, brought its cheering section to the Utah stadium by playing a tape of the Denver rooting section over a truck's loudspeakers.

FEMALE CHEERLEADERS

Documentation of women's early participation in the practice is sketchy, but the University of Minnesota has also been credited with having the first female cheerleader. Initially, school administrators resisted the notion of female participation in cheerleading, fearing that the women would become "masculinized" as a result of their involvement. The loud and deep yelling was thought to cause female cheerleaders to develop manly voices. Opponents also anticipated that female cheerleaders would adopt profanity based on their association with male squad members. Another argument for keeping women out of cheerleading was that females were considered less capable of performing the acrobatic stunts that male cheerleaders had introduced to the sport.

Resistance to female cheerleaders was so strong that some high schools and colleges

Standing on each other's shoulders to form a human pyramid, Illinois State University cheerleaders perform a routine during a home football game. (Philip Gould/Corbis)

banned them as late as the 1950s. In Redwood, California, school officials offered four arguments in support of a ban on female cheerleading at its high school: (1) girls' voices were too shrill for cheering; (2) girls did not know the subtleties of sports well enough to lead cheers; (3) girls could not control the rooters successfully; and (4) the boys wanted to get back into the act.

Although some female cheerleaders encountered opposition when they entered the sport, others added new twists and promoted cheerleading in a variety of ways. In 1940, rhythmnastics, a combination of gymnastics and dance movements, was created by Joyce Wargo, Gloria Huenger, and Nancy Johnson at Whiting High School in Indiana. These women incorporated the jazz and swing music of the time to create a new style of cheerleading.

ON TO VICTORY

Excerpt from a 1955 Rockford, Illinois, High School Yearbook

"On with Lincoln," and "Go, Go, Go," are sounds that you would hear coming from the Lincoln gym if you happened to be passing during one of the athletic contests held here at the school. On entering the gym you would see the cheerleaders out on the floor helping the teams realize that the student body is behind them, and cheering them onto victory.

To become a cheerleader at Lincoln a girl has to out-perform most of the other applicants, who sometimes number in the hundreds. She has to prove herself one of the six best in the school. When she has successfully passed the first tryouts, she must still sweat out the second and third attempts. If she is chosen by the judges, who are faculty members, pep club officers, and the old cheerleaders, she then enters a rigid schedule of practices. These practices are held before school, and are only part of the requirements for the maintenance of the position. The cheerleaders must maintain passing grades, and are not allowed to garner any zero hours during the year.

Rockford High School Yearbook (1955). Rockford, IL.

Cheerleading increased in popularity for females throughout the 1940s and 1950s despite the occasional banning. In 1946, cheerleading clinics were initiated by Bruce Turvold in Northwood, Iowa. In 1950, the University of Minnesota hosted a cheer clinic for 200 cheerleaders. The University of Michigan's cheerleading squad conducted cheer clinics in five different locations, with 2,000 to 2,500 participants per clinic. Cheerleading associations emerged in 1948 in Dallas, Texas, when Larry Herkimer, who gave the sport the term "herky" jump, started the National Cheerleading Association (NCA). The NCA provided cheerleading camps, week-long clinics for cheerleaders to train and compete; they were also an opportunity for cheerleading to become nationally organized. Cheerleading competitions have been documented in the early 1950s in New York's Westchester County. Twenty-five high school squads competed annually in front of large crowds for a single championship title. A roundtable discussion followed these competitions to develop a list of recommendations for cheerleader selection, the types of cheers, precision and timing in cheerleading, uniform problems, and sportsmanship.

Cheerleading college courses were also in existence during the 1940s and 1950s. Purdue University offered a college cheerleading course in 1942, in which thirty students learned about crowd psychology and tumbling. The University of Michigan provided a course for potential cheerleading advisers in 1952 that was limited to senior women physical education majors. In the 1950s and 1960s, cheerleaders often served as representatives of their school class. Many high school students tried out in front of the student body or faculty. These tryouts often drew between ninety and a hundred aspirants. Throughout this time, most high school squads were all-female, while most college squads were coed. In the 1960s, African American and hippie yell leaders were nominated to squads, reflecting the civil rights and antiwar sentiments of the time. A yell leader at the University of California at Berkeley, who was elected in 1969 on an antiwar platform, would yell "End the war! End the war!" during football games. African American athletes in Oklahoma fought to elect an African American cheerleader. In the 1960s, some of the first African American cheerleaders introduced soul-dance movements into cheerleading that involved more stomping and clapping as opposed to traditional cheers with straight-arm motions.

CHEERLEADING SINCE TITLE IX

Prior to the enactment of Title IX in 1972, cheerleading was often one of the few sports opportunities for women. When schools deemed cheerleading a varsity sport for funding purposes, feminists were, perhaps understandably, outraged, and cheerleading came to be resented by many women who were trying to promote what they viewed as more serious women's athletics. In the late 1960s and early 1970s, professional cheerleading squads, such as the Dallas Cowboy cheerleaders, emerged to support American football and basketball teams and to add an element of entertainment to the games. Professional cheerleading squads have typically been all-female groups whose members have exceptional dancing and entertaining ability. The financial gain for cheerleading is not the same as for players, however; most women cheerleaders have full-time jobs and do their cheering on the side.

CHEERLEADING BY COUNTRY AND REGION

Cheerleading remained a strictly U.S. phenomenon until 1982, when the introduction of American football in Great Britain led to the parallel establishment of cheerleading in that nation. The development of the World Football League in 1991 led to an international expansion of both American football and cheerleading. The style of cheerleading across the world is modeled on the version developed in the United States. Today, cheerleading associations, camps, and competitions are organized in Canada, Sweden, Germany, Japan, and elsewhere. Nations unfamiliar with the history of cheerleading and its development, however, do not always view it as a sport. Many cheerleaders outside the United States, and some within it, are seen as sex symbols rather than as athletes.

Nevertheless, cheerleading remains readily available in the United States, where little girls may begin cheering in elementary school as Pop Warner league football cheerleaders, by attending cheerleading camps or by training at a local cheer gym. Cheerleading tryouts are held at junior and senior high school and college levels for both all-female and coed squads. The popularity and competitiveness of cheerleading in the United States tends to vary by geographic location. While the sport has lost ground in some northeastern schools, as more girls choose to participate in field hockey or other sports, cheerleading remains popular in Kentucky, North Carolina, Texas, and other southern states.

COMPETITIONS

Cheerleaders still focus on crowd response during games, although they are also involved in competitions outside of games. Since the 1950s, cheerleading competitions in the United States have increased in number and are often televised by all-sports cable channels. The competitions separate all-female from coed squads and small from large squads into different categories. Most squads have from ten to twelve members, with coed squads striving for equal representation of males and females so that they can perform partner stunts.

Tumbling has reemerged as a crowd-pleasing and competitive element of cheerleading. Since the 1980s, many former gymnasts have joined high school and college cheerleading squads, as back handsprings and other gymnastics skills have increasingly become tryout requirements.

CONCLUSION

Only a century after cheerleading's inception as a white, male sport, athletes of all nationalities, ages, and colors, as well as both genders, now

CHEERLEADERS WHO BECAME FAMOUS

Female celebrities who were cheerleaders in high school are singer and actress Madonna, talk show host Kathie Lee Gifford, newswoman Katie Couric, actress Calista Flockhart, actress Sally Field, and actress Cameron Diaz. Two well-known men who were cheerleaders are Senate Majority Leader Trent Lott (in college) and financier Michael Milken, who cheered with Sally Field.

participate in a universal style of cheerleading. While the sport has engendered controversy at various stages of its development, it has remained popular and enjoyable for many individuals across the world.

Justine J. Reel

Bibliography

Birrell, Susan, and Cheryl Cole. (1994) *Women, Sport, and Culture.* Champaign, IL: Human Kinetics.

Bruce, Carolyn. (1960) *Cheerleader Handbook.* Fond du Lac, WI: National Sports.

Chappell, Lynn. (1997) *Coaching Cheerleading Successfully.* Champaign, IL: Human Kinetics.

Evans, Mary. (1982) *A Decade of Dreams.* Dallas, TX: Taylor.

Gach, John. (1938) "The Case for and Against Girl Cheerleaders." *School Activities* 9, 7: 301–302.

Gonzales, Arthur. (1956) "The First College Cheer." *The American Mercury* 83: 101–104.

Griffin, Patricia. (1984) "Girls' Participation Patterns in a Middle School Team Sports Unit." *Journal of Teaching in Physical Education* 4: 30–38.

Hanson, Mary Ellen. (1995) *Go! Fight! Win! Cheerleading in American Culture.* Bowling Green, OH: Bowling Green State University.

Hatton, Charles, and R. W. Hatton. (1978) "The Sideline Show." *Journal of the National Association for Women Deans, Administrators, & Counselors* 42, 1: 23–28.

Herkimer, Larry, and Phyllis Hollander. (1975) *The Complete Book of Cheerleading.* Garden City, NY: Doubleday.

Kinzer, Dianne, and Drue Thompson. (1985) "Obtaining Cheerleading and Drill Team Compatibility." *Interscholastic Athletic Administration* 11, 3: 21–23.

Kurman, George. (1986) "What Does Girls' Cheerleading Communicate." *Journal of Popular Culture* 20, 2: 57–64.

Loken, Newt. (1953) "Modern Cheerleading." *The Journal of the American Association for Health, Physical Education, and Health* 12–13.

Loken, Newt and Otis Dypwich. (1945) *Cheerleading and Marching Bands.* New York: A. S. Barnes and Company.

Manfredi, Jacqueline. (1983) "Peptalk: The History of Cheerleading." *Seventeen* 42: 94.

Morton, Charles. (1952) "Accent on Living." *Atlantic Monthly* 189: 92–93.

"Organized Cheering." (1911) *The Nation* 92: 5–6.

Reel, Justine, and Diane Gill. (1996) "Psychosocial Factors Related to Eating Disorders Among High School and College Female Cheerleaders." *The Sport Psychologist* 10: 195–206.

Schmid, Sue. (1995) "Safe Cheering." *Athletic Business* 19, 7: 20.

Suitor, Jill, and Rebel Reavis. (1995) "Football, Fast Cars, and Cheerleading: Adolescent Gender Norms, 1978–1989." *Adolescence* 30, 118: 265–267.

Webb, Gregg. (1984) "Cheerleaders—Spirit Leaders and Then Some." *Interscholastic Athletic Administration* 11, 1: 18–19.

Webb, Gregg. (1992) "Cheerleaders: A Unique Combination of Leadership and Athleticism." *Applied Research in Coaching and Athletics Annual:* 224–225.

CHI CHENG

(1944–)

TAIWANESE SPRINTER AND HURDLER

Chi Cheng is considered by some experts to be the greatest woman athlete in Asia in the second half of the twentieth century and certainly one of the greatest track athletes of all time. Although she enjoyed great success only in 1969 and 1970, the number of races she won during those two years and the three world records she held simultaneously in the 100-yard and 200-meter sprints and the 80-meter hurdles constitute a unique achievement in track competition.

Chi was born the third of seven children on 15 March 1944 in Hsinchu, Taiwan. Tall and athletic, she began running in high school and quickly emerged as Taiwan's best female athlete as she added hurdling and the pentathlon to her repertoire of events. She competed in the Olympic Games in 1960, 1964, and 1968, but managed only a bronze medal in the 80-meter hurdles in Mexico City in 1968. At the 1960 Games, she met U.S. track coach Vince Reel, who was coaching the Indian track team. Two years later, when he was in Taiwan to help that team prepare for the 1962 Asian Games, Chi came under his guidance. The following year, with the financial support of the Taiwan government, she then moved to Califor-

Chi Cheng setting the world record in the 200-meter sprint in 1970. (AP Photos)

nia, enrolling as a physical education student at California State Polytechnic University (Cal Tech). She and Reel later married and subsequently divorced.

Living and training in the United States improved her performances; from 1964 to 1970 she set a series of Taiwanese and Asian records in the sprints and hurdles. Her performances in the 1964 and 1968 Olympics were disappointing, but in 1969 she won sixty-six of sixty-seven outdoor races and in 1970 was undefeated in eighty-three races. The latter season was especially notable as she set world records in the 100-yard and the 200-meter sprints on the same day and in the 80-meter hurdles six days later; she also set new world records in the 100-meter sprint and the 200-meter hurdles. The 1971 season began with a string of victories but was cut short by a hip injury that kept her out of the 1972 Olympics and ultimately ended her career in 1973 after a series of operations, acupuncture, and rehabilitation failed to correct the problem.

In 1980, Chi returned to Taiwan as a national celebrity. In 1981, she was elected to the Taiwan Senate, winning 67 percent of the vote. In addi-

tion, she wrote a newspaper column, and, in 1998, she became head of the Taiwan Track and Field Federation and a member of Taiwan's National Olympic Committee.

David Levinson

Bibliography

Hanley, Reid M. (1973) *Who's Who in Track and Field.* New Rochelle, NY: Arlington House.

Lawson, Gerald. (1997) *World Record Breakers in Track & Field Athletics.* Urbana, IL: Human Kinetics.

Verschoth, Anita. (1970) "Fortune Smiles on the Cookie." *Sports Illustrated* (22 June): 48, 53.

CHILDREN'S SPORTS
see Youth Sports

CHILE

Chile is located along the Pacific coast of western South America and has a population of about 15 million. It was a Spanish colony until it achieved independence in 1810, and various traditions of Spanish society, especially the Spanish language and Roman Catholicism, continue to define life in Chile. Equally influential is an ethos that places much value on "machismo," which has tended to limit women's participation in sports as well as in other domains of public life.

Although participation by women in public life and sports has increased since the 1980s, only a minority of women participate in sports outside of the schools. Women continue to be expected to devote themselves to their homes, husbands, and children, and even women who work outside the home are expected to continue to handle these traditional responsibilities. Thus, most women have little time to participate in sports. In addition, the two most popular sports in Chile—soccer and the traditional game of *rayuela*—are considered to be men's sports (although girls now play soccer in the schools and in universities), which further limits the opportunity for women to participate. While Chile's constitution grants men and women equal rights, no laws govern the rights of women in sports.

SCHOOL SPORTS

Females in Chile participate in sports mainly in school. Physical education is mandatory from elementary school through high school and in college as well. Up to the age of about twelve, boys and girls seem to participate in physical education activities and sports in about equal numbers. From that point on, however, participation by girls declines markedly as cultural definitions of what it means to be a young man or young women begin to encourage boys to take part in sports and discourage women from doing so. By age thirteen, sports participation by young women declines by 50 percent. Those who remain active often are girls from families with a sports-participation history and young women in universities. A social-class bias affects women's sports participation; most women who take part in sports come from wealthier families, which frees them from some of the work and family responsibilities of women from poorer families. The major sports for women are tennis, aerobics, gymnastics, basketball, and volleyball. Although soccer is popular with schoolgirls, it is not popular with older women.

OLYMPIC PARTICIPATION

The relatively low value placed on women's sports is reflected in the low level of Chilean women's participation in the Olympics. Between 1936, when Chilean women first participated in the Games, and 1996, only twenty-five women in total were members of the Chilean national teams. The year of greatest participation was 1996, with five members; in 1964, 1976, and 1980, there were no women members. The best known of the Chilean female Olympic athletes is Marlene Arens, who won the silver medal in the javelin throw at the 1956 Games in Melbourne. Other notable athletes are tennis player Anita Lizana, who won the U.S. Open in 1937 and had a successful international career in the 1930s, and the basketball player Ismenia Pouchard, who starred in the Chilean women's basketball league in the 1960s. Those were the greatest years for the women's basketball team. They won the South American

Championship and placed second in the Pan-American Championship as well as the 1963 World Championship. However, the basketball league never attained professional status, and at the end of the twentieth century there were no professional sports for women in Chile.

THE CURRENT SITUATION AND FUTURE

A survey of Chilean sports participation conducted in 1996 indicated that, despite low participation by women, many of them wanted to participate more. The survey found that while 35 percent of Chileans participated in sports, the percentage of women taking part was only 19 percent. However, 63 percent of the women who classified themselves as nonparticipants said that they would like to participate in sports, especially recreational on weekends. They also said that time, availability, and money were not factors preventing their participation. In the view of women's sports advocates, greater opportunities for participation in sports by women in Chile will require a fundamental change in Chilean attitudes about the role of women in society.

Laura Gajardo Ghilardi

Bibliography

Arbena, Joseph L. (1996) "In Search of the Latin American Female Athlete: A Bibliographic Odyssey." Paper presented at the meeting of the North American Society for Sports History, Auburn, AL, May 24–27.

CHINA

China is an enormous nation with a population of 1.1 billion people, most of whom live in what is now the People's Republic of China. Chinese women's sports have developed under complex and unique social, cultural, and political circumstances.

HISTORY

In more than 5,000 years of feudal history, there were some traditional forms of women's physical exercise and entertainment. Among these were

THE GOLDEN LILIES (1890)

A Nineteenth-Century Westerner Describes Chinese Footbinding

The most important part of a young girl's dress in China is her shoes. Such tiny shoes they are, of coloured silk or satin, most tastefully embroidered, with brightly painted heels, just peeping beneath the neat pantalette; the feet are supposed to merit the poetical name bestowed upon them of "golden lilies." But how sad it is to discover that such a result is produced by indescribable torture, and that the part of the foot which is not seen is nothing but a mass of distorted or broken bones! . . .

Three inches is the correct length of the fashionable shoes in which Chinese Ladies toddle and limp, supporting themselves on a child's shoulder, or by means of a strong staff. Some very wealthy ladies are the possessors of feet which are almost useless, and, as they can hardly walk from one room to another in their spacious mansions, they are not unfrequently carried, especially about their gardens, on the backs of their large-footed attendants. Women whose feet are not quite so small, though still tightly bound, manage to walk occasionally, with great difficulty, a distance of several miles. 'Their movements are as the waving the willows,' says a Chinese poet in reference to these tiny feet; but to English eyes the gait appears to be by no means elegant, and bears a strong resemblance to what would be obtained by walking on our heels.

MARY ISABELLA BRYSON
(*c. 1890*) Child Life in China. *London: The London Missionary Society.*

taqin (gentle walk in the spring), *fang fengzheng* (flying a kite), and *tijianzi* (kicking the shuttlecock). Some court games were played by women but aimed at entertaining men. The "Grove of Violets" scroll from the Ming Dynasty, for instance, shows elegantly dressed ladies playing ball. On the whole, however, women in feudal society were valued principally as mothers and as agricultural laborers. They were very often victimized by the male-dominated society with its values deeply rooted in Chinese cultural tradition.

Women were subjugated, physically and psychologically, first and foremost through the institution of footbinding—an ingenious and brutal instrument of control used on aristocratic girls and women. Women unable to walk adequately were easy to control and to restrain. Added to this was the cultural conditioning brought about by the principles and practices of Confucianism. Prior to 1840, the life of virtually every Chinese woman from every class was a life of dependence systematized and sanctioned by the Confucian hierarchy that placed men above women. This dependence was gradually but spasmodically re-duced by both internal and external changes after 1840.

The first influential movement of modern women's assertion occurred in the mid-nineteenth century when Western powers invaded China, not only with military forces but also with strong ideological forces in the form of religious dogma. The Christian missionaries' primary purpose was to convert the Chinese to a superior worldview. The missionaries also, as it turned out, helped transmit new ideas and images to Chinese women and to free at least a few women from feudal bondage. They initiated the anti-footbinding movement in order to provide physical mobility, a prerequisite of equality. In 1844 the first school for girls was opened in Ningpo by a missionary woman. By 1902 more than 4,000 women students were studying in missionary girls' schools, and physical education became part of the modern school curriculum.

Women's education was made available to a larger group—although still a minute fraction of the population—in 1907 when the government put in place laws that would establish girls'

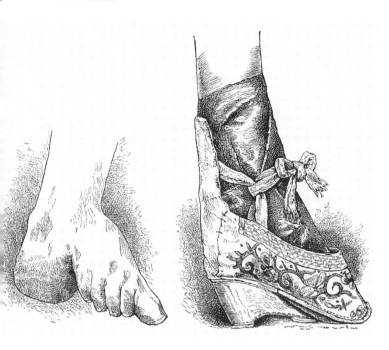

Golden Lilies—bare and shod. (Public Domain)

schools and a women's normal college. These acts stated that "the good education of the citizens of [the] empire depends upon the good education of its women." Provision was now made for establishing government-sponsored schools for girls. These new schools were expected to emphasize students' physical, as well as intellectual and moral, development. Gymnastics and physical exercise were part of the curriculum.

The development and rapid expansion of physical exercise in girls' schools called for a scientific approach and an adequate number of qualified teachers of games and gymnastics. Educators and reformers founded private women's colleges based on Western theories and practices of physical education in order to train urgently needed teachers. There soon came into being the Shanghai Chinese Gymnastics School for Women (1908), The Chinese Physical Education Teachers' College for Women (1908), and the Shanghai Liangjiang Women's College for Physical Education and Sport (1909). This marked the beginning of physical education as a discipline and stimulated the development of modern sports.

The establishment of the Chinese Communist party in 1921 was a watershed in modern Chinese history in general and had a tremendous effect on women's sports. After this date women's physical education and sports divided into two parts, reflecting two ideologies and two practices: communist and nationalist.

Between 1929 and 1934, the Chinese Communist party and its Red Army, in retreat from cities held by the nationalist army, established the Chinese Soviet Republic in the mountainous area of Jiangxi province in southeast China. They created a formal system of physical exercise for women, which for the first time reached both peasants and urban workers. This system was the "Red Sport Movement." The Communist party promoted their movement in the Soviet-controlled area from 1927 to 1934, a mass movement in which exercise was viewed as a basic aspect of the physical, cultural, and military training of people in Soviet areas. Women of every social background were made to exercise with a single purpose—military survival. Female exercise was transformed from a prerogative of the privileged into a pragmatic tool of the proletariat. A radical female role model was established: the "iron woman."

The Jiangxi era ended in October 1934 when the nationalists occupied the Red, or Soviet-controlled, area. The communists established a new base in distant Yan'an. They further institutionalized their policy toward women's sports. Physical education was systematically promoted in armies and in schools at the village and at the county levels. A physical education and sports committee was established under the leadership of the Communist party. This committee supervised clubs and groups, ratified the regulations for games, and organized sports events. The structure and principles of post-1949 physical exercise were pioneered in Yan'an. In the communist area, for the first time, female athletes competed at sports meetings, for example, the Yan'an Women's Sports Meeting in 1940 and the Yan'an Sports Meeting in 1942.

At the same time, in the nationalist-controlled area (two-thirds of China) women's exercise expanded. From 1928 to 1949, the nationalist government developed an entire national physical training system for both men and women. The government was committed to the longstanding view that the only way to restore the nation's morale was by promoting the spirit of nationalism and creating strong bodies. The Nationalist party,

WOMEN AND POPULAR DANCE FORMS IN CHINA

After the era of reform in China began (1978), three major waves of recreational dancing took over the parks, parking lots, and streets of Beijing and other major Chinese cities: disco flourished in the late 1980s, ballroom dancing in the early 1990s, and *yangge* (also spelled yangko) in the mid-1990s. Each reflected the prevailing trends in Chinese popular culture as a whole in those time periods, and each counted elderly women as its most numerous participants.

Disike, a phonetic approximation of the English word "disco," appeared around 1985. Chinese people perceived it as a modern, Western activity. Hip-swiveling and shoulder-rolling were key defining elements, but they seemed to lack explicit sexual connotations. The music tended to be slightly outdated Western pop music, which was lively by Chinese standards of the time. The Chinese version was influenced by the mass calisthenics that had been promulgated for the previous thirty years: disco dancers commonly danced in unison, in rows and columns. Women usually outnumbered men by quite a bit. Disco was quickly integrated into the official structures for mass exercise. Most work units and educational institutions substituted disco or some version of it for the traditional radio broadcast calisthenics. It was also used in the mass calisthenics displays in opening ceremonies at sports meets.

"Old people's disco," practiced by retirees around age sixty and older, attracted more media attention and public curiosity than that involving other age groups, because these elderly disco dancers challenged rigid customs for the elderly. These included the prescription of sedate bodily deportment and, for women, the taboo against wearing red, shiny, or brightly colored clothes after the age of about thirty. The breaking of modern political taboos was not as openly acknowledged as the breaking of traditional Confucian taboos, but it occurred as well. Since the Cultural Revolution, dancing had often been forbidden. Commercial ballrooms had been allowed in Beijing only since May 1987. Disco was one example of the general fascination with things that were Western and modern, the consumption of which had been forbidden for so long. Through the body, not words, it expressed a quiet resistance to the state's repression of popular culture.

Unlike disco, with its rigid group format, ballroom dancing was linked to individual self-cultivation. In Mandarin, ballroom dancing was called "social dance" (jiaoyi wu or shejiao wu) or "international dance" (guoji biaozhun wu or guoji wu). Unlike disco and yangge, it was danced by mixed-sex pairs, which meant that there was relatively equal participation by men and women. In Beijing in the mid 1990s, the main location for ballroom dancing was the large parking lot across from the Capitol Gymnasium, where several hundred dancers could be seen in the early hours of the morning until about 8:00 a.m.

This reflected the latest turn in Chinese popular culture, which had progressed from an indiscriminate fascination with everything "Western" to more selective appropriation. Ballroom dancing was considered to be culturally refined, and it played a role in emerging class distinctions. It was offered as a physical education course at colleges in order to teach students "civilized" behavior, with an emphasis on the proper etiquette for contact between the sexes. In these classes, males danced with females-unlike at the school dances that had been going on since the 1980s, where the majority of females danced with females and males with males. The instructors believed these classes would help students in the newly competitive job market by developing their social skills.

Elderly dancers dominated the public spaces, since they had little access to gymnasiums. Teachers were brought in by the offices at work units or schools in charge of arranging activities for retired employees. Old people's ballroom dancing was further given an official stamp with the organization of the first "National Fitness Dance Exhibition for the Middle-Aged and Elderly" in Beijing in 1994, which also included fitness dancing (such as disco) and folk dancing.

By contrast, yangge (literally, "the sprout song") was never successfully brought into the official fold. A dance from rural northern China, it was distinguished by its folk origins from the Western disco and ballroom dancing. It reflected the "seeking roots" (xungen) movement in Chinese

(continues)

popular culture, a search for "authentic" Chinese traditions to revitalize Chinese culture. Yangge involves slow dancing in a circle to the accompaniment of a large drum and cymbals. Typically, the majority of dancers were elderly women and the drummer a man. The women danced in pastel-colored gauze dresses and waved matching silk scarves. For the first time, elderly dancers were taking over not just the parks and parking lots of Beijing, but even the sidewalks and streets. By 1996, it was estimated that more than 60,000 elderly, from some 200 informal dance troupes, were dancing yangge each night all around the city. Almost anywhere in the city in fair weather, the drums could be heard starting up as dusk began to fall, and they would continue well into the night. In March 1997, the Beijing government banned most outdoor performances under anti-noise pollution regulations. Yangge groups, however, were vocal about their opposition to the ban and their right to spaces for exercise. Gymnasiums and parks charged fees and could not accommodate their

numbers; they had nowhere else to go. Yangge became one of the increasingly bold grassroots movements demanding a response to people's needs.

Most surprising about each of these trends is that they were led by elderly women. Often, change comes from the social margins, particularly in totalitarian regimes, and elderly women had been increasingly marginalized by economic modernization and the weakening of family structure. The social reasons were complex, but on an individual level these were women who refused to yield to the loneliness of retirement, instead actively seeking venues for sociability and exercise. Perhaps they were more successful than retired men in grassroots organizing because they were more accustomed to forming informal networks outside work. Popularly characterized as "timid" because of their past sufferings, this was the generation who had lived through the worst extremes of the Maoist period. Their lives had perhaps given them a sensitive understanding of what they could get away with in uncertain political situations.

therefore, made special efforts to encourage women's participation in exercise. The nationalists issued more than forty laws and regulations covering sports, sports administration, and physical education in the schools.

Meanwhile, sports competitions for women were developing rapidly. In 1922 Beijing Women's Normal University held an internal sports competition. In 1923 the first women's championships in volleyball, basketball, and athletics were held in Beijing. Although Chinese women did not compete in the first YMCA-sponsored Far Eastern Games in 1913, they participated in 1923, 1925, 1927, 1930, and 1934. Female athletes also took part in the fourth, fifth, sixth, and seventh national games in 1930, 1933, 1935, and 1948, respectively. Their events included basketball, volleyball, tennis, swimming, softball, martial arts, table tennis, and archery. The Chinese women first appeared at the Olympics in Berlin in 1936, including star swimmer Yang Xiuquiong, the "Chinese mermaid."

The growth in participation accelerated after 1949 when the People's Republic of China began

to implement its promise of full equality of the sexes. Chinese women athletes, for the first time, became sports superstars. The communists believed, from their early experience, that exercise would produce a strong and healthy female labor force for the construction of the new China. According to the Communist Common Program (1949), women had equal rights in physical education and sports. In the years between 1956 and 1979, the Chinese government withdrew from eight international sports federations and did not send athletes to the Olympic Games because of the "two Chinas" question (that is, the troubled relations between mainland China and Taiwan). But in China the mass sports movement, the legacy of Jiangxi and Yan'an, developed rapidly. "To develop sport and build and defend the motherland" was the slogan of the era. Women were encouraged to participate in all exercises and events. A ten-year plan for exercise and sports was formulated in 1958, in which 200 million men and women were expected to pass physical tests and earn fitness badges in the "People's Labor and Defense System."

PHYSICAL EDUCATION IN THE PEOPLE'S REPUBLIC

From the beginning of the People's Republic, physical education was a central part of the school curriculum. Boys and girls in primary and middle schools received at least two hours of physical education coursework every week and exercised for at least one hour each day. In 1979 the Ministry of Education issued "Regulations for Primary and Middle Schools' Physical Education" to reinforce this practice. In 1990 the State Council issued "Rules of Physical Education in Schools," which affirmed that "physical education is an examination course for students." From 1949 to 1995 there were 170 physical education institutes and physical education departments and more than 200 physical education colleges to train physical education teachers.

The Cultural Revolution (1966–1976) had an adverse effect on some major sports competitions, which were condemned as manifestations of elitism. On the other hand, the revolution brought the mass sports movement to its zenith. Most cities and villages had local sports activities. Factories, too, supported sports events for their employees. Women were particularly encouraged to participate in physical activities, as a symbol of China's refuting Confucian tradition and establishing revolutionary culture.

ELITE SPORTS

Chinese women and men have had equal opportunities to participate in elite sports since the establishment of the leisure-time or special sports schools in 1955. They have benefited from these opportunities. Zheng Fengyong became the first Chinese woman to break the world high-jump record in 1957. Qiu Zonghui was the first Chinese woman to win the table tennis world championships in 1965. Pan Duo was the first Chinese woman to climb Mount Everest in 1975, setting a world women's mountain-climbing record. Ma Yanhong, the first Chinese woman to win the gymnastics world championships, in 1979, was the winner of an Olympic gold medal in 1984. Women also emerged in administrative and coaching positions. Female administrators work at international, national, and regional sports councils and associations, and there are more than 3,000 professional female coaches in China.

China's female athletes have provided some stunning achievements since 1979, when China rejoined the international athletic community. In almost every sport, the women have done better in international competitions than the men. From 1985 to 1993, China had 404 top sportswomen at the international level, accounting for 51 percent of all Chinese athletes at that rank. Between 1949 and 1993, Chinese athletes won 775 world championships, of which women won 460, or 59 percent. Chinese athletes broke world records 725 times, with women accounting for 458 of these, or about 63 percent of the total. Although the disqualification of a number of elite athletes for using illicit drugs has occasionally tarnished this record, the overall accomplishment is impressive.

Hu Yiaobang, the general-secretary of the Chinese Communist party, has proclaimed that the indomitable and tenacious character displayed by Chinese women athletes embodies the new Chinese nation and has brought it to the notice of the whole world. In 1981 the State Council announced that the entire nation should learn from women athletes and use their spirit in sports to

THE MAN BEHIND THE SUCCESS OF CHINESE RUNNERS

In the 1990s, Chinese women runners emerged as the dominant performers in middle- and long-distance races in international competitions. The person credited with this success is their coach, Ma Junren. The team's success has been attributed to his use of traditional Chinese herbal medicine, to his belief that his mother is a deer spirit, and to his rigorous training regimen. Ma has also been accused of physically abusing athletes and controlling all aspects of their lives, although the national sports establishment has come to his defense.

create the new face of socialist modernization and reconstruction. The Sports Ministry announced proudly in 1990 that women athletes had established a new inspirational femininity.

CONCLUSION

A frequent topic for discussion in China in the 1990s has been why "the Phoenix" (the symbol for women) can fly higher than "the dragon" (the symbol for men) in international sports. The victories of today's Chinese women athletes are the consequence of the efforts of generations of Chinese women who struggled for the emancipation of their bodies and for opportunities in sport.

Fan Hong

Bibliography

Brownell, Susan. (1995) *Training the Body for China.* Chicago: University of Chicago Press.

Chinese Society for History of PE and Sport, ed. (1989) *Zhongguo jindai tiyu shi* [*Modern Chinese Sports History*]. Beijing: Beijing tiyu xueyuan chubanshe.

————. (1990) *Zhongguo gudai tiyu shi* [*Physical Education and Sport in Ancient China*]. Beijing: Beijing tiyu xueyuan chubanshe.

Fan, Hong. (1997) *Footbinding, Feminism and Freedom: The Liberation of Women's Bodies in Modern China.* London: Cass.

Gu, Shiquan, and Lin Boyuan. (1989) *Zhongguo tiyu shi* [*History of Chinese Physical Education and Sport*]. Beijing: Beijing tiyu xueyuan chubanshe.

Guan, Weimin, et al., eds. (1996) *Tiyui shi* [*Sports History*]. Beijing: Gaodenjiaoyu chubanshe.

Policy Department, the Ministry of Sports, ed. (1990) *Zouhua titan sishi chun* [*Forty Years of Sports Achievements in China*]. Beijing: Renmin tiyu chubanshe.

Research Centre of Sports History, Chengdu Physical Education Institute, ed. (1989) *Zhongguo jindai tiyu shi zhiliao* [*Historical Archives of Modern Chinese Sports History*]. Chengdu: Sichuan jiaoyu chubanshe.

Wang, Daping, and Hong Fan. (1990) *Tiyu shihua* [*Sport, a Social History*]. Beijing: Kexue puji chubanshe.

Wang, Zengming, et al. (1990) *Shan-Gan-Ning bianqu tiyu shi* [*History of Physical Education and Sport in the Border Area*]. Xi'an: Shanxi renmin chubanshe.

Xie, Yalong, et al. (1993) *Aulinpike yanjiu* [*Olympic Studies*]. Beijing: Beijing tiyu daxue chubanshe.

Yan, Shaolu, and Xikuan Zhou. (1990). *Tiyu yundong shi* [*History of Sport*]. Beijing: Renmin tiyu chubanshe.

Yong, Gaoling, et al., eds. (1987) *Dangdai Zhongguo tiyu* [*Contemporary Chinese Sport*]. Beijing: Zhongguo kexue chubanshe.

Zeng, Biao. (1985) *Suqu tiyu zhiliao xuanbian* [*Selected Material on Physical Education and Sport in the Soviet Area*]. Anhui: Anhui tiyu shizhi bianjishi.

CINTRÓN, CONCHITÁ

(1922–)

PERUVIAN BULLFIGHTER

Concepción (Conchita) Cintrón Verill is perhaps history's best-known and most respected female bullfighter. She grew up in Peru, where, as a teenager, she studied mounted bullfighting (*el rejoneo*) under the Portuguese *rejoneador* (mounted bullfighter) Ruy da Camara.

Cintrón was born on 9 August 1922. Her first public performance, as a fourteen-year-old, was in 1936 in the bullring of Ancho de Lima. Her success led to a series of performances in the Portuguese bullrings of Algés and Lisbon. In 1937 she performed as a *rejoneadora* in Lima's bullring, where she returned in 1938 to take the *alternativa* (the ritual of transition to being a mounted bullfighter), graduating as a professional *rejoneadora*. The same year she had her debut in *el toreo* (bullfighting on foot) in Tarma, Peru. During the following years her popularity grew with regular performances in Latin America. She reached a mass audience when she starred in the film *Maravilla del Toreo*.

From 1944 to 1948, Cintrón performed *el rejoneo* in Spain, Portugal, and France. However, since women were prohibited from performing *el toreo* in public in Spain, she performed on foot only on the private lands of bullfight aficionados or in "closed-door" performances. In her final public performance in Jaén, Spain, in 1950, she made her most significant contribution to women's bullfighting. She dismounted from her horse to complete her performance, killing her bull on foot. The audience's enormous support for her at this moment persuaded the officials governing the performance not to arrest her, allowing her career to end in triumph. Her retirement from bullfighting, at the age of twenty-eight, was precipitated by her engagement and marriage in 1951 to Francisco de Casteo Branco, nephew of Ruy da Camera, the mounted bullfighter she had trained with in Peru. She maintained links with bullfighting as a spectator and a writer. She reappeared in the ring in 1991 on horseback for the *alternativa* of French *rejoneadora* Maria Sara, though she did not perform as a *rejoneadora* on this occasion.

Sarah Pink

Bibliography

Boada, Emelia, and Fermin Cebolla. (1976) *Las senoritas toreras: Historia, erotica y politica del toreo feminino.* Madrid: Ediciones Felmar.

Feiner, Muriel. (1995) *La Mujer en el Mundo del Toro.* Madrid: Alianza Editorial.

Montero, P. (1948) *Vida y Arte de Conchita Cintron.* Seville: La Editorial Catolica.

Verill Cintron, L. (1960) *Goddess of the Bullring: The Story of Conchita Cintron, the World's Greatest Matadora.* London: Frederick Muller.

CLOTHING *see* Fashion, Sportswear Industry

COACHING

Coaching is a profession. As such, it requires that coaches receive preparation and certification. The move to professionalize coaching has taken a number of different shapes depending on the national context. At different times it has responded to a range of concerns, including improving the performance of national teams, eliminating the abusive and harassing behavior of coaches, and improving the sport experience for athletes. The professionalization of coaching has particular implications for women. In the past, the professionalization of a discipline, such as medicine in the nineteenth century, led to the exclusion of women practitioners, such as the exclusion of women from medical schools. On the other hand, professionalization means the adoption of recognized, impartial standards for judging the quality of work, and this ideally should help eliminate arbitrary discrimination against any group based on factors such as gender and race. The question becomes: Will the efforts to professionalize coaching open new opportunities for women to gain the training and recognition that will improve their access to careers in coaching?

WOMEN IN COACHING

One of the ironies of the greater participation opportunities for girls and women in sports since the 1970s has been a decrease in the number of women employed as coaches of women's sport teams. Even with the ever-increasing number of women with elite athletic experience, there is a relative dearth of highly visible, well-publicized female coaches to serve as role models for girls. The lack of role models weakens the supportive environment for girls' involvement in organized sports and may provide partial explanation for the decline of the number of females involved in physical activity and sports during adolescence.

In Europe, coaches are employed by club or sport federations, while in the United States sports for girls and women are principally organized inside the educational system. According to a recent study by R. Vivian Acosta and Linda Jean Carpenter reported in the 2 May 2000 Issue of *The Chronicle of Higher Education*, only 45.6 percent of the women's teams in the National Collegiate Athletic Association were coached by women in 2000. This is the lowest percentage of women coaches in the NCAA in twenty years. Additionally, the study also found that of the 534 head-coaching positions created for new women's teams in the last two years, 80 percent were filled by men. Whether they are male or female, coaches of women's teams are paid less than coaches of men's teams. Recent statistics indicate that in the soccer (association football), federations in Norway, Germany, and Sweden in 1995, only 25 percent of German, 20 percent of Swedish, and 10 percent of Norwegian female soccer teams in the first division were coached by women. This and

A coach instructs members of a youth soccer team. (Richard Cummins)

other findings suggest an international trend whereby the higher the performance level of female or male athletes, the greater the chance that they will be coached by a man. In Germany, only 6 out of 120 coaches for national sports teams were women in 1995, in Britain only 6–8 percent of full-salaried coaches were women, in Norway only 13 percent of the elite-level coaches were women, in Canada 25 percent of high-performance coaches were women, and only 11 percent of high-performance coaches across Australia were women.

Researchers suggest that women's disadvantaged place in coaching is the result of several factors: (1) the increase in the number of paid coaching positions for women's teams has attracted men to these positions; (2) an "old boys' network" among collegiate athletic directors and leaders of sports federations has excluded women; (3) there is the perception that men's sports experiences make men more qualified to be coaches; and (4) the belief persists that women have other responsibilities, such as child rearing, that interfere with coaching responsibilities.

Experts agree that in order to sustain and enhance the quality of female participation in sports from childhood through adulthood, there must be trained female coaches as role models. In addition, there is also research evidence that females prefer female coaches. In the 1980s, surveys showed that female high school and college athletes in the United States and Canada accepted male coaches as readily as they did female coaches. But surveys in the late 1990s indicate that they now prefer female coaches. It may well be that the formal education and certification of volunteer and paid coaches are essential for the future progress of girls and women in sport. Credentialing and licensing of coaches may be one way to solve some of the problems in coaching, such as the psychological abuse of athletes, the failure to develop basic skills, and various legal and liability issues. Research conducted principally in the United States, Australia, and Canada has shown that as many as one out of three youth participants will drop out of sports because of a coach. This is usually related to failure to get enough playing time or claims that the coach has favorites, is a poor instructor, or puts too heavy an emphasis on "winning at all costs."

The use of untrained coaches regardless of gender can present various kinds of problems: (1) lack of basic principles of child development may result in the use of inappropriate strategies for teaching and motivating young athletes; (2) lack of knowledge of proper training and conditioning principles may result in increased injuries; and (3) lack of knowledge about adolescent growth and development may lead to misleading and inaccurate decisions with regard to skill development, nutrition, and motivational levels.

COACHING EDUCATION

Because many experts believe that professional coaching is important for the future development of sports, effort has gone into and continues to go into the development of coaching education programs around the world. These programs range from courses to train the unskilled volunteer coach to highly technical programs for the elite, national-level coach.

Canada has been a leader in the area of coaching education since the 1974 initiation of the Canadian National Coaching Certification Program (NCCP) by the Coaching Association of Canada. The NCCP attempts to foster an athlete-centered approach to coaching through a program that consists of three components: theoretical, technical, and practical. The theoretical component presents general information pertinent to all coaches (e.g., the psychology and philosophy of coaching and the physiology of training). The technical component offers sport-specific information in conjunction with the different sports associations. The practical component requires that coaches work in an actual coaching situation with an experienced coach. Sports organizations and sports clubs now request specified levels of certification for their coaches. A major evaluation of NCCP-trained coaches has been conducted recently and will result in a review and revision of the coaching education program at all levels.

In the United States there are several commercial coaching education programs, including the American Sport Education Program (ASEP), the Program for Athletic Coaches' Education (PACE), and the National Youth Sports Coaches' Association (NYSCA). These programs provide coaching workshops in community-based and school-sponsored sports. As of 1999 there was no accreditation agency to determine whether college and university coaching education programs provide the curriculum and experiences necessary to develop qualified and competent coaches in the United States. Each U.S. college or university determined the content and value of its own coaching education program. One survey found at least 179 U.S. colleges and universities that offer coaching education programs (148 undergraduate minors, 10 undergraduate majors, and 21 master's degree programs). The National Association for Sport and Physical Education (NASPE) and the National Association for Girls and Women in Sport (NAGWS) were working to develop an accreditation process based on the established National Standards for Athletic Coaches.

The structure for coach education in Australia is the National Coach Accreditation Scheme (NCAS), set up in 1980 and run by the Australian Coaching Council (ACC). In 1999 there were approximately 100,000 accredited coaches active in the NCAS database. Each sport developed Level 1, 2, and 3, and High Performance Level coach accreditation courses. Following accreditation under the NCAS, coaches were required to fulfill updating requirements over a four-year period in order to stay abreast of rule changes, coaching techniques, and strategies. In addition, many of the individual sports associations offered intro-

The rising number of women's sports teams has not seen a similar increase in the number of women coaches, meaning this coach of the women's basketball team for the 1990 Goodwill Games in Seattle, Washington, has fewer female colleagues. (Kevin R. Morris/Corbis)

ductory coaching courses for beginning community coaches. Aussie Sport (coordinated nationally by the Australia Sports Commission) and the Coaching Council in conjunction with state departments of sport and recreation have established coaching centers in each state to provide better support for the delivery of coaching education courses. The Coaching Council and national sports organizations have also developed numerous coaching support resources, including coaching manuals and instructional skill videos.

The Hillary Commission for Sport in New Zealand, in its 1993 strategic plan "Moving a Nation," specified as a target "to assist all major sports to enhance their performance via coaching academies" by 1997–98. Coaching New Zealand (CNZ) is the national association for coaches: it provides coaching courses and assists national bodies in preparing and running coaching courses.

Israel's three major sports organizations—the Sport and Physical Education Authority, the Israel Olympic Committee, and the National Sport Federation—established the Unit of Youth Sport (UYS) in 1974. The UYS values and insists on certification of coaches and professionals working with Israeli youth. Another institution that prepares and educates coaches is the Nat Holman National School of Coaches and Instructors at the Wingate Institute in Netanya, Israel. Students are trained in sports centers and clubs in order to enhance coaching skills.

In the Netherlands the sport federations and associations work in conjunction with the Netherlands Sport Confederation and physical education teacher-training colleges to educate and train coaches. There are four tracks for the education of coaches: (1) voluntary course for youth sports coaches and tutors; (2) courses for recreational sport, organized mainly by local governments; (3) professional sports coach schools, five of which educated about 500 professional sports leaders yearly in the 1990s; and (4) schools for teachers in physical education, whose graduates work part time as sports coaches.

In Austria, professional coach education is called the *Diplomtrainerausbildung*, or "trainer diploma." This is a program for the best coaches in the countries who have already completed more basic training. There are only a few coaches selected each year to participate in the trainer diploma program of professional coach education to become qualified to coach at the national and international level.

CONCLUSION

The coach plays a major role in defining, creating, providing, and delivering the sports experience to the athlete. There is an untapped pool of women around the world who have skills to offer as coaches. The challenge is to recruit and train them to enter the coaching profession for both women's and men's teams. The future of national sports development will depend to a large extent on a nation's ability to provide professional training for all levels of coaching. If women are to become sports leaders as coaches they must have access to courses and practical supervised coaching experience. The International Working Group on Women and Sport (IWG, formed after the Brighton Conference on Women and Sport in 1994) aims to accelerate the process of change in order to redress the imbalances that women face in their participation and involvement in sport. In the *International Women and Sport Strategy*, under section 10.4, "National Government and Non-Government Organizations," the IWG gives nations encouragement to: "Sponsor women to attend international training courses and seminar programs, especially in coaching, and provide places in training courses domestically for women from nearby developing countries."

There is a need for global coaching education that will move the profession in a positive direction away from individuals learning how to coach from their own experiences as players or through observation, live or via television, of top-level coaches toward having a systematic program of study for all coaches.

Christine M. Shelton

See also Administration; Management; Sexual Harassment

Bibliography

Brackenridge, Celia. (1997) " 'He Owned Me Basically': Women's Experience of Sexual Abuse in Sport." *International Review of Sport Sociology* 32, 2: 115–30.

DeKnop, P., L. M. Engstrom, B. Skirstad, and M. R. Weiss. (1996) *Worldwide Trends in Youth Sport.* Champaign, IL: Human Kinetics.

Fasting, Kari, and Gertrud Pfister. (1999) "Female and Male Coaches in the Eyes of Female Elite Soccer Players." *European Physical Education Review* (in press).

Griffin, Pat. (1998) *Strong Women, Deep Closets.* Champaign, IL: Human Kinetics.

Kane, Mary Jo, and Jane Marie Stangl. (1991) "Employment Patterns of Female Coaches in Men's Athletics." *Journal of Sport and Social Issues* 15, 1: 21–41.

Knoppers, Annelies. (1988) "Men Working: Coaching as Male Dominated and Sex Segregated Occupation." *Arena Review* 12, 2: 69–80.

Knoppers, Annelies, Barbara Bedker Meyer, Martha Ewing, and Linda Forrest. (1989) "Gender and the Salaries of Coaches." *Sociology of Sport Journal* 6, 4: 348–361.

———. (1991) "Opportunity and Work Behavior in College Coaching." *Journal of Sport and Social Issues* 15, 1: 1–20.

McMillin, C. J., and C. Reffner, eds. (1999) *Directory of College and University Coaching Education Programs.* Morgantown, WV: Fitness Information Technology.

Millard, Linda. (1996) "Differences in Coaching Behaviors of Male and Female High School Soccer Coaches." *Journal of Sport Behavior* 19, 1: 19–31.

Officer, Sara A., and Lawrence B. Rosenfeld. (1985) "Self-Disclosure to Male and Female Coaches by Female High School Athletes." *Journal of Sport Psychology* 7, 4: 360–370.

Sabo, Donald. (1997) *The Women's Sport Foundation Gender Equity Report Card.* East Meadow, NY: Women's Sport Foundation.

Seefeldt, V. (1996) "The Future of Youth Sports in America." In *Children in Sport: A Biopsychosocial Perspective,* edited by F. L. Smoll and R. E. Smith. Indianapolis, IN: Brown & Benchmark, 423–435.

Stangl, Jane Marie, and Mary Jo Kane. (1991) "Structural Variables That Offer Explanatory Power for the Underrepresentation of Women Coaches Since Title IX." *Sociology of Sport Journal* 8, 1: 47–60.

Theberge, Nancy. (1984) "The Status of Women in Coaching in Canada." *Sport et Societes contemporaines.* Paris: S.F.S.S., 163–168.

———. (1988) "Making a Career in a Man's World." *Arena Review* 12, 2: 116–127.

Tomlinson, Alan, and Ilkay Yorganci. (1997) "Male Coach/Female Athlete Relations." *Journal of Sport and Social Issues* 21, 2: 135–155.

Weinberg, Robert, Margie Reveles, and Allen Jackson. (1984) "Attitudes of Male and Female Athletes Toward Male and Female Coaches." *Journal of Sport Psychology* 6, 4: 448–453.

Whitson, David, and Donald MacIntosh. (1989) "Gender and Power." *International Review of Sport Sociology* 24, 2: 137–149.

COACHMAN, ALICE

(1923–)

U.S. TRACK AND FIELD ATHLETE

Alice Coachman was the first African-American woman to win a gold medal in the Olympic Games and the first American woman to win a gold medal in a track and field event.

The fifth of ten children, Coachman was born on 9 November 1923 and raised in Albany, Georgia, by her mother, Evelyn. She attended Tuskegee Institute High School in Tuskegee, Alabama; in her freshman year of high school, Coachman tried out for the 1936 Olympic Games but failed to make the team. After high school, she continued her education at Tuskegee Institute, which had an excellent track program with a reputation for developing numerous talented young women in the sport. Cleveland Abbott, the force behind the program, organized the Tuskegee Relays, which provided an opportunity for elite competition in the sport. Coachman was Abbott's star performer. Between 1939 and 1948, she won ten Amateur Athletic Union (AAU) high-jump titles. In 1943, she won the AAU's national title in the running high jump and the 50-yard dash. In total, she won twenty-six national titles.

After World War II, when the Olympic games resumed in London, Coachman was a member of the U.S. team. The U.S. women's track and field team consisted of eleven athletes, four of them from Tuskegee: Alice Coachman, Nell Jackson,

Alice Coachman, high jumper from Albany, Georgia, and the first African American woman to win a gold medal, is shown clearing the bar with an Olympic record breaking leap of 5 feet, 6 1/8 inches. (Bettmann/Corbis)

Theresa Manuel, and Mabel Walker. These women traveled to England by ship and faced stiff competition from Fanny Blankers-Koen of the Netherlands, the outstanding female track and field athlete of the era. Coachman was the only member of the team to earn a gold medal, setting an Olympic record. Upon her return home, she was invited to the White House to meet President Harry Truman.

Coachman completed her studies at Tuskegee Institute in the dressmaking trade program in 1946 and continued her education at Albany State College. There, she earned an undergraduate degree in home economics in 1949 while she continued competing in track and field. After the 1948 Olympics, she taught physical education in her home town of Albany, Georgia.

Throughout her track career, she was admired for her strong work ethic and her deep desire to win, qualities that made her an appropriate role model for younger athletes. She founded the Alice Coachman Track and Field Foundation. Since her Olympic performance, African American women have dominated the U.S. women's track and field teams. Coachman was honored by induction into the National Track and Field Hall of Fame and the International Women's Sports Hall of Fame.

Shawn Ladda

Bibliography

Davis, Michael. (1992) *Black American Women in Olympic Track and Field*. Jefferson, NC: McFarland.

Plowden, Martha Ward. (1995) *Olympic Black Women*. Gretna, LA: Pelican Publishing.

COCKFIGHTING

Cockfighting is a sport in which participants arm gamecocks with razor-sharp weapons, or gaffs, and pit them in battle. Women's participation in the sport is quite limited, but it is greater than many people believe. Women are most often found in supporting or behind-the-scenes roles, taking care of tasks that make the sport run smoothly.

HISTORY

Cockfighting is perhaps one of the oldest sports, originating in ritual sacrifices that date back to the domestication of chickens several thousand years ago. The ancient Greeks encouraged the sport among their soldiers to teach bravery, tenacity, and courage, traits aptly exemplified in the gamecock. It was the Romans, however, who refined cockfighting as a blood sport, "sports that depend largely on a relationship of bloodletting or the likelihood of being hurt or blooded or of killing."

In the southern United States, cockfights, decidedly masculine and aggressive activities, were arenas for men to teach their sons a manly art. The gender implications of the term "sportsmanship" and what was viewed as gentlemanly conduct were not lost on these "cockers." Cockfights allowed southern sporting gentlemen to display their manliness, honor, and status in exclusively male company. Similarly, in northern urban centers, men from all social ranks gathered in taverns, saloons, and sporting halls to enjoy the gambling, drinking, swearing, and fighting associated with cockfighting.

In his pioneering article on Balinese cockfighting, the anthropologist Clifford Geertz (1973) argues that the cockfight is more than a battle between cocks; it is a battle between men that brings together the themes of "death, masculinity, rage, pride, loss, beneficence, and chance." Cockers applaud the manly qualities of their birds and live vicariously through them. In Bali, women do not attend cockfights, and in most other nations they are present primarily as spectators.

Although a popular activity throughout India, Thailand, the Philippines, Indonesia, Mexico, Peru, Cuba, Guatemala, and the Dominican Republic, cockfighting is illegal in most European and North American countries. In the United States, despite its largely illegal and deviant subcultural status, cockfighting is common in rural areas of Texas, Missouri, Oklahoma, Arizona, New Mexico, most of the Southeast, and Hawaii, and in the inner cities of New York and Los Angeles. It is particularly popular among Puerto Ricans, Mexican Americans, African Americans in the Delta region, Cajuns, and rural whites. Cockfighting has historically been regarded as a man's sport.

Not only gamecocks, but cockers themselves have become symbols of masculinity. Those who fight gamecocks often refer to themselves as members of a fraternity. They regard themselves as the best sort of men and consider outsiders to be effete. U.S. cockers boast that George Washington, Thomas Jefferson, Andrew Jackson, and Abraham Lincoln were cockers, although the historical record does not support this claim. Understandably, with the exception of Queen Anne of England, who engaged in cockfighting in the early eighteenth century, the names of few women are connected with cockfighting.

WOMEN IN COCKFIGHTING

Women's participation as actual cockers depends on the goodwill of the men involved. Generally once a year, U.S. game clubs hold all-women events called powder-puff derbies. At these rare

Woman tending to a wounded fighting bird. (Paul A. Souders/Corbis)

events, women heel (attach the gaffs to the bird) and handle (pit the birds and separate them when entangled) their own gamecocks.

The conditioning, heeling, and handling of gamecocks are duties that men usually assume. The referee and the pooler (the person entrusted with the money collected from the backers of each bird) are generally older, well-respected men. Women play a maternal role in caring for eggs and chicks and preparing meals for the cockpit's concession stands.

Although some women actively participate in the raising and fighting of gamecocks, mostly they are spectators. This, however, is not a passive role. Gambling, an integral aspect of cockfighting, is actively engaged in by both male and female spectators. Wives or female companions of cockers are often responsible for taking odds and noting wagers. They can also be found loudly cheering "kill'em, kill'em" to a favorite gamecock. Such women are, however, a small minority among all women. Some male cockers are said to have trouble finding female companions who are appreciative and supportive of the sport.

The wives, daughters, and girlfriends who stand behind the men involved often play an active role in the organization and promotion of the multimillion-dollar gamecock industry. For example, game-fowl breeding farms are often run by husband-and-wife teams, with wives responsible for the feeding and raising of the fowl. Women also hold secretary-treasurer positions in several state game breeders associations and are responsible for the organization of annual meetings. Women are also involved in the three major sport publications—*The Gamecock, The Feathered Warrior,* and *Grit and Steel*—as editors, assistant editors, advertising salespersons, and secretaries. These women may have little involvement with the actual cockpit.

WOMEN AGAINST COCKFIGHTING

Historically, women have played a more aggressive role in suppressing cockfighting than in promoting it. Beginning in the nineteenth century, women were often the instigators of anticruelty campaigns that labeled the sport "barbaric." Their efforts resulted in the banning of cockfighting in Britain, Canada, and most of the United States. Women were offended not only by the cruelty to the birds but also by the gambling, drinking, and rowdy behavior that was part of the largely male bachelor subculture of cockfighting. Female evangelists were said to have believed that cockfights posed a threat to the moral purity of the home. To lessen the threat, reform-minded evangelists tried to discourage cockfighting and impose a female piety upon its followers.

RULES AND PLAY

Cockfighting takes place in a ring or pit. Bets are placed before the fight. The birds themselves are treated very well, fed special meals before fights, and examined by fight officials. They are paired by weight and by the type of sharp weapon attached to them. In the ring, they assume fighting stances. The fight may continue until one bird is dead.

A statistical study of modern cockers found that the media often perpetuates the idea that the cockers in the United States are deviant and ad-

here to values that do not mesh with those of U.S. society in general. This impression is wrong; the values of cockers are not unlike those of noncockers; they place high priority on family security, self-respect, freedom, and independence. Today, cockers promote their sport as a family activity. Gamecock journals are replete with photos of happy families posed in front of cockfighting trophies. To ensure the family atmosphere, many cockpits explicitly prohibit drugs, guns, alcohol, rowdy behavior, and foul language. Rather than the male arenas of yesteryear, cockpits have become social environments for the entire family.

CONCLUSION

These wholesome shifts notwithstanding, however, the sport remains illegal in most parts of the United States and many other nations. Given the growing number of supporters of animal rights in the United States and in other nations, it seems unlikely that this situation will change in the foreseeable future.

Barbara Pinto Green

Bibliography

Bryant, Clifton, and Li Li. (1991) "A Statistical Value Profile of Cockfighters." *Social Science Research* 75, 4(July): 199–209.

Del Sesto, Steven L. (1975) "Roles, Rules, and Organization: A Descriptive Account of Cockfighting in Rural Louisiana." *Southern Folklore Quarterly* 39, 1: 1–14.

Donlon, Jon. (1990) "Fighting Cocks, Feathered Warriors, and Little Heroes." *Play & Culture* 3: 273–285.

Geertz, Clifford. (1973) "Deep Play: Notes on the Balinese Cockfight." *The Interpretation of Cultures: Selected Essays.* New York: Basic Books, 412–453.

Guttmann, Allen. (1986) *Spectator Sports.* New York: Columbia University Press.

Hawley, Francis Frederick. (1982) "Organized Cockfighting: A Deviant Recreational Subculture." Unpublished doctoral dissertation, Florida State University, Tallahassee.

———. (1987) "Cockfighting in the Piney Woods: Gameness in the New South." *Sport Place* (Fall): 18–26.

———. (1989) "Cockfight in the Cotton: A Moral Crusade in Microcosm." *Contemporary Crises* 13: 129–144.

Hunter, David. (1990) "To the Death" *Tennessee Illustrated* 3, 4 (Summer):13–17.

McCaghy, Charles H., and Arthur G. Neal (1974) "The Fraternity of Cockfighters: Ethical Embellishments of an Illegal Sport." *Journal of Popular Culture* 13, 8: 557–569.

Ownby, Ted. (1990) *Subduing Satan: Religion, Recreation, and Manhood in the Rural South, 1865–1920.* Chapel Hill: University of North Carolina Press.

COEDUCATIONAL SPORT

Coeducational sports are any sports that have males and females playing on the same team or competing against each other. Other than in a casual playground setting, coed sports were once virtually unheard of, both because many boys' sports were viewed as too rough for girls and because girls' sports seemed too soft for boys. If one gender took part in the sports of the opposite gender, it was feared, characteristics of the latter might somehow rub off—a girl would become rough and boyish, a boy too soft and feminine. Like most stereotypes, this one has been hard to kill, but it is indeed slowly dying as girls and young women join boys and young men on playing fields and on courts.

Various factors have contributed to the demise of sport stereotyping—the feminist movement in general and a general broadening of society's views of appropriate behavior for males and females. Perhaps the key change was the enactment of Title IX of the Education Amendments of 1972. With that law, coed recreational sports became more common, and boys and girls also began participating on the same interscholastic teams, although this remained relatively uncommon. Coed sport represents a unique set of challenges for children, parents, youth league administrators, recreation directors, high school administrators, and coaches. For instance, administrators will have to decide whether or not to offer both coed and same-sex teams, or at what level/age, if any, teams should be split by gender. Simply "selling" coed sports to parents may require philosophical adjustments on the part of those in charge. To date, researchers have done few studies of coeducational sport. What little has been done has been done in the classroom, with a few forays into the gymnasium, in physical education classes.

THE NATURE OF COEDUCATIONAL PHYSICAL EDUCATION

Research suggests that full participation by girls in coeducational sports situations is limited. Solomons (1980) observed an elementary physical education unit where children were taught newcombe (one-bounce volleyball). She found that boys of high ability—those who were good at sports—were more active in that class and received more passes than skillful female players, while girls who could play well gave away twice as many passes rather than trying to score than did their male counterparts. Skilled boys encouraged and helped low-ability boys, but girls, regardless of their abilities, did not receive the boys' encouragement.

Lowest in the pecking order, however, were the boys of very low ability. They were subjected to the most vicious verbal attacks, especially by the girls. In a second study, again observing newcombe at the elementary physical education level, she also found that girls' only contact with the ball was when they served; and so they had to make relatively few decisions about whether to pass or try to score. Overall, the girls received only about one-third as many passes as did the boys. Even girls who were successful when they tried to score did not continue to receive passes, while boys who failed in their attempts were still supplied with opportunities to pass and score. Both the girls and the boys perceived the boys as more highly skilled, even when actual performance did not support this perception.

Other research has identified similar patterns of exclusion. In the early 1980s Griffin examined participation patterns in a gymnastics unit and found that boys limited girls' opportunities to learn by hassling them (for example, making fun of them, fooling around so that girls could not get a turn). Girls, however, did not limit the boys' opportunities through similar behavior. In general, the class environment was not conducive to learning gymnastics, mainly because of the boys' behavior.

DROP THE CAP AND BARLEY BRIDGE
Elizabethan Co-Ed Games

Games at which little boys might become rough were sham fights, running, leaping, wrestling, stone-casting, flinging bucklers, sliding, skating on bones, and whatever in these simple tests of skill developed or challenged the competitive spirit. Games that both boys and girls played, sometimes with much hilarity, were Drop the Cap (like Drop the Handkerchief) and Barley Bridge (like London Bridge). The singing and excitement of Drop the Cap culminated in the chase as the child behind whom the cap was dropped pursued the one who had dropped it. Sometimes when the caught person was kissed as penalty for being caught, there was a sharp contest that might become quite rough. Barley Bridge ended in a tug-of-war that strained muscles in the effort of the two sides to outtug each other and often was extremely rough. Drop the Cap was quite a different game when played by men and women on the village green, for they could engage in much pretty dalliance, but with children it was almost always an exciting game that might end in tears or squabbles.

LU EMILY PEARSON
(1957) Elizabethans at Home. *Stanford, CA: Stanford University Press.*

Because teachers ultimately control what occurs in the classroom, researchers have also looked at their behavior. In Germany, in the early 1980s, Pfister found that boys were noticed, attended to, rewarded, and punished more than girls in coeducational physical instruction. Also, teachers tended to accommodate the interests of boys more than those of girls, in part to keep boys from becoming troublemakers. Solomons observed, too, that teachers would provide extra practice for boys who were not very skilled, but not for girls in the same situation. Teachers congratulated girls for doing something that they had done not nearly as well as boys were expected to do. When a girl performed poorly, teachers either ignored it or patronized them (that is: "nice try"). In contrast, teachers criticized and corrected boys who did not perform well. Griffin found, through interviews, that even when teachers were sincerely trying to be fair, they formed stereotypes based on their students' gender roles. One teacher explained that she divided her coed class in basketball by sex because she felt that the girls were not skillful in handling the ball; consequently, they had few opportunities to handle the ball, and therefore could not learn to play the game.

In the early 1990s, Lirgg examined how students perceived themselves and how they perceived the climate of same-sex and coeducational physical education at the middle and high school levels during a ten-week unit on basketball. Boys in coed classes reported being more confident in their abilities to learn basketball skills than those in same-sex classes. Girls in same-sex classes tended to be more confident than their coeducational counterparts, although not significantly so. However, boys and girls showed marked differences in their confidence in coeducational classes. Boys were much more confident than girls, a situation that could lead them to dominate the class activities. Overall, girls' same-sex classes were perceived most favorably by the girls, while boys' same-sex classes were perceived least favorably by the boys. For example, girls in same-sex classes believed that students in their classes helped one another more than did girls in coeducational classes or boys in either type of class. Also, girls felt that they received more teacher support than did boys, especially girls in same-sex classes. Finally, both boys and girls believed that students in same-sex classes were more involved in the class than did those in coeducational ones.

Duluth-Superior Dukes pitcher Ila Borders and her teammates watch the game from the dugout, c. 1998. Borders was the first woman to sign a contract with a men's professional baseball team, the St. Paul Saints, in 1997. (Layne Kennedy)

Students' feelings about their classes have also been studied. High school students seemed to prefer coeducational activities more often than did middle school students. Pfister noted that girls who were anxious and less skilled in sports tended to reject coeducation because they feared that they would fail to meet high standards and that other students would ridicule them.

Both Griffin and Pfister contend that the teacher holds the key to the success of coeducational physical education classes. In Germany, many projects in coeducation have produced consistently positive results, including changes in students' attitudes. However, teachers and group leaders receive much of the credit for the success of these experimental programs because they had positive attitudes toward coeducational physical education. Most important, teachers took into account the needs and wishes of the students before they introduced mixed physical education lessons. Pfister emphasizes that if teachers lack a pos-

itive attitude, then coeducational physical education is a liability for both sexes, especially for girls.

COEDUCATIONAL SPORTS OPPORTUNITIES

The enactment of Title IX in the United States helped to advance girls' sports opportunities in two major ways. The first was that girls began to challenge their exclusion from boys' teams (such as Little League baseball) because no teams existed for them. The second, an outgrowth of the first, was that more and more girls' teams were created. Because girls' sports had lagged so far behind boys' sports, many girls were not in fact particularly adept at many of these sports which were new to them. At the same time, many skilled girls found that girls' teams did not challenge them enough. They sought out teams that would match their abilities. Often girls would play on boys' teams; at younger ages, recreation departments offered coeducational teams.

BREAKING GENDER BARRIERS IN HOCKEY

In 1999, Angela Ruggiero was not allowed to play in a pick-up ice hockey league on a municipal rink near her home in St. Claire Shores, Michigan. Although a member of the gold medal 1998 Olympic ice hockey team, she was banned from the ice because the league was open to "men only." That she was an Olympian and had previously played with men did nothing to change the minds of the rink officials. To gain access and change the rink policy, Ruggiero hired an attorney and was aided by local news coverage.

Until they reach adolescence, boys and girls should have relatively similar physical capabilities. As children grow, boys, on average, will become stronger and more powerful than girls, which means that fewer girls will excel on coed teams that demand those characteristics. As with physical education classes, even preadolescent boys can limit girls' opportunities if only boys are allowed to play the skilled positions. The youth league coach is a vitally important cog in the success of a coeducational youth sports team.

ADOLESCENT SPORTS TEAMS

Coeducational teams in adolescence are not as common as they are for younger children. For example, the development of secondary sex characteristics such as breasts may make a female adolescent uncomfortable with her physical appearance. Body-fat percentage in adolescent girls also increases, with the added weight generally being distributed lower on the body than with boys. Therefore, although girls are better equipped for balance activities, they are put at a disadvantage, compared to boys, in sports that require upper-body strength and speed. However, some girls will possess the necessary physical attributes to compete, and in some instances girls have competed successfully on boys' baseball, soccer (association football), wrestling, and even football teams. Of those sports, only soccer offers a comparable girls' team.

The debate about allowing girls on boys' teams has often centered not on the relative abilities of the two groups but rather on other emotionally charged issues. For example, some administrators, coaches, and parents worry about girls beating boys, although they may hide this concern and argue instead that they are worried about the girls getting hurt. Others argue that if girls can play on boys' teams, boys should be allowed to play on girls' teams (such as volleyball and field hockey). This argument ignores the reality that most boys are stronger than girls and might dominate those sports, thus limiting girls' opportunities to make the team in the first place.

The basic question remains: Should girls be allowed to compete against boys? Many women's sports advocates argue that if a girl's skill levels are comparable, it is only a sexist ideology that bars her from competing. As more and more girls have opportunities to increase their skills at younger ages, girls' teams will improve. As an example, witness the increased skill level in girls' basketball and soccer today, an improvement that has occurred over a relatively short period of time. It is possible that more and more girls may even become more interested in previously all-boy sports, such as baseball and wrestling.

ADULT COEDUCATIONAL TEAMS

As adults, men's superiority in strength and power are more obvious. At the same time, in adult leagues, participants are often looking more for social activities than for competition. Coed bowling leagues are quite common and do not require any unusual rule changes. Coed softball and volleyball leagues are plentiful. However, rules are usually made in these sports to level the playing field. For example, in volleyball, if more than one hit on a side is needed, a woman must make one of the hits. Often, power volleyball (spiking) is not permitted. In softball, several rule changes exist. One is that women hit a smaller (eleven-inch instead of twelve-inch) ball. Batting order is arranged alternately by gender. The same number of women and men must be used in the infield and outfield, respectively. Also, the battery (pitcher and catcher) must be coed. Under some rules (such as those of the United States Slowpitch Softball Association), the outfielders must stay behind a designated line until the female batter hits the ball to prevent playing up close and thus limiting the opportunity for a woman to get a hit.

Problems in coeducational adult leagues occur in two areas. As in youth leagues, men sometimes limit women by playing out of position. For example, the pitcher, if a man, will frequently cover home plate on a play there if the catcher is a woman. Similarly, male outfielders may extend their field coverage to a female's area. Situations like these develop when the man perceives that the woman is less skilled and he is concerned primarily with winning the game.

Coed recreational sport for adults may pose increased risk of injury because men and women often differ in their levels of ability. Although this is also true for all-male or all-female teams with players of varying ability, it occurs more often in coed recreational sports. Balls hit or thrown harder than can be fielded by a player of a lesser skill level are dangerous. Most recreation programs offer different levels of competition for same-gender teams. Many highly skilled women (and men) greatly enjoy the atmosphere and competition that a high-level coed team affords. In the case of adult recreational teams, the leadership of the recreation director (instead of the coach) is the important factor in the participants' enjoyment.

ELITE AND PROFESSIONAL COED TEAMS

As skill levels increase, men and women rarely compete on the same teams. At the Olympic level, only one event is truly coed—the equestrian competition. Other competitions, such as shooting and yachting, have some mixed events at the team level. Individual professional sports have created competitions that include direct competition between men and women. Tennis and badminton have mixed doubles competitions. Golf has a provision (separate tee areas) that allows equitable pairings for men and women, although at the elite level almost all competitions are restricted to men- or women-only events.

On the professional level in team sports, few women have gained access to men's sports. Although women have been allowed to try out in the National Basketball Association (NBA), for example, or played in the minor leagues (ice hockey), they have not been able to secure positions on men's professional teams. Women are, however, breaking barriers in officiating, as evidenced by the addition of two female referees in the NBA in the late 1990s. Men have long officiated in women's sports; the time is coming when female officials will be common in all men's and women's sports.

CONCLUSION

Success in any youth league can often be measured by how many players return the following year to compete. This simple assessment should be applied to both coed and same-gender teams. Before children will return, they must experience personal success, not merely play on a winning team. Children need coaches who will help them improve their skills and who will give them chances to practice those skills in games. Children also need coaches who will be sensitive to their individual needs and emotions, and who will not berate their mistakes. In short, children need coaches who will have similar expectations for boys and girls.

As individuals get older, coeducational activities will involve much greater variation in skill level among participants. Recreation directors should be aware of this and create leagues that are safe as well as fair. They may need to maintain more than one coed division to ensure that individuals are participating on teams that reflect their skill level.

Finally, women should have the opportunity to compete at the highest levels in any sport if they are capable of doing so. Ideally, women's teams should exist for all sports in which women are interested. However, if a woman can kick 50-yard field goals, she should be allowed to participate in men's football if this sport is important to her and no women's teams exist.

Cathy D. Lirgg

See also Korfball

Bibliography

Griffin, Patricia S. (1983) " 'Gymnastics Is a Girl's Thing': Student Participation and Interaction Patterns in a Middle School Gymnastics Unit." In

Teaching Physical Education, edited by T. S. Templin and J. Olson. Champaign, IL: Human Kinetics Publishers, 71–85.

————. (1984) "Co-ed Physical Education: Problems and Promise." *Journal of Physical Education, Recreation, & Dance* 55, 6: 36–37.

————. (1985) "Girls' and Boys' Participation Styles in Middle School Physical Education Team Sport Classes: A Description and Practical Applications." *The Physical Educator* 42: 3–8.

Lirgg, Cathy D. (1993) "Effects of Same-Sex Versus Co-educational Physical Education on the Self-Perceptions of Middle and High School Students." *Research Quarterly for Exercise and Science* 64: 324–334.

————. (1994) "Environmental Perceptions of Students in Same-Sex and Co-educational Physical Education Classes." *Journal of Educational Psychology* 86: 183–192.

Mikkelson, Mary Doub. (1979) "Co-ed Gym: It's a Whole New Ballgame." *Journal of Physical Education, Recreation, and Dance* 50, 8: 63–64.

Payne, V. Gregory, and Larry D. Isaacs. (1995) *Human Motor Development: A Lifespan Approach.* Mountain View, CA: Mayfield.

Pfister, Gertrud. (1983) *Geschlechtsspezifische Sozialisation und Koedukation im Sport.* Berlin: Bartels and Wernitz.

————. (1985) "Zur Ausgrenzung von Weiblichkeit: Entwicklungen und Verhinderungen des Koedukativen Unterrichts." In *Nachdenken uber Koedukation im Sport,* edited by S. Kröner and G. Pfister. Ahrensburg: Czwalina, 11–37.

————. (1985) "Als mädchen darf mann kein fußball spielen: Über das Eiüben der Geschlechterrollen im Sportunterricht." In *Fauen machen Schule,* edited by R. Valtin and U. Warm. Frankfort: Bartels and Wernitz, 42–52.

Rice, Pamela L. (1988) "Attitudes of High School Students Toward Physical Education, Education Activities, Teachers, and Personal Health." *The Physical Educator* (Spring): 94–99.

Solomons, Helen H. (1980) "Sex Role Mediation of Achievement Behaviors and Interpersonal Interactions in Sex-Integrated Team Games." In *Children in Cooperation and Competition: Toward a Developmental Social Psychology,* edited by E. A. Pepitone. Lexington, MA: Lexington Books, 321–364.

Tannehill, Deborah, Jan-Erik Romar, Mary O'Sullivan, Kathy England, and Daniel Rosenburg. (1994) "Attitudes Toward Physical Education: Their Impact on How Physical Education Teachers Make Sense of Their Work." *Journal of Teaching in Physical Education* 13: 406–420.

COLLETT VARE, GLENNA

(1903–1985)
U.S. GOLFER

Glenna Collett Vare is known as one of the greatest women golfers of all time and one of the Big Four of women's golf of the 1920s and 1930s. Commemorating Collett Vare's high standards of skill and sportsmanship, the Ladies Professional Golf Association (LPGA) annually awards its most prestigious award, the Vare trophy, to honor the player with the lowest average of the season. Further signifying Collett Vare's greatness, the U.S. Junior Girls' Championships award their champion the Glenna Collett Vare trophy, noting that during her career Vare exemplified the standards to which all young champions should aspire. Along with Britain's Joyce Wethered (Lady Heathcoat-Armory), Collett is credited with setting new standards of excellence for modern women's golf.

Glenna Collett was born in New Haven, Connecticut, on 20 June 1903. In her early years, she excelled at swimming, diving, and tennis. At fourteen, she was introduced to golf by her father. She instantly found golf so exciting and challenging that she quit high school to pursue the game full time. Two years later, she won the U.S. Girls' Championship, the first of her forty-nine national and international championships.

Referred to as the "Queen of American Golf" by some and the "Female Bobby Jones" by others, Collett won her first U.S. Women's Championship at the age of nineteen, in 1922, defeating three-time champion Alexa Stirling. Collett was, and still is (as of 1999), the youngest woman to have held that title. That same year she won both the North and South Championships (which she eventually won six times) and the Eastern Championship. In 1924, she won fifty-nine out of sixty consecutive matches in tournament play and set a record-low qualifying score of 79 in a women's amateur tournament.

Collett repeated as the U.S. national champion in 1925, and then won the title for another three years in a row (1928–1930). Between her first and last U.S. amateur titles, she won six times, finished second twice, and advanced to the quarterfinals or semifinals on three other occasions. In the world of golf, only Bobby Jones has surpassed her record of three consecutive national championships and her overall record of six national championships. (Alexa Stirling also won three consecutive U.S. women's amateur titles in 1916, 1919, and 1920; there were no championships in 1917 or 1918 because of World War I. Virginia Van Wie tied the record in 1932–1934.)

In 1931, Collett married Edwin H. Vare, Jr., and began the delicate balancing of golf, household duties, and motherhood. (She had a son, Ned, and a daughter, Glenna.) Van Wie took the national titles in 1932 and 1934, but in 1935, Collett Vare came back to claim her sixth and last U.S. amateur championship, defeating seventeen-year-old Patty Berg. In her autobiography, *Ladies in the Rough,* written when she was only twenty-four, Collett emerged as one of the first sports feminists by suggesting that women should keep their maiden names in competition. This statement came at a time when women were identified in tournaments only by their husbands' names (e.g., Mrs. Edwin H. Vare, Jr.). In her autobiography, she also revealed her views on combining the roles of woman and golfer: "I do not wish I were a man, except sometimes, when my drives only come within a full shot of my opponent's. I envy him his spirit of freedom, his independence of trifles, his disdain of convention, his disregard of appearances, and his childlike conviction, if he is a golfer, that golf is the most important thing on this bunkered sphere."

Collett Vare obviously enjoyed her sport and kept her life in balance throughout her career. For that, she was revered by men and women of her time and has since been characterized by golf writer Herbert Warren Wind as "gifted with a conquering graciousness." At the time she was competing, there were no professional championships for women—that would not come until 1946, when the U.S. Women's Open in Spokane, Washington, awarded the winner $5,600 (of a total purse of $19,700). Before the formation of the Women's Professional Golf Association in 1948, Collett Vare worked to raise public interest in the game, playing standards, and corporate funding for women's golf matches. She worked alongside

Golfer D.E. Chambers (center) and Glenna Collett (right) drink from the cup after the joint presentation of the 1936 Curtis Cup. The match was a draw between the previous holders, USA and Great Britain. (Hulton-Deutsch Collection/Corbis)

the Curtis sisters, Harriet and Margaret, to set the stage for regular international competition between the United States and Great Britain/Ireland.

Unofficial matches had been staged as early as 1898, but no formal agreement or sponsorship existed at that time. Early in the twentieth century, several Americans competed in the British Amateur Championship, while British golfers made the journey to the United States. In 1930, Collett was able to arrange an informal match between the United States and Great Britain. This first international competition was financed by a travel agency, but in 1931, the USGA and the Ladies Golf Union agreed to hold a regular biannual competition between the United States and Great Britain, alternating the site between the two nations. France was invited, but did not participate in the early matches. The first official Curtis Cup match, which drew 15,000 spectators, was staged in May 1932 at England's Wentworth Golf Club. Wethered captained the British team, which included Van Wie, Wanda Morgan, Enid Wilson, Mrs. J. B. Watson, Molly Gourlay, Doris Park, Diana Fishwick, and Elsie Corbett. U.S. members were Marion Hollins (captain), Collett Vare, Opal Hill, Virginia Helen Hicks, Maureen Orcutt, Leona Cheney, and Dorothy Higbie (alternate). The Collett Vare–Hill defeat of the Wethered–Morgan team led the

United States to a sweep of the foursomes. Although Wethered defeated Collett Vare in the singles, the U.S. team won the match 5.5 to 3.5, bringing home the first Curtis Cup to the United States. Collett Vare played in and captained the U.S. Curtis Cup team in 1934, 1936, and 1948. She served as nonplaying captain in 1950.

Other notable Collett Vare victories included winning the Women's Eastern Championship six times and winning the Canadian (1923, 1924) and French (1925) women's opens. She reached the finals of the British Women's Amateur in 1929 and 1930, losing each time to Wethered. Golf historians have dubbed the 1929 match between the British and the U.S. champions as the greatest women's match of all time. In 1959, at age fifty-six, Collett Vare culminated her championship career with a victory in the Rhode Island Women's Golf Association Championship.

Glenna Collett Vare was recognized not only for her consistent and superb play but also as a model sportsperson, admired for her positive, competitive attitude and her sense of humor. In recognition of her many accomplishments, she was one of the six women selected in 1950 as charter members of the Women's Golf Hall of Fame. In 1952, Betty Jameson, LPGA founder, charter and Hall of Fame member, donated the Vare trophy to the LPGA Tour to honor the player with the lowest average at the end of each season. Collett Vare was inducted into the World Golf Hall of Fame in 1975, the same year as her great British rival Wethered, the only competitor of her time whom she never defeated in head-to-head competition. Perhaps there was some solace in the fact that Wethered's career had spanned only ten years, while Collett Vare's continued for more than sixty years. She was still playing golf into her eighties, shooting scores to match her age. She played in the Rhode Island Point Judith Invitational for sixty-two years. She completed her final rounds of life at her winter home in Gulfstream, Florida, and died on 3 February 1985.

Debra Ann Ballinger

Bibliography

Chambers, Marcia. (1995) *The Unplayable Lie: The Untold Story of Women and Discrimination in American Golf.* New York: Golf Digest Pocket Books.

Crosset, Todd, W. (1995) *Outsiders in the Clubhouse: The World of Women's Professional Golf.* Albany: State University of New York Press.

Dodson, James. (1995) *Final Rounds.* New York: Bantam.

Golf Journal. Features. <http://www.golfjournal.com/features/95/centennial moments.html>. 1995.

GolfWeb. "World Golf Hall of Fame Inductees." <http://www.golfweb.com/library/ap/hallinductees 980516.htm>. 1998.

Wind, Herbert Warren and Robert MacDonald, eds. (1995). The Great Women Golfers. <www.classics of golf.com/GWG-CP.HTM>.

COLOMBIA

Colombia is a Latin American nation with a population of about 36 million located on the northwest coast of South America. Women in Colombia have traditionally had a limited role in the public sphere (only 22 percent of women are in the labor force, and they form only 23 percent of that force), and that pattern is obvious in the relatively low level of women's involvement in sports. Only in the late 1990s has a movement for women's sports emerged in Colombia, and it has met with mixed results. Barriers to women's sports include the traditional views that women belong in the home, that sports activity is a masculine pursuit, and that women who are athletes are not feminine. There is also a lack of resources and support for women's sports, and few career opportunities exist for women as athletes, coaches, administrators, physical education teachers, or sports journalists.

Despite the lack of opportunities for women, many girls and fewer young women in Colombia participate in sports in schools. Soccer, basketball, volleyball, swimming (especially synchronized swimming), gymnastics, and roller skating are the most popular sports at this level. However, most girls stop participating when they reach puberty. For women who continue on with sports, soccer, volleyball, and softball are popular, with upper-class women also involved in equestrian sports and shooting, and a few women involved in major international sports such as weightlifting and track.

The best known Colombian female athletes in the 1990s were Maria Isabel Urutia in weightlifting, Monica Fernandez in volleyball, Maria Teresa

Rueda in shooting, Ana Maria Jaillier in softball, and Ximena Restrepo in track. In addition, equestrian and attorney Yolanda Matallana Tribino was the sole woman on the Colombian Olympic Committee, and Margarita Maria Martinez was the unpaid coach of the national women's soccer team, which played its first international match in California in 1998. As is the case with soccer, the level of women's participation in most sports at the international level has been low. Women first participated for Colombia in the Olympics in 1968, with nine women on the team. From 1972 to 1992, no more than six women participated in each Olympics, but in 1996 the number increased again to nine.

The 1994 Brighton Declaration supporting the international development of women's sport was an important factor in stimulating action among women's sport advocates in Colombia. A leader of the initial movement was Guillermo Gonzalez, president of the Colombian Roller Skating Federation, who represented Colombia at the Brighton Conference. In November 1996 the first Conference on Women and Sports was organized by Clemencia Anaya Maya, director of the Olympic Education Academy of the Coldeportes (Colombian National Sport Federation), and was attended by 200 men and women in Bogota. Clemencia Anaya set the agenda for the conference when she posed the following challenge: "Sport as it relates to culture is an integral aspect of the culture of each nation. Women are represented in the most minimal form in areas of decision-making and leadership in sport in Colombia. How can we change this so that women are integral to the culture of sport in our nation?" A major result of the conference was the formation of the Association Colombiana de Mujer y Deporte (Colombian Women in Sport Association; ACMD), with Anaya as its president. The conference and the ACMD were welcomed by international women's sports organizations but were criticized in Colombia by both Coldeportes (and Guillermo Gonzalez) and the Colombian Olympic Committee as "*feministas* who were trying to form a *syndicato* [union] to cause trouble."

In March 1998, a second conference was convened in Medellin, with a focus on research on women in sports, including issues such as nutrition, exercise, recreation, disabilities sport, homo-

Colombian high divers practice in Ibagué, Colombia. (Jeremy Homer/Corbis)

phobia, masculinization, rural sport, and sport and the family. The conference attracted 100 men and women, including several prominent female athletes. It also attracted the media and produced conflict between reporters and panelists, with some reporters suggesting that all female soccer players were lesbians (the soccer team had just played its first international match in California) and that Colombians were not interested in women's sports. The media attacks led some participants to wonder whether relations with Coldeportes and the National Olympic Committee, which had been repaired after the 1996 conference, were again badly damaged and would lead these organizations to withhold support for the ACMD.

In 1999 the ACMD continued to adhere to the principles set forth in the Brighton Declaration and to use those principles to develop women's sports in Colombia. However, its efforts were still hindered by a lack of institutional support, by traditional values, and by media hostility.

Christina Shelton

Bibliography

Seager, Joni (1997) *The State of Women in the World Atlas.* Harmondsworth, UK: Penguin.

COLÓN, MARIÁ CARIDAD

(1958–)

CUBAN FIELD ATHLETE

Mariá Caridad Colón, the first Latin American woman to win Olympic gold, was born on 25 March 1958 in Baracoa, Cuba. When Colón was six, her mother completed a course qualifying her to teach physical education. Colón was an apt pupil, distinguishing herself in the track and field contests of the Juegos Escolares Nacionales (National Students Games). Following her mother's path, Colón began to study physical education at the Escuela de Iniciación Deportiva in Oriente Province. In 1975, she advanced to the national sports school in Havana.

Mariá Colón throwing the javelin at the 1980 Olympics in Moscow. (AP Photos)

In 1977, competing in Havana's Pedro Marrero Stadium, Colón threw her javelin an impressive 54.32 meters, (178.21 feet) but was beaten by Mariá Antonia Beltrán's 54.40 meters (178.48 feet), a new national record. A year later, Colón surpassed Beltrán. Competing at Santiago de Cuba on 20 May 1978, she hurled her javelin 60.62 meters (198.88 feet). The two women placed first and second at that year's Central American and Caribbean Games at Medellin, Colombia. The following year, with a throw of 62.30 meters (204.39 feet), Colón defeated Lynn Cannon and Cathy Sulinski, both representing the United States, and won the gold at the Pan-American Games in San Juan, Puerto Rico. That same year, at the world championships in Montreal, she bettered her own record with 63.50 meters (208.33 feet) but was outperformed by Ruth Fuchs of East Germany and Eva Raduly-Zorgo of Romania.

Colón's greatest moment came at the Moscow Olympics of 1980. Fuchs, who had won the gold in 1972 and 1976, was unable to match Colón's winning throw of 68.40 meters (224.41 feet). In 1982, Sofia Sakorafa of Greece raised the world record to 74.20 meters (243.44 feet), a distance beyond Caridad Colón's ability.

In 1981, Colón, who had married her coach Angel Salcedo in 1979, bore her first child, whom she named for his father.

Allen Guttmann

Bibliography

Guiral, Frank. (1986) *Mariá Caridad Colón: La Jabalina de Oro.* Havana: Editorial Cientifico-Technica.

COMANECI, NADIA

(1961–)

ROMANIAN GYMNAST

At the 1976 Olympics in Montreal, fourteen-year-old Nadia Comaneci became the first woman to score a 10 in Olympic competition. This was a theoretical impossibility. The world of gymnastics had not yet conceived of such a score, nor did it have the electronic capability to display a 10.0. The best the organizers could do was to flash a "1.0." After a few seconds' pause, those attending understood that this was a historic moment for gymnastics, Comaneci, her coaches, and Romania. Romania had previously won only one gold medal in an international gymnastics open competition; Dan Grecu won the gold on rings at the 1974 world championships. No Romanian, male or female, had ever won the coveted all-around championship. Had it not been for the excellence of the Soviet team in the floor exercise and vaulting events, Comaneci may well have swept the gold medals and a team victory. However, since the Soviet Union no longer exists, the Soviet women's gymnastics team remains the only one never beaten in Olympic competition.

Nadia Comaneci was born in Onesti, Romania, on 12 November 1961. She was discovered in kindergarten by her future coach, Bela Karolyi, a former boxer, hammer thrower, and team handball player. At the time, he was assisting his wife, Marta, who was head coach at a local gymnastics club. Comaneci won her first national championship in 1970 as a junior and made her European debut at an exhibition of Europe's best gymnasts in 1974 in Paris. Although she and her close friend, Teodora Ungureanu, were scheduled to perform with a younger group of promising gymnasts at another Parisian gym, Karolyi was convinced that Comaneci should be allowed to perform with the other top women of Europe, a group that included Ludmilla Tourischeva of the Soviet Union. The previous year, Tourischeva had swept the European championships and objected to appearing with a "child." Never one to be intimidated by authority, Karolyi told Comaneci to vault without the permission of the organizers. Eventually, noting the talent of the youngster, they permitted her to continue. The next year (1975), she bested the elite women of Europe, including Tourischeva and her Soviet teammate, Nelli Kim. This was the first of three European championship overall gold medals for Comaneci, with others in 1977 and 1979. Comaneci was the first Romanian woman to rise to the top level of European gymnastics.

Prior to the Montreal Olympics in 1976, Comaneci was entered in and won the first American Cup invitational. She performed brilliantly,

Nadia Comaneci of Romania shows her perfect balance on the beam in the women's individual overall competition in the 1979 World Cup Gymnastics Championships. (Bettmann/Corbis)

with her Tsukahara vault awarded a 10.0. She shared the victory podium with Bart Conner of the United States, who won the men's all-around cup. Conner and Comaneci were married twenty years later. She won the prestigious Chunichi Cup in 1977 and defended her title at the European championships in Prague, Czechoslovakia. Trouble developed over judging in the individual events, however, and Karolyi withdrew the Romanians from the meet despite Comaneci's gold on the uneven parallel bars. The Romanians were disqualified in the individual events as a result and lost some medals, including Comaneci's gold. Karolyi was removed as national coach but later reinstated prior to the world championships in Strasbourg, France, in 1978.

Comaneci won the gold and silver medals in Strasbourg and defended her all-around title at the European championships in Copenhagen, Denmark, in 1979. Later that year at the Fort Worth world championships, the first ever in the

United States, the Romanian women challenged the Soviets and won despite a severe infection in Comaneci's wrist. She had to sit on the sidelines for most of the meet but rallied to produce a 9.95 beam performance, thus helping her team to narrowly win the team medal by little more than half a point. Despite this score, she did not win an individual medal since she was unable to compete during the compulsory events. But her teammates Melita Rühn, Emilia Eberle, Rodica Dunca, Dumitrita Turner, and Marilena Vladarau did well and took the gold medal for Romania.

At the 1980 Moscow Olympics, Comaneci was suffering from sciatica and was unable to perform elements that placed a great deal of stress on the legs and lower back. The Romanians remained undaunted despite Comaneci's condition, in the face of the Soviet's "home advantage" in judging and the Romanian team's placement in a weaker team rotation with the prospect of lower scores. Despite the obstacles, the Soviet team beat the Romanians by only 1.4 points. Comaneci tied Maxi Gnauck for the silver all-around medal and competed in three of the four individual event finals, winning the beam title outright and tying Nelli Kim for the gold in floor exercise. Her last international competition was the Universiade, or World University Games, in 1981, declared a "fiasco" due to judging errors by no less than gymnastics' premier historian, Josef Goehler of Germany. Comaneci won the all-around gold, two individual golds, and a silver; a nice way to end a career despite the quality of the meet administration.

Comaneci retired in 1984 prior to the Los Angeles Olympics, which she then attended as a guest of the International Olympic Committee. Thereafter, she was not allowed to travel outside the Soviet bloc countries and was denied permission to travel to the Seoul Olympics. She began to search for a way to defect. Her coaches Bela and Marta Karolyi had defected in 1981, along with Geza Posar, a Romanian gymnastics choreographer. In 1989, she defected with six other athletes because they could no longer suffer the repression of the Nicolae Ceausescu dictatorship. They made their way to Hungary by train and then crossed the border on foot, struggling through barbed wire in the cold and mud. In Hungary, they were offered asylum but were warned that they could be deported to Romania if they tried to leave. Ignoring the warning, Comaneci traveled to Vienna and was offered asylum by the Austrian government. All of this took place just weeks prior to the Romanian revolution and the subsequent execution of Ceausescu. Comaneci's family was detained by the government and faced a dark future, but their freedom was assured following the revolution. Some believe that Comaneci's defection accelerated the revolution because she was and remains a national heroine. Comaneci was given asylum in the United States, arriving at New York's Kennedy Airport on 28 November 1989.

Comaneci's legacy in gymnastics, her presence as a modern sports icon, and her heroism have been recognized by almost every group empowered to make awards. She is one of the greatest gymnasts who ever lived, and she is without doubt the most celebrated. She was voted female athlete of the year (1975 and 1976) by United Press International and Associated Press, and the BBC's named her "overseas personality of the year" (1976). She was inducted into the International Women's Sports Hall of Fame in 1990 and the International Gymnastics Hall of Fame in 1993. She is one of few to have received the Olympic Order of the International Olympic Committee. But it is her pioneering gymnastics accomplishments that mark her as one of the great athletes. First, she achieved a perfect score, the first one awarded in Olympic competition. Second, she displayed the ability to perform more than two consecutive acrobatic elements on the balance beam. Third, she created the "Comaneci" dismount on the uneven parallel bars. The dismount is named for her in accord with the practice of naming a new element performed for the first time in an international open competition (e.g., Olympic Games, world championships) after the gymnast who performs it. It is then so listed in the Code of Points, the official rules of gymnastics designated by the International Gymnastics Federation (FIG). And, fourth, she is the only woman to to have won three consecutive European championship all-around titles.

In 1998, Comaneci was the recipient of the Flo Hyman Memorial Award of the Women's Sports Foundation. Hyman died suddenly of a heart attack in 1986, during a volleyball match, at age thirty-two. The award is given annually to the athlete who captures the "dignity, spirit, and commitment to excellence" that characterized Flo

Hyman's career. Comaneci has also given time to a number of charities, some of which are in her native Romania. For example, she helped Romanian orphans find homes in the United States. Her home club in Onesti is now named for her. She and her husband, Bart Conner, operate a gym, the Bart Conner Gymnastics Academy, in Norman, Oklahoma, and both write a column, "Ask Bart and Nadia," for *International Gymnast* magazine.

A. B. Frederick

Bibliography

Deford, Frank. (1976) "Nadia Awed Ya." *Sports Illustrated* 2 (August): 28–31.

Goehler, Josef. (1981) "Fiasco in Bucharest." *International Gymnast* (October): 13–14.

Grumeza, Ion. (1977) *Nadia.* Ft. Lauderdale, FL: SLT Publishing.

Gutman, Dan. (1996) *Gymnastics.* New York: Viking.

Karolyi, Bela, with N. A. Richardson. (1994) *Feel No Fear.* New York: Hyperion.

Lessa, Christina. (1997) *Gymnastics Balancing Acts.* New York: Universe.

Macovei, Constantin. (1977) *Nadia Comaneci: The Gold Medal Winning Gymnast.* New York: Grosset and Dunlap.

Marshall, Nancy Thies, and Pam Vredevelt. (1988) *Women Who Compete.* Old Tappen, NJ: F.H. Revell Co.

Moran, Lyn. (1978) *The Young Gymnasts.* New York: K.S. Giniger.

Ryan, Joan. (1995) *Little Girls in Pretty Boxes.* New York: Doubleday.

Simons II, Minot. (1995) *Women's Gymnastics: A History.* Carmel, CA: Welwyn.

Straus, Hal. (1978) *Gymnastics Guide.* Mountain View, CA: World Publications.

COMMODIFICATION AND COMMERCIALIZATION

Commodification is the process by which a product or activity that once existed for utility or pleasure becomes a commodity, something used to make money, to buy and sell, through promotion or exploitation. *Commercialization* is the application of business practices where they were not formerly applied. Sports are a prime example of an activity that has, at its higher levels, become a highly commercialized commodity.

Sports have been a form of public entertainment in many societies, but commercial sports have never been more pervasive than they are today. Money is both a motivator and an elevator of athletes. Playing for high monetary stakes also excites fans. Television money dictates everything from team schedules to the scheduling of time-outs. Exceptional athletes become millionaires with their sports earnings and endorsements. In essence, modern sports have become corporate sports.

Unquestionably, commodification and commercialization have changed sports dramatically. Women figure into this phenomenon in two ways. As professional athletes, they, too, become, in essence, commodities, like their male counterparts. As spectators and amateur participants, they increase the market for sports-related products and advertising.

The commercial success of sports has relied upon their ability to generate revenues. Sources of revenue typically include gate receipts, the sale of broadcasting rights, and the sale of licensed merchandise. Successful commercialization occurs most often in or near large cities with many potential spectators who will spend money attending events and buying related goods. Cities themselves, however, are not enough. People in urban areas must have the time, discretionary income, and means to travel to competitions. Commercialization of sports is the product of both urbanization and sophistication.

FACTORS RELATED TO COMMERCIAL SUCCESS

Commercial sports require strong spectator interest. This, too, is related to the kind of community. Spectator interest seems to be highest in places where the people value achievement, where a widespread system of youth sports programs exist, and where there is general access to newspapers, radio, and television.

Spectator interest has increased worldwide, a phenomenon that includes women in many industrialized countries. As more women have entered occupations with a strong emphasis on advancement and upward mobility, they have become more interested in watching sports and attending games. Often, spectators see sports as a model of the way they would like the rest of the world to operate. As they watch a sports event, they can see that hard work and the pursuit of excellence still lead to success and prosperity.

COMMODIFICATION OF WOMEN'S SPORTS

By the 1920s commercial spectator sports were a global phenomenon. Australian swimmer Annette Kellermann performed live and in the movies. French tennis player Suzanne Lenglen attracted thousands to her matches. Women began to compete in the Olympics, and the African American track and field star of the 1940s, Alice Coachman, was featured in Coca-Cola advertisements.

Other changes contributed to women's increased involvement in sports. Suddenly, women's bodies were viewed in a new way. As Twin observes, "For the first time, the female form was becoming a marketable item, used to sell numerous products and services. The commodification of women's bodies provided a cultural opening for competitive athletics, as an industry and ambitious individuals used women to sell sports."

TRENDS IN COMMERCIAL SPORT DEVELOPMENT

Two major trends characterize the development of commercial sports: the phenomenal expansion of amateur and professional spectator sports and the increase in sports participation. Children who participate in sports often grow up to become adults who like to watch sports. As a result, the number of potential spectators in a given place increases when young people have many opportunities to take part in sports programs.

Participation in sports by a young person is strongly correlated with that person's later participation and spectator interest throughout life. Such people tend to want to watch the experts, who then become models for young people to improve their own skills and maintain their interests in participation.

Youth sports, as well as high school and college programs, are considered amateur, but they are closely tied to the production of capital in the sports industry. Local businesses use youth teams to advertise their goods and services, while high school and college games are magnets for television advertising money.

Many of the world's most famous sports events were created by commercial interests. Among the examples are the Tour de France, invented by *L'Auto* magazine, and Japan's schoolboy baseball tournament, sponsored by the *Mainichi* and the *Asahi* newspapers.

WOMEN AND THE SPORTS INDUSTRY

Throughout the industrialized world, sports are a massive commercialized enterprise. In 1987, the part of the U.S. economy related to sports was calculated at $50 billion (of a $4.52 trillion gross national product). This figure established sports as the twenty-third-largest general business enter-

---

LOW RATINGS FOR WOMEN'S SPORTS

Statistics compiled by the Nielsen Media research organization for 1998 and 1999 show that of the top 74 rated sports shows on American television, only one was a women's sport, the Women's World Cup on 10 July 1999 rated #57. Most top-rated shows were professional football games followed by professional baseball games. The lack of coverage on television and lower ratings for televised women's sports are major impediments to the commercialization of women's sports because higher ratings mean more viewers which in turn attract more advertisers who will pay higher rates for television time. The major exception to this pattern is figure skating, a women's sport which is regularly televised.

prise in the United States. Sports directly contribute more than 1 percent of the value of all goods and services produced in the United States.

The gross national sport product can be broken down into categories. These include recreational and participant sport; sporting goods and apparel; sport receipts; concessions and licensed merchandise; fees for television and radio rights; and stadium and arena construction. In each of these categories, women are significantly influencing the direction of the sport industry. Just as they have infiltrated law, medicine, and other fields, women have secured positions as executives in a variety of roles within the sports industry.

The 1990s working woman has also achieved status in the sport marketplace. As women's income has increased, so has their buying power. In most families, women are sharing or controlling major purchase decisions. In addition, children have traditionally been introduced to sports by parents. Sport marketers have acknowledged that children's spectatorship and participation encourage future adult spectatorship and consumption. The result has been a growing awareness in the industry of the need to address mothers in sports marketing efforts. Stock car racing as well as professional soccer (association football), basketball, football, and ice hockey have large female audiences and have successfully attracted sponsors and advertisers for this reason.

THE EVOLUTION OF WOMEN'S SPORTS

Since the early 1980s, there have been increasing numbers of knowledgeable women fans, in part because women have had more opportunities to take part in competitive sports. In 1971 only 300,000 girls participated in high school sports. By the mid-1990s that figure was approaching 3 million. These increases have brought a parallel increase in corporate attention to this market.

As a result of the years of growing participation and improved quality of coaching and competition, women's sports have reached a new level. The 1996 and 1998 Olympic Games showcased women's sports and created the major impetus for forming new professional leagues for women in such team sports as basketball, softball, soccer, and ice hockey. Previous attempts to create basketball leagues had failed, but in the 1990s the

interest, the fan base, and the quality of athletes led to the establishment of two women's leagues, although one folded in 1998.

TELEVISION COVERAGE OF WOMEN'S SPORTS

Women's sports have always had to compete—often unsuccessfully—for television coverage. Television is critical to the success of a sport because people who like the sport or play it can then watch it and, in turn, become consumers. Today, television is a necessary ingredient for successful merchandising programs, as well as sales of corporate sponsorships. In the sports industry, television has become the primary source of revenue, earning event promoters and organizers millions of dollars.

One of the first major sporting events involving a high-profile female athlete to be commercialized was the so-called battle of the sexes, a tennis match on 20 September 1973 between Billie Jean King and Bobby Riggs, both of the United States. The prize for the winner of the match was $100,000. Yet this paled in comparison to the $3 million gross income generated by the event. For corporate sponsors and advertisers, the commercial value offered by this unique marketing approach was enormously attractive. By the mid-1970s major corporations such as Colgate-Palmolive, Phillip Morris, L'eggs, Avon, and others decided to use women's sports as a vehicle for advertising their products. These sponsorships enabled specific women's tournaments to be covered on television. However, during this period corporations were willing to sponsor only socially acceptable women's sports such as tennis, golf, figure skating, and gymnastics.

Team and contact sports struggled for financial backing because they did not present women in a traditional way. The first amateur sport to break through the stereotyping and gain television coverage was women's intercollegiate basketball. In the 1990s, women's intercollegiate basketball programs recorded sellout crowds, gained corporate sponsorship for individual programs, and received television coverage on a variety of networks throughout the regular season. By 1994, the rights to broadcast the National Collegiate Athletic Association (NCAA) women's basketball tournament had been purchased by ESPN, making it the

Billie Jean King and Bobby Riggs played an historic "battle of the sexes" tennis match which became a much-hyped media event in 1973. (Bettmann/Corbis)

portunities for women to compete professionally in basketball in the United States and to allow fans to follow their favorite college players after college. Both leagues secured financial backing from sponsors. The WNBA, however, had much greater national exposure because of the established relationship between NBC and the NBA.

In its first year, the WNBA attracted more than 1 million fans to arenas for games, which were watched on television by more than 65 million fans in the United States and 165 other countries. The second season began 11 June 1998, accompanied by television, print, and radio campaigns to promote athletes, teams, and the league. The second-year campaign was developed to provide exposure via media outlets such as NBC, TBS, and TNT. Commercials were scheduled to run on ESPN, ESPN2, MTV, Classic Sports Network, and Fox Sports Net. Print ads were set for *USA Today, Hoop,* and all NBA team magazines.

LEAGUES FOR OTHER SPORTS

Attempts to establish new professional leagues for women in fastpitch softball, soccer, and ice hockey were in various stages of development at the end of the 1990s. Undoubtedly, the success of these new ventures will depend on their ability to generate commercial interest. In today's professional sport environment, the packaging of a sport product must include lucrative sponsorship relationships, media attention including national television exposure, and a strong following of fans who will pay to watch their favorite teams and players.

COMMERCIALIZING ATHLETES

In a separate category, sport apparel and shoe manufacturers such as Reebok, Nike, and FILA have provided the contemporary model for success via commercialization. Companies use star athletes to represent their products, thereby increasing the product's appeal. Endorsements by star athletes have been the most effective way to link brand-name recognition and product quality. In turn, stars' appearances in major advertising campaigns have contributed to the recognition of successful athletes. The symbiotic relationship of the media and sport has served as a model for the new commercial relationship between athletes and sponsors. Successful ventures for both parties rely on successful commercialization. One result

first women's team sport to gain national exposure and recognition.

The first professional women's basketball league in the United States was formed in 1976, but it collapsed before the first game. Other attempts were made in 1978, 1984, and 1986, but each league eventually failed. However, two women's professional basketball leagues, the ABL (American Basketball League) and WNBA (Women's National Basketball Association), each completed successful seasons in the 1990s, although the former went bankrupt in 1998.

In its inaugural season, the WNBA was reported to have spent $15 million in marketing the new league and players. The new league garnered national attention largely due to the clout and sports industry backing from the National Basketball Association (NBA). The ABL was a separate venture initiated a year earlier to create opof this commercialization is that athletes often compete in uniforms that display a medley of advertisements for everything from spark plugs to Gatorade.

Endorsement dollars are closely tied to television exposure. As an example, Nikki McCray of the United States, the 1997 ABL Most Valuable Player, moved to the WNBA despite offers to increase her salary significantly if she remained with the ABL. Soon after her move, an agreement was announced in which FILA contracted to pay McCray $1 million over four years if she played for the WNBA. FILA admitted that they wanted high-profile athletes to wear their shoes and clothes. That high-profile status is most likely achieved through television coverage and media exposure.

The commercialization of women's sports and women athletes has been criticized by some because it makes objects out of women's bodies and thereby creates a barrier to the acceptance of the accomplishments of women athletes. For example, the advertisement that showed volleyball player Gabrielle Reece lying on a bed of silk sheets to promote footwear was unrelated to her athletic skill. Advertisers' insistence on stories about fashion, beauty, and fitness in women's sports magazines similarly places appearance over ability.

The loudest public criticism of the commercialization of sport was aimed at the 1996 Olympic Games in Atlanta. Spectators both in Atlanta and around the world (via television) were unable to escape the pervasive advertising and commercial links used to promote the Games. Yet, for American Olympians, the 1996 Games established women's sport as a valuable commodity worthy of financial investment. With gold medal–winning teams in basketball, soccer, softball, and gymnastics, women athletes proved the appeal of their sports in the marketplace.

CONCLUSION

The lure of the American market is so great that many European athletes—such as Martina Navralitova and Katarina Witt—have centered their careers in the United States. American sport has established a model in which there are many beneficiaries of the commodification and commercialization of women's sports. Through commercialization, corporate sponsors have realized a

profit from wise sport investments. In turn, fans, athletes, leagues, and owners have been able to benefit as their sports received the financial backing that allowed them to flourish. For women in sport, the opportunity to take part in this highly sophisticated enterprise is rapidly evolving. Whether as fans, athletes, or corporate executives, women in sport have never before had such a bright future.

Nancy L. Lough

See also Advertising; Fashion; Management; Marketing; Media; Ownership; Sexuality

Bibliography

Boutilier, Mary A., and Lucinda SanGiovanni. (1983) *The Sporting Woman*. Urbana, IL: Human Kinetics.

Coakley, Jay J. (1986) *Sport in Society: Issues and Controversies*. St. Louis, MO: Times Mirror/Mosby College Publishing.

Guttman, Allen. (1986) *Sports Spectators*. New York: Columbia University Press.

Sage, George H. (1990) *Power and Ideology in American Sport*. Urbana, IL: Human Kinetics.

Sandomir, Richard. (1988) "The $50 Billion Sports Industry." *Sports Inc.* (14 November): 11–23.

Twin, Stephanie L. (1979) *Out of the Bleachers: Writings on Women and Sport*. New York: McGraw-Hill.

Wagner, R. (1988) "An Investigation of Corporate Sponsorship of Women's Sports Events." Unpublished master's thesis, Pennsylvania State University.

COMMONWEALTH GAMES

The Commonwealth Games were inaugurated as the British Empire Games in Hamilton, Ontario, Canada, in 1930 as a sports competition for athletes from Great Britain and other nations that were former colonies of Great Britain. Since then, there have been sixteen games, and they rank second only to the Olympic Games as an international multisport competition. The sixteenth

COMMONWEALTH GAMES CONTROVERSY

After the boycott of three previous Commonwealth Games, the 1994 Celebrations at Victoria, Canada, provided an upbeat occasion, largely for two reasons. First, post-apartheid South Africa returned to the Commonwealth fold after an absence of 33 years. Also, 55 disabled athletes were included among the more than 3,300 participants, regarded as a positive step by most observers. But this innovation provided one of the most startling controversies in the Games' history, when an Australian official publicly attacked their inclusion before the Games began.

At a press conference, Australian Chef de Mission Arthur Turnstall described the presence of disabled athletes in the XV Games as an "embarrassment" to able-bodied athletes. Former boxer Turnstall added to the controversy by his late-night scuffle with a reporter in the lobby of the landmark Empress Hotel. Fortunately, Turnstall himself defused the anger by a full-page written apology. At the opening ceremonies, Australian officials pointedly placed three wheelchair athletes at the front of their team as it marched into the stadium.

games were held in Kuala Lumpur, Malaysia, in 1998, and the 2002 games were scheduled to take place in Manchester, England. Called the Commonwealth Games since 1978, they were previously called the British Empire Games, the British Empire and Commonwealth Games, and the British Commonwealth Games. These name changes reflected the transformation of the British Empire, since nearly all colonies had become independent nations by the 1960s.

HISTORY

In 1891, Englishman John Astley Cooper (1858–1930) proposed an "Anglo-Saxon Olympiad" to celebrate the achievements of the English-speaking world, including the United States. Efforts to turn the idea into reality foundered with the establishment of the modern Olympic Games in 1896 and its success thereafter. However, a celebration somewhat similar to the games got underway in 1911 as the "Inter-Empire Sports Meeting" in London as part of the coronation celebrations for George V, with teams from Australia, Canada, New Zealand, South Africa, and the United Kingdom. Over the next two decades several leaders of sports in different countries lent their support to the idea of a British Empire Games, and in 1928 it was agreed that the first British Empire Games would be held in Hamilton.

Although not a single woman competed at the first Olympic Games, by 1928 at Amsterdam women were competing in five sports and comprised nearly 10 percent of the competing athletes. It is not surprising, therefore, that women did compete in the first British Empire Games. But it was surprising that they competed only in the swimming and diving events, especially given the success of the Canadian women in the Olympic track and field events two years earlier at Amsterdam, where they won two gold medals, a silver, and a bronze. The female stars of the inaugural British Empire Games were undoubtedly Joyce Cooper of England, who won three of the four individual events in the pool, and her teammate Celia Wostenholme, who improved her own world record in winning the 220-yard (200-meter) breaststroke event.

These pioneer female swimmers began an unbroken tradition of swimming excellence at these games; future celebrations featured some of the greatest performers in the sport—familiar names such as Linda Ludgrove and Anita Lonsborough (England) and Tracey Wickham and Michelle Ford (Australia). Many of them were world record-holders and also became Olympic champions, notably the incomparable Australian Dawn Fraser. She won the 100-meter freestyle at the Cardiff Games of 1958 and again at the Perth Games in 1962 (as well as the 400-meter freestyle there), the year in which she became the first woman to swim 100 meters in less than a minute (59.5 seconds). But she is best remembered for the eight medals (four gold and four silver) she picked up at the Olympic Games of 1956, 1960, and 1964.

Over the years, these games have provided Commonwealth athletes with invaluable competition before the more prestigious Olympics. For various reasons, some world and Commonwealth Games champions have not attained an Olympic gold medal. A famous example was the small Canadian fifteen-year-old Elaine Tanner, nicknamed "Mighty Mouse," who won four gold and three silver medals at the 1966 Commonwealth Games, two gold and two silver medals at the 1967 Pan-American Games, but only two silver and one bronze at the 1968 Olympic Games. She was undoubtedly one of the greatest swimmers ever, despite her Olympic "disappointment."

GROWTH OF THE GAMES

The number of swimming events for women in the Commonwealth Games increased substantially over the years, and other sports were added. These sports expanded at different rates in the program, reflecting differential growth in women's sporting participation. The eight track and field events for women included at the 1934 games were expanded threefold by the 1990s. There had been a somewhat hysterical controversy at the 1928 Olympics over the women's 800-meter event, after which several exhausted "wretched women" were strewn upon the cinder track, according to the *Times of London* report. It is some measure of women's sporting progress, seventy years later, to note inclusion of 500-meter, 10,000-meter, and marathon events for women in the 1998 Commonwealth Games in Malaysia.

As with other multisport festivals, the Commonwealth Games have endured various economic and political problems. In particular, the South African policy of apartheid provided a point of contention for almost forty years. At the 1958 Games in Cardiff—where thirty-five nations were represented by 1,100 athletes, and ten world records were broken—there were demonstrations protesting this policy. In 1961, South Africa withdrew from the Commonwealth and did not compete in the games again until 1994. The eleventh games in Edmonton were threatened with a boycott by African nations over the simmering issue of continuing sporting contacts with South Africa, particularly its rugby rivalry with New Zealand,

Jacqueline Edwards of the Bahamas competing in the long jump at the 1998 Commonwealth Games in Kuala Lumpur, Malaysia. (AP Photos)

in spite of the fact that the Commonwealth nations were committed to the Gleneagles Agreement of 1977, which prohibited sporting contacts with South Africa. Although Nigeria stayed away, diplomacy allowed the other African nations to participate. Another boycott was avoided at the successful 1982 Brisbane Games; but more nations boycotted than took part in 1986 Edinburgh Games, where the issue was the British government's refusal to implement sanctions against South Africa. Fortunately, boycott threats were not realized at Auckland for the 1990 celebration there; and the process of renewal continued at the Victoria Games four years later, aided by the return of South Africa to the competition less than three months after it rejoined the Commonwealth.

Some noteworthy events in 1994 signified women's sporting emancipation in these games. The South African team captain was swimmer Marian Kriel, and the flag-bearer for the host nation Canada at the opening ceremonies was runner Angela Chalmers, a First Nations Sioux. Beyond the 1990s women's representation was no longer regarded as a major issue in the Commonwealth

Games. A larger concern was how to spread the celebrations more equitably among this large family of nations in the twenty-first century and to avoid the appearance of an elite "old boy's club" of predominantly white nations. In this regard, the staging of the 1998 Games in Kuala Lumpur was a significant step.

Gerald Redmond

Bibliography

Agbogun, Jacob B. (1970) "A History of the British Commonwealth Games." Unpublished master's thesis, University of Alberta, Canada.

Bateman, Derek, and Derek Douglas. (1986) *Unfriendly Games: Boycotted and Broke, the Inside Story of the 1986 Commonwealth Games.* Glasgow: Mainstream Publishing Projects and *Glasgow Herald.*

Dheensaw, Cleve. (1994) *The Commonwealth Games.* Victoria, BC: Orca Book Publishers.

Guttmann, Allen. (1991) *Women's Sports: A History.* New York: Columbia University Press.

Mathews, Peter, ed. (1986) *The Official Commonwealth Games Book.* Preston, UK: Opax Publishing and the Commonwealth Games Consortium.

Moore, Katharine Elizabeth. (1986) "The Concept of British Empire Games: An Analysis of Its Origin and Evolution from 1891 to 1930." Unpublished doctoral dissertation, University of Queensland, Australia.

———, ed. *Edmonton '78: The Official Pictorial Record of the XI Commonwealth Games.* Edmonton, Alb.: Executive Sport Publications.

Victoria Commonwealth Games Society. (1994) *Let the Spirit Live On: Fifteenth Commonwealth Games.* Victoria, BC: Victoria Commonwealth Games Society.

COMMUNITY

Communities are groups of people, bound by space and time, who share identities and interests. Women, sport, and community are linked together in two basic ways. The first is by exclusion. Sport has historically been a masculine preserve, one that brought men together into a community. With few exceptions, women were excluded from this community. The second link is inclusion, a link that has become more common over the past decades as women's participation in sport increased. This process brought them together and was the basis for the construction of women's communities.

SPORT AND COMMUNITY IDENTIFICATION

Sport's ability to bring people together is one of its most important characteristics. Sport has considerable power to express people's identities, define their relationships, and create membership in a community. Examples are many: the organization of the Olympics on the basis of national representation, identification with professional and university teams, the meanings of such events as the Gay Games.

Although sport expresses varied attachments and meanings, perhaps the most significant have to do with gender. History has shown that the rise of modern sport was, in effect, the triumph of an institution that was dominated by men and that celebrated masculinity. In Canada, for example, sociologists Richard Gruneau and David Whitson (1993) note that toward the end of the nineteenth century, organized sports were a way of "speaking metaphorically" about relationships, status, and identity in Canadian life. "The most encompassing, and most traditional of these identities was the obsessive concern for manliness in sporting competition" (67).

In contrast, the story of women in sport has historically been one of exclusion, with some exceptions. In the limited instances in which they were admitted, their participation has often been ignored or made to seem trivial. Keeping women out has been crucial to maintaining sport as a male preserve and the broader relationship between sport and community. Communities are a social setting in which individuals feel they have a place. The public celebration of the masculine preserve of sport is a powerful statement about women's place in—or absence from—the construction of communities.

From time to time, women have disrupted the sanctity of the male preserve of sport in ways that were important challenges to the historical association of sport, gender, and community. Some of the most significant challenges were in the form of community-based women's sports teams and leagues that became the basis of popular identifi-

A LOYAL DODGERS FAN

In her best-selling memoir, *Wait Until Next Year: A Memoir* (1997), award-winning historian Doris Kearns Goodwin writes about baseball's importance during her childhood in Brooklyn and then in suburban Long Island after World War II. She and her father were Brooklyn Dodgers fans, and they closely followed the team's success and failures, as well as the exploits of the rival Giants and Yankees. Goodwin points out how loyalty to the Dodgers was a powerful source of community pride and cohesion which transcended religion, ethnicity, and neighborhood, and gave local people a common bond and language.

cation and association. In the early decades of the twentieth century, women's ice hockey flourished in some Canadian communities, where teams played before large and appreciative audiences. In the 1940s and 1950s, the All-American Girls Professional Baseball League (the subject of the 1992 film, *A League of Their Own*) captured the interest of fans in midwestern communities in the United States and offered an alternative to men's professional baseball for the brief period that it enjoyed commercial success. In the 1950s, women's basketball also prospered briefly, when industrial teams playing under the auspices of the Amateur Athletic Union (AAU) were the focus of interest in some American communities.

These examples illustrate the way that women's teams have both resisted and conformed to views of sport based on gender. Although these women were respected for their athletic abilities, they were expected to present a feminine image off the ice, field, and court. At the same time, as skilled and committed athletes whose involvement in a sport became a focus of local interest and pride, these women offered an important challenge to the prevailing image of sport as a male domain and to the meaning of community that sport has historically expressed.

In the decades from 1920 to 1960, the African-American community offered another example of the relationship between women's sport and community. Some black physical educators and sports leaders rejected the model of feminized athleticism that prevailed among established women's sports associations during this period. They saw no reason to construct women's sport as an alter-native to men's. As a result, competitive women's sport gained a stronghold among African Americans when it was largely rejected in the dominant women's sporting institutions.

Basketball and track and field were among the sports that were particularly well developed in the African American community. In the United States, black women dominated track and field in the 1930s and 1940s. Although largely ignored by the white media and the athletic establishment, black women's accomplishments were a source of pride and community identification among African Americans. During the 1950s, tennis player (and later professional golfer) Althea Gibson rose to prominence as the first African-American sportswoman to receive extensive coverage in the establishment press. She became a symbol of aspirations and accomplishments within the African-American community.

The relationship between African-American sportswomen and the broader community was defined in the context of race and gender relations of the time. The connections between race and gender were complex. Black women faced sexism at the hands of black men. Nevertheless, racial segregation and discrimination in the United States divided black and white women and, at times, forged alliances between black women and men. Additionally, the African-American community rejected the philosophy of separation from men's programs that was dominant in the elite women's colleges. Black women relied on Black men to cooperate with them and support them in national organizations, educational institutions, and local athletic clubs. That men's and

Successful athletes are often a symbol of community pride. This wall painting in downtown Philadelphia depicts Dawn Staley, a native Philadelphian, who plays for the Philadelphia women's professional basketball team. (Karen Christensen)

women's sports were closely associated probably increased community interest and pride in the accomplishments of African-American women.

THE MODERN ERA

Recent decades have seen more and greater challenges to the masculine preserve of sport. These challenges are the product of various factors. One is changing ideals of gender. Legal and political initiatives have also played a role, as in the 1972 passage of Title IX of the Educational Amendments Act in the United States, which increased women's opportunities in sport. More recently women have been identified as a target group for commercial fitness and sport—this, too, has led to important changes in the landscape of sport.

Two of the settings in which the growth of women's sport is most dramatically evident are collegiate sport in the United States and the Olympics. In colleges and universities in the United States, men's sport remains the dominant focus of support and interest in athletics. The dominance of men's sport has been challenged somewhat, however, most notably in women's basketball, which has become the principal women's sport in many American universities. On a number of U.S. university campuses, it is now common to see thousands of fans assemble to cheer the women's basketball team—a team that is encouraged by the university pep band and cheerleaders and targeted by the determined promotional efforts of the university athletics department. These events represent a new era in the relationship between sport and community.

The Olympics, too, have seen dramatic change in the relationship among sport, gender, and community. The 1996 Summer Olympics were described by some as the women's games, in large part because of the successful performances of U.S. women's teams, which won gold medals in soccer, softball, and basketball. (There is a particular power to community identification with team sports.) Competing in their home country, the American athletes generated a degree of public and media interest that was unprecedented for women's team sports.

The American women's basketball team received particular attention. In the fall of 1995 the U.S. national team completed an exhibition tour against major college teams. Local media covered these extensively, and the events drew large and enthusiastic crowds. The tour included games against the alma maters of many of the national team players, who were received as returning heroines.

The U.S. national team went undefeated in the tour against college competition, on a subsequent international tour, and at the Olympics. Following the spectacular success of the team in the pre-Olympic tours and at the Olympics, two professional women's basketball leagues were established in the United States, the American Basketball League (ABL), which began play in the fall of 1996, and the Women's National Basketball Association (WNBA), which began play in the summer of 1997. Benefiting from its sponsorship by the established men's National Basketball Association (NBA), the WNBA achieved greater visibility, including, most crucially, television exposure. Both leagues generated considerable interest in women's sport in the local communities in which teams played, as well as nationally, through television coverage. Observers doubted whether the two leagues would survive in the long term, and in fact the ABL ceased operation in December 1998. That these leagues existed at all is another important development on the gendered landscape of sport and indicates further change in the relationships among gender, sport, and community.

Women's ice hockey is another sport that has seen increased visibility and interest associated with Olympic participation, and hence an increased sense of community. After a brief period of prosperity earlier in the twentieth century, women's hockey lingered in obscurity for decades. As part of the general resurgence of interest in women's sport that began in the late 1960s, the sport experienced a revival. This revival began in community-based clubs and universities and led eventually to international competition, with the first world championships held in 1990. The increased popularity of the sport, together with pressures to redress the gender imbalance in the Winter Olympics in team sports, led to the inclusion of women's hockey on the Olympic program for the 1998 Games in Nagano, Japan.

Further public interest in women's hockey in North America was generated in the months preceding the Nagano Olympics, when teams from the United States and Canada played each other thirteen times in exhibitions and tournaments. One of these games was played before an audience of more than 15,000 in Vancouver as part of the National Hockey League's All-Star Weekend festivities. The Olympics brought even greater exposure. In Canada, women's hockey received regular print and television coverage throughout the Games, including complete broadcast of the Canada–United States game in the preliminary round and again when the two teams met in the gold-medal game. Hockey has historically been one of the most powerful examples of the symbolic association of sport and masculinity. While hockey retains considerable status as a symbol of masculinity, this is being chal-

Sports are often referred to as an activity that builds a sense of community. Here, high school basketball players come together to share a victory. (Geoffrey Bluh)

lenged by the rising interest in and support for women's hockey, most notably around Olympic competition. A challenge to male dominance of hockey is, in effect, a challenge to the historical association of sport, gender, and community.

SPORT AND WOMEN'S COMMUNITIES

Sport gives women the opportunity to build communities around shared interests and collective goals, and this, too, causes further disruption of men's dominance. The formation of lesbian communities in sport represents one of the most important historical instances of this. These communities formed during periods when pressures for lesbians to remain closeted were considerable. Throughout most of the twentieth century, when women's sport received little public or media interest, sport provided a safe place where lesbians were free to claim their identities and form communities.

Increased acceptance of women's sport in recent years has changed the climate for community formation among women, both lesbian and heterosexual. This acceptance has brought greater scrutiny of athletes' personal lives and pressures on lesbians to remain invisible. On some university campuses and on the professional tours, closeted communities of lesbian athletes provide important support for many women.

Homophobia—irrational fear of gays, lesbians, or bisexuals—continues to diminish the climate of support for women athletes. At the same time, other social changes have made women's sports more acceptable and provided opportunities for many women to experience the pleasure and support of the company of other women. The possibility for group bonding is a particular feature of team sports, where team members pursue a common goal. Various accounts of women's teams have offered insightful discussions of bonding among women athletes. Several books have been written on women's basketball teams, including Blais's chronicle of the Amherst (Massachusetts) Regional High School team, Kessler's story of the University of Oregon team, and Corbett's account of the U.S. Olympic women's team.

Many women are interested in sport simply to improve fitness or athletic skills and because they enjoy the sociable interaction. Others, however, have used sport to pursue a specifically feminist agenda. One of the best discussions of this is Birrell and Richter's examination of how feminists attempted to develop an alternative model of sport. The researchers interviewed women who were self-defined feminists, playing in a community softball league in the U.S. Midwest. These women criticized the dominant model of sport, which many labeled the male model, as elitist, hierarchical, authoritarian, socially exclusionary, and marked by an ethic of endangerment to self and opponents. They actively worked to develop an alternative model that was inclusive, process-oriented, and incorporated an ethic of care.

Women-centered sport and recreation programs have proliferated in the 1990s. The range of activities and interests is broad. In some cases women seek a context in which to pursue fitness without the pressure of idealized models of slimness and a concern with weight loss. In others, they want to develop their athletic skills and potential in a setting that is free of the structure and authoritarianism that characterizes much of organized sport. In a few instances, women's sport programs have been organized in a way that attempts to overcome biases of class, race, and heterosexuality still common in mainstream sport.

In all these cases women seek an alternative to the values and organizing principles of mainstream and male-dominated sport. In pursuit of alternatives, they have established programs and organizations outside the dominant sport system. In separating from the mainstream, they have gained autonomy and helped develop women-centered activities and, in some cases, women's communities.

CONCLUSION

The relationships among women, sport, and community are changing. Women are challenging the world of sport, which has long been dominated by men, and in doing so, they are disrupting the male sport community. At the same time, they are building their own communities through sport. In some cases, this involves deliberate efforts to move away from the competitive nature of men's sport toward a more cooperative and inclusive enterprise. Both point to the important connections between community and sport.

Nancy Theberge

Bibliography

Birrell, Susan, and Diana Richter. (1987) "Is a Diamond Forever? Feminist Transformations of Sport." *Women's Studies International Forum* 10, 4: 395–409.

Birrell, Susan, and Nancy Theberge. (1994) "Ideological Control of Women in Sport." In *Women and Sport: Interdisciplinary Perspectives,* edited by D. Margaret Costa and Sharon Guthrie. Champaign, IL: Human Kinetics, 341–359.

Blais, Madeleine. (1995) *In These Girls, Hope Is a Muscle.* New York: Atlantic Monthly Press.

Bryson, Lois. (1990) "Challenges to Male Hegemony in Sport." In *Sport, Men, and the Gender Order,* edited by Michael Messner and Donald Sabo. Champaign, IL: Human Kinetics, 173–184.

Cahn, Susan. (1994) *Coming On Strong: Gender and Sexuality in Twentieth Century Women's Sport.* Cambridge, MA: Harvard University Press.

Corbett, Sara. (1997) *Venus to the Hoop: A Gold-Medal Year in Women's Basketball.* New York: Doubleday.

Festle, Joan. (1996) *Playing Nice: Politics and Apologies in Women's Sports.* New York: Columbia University Press.

Gissendanner, Cindy Himes. (1994) "African-American Women and Competitive Sport, 1920–1960." In *Women, Sport, and Culture,* edited by Susan Birrell and Cheryl Cole. Champaign, IL: Human Kinetics, 81–92.

Griffin, Pat. (1998) *Strong Women, Deep Closets: Lesbians and Homophobia in Sport.* Champaign, IL: Human Kinetics.

Gruneau, Richard, and David Whitson. (1993) *Hockey Night in Canada: Sport, Identity and Cultural Politics.* Toronto: Garamond.

Hargreaves, Jennifer. (1994) *Sporting Females: Critical Issues in the History and Sociology of Women's Sports.* London: Routledge.

Kessler, Lauren. (1997) *Fullcourt Press: A Season in the Life of a Winning Basketball Team and the Women Who Made It Happen.* New York: Dutton.

Kimmel, Michael. (1990) "Baseball and the Reconstitution of American Masculinity, 1880–1920." In *Sport, Men, and the Gender Order,* edited by Michael Messner and Donald Sabo. Champaign, IL: Human Kinetics, 55–65.

McFarlane, John. (1994) *Proud Past, Bright Future: One Hundred Years of Canadian Women's Hockey.* Toronto: Stoddart.

Messner, Michael. (1998) "Sports and Male Domination: The Female Athlete as Contested Ideological Terrain." *Sociology of Sport Journal* 5, 3: 197–211.

Theberge, Nancy. (1995) "Gender, Sport, and the Construction of Community: A Case Study from Women's Ice Hockey." *Sociology of Sport Journal* 12, 4: 389–402.

———. (2000) *Higher Goals: Women, Ice Hockey, and Gender.* Albany: State University of New York Press.

COMPAGNONI, DEBORAH

(1970–)

ITALIAN ALPINE SKIER

Deborah Compagnoni is one of the most successful Alpine skiers of all time, a winner of multiple Olympic gold medals, and the best known and most popular sportswoman in Italy. She was born in Santa Caterina Valfurva, Sondrio, Italy, on 4 June 1970. Compagnoni began competing in the World Cup at the age of seventeen, but her early career was marred by a series of serious injuries and medical problems, including emergency intestinal surgery in 1990 that saved her life. As a result, she took a few years longer than expected to fulfill her early promise as a fast downhill skier

Deborah Compagnoni negotiates a gate during the giant slalom event at the 1998 Winter Olympics in Nagano, Japan. (TempSport)

and produce results at the top level of world competition. Finally, in the 1991–1992 season, she won the first of her sixteen World Cup competitions, this one in the super-giant slalom in Morzine, France. She followed with a gold medal in the super-giant slalom at the Albertville Olympics in 1992. Unfortunately, a day after winning the gold, she tore knee ligaments in the giant slalom competition and was put out of action again, for the third time in her short career.

Recovered from her latest injury, she was back on the World Cup circuit in 1993 and took a second Olympic gold medal in Lillehammer, Norway, in 1994, dominating the giant slalom event by winning both heats and defeating second-place finisher Martina Ertl of Germany by more than one second. Having achieved steady success in the downhill and super-giant slalom speed events, she moved on to the more technically challenging slalom events. Avoiding the serious injuries that had delayed her career earlier, she went on to win the giant slalom at the world championships in 1996 and in 1997 and took the slalom as well in 1997. She won the World Cup giant slalom in 1996–1997, establishing a new record of straight victories in the event, with eight wins over the 1996–1997 and 1997–1998 seasons. At the Olympics in Nagano, Japan, in 1998, she won the gold medal in giant slalom and silver in slalom, in the process becoming the first Alpine skier (male or female) to win a gold medal in three straight Winter Olympics, the first woman Alpine skier to win the giant slalom in two straight Olympics, and one of only six skiers (three men and three women) to win three Olympic gold medals in Alpine skiing. The three men are Toni Sailer of Austria, Jean-Claude Killy of France, and Alberto Tomba of Italy, and the other two women are Vreni Schneider of Switzerland and Katja Seizinger of Germany.

Her victories in the Olympics and in the world championships have made her the most successful and best-known Italian sportswoman of all time. They have also made her an enormously popular figure in Italy. Italians especially like the combination of her determination and competitiveness on the slopes and her quiet modesty and seriousness in daily life. When not skiing, she keeps a low profile and works in her family's restaurant. Her life-style provides an interesting counterpoint to the celebrity status cultivated and enjoyed by Italian male skier Alberto Tomba (known as "La Bomba"), whose international skiing career has paralleled hers.

Gherardo Bonini

Bibliography

Matteo, Pacor. "Compagnoni." <http://ourworld.compuserve.com/home-pages/pacor/>. 1999.

Wallechinsky, David. (1998) *The Complete Book of the Winter Olympics 1998*. New York: Overlook Press.

COMPETITION

The word "compete" means to strive or vie for something for which others are also contending. Without others, competition does not occur. Competition is unlike cooperation, which involves working together toward a common goal with rewards shared equally by all. It is also unlike individual activities, which are performed alone or in proximity to others who are not aware of the individual's standard for performance. Competition is a process that is influenced by society and

motivated by personal enjoyment and external and unequal rewards.

Women and men, however, differ in their interpretations of the process of competition and the structure of cooperation. Generally, female athletes value the interdependence between cooperation and competition both within a team and between opponents, while male athletes are more concerned with the outcome of competition.

DEFINING *COMPETITION*

Sport psychologist Rainer Martens used a social evaluation approach to define competition, describing it as a process involving four stages. In the first stage, the objective competitive situation, "an individual's performance is compared with some standard of excellence, in the presence of at least one other person who is aware of the criterion for comparison." The second stage, the subjective competitive situation, refers to how the person perceives, accepts, and appraises the competitive situation. Highly competitive individuals will interpret situations differently than those who are not very competitive. The third stage is response, which refers to performance (goal achievement) and nonperformance (competitive anxiety) behaviors that occur in competitive situations. In the fourth stage, the individual compares her perception of the consequences of her responses (win or lose) to her standard of comparison for evaluation, as successful or unsuccessful. In this model, competition is described as a "learned" social process that is influenced by the social environment.

Competition in sport can be direct, with confrontation between individual opponents (tennis singles) or teams (soccer). When opponents compete by taking turns (long jump) or performing in different locations (golf), competition is termed *parallel*. Another type of competition involves *comparison* of performance to a standard, as when gymnasts perform routines on the balance beam.

SOCIALIZATION PATTERNS

The patterns of play that girls develop result from the influence of socializing agents and institutions. Family, friends, teachers, and role models are socializing agents; institutions of socialization include education, government, religion, the media, and sport. The social and cultural con-

THE COMPETITIVE SPIRIT (1912)

Now, what are athletics and how are women affected by them? An athlete is one who contends against another for a victory; athletics are the events in which one contends. A gymnasium is a place for the performance of athletic exercises; a gymnast is a person who trains athletes, and gymnastics are the exercises practiced in the gymnasium for the purpose of putting one's self in proper condition for competing in the athletic contests. In our times the terms athletics, gymnastics and physical training are often used synonymously, while actually they are not alike and may bring about very different results.

If a schoolgirl practices jumping a bar with other girls, as one of the physical exercises prescribed for general development, she is engaging in gymnastics. If, however, the bar is jumped with the purpose of finding out which girl can clear the bar at the greatest height the performance becomes an athletic one. In the first instance the exercise would be undertaken as a means of physical improvement for its owns sake. In the second instance, if the spirit of emulation ran high the girls would be engaging in a course of special physical training, not primarily to benefit themselves physically, but for the set purpose of improving their jumping powers so as to vanquish their nearest competitor.

This distinction, that gymnastics are pursued as a means to an end, and athletics as an end in themselves, would apply equally well to such forms of exercise as walking, running, vaulting, swimming and skating, which may be measured in time or space and thus be made competitive. The element of competition and "sport" must, therefore, enter into what we now term athletics.

DUDLEY A. SARGENT, M.D.
(1912) "Are Athletics Making Girls Masculine?"
The Ladies' Home Journal. *March.*

ditions surrounding these agents and institutions provide the structure and constraints that determine female socialization into and through competitive sport. In societies where sport is an important aspect of the culture and where no religious or other factors limit their participation, as is the case in Western countries, females are more heavily represented.

Competitive sport requires competitive behaviors. In many cultures, however, those behaviors are considered appropriate only for males. Children learn appropriate and inappropriate behaviors for their gender roles through reward and punishment. Although in the twentieth century it became much more acceptable for females to take part in sports, their participation was viewed as better and was rewarded more when they chose an activity considered feminine in nature. Competitive sports such as ice skating, gymnastics, and tennis are considered more feminine than basketball, softball, and rugby. Serious women athletes who compete in sports considered masculine or less feminine are subject to questions about their sexuality and sexual orientation.

TRAINING FOR COMPETITIVE BEHAVIOR

The former East Germany became well known for its coaching education institutions, which selected children at an early age to be trained to represent their country in elite competitions. China utilizes a similar system, in which promising children of both genders are removed from their homes to live and train together, while being taught the technical and psychological aspects of the sport. Those with the appropriate skills and competitive attitudes eventually represent China at international competitions. The Chinese gymnast Sang Lan, who was paralyzed after an accident during warm-ups at the 1998 Goodwill Games, is a product of the Chinese system. Her parents, who were

Track and field events were considered inappropriate for women's competition for many years. (AFP/Corbis)

flown to her hospital in the United States, had not seen her in four years.

COMPETITION AND COOPERATION

Competition and cooperation have been viewed as opposites, but the difference between them is more fundamental. Competition is a social process, whereas cooperation refers to structures, rather than behavior. Athletes must perform cooperative tasks so that the process of competition may occur within and between teams. Carolyn Sherif has characterized competition as "a struggle for supremacy between two or more opposing sides," while maintaining that competition and cooperation cannot occur without the other.

Around the age of four, children develop the capacity to compare themselves to others and to direct their behavior toward a standard. However, Sherif notes, "the quality and persistence in competition depends upon the nature of the activity and its significance to the child." At the same time, children also begin to display such behaviors as cooperation, helping, and discrimination. Thus, children's approach to competition is shaped by their social experiences.

In democratic countries, widespread inequality continues within society, and competition is seen as a means to achieve power and wealth. Winners are celebrated and rewarded. The "gender logic" view is that females and males are naturally different and that the "natural" characteristics of males, such as aggression and competitiveness, are superior to those of females. Males interpret competition as aggression, with an emphasis on winning; women's ways of competition, which include cooperation and connection, are considered inferior and less worthy of interest by the spectators and the media. Many societies have challenged this gender-based form of thinking, but it still exists in poorer countries with fewer educational opportunities for females.

GENDER AND COMPETITIVENESS

Early research in the areas of competition and achievement focused on biological sex differences. These studies concluded that differences in achievement were not biologically based. Gender-role research refers to the study of gender-related social and physical characteristics and behaviors. Research in this area has consistently found that female athletes possess more of the personality characteristics traditionally considered masculine than do female nonathletes. Early gender research, however, was limited because it was based on the female/male dichotomy in personality traits, which is stereotypical and biased.

Current research in gender and achievement in sport examines the areas of socialization and societal influences. Of particular interest is the sport-specific multidimensional measure known as the Sport Orientation Questionnaire (SOQ) devised by Diane Gill and Tom Deeter. The SOQ examines competitiveness, win orientation, and goal orientation in competitive sport. Studies using the SOQ revealed that while males consistently score higher than females in sport competitiveness and win orientation, females scored just as high on goal achievement. Thus, the gender differences observed do not reflect interest in competitive sport, but rather interest in winning.

Little research has been done on gender and achievement in diverse cultures. Several studies have shown gender influences in social comparison and winning in Navajo children and in Canadian children.

INTERNATIONAL AND POLITICAL IMPLICATIONS OF COMPETITION

Women's history in the Olympic Games is one window through which to look at the international status of women's competition. In the ancient Olympics, women were not allowed as competitors or as spectators. As early as the 1900s the modern Olympics allowed women to compete in a few sports, such as tennis, golf, and archery, but swimming and diving were not introduced until 1912, and track and field was delayed until 1928. Gradually, women were allowed to compete in almost every Olympic discipline. However, there has always been debate about the "appropriateness" of each new discipline. For instance, the women's marathon was not allowed until 1984; women still do not compete in pole vaulting or the hammer throw; and in fencing, women compete only in foil, which is the lightest weapon. While men compete in many sports in which women are not allowed to compete, such as boxing, weightlifting, and wrestling, synchronized swimming is the only women's event for which there is no male counterpart. In 1998 a new era for women's competition in world sport began when International Olympic Committee (IOC) president Juan Antonio Samaranch announced that any new sport introduced to the Olympics must include women's events. An indication of the shift toward greater inclusion for women's competition is the addition of the women's modern pentathlon in the 2000 Olympic Games in Sydney.

The politics of Olympic competition can be seen in the nationalistic tendencies of victories as determined by medal counts. Cultural acceptance of a sport results in a greater number of competitors and higher levels of competition. Islamic countries have traditionally denied or limited competition for women. Indeed, Noureddine Morceli, an Algerian 1500-meter medalist in the 1996 Olympics, raced with death threats against her. A move toward cultural acceptance for Islamic women competitors occurred in Qatar in 1998. Women were allowed to compete in the Grand Prix track meet, with modifications in athletic attire to meet the Islamic dress code.

GENDER VERIFICATION

Gender verification, officially sanctioned by the IOC, involves examination of a women's physical and/or genetic characteristics to determine that she is unambiguously female and so eligible to compete. The International Amateur Athletic Federation (IAAF), the Commonwealth Games Federation, and the Canadian Association for the Advancement of Women and Sport oppose gender verification as humiliating and do not enforce IOC policy. Indeed, medical doctors in Canada, France, Korea, and the United States have stated that the policy is degrading and discriminatory, as well as a waste of time and money.

Gender verification began in 1966 in international competition when anyone who wanted to compete in a women's event was required to present themselves nude in front of female gynecologists. Under particular suspicion were female competitors whose external appearance was more masculine than feminine and who had well-developed muscles. In 1968 the IOC introduced the buccal smear test, where a scrape is made on the inside of the cheek to analyze cells to confirm that each "woman" had two complete X chromosomes and no Y chromosomes. Failure meant disqualification from the Olympics and ineligibility for life for women's athletic competition. Even women who competed only in events where men and women competed against each other were examined. In 1992, the "PCR" test was introduced. This test was designed not to establish that a competitor is female but to prove that she is not a male. The practice is not restricted to international competition but is used also in such traditionally male competitions as women's professional boxing in the United States. After much discussion and controversy, in 1999 the IOC decided to end the routine use of gender verification testing.

CROSS-CULTURAL COMPETITION

To achieve a full understanding of what competition means, competition must be studied using a multidisciplinary approach that combines perspectives from sociology, psychology, and anthropology. For example, in some societies, sport participation by women is unimportant; therefore,

NEW GAMES MOVEMENT

New Games is a sports movement that began in California in the 1970s and then spread to other nations. The basic ethos of the movement is "challenge without competition." The movement advocates sexual, ethnic, and physical equality with events open to anyone who chooses to participate. New Games activities were meant to be open and generally free of the highly specialized and hierarchal features of organized sports. The New Games approach has been incorporated into youth programs in several nations but over time the emphasis has shifted from games and equality to sports and male dominance in some programs.

female competition is not important for self-fulfillment in these societies.

Sport is structured and organized differently in different countries. That is, competition in sport may be associated with the educational process (United States), organized through private clubs and federations (Western Europe), or controlled by the government (China and Cuba). In the Western world, female participation has increased in sport, both formal and organized, as well as informal and recreational. However, females rarely have the same opportunities and rights as do males in money earned, sponsorship, and media representation. In other countries, sport participation is dictated by the structural relations of gender, such as sexual division of labor and social construction of sexuality. For instance, anthropologists have noted that in some societies in Africa and the Middle East where children play an important role in the economy and there is less education, there is little play related to sport. Observations in India and the United States, which are more complex societies with schools with competitive games, indicate that competition becomes part of play.

Within many societies, current feminist theory advocates competition as a process to be enjoyed rather than a struggle to win at all costs. Cooperation, among teammates as well as between opponents, is to be shared and appreciated in the competitive process. Feminist athletes revere their bodies and their sports, and they view injury, denigration, and humiliation of others as problematic. Mariah Burton Nelson states: "She wants to win and gives herself permission to win and seeks victory unapologetically but pays attention to the process of competing, the process of ded-

icating herself to the pursuit of excellence. Remembering that competition is a relationship, [she] competes with compassion, for herself and her rivals. She doesn't have to compete all the time. She makes conscious decisions about when to compete and when not to, how to compete and how not to. She is aware of the cultural and political factors that discourage women from competing and refuses to be limited by them. Or she competes to change them."

COMPETITION AND LIFE SPAN

The phases of transition in women's lives are an important aspect of female competition. The phases include the role of the parents and peers, the search for type of sport or competitive direction, and points of dropout or change to lower-intensity activities. Gertrud Pfister noted that "values, norms and ideals in sport differ by sex, age and culture." For example, adult women participate more for enjoyment than for competition. While competition is included, it is the leisure and recreational component that is more important. Further, adult women face economic and psychological barriers, such as family and financial responsibilities, which limit their participation in competitive sport. For those women who desire to maintain a higher level of competitiveness at older ages, there is master's competition in a variety of sports. Many countries have master's competition at the local and regional levels, while the Senior Olympics are held every four years.

CONCLUSION

Women's competition in sports has been influenced by differing cultural views of women's roles within their societies and by those behaviors deemed acceptable and natural. The process of competition and the social processes involved influence how and why women choose to compete. Girls raised with different reinforcement patterns by the adults in their environment display different levels of competitive behaviors, yet there are few firm conclusions to indicate that females are less competitive than males. A great deal of evidence suggests that competition depends upon the importance of the activity, the standards of performance, and the relationship between those standards and actual performance capability and potential.

M. Karen Ruder

See also Cooperation; Socialization; Values and Ethics

Bibliography

Bem, S. L. (1974) "The Measurement of Psychological Androgyny." *Journal of Consulting and Clinical Psychology* 42: 155–162.

Birrell, S., and C. L. Cole, eds. (1994) *Women, Sport and Culture.* Champaign, IL: Human Kinetics.

Boutilier, M. A., and L. SanGiovanni. (1983) *The Sporting Woman.* Champaign, IL: Human Kinetics.

Coakley, Jay J. (1998) *Sport in Society: Issues and Controversies.* Boston: McGraw-Hill.

Costa, D. M., and S. R. Guthrie. (1994) *Women and Sport: Interdisciplinary Perspectives.* Champaign, IL: Human Kinetics.

Duda, J. L. (1986) "A Cross-Cultural Analysis of Achievement Motivation in Sport and the Classroom." In *Current Selected Research in the Psychology and Sociology of Sport,* edited by L. Vander-Velden and J. Humphrey. New York: AMS Press, 115–132.

Gill, Diane L., and Thomas E. Deeter. (1988) "Development of the Sport Orientation Questionnaire." *Research Quarterly for Exercise and Sport* 59: 191–202.

Hall, A. M. (1996) *Feminism and Sporting Bodies.* Champaign, IL: Human Kinetics.

Martens, Rainer. (1977) *Sport Competition Anxiety Test.* Champaign, IL: Human Kinetics.

Nelson, Mariah B. (1998) *Embracing Victory: Life Lessons in Competition and Compassion.* New York: William Morrow.

Pfister, Gertrud. (1998) "Development of Relationship to Sport: Sport Biographies of German Women." *Women in Sport and Physical Activity Journal* 7, 1: 151–170.

Sherif, Carolyn W. (1972) "Females and the Competitive Process." In *Women and Sport: A National Research Conference,* edited by D. Harris. University Park: Pennsylvania State University, 115–139.

———. (1976) "The Social Context of Competition." In *Social Problems in Athletics,* edited by D. Landers. Champaign, IL: Human Kinetics, 18–36.

Spence, J. T., and R. L. Helmreich. (1978) *Masculinity and Femininity.* Austin: University of Texas Press.

CONTACT SPORTS

The term "contact sports" is used to describe any sport in which the rules permit—in some cases require—participants to have physical contact with one another, whether mild, violent, or deliberately combative. Historically, women have taken part in very few such sports, but they are now doing so in increasing numbers. Girls are seeking places on all-male football squads, and all-female wrestling is well established. That these things are happening, however, is by no means universally approved, and key issues remain unresolved.

WHAT ARE CONTACT SPORTS?

Physical contact sports are in fact not always easily defined. At the more violent end of sporting contests (such as boxing, where the aim is to physically disable the opponent) it is self-evident that the sport involves a very high level of impact between the participants. In addition, some sports that fall loosely under the umbrella of martial arts require the participants to grapple with each other within a defined arena, judo being a prime example. With some sports that use an open ring, the contest may be ended with one of the contestants ejected from the defined arena. Many team sports—such as all the variants of football (association, rugby, Australian Rules, Canadian, American) and the sports of basketball, water polo, ice hockey, and lacrosse—involve a practical degree of direct physical confrontation between the players, regardless of what the rule books say.

Other sports are not so easy to categorize. For example, in both cricket and baseball, players normally have limited direct physical connection, but inherent in the game is the potential for impact

Famina Sport (white shirts) in a 1955 game of barette against the Horindelles (dark shirts) in Paris. Barette is a gentler version of rugby. (Hulton-Deutsch)

and consequent injury should the striker be hit by a leather ball traveling at a high speed. Such sports could be more accurately described as "quasi-contact sports" or "marginal contact" sports and might also include, for example, fencing, tennis, squash, and softball. In all these latter examples, the physical contact between the participants is through an intervening agent, whether ball, racket, or rapier.

Field hockey provides a prominent example of how women have developed participation within an area of "quasi-contact sport" where any contact may be peripheral or usually delivered via the ball. The development of women's hockey closely followed the men's game, with only some ten years between the formation of the relevant national associations. The original women's association (the Ladies Hockey Association) had applied for affiliation to the governing body, the

Hockey Association. After being rejected because it was not a men's club, the women's association sought to develop the women's game separately. A fundamental point is that hockey was not viewed in the same way by the public schools as the more masculine games of football and cricket. Thus, women players were not necessarily perceived as trespassing on a sacred manly preserve.

HISTORY OF CONTROVERSY

The controversy over the involvement of women in physical contact sports is essentially a microcosm of the arguments that have been aired around women's participation in sports in general. The whole issue of gender relations within sports becomes more sharply focused when contact sports are the area of examination. Disputes have arisen over not only women's participation on the field but also their role in adjudication (it had been argued that a woman was not strong enough to act as a judge and separate the male contestants in a judo bout) and even administration.

These controversies have become more sharply focused since the early 1970s, with the dramatic increase in female participation. This increase has not been confined to Western sporting cultures only but has occurred in many countries, particularly those with reasonably strong postindustrial economies. But women in developing countries are also pushing for new opportunities to play sports on their own terms and, despite resistance, are succeeding. Accounting for this new participation is a combination of new opportunities, government legislation, the women's movement, the health and fitness movement, and an increase in media coverage of women's sports.

ARGUMENTS AGAINST WOMEN IN CONTACT SPORTS

Three central issues summarize the controversy over women in contact sports. The first concerns physiology and protection. The second is whether competition should be mixed, with males and females on the same playing field or arena. The third is whether the rules for contact sports should be adapted for women to curb certain aspects, notably the more brutal ones.

The Delicate Sex

Physical exertion is one important element of contact sports that has historically been an argument used to limit women's participation. This is the case even though many sports require a high degree of physical effort without any intentional direct contact, notably swimming and running.

One argument raised during the nineteenth century to deter the incursion of women into sport (and particularly contact sports) revolved around aspects of physiology with regard to the reproductive system. This was most marked around the issues of pregnancy and menstruation. Physicians feared that women's reproductive capacity would be reduced by physical exertion. Additionally, it was long believed that menstruation was a debilitating condition and that women who engaged in strenuous exercise while menstruating risked their health further.

Because these myths are based on the hazards of exercise, the issue of contact sports brings them into high relief. There are legitimate concerns over the safety of some sportswomen, notably women boxers, but this concern extends further into the sport generally regardless of gender. Strenuous efforts have been made to improve boxer safety and tighten medical controls. While boxing remains a legitimate exercise—although its lawfulness is difficult to justify—there is no reason to discriminate by gender in terms of access.

Myths and beliefs concerning women's physiology, sports, and exercise continue despite medical evidence to the contrary. This view of women as unable to physically tolerate vigorous exercise, with the concurrent risks to the reproductive function, found a contemporary parallel when in 1998 a British boxer had her application for a professional license refused by the British Boxing Board of Control (BBBC). The BBBC issues licenses to all boxing participants, including, among others, boxers, trainers, managers, promoters, and seconds. Without a license, boxers are forced into an unregulated world of unlicensed contests, which has grave implications for safety. Jane Couch's complaint of sex discrimination succeeded before an industry tribunal, and the board of control announced that it would review its discriminatory application procedures.

Mixed Competition

Whether males and females should take part in mixed competition is the second major issue. The principal argument against this is that boys are frequently larger and stronger than girls and tend toward rougher play. Mixed play thus would increase the chances that girls would be injured. Countering this argument, proponents point out that girls who try out for a sports team and are judged by the same criteria as boys are able to hold their own on the playing field. The risks they face, then, are no greater than those experienced by their male counterparts.

Different Rules

The third issue about girls in contact sports is whether they should play under different rules or standards than do boys. This might take the form of a higher level of bodily protection being afforded to female boxers or other athletes, or contests of reduced duration. Similarly, issues of dress and appearance take on an important focus, not least for reasons of practicality; some religious beliefs do not permit exposure of the surface of the female body. This can create problems, particularly in those sports involving direct bodily contact; in sports, such as rugby football, in which players are physically tackled, loose-fitting clothes covering much of the body place players at a disadvantage if the traditional rules are maintained. There is, though, no reason why the laws of the game could not be adapted to take account of dress differences.

Interestingly, women's dress actually led to the development within cricket of overarm bowling, which created a much more potentially dangerous mode of delivery than the underarm bowling that was then used by men. The overarm style of bowling developed because women were unable to bowl underarm because their dresses impeded the action required for this type of delivery.

RESOLVING THE QUESTIONS

Given the growth in women's participation in sport in general, these issues are going to persist. This is so because the general growth in women's participation has been accompanied by a growth not only in the types of sports that women choose but also in their characteristics. As Coakley (1998) notes, "Women's programs have undergone many changes over the past twenty-five years; they have become more competitive, they are more likely to involve an emphasis on power and performance, and the stakes associated with success have increased considerably. . . . At this point we know that as the level of competition gets higher, and as women become increasingly immersed in the social world of elite sports, they become more tolerant of rule violations and aggressive behaviors on the playing field."

The strength and growth of the women's movement have undoubtedly helped to counter these anachronistic beliefs, with, for example, women from eighty countries signing a declaration of global gender-equity principles, The Brighton Declaration, in 1994. Women have made significant inroads into many of the traditional areas of masculine sporting power—for example, in 1976 women played at Lord's cricket ground, the historic home of cricket for the first time (al-

though women may still not become members of the Marylebone Cricket Club, which owns the ground). The Women's Football Association was formed in England in 1969, and even the quintessentially masculine game of Australian Rules football has begun to see some limited female participation.

It is apparent that women's team sports, many of which have elements of physical contact, are increasing worldwide, and such international competition is being recognized through World Cup competitions in rugby football, soccer (association football), and cricket. At the same time, individual participation in individual contact sports is developing, with attempts to break down historically constructed barriers based on myths concerning physiology and ability. The crucial point is that women players find enjoyment in physical contact sports. An interview with a rugby union player spells this out: "I love to pit my strength against other women and outwit my opponents. . . . I really don't care if people smirk when they know I play rugby. . . . For me, it's the best game in the world. . . . It's very physical . . . the physical contact . . . that's what gives me the buzz."

Steve Greenfield
Guy Osborn

See also Aggression; Coeducational Sport

Bibliography

Coakley, Jay. (1998) *Sport in Society. Issues and Controversies*. Boston: McGraw Hill.

Cohen, Greta, ed. (1993) *Women in Sport: Issues and Controversies*. Newbury Park, CA: Sage Publications.

Hargreaves, Jennifer. (1994) *Sporting Females*. London: Routledge.

Hess, Rob. (1996) "Women and Australian Rules Football in Colonial Melbourne." *International Journal of the History of Sport* 13, 3: 356–372.

Mangan, J. A., and Roberta Park. (1987) *From "Fair Sex" to Feminism*. London: Frank Cass.

McCrone, Kathleen. (1988) *Sport and the Physical Emancipation of English Women 1870–1914*. London: Routledge.

Williams, John, and Jackie Woodhouse. (1991) *Can Play, Will Play? Women and Football in Britain*. Leicester, UK: Sir Norman Chester Centre for Football Research (Leicester University).

COOPERATION

Cooperation is working or playing together to accomplish shared goals or common purposes. It may seem paradoxical to include an entry on cooperation in a discussion of sport, since most definitions of sport emphasize competition between opposing groups. However, sport provides countless instances where the social processes of competition and cooperation occur separately and sometimes simultaneously. Both competition and cooperation permeate sport, and many of its social facets involve cooperative actions. A complete analysis of such topics as team cohesion, intragroup cooperation, player interdependence, and related social-psychological processes is beyond the scope of this entry; for a review of this literature readers are referred to Singer, Murphy, and Tennant (1993). The focus here is on two dimensions of cooperation as it applies to women's games and sport. The first is cooperation and gender, including the socialization of children, especially the play and games of young children. The second is the history of cooperative games (or "new games") and their relationship to more formally organized sports in society.

COOPERATION AND GENDER

Social attitudes, as well as cultural expectations, influence how we behave. Social scientists refer to this process of internalizing society's attitudes and expectations as socialization. In every culture an important part of the process involves individuals learning culturally acceptable gender roles and shaping themselves to fit them. Males and females have obvious biological differences as well as similarities. Cross-cultural research has shown, however, that many cultures exaggerate male–female differences, as in the idea that men and women are polar opposites.

The meaning a society gives to these biological differences is as important as the differences themselves. In sociological terms, gender differences are social constructions, and exactly what these differences are appear to be relative to each culture. Gender roles are learned during childhood, and extensive research shows how impor-

Women's sports often stress both competition and cooperation. Here, winners and losers congratulate and console one another after a softball game. (Geoffrey Bluh)

tant play and games are to the development of a child's identity as either male or female, including the development of separate attitudes, skills, and interests between girls and boys. In essence, play and games are important ways of learning culturally appropriate conceptions of male and female.

Boys' Play, Girls' Play

Research on this topic has primarily focused on the mainstream of North American and European societies. These studies of young girls and boys at play have consistently found that although the two genders sometimes may play together, they more often play in groups of the same sex. Furthermore, boys and girls often play using very different types of playing styles and games. For example, boys' games (like sports) tend to take place outdoors and in larger groups. Boys' games, too, have more elaborate systems of rules, and they place much greater emphasis on competition. Finally, boys' games stress winners and losers, and status within the group is very much tied to winning.

In contrast, girls tend to play in smaller groups or in pairs, and they emphasize intimacy and cooperation much more. For example, in such traditional girls' games as hopscotch and jump rope, the focus is on taking turns, and winning may not be all that important. Skill, rather than winning, is the goal of many of these girls' games.

Finally, many other girls' games may not even have winners or losers, and girls more frequently ease conflicts while playing by compromising and stressing the importance of cooperation. The sex segregation of younger children's play groups is reinforced later in the schools, and, as Thorne indicates, the evidence suggests that gender separation among children is even more extensive in schools, especially in formally organized school sports.

Gender socialization and society's attitudes have very much limited women's athletic participation in many Western societies. Sports have been traditionally viewed as a more masculine activity, and different socialization practices have encouraged males to have a more competitive, serious, and professional orientation toward sports participation. Even when women do participate in sports, studies suggest that their orientations differ significantly from those of men. Research has found, for example, that competition and winning matter more to male athletes than to females.

THE ANTICOMPETITION MOVEMENT IN WOMEN'S SPORTS

The roots of the contemporary cooperative games movement can be found historically in the anticompetition movement in women's sport during the 1920s. During this period, in the United States and in many other Western countries, women athletes increased their skill, and women became more vigorous, competitive, and organized. Female athletes began to participate in national and international competition, and additional pressures from Europe led to the inclusion of women's track and field events in the 1928 Olympic Games.

American educators responded with more intense criticism of organized women's sports. Many disapproved of competitive sport for women altogether. However, their objections were not based on the earlier idea that women's sporting behaviors ran counter to the Victorian ideals of womanhood of the late 1800s. Rather, critics argued that competitive sports for women would follow the example of men's athletics and would focus attention on the elite athlete at the expense of the less skilled. They feared that further commercialization of the female athlete ultimately would discourage the wider participation of women in physical activities and sport. For example, one of the directives of the women's division of the National Amateur Athletic Federation (NAAF) stated: "The Women's Division believes in the spirit of play for its own sake and works for the promotion of physical activity for the largest possible proportion of persons in any given group." Research a half-century later has supported this belief: physical activities that place greater emphasis on high-level competition and winning are generally associated with lower rates of participation.

More recent protests about the excessive competition of contemporary sport have similarly stressed the importance of maximizing participation. Critics both within and outside sports argue that participation should be open to all—regardless of gender, physical abilities, or political philosophy. Jack Scott, first a professional athlete

THE PARTNERSHIP MODEL

In her book *Are We Winning Yet? How Women are Changing Sports and Sports are Changing Women*, former athlete Mariah Burton Nelson advocates a partnership model of sports. The partnership model rejects the idea that sports are primarily about competition and suggests that all those involved—teammates, coaches, opponents—see themselves as comrades involved in the same activity. Partnership also involves equal participation for all, with all participants, regardless of skill level, valued for their abilities and made to feel part of the team and the activity. The partnership model also suggests that taking care of one's own body and bodies of others is an important value and that playing hard and to the best of one's abilities is a key purpose of sports.

and then a critic of contemporary sports, has led a democratic movement that has argued for the restructuring of sports so as to encourage the more humanistic values of cooperation, altruism, and interpersonal responsibility, while deemphasizing the win-at-all-costs ethic of excessive competition and violence. Other critics have stressed the importance of cooperation and have recommended a more radical examination of the value of competition in general, pointing to its dangers and destructive consequences. This focus on cooperation is especially visible in discussions of the value of cooperative (or noncompetitive) games for both children and adults.

Cooperative or New Games

Cross-cultural studies have demonstrated that not all cultures value competition as much as do Western societies. The games (and sports) of some cultures place far less emphasis on competition. For example, Galliher and Hessler note that the Chinese government's efforts to promote interpersonal relations and cooperation through sports ("friendship first, competition second") allegedly resulted in greater mass participation in sports.

Central to cooperative game theory is the notion of individuals or groups working together toward mutually beneficial ends. The main difference between competitive and cooperative games is that in cooperative games, everyone cooperates, and therefore, by definition, everyone wins and no one loses. An example of this approach is the scoring rules for Infinity Volleyball as described in the *The New Games Book:*

> [T]his game is pure cooperation, and any number can play. The rules of standard volleyball still apply, including three hits per side before sending the ball over the net. The score, kept track of by both teams chanting in unison, is the number of times the ball is hit over the net to the other side without hitting the ground. Any score over 50 is good. Over 100 is phenomenal. And both teams always win.

The basic goal of the cooperative games movement is to provide a radical alternative to traditional sporting activities. The cooperative games (sometimes referred to as "new games") offer this option by stressing participation, cooperation, spontaneity, and playing for fun, as opposed to being a spectator, competition, predeter-

mined rules, and playing to win. Most importantly, cooperative games are subject to evolution—players are free to improvise and change the rules of the game as they play. Orlick credits the origins of the cooperative games movement to the special role of women in many cultures. In his studies of both traditional and contemporary North American cultures, he concludes that it is the humanistic strength of women that holds most societies together. Orlick credits women as being far more caring, considerate, dependable, and cooperative than men. As women's participation in sports increases, these qualities exert more influence on both what sports are played and how we think about sports in general.

John R. Bowman

See also Competition; Values and Ethics

Bibliography

Bascow, Susan. (1992) *Gender: Stereotypes and Roles.* Pacific Grove, CA: Brooks/Cole.

Caillois, Roger. (1958) *Les Jeux et Les Hommes.* Paris: Gallimard.

Edwards, Harry. (1973) *Sociology of Sport.* Homewood, IL: Dorsey Press.

Fluegelman, Andrew. (1976) *The New Games Book.* Garden City, NY: Doubleday.

Galliher, John, and Richard Hessler. (1979) "Sports Competition and International Capitalism." *Journal of Sport and Social Issues* 3 (Spring/Summer): 10–21.

Guttman, Allen. (1978) *From Ritual to Record.* New York: Columbia University Press.

Leonard, Wilbert. (1993) *A Sociological Perspective of Sport.* New York: Macmillan.

Orlick, Terry. (1978) *The Cooperative Sports and Games Book: Challenge Without Competition.* New York: Pantheon Books.

———. (1982) *The Second Cooperative Sports and Games Book.* New York: Pantheon Books.

Scott, Jack. (1969) *Athletics for Athletes.* Berkeley, CA: An Otherways Book.

———. (1971) *The Athletic Revolution.* New York: Free Press.

Singer, Robert, Milledge Murphy, and Keith Tennant. (1993) *Handbook of Research on Sport Psychology.* New York: Macmillan.

Synder, Eldon, and Elmer Spreitzer. (1979) "Orientations Toward Sport: Intrinsic, Normative, and Extrinsic." *Journal of Sport Psychology* 1, 2: 170–175.

Tannen, Deborah. (1990) *You Just Don't Understand: Women and Men in Conversation.* New York: Ballantine Books.

Thorne, Barrie. (1993) *Gender Play: Girls and Boys in School.* New Brunswick, NJ: Rutgers University Press.

Woolum, Janet. (1992) *Outstanding Women Athletes.* Phoenix, AZ: Oryx Press.

COSTA RICA

Costa Rica is located in Central America and has a population of about 3.5 million. Warm year-round temperatures allow Costa Ricans to enjoy a variety of outdoor sports and activities, and temperate sea and ocean waters are conducive to world-class white-water rafting, kayaking, fishing, surfing, and windsurfing. Costa Rica has a stable democratic form of government and a progressive economy, which have produced a high standard of living and relative equality for women. For example, 93 percent of men and women are literate, and the

Swimmer Claudia Poll, Costa Rica's first ever gold medal winner in any Olympic event, male or female. (AFP/Corbis)

life expectancy for women is 80.1 years, compared with 76.2 years for men.

This political and economic stability has aided the growth of women's sports, and women's sports and physical education in Costa Rica have benefited from important changes since the late 1960s. In 1966, the General Department of Physical Education and Sports was established, along with comparable physical education training for males and females in the school system. Five years later, the Ministry of Culture, Youth, and Sports was formed to further promote human development. La Comisión Interinstitucional Mujer, Salud y Deporte (the Commission for Women, Health, and Sport) has also promoted women's physical activities.

INTERNATIONAL COMPETITION

In the 1990s, Costa Rican women moved into the international arena. At the 1996 Olympic Games, swimmer Claudia Poll's victory in the 200-meter freestyle secured Costa Rica's first Olympic gold medal in the 100-year history of the modern Olympic Games. Upon returning home, she was hailed as a national hero. Her sister, Silvia, had won the silver medal in the same event in the 1988 Olympic Games. Other women who have represented Costa Rica in recent Olympic Games include swimmer Meliza Mata and track and field athlete Zoila Rosa Stewart Lee. In 1992, Lee became the first Costa Rican woman to qualify for the quarter-finals in the 400 meters, and she advanced to the 400-meter semifinals in the 1996 Olympics. Costa Rican women's soccer (association football), which gained momentum in the last two decades of the twentieth century, has also experienced much success: the team placed third in the 1998 CONCACAF Women's Championship, an event which also served as a World Cup qualifier.

Costa Rica's varied terrain and ecosystems invite many to participate in *andar en bici* (bicycling) for both leisure and competition. Each year, Costa Rica hosts the Ruta de Los Conquistadores (Route of the Conquistadors), drawing bicyclists from around the world to the 300-mile (483-kilometer) mountain-bike race. The race challenges riders with a Pacific-to-Caribbean route that includes extreme temperature changes, a climb over the nation's highest volcano, and treks through rain forests during the three-day competition. In 1997, four women finished the race, with Costa Ricans Dora Elizando and Natalia Alvarado finishing first and third respectively.

A number of women athletes from a variety of sports have been honored by induction into the Galeria del Deporte de Costa Rica (Hall of Fame of Costa Rica), established in 1969. Among them are track and field athletes Yolanda Britton (also inducted for basketball) and Mayra Soto; basketball players Cristina Lizano, Margarita Martinez, Avis McLean, Margarita Segreda, and Lidia Vargas; swimmer Maria del Milagro Paris; and volleyball player Ana Cristina Ulloa Delgado.

C. J. Lockman Hall

Bibliography

Cleland, Donna, (1980) *Education Fisica* [*Physical Education*] in Costa Rica. *Journal of Physical Education and Recreation* (September): 63–66.

"Deportes." <http://www.cr/deportes.html>. 1999.

"La Galeria del Deporte de Costa Rica." <http://www.intnet.co.cr/galcode>. 1999.

"La Nacion en Atlanta 96." <http://www.nacion.co.cr/In_ee/1996/julio/22/olimp_cables.html>. 1999.

"Route of the Conquistadors." <http://www.adventurerace.com>. 1999.

Australian Margaret Court in action at the 1972 Virginia Slims tournament at Newport, RI. (Bettmann/Corbis)

COURT, MARGARET SMITH

(1942–)

AUSTRALIAN TENNIS PLAYER

Margaret Court, the first internationally recognized Australian female tennis player, won twenty-two "Grand Slam" singles titles at the Australian Open, Wimbledon, the United States Open, and the French Open. In 1963, she won all four mixed-doubles titles; in 1970, she achieved an even more difficult goal by sweeping the singles titles.

Margaret Smith was born in New South Wales, Australia, on 16 July 1942. Her family lived across the street from the Border Tennis Association, where she often performed odd jobs in exchange for playing time. In addition to tennis, she played basketball and softball and also ran track. In fact, she was training for the Australian Olympic team in the 400- and 800-meter races when she decided to give up running because it was having a negative effect on her tennis game. In 1960, she won the Australian Open, her first Grand Slam event (and the first of her seven consecutive Australian titles). From that moment until 1973, she and Billie Jean King dominated women's tennis. Court was ranked first in the world for seven of these thirteen years. Court retired a number of times during her career, once out of boredom in 1966 and twice to have children, but she always returned to the game. Her greatest rival was King, who upset her in the opening round at Wimbledon in 1962. In their matches against each other, Court won twenty-one to King's thirteen.

Court refers to her Bobby Riggs match as a fiasco. In 1973, Bobby Riggs, the 1939 Wimbledon champion, challenged King to a match in order to make good on his boast that "any man can beat any woman." King turned down the self-styled "court jester's" challenge. Court accepted, mainly due to her annoyance that Riggs had challenged King, who, in Court's mind, was not the best tennis player at the time. Court took the match lightly while the media and Riggs turned the match into a major event. Rattled by her opponent's unorthodox play, Court lost 6–2, 6–1. Four months later King defeated Riggs in a match televised around the world and remembered as a marker on the road to "women's liberation."

In general, the charismatic King tended to receive more media attention than Court, who was more shy and reserved. As long as she was playing, Court was always the higher-ranked player of the two. Court's tennis abilities included an attacking style of play and great athleticism and endurance. She was inducted into the International Tennis Hall of Fame in 1979 and the International Women's Sports Hall of Fame in 1986.

Shawn Ladda

Bibliography

Court, Margaret Smith. (1975) *Court on Court: A Life in Tennis*. New York: Dodd, Mead.

Lumpkin, Angela. (1965) *Women's Tennis: A Historical Documentary of the Players and Their Game*. Troy, NY: Whitston Publishing Company.

Smith, Margaret. (1965) *The Margaret Smith Story*. London: Stanley Paul Publishing.

CRANZ, CHRISTL

(1914–)

GERMAN ALPINE SKIER, SKIING TEACHER, AND OFFICIAL

Probably the most famous Alpine skier of the 1930s, Christl Cranz-Borchers was the first winner of women's combined Alpine events at the 1936 Olympics. From 1934 to 1939, Cranz won a total of thirteen gold and three silver medals.

Cranz was born on 1 July 1914 in Brussels. At the age of four, she received her first pair of skis. It was in Grindelwald, Switzerland, where she

Christl Cranz of Germany crosses the line to win the 1936 Olympic slalom event at Garmisch-Partenkirchen. (Bettmann/Corbis)

lived with her parents and two brothers from 1920 to 1928, that nine-year-old Christl Cranz won her first ski competition. In 1928, the family moved to Freiburg im Breisgau, Germany; this was the starting point of her professional career, which was to lead to her first title as Schwarzwaldmeisterin (Black Forest champion).

Six years later, she won the German Women's Alpine Skiing Championship in the first event of its kind and, in doing so, qualified for the 1936 German Olympic team. Cranz retained the German title in the following years until 1941. She was also successful in the world championships from 1934 to 1941 and the Academic World Games in 1934 at St. Moritz, Switzerland, and in 1937 at Zell am See, Austria. The Alpine combination (downhill and slalom races) was a new event at the 1936 Olympic Games in Garmisch-Partenkirchen, Germany. In an exciting competition, after a tumble in the downhill race on the first day of the combination, Cranz was only in sixth position. The next day, she skied two perfect slalom races and became the first women's gold medalist in the Olympic combination event. In second place was Käthe Grasegger, also of Germany; the bronze medalist was Laila Schou-Nielsen of Norway. Cranz competed in her last international race in politically neutral Sweden in 1941.

During World War II—having finished her physical education studies at the University of Berlin—Cranz worked as a teacher at the Institute for Physical Education at the University of Freiburg, where she had been an assistant since 1936. After the war, she made her home in Steibis, Allgäu, in the German Alps. In 1947, she opened a ski school primarily for children, and during the 1950s and 1960s her ideas had an influence on the development of children's skiing in the German Ski Instructor's Union. She was adviser for women's affairs in the German Ski Federation until 1964, promoting women's skiing by her involvement. At the 1960 Olympic Games in Squaw Valley, California, Cranz took part as an official team host and umpire, and she was also umpire during the 1964 Games in Innsbruck, Austria.

Michaela Czech

Bibliography

Cranz, Christl. (1949) *Christl erzähl.* Munich: Rother Berg Verlag.

———. (1988, 1989) Unpublished interviews with the author on 15 April 1998 and 26 April 1989.

Czech, Michaela. (1994) *Frauen und Sport im nationalsozialistischen Deustchland: Eine Untersuchung zur weiblichen Sportrealität in einem patriarchalen Herrschaftsystem.* Berlin: Verlagsgesellschaft Tischler GmbH.

"Die Sieger der IV. Olympischen Winter-Spiele. Der Kampf um die Goldmedaillen von Garmsich-Partenkirchen 1936." (1936) *Neue Leipziger Zeitung.* (Leipzig: Verlag Leipziger Verlagsdruckerei AG): 7–14.

CRESTA SLEDDING *see*
Sledding–Skeleton (Cresta Run)
Tobogganing

CRICKET

Since the English team game of cricket was codified in the eighteenth century, it has mainly been defined as a male game—cricket, like association football (soccer), was considered a test of manliness. Women's role in the game was largely an auxiliary one: preparing afternoon teas for the male players and watching the game. Those women who took up the game achieved little recognition at best, and ridicule at worst.

Despite such discouragement, many women have been keen to play the game. Women have been playing organized club cricket for more than a century and international cricket for more than six decades. From the nineteenth century on, many women have been avid and knowledgeable spectators. Separate Ladies' Stands, created at many major cricket grounds in the late nineteenth century, acknowledged this role.

RULES AND PLAY

Cricket emerged as a ball-and-bat sport among the English aristocracy in the late sixteenth century and developed as a major leisure activity over the course of the seventeenth century. The basic rules were codified from the middle to the end of the eighteenth century, and they served as the basis for the formation of cricket clubs across England in the following century, when cricket also spread to English colonies such as Australia. In the twentieth century, cricket continued to spread across the British Empire, with a clear distinction emerging between amateur (upper-class) and professional (lower-class) players.

The rules of cricket are well known to be complicated and perplexing, and enthusiasts like to compare it to chess. Cricket is played between two teams of eleven players each, who take turns batting in separate innings. An inning is over when ten players have been dismissed (or are "out") because there must at all times be two batters (generally known as batsmen or batswomen), each of whom stands in a crease, a marked area at either end of a playing area 20 meters (65.6 feet) long in the center of the field. In the crease, behind the batter, is the wicket—three small wooden posts in line, topped with small, unattached wooden pegs called bails. The wicket keeper stands behind the wicket, a position similar to that of the catcher in baseball.

There are two bowlers on the field at a time, bowling in alternate "overs," or six-ball sequences of throws. The bowler delivers the ball—throws it toward the batter—overhand. Bowlers are generally "fast" or "slow," each with different techniques. Runs are scored when both batters safely reach the other end, and in the course of an inning they may run back and forth hundreds of times.

THE FIRST RECORD OF A WOMEN'S CRICKET MATCH (1891)

An Excerpt from the Derby Mercury *on an Eventful Cricket Match*

Another proof that cricket was not confined to male players is furnished in the following paragraph from the *Derby Mercury* of August 1745: "The greatest cricket match that was ever played in the south part of England was on Friday the 26th of last month, on Gosden Common, near Guildford, between eleven maids of Bramley and eleven maids of Hambledon, dressed all in white. The Bramley girls got 119 notches and the Hambledon girls 127. There was of both sexes the greatest number that ever was seen on such an occasion. The girls bowled, batted, ran, and caught as well as any men could do."

WILLIAM CONNOR SYDNEY
(1891) England and the English in the Eighteenth Century: Chapters in the Social History of the Times. *London: Ward and Downey.*

The aim of the batter is to amass as many runs as possible for her individual innings (once a batter is dismissed, she does not bat again) and to help her co-batter to accumulate runs. Batters work together to see that the stronger batter faces as many balls as possible. Batters do not have to run if they hit a ball to the boundary (four runs are scored automatically, and six if the ball crosses the boundary), and batters often bat for hours and even for days in Test (international) matches.

The aim of the bowler is to dismiss the batter—that is, to end her individual innings—by (1) bowling (throwing the ball past the batter and hitting the wicket); (2) catching the ball before it hits the ground; (3) placing a "leg before wicket" (or l.b.w.), when the batter is forced to step between the ball and the wicket; or (2) being "stumped," meaning that the wicket keeper knocks the bails off the wicket while the batter is out of the crease or safe zone. A cricket match goes on until both teams are dismissed.

EARLY HISTORY

As early as the 1740s there were many reports of games between villages involving peasant women in the English counties of Surrey and Sussex. The growth of women's cricket ran parallel to the rise of the men's game in this period. Flint and Rheinberg noted that the atmosphere at these women's cricket matches was "robust, colorful, boisterous, sometimes rowdy and certainly often inelegant, with spectators of both sexes drinking, shouting, swearing and gambling." There are many hints that women cricketers achieved more acceptance in this century than subsequently. The leading matches were advertised in the press, gate entry was charged, and sizable crowds watched. Women's matches were scheduled on prominent grounds, including the Artillery Ground in London. Some of the leading patrons of cricket, such as the third earl of Dorset, were sympathetic to women playing cricket. He quipped: "What is human life but a game of cricket and, if this be so, why shouldn't ladies play it as well as we?"

However, new definitions of femininity developed by the reforming middle class resulted in the virtual exclusion of women from many team sports. For much of the nineteenth century women's cricket was in a state of decline. Nonetheless, a woman, Christina Willes, provided the inspiration for the roundarm bowling style that was legalized in 1835. This is considered the most important change in cricket during the nineteenth century because it led to the legalization of overarm bowling in 1864. Christina Willes was the sister of John Willes, a prominent bowler from Kent. It was said that "Willes, his sister and his dog could beat any eleven in England." Finding it difficult to bowl in the current style of underarm because she wore a full skirt, she developed a high roundarm action when bowling to her brother in their Tonford barn. Christina's roundarm bowling so impressed her brother that he emulated the style, and it became common throughout the country.

ORGANIZED CLUBS

Club cricket emerged in Australia and England in the 1880s. In 1886 the Fernleas and Siroccos played several matches in aid of a "deserving charity" at the Sydney Cricket Ground. The English White Heather Club was organized in 1887.

Sizable crowds watched these first club games, but many, who came to watch for reasons of novelty, failed to return. These clubs were for men; women's cricket was treated by many as a joke. There were media reports of a match in Lahore, Pakistan, in 1887. A team of men batted with broomsticks against a team of women who played with real bats.

One way for women to avoid public criticism was to play modified cricket. From the 1870s on, many such games were invented, such as frisquette, rockley rules, vigoro, and cricko. Because such games were clearly women's sports and confirmed women's inferior status, women players could avoid public criticism. The revival of interest in women's cricket was related in part to the extension of secondary and tertiary education for women and the growth of feminism. Prominent radical Vida Goldstein, one of the first women to stand for the Australian Parliament, was elected president of the Victorian Ladies Cricket Association, launched in 1905. During the next decades similar women's cricket associations were founded in Australia, England, and New Zealand. National associations had been formed in the three countries by the time of the first international tour of 1934–1935.

INTERNATIONAL CRICKET FROM THE 1930S ONWARD

It was a bold gamble for an English team to tour Australia and New Zealand in 1934–1935, when the first women's Test matches—international competitions that often last five or six days—were played. The national associations had limited funds, and the touring English players raised their own round-trip fare to attend the Tests. They were billeted in homes to save costs. However, the tour was a great success. The women, who played cricket on some of the major grounds of the country, including the Melbourne and Sydney Cricket Grounds, attracted sizable crowds and generated much public interest. England won the series against Australia, winning the Tests 2–0 (with one draw). England then toured New Zealand, defeating New Zealand by a wide margin in the single Test match they played.

Interest in cricket was never higher than in the 1930s, when the arrival of superstar Donald Bradman coincided with the controversial Bodyline series and play-by-play radio broadcasts. The popularity of women's cricket was in part a spin-off of this boom.

The debate about an appropriate costume for women in the 1930s suggests that the acceptance of women playing cricket was a qualified one. While some women preferred to play in trousers, officials in Australia and England opted instead for culottes, a divided skirt, because it was seen to present a suitably feminine image. However, in later decades, women of other countries, such as India and New Zealand in the 1990s, opted instead to play in trousers. So from the 1970s on, international contests sometimes involved women on one side playing in skirts while the other side played in trousers. Women's cricket all but disappeared from the media and major cricket grounds after World War II, although international matches continued to be played. The lack of interest was another indication that public acceptance of women's cricket was partial and limited. The modified sport of softball, by contrast, which had been introduced to Australia by North Americans in the 1940s, experienced rapid growth.

WORLD CUP OF 1973

A casual chat in June 1971 between Rachel Heyhoe-Flint and millionaire Jack Hayward led to the first World Cup, with Hayward offering the huge sum of £40,000 to cover the accommodation expenses of players. The World Cup was a major boost for women's cricket. It generated much needed publicity for the game, the likes of which had not been seen since the 1930s. It also provided the venue for the first media personality of women's cricket, English captain Rachael Heyhoe-Flint. This imaginative concept preceded an equivalent men's World Cup, held for the first time in 1975.

The first women's World Cup involved the founding Test nations, England and Australia;

CO-ED CRICKET
IN THE EIGHTEENTH CENTURY (1891)

Cricket was much in vogue in the provinces, especially on the wide grassy commons and heaths of the southern counties of England, the first match on record being that played between Kent and England, on the Artillery Ground in London, in 1746. Four years afterwards the Hambledon Cricket Club was formed, and proved invincible until 1769. Cricket was not confined to the sterner sex. The *Annual Register* for 1775 contains the record of an extraordinary cricket match which was played at Moulsey Hurst on August 3 of that year, between six unmarried men and an equal number of unmarried women, and which was won by the former, though one of the latter ran seventeen notches.

WILLIAM CONNOR SYDNEY
(1891) England and the English in the Eighteenth Century: Chapters in the Social History of the Times. *London: Ward and Downey.*

---

two West Indian teams, Jamaica, and Trinidad and Tobago; and Young England and an International Eleven. England, which hit up a commanding 3/279, defeated Australia 9/187 in the final.

Australia has been the dominant women's cricket country since 1973, winning the World Cup four times. England won its second World Cup in 1993, when the World Cup matches were again played on its home ground.

SPREAD OF THE GAME

England toured South Africa for a four-Test series in 1960–1961 and New Zealand toured there in 1972, although there were few further international exchanges with South Africa during the apartheid years. Before the World Cup of 1973, women's cricket associations had been established in Jamaica (1966) and Trinidad and Tobago (1967). England toured in the West Indies in 1970 and 1971, playing a Test against Jamaica in February 1971. Although there have been subsequent international tours, women's cricket in the West Indies has been vastly inferior to the men's. India emerged as a fourth significant cricket power—alongside England and Australia—and the second World Cup was played there in 1978.

MEDIA ISSUES

Gaining adequate public support, sponsorship, and media attention continued to be a problem for women's cricket in the 1990s. While there was some improvement in levels of sponsorship and government support, women's cricket still suffered from some negative images.

Australian batter Denise Annetts, who was then the world record-holder, vented her frustration over her omission from the Australian team in 1994 by claiming that she was dropped because she was heterosexual. The whiff of a lesbian scandal in cricket attracted a voracious media eager to confirm a long-held suspicion that women cricketers were "closet males." Women's cricket, which had struggled to gain adequate attention for decades, was front-page news for weeks on end.

However, the emergence of a popular superstar, Australian Zoe Goss, provided a more positive image that helped promote the game. Goss accepted a last-minute invitation to play in an otherwise all-male charity match involving many international stars. She achieved instant fame when she dismissed the star West Indian cricketer Brian Lara.

FUTURE OF WOMEN'S CRICKET

The future of women's cricket looked more promising in the 1990s than at any previous time. Many cricket barriers—such as women not being allowed to play at Lord's (the home of cricket), not being admitted to the Long Room there, and not enjoying full membership of the Marylebone Cricket Club (MCC)—have disappeared. Cricket, like soccer (association football) and many other tough physical sports such as weightlifting and marathon running, is no longer regarded as exclusively male. Eleven countries were represented at the 1997 women's World Cup: Pakistan, South Africa, and Sri Lanka appeared for the first time, joining Australia, Denmark, England, India, Ireland, New Zealand, the Netherlands, and the West Indies.

However, the future of the sport will depend on how well cricket competes in an expanding and competitive sporting environment. Women, as well as men, have a greater variety of choice in regard to team games than before. Many women may chose to play basketball, netball, softball, or hockey instead of cricket.

Richard Cashman
Amanda Weaver

Bibliography

Burroughs, Angela, Leonie Seebohm, and Liz Ashburn. (1995) " 'A Leso Story': Women's Cricket and Its Media Experience." *Sporting Traditions* 12, 1 (November): 27–46.

Butcher, Betty. (1984) *The Sport of Grace: Women's Cricket in Victoria.* Melbourne: Sports Federation of Australia.

Cashman, Richard. (1995) "Defining 'Real Sport': The Question of Modified Sport for Women." In *Method and Methodology in Sport and Cultural History,* edited by K. B. Wamsley. Dubuque, IA: Wm. C. Brown, 88–101.

Cashman, Richard, and Amanda Weaver. (1991) *Wicket Women: Cricket & Women in Australia.* Kensington, New South Wales: International Specialized Book Services.

Cashman, Richard, et al, eds. (1996) *The Oxford Companion to Australian Cricket.* Flint and Rheinberg. Melbourne: Oxford University Press.

Hawes, Joan L. (1987) *Women's Test Cricket: The Golden Triangle 1934–84.* Lewes, UK: Book Guild.

Heyhoe-Flint, Rachael, and Netta Rheinberg. (1976) *Fair Play: The Story of Women's Cricket.* London: Angus & Robertson.

Joy, Nancy. (1950) *Maiden Over: A Short History of Women's Cricket and a Diary of the 1948–49 Test Tour to Australia.* London: Sporting Hardbooks.

Pollard, Marjorie. (1934) *Cricket for Women and Girls.* London: Hutchinson.

CROATIA *see* Yugoslavia

CROQUET

Croquet is a lawn game played with a mallet that is used to strike a ball along the ground through a series of arched hoops that are laid out in a prescribed course. There are six hoops on a grass lawn 31.9 meters (104.7 feet) long and 25.6 meters (84 feet) wide, with a peg at the finish. A player attempts to make it through the course and be the first to hit the peg with her ball. During play she may gain extra strokes by hitting her opponent's ball with her ball, or she may use such contact to send her opponent's ball to another location. Golf croquet is a single-shot game, where the players play in sequence one after the other. Association croquet is more like snooker, where a player earns extra strokes to keep her turn going, and a turn can consist of up to ninety-one strokes.

Croquet allowed competition between men and women before other sports did. Throughout its history, this mixed-sex competition caused the sport to suffer periodic declines, having been labeled effeminate. The sport is once again leading the way on gender equality. Modern world rankings are combined for men and women, and the United States Croquet Association does not hold separate men's and women's championships.

Gender issues permeate croquet's history. The earliest known rules for the game allowed only one hand on the mallet so that women could hold parasols while playing. It originated in the thirteenth century in Languedoc, France, where it was called *palle malle* or *jeu de mail*. French nuns took the game to Ireland in the early nineteenth century.

Nineteenth-century artwork depicted women and men playing together. These early pictures showed women holding parasols with one hand and using the other to guide a mallet toward a ball that was resting against an opponent's ball in anticipation of sending it out of the picture. Men watched these shots from the background with looks of impending castration. Sexual overtones were rich in these drawings. Women were often pictured as if flirting with their male opponents. Their breasts were accentuated, and the poses would have been considered wanton for the time.

Chinese croquet player. (Craig Lovell/Corbis)

Men and women were pictured playing together in a game that allowed women to wield power over men. This struck fear into the hearts of many men, including one who wrote to *Living Age* magazine that "who takes the mallet in his hand, has grasped naked vice; and who passes through the treacherous wire portal leaves virtue, honor and charity behind" (quoted in Guttmann 1991, 119).

It may have been a woman, a Miss Macpherson, who introduced croquet to England from Ireland in the 1850s. Men were quick to take over the marketing of the sport in England. John Jaques, who had seen the sport played in Ireland, wrote down the rules and made hoops and mallets to sell. Walter Jones Whitmore, who competed against women at his brother's home, became obsessed with croquet, organizing tournaments and eventually forming the All-England Croquet Club. This club purchased four acres of land at Wimbledon. The game grew with the increased publicity and organization. By the late 1800s, every English town had its club and most private homes with gardens had their "lawns."

Unexpectedly, the game began to decline. The "lawns" at Wimbledon were being used more and more for tennis, eventually leading to a name change to the All-England Croquet and Lawn Tennis Club. By 1882 the croquet championships had been abandoned, and in 1884 the word "croquet" was dropped from the club's title. It was a woman who saved the game from near-extinction during this decline. A Mrs. Hill organized a tournament for a challenge cup presented by F. H. Ayers. Thus in 1894, a woman was organizing a major national sporting event. Over the next three years she saw the number of club entries grow to 160, and the championships were listed with other major sporting events. By 1900 the Croquet Association (U.K.) was formed.

The former colonies of England and France adopted the game, and by 1986 the World Croquet Federation served national or regional groups from Australia, Canada, England, France, Ireland, Italy, Japan, Jersey, New Zealand, Scotland, South Africa, and the United States. World championships have been held in Australia, Egypt, England, France, Italy, and the United States. Other national croquet associations joined the World Croquet Association since 1990. These include organizations from Switzerland, Wales, Guernsey, the Netherlands, Egypt, Spain, Belgium, and Israel.

Lily Gower of Great Britain (1877–1959) was the first woman player to win the Croquet Association's British Open Championships. Self-taught from an instructional manual, she won her first tournament in 1898 and then won three women's championships from 1899 to 1901 and a fourth in 1928. The greatest woman croquet player was Dorthy Steele of Great Britain (1884–1965). She won the open titles in 1923, 1933, 1935, and 1936, fifteen women's championships, and twelve women's and mixed-doubles titles. Fifteen of the top 200 world-ranked players in June of 1998 were women. England had three, with the top-ranked woman (Debbie Cornelius) in twenty-first place. Australia had six women in the top 200, including H. Thurston, ranked fiftieth. New Zealand also had six women in the top 200.

Women in croquet face obstacles when attempting to compete openly against men. The selectors for the England team for the prestigious MacRobertson International Shield attend the British men's open and observe players and discuss their selection. In order to get this exposure, Debbie Cornelius applied to play in the men's open. This was an attempt on her part to get equal exposure and equal opportunity for selection. Since there was also a women's open, Cornelius was criticized for wanting to play in the men's. She ultimately did not play in either the men's or women's, choosing instead to play in the Sonoma-Cutrer Open Tournament. While this choice avoided conflict, it may have hindered her own career chances.

Another hindrance for world-class women players is the quality of their female opposition. Competing regularly against only women players means fewer opportunities to play against the best croquet players. This is not an obstacle for men players, who regularly face the top-ranked croquet players in their men's open tournament and in the open tournaments.

Kay Flatten

Bibliography

Birley, Derek. (1993) *Sport and the Making of Britain.* Manchester, UK: Manchester University Press.

Brash, R. (1972) *How Did Sports Begin?: A Look into the Origins of Man at Play.* London: Longman.

Guttmann, Allen. (1991) *Women's Sports: A History.* New York: Columbia University Press.

Hargreaves, Jennifer. (1994) *Sporting Females: Critical Issues in the History and Sociology of Women's Sports.* London: Routledge.

Mathews, Peter. (1995) *The Guinness Encyclopedia of International Sports Records and Results,* 4th ed. London: Guinness.

Matthews, Peter, et al. (1993) *Guinness International Who's Who of Sport.* London: Guinness.

Polly, Martin. (1998) *Moving the Goalposts: A History of Sport and Society Since 1945.* London: Routledge.

World Croquet Federation. <http://www.personal.u-net.com/~worldcroquet/home.html>. 1998.

Wymer, Norman (1949). *Sport in England.* London: George G. Harrap.

Additional information was provided by David McLaughlin.

CROSS-COUNTRY RUNNING

Cross-country running is a kind of distance running distinguished from other types by the distances run and the terrain on which the competition occurs. The sport is distinct, although it is often confused with such other forms of long-distance running as marathons, road races, and the distance events in track and field. Unlike these sports, however, there is no standardized distance for the courses run, and the terrain is rougher "offroad." Although women have participated since the 1920s, the sport became fully open to them only in the 1960s, as part of the general acceptance of women in distance events. Since then, it has become one of the few sports that is more popular with women than with men.

HISTORY

Cross-country emerged as a competitive sport in early nineteenth-century England with a game called "Hare and Hounds" or "The Paper Chase." One runner or a group of runners created a trail for a second group of runners by dropping pieces of paper or other markers that the second group, running through later, tried to follow.

The first formal competition was held at the Rugby School in 1837 and was called the Crick Run. Other public schools followed suit, and then Oxford and Cambridge Universities also began to hold competitions. While Hare and Hounds continued to be a popular pastime, in serious competition the game was transformed into a cross-country race over a course that was established in advance over rough trails and open country. English national championships were established in 1876, and two years later William C. Vosburgh, a New York native, brought the sport to the United States. The National Cross-Country Association (NCCA) was formed in 1887, along with the first U.S. championship, which the Amateur Athletic Association (AAU) began to run in 1880.

That same year, cross-country was introduced at Harvard, but was conceived as a form of fall training for distance runners who competed in track and field in the spring. Other campuses began to do the same. The first intercollegiate meet was held in 1890 between Cornell University, City College of New York, and the University of Pennsylvania. Cornell in particular developed a pronounced interest in the sport and began to organize the Intercollegiate Cross-Country Association in 1898. At the college level, the historical emergence of cross-country as a means to an end—success in track—rather than a sport in itself continues to affect attitudes today. Cross-country is still somewhat seen as the poorer, less glamorous sister to track and is for the most part given less press and attention. It is rare that an athlete is recruited for cross-country but not track, and athletes who run cross-country are always expected to run track as well.

International cross-country competition began in 1898 with a race between England and France. An annual championship meet, held at the Hamilton Park Racecourse in Glasgow, Scotland, was established in 1903 and included England, Ireland, Scotland, and Wales. *The International Amateur Athletic Foundation Magazine* notes that Alf Shrub, who led England to victory, "like most of his successors . . . was to transfer his talents to the track and during the next two years he set fourteen world records" (in track). Lack of a standardized distance for cross-country means that no world records can be set, so often serious competitors switch to a sport such as track in which they can set records. The idea of cross-country as a starting point for or stepping stone to track continued to follow the sport's growth. But it did grow, and other European countries began to take part in the 1920s.

Though it is unclear who the first woman was to run a cross-country race, women were competing at this time. F. A. M. Webster's *Athletics of Today for Women: History, Development, and Training* (1930) specifies that Rene Trente won the 1930 French women's cross-country championship for the seventh year in a row and that in the English women's cross-country championship. "Miss L. D. Styles retained her title." The author was clearly an advocate of women's sports, for he writes of an earlier race that "it was to be proven even more conclusively in 1929 that women ath-letes have not as yet by any means reached the limits of their record breaking potentialities." Contrary to any lingering stereotypes of delicate Victorian womanhood, Webster emphasizes that "despite adverse weather conditions and continuous showers of hailstones," on 13–14 May 1929 at the women's interuniversity championships in Birmingham, "the home university placed girls in every event, and carried off the Challenge Shield, which they had not held previously."

Cross-country was on the Olympic roster in 1912, 1920, and 1924 but was then dropped because it was considered a bad fit with summer competition. In the United States, the annual National Collegiate Athletic Association (NCAA) cross-country championship was established in 1938. The worldwide governing body for track and field, the International Amateur Athletic Federation (IAAF), assumed responsibility for cross-country in 1962 and established both men's and women's rules. The first international women's world championship was held in 1967, a year after the Amateur Athletic Union (AAU) held a national championship for women in the United States. Cross-country running for women emerged at roughly the same time as a national women's movement invested in securing equality of opportunity in all areas, including sports.

WOMEN'S DISTANCE RUNNING

Women's distance running in general has had a long and twisted history, and the emergence of a women's world cross-country championship in 1967 was due to developments in this larger context. Although scientific data now show that women are actually more suited than men to endurance events, medical lore of the early twentieth century stressed "moderate" exercise for women lest they compromise their reproductive capacities. This view was strongly entrenched, for although women had been running in marathons since 1926 to no visible ill effect, the audience's distress at seeing women looking "exhausted" after their 800-meter runs in the 1928 Amsterdam Olympics led to an International Olympic Committee (IOC) ban that prohibited women from running any race longer than the 200 meters until the 1960 Games in Rome.

Marathon running in the United States was itself notorious for excluding women until that exclusion was publicized and challenged by Kathrine Switzer in 1967. Switzer entered the Boston Marathon as K. Switzer, and despite the race officials' attempts to pull her entry number off her chest once they realized a woman was competing in the race, Switzer finished and called media attention to her cause, which was simply that women should be able to compete. Her quest had larger social and political implications, for the women's movement in the United States was gathering force at the time, and the push to include women in athletic events like the marathon paralleled the larger struggle for equal opportunity and revision of women's previously limiting gender roles.

Switzer's struggle, along with that of other women pursuing equal rights in running as elsewhere, cleared the way for much larger participation. When the New York Marathon was established three years later, women were included, and the Boston Marathon began to accept women entrants in 1972. With Switzer's input, Avon began to sponsor women-only road racing events of varying distances in 1978, and the Avon International Running Circuit continues as of the end of the 1990s.

The history of women's distance running had a profound effect on women's participation in cross-country. It has shifted from being primarily an intercollegiate men's sport, as it was early in the twentieth century, to a sport that has far surpassed demands for equality of opportunity. Today, women's cross-country is more widespread and popular than men's, with the NCAA listing 890 schools that sponsored women's cross-country teams in 1998 as compared to 828 schools sponsoring men's teams. (Schools struggling to comply with Title IX requirements often add women's cross-country as a sport because it has low overhead.) At the high school level, 1995–1996 statistics compiled by the National Federation of State High School Associations show cross-country as the seventh-highest participant sport for girls, with 140,187 athletes competing at 10,774 schools.

As the generalist event of distance running, cross-country is a very competitive sport, because it draws runners from all distance specialties. Competitors from events as short as the 1500 meters in track all the way through runners who compete in the marathon flock to cross-country racing in the fall, making the world cross-country championships notoriously difficult to win. A woman who wins the world championship for the 5000 meters in track (the most comparable distance) will not necessarily win in cross-country, whose variable courses and terrains makes it always a new challenge.

RULES AND PLAY

The primary difference between a cross-country race and the 5000-meter and 10,000-meter races in track and field is that cross-country events are still run on courses that are technically "offroad"—that is, they are not on a track or paved road, but rather wind through parks, forests, and golf courses. There is no standardized distance for cross-country, and courses vary from 10,000 to 12,000 meters (10,936 to 13,123 yards) for men and 2000 to 5000 meters (2187 to 5468 yards) for women. It is also more a team sport than is track and field, with five to nine runners competing in a given race. The team's order of finish is determined by adding up the places in which team members finish (1 point for first, 10 points for tenth, and so forth); the team with the lowest score wins. A latter-day derivative of cross-country running is trail running, for which special shoes began to be marketed in the mid-to late 1990s in the United States.

MAJOR COMPETITIONS

Elite women cross-country runners tend to be successful across the women's distance-running spectrum. Probably the best-known women's cross-country competitor of all time is Norway's Grete Waitz, who dominated women's distance running in the late 1970s and early 1980s. Though she is best known for her marathon victories, Waitz won five world cross-country titles, four of them consecutively between 1978 and 1981. Waitz is typical of many runners in that she ran cross-country first, and her success there motivated her to try other distances. Waitz was unbeaten in cross-country races for twelve years, until she was defeated in the 1982 world championships by Romanians Maricica Puica and Fita Lovin. Her fifth world cross-country title, however, came in 1983, when she won by more than 12 seconds. She is best known, though, for her marathon efforts, which included winning the New York Marathon nine times, setting a world record four times, and getting a silver medal in the event in the 1984 Olympic Games.

American Lynn Jennings was a formidable presence on the cross-country stage, beginning with her 1976 victory at the junior national cross-country championships. In 1985 she won the first of eight Athletics Congress national cross-country championships. She competed in every single world cross-country championship between 1986 and 1993. She placed second in her first appearance, behind Zola Budd, and then achieved two fourth places and a sixth. In 1990–1992, however, she was undefeated in three consecutive world-title races, including the 1990 race, which she led from the start. She also won a bronze in the 10,000 meters in the 1992 Olympics, finishing behind Derartu Tulu of Ethiopia and Elana Meyer of South Africa. Jennings recommends cross-country, especially for teens, telling *Runner's World* that it "provides the basis of excellence for track success . . . and most kids get their start as runners in high school cross-country. I'd like to think that my success with cross-country could serve as a kind of beacon to them." She was *Runner's World*'s American Female Runner of the Year five times. Though she decided to concentrate her energies on track in 1994 (and won the 10,000-meter event at the 1998 International Track and Field Championships), Jennings showed to a whole generation of cross-country runners that despite its usual backseat status, fame and fortune could be found in the sport.

In the 1990s, African women came to be a dominant presence in women's cross-country, and Derartu Tulu, who won the gold in Jennings's Olympics race (the first black African woman to win an Olympic gold), has been one of their leaders. She started her career in cross-country as well, beginning in 1989 on Ethiopia's women's junior cross-country team. She won the world championships in 1995 and again in 1997, winning the latter with a strong kick at the end that took her past Britain's Paula Radcliffe, who had won the junior worlds in 1992. Fellow Ethiopian Gete Wami, who also started on the Ethiopian junior team, won the world cross-country title in 1996. In the 1998 world championship, though, Irish runner Sonia O'Sullivan won the individual title;

Kenya won the team title, followed by Ethiopia. A new presence on the scene in the 1990s, Finland's Annemari Sandell, who won the junior worlds in 1995, surprised everyone by defeating Kenyan stars such as Jackline Maranga. O'Sullivan defended her title in the 1999 worlds, held on her home territory of Belfast, Ireland.

One of the underlying ideas behind the sport is reflected in the comments of IAAF president Dr. Primo Nebiolo, who hoped that the championships would make a contribution toward peace in wartorn Belfast. Nebiolo cited the way a world competition brings athletes together from every part of the world irrespective of race, religion, ideology, or gender. But such inclusiveness has been hard-won, and the efforts of women runners worldwide to establish equality for women in terms of teams, meets, and scholarships have greatly contributed to such attitudes.

In NCAA cross-country competitions in the late 1990s, Stanford won the women's national title in 1996, followed by Brigham Young University (BYU) in 1997 and Villanova in 1998, when BYU was second and Stanford third. Individually, Amy Skieresz of the University of Arizona finished second in 1995, 1997, and 1998, winning the individual title in 1996. Katie McGregor of the University of Michigan won the individual title in 1998.

THE FUTURE

Cross-country is still seen as a starting sport for runners who will later become the world's top marathoners and track and field competitors. Nevertheless, the increased rate of girls' and women's participation shows that it is an important sport for meeting the mandates of Title IX and that female competitors continue to demonstrate a facility for and interest in the sport. Two developments in the NCAA show a movement toward granting cross-country a more independent status: a move to require universities to offer scholarships to cross-country runners independently of track and a 1997 subcommittee vote that extended the distance of the women's national championships from 5000 to 6000 meters (5468 to 6561 yards); 5000 meters had been the distance since 1981. Coaches contend that the longer distance will also help make cross-country a sport with a firmer identity of its own.

The 1997 realignment of Division I schools from eight districts into nine provides a better balance in terms of the number of schools sponsoring cross-country in each district. This makes access to the championships fairer; and it increased the field sizes by 40 percent, from 184 runners in 1997 to 255 in 1998. This gives more teams and more athletes the chance to participate in a national championship, which raises the level of excitement in and commitment to the sport. With these improvements, in conjunction with the increased emphasis on separate scholarships for cross-country, it may not be long before cross-country outgrows its little-sister status and emerges as a women's sport with a distinct identity and place.

Leslie Heywood

Bibliography

Hickok, Bill. "Cross Country Running." <http://www.HickokSports.com>. 1998. *IAFF Magazine.* (1997).

Johnson, Anne Janette. (1996) *Great Women in Sports.* Detroit: Visible Ink Press.

NCAA. (1998) "Women's Cross Country" <http://www.ncaa.org>. 1998.

Webster, F. A. M. (1930) *Athletics for Women: History, Development, and Training.* New York: Fredrick Warne.

Additional information was provided by Wayne Wilson (Amateur Athletic Foundation, Los Angeles).

CURLING

Curling is a team target game played on ice with oblate granite stones weighing about 20 kilograms (44 pounds) and fitted with handles. Players throw (slide) the stones along a sheet of ice. Scottish women were some of the earliest female players, amid some controversy.

HISTORY

Most sources agree that curling developed in Scotland in the 1500s or 1600s and that Scottish women were playing sporadically by the mid-1800s, although the cumbersome clothing women

A female competitor in the 1959 outdoor Bonspiel in Scotland. (Hulton-Deutsch Collection/Corbis)

wore in that period hampered athletic movements. On these occasions, male disapproval was evident in newspaper comment about the dubious propriety of women's participation, since men believed the game not of a character befitting the female sex. By the 1890s, curling Scotswomen were no longer such curiosities, and Perth and Stirling reportedly boasted forty-two women's clubs. But the sporting world paid little attention to these players before World War I.

After the war, Scottish women joined men's curling clubs, formed women's rinks (teams) within them, and founded their own clubs. By World War II, rinks made up of Scottish women were playing in ankle-length tartan skirts, but soon, like athletic women everywhere, they wore trousers to play. Scottish women started intercity matches in 1930, and they began the transition from small 13.5-kilogram (30-pound) stones to stones the size and weight of the men's. In the 1950s four Scotswomen's rinks traveled to

Canada and the United States to play (the men had made similar trips since early in the century). In 1977 the International Curling Federation, a men's group, approved the formation of a women's committee of the federation, thus granting the women the right to play under official sanction. The Royal Bank of Scotland sponsored a Ladies World Curling Championship in 1979 in Perth, where women of eleven countries, all of them Northern European except for Canada and the United States, took part.

NORTH AMERICAN CURLING

In North America, Scottish immigrants had introduced curling at least by the mid-1700s, and the first organized club was formed in Montreal in 1807. Curling spread westward, and as provincial rivalry grew, Manitoba became the center of Canadian curling interest. By 1900, with the spread of indoor ice rinks, curling clubs had moved almost exclusively inside, and women had begun organized play in Canada. But allowing women to curl was at first considered close to revolutionary, and when a men's club discussed permitting women to join in 1913, the great majority were decidedly hostile. Only gradually did Canadian clubs yield, as it was put, not only to plain justice but to a still plainer common sense.

Between the wars the important Manitoba Curling Association, a men's group, set up a league for schoolboys, but not for adult women, although women there had been curling since the 1890s and women's leagues were already associated with several of its affiliated clubs. One Winnipeg club organized itself in the same way as the men's except that the women had no chaplain, since they believed only the men needed one.

In the era between the wars North American women who wanted to enjoy curling were advised even by other women to avoid striving for excellence or victory and to curl only for wholesome exercise. This view echoes that of college physical education teachers of the period, who discouraged athletic women from trying hard to win because they believed a competitive spirit could harm the female reproductive system. Published curling rules used the masculine pronouns *he, his,* and *him,* and as late as 1964 the Manitoba Curling Association stressed that the ultimate object of curling is to be a *Manly recreation.*

After World War II wives of male curlers who wanted to watch their husbands curl were said to be invading men's sacred premises (the clubrooms associated with the rinks). But their presence enhanced the social aspect of the clubs, inspiring dances and other affairs, altering the atmosphere of curling clubs from a world once strictly reserved for men to one more like a community center set up for social gatherings.

In 1935 Canadian men formed the Dominion Curling Association, later called the Canadian Curling Association. Canadian women, after competing in various regional playoffs, were granted an opportunity to take part in a national event in 1961, when the men's association finally provided a national women's championship. With no commercial backer, Canadian women sponsored their own championships until 1972, when the tobacco company that sponsored the men's championship backed a women's event called the Lassie. That backing lasted until 1979, after which the women were again on their own until 1982, when a paper company supported their national competition.

Canadian women's play gradually improved to the point where their skill approached that of men. Joyce McKee of Saskatchewan, skip (captain) of national championship teams in the 1960s and early 1970s, reputedly revolutionized the women's game by helping to introduce a long, sliding delivery and an aggressive approach to play. By the 1970s Canadian women had developed strong and beautiful deliveries, and their sweeping, too, was compared favorably with men's.

Among the public, however, women's curling still attracted much less interest than the men's. Mabel Mitchell of Brandon, Manitoba, recalled that in this era she curled in important women's events at which participants outnumbered spectators. The first time a women's championship featured all the ceremony and crowd enthusiasm of a major men's event, she said, was the 1968 championship, and that day tears came to her eyes because there was a pipe band, a feature of the all-important men's competitions, and the stands were full of people. Some felt that this exciting event was so well arranged because a woman, Lura McLuckie, ran it. Canadian national mixed play—men's teams playing women's teams—began in 1964 under the sponsorship of a liquor company.

Canada's passion for curling spilled over the border into the northern part of the United States, especially Minnesota and Wisconsin. In 1947, nine years before American men organized, American women curlers formed a national organization, the United States Women's Curling Association (USWCA). Most elite national and international events for both genders of Americans are, however, sponsored by the men's organization. The women agreed to affiliate with it only after long solicitation by the men's association, which, said USWCA officer Anne Winslow, "envied us our cash position and alluded to our 'full cookie jar' so often as to make us very uneasy." Over the years, the milieu of American women's curling reportedly shifted from friendly competition to stalwart competitiveness.

CURLING BECOMES GLOBAL

Women's first world curling championship in 1979 featured teams from eleven countries; besides Scotland, Canada, and the United States, it included women from Denmark, England, France, Germany, Italy, Norway, Sweden, and Switzerland. Since 1989 women's and men's world championships have been held jointly. Canadian women have dominated the world events by winning ten championships, but in 1998 the Swedish team headed by Elisabet Gustafson, a surgeon, won the honors.

When curling made its debut as a medal sport in the 1998 Winter Olympics in Nagano, Japan, Canadian women under Sandra Schmirler won the gold, defeating a Danish team headed by Helena Blach Lavrsen. The silver medal won by Danish women influenced the municipality of Copenhagen to expand city curling rinks from the one then currently available (when it was not being repaired) to two. The ten Danish women's teams practice mostly on ice hockey rinks.

Despite the World Curling Federation's continued use of *he*, *his*, and *him* in its official handbook, curling today is a women's game as well as a men's sport. Women's bonspiel (tournament) prizes are generally smaller than men's, but that doesn't mean women are discriminated against, says Linda Moore, who has played on winning Canadian teams in world competition. Prizes must be smaller when there are fewer participants, fewer because women cannot usually take as much time away from home responsibilities as can men. Prizes are also smaller because of lower entry fees. Women, because of lower wages in the workaday world, often cannot afford high entry fees or the travel and accommodation expenses related to curling with a team, although curling clubs, sponsors, and local and national associations have been very supportive of women's teams, and the Sports Network on TV has helped

JAPAN TAKES SILVER IN JUNIOR LADIES' CURLING CHAMPIONSHIP

Since 1988 young women curlers from various countries have played in a world junior ladies' championship. In 1998 in Canada a Japanese team, coached by Canadian Elaine Dagg-Jackson, won the silver. The team leader, Akiko Katoh, according to Dagg-Jackson, was "a one-woman show. . . . She won the first three games by herself" (*Victoria [British Columbia] Times-Colonist*, 6 April 1998). The Japanese finally lost 11–3 to a Canadian team from New Brunswick, but the coach anticipated her charges would find that winning momentum again.

Katoh, born in Hokkaido in 1978, has curled only since 1994. In Japan she was a member of the Tokoro Curling Club. But for six months she lived in Victoria, and trained there under Dagg-Jackson, along with the Japanese men's and women's national teams. In winning the silver, the young women curlers brought Japan its first medal in curling.

This occasion marked only the third time Japan had made the playoffs in any world curling category. The Japanese had never seen curling before an American demonstrated it in Tokyo in 1967 and a Canadian taught it in 1979. By the 1990s the World Curling Federation was regularly getting e-mail from Japanese wanting to know how they can start curling.

bring women's curling to public attention, according to Moore.

RULES AND PLAY

Each player takes a turn sliding two stones toward the house, a series of three concentric circles approximately 40 meters (130 feet) away, near the end of the ice sheet. After a stone is thrown and begins sliding with a curving trajectory, other team members sweep the ice in its path to alter direction and/or speed and to remove any pebbling or foreign objects. When all sixteen stones are delivered in each end (team turn), a team scores 1 point for each stone that finishes the closest to the button (center of the innermost circle). The team with the most points scored after an agreed-upon number of ends are played wins the game.

CONCLUSION

Women's curling can make a colorful spectacle. The carefully aimed throw, followed by the intense and skillful sweeping of other team members in their smart uniforms, is complemented by the shrill cries of the skip (captain) and the thrower giving directions to the sweepers over the bass growl of the speeding, curving rock. When the rock stops sliding, then come the admiring murmurs and polite clapping and cheering of the crowd.

Dorothy Jane Mills

Bibliography

Canadian Association for the Advancement of Women and Sport and Physical Activity (CAAWS) and Women's Program Sport Canada. (1993) *Towards Gender Equity for Women in Sport: A Handbook for Sport Organizations*. Gloucester, Ontario: CAAWS.

Creelman, William Albert. (1950) *Curling Past and Present*. Toronto: McClelland & Stewart.

Eberlein, Doris, ed. (1997) *United States Women's Curling Association: 1947–1997 Historical Review*. Wausau, WI: Presto Prints.

Komosky, Dave. (1982–1983) "Where Are They Today?" In *Curling Canada*, 24. Ottawa: Canadian Curling Association.

Lukowitch, Ed, Eigil Ramsfell, and Bud Somerville. (1990) *The Joy of Curling*. Toronto: McGraw Hill-Ryerson.

Manitoba Curling Association. (1964) *76th Annual Bonspiel 1964, Winnipeg, Monday, February 3, The Manitoba Curling Association*. Winnipeg: Manitoba Curling Association.

Messner, Michael A., and Donald F. Sabo, eds. (1990) *Sport, Men, and the Gender Order: Critical Feminist Perspectives*. Champaign, IL: Human Kinetics.

Moore, Linda. (11 May 1998) Personal Communication.

Mott, Morris K., and John Allardyce. (1989) *Curling Capital: Winnipeg and the Roarin' Game, 1876 to 1989*. Winnipeg: University of Manitoba Press.

Murray, William Hutchison. (1982) *The Curling Companion*. Toronto: Collins.

Smith, David B. (1981) *Curling, An Illustrated History*. Edinburgh: John Donald.

Smith, Peter M. "Icing." International Curling Information Group, <http://icing.org>. May 1998.

Watson, James Kenneth. (1963) "The Anniversary Story of Curling in Manitoba." In *75th Anniversary Bonspiel, Winnipeg, Monday, February 4th, The Manitoba Curling Association*. Winnipeg: Manitoba Curling Association.

Welsh, Robin. (1985) *International Guide to Curling*. London: Pelham.

World Curling Federation. "Official Handbook." <http://www.worldsport.com>. 1997.

CUTHBERT, BETTY

(1938–)

AUSTRALIAN TRACK ATHLETE

Betty Cuthbert is the holder of the most gold medals in Australian Olympic track and field history. In the 1956 Melbourne Olympic Games, she won gold medals in the 100- and 200-meter dashes as well as the 4 × 100-meter relay. In winning her first gold medal, she became the first Australian to win a gold medal on home soil.

Cuthbert was born on 20 April 1938 in Ermington, Sydney, Australia. Successful as a sprinter in school, she came to the attention of Australian coach June Ferguson, who had won a silver medal as a member of the Australian women's 4 × 100-meter relay team at the 1948 Olympics. Cuthbert set world records in the 100-yard dash in 1953 and the 200-meter dash in 1956; she became a well-known figure in Australia because her rivalry room after her, and the grandstand for the 2000 Olympics in Sydney is also named for her.

Holly Cliett

Bibliography

"Betty Cuthbert." <http://www.coolrunning.com>. 1999.

Cashman, Richard. (1997) *Australian Sport Through Time*. Sydney: Random House.

"Grandstand." <http://www.siac.nsw.gov.au/>. 1999.

"Legends." <http://www.ausport.gov.au/>. 1999.

Betty Cuthbert is shown winning the 100-meter final at the 1956 Olympic Games. (Bettmann/Corbis)

with fellow-Australian sprinter Marlene Matthews was widely publicized. Cuthbert's triumphs at the 1956 Olympics made her a national celebrity, and she was named Sportstar of the Year in 1956.

At the 1960 Olympics, Cuthbert was hampered by injuries, and American Wilma Rudolph replaced her as the premier woman Olympic sprinter. However, Cuthbert recovered and in an amazing effort moved up to the 400-meter run and took the gold at the 1964 Olympics. She considered this to be her greatest athletic accomplishment, and it was recognized by the Helms Award for the year. Cuthbert is one of the few Australian Olympians to have won four gold medals in four separate events. By the time she retired from competition after the 1964 Olympics, she had set eleven world records in sprints from 60 to 400 meters and had been a member of relay teams that set another five world records.

Following her career, Cuthbert battled multiple sclerosis and in the 1990s experienced financial problems after losing money in a bad business deal. She was swindled by a man who claimed he wanted to set up a trust fund to help the disabled and needy. Cuthbert was eager to help, and she and a friend rushed to donate what they could. This experience did not dampen her charitable spirit, and in May 1998 she donated a commemorative plaque to raise money for Australia's Commonwealth Games team. She has remained a prominent figure in the Australian running scene: The Melbourne Cricket Club named a

CYCLING

Cycling is a major form of recreation and exercise as well as a competitive sport in Western Europe and North America and a major form of transportation in many other parts of the world. Cycling as a recreational activity and sport for women has an interesting and somewhat unique history. It is one of the few sports that has involved women from the beginning of the sport, although it later declined in popularity among women. And, it is also one of the few sports associated with the women's rights movement, since access to the bicycle in the late 1880s gave women more freedom to travel away from the home and also allowed them to wear clothing other than dresses or skirts. In the 1990s cycling was a relatively minor sport for both men and women, although it drew participants from many nations and had become more popular with women than earlier in the century.

HISTORY

The exact origin of the bicycle is uncertain, and the available historical record is subject to various interpretations. Although prototypes of the modern bicycle date to 1791 in France and the early 1800s in Germany and Scotland, the main advance in what was then called the "velocipède" occurred in Paris around 1863, when Pierre Michaux and his son, Ernest, modified a client's velocipède when it was in for repair by adding a

BICYCLES BRING WOMEN EXERCISE AND FREEDOM

Unlike many other sports where women's participation was the result of increased opportunities for women, cycling in the late 1800s and early 1900s actually helped women gain more freedom. Cycling served as an inexpensive and safe form of transportation that allowed women to travel further from home than before and on a more regular basis. It was also an activity that made them healthier and afforded women the choice of wearing sportier clothing. Unfortunately, much of this progress was lost with the arrival of mass produced automobiles in the early twentieth century. Automobile ownership and driving was defined as a male domain and with the demise of cycling as a form of transportation, many women found themselves again dependent on men for traveling away from the home.

pedal crank to the front wheel. The new modification caught on, and the Michauxes built 400 velocipèdes (otherwise known as the "boneshaker" because of the rough ride) per year and could not keep up with the demand. There is some dispute about who should get credit for adding the front-wheel cranks to the cycle. The Michauxes claimed to have conceived the idea in 1861, but their employee, Pierre Lallemont, who was the technician who installed the front-wheel cranks, also claimed to have come up with the idea; he later moved to the United States and patented the invention. The popularity of the bicycle became widespread in 1885, when the safety bicycle with two wheels of equal size and a chain drive was introduced in the United States. Since then the bicycle has continued to experience continuous modification, and in the 1990s cycles came in numerous sizes, shapes, designs, weights, and prices. The old tradition of "women's bikes" and "men's bikes" has largely disappeared and both ride same-style bicycles, with variations in design and configuration based on the rider's height, weight, and purpose in riding.

Cycling became popular in France as a sport in the 1860s, and the first track races for men and then women were held in 1868 in Paris. The first road races, again for men and women, were held the following year, on the 76-mile (122-kilometer) route from Paris to Rouen. Cycling as a sport spread to England, Australia, and the United States, and its popularity spread as bicycle design was improved and the ride became safer, easier, and faster. While women continued to compete in France and, to a lesser extent, in the United States, Victorian attitudes discouraged women in England and Australia from sport cycling in the late 1800s, although cycling as a leisure pursuit remained popular for the middle class. The invention of the motorcycle and automobile, and the mass production of both, rendered the bicycle obsolete as a major form of transportation in the early twentieth century, and cycling declined as a popular sport. For the first several decades of the century, women rarely competed in races. Women began competing in the U.S. national championships in 1937 and in the international championships in 1958. Bicycling for men was introduced at the first modern Olympics in 1896 but not until 1984 for women, when they competed for the first time in a road race. In 1984 the first women's Tour de France, the 616-mile (991-kilometer) Tour de France Féminin, was held, although it has yet to compete in popularity with the men's event.

CYCLING AND WOMEN'S LIVES

The cycle (velocipède) contributed to the expansion of women's leisure activities in the late 1800s and began to change social notions about appropriate physical recreational activity and attire for women. Prior to this time, family-oriented leisure experiences were not always perceived as leisure

Female professional bicyclists in a 1989 race. (ChromaSohm)

by women, since they were usually expected to bear the burdens of the support role in making preparations, providing on-site domestic services, and cleaning up after an outing. For the most part, women's leisure engagements were restricted to rather passive but "respectable" Victorian roles of support—such as peripheral involvement in appropriate male/female social encounters; serving as spectators at horse racing, ice skating, baseball, and other male events; and providing applause.

This view began to change in England as early as 1831, when an article in *The Journal of Health* promoted the notion that physical activity was good for women, thus opening up a range of possible activities for women beyond passive forms. In addition, outdoor forms of recreation were promoted for women because they were viewed as providing healthful experiences and also because there was a lack of indoor facilities. However, a woman's participation had to be consistent with and reflect the societal ideal of womanly beauty,

aesthetics, and grace. For women this meant finding an activity that would not result in breaking "an indelicate sweat." This, of course, resulted in a relatively limited number of permissible leisure activities for women, including horseback riding, sleigh and carriage riding, ice and roller skating, swimming and bathing, and biking.

During the 1860s, some women began to ride the popular "boneshaker," and this act literally and figuratively helped to propel them out of their kitchens and limited leisure roles. In comparison to their European counterparts, American female cyclists were viewed as a bold and brazen lot. Joseph Bottomley, writing in his book from London, *The Velocipede, Its Past, Its Present, Its Future,* pointed out the differences between the American bicycle and the European tricycle designs for females. Bottomley expressed contempt for the wayward American version of the female cycle and pointedly condemned it as another example of the loose state of American morals, writing: "If French

WOMEN'S ROAD RACE CHAMPIONS OF 1999

Paris-Roubaix: Andrea Tafi, Italy
Women's Tour de France: Diana Ziliute, Lithuania

World Cup, Overall: Anna Wilson, Australia
U. S. Pro Road: Mary Jemison, United States

or English ladies are bent on velocipedestination, this [Parisian ladies' tricycle] is the machine they will have to perform on. Of course the Bloomers and Mary Walkers of the States cannot rest content with such a machine, but we in Europe are still so old-fashioned as to prefer propriety to sensation." Bottomley's writings provide insight into the stereotyped and limited niche that "nice" women were supposed to occupy.

At first, women rode sidesaddle on the bicycles as they did while horseback riding, since it was not considered proper for a women to straddle a bicycle as did the men. Sitting sidesaddle, however, did not permit women very much active involvement in the cycling experience. In the 1870s Catharine Beecher began to advocate vigorous daily exercise for women as well as men. Some women began to heed this advice as well as their own inclinations toward physical activity, pursuing cycling and other sports. As a matter of practicality and safety, there was a need for better-designed women's garments that permitted greater ease in movement. Women at this time were not usually encouraged to exercise strenuously, and their clothing was designed, with female modesty in mind, to conceal most of their body and restrict movement.

Amelia Jenks Bloomer, from Homer, New York, became an early advocate for more sensible women's clothing and experimented with a new design that included a divided skirt or loose-fitting pantaloon-style pants. These were worn under a dress to allow greater freedom of movement. This alternative outfit became known as "Bloomers" or a "Bloomers Costume." This attire was readily adopted by many women cyclists, horseback riders, gymnasts, and skaters in the United States and Europe. Women who wore this outfit were referred to as "Bloomer Girls" or "Bloomerites." Many of these women joined women's circles where they discussed social and political issues of the day. Cycling and bloomers (which spread as far as Japan as sports clothing for women) became associated with the social reform agenda of the women's rights movement. The women's suffrage leader Elizabeth Cady Stanton remarked that "many a woman is riding to suffrage on a bicycle."

RULES AND PLAY

Over the years, diversification in cycling race events has occurred in both men's and women's competitions. Short and long races, and races with different strategies and tests of abilities, as well as speed, have been added to the sport. Three main race categories existed in the 1990s: road, track, and mountain. Road races consist of individual and team trials in which the objective is to race against the clock over open roads on flat and hilly courses. An event called the criterium is a multilap race where racers compete to cross the finish line first.

Track cycling involves three components: time trials, pursuits, and sprints. Competitors use lightweight bicycles that have neither gear mechanisms nor brakes. The races are held on a banked track arena called a velodrome. Speed, skill, power, and strategy are displayed in track cycling. The pursuits event is novel and exciting, since two competitors are positioned at opposite ends of the velodrome and attempt to pursue and pass the other in order to finish first.

Mountain-bike races include three types: cross-country, downhill, and slalom. These races feature courses over open country with unpaved trails that include steep uphill and downhill slopes. Strength, skill, endurance, and nerves are put to the test. In 1996 mountain biking was added as an Olympic Games event.

Three other cycling races should be noted as well: cyclo-cross, a race that includes trails over different terrain and often requires carrying the bicycle through a body of water; the triathlon, which mixes cycling with running and swimming; and distance events, such as the Tour de France Féminin and the Race Across America.

At the 1996 Olympics, women competed in six events as compared to nine for men. For women, these were the individual sprint (three laps), 3000-meter individual pursuit, individual points race, individual race, individual time trial, and cross-country mountain-bike event. The leading women bikers came from France and Italy, as well as Australia and Germany.

Katharine A. Pawelko

See also Longo-Ciprelli, Jeannie; Triathlon

Bibliography

Dempsey, Paul. (1977) *The Bicycler's Bible*. Blue Ridge Summit, PA: TAB Books.

Gattey, Charles. (1968) *The Bloomer Girls*. New York: Coward, McCann.

Gerber, Ellen., Jan Felshin, Pearl Berline, and Waneen Wyrick. (1974) *The American Woman in Sport*. Reading, MA: Addison-Wesley.

Henderson, Karla A., M. Deborah Bialeschki, Susan M. Shaw, and Valeria J. Freysinger. (1989) *A Leisure of One's Own: A Feminist Perspective on Women's Leisure*. State College, PA: Venture Publishing.

Oliver, Smith Hempstone, and Donald H. Berkebile. (1974) *Wheels and Wheeling: The Smithsonian Cycle Collection* (Smithsonian Studies in History and Technology, Number 24). Washington, DC: Smithsonian Institution Press.

Wagenvoord, James. (1972) *Bikes and Riders*. New York: Van Nostrand Reinhold.

Welch, Paula D., and Harold A. Lerch. (1996) *History of American Physical Education and Sport*, 2d ed. Springfield, IL: Charles C. Thomas.

CYNISCA

More than any other Greek city-state, ancient Sparta emphasized athletics for girls as well as for boys. They ran races, wrestled, and proved themselves fit to bear the healthy sons who became the city's defenders. According to the not-always-reliable historian Athenaeus of Naucratis (third century CE), Spartan girls drove two-horse char-

iots and raced them at the annual festival of Hyacinthus. It was, therefore, appropriate that the first woman ever to glory in an Olympic victory was Cynisca, a Spartan princess who bred horses and was the owner (not the driver) of the winning chariots at two successive Olympics (probably those of 396 and 392 BCE). In her honor, a statue by Apelles was erected at the site. The statue's inscription, recording the first of her victories, refers to King Archidamus, her father, and to King Agesilaos, her brother: "My father and brothers were kings of Sparta. I, Cynisca, won a victory with my swift-running horses and set up this statue. I claim that I am the only woman from all Greece to have won this crown." Other women of royal birth and great wealth, among them Berenice II of Cyrene (second century BCE), entered successful chariots at the Olympics and at other Greek athletic festivals. The travel writer Pausanius, visiting Olympia more than 500 years after Cynisca's victories, discovered that none of these other women was as famous as she.

Allen Guttmann

Bibliography

Moretti, Luigi. (1953) *Iscrizioni Agonistiche Greche*. Rome: Angelo Signorelli.

Pausanias. (1918–1933) *Description of Greece*, 4 vols. Trans. by W. H. S. Jones. London: Heineman.

CZECHOSLOVAKIA; CZECH REPUBLIC; SLOVAKIAN REPUBLIC

The Czech Republic and the Slovak Republic are located in Eastern Europe and have populations of 10.3 and 5.5 million people, respectively. The two republics have a very complicated history. They were originally part of the Czechoslovakian

Czechoslovakian competitors in the 12th annual International Archery Tournament, 1948. (Hulton-Deutsch Collection/Corbis)

Republic, which was founded in 1918 as one of the successor states of the Austro-Hungarian Empire, ruled by the Hapsburg monarchy. In World War II, they were separated during the German occupation; they were reunited in 1945, forming a Czechoslovakian communist federation. With the end of communist rule after the peaceful victory of Prague's "velvet revolution," the federation dissolved in 1989. In 1993, the independent Czech and Slovak Republics came into existence. Women, who had been participating in sports in a limited way since the late nineteenth century, became increasingly active as sports generally became more acceptable for them. The decades of communist rule after World War II brought many more women into sports, and in the 1990s women remained involved in many sports.

CZECHOSLOVAKIAN REPUBLIC

The founding of the Czechoslovakian Republic had a positive influence on new sport organizations that had come into existence in the early twentieth century. At the Olympic Games in Antwerp in 1920, the Czech tennis player Milena Skrbkova won the bronze medal in the mixed-doubles competition. Soon, a handball organization was formed, as was a women's sport organiza-

zation. In 1930, these groups succeeded in bringing the third women's world games to Prague. The sprinter Marie Mejzlikova successfully defended several international records, and Czech women did well in rowing and gymnastics. At the Berlin Olympic Games in 1936, the Czechoslovakian women's team won the silver medal in the gymnastics team event.

World War II ended the first republic and disrupted the progress women were making in sports participation. However, the country's female athletes made a significant contribution to the war. In her book *Naelnice*, Marie Provazníková tells of the role the Sokol women played in the resistance movement against the Germans during the years of occupation between 1938 and 1945. The gymnastic organization became an important part of the Czech underground movement. In this case, it proved to be an advantage that this organization had always been political as well as athletic.

After World War II, the region came under Soviet control and was reunited as Czechoslovakia with a communist government. Under centralized government control and as part of the Cold War competition between the communist and Western nations, sports became an instrument to control the people and to gain international prestige through victories in the Olympics and other international competitions. The original Sokol movement was dissolved, even though the new central organization kept the old name. Sokol celebrations were turned into Spartakiads, in which women played a subordinate role, as they had in the early days of the movement. However, the emphasis on creating world-class athletes in accord with the Soviet agenda for sports enabled women to participate and excel in a wider range of sports than previously. Czech women gymnasts soon became the best in the world. At the first postwar Olympics in London in 1948, the Czech women's gymnastic team won the gold medal. The Czech track and field athlete Dana Zátopková took the gold in 1952 and the silver in 1960 in the javelin throw. Olga Fikotová took the gold in the discus throw at the Melbourne Olympics in 1956, and Miloslava Rezková won the high-jump competition in Mexico City in the 1968 Olympics. The 400- and 800-meter runner Jarmila Kratochvílová took the silver at the 1980 Olym-

WOMEN JOIN THE SOKOL MOVEMENT

Following the end of communist rule, the repressed Sokol movement re-emerged with women at the forefront. Over 50% of Sokol members in the Czech Republic are women, and they have played a leading role in promoting recreational sports, staging national sport festivals, and supporting professional sports.

pics in Moscow but lost a chance for Olympic victory when communist-bloc nations boycotted the 1984 Los Angeles Games.

The premier Czech female athlete was the gymnast Caslavska, who won three gold medals at the Tokyo Olympics in 1964 and four more in Mexico City in 1968. She also took the lead in again linking sports with Czech freedom and democracy when she signed the famous Manifesto of 2000 Words during the "Prague Spring" of 1968. She signed along with Czech sport heroes Emil Zátopek and Jírí Raka. The International Olympic Committee (IOC) ignored the Czech members' request to exclude from the Olympic Games those Warsaw Treaty nations that had just intervened militarily in Prague in August 1968.

Caslavska then gave her four Mexico City gold medals to the leaders of the "Prague Spring"-Dubcek, Smrkovsky, Svoboda, and Černik.

After the fall of communism in 1989, Caslavska became president of the National Olympic Committee of Czechoslovakia in 1990. In 1992, after the two republics formed their own Olympic committees, she became president of the Czech National Olympic Committee, a position she held until 1996. At the eighteenth congress of the IOC in Budapest, she was appointed a member of the IOC, becoming one of only a few women in that largely male body.

At the professional level, Czech women are best known for their success in tennis. Players of Czech birth such as Martina Navratilova and Martina Hingis as well as the Czech players Jana Novotná and Helena Suková have been successful on the women's professional tour. In the postcommunist years, there has also been a reemergence of the Sokol movement, which has made sports for the masses attractive again. In 1999, the Sokol had 200,000 members and offered a wide range of new opportunities and chances for women who wanted to get involved in sports. At the Atlanta Olympics in 1996, the Czech team included thirty-one women. Stepárnna Hilgertová won the gold medal in the canoe-slalom and Sárka Kaspárnová the bronze medal in the hop-skip-and-jump.

CZECH REPUBLIC

In Czech territory, the first major sports movement was the gymnastics movement, which originated in the Sokol (falcon) gymnastics club, founded in Prague in 1862. The gymnastics movement was part of a nationalistic movement within the Czech region to give it a distinct identity within the Austro-Hungarian Empire. The Sokol soon became the largest Czech gymnastics organization, always being far more popular than the workers' gymnastics club and the Orel (eagle) organizations, which were supported by the church.

In the Sokol movement, women were at first limited to such secondary activities as helping with receptions, raising money, sewing the organization's flag, and participating in the important flag ceremony, which symbolized the links between the Czech community and the national gymnastics movement. But Sokol's regulations prevented women from being members. In 1869, however, Prague's Sokol club openly supported the formation of the first Gymnastics Club of the Ladies and Girls of Prague and made the Sokol's gymnastics hall available to women. The leading members of this first Czech women's gymnastics club came from the middle class, who formed the leadership of the Sokol movement, and from the segment of the Czech community that supported the Czech nationalism movement.

Klemena Hanusová, a model pupil of the Sokol founder, became their first gymnastics teacher and wrote about women's gymnastics, including an important three-volume book *Dívcí Tlocvik* (*Girls' Gymnastics*) written between 1872 and 1887. In 1882, the club had ninety-two active members. The next major step in the development of women's gymnastics was the founding in 1890 of the first girls' college in Prague, where physical education was taught by female teachers from Prague's women's gymnastics club.

By the end of the nineteenth century, young Czech women were more eager to participate in sports. Their enthusiasm was the product of two trends. The first was the general modernization ushered in by industrialization. At the same time, many women from all over Europe were actively involved in sports, and Czech women wanted to do the same. They formed their own women's sections within the Sokol clubs. By 1893, there were sixty sections where approximately 2,000 gymnasts were coached and supervised. As women's sports became more popular, the clubs began to include young women from the lower middle class. In 1898, these women's sections had their first public performance and, three years later, some 875 female Sokol gymnasts presented themselves at the general Sokol parade in Prague. This is viewed as the traditional highlight of the movement.

Despite these developments, women became discouraged with their slow rate of progress. Under the Sokol rules, women were looked upon as juveniles, which meant that they had the status of adolescents and no equal membership rights, and thus no right of determining their participation; nor could they hold leadership positions in the organization. This situation changed shortly before World War I, when 17 percent of the Sokol members were women. This was the highest percentage of women in any organization—sport, political, or labor—in Eastern Europe at the time. During World War I, the women involved in the Sokol movement strengthened their positions in such a way that at the Sokol celebration in 1920, women were allowed to participate in the marches. And for the first time in united Czechoslovakia women were granted their own female coaches, called *náelnice*.

SLOVAKIAN REPUBLIC

From 1918 until 1993, Slovakia was part of the Czechoslovakian Republic, with the two separated only during the fictitious independence of World War II, although during this period the new republic did form a National Olympic Committee, which existed from 1939 to 1945. After World War II, the Slovakian and Czech organizations for physical education were united under one central federation. It was only after the formation of its own national Olympic committee in Bratislava in 1992 that Slovakia was accepted by the IOC one year later.

Slovakian sport has been independent for such a short time that it is difficult to say anything specific about the role and status of women. The vice president of Slovakia's national Olympic committee is a woman, Mária Mracnová. In 1994, Slovakia participated for the first time at the Winter Olympics in Lillehammer, Norway, with an independent team of forty-one athletes. There were seven women on the team competing in downhill and cross-country skiing, biathlon, and luge. At the Atlanta Olympics, twelve women and eighty-three men formed the Slovakian team. Women competed in track and field, gymnastics, swimming, table tennis, and tennis. In the Nagano Winter Olympics in 1998, the Slovakian team consisted of nine women and thirty-eight men. The women participated in biathlon, cross-country skiing, luge, and snowboarding.

Diethelm Blecking

See also Sokol Movement

Bibliography

Kössl, Jírí. (1998) "The History of the Czech Olympic Movement—A Legacy for the Future." *Bulletin of the Czech Olympic Committee,* 18–53.

Nolte, Claire. (1993) " 'Every Czech a Sokol!': Feminism and Nationalism in the Czech Sokol Movement." *Austrian History Yearbook,* Vol. 24, 79–100.

Provaznikova, Marie. (1988) *To byl sokol* [*This was the sokol*]. Munich: Ceské Slovo.

Slovak Olympic Committee. (1998) *Slovakia Nagano 98.* Bratislava: Slovak Olympic Committee.

Stumbauer, Jan, and Marek Waic. (1995) "The Origin and the Beginnings of Women's Physical Education in the Czech Lands." *Acta Universitatis Carolinae, Kinanthropologica* 31, 2: 19–28.

D

DANCE

Dance includes a wide variety of forms of rhythmic physical movement, usually performed to music, and serves as a popular leisure pursuit, important form of artistic endeavor, and competitive activity with many athletic elements. In its many forms throughout human history, it has been a vital part of religious ritual, an important performance art, and a significant form of relaxation. Dance has often played an important role in women's lives. In 1917 the New York City Board of Education's Inspector of Athletics for Girls called dance the best female sport and, in many times and places, it has been the only accepted form of vigorous physical activity for women. Dance is linked today with women's sports in both organized programs and informal participation, and many forms of dance, including ballroom dancing, are increasingly popular in schools and colleges. Although males and females today dance leading roles in modern dance, many of the most significant early pioneers were women.

DANCE IN SOCIETY

While considering vast contextual differences in time period and culture, one can identify four primary reasons why people have danced throughout history: (1) to please the gods; (2) to please others; (3) to please themselves; and (4) to build community within an ethnic group. Dances performed to please the gods include the southwestern Native American corn dance of the Jemez Pueblo, a ritualistic dance performed by the whole community; or the fifteenth-century *los seises*, a Roman Catholic choirboy dance performed during church holidays in the cathedral of Seville, Spain. Dances performed to please others range from those seen in a contemporary all-male *Kabuki* performance in Japan to the traditional Balinese *legong* for young girls to those seen in a performance by the Martha Graham

Ballerina Anna Pavlova (1882-1931). (Corbis/Hulton-Deutsch Collection)

Dance Company at the Joyce Theatre in New York City. Most people are familiar with examples of dancing to please oneself, whether through aerobic dancing for the sake of fitness or for the sheer kinesthetic pleasure of movement to music. Dances performed specifically to build a sense of community include *la marcha*, a group dance traditionally performed at Hispanic weddings; the *kalamatianos*, a Greek social dance; the *mayim*, an Israeli folk dance; and the *koko sawa*, a playful West African dance for boys and girls. Since people throughout the ages have danced, abundant examples demonstrate the breadth of reasons why people have danced—around the globe and through time.

STYLES OF DANCE

Women and men have generally had different dance styles and roles in dance. In traditional ritualistic dances, gender roles are a dominating factor. Women's dances often have such themes as planting, harvest, relationships, or child rearing, whereas men's dances deal with war, hunting, or displays of physical prowess. Female ritualistic dancing often utilizes subtlety in its use of gestures, and a compact use of space. Male dances are usually more physically mobile, with bold and energetic movements.

Styles of dance also vary from culture to culture. Around the globe, identifiable characteristics may be associated with individual cultures. Traditional Asian dance, for example, has remained closely linked with worship and has generally adhered to ancient forms and legends in its choreography, costumes, and musical accompaniment. Characteristics of Asian dance movement include a fluid body stance with a flexible use of the spine. The hips, rib cage, head, and shoulders shift from side to side, while the legs glide in a low level over the ground. The overall movement quality is multifocused, with a bound flow and a light use of weight. The arms, fingers, hands, and eyes perform subtle and expressive movements while stylized facial expressions are utilized. In most Asian dance forms, one finds a distinction between more vigorous and athletic dancing for males and more confined and subtle dancing for females.

African dance, on the other hand, has evolved through time from a religious and community-building context into a means of personal fulfillment or theatrical performance. African dance has always been closely tied to the music with which it is performed. African dance, like African music, is frequently polyrhythmic, with contrasting rhythms and musical gestures occurring simultaneously. The movement style is strong and free flowing, with the body weight rooted in the earth. The head, shoulders, rib cage, and hips move in a flexible manner, often to independent rhythms, while the legs are often bent. In African dance forms, both males and females sometimes dance in a strong and grounded manner. Some dances, such as the *adowa*, are gender-specific; the female version is more subtle and expressive and the male version more aggressive and exhibitionistic.

In contrast, most classical European dance incorporates a stable and erect spine, with hips, shoulders, and arms held framing the torso. Classical European dances often use bent legs only as a preparation to jump or to accentuate the extension of the legs. The body is generally held erect, with a light use of weight, and an emphasis on intricate footwork. High jumps and leg extensions are frequently used in ballet technique and in some forms of folk dance. Ballets often feature women in spectacular displays of exhibitionism, whereas male dancers frequently take on supporting roles.

American dance forms, with the exception of traditional Native American dances, are a fairly new addition to world dance. Jazz dance, tap dance, and modern dance are uniquely American forms and vary widely in style. Jazz dance has its roots in Africa and has developed into an eclectic mix of styles, including Broadway dance, lyrical jazz dance, and various street-dance forms (e.g., hip-hop dance). Tap dance is derived from a mix of British Isles step dancing and dances of African slaves in the colonial United States. Modern dance, which has European as well as American roots, incorporates a flexible use of the spine and a lower and stronger use of body weight than ballet technique.

WESTERN DANCE BEFORE BALLET

Since ancient times, dance has been associated with ritual and worship. In ancient Egypt, the goddess Isis was the center of a cult celebrating the rising and falling of the Nile River. Dance and music played a significant part in this agricultural ritual. Egyptian priests, who were also astronomers, imitated the movements of the sun and cosmos during ritual functions. Egyptian courts and temples maintained specially trained dancers to participate in ceremonial functions.

With regard to dance in Western civilization, the ancient Greeks have exerted a profound influence. Dance flourished among the ancient Greeks during the classical period (540–300 BCE). The Greeks viewed the union of dance, music, and poetry as symbolic of the harmony of mind and body. Dance was seen as a metaphor for order and harmony in the heavens; dance enriched theatrical presentations, as well as religious festivals. Young men were taught to dance as part of their military training; guests were entertained by professional dancers at banquets; and at many religious festivals everyone danced, men and women, young and old, aristocrats and peasants. According to Greek mythology, the cultivation and preservation of dance was entrusted to Terpsichore, the muse of dance. Two Greek gods, Apollo and Dionysus, also came to symbolize the two basic approaches to dance: virtuoso technique (Apollonian) or unrestrained emotional expression (Dionysian).

During the Roman Empire, dance became increasingly divorced from poetry and music. As a result the art form that later became known as pantomime flourished. Over time, there grew to be a lewd, violent, and sensationalistic side to Roman entertainment. Scholars have cited instances in which captured slaves and condemned prisoners were forced to dance in an arena until the flammable clothing they wore was set on fire and they died in agony. In 426, Saint Augustine denounced the cruelty of the arena games and the vulgarity of pantomime, blaming the debauched state of Roman society.

As Christianity spread slowly throughout Europe during the Middle Ages, the use of dance in public festivals became limited. Unlike traditional Asian dance, which has remained closely linked with worship, the idea of dance as worship struck many Europeans of the time as sacrilegious. The Christian church eventually adopted a policy discouraging all large public gatherings that included dance and theatrical performances and, by 744, forbade all secular forms of dance. The eighth-century English priest Alcuin characterized the situation in his admonition, "The man who brings actors and mimes and dancers to his house knows not what a bevy of unclean spirits follow them." Anyone engaging in public dancing was cast out of the church, ostracized from society, and denied Christian burial.

Although dance as public entertainment was severely limited because of restrictions imposed by the Christian church, everyday life during the Middle Ages was not devoid of dancing. Medieval guilds representing the workers in a particular profession, developed ritual activities, in-

cluding dances that were specifically related to the occupations they represented. These guilds were authorized to hold public celebrations during the pre-Lenten carnival. Musicians' guilds, founded by royal decree, not only provided music for social gatherings for the nobility but also took over the teaching of dance steps. Throughout Europe licenses were granted for the teaching of dance to persons who had demonstrated not only a thorough knowledge of music but also the ability to execute dance steps, to create new dances, and to notate dances.

With the coming of the Renaissance, members of the nobility organized an elaborate court life for themselves, their associates, and their servants. Intricate rituals of dressing, etiquette, and personal fashion evolved. Florence was the fifteenth-century cultural capital of Europe, with the Medici court a prominent cultural force. Dance masters were now in great demand. Court entertainments became lavish spectacles, usually organized around Greek or Roman mythology. These spectacles served as powerful political propaganda for the ruling class in that the nobility could display great wealth (and therefore authority), along with richly cloaked allegorical commentary on political and social matters.

In the mid-sixteenth century, Catherine de Medici married into the French court and brought with her the Italian ideals of lavish court entertainments, as well as proper culture and style. She hired Balthasar de Beaujoyeux, an Italian dance master, to create entertainments for the court. His *Ballet Comique de la Reine* (1581) became what is considered by dance historians the first identifiable ballet because of its cohesive plot, poetry, music, dance, and décor. Although Renaissance court spectacles were often elaborate, it is important to note that the performers were all amateur dancers from the nobility. Dancing was one of the few acceptable ways for women of the nobility to engage in strenuous physical activity. Many popular sixteenth- and seventeenth-century court dances survive today, preserved by the notations and descriptions made by dance masters during that time. Of these, one of the most famous dance manuals is *Orchésographie*, written in 1588 by Thoinot Arbeau. Examples of court dances from this time period include the slow and stately *pavane*, the fast and athletic *galliard*, the gracefully flowing *allemande,* the playful and running *courante,* the lively *gigue,* and the dainty and precise *minuet.* Skill in performing these dances was considered essential for a proper lady or gentleman of the nobility.

King Louis XIV of France (1638–1715) used dance as a tool of power. He built the Palace of Versailles and invited French nobility to live together under one roof. The king staged elaborate dance productions in which members of the nobility were expected to participate. Men and women spent hours each day learning dance steps so as to keep their status within the court. Missteps had grave consequences. Scholars have noted reports of persons being disgraced at court for poor dancing and having to slowly climb their way back up through the social ranks.

French court ballet reached its height during the reign of King Louis XIV. The king was himself a dancer; his teacher, Pierre Beauchamps (1631–1705), was the leading dance master of this era. Ballet fundamentals, including the five feet positions and standard arm movements, were classified under Beauchamps. As the dance steps became more complicated, the use of a ballet barre in training was developed. The barre is a railing attached to the floor or walls that ballet dancers gently grasp while practicing. Ballet turnout, an outward rotation of the hip sockets, was originally an adaptation of a fencer's stance. Dance masters found that turnout not only allowed a performer to open outward toward an audience but also increased flexibility in the hips. By the middle of the seventeenth century, ballet had reached such a technical level that the first professional dancers appeared in Europe.

During the seventeenth century, proscenium theaters began to be built, and dance moved out of the courts and onto the professional stage. Previously, audience members had sat on all sides of the performance, while proscenium theaters framed the stage as in a picture frame, with the audience seated on one side only. With the beginning of the Industrial Revolution and the rise of a new middle class, audiences flocked to these popular theaters for entertainment. The ascent of professional dancers gave rise to the first balletomanes, or devotees of ballet, and to famous rivalries among dancers. And dancing offered one of the first opportunities for respectable middle-class women to work outside the home in Europe.

BALLET AND BEYOND

As in sport, intense rivalries have always existed in dance. Apollo and Dionysus, the two Greek gods who symbolized contrasting types of art, were the prototypes for these dance rivalries. Apollo symbolizes the ideals of virtuoso technique, strength, and perfect form, ideals that also hold true for many sports. Many traditional ballets, such as *Agon* (1957), choreographed by George Balanchine, can be considered Apollonian.

Dionysus symbolizes the aspects of artistic expression that are emotional and creative and focused on content. This type of expression is present in certain sports, including figure skating, ice dancing, and rhythmic gymnastics. Although these events have demanding technical requirements, the aesthetic component of the event is part of the criteria in judging. The Neo-Expressionist Japanese dance form called *Butoh,* with its sometimes grotesque movements, is a Dionysian response to the horrors of the atomic bombs dropped on Hiroshima and Nagasaki, as well as a reaction to the traditional etiquette of Japanese society.

Dance is generally expected to include both Apollonian and Dionysian components or, stated another way, both form and content. Emphasis on dance technique alone ignores artistic expression, whereas emotional expression can rarely be effectively conveyed without a fully developed technique. Viewing dance according to its Apollonian or Dionysian elements can provide a framework for understanding contrasting artistic styles and, in many cases, one or the other characteristic can be seen to dominate a work of art.

Eighteenth-century dance rivals, Marie-Anne de Cupis de Camargo (1710–1770) and Marie Sallé (1707–1756), exemplified the prototypical ballerina rivals—one Apollian and the other Dionysian. Camargo was highly skilled in the performance of virtuoso jumps and leg beats that were the usual domain of male dancers. Although she caused a scandal by raising her skirts to ankle length to display her impressive technique and fast footwork, her athleticism and technical ability made her famous throughout Europe. Her contemporary and rival, Marie Sallé, was known for her formidable acting talent and expressive performance ability. Sallé also altered her costumes, not to display her technical abilities but to heighten her emotional intensity in portraying dramatic characters convincingly.

For many, it is difficult to find a more sentimental image than that of an otherworldly Romantic ballerina floating across the stage as an unattainable and tragic figure. During the golden age of Romantic ballet (1830–1850), female dancers rose to unprecedented prominence. Ballets such as *La Sylphide, Giselle,* and *Coppélia* feature women as the central figures; male dancers were demoted from strong and muscular figures to assistants waiting at the feet of ballerinas to assist in lifts. The most famous rival ballerinas during the height of Romantic ballet were Marie Taglioni (1804–1884) and Fanny Elssler (1810–1884). Taglioni, an Italian dancer, won her fame through a combination of great technical skill and ease of manner in performance. Her skill was the result of a demanding training regime directed by her father, Filippo Taglioni, who led his daughter through a rigorous daily physical routine until she nearly fainted and had to have help to dress after class. Her strength, graceful ease, and ethereal lightness dancing *en pointe* (on the tips of her toes) in *La Sylphide* made her internationally famous. Her rival, the Austrian dancer Fanny Elssler, was a more Dionysian dancer. Elssler had impressive technique, yet audiences were drawn to her personal magnetism and theatrical ability. One of her most famous roles was a sensual solo dance called "La Cachucha," in which she played castanets. Taglioni came to be known as the ethereal "Christian dancer," while Elssler was loved as the sensuous "pagan dancer."

In the early twentieth century, a new company emerged: the Ballets Russes commanded attention throughout Europe. Company manager Sergei Diaghilev (1872–1929) managed to hire the most talented dancers, choreographers, composers, and visual artists of his time. Important artists who created work for this company include: the painters Picasso, Matisse, Miró, Rouault, and Bakst; the composers Stravinsky, Prokofiev, Debussy, Satie, Poulenc, and Richard Strauss; and the choreographers Balanchine, Nijinsky, Massine, Fokine, and Nijinska. As before, two rival

Ballet dancers at the Sadler's Wells Theatre Ballet perfect their form during rehearsal. (Hulton-Deutsch/Corbis)

ballerinas embodying the Apollonian/Dionysian contrast arose. Anna Pavlova (1881–1931), who trained at the Marinsky School in St. Petersburg, had a natural delicacy, lightness, and grace. After breaking with the Ballets Russes in 1910, Pavlova formed her own company and toured the globe, often performing her celebrated piece *The Dying Swan,* choreographed for her by Michel Fokine (1880–1942). She was known for the Apollonian ideals of grace, beauty, and form. Tamara Karsavina (1885–1978), who danced as a soloist in the Imperial Ballet in St. Petersburg, was also a starring ballerina for the Ballet Russes. Although Karsavina had strong technical abilities, she impressed audiences with her dramatic and expressive qualities in ballets such as *Firebird* and *Petrouchka.*

THE REBELLION AGAINST BALLET

Modern dance began in the early twentieth century, partly as a reaction to the strict confines of ballet technique but also as a means for a new society to express its changing ideals in the wake of the world wars. This form of dance, which has German as well as American roots, has flourished in the United States in an unbroken progression since its inception, whereas the devastating effects of World War II inhibited the growth of German modern dance for many years. Early German modern dancers such as Mary Wigman (1886–1973) believed that art is most powerful when form and content are joined. She was instrumental in developing the new dance form *Ausdruckstanz,* or "expressive dance." Wigman's dances were often about the struggles between conflicting powers, in which opposing forces were given corporeal shape. She studied with Émile Jaques-Dalcroze (1865–1950), who developed a system of expressing rhythm through bodily movements called *eurhythmics,* and with the important dance theorist Rudolph von Laban (1879–1958).

Laban, who was also a dancer and choreographer, is perhaps best known for his work in the analysis of human motion and his development of a dance notation system. His Labanotation system is the most widely used dance notation system today. By the end of World War II, German modern dance had been artistically weakened by the Nazi oppression and was not to see an artistic phoenix until the rise of *Tanz-theater* in the early 1970s. Perhaps the best known of these *Tanz-theater* artists is Pina Bausch (b. 1940), whose productions are known for their dreamlike imagery, dramatic intensity, and preoccupation with the struggles between women and men.

During the early twentieth century, several American dancers made their name in Europe. Among these are Loie Fuller (1862–1928), Josephine Baker (1906–1975), and Isadora Duncan (1877–1927). Fuller, a pioneer of modern dance, experimented with the effects of stage lighting on voluminous costumes of silk, which she manipulated through movement. Baker devoted herself more to musical theater and cabaret. Her performances were considered rather suggestive in early-twentieth-century America, and so Paris became the center of her activities while her international fame grew. Duncan is considered one of the most important pioneers of modern dance in that she reduced costuming to silky tunics, performed barefoot, and used freely flowing movements inspired by nature, great classical music, and Grecian art. Duncan often performed solo dances to music by such composers as Beethoven, Wagner, Chopin, and Scriabin and sometimes burst into impromptu speeches on the issues of the day. All three women enjoyed international fame, albeit for differing approaches to artistic expression through dance.

Two of the most influential American founders of modern dance, Doris Humphrey (1895–1958) and Martha Graham (1894–1991), may also be discussed in the context of form versus content. Humphrey based her movement vocabulary on a reaction to gravity, yielding and resisting gravity in a "fall and recovery." Her choreography centered around designs in space. Although she believed in a clear motivation for her dances, it is the manner in which her dancers interact in space that suggests these motivations. Her works are seldom literal depictions; and many of her earlier works can be aptly described as abstract "music visualizations." In contrast, Martha Graham based her movement vocabulary on the breath, or "contraction and release." For Graham, movement was a mirror into the expressive soul. Her choreography is angular, expressionistic, and charged with tension and passion. She created an impressive body of choreographic work over a sixty-year period and was the first dancer to receive the Medal of Freedom, the United States' highest civilian honor.

Later modern dancers had different aesthetic concerns. Choreographers such as Merce Cunningham (1919–) rejected the notion of dance as expressing emotions or stories. His work is abstract, and his experiments with chance choreography, the treatment of stage space as an open field for movement, and his regard for all components in a dance production (choreography, costuming, scenic design, lighting design) as independent entities have made him an influential choreographer. He is also known for his collaborations with the foremost contemporary artists of the era, including the painters Andy Warhol, Jasper Johns, and Robert Rauschenberg, and his long-term collaboration with the experimental composer John Cage. In the early 1960s, experimental choreographers from the Judson Dance Theatre explored the idea that everyday movements ordered in time and space can function as dance. Pedestrian movements, those that can be performed by nondancers in everyday situations, quickly came into vogue on the concert stage. Choreographers such as Yvonne Rainer, Steve Paxton, Deborah Hay, and David Gordon accepted the concept that almost any movement,

DANCE EDUCATION IN AUSTRALIA: IT'S AN ART

In Australia education focuses on eight areas: English, mathematics, science, technology, languages other than English, health and physical education, studies of society and the environment, and the arts. Dance falls in the arts (along with drama, media, music, and the visual arts), and not in physical education as often is the case in western countries.

However, that was not always the case. Originally, dance was seen as a way to develop physical skills needed for a healthy lifestyle. Teachers included folk dancing and creative dance in their instruction. Then, in the 1960s and 1970s, leading dance educators in Australia worked with prominent professional artists to move dance education out of its traditional role as a tool for skills development and into an artistic and aesthetic framework. After four seminal conferences held between 1967 and 1976 at the University of New

England in New South Wales, this group formed the Australian Association for Dance Education (AADE, now the Australian Dance Council or Ausdance) in 1977. The new AADE quickly established a profile for dance education in Australia and by 1984 had made the case for having dance recognized as an art form in the curriculum rather than as part of a physical education syllabus. Subsequently, the National Affiliation of Arts Educators (NAAE), a lobby group for arts education in Australian schools, succeeded in reaching agreement with the federal government about "mapping" the arts in schools, accepting the arts as a "key learning area," and determining the five discrete art forms, each with its own body of knowledge, which art education includes. Dance has thus been designated since the mid-1980s as one of the key learning areas in all Australian educations systems.

from the simplest to the most complex, may legitimately function as dance movement.

DANCE TODAY

Dance today has progressed dramatically from its roots. In the early part of this century, American choreographer Ted Shawn characterized the relationship between dance and athletics by explaining, "Dancing is a manly sport, more strenuous than golf or tennis, more exciting than boxing or wrestling and more beneficial than gymnastics." Today, as in early tribal rituals, dance engages persons of both genders in vigorous activity. Although women now have varied opportunities to engage in sports—unlike their great grandmothers, for whom dance may have been the only socially acceptable way to engage in strenuous physical activity—dance remains popular all over the world. And dance is often considered a part of the world of women's sports: major organizations have "Dance" in their names and dance education as part of their work. These include the International Council for Health, Physical Education, Recreation, Sport and Dance (ICHPERSD) and

American Alliance for Physical Education, Recreation and Dance (AAHPERD).

Dance training today has much in common with athletics: for instance, a repetitive training schedule focusing on specific muscular patterns; practice sessions emphasizing strength, coordination, and balance; and the need for both individual and group training sessions. Most professional dancers attend daily dance technique classes in addition to three to six hours of daily rehearsal for specific choreographic works. Many professional dance companies provide technique classes for company members, whereas others expect dancers to arrange their own personal training schedule.

The need for rigorous training, as well as an aesthetic based on leanness, has caused some dancers to develop eating disorders and other addictive problems. A famous dancer who suffered such problems is Gelsey Kirkland (b. 1953), who shocked balletomanes by leaving the New York City Ballet, where she worked with George Balanchine (1904–1983), and joining the American Ballet Theatre to work with Mikhail Baryshnikov

Members of the Little Angels, a Korean children's dance group, performing in traditional dress. (Stephanie Maze/Corbis)

(b. 1948). After leaving the American Ballet Theatre, Kirkland revealed in her autobiography, *Dancing on My Grave,* that she was able to maintain such a svelte physique and perform with such speed and brilliance as a result of a cocaine addiction and an accompanying eating disorder. Many critics cite George Balanchine, founder of the New York City Ballet, for contributing to the problem of dancers' eating disorders. Balanchine, a seminal figure in American ballet, idolized an extremely thin female form.

Some choreographers who desire to find new sources for virtuosic steps turn away from standard dance techniques to sports, acrobatics, weightlifting, and gymnastics. The American company Pilobolus combines gymnastic movements with modern dance in witty, sculptural dances. Contemporary American choreographers such as Molissa Fenley and Elizabeth Streb are interested in athletics. Fenley's grueling dances require great endurance, so much so that her training routine has included running and weightlifting instead of the standard dance technique class. Streb's company, based in New York City, regularly performs on a series of trapezes and mats, presenting movements related to circus acrobatics and gymnastics.

However inclined choreographers may be to emphasize athletic movements, dancers are still refining their dance technique in traditional ways. To gain strength and versatility, professional dancers often train in both modern dance and ballet technique. Ballet technique develops speed, line, lightness, and articulate footwork, whereas modern dance emphasizes strength, weight, a flexible use of the spine, and asymmetrical and off-balance movements. In contemporary dance, both women and men are expected to have the strength and flexibility to lift other dancers and to be lifted themselves. Although gender roles in dance have expanded in most Western concert dance forms, traditional forms such as classical ballet, flamenco, and some folk dances retain their historical gender role divisions.

Professional dance is a competitive field. Dancers usually audition for specific roles or openings in professional companies through highly competitive auditions. Additionally, dancers sometimes compete for prizes and titles in events such as the USA International Ballet Competition, held every four years or so in Jackson, Mississippi. In 1998, eighty-seven dancers from twenty-six countries competed not only for prizes but also for attention as they exhibited their technique before dance companies that might employ them. Nonprofessional dance studios and dance teams frequently compete in regional and national competitions. Athletes and their coaches increasingly utilize dance training to improve coordination, flexibility, agility, alignment, and balance, with professional football teams in the United States sometimes requiring their players to attend ballet class. Research clearly shows that dance technique has benefits for athletes in other sports as well, such as diving, women's track and field, and synchronized swimming. Although dance training can benefit athletes, its primary focus historically has been on aesthetics rather than competition.

Among the current trends in dance is a return to content and expressionism with such artists as Anne Teresa de Keersmaeker (Belgium, 1960–), Meredith Monk (United States, 1943–), Pina Bausch (Germany, 1940–), and Kazuo Ohno (Japan, 1906–), among others. Other choreographers and dance companies, such as Bill T. Jones (United States, 1952–), Anna Halprin (United States, 1920–), and a group called Urban Bush Women, are more concerned with exploring social issues. National folk dance companies have become common and tour to concert stages around the globe. Recreational dance enjoys increased interest with its cultivation of physical fitness and social enjoyment. Ballroom and other social dance forms are now popular as both recreational and competitive activities, and competitive dancing, known as DanceSport, in 1999 was being considered as a possible Olympic sport—to mixed reactions in both the sports and dance worlds.

Helen Myers

See also DanceSport; Eating Disorders; Graham, Martha

Bibliography

Adshead-Lansdale, Janet, and June Layson, eds. (1994) *Dance History: An Introduction.* 2d ed. London: Routledge.

Anderson, Jack. (1997) *Art Without Boundaries: The World of Modern Dance.* Iowa City: University of Iowa Press.

———. (1992) *Ballet and Modern Dance: A Concise History.* 2d ed. Pennington, NJ: Princeton Book Company.

Banes, Sally. (1994) *Writing Dance in the Age of Postmodernism.* Middletown: Wesleyan University Press.

Bond, Chrystelle Trump. (1990) "An Aesthetic Framework for Dance." In *Encores II: Travels through the Spectrum of Dance,* edited by Ann Severance Akins and Janice LaPointe-Crump. Reston, VA: American Alliance for Health, Physical Education, Recreation and Dance.

Cass, Joan. (1993) *Dancing Through History.* Englewood Cliffs, NJ: Prentice-Hall.

Dance at Court. (1993) Produced by Rhoda Grauer, Thirteen/WNET in association with RM Arts and BBC-TV. Program four of eight-part series. 58 mins. Videocassette.

Dyke, Jan Van. (1992) *Modern Dance in a Postmodern World.* Reston, VA: American Alliance for Health, Physical Education, Recreation and Dance.

Foster, Susan Leigh. (1986) *Reading Dancing.* Berkeley, CA: University of California Press.

Lee, Carol. (1999) *Ballet in Western Culture: A History of Its Origins and Evolution.* Needham Heights, MA: Allyn and Bacon.

Pruett, Diane Milhan. (1990) "Ballet for Divers." In *Encores II: Travels through the Spectrum of Dance,* edited by Ann Severance Akins, and Janice LaPointe-Crump. Reston, VA: American Alliance for Health, Physical Education, Recreation and Dance.

Stearns, Marshall, and Jean Stearns. (1968) *Jazz Dance: The Story of American Vernacular Dance.* New York: Da Capo Press.

DANCESPORT

DanceSport is the competitive version of ballroom dancing. It is similar to ice or roller dancing in that it requires athleticism and technical and artistic skills; in addition, the winners are selected by a panel of judges. Because competitions involve couples, the sport attracts equal numbers of women and men, and gender bias is not an issue. DanceSport increased in popularity during the 1990s. The primary issue for both the international and U.S. DanceSport athletes and their organizations is to have it accepted as an Olympic sport.

HISTORY

Modern ballroom dancing has its origins in the dance styles of medieval Europe. From the medieval choral dance emerged the practice of dancing in couples, leading to the popular court dances of Renaissance Europe. These dances derived their aristocratic pomp and pageantry from traditional peasant-style patterns, but the dance masters of the day created a dignified new style of dance exclusively for the upper classes. In the seventeenth century, the stately minuet was ushered in, but it was the waltz that would change couple dancing forever. Known as wild and risqué, the waltz became the rage in Europe during the eighteenth century. Interestingly enough, all segments of society engaged in the waltz, especially in Germany. France and Austria followed their neighbor's lead, and the waltz (notably the Viennese waltz, a particular style associated with that Austrian city) soon became the classical, whirling favorite of European ballrooms.

In the mid-1800s the polka joined the waltz in popularity, rising from the rank of a Bohemian folk dance to ballroom status. Other countries followed European leadership and contributed to the ballroom scene in the twentieth century. Ultimately, these various national dances became incorporated into the content of DanceSport today. Argentina is linked to the tango, an erotic dance popularized in the barrios of Buenos Aires and originally ignored by those in the upper classes. The United States contributed the fox-trot and jit-terbug (swing, lindy, jive, boogie-woogie), while Cuba and the Caribbean islands delighted the world with Latin dances—rumba, cha-cha, mambo, and merengue. Brazil's sensual gift to the ballroom scene was the samba, and Spain added the paso doble. Not to be outdone, England created the quickstep, the English version of the quick fox-trot.

Early competitive ballroom dancing began in European cities (such as Paris, Berlin, and Baden-Baden in Germany) prior to World War I, but no international organization for either amateurs or professionals existed at the time. The first international amateur association was founded in 1935 in Prague; this Fédération Internationale de Dance pour Amateurs (FIDA) was active until the outbreak of World War II in 1939. FIDA did, however, organize and hold the first official world championships at Bad Nauheim, Germany, just prior to the 1936 Olympic Games in Berlin.

By 1950 the International Council of Ballroom Dancing (ICBD) was created in Edinburgh, Scotland, as the first international professional dance organization. Because the interests of FIDA and ICBD were so diverse, the two organizations did not cooperate, and in 1956 FIDA activities were suspended. By 1964 FIDA had ceased its work altogether. In the meantime, the International Council of Amateur Dancers (ICAD) was established in 1957 in Wiesbaden, Germany. ICBD had given its approval to the formation of ICAD, and by 1958 fourteen national associations from twelve countries claimed membership in this new amateur association.

The two organizations, ICBD and ICAD, worked together over the years, and in 1990 the International Council of Amateur Dancers changed its name to the International DanceSport Federation (IDSF). Recognition of ballroom dancing as a "sport" within the International Olympic Committee (IOC) was a prime objective at this time as a condition of DanceSport's entry into the Olympic Games.

Many changes occurred in the early 1990s. Eastern European countries added to the growing IDSF membership, as did Asian countries. By the late 1990s, IDSF was composed of more than seventy member countries on five continents and had become the governing body for all international competition for amateur DanceSport.

IDSF was welcomed, with provisional status, into the Olympic family by IOC President Juan Antonio Samaranch on 6 April 1995; the federation's ultimate goal was realized on 4 September 1997 at the 106th session of the IOC in Lausanne, Switzerland, when IDSF was granted full Olympic status although DanceSport was not yet scheduled as an Olympic sport.

UNITED STATES

The United States Amateur Ballroom Dancers Association (USABDA) was established in 1965 to promote the acceptance of ballroom dancing into the Olympic Games. In 1987 it became the sole governing body for amateur ballroom dancing in the United States. In 1998 USABDA had 16,000 dance members, with 33 percent of them Dance-Sport athletes and 67 percent recreational dancers. The advent of films highlighting ballroom dance, such as Australia's *Strictly Ballroom* (1992) and Japan's *Shall We Dance?* (1998), added to public awareness of DanceSport in the United States; and the Public Broadcasting System's "Championship Ballroom Dancing" television program continues to draw audiences. Ballroom dancing also became popular as both a course and a social activity on many U.S. college campuses in the 1990s, although it was not clear if this popularity would produce a new generation of DanceSport athletes.

In addition to its administrative role, USABDA promotes local social and recreational opportunities by organizing affordable dances, lessons, and workshops; the group also provides financial support to amateur dancers for world competitions. In addition, the association develops the Youth College Network by introducing ballroom dance to all educational levels (primary through college) and by encouraging the competitive aspect of DanceSport.

RULES AND PLAY

The rules for DanceSport vary according to type of competition. Variations in competition include those based on breadth of competition from local to international; eligibility (amateur, professional, pro-am, team, and others); dance style (International, Latin, American Smooth, among others), proficiency level (novice, prechampionship, championship); and age level of competitors (ju-

U.S. Champions Olga Foraponova and David Hamilton dance the waltz at the 1998 U.S. Dance Sport Championships in San Diego. (AP Photo)

nior, senior, adult). Competitions may involve solo and/or group events. Solo events are those in which only one couple dances at a time, performing a choreographed routine to the music of their choice. Group events have two or more couples dancing simultaneously in competition with each other.

Specific dances may include the waltz, tango, Viennese waltz, slow fox-trot, quickstep, cha-cha, samba, rumba, paso doble, jive, swing, and others. Time and tempo for each dance are specified according to the competition. Each dance possesses its own unique style, from the sharp, almost aloof, movements of the tango to the effortless glide of the waltz. Appropriate costuming enhances and highlights each dance, as well as its unique style—a plus for spectators at any competition.

The structure of competitions has recently undergone a major change. The first IDSF competition including professional couples was held as part of the Asian Games in Bangkok, Thailand, on 7 December 1998, under the umbrella of the Asian Olympic Council and the International Olympic Committee. The organization of this competition was under the aegis of the IDSF Asian DanceSport Federation; the integration of professional and amateur competitions, judged by professional and amateur adjudicators, was deemed a success,

THE DANCESPORT DEBATE

The key goal for proponents of DanceSport in 2000 is having it recognized as an Olympic sport and scheduled for Olympic competition, perhaps as early as 2008. These proponents argue DanceSport is a sport, is similar to other Olympic sports such as ice dancing and synchro- nized swimming, and is unique because it is gender neutral. Opponents argue that DanceSport is a recreational activity not a sport, that Dance- Sport participants are not athletes, that the judging system is too subjective, and that the Olympics are already burdened by too many sports.

and in 1999 the word *amateur* was deleted from all DanceSport publications. (In 1986, the Olympic Charter entirely eliminated *amateur* from its rules governing Olympic Games eligibility, and so there is no longer any reason to distinguish an amateur athlete from a professional athlete. This amendment to Olympic Bylaw 26 was effected under IOC President Samaranch, thus making it clear that "all are welcome to compete in the Olympic Games.")

Since DanceSport is the competitive aspect of ballroom dancing, it is subject to specific judging criteria. The International DanceSport Federation, the international governing body as approved by the International Olympic Committee, has chosen to use the Skating System of Judging. In all rounds of competition prior to the finals, each judge must vote for the number of couples stated by the chairman of adjudicators. During the final round, each judge must place all the competing couples in order of merit, with "1" being highest, in each of the dances performed. Judges are not permitted to "tie" couples for any place in the final of any dance. The "open" system of marking must be used in final competition. There are gen- erally seven IDSF-licensed judges for major and international competitions.

Costuming for ballroom dance competition varies greatly between men and women. Women must invest considerable amounts of money in "standard" gowns, "smooth" gowns, "Latin" dresses, and other competitive clothing. These specific categories denote the type of dance being performed; for example, standard includes waltz, tango, Vienna Waltz, slow fox-trot, and quickstep. Attire for men remains more traditional, with tail- coat suits the rule for most of the dances. The no- table exception is the Latin category, in which both male and female dancers are allowed more crea- tivity in costuming although it is preferred that a competitor's dress promote a sporting image so as not to denigrate or trivialize DanceSport.

Specific examples of costume requirements in- clude the following: preteen boys should wear dark pants and white shirt with optional tie; pre- teen girls should wear either a leotard with wrap- around skirt or a party dress without rhinestones. In contrast, the junior and youth categories allow jackets or tuxedos for the boys and cocktail dresses or ball gowns for the girls. Adult and sen- ior divisions incorporate tail suits and ball gowns, complete with decoration (such as rhinestones, se- quins, and feathers).

DANCESPORT AND THE OLYMPICS

Is DanceSport a viable event for the Olympic Games? This question is being hotly debated by devotees and detractors of the sport around the world. Since formal recognition by the IOC in 1997, the IDSF has raised its hopes that Dance- Sport will be placed on the Olympic Games pro- gram, perhaps as early as 2008. The host city, yet to be determined, must agree to the inclusion of this artistic sport before it can become part of the official program.

Those in favor of DanceSport argue that it has as much right as ice dance, rhythmic gymnastics, and synchronized swimming to be a medal status sport. DanceSport has been described as "ice dancing on hardwood" by some devotees, and the prospect of having 50 percent women athletes, as well as 50 percent men, is another positive attribute of this gender-equal sport. In addition, advocates point out that costs are negligible as special venues will not have to be built, given that suitable facilities are found nearly everywhere. DanceSport is also practiced in numerous countries around the world, does not depend on weather or climate, and can be enjoyed by all ages from young children to older adults. Devotees also argue that, from a philosophical perspective, DanceSport actually fulfills one of the basic tenets of the Olympic Movement: sport for all. There is no discrimination regarding age, race, religion, or gender. The founder of the modern Olympic Games, the Baron Pierre de Coubertin, espoused an egalitarian desire to offer sporting opportunity for everyone. This French historian and pedagogue believed in educating the entire person: body, mind, and spirit. This argument, however, has not yet convinced enough people to schedule DanceSport in the 2000 or 2004 Olympics.

Opposition to inclusion of DanceSport as a medal sport in the Olympic Games is based on a variety of beliefs, for instance, that dance is not sport, that ballroom dancers are not athletes, that judging is too subjective (with "beauty being in the eye of the beholder"), and that the Olympic program is overburdened as it is so that no new sports should be added until some others are dropped.

This debate, of course, raises many basic issues about sport, including what physical activities constitute sport, what attributes—strength, agility, speed, and so on—make an individual an athlete, and whether the Olympics are truly representative of all forms of sport.

CONCLUSION

Participation by women worldwide in DanceSport, from youngsters to seniors, is one reason for its increasing popularity; 50 percent of participants are female and 50 percent are male. It is one of the few sports without gender bias, either at the social-recreational level or at the competitive level. As an activity that incorporates discipline and coordination, poise and balance, flexibility and strength, in addition to teamwork with a partner, ballroom dancing is seen by many participants as a source of fitness for all ages. It is a lifetime activity with virtually no age limit that fits within the modern category of wellness activities.

Elizabeth A. Hanley

See also Dance

Bibliography

Buckman, Peter. (1978) *Let's Dance*. London: Paddington Press.

Hazelwood, Archie. (1998) USABDA President's Report. *Amateur Dancers* 114:20–23.

Kidane, Fekrou. (1997) "The 106th IOC Session." *Olympic Review* 26, 17:8.

Mason, Richard S. (1995) "Ballroom Dancing Inches Toward Olympics." *Danceweek* 20:14.

Pease, Doris. (1995) "Camaraderie Journey." *Dancing USA* 13, 3:2.

Rushing, Shirley, and Patrick Macmillan. (1997) *Ballroom Dance*. Dubuque, IA: Eddie Bowers Publishing.

Sachs, Curt. (1937) *World History of the Dance*. New York: Norton.

DARTS

The sport of darts has its roots in the English public house, and therein lies the key reason that, until the last third of the twentieth century, women were afforded little opportunity to play either recreationally or competitively. Dartboards were—and are—usually situated in the public bar or vault of a public house, or pub which, in many areas of Britain, is traditionally regarded as a male preserve, and the game has been emphatically male-only for most of its history. Women have, nonetheless, competed in national championships in Britain since the 1950s, and Queen Elizabeth, the Queen Mother (1900–), helped bring the game to the attention of women as long ago as the 1930s.

HISTORY

It is generally accepted that darts evolved from archery. Darts, in one form or another, has been played in English public houses since the early sixteenth century. In 1924 the National Darts Association (NDA) was founded in London, with the goal of regularizing and standardizing the sport. In 1925 the NDA ran its first major individual darts competition. This was called the Licensees Charity Cup, and women could qualify only if they were themselves pub licensees or

Woman playing darts. (Shelly Gazin/Corbis)

wives of licensees and if the pub darts club was registered with the association.

In the 1930s darts playing became a cult in Britain. In December 1937 King George VI and Queen Elizabeth (the mother of Queen Elizabeth II) visited a new community center in an English town and, during a tour of the building, they played a brief game of darts. In the short game that followed, Her Majesty beat His Majesty 21–19, although she did stand one foot closer to the dartboard. The next day, a photograph of the queen playing darts appeared in national daily papers, with the queen quoted as saying, "Do let me try. I have heard so much about this game." After that, darts became a craze, with the queen's action having a particular effect on women. Shortly afterward, the *Sunday Chronicle* banner headline read, "Women Flock to Follow the Queen's Lead at Darts," and the office of the British Darts Council was reported to be inundated with requests from women asking where they could learn to play the game. For a short time, darts appeared to break through the barriers of class and gender that had previously restricted almost all participation to working-class men, but it is unlikely that such general popularity would have lasted, given the game's usual venue. In any event, within two years, World War II had intervened.

During and after World War II, darts spread across the globe. U.S. servicemen returning home took the game back with them from England. In the United States, darts had been considered more of a children's game than an adult sport or pastime. British expatriates who decided to stay in countries where they had been stationed, such as the Netherlands and Spain, helped establish dart clubs in Europe. Darts leagues were being created at an amazing rate, particularly in Britain; they were, however, predominately male, and any incursion into this domain by female dart players or teams continued to make the headlines throughout the 1940s, 1950s, and 1960s. In 1963, for example, Pat Tymon, a housewife from Lancaster, England, applied to join the local Lancaster City Darts League, only to be told that it was men only. Despite such setbacks, women's teams and women's individual enthusiasm for darts playing continued to grow and, during the second half of the twentieth century, the inequality of opportunity began to fade.

In 1958 the National Darts Association of Great Britain (NDAGB, established in 1954) introduced the first women's pairs competition, which was won by Joan Adams and Rose Branham of the Workers Club, Kings Lynn, Norfolk. The NDAGB also organized mixed pairs championships and in 1967 introduced a women's individual championship that was won in its inaugural year by Marjorie Drabble of the Marston Moor Club, near Chesterfield, England. By the mid-1970s women's darts were beginning to be taken seriously, but even then the interest was not great enough to attract much of the all-important television coverage that brought sponsorship. It was not until 1973, the year of the founding of the British Darts Organisation (BDO), that women's darts were truly recognized and women's participation put on a footing similar to that of their male counterparts. The BDO first ran women's singles in the 1979 British Open, won by Judy Campbell of England. From the beginning the BDO structure for the county league encompassed women's darts. Women also participate in the World Darts Federation World Cup, which is held every two years. In the 1997 World Cup, twenty-nine countries were represented, including Brazil, Bermuda, Malaysia, Kenya, and Japan, each with a women's team. The top five women's teams in that year's competition were the United States, New Zealand, the Philippines, Northern Ireland, and Wales.

The *News of the World* Individual Darts Championship, which was until the late 1970s *the* darts competition to win, was first held in the 1927–1928 season. Although some evidence suggests that women played in the early rounds of this competition over the seventy-plus years of its existence, only when the competition was relaunched in 1996 was a separate event organized for women. The last eight women's finalists all hailed from Britain, and the champion was Linda Jones of Chorley, England. Jones won a first prize of £6,000. Although a valuable top prize for women's darts, it was modest compared with the £42,000 first prize for the men's champion, Phil Taylor.

In late 1995 the BDO agreed that women dart players could enter the preliminary rounds of what many darts aficionados regard as the greatest darts championship in the world, the Embassy World Darts Championship. At the turn of the twenty-first-century, no woman had made it beyond the qualifying stage of the championship.

In May 1978 ex-world professional darts champion Leighton Rees (Wales) said, "I think we'll soon see the time when the world men's champion will lose to a woman. There are some great girl players on the circuit now. . . ." Although women were able to take part in more competitions starting in the late 1970s and early 1980s, their participation has never been considered sufficiently interesting to attract television coverage or sponsors and, thus, the potential earnings for women are low. Earnings rankings published in *Darts World* magazine in February 1999 showed that Trina Gulliver of England was at the top of the table, earning a mere £4,555, excluding exhibitions, during 1998. (In comparison, the top three male dart players earned in excess of £25,000 each, excluding exhibitions.) World Darts Federation rankings, based on a points system, published that same month showed that Trina Gulliver was also the top woman player in the world, with Francis Hoenselaar of the Netherlands runner-up. The highest-ranked U.S. woman darts player was Stacy Bromberg in eleventh place.

RULES AND PLAY

Darts can be played by two or more people. It is essentially a game of precision, requiring players to throw a small, sharp, projectile at a round

English munition workers gather for a game of darts, c. 1942. (Corbis/Hulton-Deutsch Collection)

board divided into segments, each with an assigned number of points.

The standard dartboard is circular and divided into twenty scoring segments, numbered 1 to 20 but not in sequence, an outer bull's-eye scoring 25 points, and an inner bull's-eye scoring 50 points. Darts shot into the outer ring of the dartboard score double the number, and those striking the inner ring between the double ring and the outer bull's eye score treble the number. Matches normally played are 501, 401, or 301-up, where the players have to reduce the number to zero in the least number of darts, each game ending with the scoring of the required final double.

CONCLUSION

In 1999 the English Sports Council still did not recognize darts as a sport for its purposes even though darts demands the same dedication and rigid discipline, the same skilled coordination of hand and eye as any other target sport, such as archery or target-shooting, both of which are recognized as Olympic sports. Darts is played worldwide but remains especially popular in Britain, where in excess of 6 million men and women participate in the sport either competitively at country, county, local league, pub league, friendly level, or just on a casual basis. Darts remains very popular in British public houses. Major darts competitions are shown regularly on television in that country, increasingly on satellite and cable channels. In excess of 5 million viewers watched the televised final of the Embassy World Darts Championship in January 1999. Although women darts players may have fewer opportunities available to them for championship play, and thus lack the experience of men in this respect, there is no physical reason why they cannot be as proficient at darts as men.

Patrick Chaplin

Bibliography

Brown, Derek. (1981) *The Guinness Book of Darts*. Enfield, Middlesex: Guinness Superlatives Ltd.

Croft-Cooke, Rupert. (1936) *Darts*. London: Geoffrey Bles.

Mass Observation. (1987) *The Pub and the People*. London: The Cresset Library.

McClintock, Jack. (1977) *The Book of Darts*. New York: Random House.

Taylor, Arthur R. (1992) *The Guinness Book of Traditional Pub Games*. Enfield, Middlesex: Guinness Publishing.

Turner, Keith. (1980) *Darts—The Complete Book of the Game*. Newton Abbot, Devon: David & Charles.

DEAF OLYMPICS

The World Games for the Deaf (WGD) are a competitive event in which only elite athletes with deafness participate. The WGD, modeled after the Olympic Games, are held every two years, alternating summer and winter games. Women have participated in the games since their inception.

Affectionately referred to as the "Deaf Olympics," the Games were founded in 1924 and first held in Paris on 10–17 August of that year. Six countries competed (Belgium, Czechoslovakia, France, the United Kingdom, the Netherlands, and Poland). The sports included were track and field, cycling, football, shooting, and swimming. The first Winter World Games for the Deaf took place in Seefeld, Austria, from 26 to 30 January

1949. Five nations competed, with a total of thirty-three competitors. The Comité International des Sports des Sourds (CISS; International Committee of Sports for the Deaf) is the international governing body of deaf sport and controls the WGD. It is managed by an eight-member executive committee, all of whom are deaf. Membership is composed of deaf national sport governing bodies of seventy-two countries. The CISS was recognized by the International Olympic Committee (IOC) in 1955. In 1966 the IOC awarded the organization the Courbertin Cup, named for the founder of the modern Olympic Games, in recognition of its strict adherence to the Olympic ideal and its service to international sports.

The WGD is unique in that it is organized and governed by and for deaf men and women. Participation in the WGD requires that an athlete have a hearing loss of 55 decibels or more in the better ear. The deaf athlete typically considers herself not as "disabled" but rather as part of a cultural and linguistic minority. The events have no special rules or changes in competition other than visual cues instead of auditory signals (for example, flashing lights for starting signals).

The Summer Games include eight sports for women (track and field, badminton, basketball, shooting, swimming, table tennis, tennis, and volleyball) and thirteen sports for men. The Winter WGD offers Alpine and Nordic skiing for women.

The WGD, like most sporting organizations, traditionally has been dominated by men. Almost three times as many male athletes as female athletes take part in the WGD. Deaf women served in a leadership capacity, however, long before their hearing counterparts in the IOC. Marie Bendeguz of Colombia was the first deaf woman to serve on the CISS executive committee (1981–1985), followed by JoAnne Robinson of Canada (1985–1993). Donalda Ammons, who was the first woman appointed to lead the United States WGD (1990), served as second vice president (1995–1997) of the CISS Executive Committee and subsequently as the secretary general.

Outstanding female athletes of the WGD include Germany's Rita Windbrake (track and field) and Sieglinde Mayrhofer (track and field); Connie Johnson-Ruberry (track and field) of the United States; Nina Ivanova (track and field) of Russia; JoAnne Robinson (swimming) of Canada; Elisabeth Lutz (swimming), Cindy-Lu Fitzpatrick (swimming), Laurie Barber (swimming), and Carrie Miller (swimming) of the United States; and Tone Tangen (cross-country) of Norway. The United States has dominated women's basketball since its introduction into the Games in 1981, with five gold medals. Russia, the United States, and Germany (both before and after reunification) have traded gold medals in women's volleyball since 1977. Windbrake set deaf world records in every track event from the 100- to 1500-meter races since 1963 and won medals in every summer WGD from 1969 to 1994. Three of her records (400-, 800-, and 1500-meter races) still stood at the end of the 1990s.

Rebecca A. Clark

Bibliography

Clark, Rebecca A. (1995) "Team Perceptions of Cohesion among Deaf/Nondeaf Culture and Starter/Nonstarter Varsity Athletes at Gallaudet University." Doctoral dissertation, Temple University, Philadelphia, PA.

DePauw, Karen P., and Susan J. Gavron. (1995) *Disability and Sport*. Champaign, IL: Human Kinetics.

Jordan, Jerald M. (1997) "World Games for the Deaf and the Paralympic Games." Oglesby, Carole A., Doreen L. Greenberg, Ruth L. Hall, Karen L. Hill, Francis Johnston, and Sheila E. Ridley, eds. (1998) *Encyclopedia of Women and Sport in America*. Phoenix, AZ: Oryx Press.

Staff. (1998) *CISS Bulletin*. North Potomac, MD: CISS.

Stewart, David A. (1991) *Deaf Sport*. Washington, DC: Gallaudet University.

DECKER SLANEY, MARY

(1958–)

U.S. TRACK AND FIELD ATHLETE

Mary Decker Slaney was the first woman to run a 1500-meter race in less than four minutes. She has held world records in the 880-yard, 800-meter, 1000-meter, mile, and 5000-meter runs, had world championship titles in 800-meter, 1000-, 3000-, 5000-, and 10,000-meter runs, and held seven U.S. records in distances from 800 to 10,000 meters. Entering her first official cross-country race at age eleven, Slaney was still running thirty years later, qualified for five U.S. Olympic teams, amassed a total of seventeen world records, and set new American track records thirty-six times.

Born in New Jersey on 4 August 1958, Mary Decker grew up in Huntington Beach, California, where she competed for her school teams. People who knew her as a child say that she ran as much for the love of running as for the sake of competition. In 1972, at only fourteen years of age, Decker won an international race in the 800-meter race, beating the Russian woman who had won a silver medal in the 1972 Summer Olympics. By 1973 Decker had entered the record books for running an indoor mile in 4:40.1 and was ranked first in the United States and fourth in the world in the 800-meter race. In 1974 she set a U.S. high school record of 2:02.29 in the 800-meter run, and the same year she set an indoor record of 2:01.8 for that race. In 1980 Decker set a world mile pace of 4:21.68 in Auckland, New Zealand—and, in the same year, she set an unofficial indoor time of 4:17.55 on an oversized track in Houston, Texas. As fate would have it, when Decker was in her top form and running without injury, the United States became involved in a situation that mingled sports and politics, boycotting the 1980 Moscow Olympics, and she was unable to compete for the gold medal. In 1981 Decker lost the world record but reclaimed it later in the year with a time of 4:18.08 in Paris and lowered the record once again in 1985 in Zurich with a time of 4:16.71.

Decker set the 2000-meter world-record time of 5:32.7 in Eugene, Oregon, on 3 August 1982, but she was dethroned the next day by Kazankina of the Soviet Union, running in Moscow. In 1982, her greatest season ever, she was awarded the Jesse Owens Award—the first woman to win that prestigious track and field honor—setting world records for the 2000-, 3000-, 5000-, and 10,000-meter races, as well as two one-mile records. That year she also received the James E. Sullivan Memorial Trophy, which is awarded to the amateur athlete "who has done the most during the year to advance the cause of sportsmanship." In Eugene, on 5 June 1982, Decker set the 5000-meter record of

15:08.26; she held the record for exactly two years until she was unseated by Zola Budd of South Africa (running for England) in 1984. In 1983 Decker attended the first world championships of track and field and won both the 1500- and 3000-meter races. Between 1982 and 1984, she won ten consecutive 3000-meter events. Decker also was presented with *Sports Illustrated's* 1983 Sportsman of the Year Award.

This record set the stage for the event that many consider the most memorable in women's track and field competition—the 3000-meter race that paired Budd and Decker in the 1984 Olympic finals. The race was a new Olympic event that year, and there was much anticipation about the matchup in the 3000 meters between the more experienced Decker and the teenager from South Africa running under the British flag. After sitting out the 1980 games, Decker was ready to run the race of her life, on U.S. soil and in her home state of California. She was coming off the 1983 world championship victories in both the 1500- and 3000-meter races and had defeated the 1980 Olympic gold medalist.

The event that went down in history was not what the runners or the spectators could have anticipated. Decker, as was her characteristic pattern, led from the starting gun and turned the halfway mark of 1500 meters at 4:18. Wendy Sly (also running for Britain) and Budd challenged for the lead. Budd's and Decker's feet became tangled, and the two runners bumped into each other, fell, and were injured. Most spectators do not remember the winner of that race (Maricica Puica of Romania), but they retain strong images of Decker being carried off the track in pain and disappointment. Despite this loss, and not long after this 1984 Olympic incident, the Women's Sports Foundation named Decker one of the five greatest athletes of the years 1960–1984.

Decker has faced other setbacks over the years. When Decker was a teenager, she was on the warm-up area in a track meet when a race official tried to remove her. Decker's coach had to intervene, and Decker proceeded to set a new world record in the 1000-yard race. On 11 June 1997 she was banned from competition when an excessively high steroid level was found during a drug test following Olympic trials. She was cleared of those charges, but her reputation was smeared.

Mary Decker running in a race. (Corbis/Neal Preston)

In 1984 Decker married Richard Slaney, a British-born champion discus thrower. In 1985, Decker set a new record for the mile (4:16.71), which remains fourth on the All-Time Outdoor Track List for Women. In fact, in 1985 Decker held U.S. records at eight distances from 800 through 10,000 meters, records that were not broken at least to 1999.

The fall in the 1984 Games left her with permanent mental scars and physical damage to her heel bone. Decker had more than twenty operations to repair that injury, plus shin splints and an inflamed Achilles tendon from her years of running. The injuries plagued her in the 1988 Olympics, where she finished a disappointing tenth, and some thought this would convince her to retire. In 1992 she failed to make the U.S. team, and she was suffering with pain from the physical abuse her body had endured through the years. Another series of surgeries followed to relieve pressure on her Achilles tendons, and for the next three years she had difficulty even standing or walking. Nevertheless, Decker finished second in the 5000-meter race qualifier at the U.S. Track and Field Trials, giving her a spot on the 1996 team. Although she failed to qualify for the Olympic finals, Decker banished the ghosts of 1984 and re-emerged as a competitor and champion in distance running.

Decker has been described as having a biomechanically perfect stride, which many coaches attempt to recreate in their young athletes. Above all, she had the proven mental toughness to carry her through controversy and comebacks and emerge as a role model for all athletes.

Debra Ann Ballinger

Bibliography

"All-Time Outdoor Track Lists, Women." (1998) <http://www.runnersworld.com>.

Dyer, Kenneth F. (1982) *Catching Up the Men.* London: Junction Books.

Hersh, Philip. (1996) "Slaney: A Model of Courage and Perseverance." <http://interactive.phillynews.com>.

Huey, Linda. (1976) *A Running Start: An Athlete a Woman.* New York: Quadrangle.
"Greatest Olympic Competition: 3000 meters: 1984, Los Angeles." (1998) <http://www.runnersworld.com>.

Anita DeFrantz, a vice president of the International Olympic Committee in July, 1998. (AP Photo)

DEFRANTZ, ANITA

(1952–)

U.S. ROWER AND ADMINISTRATOR

Anita DeFrantz, an Olympic bronze medalist in rowing (women's eight-oared shell) for the United States at the Montreal Games in 1976, is best known as the first U.S. woman and the first African American to be appointed to the International Olympic Committee (IOC) and then to be elected in 1997 as one of its four vice-presidents. DeFrantz is dedicated to the achievement of equity and parity for women's sports in the Olympics, as well as for increased opportunities for all girls and women to participate in sports throughout their lives.

Born on 4 October 1952 in Philadelphia, Pennsylvania, DeFrantz was limited in her early sporting opportunities, as were many young girls of the time. She was introduced to the sport of rowing as a first-year college student at Connecticut College when she crossed paths with rowing coach Bart Gulong, who was walking across campus with a shell on his back. At his invitation, she joined the team and began training with the discipline and energy that had earlier earned her an academic scholarship to college. This same drive led to her admission to the University of Pennsylvania Law School, where she earned her law degree in 1977.

DeFrantz was a member of the U.S. rowing team from 1975 to 1980. She and her teammates earned the bronze medal in the 1976 Olympics, won six national rowing titles, and advanced to the finals in five world rowing championships, winning a silver medal in 1978. DeFrantz continued to train diligently with teammates for the 1980 Moscow Games but was denied the right to compete, along with the entire U.S. Olympic team, when President Jimmy Carter's administration declared a U.S. boycott of the Games. Fueled by frustration and armed with legal knowledge, DeFrantz filed suit against the government. Although the lawsuit failed to allow them to compete, the IOC, which has vigorously opposed use of the Olympics as a political forum, took notice of DeFrantz and awarded her the Medal of the Olympic Order in recognition of her contributions.

In 1984 Peter Ueberroth, organizer of the 1984 Olympics in Los Angeles, appointed DeFrantz vice-president of the 1984 Los Angeles Games' organizing committee. After the Games DeFrantz joined the Amateur Athletic Foundation and was named its president. Following the success of the 1984 Games and in recognition of DeFrantz's effectiveness in her leadership role, IOC President Juan Antonio Samaranch secured her appointment as a regular IOC member in 1986. This appointment runs through 2027. Known to be hardworking and an outspoken advocate for the purity of athletic competition, the integrity of the Games, and a greater women's presence in them, DeFrantz has been instrumental in increasing women's participation in the Olympics. She was a strong advocate for the inclusion of women's soccer and softball in the 1996 Atlanta Games. She has helped pass legislation that establishes targets to increase women's part in the leadership of the IOC to 10 percent by 2000 and 20 percent by 2005. DeFrantz also serves on the program commission, eligibility commission, and judicial commission; she has been outspoken about the need for stricter drug testing and drug guidelines and insisted that the Committee for the Atlanta Games purchase the most advanced drug-testing mechanisms to prevent use of steroids and other illicit performance-enhancing aids for Olympic athletes.

Within her sport of rowing, DeFrantz remained actively involved, and in 1993 she served as vice-president of the International Rowing Federation. She is a member of the Women's Sports Foundation's board of stewards and has been awarded the Guiding Woman in Sports Award by the National Association of Girls and Women in Sports to recognize women who work to increase opportunities for girls and women to participate in sports and sports leadership in the United States. DeFrantz has been recognized by the *Sporting News* as one of the 100 Most Powerful People in Sports, by *Ladies Home Journal* as one of the 100 Most Important Women in America, and by the *Los Angeles Sentinal* as one of the 10 Outstanding Women of the Year. Some have predicted that she will become the first female president of the IOC and that she may be chosen to replace Samaranch following his tenure. It is certain that DeFrantz will continue to be outspoken in her belief that sports are everyone's birthright and that the Olympic movement must lead the challenge to spread opportunities for girls and women in sports.

Debra Ann Ballinger

Bibliography

DeFrantz, Anita. (1993) "The Olympic Games: Our Birthright to Sports." In *Women in Sport: Issues and Controversies,* edited by Greta L. Cohen. Newbury Park, CA: Sage, 185–191.

"Female Official Breaks IOC Barrier." (1997) <http://olympics.canada.com/nagano/news_stories/olympic_notes1.html>.

Oglesby, Carole, ed. (1998) "Anita DeFrantz," in *Encyclopedia of Women and Sport in America.* Phoenix, AZ: Oryx.

Sherrow, Victoria. (1996) "Anita DeFrantz," in *Encyclopedia of Women and Sports.* Santa Barbara, CA: ABC-Clio.

DENMARK

Denmark is a Nordic nation with a population of approximately 5.2 million. Sports in Denmark—as well as their continuing evolution—is the product of a nearly 200-year-long process. Within Danish sports, women's physical education, gymnastics, and sports have been influenced in various ways by different gymnastics systems as well as by English sports.

HISTORY

Many elements contributed to the development of physical education and sports. First were the public schools, whose influence began at the start of the nineteenth century. Next were the private institutes, started in the 1850s. There were also voluntary clubs, which were established from about the 1870s. The fourth element was the folk high school, which began to exert an influence in the mid-1880s. Folk high schools, founded on private initiative, were intended to use an "educational-cultural" break of 3–5 months to give farmers' children—who lived at the school when classes were in session—a chance to be educated academically and socially and to help shape them into confident, democratic citizens.

At the same time, two distinct sport movements emerged, one rural and one centered in the towns. In rural areas, a gymnastics movement developed, supported by a strong and self-aware social class. This contrasted with the sport movement connected to the towns. This division is still visible in the current Danish sport system (*idræt-system*), which has two different national organizations with different historical traditions, cultures, and ideologies. The Danish Gymnastics and Sport Association (DGI) grew from rural roots while Denmark's Sports Federation (DIF) grew from urban beginnings. The aim of DGI is to strengthen, through sports and other cultural activity, "voluntary association work in order to promote popular enlightenment." In contrast, the aim of DIF, which is an amalgamation of Danish sports associations, is to work for the "promotion of Danish sports (*idræt*) and for the popularization of sports in Danish society." Many Danes (about 1.6 million in 1998) are active members of one of the 14,000 voluntary clubs across the country, most of which are members of both DIF and DGI. About 40 percent of the active participants are women.

SPORTS AND THE SCHOOLS

School legislation enacted in 1814 introduced gymnastics into the Danish primary schools, both in rural areas and in the towns, and initially gymnastics was meant for both sexes. The Danish pio-

neer Franz Nachtegall (1777–1847) was inspired by German philanthropic ideas and Johann Friedrich GutsMuth's German pedagogical gymnastics. In 1828, however, gymnastics was discontinued for girls, when the justification for including it in the curriculum became more closely linked with preparing boys to enter military service when they finished school.

A major initiative for girls began in 1838 with the establishment of an "experimental school for instructing female youth in body and health exercises" at the Royal Military Gymnastics Institute. The program was intended to give school mistresses and other interested people the opportunity to learn how to teach physical education to girls and women. This renewed interest in gymnastics for girls arose from physicians' concerns about deficiencies in women's physical development. Although a number of girls' schools, especially private schools, took up girls' gymnastics, it was not until 1904 that the state-run primary schools again made gymnastics mandatory.

From about 1860 to 1900, physical activity for women was reestablished through physical education classes in the schools, gymnastics and sports in private schools, private gymnastics institutes, voluntary clubs, and folk high schools. In the private schools and private institutes, the primary purpose of offering physical activities was to promote a healthy life, but there was also the more general idea of developing "citizenship" through discipline and controlled exercises. The focus of the clubs was to use games and sports as a way to socialize, whereas the folk high schools took up physical education to supplement the daily life at the school, very often to balance the time students spent sitting and listening to lectures. In the rural areas, the Swedish form of gymnastics won out over various other gymnastic systems, and from the 1880s this particular variety was taught to girls and women at school, folk high schools, and gymnastics clubs. In the towns and cities, in contrast, a system developed by a Danish teacher named Paul Petersen (1845–1906) became dominant. Petersen called his system "Danish women's gymnastics." In 1878 he started the Institute for the Education of Female Gymnastics Teachers, which is still in operation.

The 1870s also saw many young urban women begin to participate in skating, swimming, tennis, cycling, and fencing, both in clubs started for women only and in those open to males and females. Doctors, female teachers, and gymnastics teachers all acted as pioneers and champions of women's gymnastics and sport; these supporters believed that physical activities could greatly enhance women's lives, mentally as well as physically. Some doctors (and other critics), however, came out against many of the women's sport activities (as opposed to gymnastics) out of concern that such physical stress could damage a woman's reproductive system. Although these doctors believed that women should avoid sports entirely, they felt that women could safely participate in gymnastics except during their menstrual periods. Such medical opinions, combined with the contemporary norms for what women could do, definitely limited women's participation in sports.

The period from 1900 to 1945 was a time of stabilization and development in Danish sports. Danes took up many new activities, such as track and field, handball, badminton, and hockey. From the mid-1930s, about 35 percent of the participants in the voluntary clubs were women. Women were able to gain access quite easily to some sport activities, such as gymnastics, swimming, handball, tennis, and fencing. Track and field was another matter; while discussions about whether Denmark should have track and field championships for women began in the early 1930s, the event was not established until 1944.

WOMEN AND SPORT ORGANIZATIONS

From its founding in 1896, the DIF permitted women to be both members and leaders, whereas the other organization—at that time the Danish Gymnastics and Rifle Club (established in 1861)—did not permit women as members or elected officials until 1918. In 1915 Danish women were given the right to vote, an event that made it much easier and much more common for women to participate in society, including all levels of sports. In the 1920s and 1930s, women struggled in different ways to influence the sport organizations. But few women succeeded in reaching secure positions of leadership.

During these years many women became involved in teaching and some began to coach as well. In 1925 a folk and gymnastics high school was established just for women; this had great

Handball match between Danish and Korean Olympic teams during the 1996 Summer Olympics. Denmark won the gold medal. (TempSport/Corbis)

importance for the development of women's gymnastics because the school trained rural women as gymnastics teachers. The school was inspired by the Finnish gymnastics teacher Elli Bjørkstén, who focused on a new kind of femininity.

During World War II many people–including many women–joined voluntary clubs and participated in sports for the first time. During the German occupation, sport clubs were among the few places where people were allowed to gather in their leisure time. After the war, sport activity from 1945 to about 1960 was relatively quiet, as the Danes rebuilt their society after five years of occupation. The same period brought demographic changes, including increased urbanization and industrialization.

Since the mid-1960s, sports in Denmark have grown and become more international. More people, particularly women, have joined clubs and other organizations. Many women participate in jogging and running (marathon races, half-marathons, and the like), and women-only events have been introduced. In 1991 "Tøserunden" (Girls-Round), a women's bicycle race on a 115-kilometer (71.3-mile) course, was first held. The inaugural race had 1,498 participants. Each year the number of entrants increases; in 1997 approximately 7,000 women participated.

DANISH WOMEN FLOCK TO SPORTS

Denmark is among the most liberal of nations in regard to female participation in sports. Regular sports participation by women dates back to the early eighteenth century, and in 2000 women's participation continues to expand with some 700,000 women members of sports clubs in villages, towns, and cities. Nonetheless, the sports establishment continues to be dominated by men.

In 1983 an organization called Women and Sports was founded with the aim of establishing networks to increase women's participation in sports. The organization focused on specific problems for women in sports, for example, the lack of representation and influence of women in decision-making processes and women's invisibility in the media. Although the group made serious efforts to promote change, the results have been minimal except in the media, where women today are much more visible. Sport organizations still have few women at the top of the organizational hierarchy although women constitute more than 40 percent of all the active participants in the voluntary clubs.

ELITE SPORTS

Danish women have participated in the Olympic Games since 1904, when they were part of the Olympic festival in Athens. At the 1904, 1908, 1912, and 1920 Olympic Games, Danish women gymnasts performed demonstration events because gymnastics had not yet been added to the Olympic program as a competitive sport. In the period up to and including the 1920 Olympic Games in Antwerp, 202 Danish women gymnasts had participated in these demonstration events, which nearly equals the total number of women who had participated in the Olympics from all countries. In 1912, Danish women began competing in other events in the Olympics and have taken part in all subsequent Summer Games. Until 1952 swimming was the dominant discipline, with more Danish women swimmers participating than Danish athletes in any other sport. In 1968 a Danish woman participated in the Olympic Winter Games for the first time.

In 1985 Team Denmark was established to promote and support participation in sports at the international level. The goal of the new organization was to promote Danish elite sport in a socially acceptable fashion. The organization also supported female athletes, with successful results. More than half of the Danish participants at the Olympic Games in 1996 were women. The most successful Danish women athletes within recent years have been the members of the Danish handball team, which won the European championship in 1994 and 1996, the Olympic gold medal in 1996, and the world championship in 1997.

Else Trangbæk

Bibliography

Trangbæk, Else. (1996) "Danish Gymnastics: What's So Danish about the Danes?" *The International Journal of the History of Sport* 13, 2 (August): 203–214.

——. (1996) "Danish Women Gymnasts: An Olympic Success Story." In *Proceedings from the Third International Symposium for Olympic Research*. London, Ontario: The University of Western Ontario, 237–244.

——. (1996) "Discipline and Emancipation Through Sport: The Pioneers of Women's Sport in Denmark." *Scandinavian Journal of History* 21: 121–134.

——. (1997) "Gender in Modern Society: Femininity, Gymnastics, and Sport." *The Nordic World, The International Journal of the History of Sport* 14, 3 (December): 136–156.

——. (1989) "La gymnastique au Danemark 1800–1900. Identité nationale et acculturation." *Sport historie, revue internationale des sports jeux* 3: 61–81.

——. (1987) *Mellem leg og disciplin. Gymnastikken i Danmark i 1800 tallet.* Auning: Duo.

———. (1993/94) "Women, Body, and Sport in Denmark at the End of the Nineteenth Century." In *Stadion, Internationale Zeitschrift für Geschichte des Sports*. Sankt Augustin, Germany: Academia Verlag, 239–258.

Trangbæk, Else, et al. (1995) *Dansk Idrætsliv*. 2 vols. Copenhagen, Denmark: Gyldendal.

DE VARONA, DONNA

(1947–)

U.S. SWIMMER

Donna De Varona doing the butterfly stroke in 1969. (Corbis/Jack Fields)

In the 1960s Donna De Varona was one of the world's best all-around swimmers, specializing in the extremely demanding individual medley event, which requires swimming the backstroke, breaststroke, butterfly, and freestyle in a single race. Following her retirement from competitive swimming, De Varona became a sport commentator and a leader of the women's sports movement.

De Varona was born in San Diego, California, on 26 April 1947. As a child, she enjoyed many outdoor sports and was frustrated, like many female athletes of her generation, by the no-girls rule in Little League Baseball. She concentrated on competitive swimming, which led to her winning thirty-seven individual national swimming titles and setting eighteen national and world records. In 1960 the thirteen-year-old De Varona qualified as an alternate on the United States Olympic swimming team and went to Rome as the team's youngest member. After the Games she continued to train and began to set world records in the backstroke, butterfly, and freestyle. At the 1964 Olympic Games in Tokyo, she won the first-ever 400-meter Olympic medley, setting a world record. She was also a member of the winning 400-meter freestyle relay team. Soon after the 1964 Olympics, she retired from competitive swimming at the age of seventeen.

De Varona received her college degree from the University of California, Los Angeles, where she majored in political science. In 1965 she was hired by the American Broadcasting Company as the first full-time female sportscaster in the United States. In 1968 she became the first woman to cover the Olympics for a U.S. television network.

Throughout her life De Varona has worked toward promoting sports for all. This was demonstrated in 1974 when she joined Billie Jean King in founding the Women's Sports Foundation, an organization dedicated to increasing opportunities for girls and women in sports and fitness. In addition to serving as president of the foundation, De Varona helped gain passage of Title IX in 1972 and the Amateur Sports Act of 1978. Before congressional committees she was a skillful and persuasive speaker.

De Varona's involvement with sports also included service on two presidential commissions: Gerald Ford's Commission on Olympic Sports and Jimmy Carter's Women's Advisory Commission. She also served on the President's Council on Physical Fitness and Sports. In 1999 she chaired the organizing committee for the Women's World Cup Soccer Tournament, which was held in the United States.

De Varona's swimming prowess was acknowledged by her induction into the International Swimming Hall of Fame, the International Women's Sports Hall of Fame, and the United States Olympic Hall of Fame.

Shawn Ladda

Bibliography

Johnson, Anne. (1996) *Great Women in Sports*. Detroit, MI: Visible Ink Press.

Additional information provided by the ABC Television Network (New York).

DIDRIKSON ZAHARIAS, MILDRED (BABE)

(1911–1956)

U.S. MULTISPORT ATHLETE

Babe Didrikson throwing the discus. (Corbis/Bettmann)

In 1950 the Associated Press named Mildred (Babe) Didrikson Zaharias the outstanding female athlete of the first half of the twentieth century (the legendary Jim Thorpe was her male counterpart). She may well be the greatest female athlete of all time; modern challengers, such as Jackie Joyner-Kersee, are quite accomplished, but they pale in terms of overall athletic accomplishment.

Mildred Ella Didrikson was born on 26 June 1911 in Port Arthur, Texas, and spent most of her childhood in nearby Beaumont. Her parents were Norwegian immigrants, and she was the sixth of their seven children. She was known from her earliest days as "Baby," a nickname amended to "Babe" as her athletic accomplishments began to parallel—at least from a provincial hometown perspective—the feats of the New York Yankee baseball great, George Herman (Babe) Ruth.

Athletics were a big part of Didrikson's life, and she competed throughout high school in baseball, basketball, swimming and diving, and track and field. Her track specialties were the hurdles and the javelin, and her skills in these events were to serve her well at a later point in her athletic career.

In 1930 Didrikson was offered a job by the Employers Casualty Company of Dallas, Texas, ostensibly as a stenographer, but her real function was to represent the company in national basketball competition. The Employers Casualty team, the Golden Cyclones, won the Amateur Athletic Union (AAU) championship in 1931, with Didrikson named to the All-American team in 1930, 1931, and 1932. In the 1930 national tournament, she averaged 42 points per game; the following year, she scored 35 points per game and led the Golden Cyclones to the national title. In her spare time Didrikson was an all-star softball player in Dallas.

Excelling in basketball and softball did not quench her thirst for competitive excellence. Her employer and mentor in Dallas, retired Army Colonel Melvin Jackson McCombs, subsequently suggested that she might next try track and field. Picking up that challenge, Didrikson won both the baseball throw and the javelin at the 1930 AAU meet; the 80-meter hurdles, the long jump, and the baseball throw in 1931; and the shot put and the baseball throw in 1932. Didrikson also won gold medals in the 80-meter hurdles and the javelin and a silver medal in the high jump at the Los Angeles Olympic Games in 1932. In the high jump, Didrikson actually won but was awarded second place because she used a style of high

GOOD AT ALMOST EVERYTHING

At the close of the twentieth century, Babe Didrikson appeared on every list of the best athletes of the twentieth century and near the top of the list of female athletes. What separated Didrikson from the other women on the lists, such as Martina Navratilova, Billie Jean King, Nadia Comaneci, Chris Evert, Sonja Henie, Wilma Rudolph, and Jackie Joyner-Kersee, was that Didrikson was a multi-sport athlete who excelled in track and field, basketball, softball, and golf.

jump that was new and unaccepted at that time, diving or going over the bar head first instead of straddling it. Her style was really a precursor of the western roll, which was to become the approach of choice for several decades for both men and women high jumpers.

Despite all her success in basketball and track, it was the sport of golf that truly put Didrikson on the sport map; golf provided the challenge to her athletic skills and personal tenacity that she had so long sought. She had played golf briefly as a teen under the informal tutelage of a high school teacher and coach but had not given the game much thought in the basketball and track and field years. As her fascination with those two sports waned, Didrikson immersed herself in this new obsession, which eventually led to practices lasting as long as ten to fourteen hours. She might hit up to 1,000 balls per session. Often, she had to wrap her hands because of blisters and bleeding from her grueling practice regimen. By 1934, at the age of twenty-three, she had honed her game sufficiently to enter her first tournament, where she shot an opening round of 92. Soon thereafter, she was booming drives for an average of 240 to 250 yards; her longest drive was 408 yards. Within a short time she became a complete player and the dominant force in women's golf. As an amateur, Didrikson was the first to win both the United States Women's Amateur and British Women's Amateur championships. As a professional, she won the United States Women's Open three times (1948, 1950, and 1954). Didrikson was the leading money winner on the women's tour in 1948 through 1951 and the first woman athlete to earn a six-figure annual income. By the time her career ended, Didrikson had won eighty-two amateur and professional golf championships, including seventeen in a row in 1946 and 1947. Part of Didrikson's success as a golfer is attributable to the financial and psychological support she received from George Zaharias, a professional wrestler and successful businessman whom she married in 1938.

In April of 1953, Didrikson was diagnosed with colon cancer and underwent a colostomy, which allowed her to resume a relatively normal life. Testimony to her recovery were the five professional tour events she won in 1954, including a convincing victory at the U.S. Open, where her margin of victory was twelve strokes. Early in 1955, the cancer returned and ultimately was found to be inoperable. Always the fighter, Didrikson remained undaunted by her illness and continued to play golf into early 1956, when the pain became unbearable and ultimately forced her out of competition. The ravages of the disease dropped her weight from the normal 145 to about 80 pounds. Didrikson died in Galveston, Texas, on 27 September 1956 at the age of forty-five.

Arnold LeUnes

Bibliography

Cayleff, Susan E. (1995) *Babe: The Life and Legend of Babe Didrikson Zaharias.* Urbana, IL: University of Illinois Press.

Hicks, B. (1993) "The Legendary Babe Didrikson Zaharias." In *Women in Sport: Issues and Controversies,* edited by Greta L. Cohen. Thousand Oaks, CA: Sage.

Johnson, William, and Nancy Johnson. (1977). *Whatta Gal! The Babe Didrikson Story.* Boston: Little, Brown.

Knudson, R. R. (1985) *Babe Didrikson: Athlete of the Century.* New York: Viking Press.

Zaharias, Babe. (1955) *This Life I've Led: My Autobiography.* New York: A. S. Barnes.

DIEM, LISELOTT

(1906–1992)

GERMAN ATHLETE, OFFICIAL, PROFESSOR

Liselott Diem advocated full participation by women in sports, and her research focused on sports and physical education for girls and women. Her efforts helped reduce discrimination against women in Germany and in international sport organizations after World War II.

Born in 1906 Liselott Bail grew up in an upper-middle-class home in Berlin. Her father, who had a high position in the Prussian ministry for trade and commerce, was her model and aroused her passion for sports. In 1924 she enrolled in the recently founded (1920) German Sport University in Berlin, where she was one of only a few women students. There she met her future husband, the German sport official Carl Diem, who was one of her teachers. She was active in motor biking, rowing, and skiing. In 1927 she finished her studies (she was the best student in her class) and was awarded the August Bier Plaque. Her master's thesis was titled "The Importance of Physical Activities for Gainfully Employed Women."

From 1927 to 1933, she worked as a teacher and the head of the women's education division at the Sport University. She married Carl Diem in 1930. They had three daughters and one son. During Hitler's regime she was a physical education teacher at various schools, and she also qualified as a gymnastic teacher. After World War II, it was not possible to reopen the Sport University in Berlin because the city was destroyed and divided. Diem followed her husband to Cologne, where he created a new Sport University. She headed the women's program from 1947 to 1965 and was promoted to full professor in 1965, the only woman on the faculty at that time to attain that rank. From 1967 to 1969, she was the rector of the Sports University in Cologne. As a scholar and professor, Diem was highly regarded. Her several hundred publications deal with physical education in elementary schools, play and games, physical activities for older people, and physical education and sports for girls and women.

LISELOTT DIEM ON WOMEN IN SPORTS IN GERMANY (1920s)

We sports students wore short pants all winter long. Athletic shorts came along much later, introduced by American athletes. Our first long pants were sewn by our mothers. We bought knickerbockers and wore them for skiing and motorbike riding. Together with five other female students at the German Sports University I rode a motorbike and roared around the bends of the concrete wall that enclosed the sports field.

We were ready for anything from weightlifting to pole-vaulting. We dove from the ten-meter platform and got black-and-blue marks. We were the first competitive rowers and called ourselves the Valkyries. And whenever we competed, we won in the boats for one, two, and four rowers. The officials were annoyed that we didn't row "properly" and they gave us the lowest possible scores for style, but we finished ahead of the others.

We were the first to play team handball and we competed for the club of the founder, Carl Schelenz, who worked for the Siemens company. I played as right stormer three weeks after the birth of my children. The team needed someone who threw the ball hard.

From Gertrud Pfister, ed., Frau und Sport. *Frankfurt: Fischer, 1980. Translated by Allen Guttmann.*

Diem served on important committees of numerous national and international organizations. She was especially involved in physical education for girls and women. From 1965 to 1981, she was president of the International Association of Physical Education and Sport for Girls and Women (IAPESGW) and strongly influenced its ideas and initiatives.

Her lifelong engagement in sports was recognized by numerous awards, among them the Grosse Bundesverdienstkreuz (Germany), the Ehrenplakette des the Philip-Noel-Baker-Award (International Council of Sport and Physical Education), and the Olympic Order.

Aside from her numerous books and articles, Diem lectured, organized meetings and conferences, traveled around the world, gave speeches, and organized workshops and demonstrations. One of her favorite topics was women and sport, on which she had the quite progressive view that women could compete in every sport. Later she studied children and their motor development, which led her to stress the importance of free and natural movements and to support the "fun" element in physical education through participation in play and games. In her later years she began writing on fitness and health, in particular about the physical activities of elderly people.

Gertrud Pfister

Bibliography

Carl Diem Institut, ed. (1986) *Liselott Diem. Leben als Herausforderung.* 3 vols. St. Augustin, Germany: Academia Verlag.

DISABILITY SPORT

Disability sport refers to a sport that has been designed for, or is specifically practiced by, male or female athletes with disabilities.

Since the 1950s various terms have been used to describe the participation of individuals with disabilities in sports: handicapped sports, sports for the disabled, adapted sports, blind sports, wheelchair sports, deaf sports, and more. In the 1990s, *disability sports* became the accepted term used to describe the general sports movement for athletes with disabilities.

Disability sports encompass sports configured for a selected disability group (for example, goal ball for athletes who are blind or visually impaired and, for athletes with lower limb impairments, wheelchair basketball and sitting volleyball). Disability sports also include sports practiced by able-bodied individuals that have been modified or adapted to include athletes with disabilities (for example, wheelchair tennis or tandem cycling) as well as sports that require little or no modification to allow individuals with disabilities to participate (track and field, wrestling, and swimming). In the most general sense, disability sports encompass opportunities and competitions for athletes with physical, sensory, and mental impairments. However, Deaf Sports and Special Olympics are often viewed as separate entities.

HISTORY

Before the two world wars, most athletes with disabilities had virtually no opportunities for organized sport competition. The exceptions were the deaf (Sports Club for the Deaf, founded in Berlin in 1888), single-arm amputee golfers (British Society of One-Armed Golfers, founded in 1932), and a few self-selected individuals. In 1924 the first International Silent Games were held in France, and the Comité International des Sports des Sourds (CISS; International Committee of Sports for the Deaf) became the first international organization to provide sport competition for any disability group.

World War II significantly influenced the treatment of individuals with disabilities, especially in terms of the rehabilitation needs of disabled veterans. The British government, credited as the first to recognize these needs, opened the Spinal Injuries Center at Stoke Mandeville Hospital in Aylesbury, England, in 1944. Sir Ludwig Guttmann, director of this center, first introduced competitive sports as an integral part of the rehabilitation of disabled veterans in 1948. In 1952 Guttman organized the first international competition for wheelchair athletes at Stoke Mandeville with competition between the British team and a team from the Netherlands. Although originally sanctioned for those with spinal cord injuries, in

1976 the Games were expanded to include people with other physical impairments, including blind and amputee athletes.

During the 1960s, international sport competitions were extended to include other disability groups not eligible for the World Games for the Deaf or the International Stoke Mandeville Games. The leadership for these additional disability sport competitions came in the form of the International Sports Organization for the Disabled (ISOD). In Paris in 1964, the ISOD was officially formed to provide international sport opportunities for blind people, amputees, and athletes with locomotor disabilities. The Special Olympics, founded in 1968 by Eunice Kennedy Shriver—who wanted to provide sport opportunities for individuals with mental retardation—held its first games in Chicago, Illinois. In 1960 the first International Games for the Disabled were held in Rome. These games would later be known as the Paralympic Games, which provided international competition for athletes with physical and visual impairments.

The International Cerebral Palsy Society (ICPS) was founded in part because individuals with cerebral palsy were dissatisfied with existing competitions. A sport and leisure subcommittee formed in the mid-1960s sponsored the first international games for athletes with cerebral palsy, which were held in France in 1968. The ICPS continued to sponsor this international competition every two years until 1978, when Cerebral Palsy–International Sports and Recreation Association (CP-ISRA) became recognized by the ISOD as the official sanctioning body for cerebral palsy sports.

Similarly, the International Blind Sports Association (IBSA) was formed in 1981 in response to increasing interest and expanding opportunities for competitions for blind athletes.

FEMALE ATHLETES WITH DISABILITIES

In the early to mid-1900s, female athletes with disabilities first entered the competitive sporting arena. Specifically, women with hearing impairments were among the pioneering competitors at the first World Games for the Deaf in Paris in 1924. Two women (and sixteen men) competed in wheelchair archery at the Stoke Mandeville Hospital in England, and this event marked the beginning of wheelchair sport. In 1952 Liz Hartel (postpolio) won a silver medal in dressage at the Summer Olympic Games.

Despite these exceptions, it was not until the 1960s that women with disabilities truly began to gain access to the world of sport through disability sport. The international disability sport organizations provided opportunities and competitions to females as well as males. Special Olympics, founded in 1968, allowed females with mental retardation to compete internationally. At the 1968 Paralympics in Tel Aviv, Israel, women's wheelchair basketball was introduced; this move provided the impetus for the U.S. National Wheelchair Basketball Association (NWBA) to host the first women's national wheelchair basketball tournament in 1975. Since the 1970s, girls and women with disabilities have been active participants in disability sports at local, national, and international levels.

JOINING FORCES

In 1982 mutual interest in expanded international sport for individuals with disabilities brought the CP-ISRA, IBSA, the International Stoke Mandeville Games Federation (ISMGF), and the ISOD

RUNNING BLIND

Probably the most successful disabled athlete is runner Maria Runyan of the United States. Although legally blind, Runyan competes in major 1,500 meter races against fully-sighted runners. In June, 1999 she finished fourth in the 1,500 meter run at the U.S. Track and Field Outdoor Championships, and in July 1999 she took the gold medal in the 1,500 meter run at the Pan American Games.

together to form a new umbrella organization. The International Coordinating Committee of the World Sports Organizations (ICC) was established to coordinate disability sport worldwide and to negotiate with the International Olympic Committee (IOC) on behalf of athletes with disabilities. In addition, CISS (for deaf sports) and the International Federation for Sports for Persons with Mental Handicaps (INAS-FMH) joined the ICC in 1986. The ICC, however, served as a fragile alliance of international sport federations, with an uneasy history from 1982 to 1987.

In March 1987 in Arnhem, the Netherlands, representatives of thirty-nine countries and six international federations met to determine the future of international disability sport. The participants of the Arnhem meeting decided to form a new organization with national representation from every nation with a disability sports program. The organization would govern itself through a council of nations. Thus, in Düsseldorf, Germany, on 21 and 22 September 1989, the International Paralympic Committee (IPC) was born.

The founding of the IPC began a significant chapter in the history of sports and disability. The organization was designed to serve as the international governing body for disability sport; it became the IOC of sport for individuals with disabilities. The IPC has been recognized by the IOC and currently serves as a liaison to the IOC on behalf of athletes with disabilities. Among its many activities, the IPC sanctions international competitions, including the Summer and Winter Paralympic Games.

INTERNATIONAL COMPETITIONS FOR ATHLETES WITH DISABILITIES

Multisport, multidisability world championships, as well as single-sport, single-disability international competitions, are held regularly. Some are specific to the disability type as well as the sport, such as International Wheelchair Archery Tournaments and World Goal Ball Championships International Wheelchair Marathons. In addition, multisport and multidisability competitions are included in the Pan American Wheelchair Games, World Cup Alpine Disabled Skiing Championships, and European Championships for Athletics and Swimming. Multisport, single-disability events include the European Special

Olympics and competitions offered under the auspices of the North American Deaf Sports Association.

OLYMPIAN COMPETITION

International competitions similar to the Olympics are held for individuals with disabilities. These include the Paralympics, World Games for the Deaf, and International Special Olympics.

Paralympics

The Paralympics can be considered the equivalent of the Olympic Games for elite physically and visually impaired athletes. Both summer and winter Games are held every four years, currently in the same host country as the Olympics. The Paralympic Games include many of the sports found on the program of the Olympic Games and are open to athletes who are paraplegic and quadriplegic, blind, amputee, have cerebral palsy, or have other physical conditions (termed *les autres,* or "the others"). The first Games were held in 1952 at Stoke Mandeville, England, and in 1960 in Rome. The term *paralympic* has been used to describe the Games only since the 1964 Games in Tokyo.

A significant milestone in Paralympic history occurred during the Summer Paralympics in 1988 in Seoul, South Korea. The Games included some 3,200 athletes from sixty-two countries who competed in 732 different events. These Games made use of the facilities, housing, and competition sites of the 1988 Olympics. The opening and closing ceremonies were identical to the Olympics as well. Competition was held in sixteen different sports, including archery, athletics, basketball, boccie, cycling, equestrian, fencing, goal ball, judo, shooting, volleyball, soccer, swimming, table tennis, weightlifting/powerlifting, lawn bowling, and snooker. The momentum of Seoul continued into the 1992 Paralympic Games in Barcelona and the 1996 Paralympic Games in Atlanta, and it is expected to continue.

The Winter Paralympics are also held every four years and include competitions in a variety of Alpine and Nordic events, skating, ice picking, and more. Physically impaired (amputee, cerebral palsy, *les autres*) athletes and visually impaired/blind athletes compete in these Games. As is the case with the Summer Paralympics, these Games are to be held in the Olympic host city near the time of the Olympic Games. The 1992 Winter Paralympics were held in Albertville/Tigne, France. Lillehammer, Norway, served as the host city for both the 1994 Olympics and 1994 Paralympics; Nagano, Japan, hosted the Olympic and Paralympics in 1998. As with the Summer Games, the connection between the Olympic and Paralympic Games will continue.

World Games for the Deaf

World Games for the Deaf have been held regularly in locations throughout the world since the first World Summer Games for the Deaf in 1924 in Paris. The first World Winter Games for the Deaf were held in Seefeld, Austria in 1949. Since then, the World Games have been held every four years, the year following the Olympic year and, if possible, in the same host country or city. For example, the 1985 World Games for the Deaf (WGD) were held in Los Angeles and used many of the Olympic venues. Deaf athletes have also been able to compete in Pan American Games for the Deaf.

Events on the program of the Summer World Games for the Deaf include men's basketball, women's basketball, cycling, soccer, swimming, tennis, water polo, badminton, shooting, table tennis, team handball, men's athletics, women's athletics, men's volleyball, women's volleyball, and wrestling. For the Winter World Games for the Deaf, athletes compete in Alpine events (men's and women's downhill skiing, giant slalom, slalom, and parallel slalom), Nordic skiing events (men's 15- and 30-meter, and 3 × 10-kilometer relay; women's 5- and 10-meter and 3 × 5-kilometer relay), speed skating (500-, 1000-, 1500-, and 3000-meter races), and ice hockey.

One distinctive aspect of the World Games for the Deaf is the concerted effort to provide an international forum for the exchange of culturally relevant information. The Games offer participants the opportunity to experience the unique cultural identify of people who are deaf. The Games are much more than athletic competition; they represent a celebration of community.

International Special Olympics

International Special Olympics sponsors both Summer and Winter Games for individuals who are developmentally delayed. The first Special Olympics were held at Soldier's Field in Chicago; 1,000 athletes from twenty-six states and Canada participated. International Special Olympics competitions are held every two years, alternating Winter and Summer Games. Typical Summer Games held in the United States have included more than 5,000 athletes from seventy countries. Official sports include aquatics, athletics, basketball, bowling, equestrian, soccer, gymnastics, roller skating, softball, and volleyball; demonstration events include cycling, powerlifting, table tennis, team handball, and tennis. In addition to competitions held regularly in the United States, European Summer Special Olympics were started in the 1980s (Belgium in 1981 and Dublin in 1985).

In March 1993 the Fifth International Special Olympics World Winter Games were held in Schladming, Austria. These Games were the first International Special Olympics held outside the United States. Approximately 1,600 athletes from sixty-three countries attended, competing in Alpine and cross-country skiing, figure skating, speed skating, and floor hockey.

Unlike the World Games for the Deaf and the Paralympics, media coverage is extensive for International Special Olympic events; thus, the public has been more aware of Special Olympics than any other athletic events for athletes with a disability.

WOMEN WITH DISABILITIES IN OTHER COMPETITIONS

Women with disabilities have participated as fully accepted Olympians in both the Summer and Winter Olympic Games. For example, Liz Hartel and Nerol Fairhall, representing New Zealand, competed in archery from wheelchairs during the 1984 Olympics in Los Angeles. Women with disabilities have also competed in exhibition events at the Olympic Games since 1984. These events include downhill skiing and Nordic events in Sarajevo (1984), Calgary (1988), and Albertville (1992); and the 800-meter wheelchair race for women and 1500-meter wheelchair race for men in Los Angeles (1984), Seoul (1988), Barcelona (1992), and Atlanta (1996).

Athletes with disabilities regularly compete in marathons around the world, most notably the Boston Marathon, which included male wheelchair athletes as early as 1974. The first female wheelchair athlete to compete, Sharon Rahn (Hedrick), entered the race in 1977 and won her division with a time of 3:48:51. Since then, the winning times for men and women have dramatically improved; men in wheelchairs often finish under 1:30 and women under 1:45. Jean Driscoll is the only individual to win the women's wheelchair division of the Boston Marathon seven times.

Now increasingly visible and accepted, athletes with disabilities are more and more able to pursue athletic careers. Wheelchair divisions in major road races allow wheelchair athletes to compete professionally for substantial prize money. Today, athletes with disabilities are able to attract major corporate sponsors to assist with their careers (two examples of such sponsored athletes are Diana Golden, three-track skier, and Boston Marathon winner Jean Driscoll). Additionally, selected colleges and universities offer intercollegiate athletics and athletic scholarships for individuals with disabilities.

Today, disability sport organizations around the world provide a valuable resource for girls and women. They often provide educational and training programs for athletes and coaches, training tips, sport medicine information, nutrition counseling, and instruction on assisted technology. Through these organizations, girls and women with disabilities can gain access to state, regional, national, and international competitions.

CONCLUSION

Convergence of the sport movement for athletes with disabilities with the Olympic sport movement was inevitable. As a result of the successful history of international competitions for athletes with disabilities (such as the Paralympics, World Games for the Deaf, and Special Olympics), it has become an accepted fact that sport is no longer the sole prerogative of able-bodied male athletes. Once exclusively the domain of those free of physical impairments, sports—and society's view of sports—have now been altered for more inclusion and greater acceptance of individuals with disabilities, including girls and women with disabilities. Although sport remains a forum for the expression of physical prowess, strength, endurance, and grace, society's view of these has been expanded to include athletes using wheelchairs and others with physical, mental, or sensory im-

pairments. Although equity in sport is still a distant reality, sport for and including athletes with disabilities is a movement whose time has come.

Karen P. DePauw

See also Deaf Olympics; Goalball; Paralympics; Special Olympics

Bibliography

Cowan, Jay. (1993) "Brave in the Attempt." *Olympian* 19, 23.

DePauw, Karen P. (1988) "Female Athletes with Disabilities." In *Encyclopedia of Women and Sport in America,* edited by Carole A. Oglesby, Doreen L. Greenberg, Ruth L. Hall, Karen L. Hill, Francis Johnston, and Sheila E. Ridley. Phoenix, AZ: Oryx Press.

DePauw, Karen P., and Susan J. Gavron. (1995) *Disability and Sport.* Champaign, IL: Human Kinetics.

Guttmann, Ludwig. (1976) *Textbook of Sport for the Disabled.* Oxford: H.M. & M. Publishers.

Landry, Fernand. (1992) "Olympism, Olympics, Paralympism, Paralympics: Converging or Diverging Notions and Courses on the Eve of the Third Millennium?" Paper presented at the 1st Paralympic Congress, Barcelona, Spain (31 August).

Lindstrom, Hans. (1984) "Sports for Disabled: Alive and Well." *Rehabilitation World* 8: 12–16.

Stewart, David A. (1991) *Deaf Sport.* Washington, DC: Gallaudet University Press.

DIVING

Diving is a modern sport in which participants attempt complex maneuvers between the time they propel themselves off the diving platform and the moment they hit the water. Women have gained considerable recognition in the sport, but they have not achieved complete equality with their male counterparts. Modern competitions continue to reflect traditional attitudes that view men as stronger and more acrobatic and women as more graceful.

HISTORY

In ancient times, diving was rarely performed as a competitive event although archaeological evidence shows that women did dive in both the Greek and Roman eras. In general, diving was limited to pools and other sites deep enough for safety and also to the relatively few occasions for outside competitions. During the Middle Ages and the Renaissance, water sports were not popular, and so diving was not a major athletic activity.

Diving became a competitive sport in the nineteenth century. It originated as a sport in England, where divers were graded for the depth of their dives and their technical merit. One form was *plunging,* in which the athlete dived into the water, and the judges measured the distance between the takeoff and the depth of the dive from a track floated underwater. The governing body of English swimming, the Amateur Swimming Association (ASA), organized the first English championship for male plunging in 1883 but never established one for women although in 1913 the ASA recognized the first women's record in plunging.

Platform diving became popular around the turn of the century. Professional diving associations were open to women, and stars such as Agnes Beckwith and Ada Webb performed high dives from bridges, cliffs, and riverbanks. Because the events were more entertainment than sport competition, artificial platforms were rarely used. At about the same time in Sweden, a form of artistic diving called *plain diving,* derived from gymnastics, flourished. The core of plain diving was the swallow dive, a static dive that must demonstrate aesthetic entry into the water with few movements. In the swallow dive, when the diver took off, she assumed the figure of a swallow and held the position until entering the water. The artistic element of the dive was based on the line of the dive and the ability of the diver to hold the position. In Sweden, women competed in sanctioned diving contests as early as 1884, and the Swedish Swimming Federation organized the first national women's championship for plain diving in 1910.

Plain diving did not include somersaults or acrobatic moves. In Germany, however, fancy diving that did include acrobatic moves and somersaults was popular. The first women's diving organization, the Ladies Diving Association (LDA), was established in England in 1908. Its separate status from the established Amateur Diving As-

Pat McCormick. (Bettmann/Corbis)

sociation (ADA), which had been founded in 1901 and was (theoretically) open to men and women, implied that it had a more marginal status, although women officials of the ADA (or later, of the ASA) did judge women's events. Nevertheless, when the LDA and ADA were absorbed by the ASA in 1935, the official English champion of the LDA was not recognized.

In general, women divers were excluded from swimming meets early in the twentieth century. Often it was left to women's clubs to organize diving contests for women, but these events had few spectators, limited space, and little coverage by the sport press. Still, many women's clubs recruited and trained girls for diving; but financial pressures (increased by the expenses of recruiting and training) led many of these clubs to close or merge with the dominant male associations. The women's associations did sponsor some competitions. For example, in Austria in 1904, the First Vienna Ladies Swim Club organized an overall diving contest, with a plunging event, an immersion competition (a time test of how long a swimmer could remain under water), and a fancy diving event from the springboard. And in Germany in the early twentieth century, groups of male and female divers participated in joint exhibitions, with women diving from lower platforms than those used by the men.

Critics of women's diving claimed that, because women have breasts, they could not rotate

AN EXAGGERATED SENSE OF FAIR PLAY

In the women's springboard event of the 1952 Olympics in Helsinki, U.S. athlete Zoe Ann Olsen-Jensen (1931–) planned a double and half somersault. She completely missed the take-off and badly splashed into the water, consequently receiving a low score. She protested, but the referee rejected the complaint; the only official who tried to help her was the Finnish technical representative, who said that the fulcrum was in movement at the moment of her take-off and that the athlete's performance was therefore affected. The jury allowed Olsen-Jensen to redo her dive, but afterward, in what diving expert Pat Besford calls a "wise and fair decision," the previous low score was recognized. This final decision was an important event in women's sports as it showed that a woman athlete could make technical errors like her male colleagues and could continue to compete without the benefit of a compassionate—but false or misplaced—excuse or justification. Despite the one bad dive, Olsen-Jensen won the bronze medal.

their bodies in the air as easily or as completely as men and therefore risked injury. Moreover, the promoters of diving shows stressed that courage and determination, as well as quick reactions, were needed to perform high dives and acrobatic dives—and these were viewed as male attributes. Beyond these cultural factors, women were also thought to be too weak or nervous and thus unable to maintain the high degree of concentration necessary to perform the most difficult stunts. In reality, though, the limits placed on women's participation were due to cultural biases against women performing athletic exercises in public.

Apparently, the sporting press was enthusiastic when women performed the most difficult dives, but often promoters and the same reporters were much more interested in another aspect of women's diving, its visual appeal. Consequently, women were directed toward exhibition diving.

WOMEN DIVERS EMERGE

As modern diving developed in the twentieth century, physiologists recognized that women were indeed able to dive, but women's diving remained limited because of continuing concerns about women displaying their bodies in public. In 1907 the Australian swimmer and diver Annette Kellermann (1886–1953), whose skill was universally recognized, was placed on trial for offending the public decency; as she dived, her costume had shown her leg completely uncovered from her thigh down, and she had also displayed her bare back and upper arms. A compromise was reached with Kellerman agreeing to wear a jersey under the costume and pants slightly above the knee. It was not until the 1920s that women began to show bare upper arms, thighs, and backs. The media stressed that, in diving, women were better when they displayed grace, softness, and elegance. Men, in contrast, were not required to be graceful.

The tendency to consider women's diving as a theatrical as well as an athletic event persisted during the period between the two world wars. It was reinforced by the appearance of women in Hollywood films and swimming circuses. Showy costumes and exotic headgear transformed the divers into modern nymphs, who captivated the spectators with their beauty and glamour. In some movies, women divers were displayed in beauty parades that had nothing to do with competition as they performed few or no stunts. When women were permitted to dive, they were restricted to the springboard until after World War II.

COMPETITIVE DIVING

Through the first half of the twentieth century, women's diving was most often seen as entertainment, but women did dive competitively, and women's diving was an event at national and international meets and at the Olympics, where women first dived in 1912.

For both women and men, the associations that scouted swish clubs for new talent emphasized recruiting and training boys and girls for diving. Training focused on acrobatic moves, speed, and technique, and special attention was given to training girls who would become international champions in their early teens (this is still a major focus). Diving preceded other women's sports such as tennis, gymnastics, and swimming in its emphasis on the training of young athletes. The U.S. diver Aileen Riggin (1906–) won the springboard event in the Olympics at Antwerp in 1920 when she was fourteen years old. Marjorie Gestring (1922–1992), also of the United States, won the 1936 springboard Olympic contest in Berlin at the age of thirteen.

After World War II, however, the abilities of mature women were emphasized, and older U.S. women began to dive competitively. For example, Patricia McCormick (1930–) won the Olympics at Melbourne in 1956, in both springboard and platform, when she was twenty-six years old. This trend was later replaced by a resumption of recruiting and training the very young, a preference that continued into the 1990s, as Germany, Russia (and other nations of the former Soviet Union), and China joined the United States in dominating top-level competitions. In general, since the 1950s, women's diving has become more international, with divers from Sweden, Denmark, Canada, the United Kingdom, France, and Australia joining those from China, Germany, Russia, and the United States on the lists of Olympic medal winners.

NEARING EQUALITY

The Olympics have been the venue for the continuing fight by women divers for equality. Women first competed in Olympic diving in 1912 in Stockholm, in the platform events, with ten compulsory plain dives, that is, without the acrobatic moves used by the men. Women's springboard diving became an event in the 1920 Olympics in Antwerp, whereas in platform diving, a plain diving program was used by women. Men made two dives from 5 meters (16.5 feet) and three from 10 meters (33 feet); women made two

Platform diver Li Na at the 1998 Asian Games. (Corbis/AFP)

dives from 4 meters (13.2 feet) and three from 8 meters (26.4 feet). At Paris in 1924, women gained equality in distance, with dives from 5 and 10 meters, but still only plain diving was allowed. In 1925 the Fédération Internationale de Natation Amateur (FINA; International Federation of Amateur Swimming) ended the distinction between plain and fancy diving and established a new official program that distinguished only between springboard and platform events. Still, at the 1928 Olympics in Amsterdam, dives from the platform remained compulsory for women, with less attention given to the degree of difficulty of the dive for women than for the men. The situation remained the same at the Olympics at Los Angeles in 1932, but in the springboard event Georgia Coleman (1912–1940) was daring enough to attempt and complete a double somersault and a half in the voluntary dives. Finally, at the 1936 Olympics a compulsory backward dive from 5 meters (16.5 feet) was allowed for women in the platform event. In the 1948 Olympics in London, more complex dives were allowed for both sexes, but the maximum degree of difficulty tolerated for women was less, even though the women were allowed to perform voluntary platform dives for the first time and women officials served as judges.

For the 1996 Olympics in Atlanta, the rules for women's dives were changed again. In the springboard event, women made five dives, and the twelve finalists made five dives in the final round, with no limit on the degree of difficulty. In the platform event, women made four dives in the preliminary round, and then the finalists made five dives with no limit on the degree of difficulty.

CONCLUSION

By the end of the 1990s, women divers had neared equality with men as women were allowed to perform all types of dives, but in the compulsory dives women's dives were as a group still less difficult than men's. This easier compulsory schedule continues to reflect the old view that women are unable to perform the most acrobatic dives. Another vestige of the past is that, in the final phase of the platform competition, women continue to perform fewer dives than the men do. Nonetheless, competitive diving by women is now a full sport that has fully replaced the earlier entertainment diving and has become a major competitive sport for women around the world. The trend in the late 1990s returned to the recruitment of younger divers, with some of the best in the world being in their mid-teens.

Gherardo Bonini

Bibliography

Besford, Pat. (1952) "Swimming," in *Olympic Games 1952*. British Olympic Association Official Report. London: World Sports.

Cryer, Jon. (1996) "Olympic Diving." <http://www.members.aol.com>.

Domenico, Maiello, and Carlo Cuccioletta. (1994) *II nuoto dalle origini all'Impero Romano. (Swimming from the Beginning to the Roman Empire)*. Rome: Nemi.

Keil, Ian, and Don Wix. (1996) *In the Swim: The Amateur Swimming Association from 1869 to 1994*. Loughborough: Swimming Times.

Lechnir, Josef, and Hanns Kefer (1936) *Die Schule des Wassersprings*. Berlin: Limpert.

Mallon, Bill, and Erich Kamper. (1992) *II libro d'oro delle Olimpiadi*. Milan: Vallardi & Associates.

Volker, Kluge. (1997) "Olympische Sommerspiele. 1896–1936 (I)." *Die Chronik*. Berlin: Sportverlag.

DOD, CHARLOTTE

(1871–1960)

BRITISH MULTISPORT ATHLETE

Charlotte "Lottie" Dod is considered the best all-around British female athlete of all time. Best known as a champion tennis player, she also excelled at golf, archery, and field hockey, as well as luge and ice skating. Growing up in the Victorian era, she defied most standards of appropriate behavior for women and, in the process, opened up opportunities for other women to participate in sports.

Dod was born in Cheshire, England, on 21 September 1871 as the fourth child of a retired cotton broker. After demonstrating her talent for lawn tennis (a sport then open to women), she was nicknamed the "Little Wonder." During her eleven-year tennis career, she won five ladies' singles titles at Wimbledon and thirty-three in other tournaments in singles, doubles, and mixed doubles, frequently accompanied by her two brothers or her sister. She lost only five singles matches in her career and is the youngest woman or man to win Wimbledon, having won for the first time in 1887 at the age of fifteen years and nine months.

She was known not just for her victories but also for her style of play and dress. Unlike the other women who stroked the ball back and forth from their baselines, Dod played an aggressive, men's style of game, featuring powerful ground strokes and charges to the net to finish the point off with overhead smashes. Part of her success was also due to her unorthodox attire. Again, she ignored the norms of women's behavior; instead of wearing the cumbersome skirts of the disciplined Victorian tennis ladies, she played in her calf-length school uniform skirt. With the less restrictive clothing, she was able to use to full advantage her dynamic, attacking style. Her choice of more practical attire made it clear to others that the right to dress appropriately for sports needed to be an important component of the effort to allow women to participate freely in sports. A fierce competitor, Dod also took on male opponents; in an 1888 handicap match, in which Dod started each game with a 30–0 advantage, she beat the men's Wimbledon champion Ernest Renshaw—and later in the year she also beat her brother William, another prominent tennis player.

In 1889, when Dod was only eighteen years of age, she temporarily left tennis to dedicate herself to golf, which she had been playing since she was thirteen. (In 1891 she returned briefly to tennis, quickly demonstrating her superiority over the other women players and winning Wimbledon again in 1882). During her golf career, Dod won the British Amateur Championship in 1904 and represented England at the international level. To tennis and golf she added field hockey and archery. She was a member of the Spital Hockey Club and was twice selected to play on the English national team. In archery she won a silver medal at the 1908 Olympics while her brother William took the gold in the men's event. She was also an accomplished ice skater and the first woman to make a run down the bobsled course at Saint-Moritz. Dod remained an active sportswoman until the outbreak of World War I. She died at the age of eighty-eight on 27 June 1960. In 1986 she was elected to the International Women's Sports Hall of Fame.

Gherardo Bonini

Bibliography

Kamper, Erich, and Bill Mallon. (1992) *Il libro d'oro delle Olimpiadi.* Milan: Vallardi & Associates.

Little, Alan. (1983) *Lottie Dod: Wimbledon Champion and All-rounder Extraordinary.* London: Kenneth Ritchie Wimbledon Library.

Pollard, Marjorie. (1946) *Fifty Years of All England Women's Field Hockey Association (1895–1945).* Harcourt, England: Christopher Press.

Wymer, Norman. (1949) *Sport in England.* London: Harrap.

DOUBLE DUTCH

Jumping rope, one of the most venerable of traditional children's activities, can be done by one person or several. In its simplest form it is a matter of holding both ends of a rope, swinging the rope around, and jumping over it as it reaches its lowest point. Double Dutch is a specialized form of jumping rope involving two ropes turned independently in synchrony—popular as an inexpensive and easily accessible activity played primarily by girls. Double Dutch has been transformed into an increasingly popular sport that can be played for fun or competition.

HISTORY

The origins of jumping rope can be traced back to ancient Phoenicia and Egypt. Rope makers at that time plied their trade in large work areas in seaports. As the spinners spun the fiber into rope, runners would jump over and through the strands in order to fetch additional hemp. It is likely that the rope makers created a series of games with two pairs of rope and the games were passed on through the generations and carried to the places to which the trading ships traveled. During the 1600s the Dutch colonists brought the game to the New World, and especially to New

Double Dutch on Harlem sidewalk. (Corbis/Michael S. Yamashita)

THE JOYS OF SKIPPING

Excerpt from The Secret Garden *by Frances Hodgson Burnett*

The skipping-rope was a wonderful thing. [Mary] counted and skipped, and skipped and counted, until her cheeks were quite red, and she was more interested than she had ever been since she was born. The sun was shining and a little wind was blowing—not a rough wind, but one which came in delightful little gusts and brought a fresh scent of newly turned earth with it. . . . She skipped at last into the kitchen-garden and saw Ben Weatherstaff digging and talking to his robin, which was hopping about him. She skipped down the walk towards him and he lifted his head and looked at her with a curious expression. She had wondered if he would notice her. She really wanted him to see her skip.

'Well!' he exclaimed. 'Upon my word! P'raps tha' art a young 'un, after all, an' p'raps tha's got child's blood in they veins instead of sour buttermilk. Tha's skipped red into thy cheeks as sure as my name's Ben Weatherstaff. I wouldn't have believed tha' could do it.'

'I never skipped before,' Mary said. 'I'm just beginning. I can only go up to twenty.'

'Tha' keep on,' said Ben. 'Tha' shapes well enough at it for a young 'un that's lived with heathen. . . ."

Mary skipped round all the gardens and round the orchard, resting every few minutes. At length she went to her own special walk and made up her mind to try if she could skip the whole length of it. It was a good long skip, and she began slowly, but before she had gone halfway down the path she was so hot and breathless that she was obliged to stop. She did not mind much, because she had already counted up to thirty. She stopped with a little laugh of pleasure, and there, lo and behold, was the robin swaying on a long branch of ivy.

FRANCES HODGSON BURNETT
(1911) The Secret Garden.

Amsterdam. When the English took control of the colony and renamed the city New York, they began using the term "Double Dutch" to describe any Dutch words or customs that seemed confusing or difficult to understand. The rope-jumping games later took root in the United States and became an enduring game of childhood.

In 1973 David A. Walker, a New York City police officer working in the community affairs department, institutionalized the sport of Double Dutch. With Detective Ulysses Williams, he founded the American Double Dutch League. Walker saw the sport as a way to involve and energize the many girls and young women he worked with who had few opportunities to participate in competitive sports. As Walker explained, "One Christmas . . . I started a bike training program. After noticing that it was only boys who turned up, I figured that I needed to come up with something for girls. When I saw a group of kids doing Double Dutch in the street, bells suddenly went off in my head. I thought it could be developed as a sport."

Although his superiors were skeptical, Walker persevered. He asked, "Aren't there lessons to be learned from practicing teamwork and competition? What better way to protect our future mothers, aunts, and godmothers than to teach them to respect and love themselves—and each other?" The following year, in 1974, 700 young girls from the Harlem section of Manhattan participated in the first Double Dutch tournament. In the 1990s more than 250,000 youngsters were jumping Double Dutch in cities across the United States, and the International Double Dutch Federation coordinated activities in nations around the world, including the Netherlands, Germany, Great Britain, Japan, Sweden, and France. On 7 December 1997 the sixth annual Double Dutch Holiday Classic was held at the Apollo Theater in Harlem, with more than 250 competitors from as far away as Japan; the participants showed extraordinary dexterity as they danced over two ropes twirling in opposite directions.

RULES AND PLAY

There are two forms of Double Dutch teams. Singles teams consist of two rope turners and one rope jumper; a doubles team requires two rope turners and two jumpers. Equipment needs are minimal: a set of Double Dutch jump ropes, comfortable clothing, and a flat surface with enough room for the rope and players to move about safely.

The basic piece of equipment is the recreational Double Dutch rope, which is made from number 9 or number 10 weight sash rope. Four equal-length pieces of identical rope are used to make a Double Dutch rope set. For a singles team set, the length of the four pieces is 2.2 to 2.7 meters long (10 to 12 feet); for a doubles team set, the length is 2.7 to 4 meters (12 to 14 feet).

Double Dutch competitions are always played on hard, flat surfaces such as a gymnasium floor. The floors are marked for competition to provide space for the teams to turn ropes and to allow room for the judges and counters. A mechanical tally counter is used for the speed test category. A time clock is used to set and control the speed, compulsory, and freestyle events, and a whistle or buzzer is used to start and end all competitive events.

Tournament officials include the floor judge, recorder, floor counter, freestyle judge, scorekeeper, and timekeeper. The floor judge verifies the team members' names, checks the conditions of the ropes and the equipment, and is responsible for making sure there are no violations of the rules during the competition. The recorder assists the floor judge and keeps a record of violations. During the singles and doubles two-minute speed tests, the floor counter, using a mechanical tally counter, counts the number of completed jumps by carefully counting each time the jumper's left foot correctly hits the floor. If a violation occurs, the floor counter stops counting until the jumper resumes the correct jumping procedure. Points are deducted for every violation. Freestyle judges, usually physical education instructors, dance instructors, or trained Double Dutch judges, check to see that the routine expresses the three main criteria: intricate rope turning, dance, and strength.

Competition begins when the turners hold their ropes at a still position touching the tournament floor. They must maintain an upright position while turning. If the ropes stop, the turners must resume turning within five seconds. A singles team jumper or doubles team jumpers must enter the inwardly moving ropes from either end of where a turner is standing within five seconds of the starting whistle and without touching the ropes. If the rope touches a jumper or the other rope, a bad entry violation is charged, and points are deducted.

During the speed test, the jumpers must use alternating steps (the jumper's legs moving one after the other and jumping at least four inches off the floor). Once within the ropes, the jumpers must stand erect, with arms held waist-high, on hips, crossed at the waist, or straight down. A jumper must remain in the center of the rope's arc during the speed test, and the jumper must exit cleanly without touching the ropes within five seconds of the closing whistle. The exit must be at an oblique angle off the right or left shoulder of the turner the jumper is facing.

There are several competitive Double Dutch tests, including speed tests and freestyle tricks, as well as the compulsory tricks jumper test, which involves the following sequence: two right jumps on the right foot; two left turn jumps on the left foot; two right foot crisscross jumps (right foot passing over the left); two left foot crisscross jumps (left foot passing over the right); and ten high steps (alternating jumps in which the jumper's knee is lifted waist-high with the thigh parallel to the floor).

These tricks must be completed within 30 seconds for the singles team and 40 seconds for the doubles team. Freestyle routines are judged by the agility of the participants, their coordination and dance movements, and the degree of difficulty of execution.

There are Double Dutch teams in a variety of competition levels from the amateur, school grade, and parks and recreation divisions, to the advanced professional division. Double Dutch competitors range in age from eight to thirty and, although the participants are predominantly female, boys and men jump as well. As part of its worldwide expansion, a Double Dutch exhibition was scheduled for the 2000 Olympic Games in

Sydney, Australia. Proponents hope that the Olympics will soon welcome Double Dutch as a competitive event.

Mickey Friedman

Bibliography

New York Sports OnLine (1999) <http://www.nynow.com/nysol/ddutch2.html>.

Walker, David A. (1997) *Double Dutch: Official Rule Book.* Bronx, New York: National Double Dutch League.

Additional information was provided by David A. Walker and the National Double Dutch League.

DRUGS AND DRUG TESTING

The use of drugs or other illegal methods to improve performance is a major ethical issue in modern sports. Many people believe that the use of drugs to enhance performance destroys the

Russian runner Marina Trandenkova leads Colombian runner Zandra Borrero in a 100-meter race at the 1996 Olympics. Trandenkova qualifed for the finals but was subsequently disqualified when she tested positive for a banned substance. (Corbis/Wally McNamee)

basic rationale for competitive sport—to determine the best through a fair competition. Drug use, or "doping" as it is commonly called in the sports world, is an issue for both men and women, and some of the best-known cases of doping or suspected doping have involved women. These include the East German swimmers in the 1970s, the Chinese swimmers in the 1990s, and the Irish swimmer Michelle Smith at the 1996 Olympics.

HISTORY

Accusations that athletes used performance-enhancing substances date back as far as ancient Greece. The issue became central to modern sports only in the 1960s, when several European sport organizations and the International Olympic Committee (IOC) became concerned about the practice. The IOC created a medical commission and initiated an antidoping program to protect the health of the athletes, to respect medical and sport ethics, and to ensure fair competition for all athletes. In the 1960s, after cardiovascular problems and even deaths were attributed to amphetamine use, some stimulants and narcotics were the first drugs to be prohibited.

Since that time, the IOC has been the central organization involved in the drug testing of athletes. The IOC provides lists of banned drugs and has established a network of testing laboratories that grew from six in 1984 to twenty-five in 1998. In addition, most sport associations now have their own regulations to control doping. However, these regulations are not the same across organizations, and substances that are banned in one sport may not be banned in another. In addition, the testing programs often differ from one country to another and from one federation to the other, and the sanctions for a given doping offense may vary from a public warning to a four-year ban on participation.

Only a few international federations have implemented a serious and extensive out-of-competition testing program, the only approach to control that many experts believe can be effective. Unfortunately, collection of urine samples without prior notification to the athletes represents a formidable task. For example, the testing organizations that collect samples must know the athletes' whereabouts at all times.

SOME TEENAGE GIRLS RELY ON STEROIDS

A study conducted by Charles Yesaltis of Pennsylvania State University shows that in the 1990s the use of steroids by eighth-grade girls increased dramatically while it declined for boys. The increased use reflected both a low level of use by girls in the past and a recent increase in the level of girls' participation in sports requiring strength.

CONTROLLED DRUGS IN SPORTS

Some athletes take banned substances—and risk exposing themselves to suspension, disqualification, and health problems—to excel and reap the rewards of sports competition. In some sports, athletes believe that because other athletes use drugs, they can compete successfully only if they also use drugs. For some athletes, the drugs' benefits seem to take precedence over the remote possibility of getting caught or the prospect of dangerous side effects.

The drug arsenal is highly diversified and it is expanding. The agents used include stimulants, which are used to mask fatigue, increase alertness, and stimulate the metabolism; diuretics, taken to control body weight; anabolic agents, used to speed recovery from injury, raise hormone levels, and increase muscle mass and strength; and masking agents to dilute urine samples or retard the excretion of other drugs, making their detection more difficult.

Many medications and drugs are either prohibited or restricted by international sport authorities. The authorities are constantly modifying the list of banned substances and methods to incorporate other classes of drugs, following methodological improvements in detection and reports of abuse by athletes. Anabolic steroids were added to the list in 1976; blood doping, masking agents, diuretics and beta-blockers in 1988; and peptide hormones and beta-2 agonists as anabolic agents in 1992. Substances of restricted use, meaning that they are permitted under certain conditions in certain circumstances, are the corticosteroids (anti-inflammatory agents) and the local anesthetics. For example, in the meat industry, clenbuterol and other beta-2-agonists may be illegally administered to promote animal growth. It was found in the early 1990s that athletes were using clenbuterol during training and competitions. As a result beta-2 agonists were banned, but a few of them are permitted as asthma medications by inhalation only. In the late 1990s, marijuana and alcohol use were prohibited by a few sport federations, but the IOC has not banned the use of marijuana although it wished to prohibit its use during the Sydney Olympics in 2000.

Russian scientists have added to this collection in the 1990s through the development of the stimulants mesocarb, bromantan, and carphedon. Just before the 1996 Olympic Games, through the joint efforts of five IOC-accredited laboratories and the International Amateur Athletic Federation (IAAF), a new doping agent, bromantan, was identified. The metabolite (that is, the by-product of metabolism) of this unknown substance was found, from the end of 1994 through 1996, in the urine samples of many competitors, the vast majority of whom were female athletes from Russia, along with a few from some of the former Eastern European communist nations. Reportedly, an agent that modifies immune function and a thermoprotective agent, bromantan is also considered a stimulant. A year later, another unknown Russian drug that had been synthesized four years earlier, carphedon, was added to the list of banned stimulants after it was identified in athletes' urine samples.

METHODS OF DRUG TESTING

Doping controls during competition were first applied in the late 1960s and focused mainly on stimulants. The first comprehensive gas chromatographic method for the detection of stimulants and narcotics was implemented during the Munich Olympics (1972) by Manfred Donike.

Table 1. IOC List of banned substances and methods as of 1998

Prohibited classes of substances and examples

Stimulants	Amineptine, amphetamines, bromantan, caffeine, carphedon, cocaine, ephedrines, mesocarb, methylphenidate, nicetamide, pemoline, phentermine, salbutamol, selegiline, strychnine, and others
Narcotics	Heroin, hydrocodone, methadone, morphine, pethidine, and others
Anabolic agents	Androstenedione, boldenone, clenbuterol, dehydrochlormethyltestosterone, dihydroepiandrosterone, fluoxymesterone, methandienone, methenolone, methyltestosterone, nandrolone, oxandrolone, oxymetholone, stanozolol, testosterone, and others
Diuretics	Canrenone, furosemide, hydrochlorothiazide, indapamide, triamterene, and others
Peptide and glycoprotein hormones and analogues	Human chorionic gonadotrophin (hCG), corticotrophin (ACTH), human growth hormone (hGH), erythropoietin (EPO)

Prohibited methods

Blood doping	Administration of blood, red blood cells, and related blood products
Pharmaceutical, chemical, and physical manipulation	Catheterization, urine substitution/tampering, inhibition of renal excretion, probenecide, epitestosterone, bromantan, diuretics

Classes of drugs subject to certain restrictions

Alcohol

Marijuana

Local anesthetics

Corticosteroids

Beta-blockers

More than 2,000 samples were analyzed. During the Montreal Olympic Games (1976) authorities tested for some anabolic androgenic steroids in about 200 samples by a combination of immunoassays and mass spectrometry. The procedure was obviously less sensitive than it is now because of limited knowledge of anabolic androgenic steroids' metabolism, the lack of specificity of the immunoassays, and the restricted capabilities of the 1970s gas chromatograph–mass spectrometer analysis. Analytical instrumentation was significantly improved in the mid-1980s and finally provided the versatile tool needed to efficiently detect traces of anabolic agents in urine samples.

Both human and veterinary substances are included in the class of anabolic agents and, in fact, are taken by some athletes. For example, zeranol, a nonsteroidal estrogenic agent and a growth promoter in the veterinary practice, was once reported present in an athlete's specimen. Scientists of many laboratories worked hard to gain knowledge of the excretion of steroids metabolites and to develop sensitive and comprehensive gas chromatographic–mass spectrometric methods. The detection of some anabolic agents represented a real challenge. For many years, stanozolol, for example, was reputed to be invisible, and indeed sensitive detection was not achieved until the end of the 1980s. The laboratories' ability to detect traces of metabolites steadily improved. The IOC now requires that laboratories use high-sensitivity techniques such as those afforded by high-resolution or tandem mass spectrometry.

PROCEDURES FOR DRUG TESTING

Samples collected during competition are tested for the presence of all banned and restricted substances. The out-of-competition program focuses mainly on the anabolic agents, including the beta-2 agonists, the masking agents such as probenecide, epitestosterone, and the diuretics.

Testing requires a rigorous procedure to ensure that neither athletes nor anyone else tampers with the samples. The specimens are divided in two coded and sealed bottles, labeled A and B.

The laboratory receives both A and B samples but does the testing procedures on the A sample only while the B container is kept intact. An athlete notified that the laboratory has confirmed a positive result can request that the B-sample analysis be made in the presence of his or her representatives.

The vast majority of banned or restricted substances are synthetic compounds. Even if some stimulants such as the ephedrines, caffeine, cocaine, strychnine, the narcotic morphine, and marijuana are natural, their presence in human body fluids reflects the intake of a given preparation. Since more than one hundred drugs and medications must be tested simultaneously, the doping control laboratories developed different screening procedures to group substances of similar physicochemical nature and properties. Different analytical strategies are applied, but in most instances the substances are extracted from urine and analyzed by gas chromatography with selective detection, immunoassays, high-pressure liquid chromatography, or gas chromatography–mass spectrometry. A positive finding consists of confirmation of the presence of the doping agents or their metabolites in the specimen as measured against authentic standards or reference urine samples. This finding must be confirmed by mass spectrometry, the only exception being peptide hormones such as hCG (human growth hormone).

The stimulants, the beta-blockers, and the narcotics taken to exert their action during the competition will most of the time be present in amounts higher than the detection limit of the procedure. More sensitive techniques are required for anabolic agents that athletes took during training and stopped taking prior to the competition testing. The detection periods are extremely variable depending on the steroid metabolism, the pharmaceutical preparation, and its mode of administration ranging from one day to several months.

Now that purely synthetic substances can be detected quite effectively, some athletes are turning to the natural steroids. Testing to prove the use of substances that are normally present in human body fluids represents a more complex task. Dihydrotestosterone (DHT), testosterone and its precursors, androstenedione, androstenediol, and dehydroepiandrosterone (DHEA), banned in sport as anabolic agents, are naturally found in humans of both genders in greater or smaller quantities. Some may be purchased as nutritional supplements in the United States. The administration of these steroids which alter the normal urinary steroid profile by either suppressing or increasing the excretion of some metabolites, can be identified in the laboratory.

Since 1982 and following the work of Manfred Donike, laboratories now detect the use of testosterone through the increased value of the testosterone-epitestosterone ratio in urine. Fifteen years later and following many attempts to question its diagnostic value, the testosterone-epitestosterone ratio has proved its usefulness. Analyses of thousands of samples were made to measure the normal ranges of testosterone-epitestosterone values in male and female athletes. Research also showed that, if no steroids are used, the values of the testosterone-epitestosterone ratios of a given individual are stable. Comparing the reported elevated testosterone-epitestosterone value to the athlete's individual normal value allows the laboratory to distinguish between a normal systematic excretion of elevated values and the sudden increase related to the use of testosterone or its precursors.

It is now possible to test for all natural substances thought to be used as performance enhancers but not yet for EPO (erythropoietin) and hGH.

DRUGS AND SPORTS

In the 1990s, media coverage of sports suggested that athletes could reach the top of their sport only if they used performance-enhancing drugs. Superior athletic performances are often overshadowed by rumors of doping spread by observers and other competitors. In fact, the prevalence of doping in Olympic sports cannot be precisely estimated. According to the yearly statistics of the testing activities in IOC-accredited laboratories, positive findings are reported in around 1 to 2 percent of the 50,000 to 60,000 A samples analyzed, with not all positive findings resulting from illegal drug use. For example, the presence of salbutamol (an asthma control medication) in the specimen is reported by the laboratory, but the sport authorities do not sanction the athlete if they were properly notified in

On December 22, 1999, three former East German sports officials were convicted of causing bodily harm to female teenage swimmers from 1975 to 1989. The three were charged with giving the swimmers anabolic steroids to improve the swimmers' performances. The three officials were Jargon Tanneberger, the former East German women's swimming coach; another coach Wolfgang Richter; and Egon Muller, former general-secretary of the East German sports federation. Each was placed on one year's probation and fined $2,600 which was donated to a women's sports organization. World champion swimmers, such as Kornelia Ender and Kristin Otto, were given steroids and other drugs as part of the East German program.

advance that the athlete used this medication. Including non-Olympic sports for which tests are conducted, the highest number of positive findings are due to the use of anabolic agents (testosterone, nandrolone, methandienone, stanozolol, and clenbuterol) followed by the stimulants (ephedrines, amphetamine, caffeine, and cocaine).

Thirty years after the testing was first used at Olympic events, some people are ready to describe the control programs in Olympic sports as a total failure and suggest publicly that the ban on drug use in sport be lifted. Those who take this position argue that the use of performance-enhancing substances in elite sports is so widespread that nothing can reverse the situation. They describe the existing control programs as motivated by paternalism; as ineffective, costly, and flawed; and even as endangering the health of athletes by pushing them to turn to black-market sources, undetectable substances, or masking agents. They further argue that doping would not mean cheating in sports if authorities had not taken the view that it is unethical. They believe that there are no proven serious health problems associated with the use of these substances when administered under the supervision of a physician and that, as far as competent consenting adults are concerned, doping-control programs conducted by sports authorities constitute an unacceptable interference in their personal lives.

Critics of this accepting view cite what is now known about the doping program in the former East Germany. In 1999 four coaches and two doctors stood accused of causing grievous bodily harm in a spectacular trial revealing how, in the former East Germany, female athletes as young as eleven and thirteen were forced to take pills and receive injections of male hormones (dehydrochlormethyltestosterone, testosterone, and mesterolone), referred to as "supporting means." Secret police files show that probably thousands of athletes, including minors, were used since the 1960s in what is believed to be a methodically planned system driven by one goal: proving the superiority of the East German communist state through astonishing athletic performances. The program focused primarily on girls and women athletes because developing strength and endurance in these athletes would lead to the greatest achievements in sports. Physicians have documented the side effects in these girls, which range from a deepening of the voice and muscle cramps and tightness to steroid acne, hirsutism (excessive bodily hair), and irregular menstruation to polycystic ovarian syndrome and liver damage in a few cases. Although the program went on for nearly thirty years, very few female athletes were ever caught. The scientists developed ways to avoid positive test results by designing new undetectable drugs, monitoring the elimination of urinary metabolites, and even manipulating urine samples. But the drugs did help in competition: some records established by East German female athletes in the 1970s and 1980s have never been matched.

China provides another example of a mass doping program, again for the purpose of enhancing the nation's performance in international competitions. China was suspected of practicing organized doping because female swimmers in the 1990s had the powerful muscles and broad shoulders that brought back memories of the East German swimmers at the Montreal Olympic Games in 1976. During the Asian Games in 1994, some Chinese male and female athletes' urine samples contained a banned anabolic androgenic steroid, dihydrotestosterone and, four years later at the Perth world swimming championships, the presence of the diuretic-masking agent triamterene was found in four Chinese swimmers' samples. Adding to the scandal, a female athlete was caught at Australian customs smuggling vials of human growth hormone. As a result, Chinese sport authorities had to take a strong stand against doping and implement stringent educational and control programs.

THE CURRENT SITUATION AND THE FUTURE

Doping has no frontiers, and it should never be assumed to be restricted to certain countries or sports. Male and female athletes from many different nations, in a wide range of sports, and as young as fifteen have tested positive. Although in Western countries doping is viewed as an individual decision, undoubtedly the pressure on athletes in some sports to use performance-enhancing substances is very great. The risks to wealthy athletes may be less than those for other athletes as they can rely on a physician to monitor the potentially harmful side effects of the drug and can afford legal representation to contest a positive finding.

The pressure to use drugs is not restricted to the elite nor to one gender; boys and girls are using these substances. While the level of steroid use in boys seems stable, the level of use among teenage girls in the United States has doubled since 1991. This development may reflect the increased athletic opportunities for women as well as the desire for a leaner body. Education programs to control drug use are designed mainly for boys, and teenage girls are not receiving proper counseling. Although in many countries the traffic and importation of drugs and anabolic agents are controlled, it is relatively easy to buy them, and the Internet is an endless resource for regimens designed by sports gurus to enhance muscle mass and stimulate the body.

The summer of 1998 will be remembered as a tragic period in the use of performance-enhancing substances. During the 1998 Tour de France, the month-long cycling race, the athletic performances were barely noticed as a team of professional cyclists had to be removed from the Tour after it was learned that the athletes took drugs under medical supervision. As reported by the press, a member of the staff was caught at customs with vials and pills of erythropoietin, human growth hormone, anabolic agents, and stimulants. Women's sports were also tainted in August 1998, when Irish swimmer Michelle Smith was suspended from international competition by the FINA when an out-of-competition sample provided eight months before showed "unequivocal signs of adulteration." She is appealing this decision. Although her tests were always negative, Smith's gold medal performances at the Atlanta Olympic Games were openly criticized and attacked by other competitors and observers as the products of drug use.

These embarrassments and others refueled the debate about drug use and especially about the effectiveness of control programs, with some experts calling for the legalization of drug use and others calling for more testing and even criminal sanctions. In addition, appeals by athletes because of positive test results have led to hearings and arbitration sessions during which all aspects of drug testing protocols are challenged in an attempt to find a mistake that can be used to clear the athlete.

The IOC and most international sport federations have committed themselves to fight doping, and the IOC held a conference on the issue in February 1999. However, the conference produced few tangible results because delegates were divided over whether the IOC or an independent agency should control the international program and supervise the effort to harmonize all aspects of the doping control programs, including regulations and sanctions, as well as research and laboratory accreditation. At the conference the authority of the IOC was weakened by the then-recent scandal of over payments to IOC members from cities seeking to host the Olympics.

Christiane Ayotte

Bibliography

Ayotte, Christiane. (1997) "Evaluation of Elevated Testosterone/Epitestosterone Values in Athletes' Urine Samples." *IAF New Studies in Athletics*, 12: 2–3.

Ayotte, Christiane, Danielle Goudreault, and Alain Charlebois. (1996) "Testing for Natural and Synthetic Anabolic Agents in Human Urine." *Journal of Chromatography B* 687: 3–25.

Canadian Centre for Drug-free Sport. (1993) Étude Scolaire Nationale sur la Drogue et le Sport, Final Report. Ottawa, Canada: Canadian Centre for Drug-free Sport.

Faigenbaum, Avery D., Leonard D. Zaichkowsky, Douglas E. Bardner, and Lyle J. Micheli. (1998) "Anabolic Steroid Use by Male and Female Middle School Students." *Pediatrics* 101, 5:6.

Franke Werner W., and Brigitte Berendonk. (1997) "Hormonal Doping and Androgenization of Athletes: A Secret Program of the German Democratic Republic Government, Doping in Sports Symposium." *Clinical Chemistry* 43, 7: 1262–1279.

Hemmersbach, Peter, and Raphael de la Torre. (1996) "Stimulants, Narcotics and b-Blockers: 25 Years of Development in Analytical Techniques for Doping Control." *Journal of Chromatography B* 687: 221–238.

International Olympic Committee. (1995) *IOC Medical Code*. Lausanne: IOC.

Ventura, Rosa, and Jordi Segura. (1996) "Detection of Diuretic Agents in Doping Control." *Journal of Chromatography B* 687: 127–144.

Voy, Robert, and Kirk Deeter. (1991) *Drugs, Sport, and Politics*. Champaign, IL: Leisure Press.

Yesalis, Charles. (1993) *Anabolic Steroids in Sport and Exercise*. Champaign, IL: Human Kinetics.

Yesalis, Charles, C. Barsukiewicz, Andrea N. Kopstein, and Michael S. Bahrke. (1997) "Trends in Anabolic-Androgenic Steroid Use Among Adolescents." *Archives of Pediatric and Adolescent Medicine* 151, 1197–1206.

DUATHLON

Duathlon is an endurance racing sport that most often involves a combination of running and bicycling, although technically a duathlon may be made up of any pair of the component disciplines of triathlon (swimming, biking, and running). Women have both participated and been influential in the duathlon since its beginning as a formal sport.

HISTORY

The biathlon—the original name of the duathlon—together with the related sport of triathlon, developed in California in the 1970s. The multisport movement originated in California, where an active life-style leads many residents to bike, run, and swim to maintain fitness and health. Children often do all three in the same day. The multisport pioneer Scott Tinley suggests that the earliest informal races were dual-discipline events. Endurance runners, for example, would jump in for a refreshing (but perhaps competitive) swim immediately following a run.

The earliest quasi-organized multisport race is believed to have been assembled by David Pain in San Diego on his fiftieth birthday. Pain threw himself a party, at which he had guests compete in a "biathlon." In this version they ran a 10-kilometer (6.2-mile) race before swimming 750 meters (0.5 miles). Within two years, two of Pain's friends, Don Shannahan and Jack Johnstone, had created the first formal triathlon by adding a bike portion to Pain's original mixture.

Starting in the late 1970s, triathlon received a good deal of publicity. Adherents flocked to the sport, many as a result of Julie Moss's heroic finish in the 1982 Hawaii Ironman Triathlon. Moss finished a full day of racing by collapsing several hundred meters from the finish in extreme glycogen depletion. Eventually she crawled across the finish line by a sheer act of will.

The Triathlon Federation of the United States emerged as the national governing board for multisport endurance events (triathlon and duathlon) in 1982. A confederation of these national boards, known as the International Triathlon Union (ITU), arose in 1989 with the avowed purposes of making triathlon—rather than duathlon—an Olympic sport and both developing and enhancing professional competition. Through this politicization of the sport, duathlon, the first of the multisport events to be contested, became the poor relation of the movement that it originated. For example, the name of the sport is in no way included in the names of the major national or international governing boards. Still, duathlon has maintained its popularity throughout the world.

MULTISPORT RACING: THE POWER (WO)MAN DUATHLON SERIES

The Powerman Duathlon series, with Swiss organizers Dr. Urs Linsi and newspaper publisher Bruno Imfeld, boasts one of multisport's richest purses. The original Powerman race was held in Zofingen, Switzerland, in 1989. In 1993, the race was expanded into a worldwide series similar to the Ironman Triathlons. Duathletes must qualify to race at Zofingen, just as triathletes compete for slots at the Hawaii Ironman. The series now offers fifteen to twenty races per year. Along with professional triathletes competing in the Powerman events, there are also duathlon specialists such as Natascha Badmann and Maddy Tormoen and Michael Tobin and Ken Souza.

The more grueling 13-kilometer (8-mile) run, 150-kilometer (93-mile) bike, and 30-kilometer (18.6-mile) run course for the elites has been characterized as one of the most demanding in the world (even in recent years, when 4.5 kilometers [2.8 miles] has been eliminated from the initial run).

In contrast to Hawaii's oppressive heat, Zofingen races entail occasional snow and cold and the legendary Swiss hills and mountains. One competitor noted that when he completed the course, more than one-third of the racers had dropped out; in Hawaii, only about 2 percent typically fail to finish.

Powerman organizers want to increase women's participation in their events. The races offer equal prize money to men and women despite clear imbalances in the ratio of male to female participants. The race offers $20,000 in prize money that is distributed among the first twenty-five men and the first fifteen women. The top fifteen men and women earn the same amount. Officials also apply a "handicap," in which elite women start at an earlier time than the men, allowing them the opportunity to finish together. The series is also called the Power(Wo)man in many contexts, especially when talking about female contestants.

The ITU's acceptance of duathlon's most common form of running and cycling reflects several factors. Although running and cycling are popular around the world, in some countries there are few competitive swimmers. Distance swimming is also affected by climate. Colder regions and desert environments provide difficult venues for distance swimmers and high levels of water pollution in some locations present severe health risks for swimmers.

When the ITU emerged as the uncompromising advocate of triathlon as an Olympic sport, dual-sport athletes referred to their sport as *biathlon*. The sport changed its name to *duathlon* at the request of ITU president Les McDonald, who thought that the term *biathlon*—which already was an Olympic sport, combining skiing and shooting—would harm triathlon's chances for acceptance by the International Olympic Committee. Moreover, McDonald noted that the international federation of the athletes who ski and shoot had formally requested that endurance multisporters not usurp their name.

RULES AND PLAY

Although the term *duathlon* can refer to any combination of two endurance disciplines, typical events are run-bike-run affairs, in which contestants run a specified distance and bike for a longer distance before running another distance to complete the race. On occasion, an uncommon (non-triathlon) sport (for example, in-line skating) may be included in a multisport race like duathlon. The winner is the participant who gets through the entire race course in the shortest time. Racers commonly receive awards for top performances by gender and by five-year age groups. Another popular form consists of a run followed by a bike segment that ends the race. The runs in duathlons are generally 3 to 7 miles (4.8 to 11.2 kilometers), and the bike rides are three to four times the distance of the run. Athletes involved in the sport regard the most common form as similar to triathlon but more difficult; running immediately after biking is more problematic because of the different muscle groups involved in the two disciplines.

Most multisport athletes regard these races as tests of individual fitness and preparedness. Many believe that the raison d'être of multisport events is the intensely personal struggle to overcome self-doubt. Races involve dedication and fortitude, which place the greatest premium on individual effort. For this reason, only race officials are permitted to assist athletes on the racecourse. Similar concerns explain why both race personnel and the athletes are interested in preventing bike drafting.

Drafting occurs when one duathlete follows another too closely. The trailing athlete obtains a measurable advantage because the lead individual works harder in bearing the brunt of the wind's physical impact. Bike drafting has been highly regulated by the national governing boards, and it is illegal to draft in most sanctioned races. Much of the effort of multisport officials (that is, referees) is devoted to the prevention and elimination of bike drafting. The orientation toward individual performance also explains why the nonbiking event (usually a run) comes before the bike segment: to spread the field and thus help prevent drafting on the bike.

At one point the ITU had a membership that included about 120 national governing boards representing more than 2 million affiliated triathletes worldwide. The governing boards vary greatly in size and activity level.

During the ITU Congress associated with the earliest world triathlon championships in Avignon, France, in 1989, a dispute arose regarding the award of equal prize money for women. Several national governing boards and athletes, led by such rising stars as New Zealand's Erin Baker (two-time winner at the duathlon events in Zofingen, 1992 and 1994) and Mark Allen of the United States (six-time Hawaii Ironman winner and husband of Julie Moss), threatened to leave the championships unless the awards were equalized. The congress yielded. The following year the ITU women's committee was born. The committee worked with ITU's executive board to achieve equality for women and to put mechanisms in place to allow them to achieve their full potential.

In 1993 the first representatives of the women's committee were named to ITU's executive board. A year later the ITU became the first international sports organization to adopt the Brighton Declaration on women's participation in sports. The declaration reflected the work of the First World Conference of Women and Sport held in Brighton, England, in May 1994. The ten principles of the declaration dealt with various items aimed at promoting equality, equity, and ease of entry to, and continuation in, sports for women worldwide. The women's committee has continued working on several projects to promote these principles.

Among the committee's goals has been an increase in the number of women serving on the executive boards of national governing boards. The woman's committee has also sought to encourage women's multisport participation by disseminating information, ranging from stories about the experience of duathlon to advice on the effects of training, both physiological and psychological. Committee members have also considered factors such as economics (given the price of competitive bicycles) and cultural and religious taboos on acceptable behavior among women, to determine how best to stimulate multisport participation among women in developing countries.

The committee has also encouraged women-only multisport events. The appeal is simple; women have exclusive media attention and can avoid situations in which the presence or actions of men may inhibit women participants from reaching their full potential. In an all-women's event, the women are not deviant. All-women triathlon series exist in Australia and the United States (the very successful Danskin Series). Individual women-only events also have been staged in Canada, Denmark, Hong Kong, Japan, and Switzerland. Typically these have significantly more female participants than the unrestricted events in the same locations.

The first all-women's duathlon in the United States is believed to be the Ultratech Orlon Women's Biathlon, held in New York's Central Park in mid-September 1989. About one-third of the women were first-time duathletes. Worldwide, women's participation in the unrestricted events typically varies from 2 percent to 33 percent.

Women's committees have caught on with many national boards. Boards in countries with broader women's movements have been quickest to respond, whereas countries in which women's behavior is more limited by cultural and religious factors have been slower to include women's committees.

In much of the world, there seem to be from 20 to 50 percent as many duathlons as triathlons. Moreover, twice as many countries send contestants to the ITU World Triathlon Championships as send athletes to the duathlon championships. With triathlon an event at the 2000 Olympic Games in Sydney, duathlon may become even less salient for the various national governing boards. Nevertheless, although there is great commerce between the two major multisports, people have made their reputations with a primary (or even exclusive) emphasis on duathlon.

FEMALE DUATHLETES

Among the women, Erin Baker, Maddy Tormoen, and most recently Natascha Badmann have been repeat winners at Power(Wo)man Zofingen. Tormoen, a duathlon specialist from the United States, took the Zofingen title in 1993 and 1995 and was runner-up in 1994. As is true with many top multisporters, Tormoen has dispensed training advice both at multisport camps and in magazines. In 1998, following several years off, Tormoen dropped out of Power(Wo)man Alabama after suffering leg cramps in the bike segment.

Baker, who helped lead the 1989 prize protest, won the Hawaii Ironman Triathlon in 1987 and 1990 and Zofingen in 1992 and 1994. In 1990 Baker also won the Ironman series and was runner-up in Hawaii in 1988, 1991, and 1993. In each of these instances, she was beaten only by the unrivaled eight-time champion Paula Newby-Fraser (who won Zofingen in 1991). In 1993 Baker recorded a personal best (9:08:04) on the Ironman course five months after giving birth to a son.

Natascha Badmann of Switzerland is a more recent draw on the duathlon circuit. The only back-to-back winner ever at Zofingen (1996, 1997), Badmann made an attempt at the Hawaii Ironman in 1996. She stunned the field with a second-place finish of 4:30 behind the redoubtable Newby-Fraser, who ran the rookie Badmann down during the marathon. In 1998 Badman won the Hawaii Ironman handily. In 1997 Badmann won Zofingen by more than 16 minutes, a margin surpassed only by Newby-Fraser (in a slightly longer version of the race).

CONCLUSION

Duathlon has, in some ways, been eclipsed by the more spectacular multisport event of triathlon. As an athletic competition, duathlon offers different challenges and competition on a different scale than triathlon. Swimming is perceived as a difficult sport because of the absence of swim venues, possible drowning dangers, and skills that many people believe are more difficult to develop. In contrast, because biking is a means of transportation worldwide, biking skills are seen as ordinary. Thus, the common (bike-and-run) form of duathlon is likely to continue to draw adherents worldwide.

B. James Starr

See also Triathlon

Bibliography

Almekinders, Louis, Sally Almekinders, and Tom Roberts. (1991) *Triathlon Training*. Winston-Salem, NC: Hunter Textbooks.

Blanchard, Kendall, and Alyce Cheska. (1985) *The Anthropology of Sport: An Introduction*. South Hadley, MA: Bergin & Garvey.

Bragg, Patricia. (1985) *The Complete Triathlon—Swim, Bike, Run Endurance Training Manual*. Santa Barbara, CA: Health Science.

Cook, Jeff S. (1992) *The Triathletes: A Season in the Life of Four Women in the Toughest Sport of All*. New York: St. Martin's Press.

Edwards, Sally. (1983) *Triathlon, a Triple Fitness Sport: The First Complete Guide to Challenge You to a New Total Fitness*. Chicago: Contemporary Books.

——. (1985) *The Triathlon Training and Racing Book*. Chicago: Contemporary Books.

——. (1987) *The Equilibrium Plan: Balancing Diet and Exercise for Lifetime Fitness*. New York: Arbor House.

——. (1992) *The Heart Rate Monitor Book*. Sacramento, CA: Fleet Feet Press.

——. (1996) *Heart Zone Training*. Holbrook, MA: Adams Media Corp.

Habernicht, Jorg. (1991) *Triathlon Sportgeschichte*. Bochum, Germany: N. Brockmeyer.

Ingham, Alan G., and John W. Loy, eds. (1993) *Sport in Social Development: Traditions, Transitions, and Transformations*. Champaign, IL: Human Kinetics Press.

Lehenaff, Didier D. A. (1987) *Votre sport le triathlon*. Paris: Bertrand.

Miles, Rick. (1997) *Time-saving Training for Multisports Athletes*. Champaign, IL: Human Kinetics Press.

Newby-Fraser, Paula. (1995) *Peak Fitness for Women.* Champaign: IL: Human Kinetics Press.

Sisson, Mark. (1989) *Training and Racing Biathlons.* Los Angeles: Primal Urge Press.

Souza, Ken, with Bob Babbitt. (1989) *Biathlon: Training and Racing Techniques.* Chicago: Contemporary Books.

Tinley, Scott, with Mike Plant. (1986) *Winning Triathlon.* Chicago: Contemporary Books.

Vaz, Katherine. (1984) *Cross-training: The Complete Book of Triathlon.* New York: Avon.

Vaz, Katherine, and Barclay Kruse. (1985) *The High-performance Triathlete.* Chicago: Contemporary Books.

DURACK, FANNY

(1889–1956)

AUSTRALIAN SWIMMER

Sarah "Fanny" Durack was the first Australian woman to win an Olympic gold medal. Her swimming career, which was marked by many controversies, spanned a time of change for

Fanny Durack in center, after taking the 100-meter freestyle at the 1912 Olympics. (International Olympic Museum)

women not only in sports but in society as a whole.

Born in Sydney, Australia, in 1889, Durack taught herself to swim during the "ladies hour" at the Coogee Baths in her hometown. Although swimming competitions for women were few, Durack managed to participate as a school girl, eventually winning the New South Wales 100-yard title in 1906. For the next four years, she dominated Australian women's swimming. Durack did not perform well the following season, but she was back to her old form in 1911 and 1912, breaking three world records.

Her swimming prowess made her a natural choice to represent Australia in the 1912 Olympics in Stockholm. It was the first Olympics to include women's swimming events (the 100-meter and 4 × 100-meter relay). Five men were selected from Australia to go to the Olympics to participate in the seven events open to them, but no women were chosen to represent the country. When the all-male selection panel was berated for not having chosen any Australian women, their argument was that it was far too expensive to send two women for one event. Furthermore, since young women of that period were not allowed to travel without a chaperone, the numbers would be instantly doubled if women were to participate in Stockholm. (The chaperone also doubled as a "cloak-maid." All female swimmers had to wear long cloaks, which were thrown to their cloak-maids just before the starting gun went off.) Funds were raised for Durack by various organizations, but Fanny's sister, who acted as chaperone, had to pay her own way to Stockholm. Durack had problems not only with the selection panel but also with the New South Wales Women's Swimming Association. There was a rule stating that members could not appear in competition if men were present. Furious debate ensued, and the rule was rescinded. Ironically, Durack had perfected her stroke by training with the Australian men's team, which is how she progressed from the breaststroke to the trudgen (sidestroke) and then to the more familiar "Australian crawl."

Despite all the controversy, Durack and her teammate Wilhelmina Wylie swam in the Olympic 100-meter final. Even though she ran into the side of the pool, Durack won the gold medal and

Wylie took the silver. After the Olympics, Durack continued her strong performance, breaking eleven world records between 1912 and 1918. In 1913 Durack and Wylie attempted a swimming tour of the United States. Disputes with the U.S. organizers and an alleged "willfulness" on Durack's part rendered the tour unsuccessful. World War I caused the cancellation of the 1916 Olympics, and so Durack concentrated on the 1920 Antwerp Games. Just before the Olympics, Durack's appendix burst. Her illness was further complicated by typhoid fever and pneumonia, and it became impossible for her to defend her title in Antwerp.

Fanny Durack married in 1921 and spent the rest of her life coaching swimming. She was mentor and friend to many successful Australian female swimmers. She died of cancer on 20 March 1956 and was elected to the International Swimming Hall of Fame in 1967.

J. P. Anderson

Bibliography

Carlile, Forbes. (1963) *On Swimming.* London: Pelham Books.

Chronicle of the Olympics. (1998) London: DK Publishing.

Howell, Reet A. (1985) "Australia's First Female Olympians." In *Olympic Scientific Congress: Sport History,* edited by Norbert Müller and Joachim K. Rühl. Niedernhausen, Germany: Schors-Verlag.

Lucas, John A., and Ian Jobling. (1995) "Troubled Waters: Fanny Durack's 1919 Swimming Tour of America, Amid Transnational Amateur Athletic Prudery and Bureaucracy." *Olympika: The International Journal of Olympic Studies* 4:93–112.

EARHART, AMELIA

(1897–1937)

U.S. AVIATOR

Best remembered for her fatal last attempt to circle the globe in a continuous flight, Amelia Earhart had already set several long-standing aviation records and had been involved in efforts to develop and promote women's aviation.

Amelia Mary Earhart was born on 24 July 1897, in Atchison, Kansas, to Amy and Edwin Earhart. Amelia had one sister, Muriel. Her father was a lawyer, and his work took him to Des Moines, Iowa, in 1905. The girls stayed behind with their grandparents until 1908 when they rejoined their parents. In 1914 the girls moved with their mother to Chicago because their father had an alcohol problem and was unable to care for his family. Here Amelia was able to graduate from Hyde Park High School in 1916.

By 1917 Earhart was ready to branch out on her own. She became a nurse's aide and served in the military hospital in Toronto until November 1918. After this wartime nursing experience, Earhart went to New York City and entered Columbia University to study medicine. Her vocational direction changed when she got a chance to take flying lessons. She purchased her first plane in January 1921 and made her first solo flight shortly after. In her own plane Earhart flew a number of solo flights that included a record-breaking altitude flight in 1922. Her record of 14,000 feet stood for women until Ruth Nichols broke it in 1931. Not content just flying planes, in 1925 she took a job in Boston as a social worker at Denison House.

A chance meeting in 1926 changed Earhart's life. New York publisher G. P. Putnam was looking for a woman to fly as a passenger on a flight across the Atlantic and thought she would be perfect for this journey. The flight took place two

Amelia Earhart in the cockpit of her autogrio, in Philadelphia in 1931 after setting a new altitude record for women in planes of this type. (Bettmann/Corbis)

years later, on 17–18 June 1928. The pilots were Wilber Stultz and Louis Gordon. The Friendship, as the plane was called, took off from Trepessy, Newfoundland, and landed in Burry Port, South Wales, some twenty-one hours later. Earhart immediately became a media darling. She was hailed by the press, which compared her to the great Charles Lindbergh and called her "Lady Lindy."

Earhart was only a passenger on that 1928 flight and she wanted to earn the accolades from the press for her own flight. During September 1928 Earhart flew a solo flight from the Atlantic to the Pacific coast. This was followed by the publication of her book, *20 Hours, 40 Minutes*, describing her Atlantic crossing. G. P. Putnam used his promotional knowledge to keep Earhart's name in the press. In 1929 Earhart participated in the Los Angeles-to-Cleveland Women's Air Derby, the inaugural running of this cross-country air race for women. In Cleveland, Earhart and ninety-eight other female pilots organized the Ninety-Nines, an organization to help promote women pilots. Earhart served as the group's first president.

Earhart married G. P. Putnam on 7 February 1931, and he continued to promote her. She completed her solo flight across the Atlantic in May 1932 flying from Newfoundland to Northern Ireland. In response, President Franklin Roosevelt presented her with a special gold medal from the National Geographic Society. She was also named Outstanding Woman of the Year in 1932. She was the recipient of the Distinguished Flying Cross from the United States as well as the Cross of the Legion of Honor from France.

By 1935 Earhart was ready for a new challenge. She prepared for a flight around the world with Fred Noonan as her navigator. On 21 May 1937 they took off from Los Angeles in a Lockheed Electra 10E, and by 29 June they had covered 22,000 miles, only 7,000 miles to journey's end. Earhart sent regular letters to her husband and also wrote a series of articles for the *Herald Tribune.* The plane disappeared on 2 July 1937, after the aviators had reported several times that they were having difficulty in finding their landing target. They last reported from somewhere off the coast of Howland Island in the Pacific Ocean, but no trace has ever been found of their plane.

As a result of the complete disappearance of her plane, Earhart has remained a constant source of investigation. Many have tried to find the plane by tracing her route, by examining all the radio messages, and sending out teams to investigate. Earhart was selected as one of the original inductees in the International Women's Sports Hall of Fame in 1980. A stamp was issued in her honor on 24 July 1963, commemorating all that she contributed to aviation and women's history.

Leslie Heaphy

Bibliography

Earhart, Amelia. (1977) *For the Fun of It.* Chicago: Academy Press.

Garst, Shannon. (1947) *Amelia Earhart, Heroine of the Skies.* New York: J. Messner.

Kerby, Mona. (1990) *Amelia Earhart: Courage in the Sky.* New York: Viking Press.

Randolph, Blythe. (1987) *Biography: Amelia Earhart.* New York: Franklin Watts.

Rich, Doris L. (1989) *Amelia Earhart: A Biography.* Washington, DC: Smithsonian Institution.

Ware, Susan. (1993) *Still Missing: Amelia Earhart and the Search for Modern Feminism.* New York: W.W. Norton.

EATING DISORDERS

Many women do not consider training or exercise sufficient to accomplish their idealized body shape or level of thinness. A significant number diet and try to meet their goals by using harmful, though ineffective, weight-loss practices such as restrictive eating, vomiting, laxatives, and diuretics (medications that help to eliminate water from the body). The problems that result when these behaviors become habitual or compulsive are called, collectively, eating disorders. Anorexia nervosa—a pathological fear or concern with weight gain—and bulimia—a constant craving or compulsion to eat—are the most common. Eating disorders can result in short- and long-term medical problems, decreased performance, amenorrhea (absence of menstrual periods for several months or longer), and, in extreme cases, death. Signs and symptoms of eating disorders in competitive and elite athletes are often ignored. Subclinical cases—with symptoms that are not apparent—are simply not noticed. In some sports, disordered eating even seems to be regarded as a natural part of being an athlete. Some investigators also argue that female athletes, compared to nonathletes, are at increased risk for developing eating disorders because of the focus on low body weight as a performance enhancer, comments from coaches or important others, and the pressure to perform. Whether these factors or others explain the difference, symptoms of eating disorders are more prevalent among female athletes than nonathletes.

Estimates of the prevalence of eating disorders among female athletes vary widely—from less than 1 percent to as high as 75 percent. The prevalence of anorexia nervosa in female elite athletes (1.3 percent) is similar to the range reported among nonathletes, whereas bulimia (8.2 percent) and subclinical eating disorders (8 percent) seem to be more prevalent among athletes than non-athletes. Eating disorders together with amenorrhea and osteoporosis (bone loss) are known as the "female athlete triad," a group of related medical problems seen in some female athletes.

Eating disorders are significantly more frequent among athletes competing in aesthetic and weight-class sports than among other sport groups where leanness is considered less important, such as power sports, ball sports, endurance sports, and technical skill sports.

THE NATURE OF EATING DISORDERS

Eating disorders are characterized by disturbances in eating behavior, body image, emotions, and relations. Athletes constitute a unique population, and medical personnel need to take into account special diagnostic considerations when working with this group. Despite similar symptoms, subclinical cases of eating disorders among athletes are easier to identify than those of non-athletes. This is true because at least at the elite level, coaches evaluate athletes almost every day and are more likely to notice changes in behavior and physical symptoms. Nevertheless, too often coaches ignore or fail to detect symptoms of eating disorders. One reason for this is that they lack knowledge about symptoms and the strategies that have been developed to help athletes with eating disorders.

Medical Diagnoses

The *Diagnostic and Statistical Manual* of the American Psychiatric Association (DSM-IV) summarizes the symptoms that physicians use to make a diagnosis of anorexia nervosa (bulimia and other eating disorders are not specified). The diagnostic criteria, in general, describe a person who no longer has a normal perspective on eating, on her weight, or on how she appears. The first sign is the refusal to maintain body weight at 85 percent or more of the minimum normal weight for a person's age and height. A person with anorexia nervosa also shows an intense fear of gaining weight or becoming fat, even though she is in fact underweight. When she views her body, she does not see it objectively and may deny that her weight is in fact too low. If a young woman has reached menarche, a health care pro-

The extreme fear of eating and gaining weight is the hallmark of anorexia nervosa. (Custom Medical Stock Photo, Inc.)

vider will find out if she is experiencing amenorrhea, or the absence of at least three menstrual cycles. Anorexia nervosa has been broken down into two types, the restricting type—those who simply do not eat enough—and the binge eating/purging type.

The symptoms of bulimia nervosa also center on a person's fixation on low weight. As with anorexia nervosa, the woman places excessive emphasis on her weight in her self-image. It differs, however, in that she additionally engages in recurrent episodes of binge eating. Binge eating, in this sense, is defined as eating within a given period (two hours, for example) an amount of food that is definitely larger than most people would eat during a similar period of time in similar circumstances. At the same time, the person feels that she can neither stop eating nor control how much or what she is eating. To compensate for this out-of-control eating and to keep from gaining weight, she adopts one of two general strategies.

STARVING FOR THE GOLD
The Tragedy of Eating Disorders

"It feels like there's a beast inside me,
like a monster. It feels evil."
—Christy Henrich, elite gymnast

When she looked in her mirror, she saw a loser.
A fat loser. She carried this failure
in the heft of her thighs,
the curve of her cheeks.
Anywhere she couldn't see bone.
That night, she stopped eating,
but then, she never did anything
half way. Some days she only ate an apple.
Some days she only ate one slice of an apple.
She took her emotions, placed them in a
    wooden box,
locked tight with a gold key. She wanted to stand
in the spotlight, which shone round and full
as the moon, or a medal.
The moon, ruler of women's lives, waxes
and wanes, ebbs and flows. She knew
the moon, all right. It was the clock that ticks,
puberty, menarche.
She had to starve herself to shut it down,
stop estrogen, look like a boy, no breasts
or butt, see her ribs emerge like a sunken boat.
Pared to muscle and bone, a body light enough
to spin and twirl, free of gravity, a body that
    could

now break more easily as bones thinned,
a body bound as Victorian women in whale-
    bone,
as Chinese women's golden lilies,
crushed bones in red lacquer shoes.
She taught herself not to feel pain,
to compete with stress fractures, shin splints.
She taught herself
not to feel
anything at all.
She couldn't stop.
Her mind had hooked
itself to perfection's fish:
a body with no disfiguring fat,
lighter than the Russians,
lighter than air.
She wanted to be a swan.
She wanted to have
elastic bands for bones,
no nerves,
a body light and fluid
as a pink satin ribbon
floating in the wind.
She wanted to let go
the bounds of earth.
And did.

BARBARA CROOKER

The purging sufferer forces vomiting or misuses laxatives, diuretics, or enemas. The nonpurger fasts or exercises in excess to compensate for overeating. Either may do these things during times other than episodes of anorexia nervosa, when body weight is too low.

Risk Factors for the Development of Eating Disorders

Eating disorders, in general, develop for a variety of reasons. Among elite athletes, the additional stress associated with the athletic environment appears to make them more vulnerable to eating disorders than the general female population. Furthermore, studies suggest that some sport settings contain specific risk factors for the development of eating disorders. One retrospective study indicates that a sudden increase in training load may induce a caloric deprivation in endurance athletes. Reinforced both biologically and socially, this may lead to the development of eating disorders. The role played by different sports in the development of eating disorders will remain uncertain in the absence of longitudinal studies (that is, studies over a period of time) that closely monitor various sport-specific factors such as amount, type, and intensity of training in comparison with other characteristics such as clothing, weight classes, physical and psychological demands, rules, subjective judging, and coaching behavior. Another factor to consider is when athletes start sport-specific training. Those who begin before puberty may have chosen a sport not suitable for their adult body type. Studies have shown that athletes with eating disorders often started sport-specific training at an earlier age than athletes without eating disorders.

Further complexities may be inferred from athletes who reported that they developed eating disorders in response to events that they perceived as traumatic, such as the loss or change of a coach, or an injury or illness that left them temporarily unable to continue their normal level of training. As a result, the athlete may expend less energy and so gain weight, which in some cases may develop into an irrational fear of further weight gain, or the athlete may begin to diet to compensate for the lack of exercise.

Pressure to reduce weight has been the common explanation for the increased prevalence of eating-related problems among athletes. The important factor may not be dieting as such but rather the situation in which the athlete is told to lose weight, the words used, and whether the athlete received guidance or not. In addition to the pressure to reduce weight, athletes are often pressed for time, and they have to lose weight rapidly to make or stay on the team. As a result they often go on extreme diets or experience weight cycling (repeated loss and gain of weight). Weight cycling has been suggested as an important risk or trigger factor for the development of eating disorders in athletes.

Personality and Sport-Specific Issues

Some authors have argued that specific sports attract individuals who are anorectic, at least in attitude if not in behavior or weight, before they begin their participation in sports. The attraction-to-sport hypothesis might be true for the general population, but athletes generally do not achieve the elite level if weight loss is their only motivation. Therefore, this hypothesis may be more applicable to lower-level athletes.

In a Norwegian study, athletes with eating disorders gave various and multiple reasons for their disorder. The most common cause was prolonged periods of dieting, listed by 37 percent. Having a new coach as a factor was given by 30 percent. Injury or illness—times when they might

be expected to gain weight—were given as reasons by 23 percent. Casual comments, presumably of the "have you gained weight" variety, were listed by 19 percent. Leaving home or failing in schoolwork, problems in a relationship, family problems, and illness or injury to family members were each listed by 10 percent. Death of significant others or sexual abuse by a coach were both listed by 4 percent of the athletes surveyed.

Most researchers agree that coaches do not cause eating disorders in athletes, although inappropriate coaching may trigger or worsen the problem in vulnerable individuals. In most cases then, the role of coaches in the development of eating disorders in athletes should be seen as a part of a larger, complex interplay of factors.

Though research has suggested some connections, no hard evidence exists for sport-specific risk factors for eating disorders. Studies are clearly needed.

Medical Issues

For both athletes and nonathletes eating disorders may cause serious medical problems and can even be fatal. Whereas most complications of anorexia nervosa occur as a direct or indirect result of starvation, complications of bulimia are a result of binge-eating and purging. Anorexia nervosa patients display a mortality rate up to six times higher than the general population; mortality is uncertain among bulimic patients. Death is usually attributable to fluid and electrolyte abnormalities, or suicide. Mortality in bulimia is less studied, but deaths do occur, usually secondary to the complications of the binge-purge cycle or suicide.

The long-term effects of weight cycling and eating disorders in athletes are unclear. Biological maturation and growth have been studied in girl gymnasts before and during puberty, and the results suggest that young female gymnasts are smaller, and that they mature later, than females from sports that do not require extreme leanness, such as swimming. It is difficult to separate the effects of physical strain, energy restriction, and genetic predisposition to delayed puberty. Mortality rates of eating disorders among athletes are not known. A number of deaths of top-level athletes representing gymnastics, running, alpine skiing, and cycling have been reported in the media. Five percent of those diagnosed in the Norwegian study reported suicide attempts.

Besides increasing the likelihood of amenorrhea and stress fractures, early bone loss may keep athletes from achieving their normal peak bone mass. Thus, athletes with frequent or longer periods of amenorrhea may be at high risk of sustaining fractures. There is a clear need for studies that provide longitudinal data on fast and gradual body weight reduction and cycling in relation to the health and performance of different groups of athletes.

The nature and the magnitude of the effect of eating disorders on athletic performance are influenced by how severe and chronic the eating disorder is, as well as the physical and psychological demands of the sport. No studies have appeared looking at specific tests and the results of shorter or longer periods of disordered eating. To be sure, dehydration affects endurance and impairs exercise performance. Mental performance may also be affected, as Norwegian female elite athletes reported increased fatigue, anger, or anxiety when attempting to rapidly lose body weight.

IDENTIFYING ATHLETES WITH EATING DISORDERS

Most individuals with eating disorders do not realize that they have a problem and therefore do not seek treatment on their own. Athletes may consider seeking help only if they note that their performance is leveling off.

Symptoms of Anorexia Nervosa in Athletes

Coaches and others around the athlete may detect abnormalities. Anorexia nervosa and bulimia nervosa both display characteristic physical symptoms and psychological and behavioral characteristics. For anorexia nervosa, the physical symptoms include significant weight loss beyond what is necessary for adequate sports performance, amenorrhea or menstrual dysfunction, dehydration, and fatigue beyond what would normally be expected during training or competition. Other symptoms could be constipation, diarrhea, bloating, or discomfort after eating. The athlete may be hyperactive or have an abnormally low body temperature (hypothermia). Her heartbeat may be abnormally slow (bradycardia). She may

develop abnormal hair growth, called lanugo, a short, downy growth. Her muscles may grow weak, and her bone-mineral density may drop. She may be subject to stress fractures.

Anorexia nervosa has characteristic psychological symptoms and behavior as well. The athlete may be anxious, perhaps about her sport performance, but also about other matters. She may be depressed and suffer from insomnia, withdraw socially, and feel very restless, as if she cannot relax. She is abnormally aware of weight in various ways. She may claim that she "feels fat" although she is thin. Coaches or others may recommend that she gain weight or at least not lose any further weight, but she will resist these suggestions. She may weigh herself constantly or object to being weighed to the point that she refuses. Her behavior about exercise is equally fixed; she becomes compulsive and rigid, and may exercise beyond what is necessary for a particular sport.

Symptoms of Bulimia Nervosa in Athletes

The athlete with bulimia nervosa also shows distinctive physical symptoms. On the back of her hand, she may have calluses or abrasions from inducing vomiting. Induced vomiting or other forms of purging may also lead to dehydration. Dental and gum problems are common, as are electrolyte abnormalities. Her weight may go up and down frequently and often extremely, with her mood worsening as her weight rises, although her weight will likely remain low even if she eats large amounts of food. She may feel bloated and/or have gastrointestinal problems; have muscle cramps; or feel weak. Her parotid (salivary) glands may be swollen. And as in anorexia nervosa, she may have menstrual irregularities.

The physical symptoms are matched by a whole constellation of psychological and behavioral symptoms. She may be depressed and critical of herself, especially of her weight and athletic performance. Her eating behavior is not normal. She may diet when it is not necessary. She may eat in secret. She may vomit when she is not ill. A person who is purging spends abnormal amounts of time in the bathroom, often vanishing into it after eating. Substance abuse may also be part of the picture—drugs, legal or illegal, prescription or nonprescription, particularly laxatives and diuretics.

In contrast to the athletes with anorectic symptoms, most athletes suffering from bulimia are at or near normal weight and therefore difficult to detect. Hence, team staffs must be able to recognize these physical symptoms and psychological characteristics. The presence of some of these characteristics does not necessarily indicate the presence of the disorder. However, the likelihood of the disorder increases as the number of presenting characteristics increases.

TREATMENT AND PREVENTION OF EATING DISORDERS

Eating-disordered athletes seem more likely to accept the idea of going for a single consultation than committing themselves to prolonged treatment. The treatment of athletes with eating disorders should be undertaken by health care professionals. For an athlete with an eating disorder, it is easier to establish a trusting relationship with a therapist who knows the sport, as well as being trained in treating eating-disordered patients. Therapists who have good knowledge about eating disorders and know the various sports will better understand the athletes' training setting, daily demands, and relations that are specific to the sport. To build such a relationship the therapist must respect the athlete's desire to be lean for athletic performance, and express a willingness to work together to help the eating-disordered athlete become lean and healthy. The treatment team needs to accept the athlete's fears and irrational thoughts about food and weight, and then present a rational approach for achieving self-management of healthy diet, weight, and training program.

Experience has shown that a total suspension of training during treatment is not a good solution. Unless severe medical complications are present, the athlete should be allowed to train at a lower amount and decreased intensity. In general, it is recommended that athletes not compete during treatment to avoid the message that the sport performance is more important than their health. Nevertheless, competitions during treatment might be considered for individuals with less severe eating disorders engaged in low-risk sports.

Prevention of Eating Disorders in Athletes

In contrast to findings from the general adolescent population, advice to competitive athletes and coaches about eating disorders and related problems such as menstrual dysfunction and bone loss prevents eating disorders in that population. Coaches, trainers, administrators, and parents should receive information about eating disorders and related issues such as growth and development, the relationship between body composition, health and performance, and nutrition. Coaches should realize that they can strongly influence their athletes. Coaches or others involved with young athletes should not comment on an individual's body size, or require weight loss in young and still-growing athletes. Without offering further guidance, dieting may result in unhealthy eating behavior or eating disorders in highly motivated and uninformed athletes.

Early intervention is also important, since eating disorders are more difficult to treat the longer they progress. Professionals working with athletes should be informed about the possible risk factors for the development, early signs, and symptoms of eating disorders, the medical, psychological, and social consequences of these disorders; how to approach the problem if it occurs; and what treatment options are available.

CONCLUSION

The diagnosis of eating disorders in female athletes can easily be missed unless specifically searched for. If untreated, eating disorders can have long-lasting physiological and psychological effects and may even be fatal. Treating athletes with eating disorders should be undertaken only by qualified health care professionals. Ideally, these individuals should also be familiar with and have an appreciation for the sport environment.

Jorunn Sundgot-Borgen

See also Amenorrhea; Body Image; Nutrition; Osteoporosis; Self-Esteem; Sexuality

Bibliography

American Psychiatric Association. (1987) *Diagnostic and Statistical Manual of Mental Disorders*. 3d ed. Washington DC, 65–60.

Beumont, P. J. V., J. D. Russell, and S. W. Touyz. (1993) "Treatment of Anorexia Nervosa." *The Lancet* 26: 1635–1640.

Brownell, Kelley D., Judith Rodin, and Jack H. Wilmore. (1992) *Eating, Body Weight and Performance in Athletes. Disorders of Modern Society.* Philadelphia: Lea and Febiger.

Clark, Nancy. (1993) "How to Help the Athlete with Bulimia: Practical Tips and Case Study." *International Journal of Sport Nutrition* 3: 450–460.

Dummer, G. M., L. W. Rosen, and W. W. Heusner. (1987) "Pathogenic Weight-Control Behaviors of Young Competitive Swimmers." *Physician and Sportsmedicine* 5: 75–86.

Eisenman, P. A., S. C. Johnson, and J. E. Benson. (1990) *Coaches' Guide to Nutrition and Weight Control.* 2d ed. Champaign, IL: Leisure Press.

Fogelholm, Michael. (1994) "Effects of Bodyweight Reduction on Sports Performance." *Sports Medicine* 4: 249–267.

Gadpalle, W. J., C. F. Sandborn, and W. W. Wagner. (1987) "Athletic Amenorrhea, Major Affective Disorders and Eating Disorders." *American Journal of Psychiatry* 144: 9399–43.

Gresko, Runi Børresen, and Jan H. Rosenvinge. (1998) "The Norwegian School-Based Prevention Model: Development and Validation." In *The Prevention of Eating Disorders,* edited by W. Vandereycken and G. Noordenbos. New York: New York University Press.

Hsu, L. K. G. (1990) *Eating Disorders.* New York: Guilford Press.

Johnson, C., and S. M. Connor. (1987) *The Etiology and Treatment of Bulimia Nervosa.* New York: Basic Books.

Katz, J. L. (1985) "Some Reflections on the Nature of the Eating Disorders." *International Journal of Eating Disorders* 4: 617–626.

Mansfield, M. J., and S. J. Emans. (1993) "Growth in Female Gymnasts: Should Training Decrease During Puberty?" *Pediatrics* 122: 237–240.

Mitchell, J. E. (1990) *Bulimia Nervosa.* Minneapolis: University of Minnesota Press.

Nielsen, S., S. Møller-Madsen, T. Isager, J. Jørgensen, K. Pagsberg, and S. Theander. (1998) "Standardized Mortality in Eating Disorders—A Qualitative Summary of Previously Published and New Evidence." *Journal of Psychosomatic Research* 44: 413–434.

Rosen, L. W., D. B. McKeag, and D. O. Hough. (1986) "Pathogenic Weight-Control Behaviors in Female Athletes." *Physician and Sportsmedicine* 14: 79–86.

Rosenvinge, Jan H., and Runi Barresen Gresko. (1997) "Do We Need a Prevention Model for Eating Disorders?" *Eating Disorders: The Journal of Treatment and Prevention* 5: 110–118.

Rucinski, A. (1989) "Relationship of Body Image and Dietary Intake of Competitive Ice Skaters." *Journal of American Dietetic Association* 89: 98–100.

Sacks, M. H. (1990) "Psychiatry and Sports." *Annals of Sports Medicine* 5: 47–52.

———. (1993) "Prevalence of Eating Disorders in Female Elite Athletes." *International Journal of Sport Nutrition* 3: 29–40.

———. (1994) "Risk and Trigger Factors for the Development of Eating Disorders in Female Elite Athletes." *Medicine and Science in Sports and Exercise* 4: 414–419.

———. (1996) "Eating Disorders, Energy Intake, Training Volume, and Menstrual Function in High-Level Modern Rhythmic Gymnasts." *International Journal of Sport Nutrition* 6: 100–109.

Sundgot-Borgen, Jorunn, and Monica Klungland. (1998) "The Female Athlete Triad and the Effect of Preventive Work." *Medicine and Science in Sports and Exercise* Supl 5: 181.

———, and S. Larsen. (1993) "Nutrient Intake and Eating Behavior of Female Elite Athletes Suffering from Anorexia Nervosa, Anorexia Athletica and Bulimia Nervosa." *International Journal of Sport Nutrition* 3: 431–442.

Theintz, M. J., H. Howald, and U. Weiss. (1993) "Evidence of a Reduction of Growth Potential in Adolescent Female Gymnasts." *Journal of Pediatric* 122: 306–313.

Thompson, R. A., and R. Trattner-Sherman. (1993) *Helping Athletes with Eating Disorders.* Champaign, IL: Human Kinetic.

Warren, B. J., A. L. Stanton, and D. L. Blessing. (1990) "Disordered Eating Patterns in Competitive Female Athletes." *International Journal of Eating Disorders* 5: 565–569.

Wilmore, J. H. (1991) "Eating and Weight Disorders in Female Athletes." *International Journal of Sport Nutrition* 1: 104–117.

EDERLE, GERTRUDE

(1906–)

U.S. SWIMMER

Between 1921 and 1925 Gertrude Ederle held twenty-nine national and world swimming records, most of them achieved in 1924. Her greatest feat was a personal one as she was the first woman to swim the English Channel.

Gertrude (Trudy) Caroline Ederle was born on 23 October 1906 in New York City to German immigrant parents. She was one of six children. Her father was a butcher. Early in her life Trudy developed an interest in swimming and she learned to swim on the New Jersey shore. Trudy quickly discovered she had an affinity for the water, and with her sister Margaret's support she began to swim competitively.

In 1922 Ederle participated in the International Joseph P. Day Cup race with fifty other competitive swimmers, placing first. This victory launched her brief but important career. Ederle followed this win with a triumph in the 500-meter freestyle at the Amateur Athletic Union Outdoor Championships in 1922. Ederle became internationally known when she was chosen to represent the United States as part of the 1924 women's Olympic swim team. In Paris, Ederle won gold in the 400-meter freestyle relay race and bronze in both the 100-meter and 400-meter freestyle races.

Following her Olympic success, Ederle wanted to find some long distance records she could break. In 1925 she set a record by swimming the 17.5 miles from lower Manhattan to Sandy Hook, New Jersey, in seven hours. Her next target became the English Channel as she wanted to accomplish what no other woman had done. There were many who thought she could not accomplish this feat because as a woman she would not be strong enough to complete the grueling swim.

It seemed that her critics were right when her first effort in 1925 failed. She had to be pulled from the water after about nine hours because she was suffering from cold and exhaustion. Ederle was not deterred by the failure and she recruited William Burgess to help her train. Burgess had successfully swum the channel in 1911 and knew what was needed to keep a swimmer moving through the cold, strong waters. For the actual swim, Ederle would be followed by a support boat carrying Burgess, Ederle's father, and her sister Margaret. A number of photographers and reporters went along for the ride. They were there to record what most expected to be her failure, but Ederle proved them all wrong.

Gertrude Ederle. (Archive)

On 6 August 1926 at Cape Gris-Nez in France, Ederle entered the cold channel waters at 7:09 A.M. Fourteen hours and thirty-one minutes later she stepped ashore near Dover, England. Ederle thus became the first woman to swim the 56 kilometers (35 miles) from Cape Gris-Nez to England and also broke the existing men's record by over two hours. Her record would stand among women swimmers until 1950 when Florence Chadwick swam the channel in thirteen hours, twenty minutes.

Ederle's record-breaking swim earned her international acclaim. Her picture was on the front page of newspapers in France, England, and the United States. President Coolidge referred to her as "America's Best Girl." A ticker tape parade greeted her return to New York City, with over two million coming out to cheer for her. New York City Mayor Jimmy Walker compared her swim to other great historical crossings like those of Washington, Moses, and Caesar.

Her victory was not without cost as Ederle suffered a loss of hearing. Following her short period of international acclaim Ederle faded from the public's eye. She moved to Flushing, New York, where she taught swimming lessons at the Lexington School for the Deaf. She also took up a fashion design career for a short time.

Though she was out of the public eye for the remainder of her life, Ederle's accomplishments did not go unnoticed. In 1980 she was selected as one of the first inductees into the International Women's Sports Hall of Fame. Her record-breaking swim in 1926 opened many doors for girls and women in sports of all kinds as she proved that women were fully capable of participating in even the most rigorous of sports activities.

Leslie Heaphy

Bibliography

Condon, Robert J. (1991) *Great Women Athletes of the Twentieth Century.* Jefferson, NC: McFarland.

Ware, Susan, ed. (1998) *Forgotten Heroes: Inspiring American Portraits from our Leading Historians.* New York: Free Press.

EGYPT

Egypt is located in the northeast corner of Africa and has a population of about 52 million. Located at the crossroads of Africa, Asia, and Europe, modern Egyptian society has been influenced by developments in all three regions. Thus Egypt is in some ways North African, in other ways European, and in other ways Middle Eastern. Since the seventh century Egypt has been an Islamic nation, and Islamic beliefs about women's role and appropriate sport activity have had a major influence on sport participation in Egyptian society. At the same time, Egypt has been in contact with European society since the early 1800s and in the nineteenth and early twentieth centuries was under British control. This contact has also shaped Egyptian sport, primarily by involving men in traditional European sports such as soccer (association football). A final major influence on sport since the mid-twentieth century has been Egypt's participation in regional tournaments and sport programs. In Egypt, in 1998, this emphasis finally involved women's as well as men's sports.

HISTORY

Some of the oldest evidence of physical fitness activity and sport participation by women in human history is from ancient Egypt. This evidence comes from the archaeological record, which includes writings, sculpture, carvings, drawings, and paintings of women involved in gymnastics, swimming, archery, horseback riding, and dance. For example, an Eighteenth Dynasty (1570–1342 BCE) illustration from the Luxor tomb of Nub Amon shows two women dancing, and the walls of the temple of Bani Hassan from the Eleventh Dynasty (2134–2000 BCE) show a group of women exercising and playing with balls stuffed with hay and thread, and covered with animal skin. Physical fitness was also important to the ancient Egyptian rulers, both men and women. Statues of Queen Hatshepsut (1490–1468 BCE) and Queen Nefertiti (1364–1306 BCE) show them both as physically active. However, it is unlikely that most Egyptians, male or female, participated in sport because these activities were the privilege of the ruling and priestly classes only.

As Egypt declined and then came under Roman rule, sports were mainly limited to large Roman-style public tournaments, which did not involve women except as spectators. In the seventh century, Egypt was conquered by Muslims from Arabia and became an Islamic society. In Islam, physical fitness is considered an important factor in maintaining health and strength. The scholars of Islam, the "ullamas," affirmed that fitness was connected to creating an integrated, well-rounded personality, and that one should become physically fit through sport, mentally fit through culture, morally fit through virtue, spiritually fit through worship, socially fit through social service, and politically fit through community involvement. Some of the central activities of Islamic life help to promote fitness: prayer, which involves physical movements that resemble common exercises; the practice of fasting, which involves several characteristics necessary for success in sport, including self-control, patience, and discipline; and pilgrimage, which often requires physical activity and hardship. The role of women in Egyptian Muslim society meant that they were generally not allowed to participate in physical fitness activities or sport with men, or in public.

PHYSICAL EDUCATION

Physical education programs for girls were first instituted during the Ottoman rule of Egypt in the nineteenth century and were also encouraged during the period of British control from 1882 to 1920. The interest in physical education for girls was part of a heightened concern about education that also led to the building of many new schools. However, progress in developing women's programs was slow, and it was not until 1937 that the Ministry of Education established formal training programs for physical education teachers and more women became involved as instructors. In accord with Islam, separate departments were established for male teachers and female teachers at the Princess Fawzeya School for Girls. In order to be accepted, applicants needed a high school diploma, be between eighteen and twenty-four years of age, be physically fit, show good behavior, and pass an exam. In 1939 the Ministry established two physical education departments, one for men, which remained a part of the Educational Institute for teachers, and one for women, which became a part of the Institute for Art Teachers.

The 1952 revolution, which created a republic and ended the monarchy, brought significant change to Egypt. The new government placed great emphasis on education, and women's education was especially encouraged. In 1955 two physical education institutes were established in Alexandria, one for men and one for women, with a four-year course of study that led to a bachelor's degree in physical education. In 1974 graduate programs were developed that led to master's and doctoral degrees.

By the 1990s, sport had become an important activity in African and Muslim nations, and Egypt was part of this movement. In 1993 the physical education program established at Tanta University became the first coed physical education faculty in Egypt. The El Minya University physical education program became coed in 1994, followed by Monofaya University in 1995 and Assuit University in 1996. The understand-ing was that boys and girls and men and women would share classrooms for their academic studies but participate separately in physical activities and sports.

MODERN SPORT ORGANIZATION

Although Egyptian women have had more opportunities since the 1950s to be involved in physical fitness activities and sport at the school level (soccer, basketball), it was not until 1998 that they were able to take part in organized national team sports, when the gender barrier was broken on the soccer field. Soccer was a men-only sport until the establishment of Egypt's first national team for women in 1994 and the creation of the Egyptian Association for Women's Football (EAWF). This was the doing of an Egyptian woman, Sahar al-Hawari, on her own time and with her own money, despite opposition from some in the sport establishment and from parents who did not want their daughters to participate in public or in a rough sport. In 1998 the Egyptian women competed in the Africa Cup for Women. Nevertheless, women's participation remained very low compared with that of men, who participated in hundreds of soccer teams, as well as other sports, while there were only fifteen women's soccer teams. Men hold the most positions on the EAWF board of directors and fathers still have a say in whether their daughters are allowed to participate.

Perhaps the major problem facing women's soccer has been parental attitudes about the appropriate role for young women in Egyptian society. Coaches and trainers have had to overcome parental prejudice and discomfort. Progress has been slow. There is now a training program for female referees, and the first female tournaments were scheduled for 1999. The Sports and Youth Authority announced in 1999 that it would establish a special sports school for girls.

Nabila Ahmed Abdel Rahman
Mickey Friedman

Bibliography

Rahman, Nabila Ahmed Abdel. (1998) "Physical Education in Egypt: From Past to Future." Paper presented at the Second World Conference on Women and Sport. Windhoek, Namibia.

EL MOUTAWAKEL, NAWAL

(1962–)

MOROCCAN HURDLER AND SPORTS ADMINISTRATOR

Nawal El Moutawakel was the first Arab woman to win an Olympic gold medal, the first Moroccan to win an Olympic gold medal, and the first woman from a predominantly Islamic nation to be elected to the International Olympic Committee (IOC). A native of Casablanca, El Moutawakel showed promise as a young runner and was encouraged by her father to develop her talent. She received a grant in 1982 from the king of Morocco to support her training as a hurdles specialist. El Moutawakel dominated national and regional hurdle competitions in the early 1980s, winning titles at every distance from 100 to 400 meters. She won the African 400-meter hurdles crown in 1983. Her success attracted the attention of a track coach at Iowa State University in the United States. The university offered El Moutawakel an athletic scholarship. She enrolled there in 1983, and won the 1984 National Collegiate Athletic Association (NCAA) Division I championship in the 400-meter hurdles, defeating 1992 Olympic silver medalist Sandra Farmer.

Despite her NCAA victory El Moutawakel was not considered the gold-medal favorite going into the 1984 Olympic Games, even after several top competitors dropped out of contention due to the Soviet-led boycott of the Los Angeles Games. She ran impressively, however, in the preliminary rounds. In the finals, El Moutawakel led the race from the first hurdle to the finish, posting a winning time of 54.61 seconds. Moroccan television viewers watched the race after midnight and took to the streets in celebration.

Following the Los Angeles Games, El Moutawakel continued to compete for Iowa State, where she studied physical education and physiotherapy. A knee injury, however, hampered her train-

Nawal El Moutawakel celebrating a hurdles victory in the 1984 Summer Olympics. (LPI/AAF)

ing, and she never again achieved her 1984 level of excellence. She retired from competition after the 1987 world championships.

El Moutawakel remained active in sport after her athletic career ended. She served as sprint and hurdles coach in Morocco; organized the first women's road race in Casablanca, in 1993; and accepted a government post, reporting to the minister of youth and sport. Fluent in Arabic, French, and English, El Moutawakel also became increasingly active in international sport governance during the 1990s. She became a member of the executive board of the International Amateur Athletic Federation, the international governing body of track and field, in 1995. Three years later, El Moutawakel was elected to the International Olympic Committee.

Wayne Wilson

Bibliography

International Olympic Committee. (1998) Biographies of the active and honorary IOC members. Lausanne, Switzerland: IOC.

ENDER, KORNELIA

(1958–)

GERMAN SWIMMER

Kornelia Ender was one of the most successful of a group of very successful East German swimmers of the 1970s. Throughout her career, she and other German swimmers were burdened by charges that they had used illegal performance-enhancing drugs. Although East German sports officials denied the charges at the time, they were proved true in the 1990s following the reunification of East and West Germany and scrutiny of East German records.

Ender was born in Plauen im Vogtland in the former East Germany, on 25 October 1958. An athletic career seemed unlikely because she was born with misaligned hips. However, part of the treatment for her condition was daily swimming, and her family signed her up at the local swim club. Swimming became more than a form of physical therapy, and Ender began to swim competitively. Big, strong, and supported by the East German government sports establishment, Ender soon emerged as a contender at the national level.

In 1972, at the age of fourteen, she was on the East German team at the Olympics in Munich and won three silver medals, one in the 200-meter individual medley and two others with her teammates in medleys. In 1973, still only fourteen, she set her first world record of 58.25 seconds in the 100-meter freestyle. Over the next three years, she broke another twenty-two world records, the largest number of world records ever held by a female swimmer. The years from 1973 to 1976 were the high point of her career, when she won dozens of medals in the German, European, and world championships in the freestyle, butterfly, and backstroke. She also emerged as the leader of the

Kornelia Ender at the 1976 Olympics in Montreal, Canada. (Sussex Archeological Society)

East German women's swim team and was nick-named "Divine" for her dedication to practice, the apparent ease of her victories, and her outgoing personality, which stood in marked contrast to the serious demeanor of her teammates.

Ender's career ended with the 1976 Olympics in Montreal where she won gold medals in the 100- and 200-meter freestyle events, the 100-meter butterfly, and as a member of the medley relay. She also took a silver medal in the 400-meter freestyle relay. Perhaps her most remarkable achievement at the Games was winning the 100-meter freestyle and 200-meter butterfly, because the racing schedule allowed her only twenty minutes between the two races. In her entire career, an even more remarkable achievement was that she had lost only two races in individual competition. The first was in the 200-meter individual medley to her teammate Ulrike Tauber at the world championships in 1975 and the second in the 200-meter freestyle at the same world championships to Shirley Babashoff of the United States.

Ender was married to East German backstroker and four-time Olympic champion Roland Matthes. They were a celebrity couple and had a daughter who competed against Ender in an exhibition in 1992. After her divorce from Matthes, she married Steffan Gummt, a decathlete and bobsledder. As with other East German swimmers of her time, the validity of her victories and records were questioned in the 1990s, as evidence became public that the East German athletes did use performance-enhancing drugs. Unlike some other athletes, Ender has admitted her involvement in the mass drug program supported by the government. Despite the drug use, some experts believe that Ender's accomplishments should continue to be viewed as legitimate because she was successful for a long period of time and broke more records than any of her competitors, whether or not they used the drugs. Others argue that while Ender's and other East German swimmers' medals should not be taken from them, alternative lists of winners for those years should also be published.

Gherardo Bonini

Bibliography

Enciclopedia dello Sport. Vol. 1, *Gli sports olimpici.* (1980) Rome: Peruzzo Editore.

Umminger, Walter, ed. (1992) *Die Chronik des Sports.* Harenbeg, Germany: Chronik Verlag.

ENDURANCE

All sports require muscular activity, which can occur only with a supply of energy. The key to athletic success, then, is to train muscles to become as strong as possible, and to train the cardiorespiratory system to supply energy efficiently. The belief that women are indeed capable of improving their strength and endurance is of relatively recent origin.

As late as the 1920s, it was believed that women were physiologically incapable of pro-longed physical activity, and they were considered too weak to participate in most Olympic events. With the addition of the women's marathon in the 1984 Olympic Games in Los Angeles, these myths were officially laid to rest. In the 1980s and 1990s, many studies compared the physiological bases of strength and endurance in men and women, and confirmed the popular sense that had emerged after watching women participate in the Olympics.

Women perform better than men in running events longer than 42.2 kilometers (26 miles, or marathon length). One possible explanation for this is that women have a greater resistance to muscle fatigue than do men. One study of men reported an inverse relationship between strength and how long it took for the muscles to become fatigued. Whether the fact that similarly trained men have a greater absolute strength (due to larger absolute muscle mass) than women contributes to this possible disadvantage in resistance to fatigue when compared to women is unknown.

STRENGTH

Muscular strength is the maximum force or tension that a muscle can generate. Multiple factors work toward the development of muscular strength. These include adaptations of neuromuscular activity, an increase in muscle size (hypertrophy), changes in muscle fiber composition, and hormonal activities. Although most studies investigating how training affects muscular strength have focused on men, research on women increased in the 1980s and thereafter.

Whole Muscle Growth

Earlier studies of resistance training in women had reported minimal changes in muscle size, or gains that were only about 50 percent as great as those observed in men. Studies in the 1990s using more sophisticated techniques challenged these findings. Although women do not achieve the same maximal size or strength as similarly trained men, this new research indicates that the muscles of women who do heavy resistance training adapt in a similar manner. After two to eight weeks of training, gains in muscular strength through resistance training are due mostly to neural alterations. Muscle size remains essentially unchanged. Researchers have confirmed that neural factors in-

GOING THE DISTANCE

While men perform better in physical activities that require strength because of their larger muscle mass, women perform better at activities that require endurance such as long distance running. Evidence suggests women have more endurance because their muscles do not tire as quickly as men's.

fluence the maximum strength gain in both men and women, and that women gain strength at about the same rate as men.

Muscle Fiber Type and Size

How resistance training affects muscle fiber in women was not studied extensively until the 1990s. A 1990 study looked at women who participated in a heavy resistance training program designed to increase thigh muscle strength. In addition to the expected improvements in strength, increases were found in the size and distribution of various (but not all) muscle fiber types. Women who stopped training for between thirty and thirty-two weeks did lose strength and their muscle fibers became smaller, but the women in both groups remained stronger than before the training. If they then trained again for six weeks, they regained the same strength and muscle fiber that had required the much more extended training the first time. This suggests that the gains women make through resistance training endure over a relatively long period of time, and they can regain them relatively quickly.

Hormonal Factors

Various hormones specific to males and females regulate the muscle growth that accompanies heavy resistance training. In men, anabolic hormones, including testosterone and human growth hormone predominate. A comparative study of heavy resistance training performed by men and women showed a correlation between the early changes in muscle fiber types and increased testosterone and decreased cortisol levels in men. Women did not show these same endocrine responses, although the changes in their muscles were similar.

Few studies have found that the level of testosterone in women's blood increases during resistance training, though some research has shown that human growth hormone may increase while women engage in heavy resistance training. Lactic acid levels in the muscles rise during this type of training, and some investigators theorize that this rise plays a role in the release of human growth hormone and other hormonal responses.

CARDIORESPIRATORY ENDURANCE

Dramatic improvements in performance times of women, especially in running events, have led to the speculation that in the near future women's and men's running times will converge. Not all researchers agree with this, but studies of ultraendurance athletes, both male and female, suggest that it is true. In equally trained men and women, one study showed that men and women ran at virtually the same speed at distances over marathon length. These investigations suggested that women may outperform men at distances greater than 70 kilometers (43 miles, the distance commonly called an "ultramarathon"). Studies of comparably performing male and female marathon runners have observed that the women performed better at a longer distance of 90 kilometers (56 miles) than their male counterparts. While women's running performance may indeed be equal to that of men at some time, biological differences will probably keep women from surpassing men in events that rely most on strength and power.

Endurance performance results from the complex interactions of multiple physiological factors. These include maximal oxygen uptake, economy of movement (how efficiently the athlete moves), and lactate threshold (ability to tolerate the lactic acid produced by contracting muscles, which causes an overworked muscle to "shut down"). These components are influenced by structural and functional characteristics that are, to some extent, genetically determined. In addition, the ability to sustain relatively high exercise intensities over long periods, a goal of endurance athletes, is also dependent on the utilization and availability of energy.

Determinants of VO2max

"VO2max" is the maximum volume of oxygen utilized by the body during each minute of exercise. In essence, it is a measure of a person's aerobic capabilities. VO2max of women athletes is typically reported to be 10 to 15 percent lower than for comparably trained men, except among competitive triathletes. Higher body fat has been implicated in the lower aerobic power measured in endurance-trained women when compared with men. Other factors, as yet undetermined, are also implicated.

Hemoglobin concentration (responsible for oxygen transport in the blood) and blood volume are also lower in women, which may contribute to differences in oxygen delivery and ultimately VO2max. However, researchers have found higher concentrations of 2,3 DPG—a phosphate compound that enhances the release of oxygen to the tissues—in women runners that may compensate for lower hemoglobin values.

The smaller heart volume in women results in lower maximal cardiac output (the volume of blood that circulates through the body each minute) and stroke volume (the volume of blood passed through the left ventricle with each beat) when compared with men. The cardiovascular systems of men and women adapt the same way to exercise training; maximal cardiac output and stroke volume both increase. One study, however, reported sex differences in the contribution of these cardiovascular alterations to VO2max. Women have smaller left ventricles, which researchers have found accounts for 68 percent of the difference in the oxygen uptake, compared to men. This difference in size along with more body fat, probably accounts for the gender differences in VO2max.

Lactate Threshold (LT)

Researchers have reported a strong relationship between the LT, which is the percentage of VO2max corresponding to an increase in lactic acid measured in the blood, and endurance performance in trained male cyclists who had normally high values for VO2max. Similar values for LT are reported in male and female endurance athletes. LT is influenced by enzymes important for aerobic metabolism, and endurance training results in similar adaptations in these aerobic enzymes for men and women.

A study of an elite marathoner who trained for sixteen weeks following childbirth demonstrates the trainability of LT. An increase in LT from 68 percent VO2max at four weeks postpartum to 82 percent VO2max at eight weeks postpartum was evident even though minimal changes were observed in VO2max.

Economy of Movement

The economy of movement, which is the oxygen cost required to maintain a given velocity, combines with VO2max and LT to influence endurance performance. It appears that highly trained men and women demonstrate similar running economies. Although the biomechanics of running (e.g., stride length, vertical displacement, pelvic width) may theoretically have an impact on running economy, only minimal correlations were found between biomechanical properties and running economy in elite female distance runners. One investigation of 10-kilometer performance in endurance-trained women found that LT and VO2max, but not running economy, were significantly related to performance. Another study of performance-matched men and women marathoners with similar VO2max found a reduced running economy among the women. Others have reported a high correlation between running economy and endurance performance in trained women.

Cycling efficiency in women has been found to relate to body mass, work rate, and pedal frequency—correlates previously demonstrated in men. Similarities in mechanical efficiency between trained men and women cyclists is not surprising since the percentage of a certain muscle fiber type has been linked to cycling efficiency, and muscle fiber type distribution is similar in sport-matched elite male and female athletes.

Substrate (Energy) Utilization

In the biological sciences, "substrate" is the base upon which an organism lives. In this context, it refers to stored and available fats and sugars that may be converted to energy. The availability of muscle glycogen (stored carbohydrates) and blood glucose (free or available carbohydrates) is also an important determinant of endurance performance. Because the female sex hormones (especially estradiol) may potentially influence fat metabolism, substrate utilization during endurance exercise may be affected. It has been suggested that better performances in women beyond 42.2-kilometer (26 mile) races may be partially explained by a lesser reliance on glycogen due to increased fat oxidation. The use of lipids (fats) for fuel during moderate-intensity exercise is apparently greater in women runners when compared with men and accounts for a smaller measurable reduction in muscle glycogen. On the other hand, there are apparently no gender differences in fat metabolism or the hormones that regulate it at 80 percent VO2max in endurance-trained women and men. The impact of gender differences in glycogen sparing on substrate metabolism during endurance exercise, with and without carbohydrate (CHO) loading, has also been studied. Although it appears that women utilize carbohydrates differently than men during endurance exercise, further research is warranted.

The oxidation of protein during prolonged exercise has also been reported to be lower in women when compared with similarly trained men. Although the contribution of protein to total energy metabolism during prolonged exercise is relatively small, the relationship between carbohydrate, fat, and protein availability may influence fatigue during prolonged exercise due to altered central nervous system function.

SUMMARY

The gains in muscle strength and cardiorespiratory endurance with exercise training is, with minor exceptions, similar for men and women. As young girls begin to participate in exercise and sport at an early age and continue through their formative years, many of the previously noted sex differences may be reduced to only such basic biological differences as size and mass. These determinants notwithstanding, women are as able as men to develop endurance and to push their bodies to their respective limits.

Karen D. Mittleman

Bibliography

Bam, Jenifer, Timothy D. Noakes, June Juritz, and Steven C. Dennis. (1997) "Could Women Outrun Men in Ultramarathon Races?" *Medicine and Science in Sports and Exercise* 29: 244–247.

Bouchard, Claude, Francois T. Dionne, Jeane-Aime Simoneau, and Marcel R. Boulay. (1992) "Genetics of Aerobic and Anaerobic Performances." *Exercise and Sport Sciences Reviews* 20: 27–58.

Coyle, Edward F. (1995) "Integration of the Physiological Factors Determining Endurance Performance Ability." *Exercise and Sport Sciences Reviews* 23: 25–63.

Drinkwater, Barbara L. (1973) "Physiological Responses of Women to Exercise." *Exercise and Sport Sciences Reviews* 1: 125–153.

———. (1984) "Women and Exercise: Physiological Aspects." *Exercise and Sport Sciences Reviews* 12: 339–372.

Gollnick, Phillip D. (1988) "Energy Metabolism and Prolonged Exercise." In *Perspectives in Exercise Science and Sports Medicine*, edited by D. R. Lamb and R. Murray. Indianapolis, IN: Benchmark Press, 1–42.

Joyner, Michael J. (1993) "Physiological Limiting Factors and Distance Running: Influence of Gender and Age on Record Performances." *Exercise and Sport Sciences Reviews* 21: 103–133.

Kraemer, William J., Steven J. Fleck, and William J. Evans. (1996) "Strength and Power Training: Physiological Mechanisms of Adaptation." *Exercise and Sport Sciences Reviews* 24: 363–397.

Lucas, John A., and R. A. Smith. (1982) "Women's Sport: A Trial of Equality." In *Her Story in Sport: A Historical Anthology of Women in Sports*, edited by R. Howell. West Point, NY: Leisure Press, 239–265.

Plowman, Sharon A., and Denise L. Smith. (1997) *Exercise Physiology for Health, Fitness, and Performance.* Boston, MA: Allyn and Bacon.

Seiler, Stephen. (1998) "Masters Athlete Physiology and Performance." <http://www.krs.hia.no/~stephens/>.

Wells, Christine L. (1991) *Women, Sport and Performance.* Champaign, IL: Human Kinetics.

ENGLAND *see* United Kingdom

ENVIRONMENT

The physical environment in which women live, work, and play can affect their bodies and physiological responses. Environmental temperature, humidity, wind velocity, barometric pressure, and air pollutants can alter normal responses both at rest and during physical activity. Indoor environments are usually well regulated to maintain air temperature, humidity, and wind within a narrow range. Outdoor air temperatures can range from –40 degrees Fahrenheit to 120 degrees Fahrenheit; the humidity from less than 10 percent to 100 percent; and wind from 0 to more than 40 miles per hour. Such broad ranges in these variables can affect both how women feel during physical activity and how well they perform.

COMFORTABLE (THERMONEUTRAL) ENVIRONMENTS

Body core temperature in humans is regulated around a set temperature of 37°C (98.6°F). During physical activity humans expend more energy than usual, which results in increased body heat production and an elevation in body temperature. As the body core temperature rises, blood flow is diverted to the superficial blood vessels in the skin, which have dilated. This allows heat produced by skeletal muscles to be transported to the skin where it can be transferred to the air (convective heat loss). A person begins to sweat when the core temperature reaches a certain point (threshold). Heat is also lost when sweat is changed from a liquid to a gaseous state (evaporative heat loss). During continuous physical activity (such as walking or running), a person's body core temperature will reach a plateau after twenty to thirty minutes over a broad range of air temperatures, humidities, and air velocities. Several factors, however, influence how high the core temperature will rise and whether a plateau will occur. One of the most important is the intensity of the physical activity. The more intense the exercise, the more

heat the body is producing, and the higher the core temperature will be when it plateaus. As a result of the increased heat production, the range of air temperatures and humidities where a core temperature plateau will occur is smaller during higher intensities of physical activity.

HEAT AND HUMIDITY

In hot environments convective heat loss will not occur if the air temperature is greater than skin temperatures. Instead, the body will gain heat from the air. This is usually the situation when air temperatures exceed 35°C (95°F). The body compensates by increasing the rate of sweating and evaporative heat loss in hot environments. After a certain point, however, no additional heat can be lost. The relative humidity of the environment is the major determinant of the maximal evaporative rate. Air that is already saturated with water vapor (100% relative humidity) cannot absorb additional evaporated sweat. The result will be visible sweat standing on the skin and dripping from the body. Several indexes are used to evaluate the environmental heat stress produced by combinations of air temperatures and humidities. The two most widely used are the Heat Stress Index (HSI) and the Wet Bulb Globe Temperature (WBGT) Index that also takes into account heat from the sun.

Hot, arid environments, typical of the southwestern United States, where the air temperature may exceed 100°F and the humidity is low (less than 20%), produce the highest sweat and evaporative rates during physical activity. Because the sweat rate is elevated, dehydration is a common problem during physical activity and can lead to serious heat illnesses. Adequate fluid replacement (150–300 milliliters, about one-half pint) must occur every fifteen minutes to reduce the risk of heat illness. Evaporative heat loss is very similar in well-trained men and women exercising in hot, dry environments. In women, however, a slightly greater degree of dehydration will occur due to their smaller body size and total body water. Female athletes should consume up to 500 ml (one pint) of fluid before exercising to reduce the amount of dehydration. Because most females consume fewer fluids than they lose during physical activity, they must continue to replace fluids—that is, drink liquids—after they stop exercising.

Physical activity in warm humid environments is also stressful even though air temperatures are lower. For example, the heat stress at an air temperature of 90°F with a relative humidity of 70 percent will be the same as an air temperature of 105°F with a relative humidity of 20 percent. In humid environments, males sweat more than females but most of the additional sweat is not evaporated. Males' additional loss of body fluids causes them to have higher heart rates than females during physical activity in warm, humid environments.

Females' core and skin temperatures fluctuate during the menstrual cycle. Following ovulation both core and skin temperature increase from the influence of the hormone progesterone. The threshold core temperatures for the onset of sweating and skin vasodilation also increase after ovulation. During physical activity core temperature will be higher after ovulation (the luteal phase) than between the beginning of the menses and ovulation (the follicular phase). No evidence suggests, however, that females are less tolerant of physical activity in hot environments or at greater risk of heat illness during the luteal phase than males are in general.

COLD

During physical activity in cold environments, superficial blood vessels in arms and legs constrict, thus shunting blood flow into deeper vessels. This helps to protect the core temperature and reduces the rate of heat loss. If the core temperature decreases, a person begins to shiver, and her metabolic rate increases. In cold environments, females' relatively greater subcutaneous fat thickness is advantageous because it provides more insulation and reduces the rate of heat loss from the body. During cold water immersion, female skin-divers had thicker tissue insulation and thus were able to tolerate colder water temperatures before they began to shiver than males. Similar responses have been observed during exercise in cold water.

In cold environments, heat produced during physical activity can offset the heat lost. At lower air temperatures, a person will have to increase the intensity of their exercise for heat production to balance heat loss. If males and females exercise at the same relative intensity (that is, the same percentage of maximal oxygen uptake), the males will usually produce more heat because they have larger maximal oxygen uptakes. During prolonged physical activity in the cold, females may have lower core temperatures because they produce less heat. This is most likely to happen during low-intensity physical activities.

Women begin to shiver at higher core temperatures after ovulation than before, but the increase in the amount of heat they produce is the same before ovulation as after. Females who are iron deficient have lower core temperatures in the cold and begin to shiver sooner than do those with normal iron stores.

ALTITUDE

Participation in sports and physical activities at higher altitudes (skiing, hiking, mountain climbing) presents a different type of stress because barometric pressure decreases as altitude increases. As a result, the oxygen pressure is lower at a higher altitude, and respiration will increase. At altitudes above 1,500 meters (4,950 feet), maximal oxygen uptake will be significantly reduced by 1 percent for every 100-meter (330-feet) increase in altitude. In endurance sports (distance running, cross-country skiing), participants will be forced to reduce their speed (intensity) at altitude. Air is less dense at greater heights, which will reduce air resistance. In sprint-type events (running, cycling, speed skating), the reduction in air resistance allows the performer to move faster. Many world records in sprint events were set at the 1968 Olympics in Mexico City, which has an altitude of 2,300 meters (7,590 feet).

As a person stays at altitude over a period of time (days, weeks, months), many physiological changes occur. This process is known as acclimatization. Two of the more important changes are increases in hemoglobin concentration and red cell volume. Because hemoglobin carries almost all of the oxygen in the blood, these changes improve oxygen delivery to the tissues. This is one of the reasons performance in endurance activities usually improves with acclimatization. Increases in hemoglobin concentration in female mountaineers are not as large during acclimatization as reported in males. However, smaller increases in hemoglobin do not appear to impair female mountaineers' ability to climb the highest peaks in the Himalayas. Researchers have also ob-

Water and air pollution can both adversely affect an athlete's performance. Here two women taking part in trials for a canoe race on the River Medway in England in 1932 don masks as protection. (Hulton-Deutsch Collection/Corbis)

served that red cell volume does not increase in iron-deficient individuals after four weeks at altitude. As a result, improvements in endurance at altitude may occur more slowly in individuals who are iron deficient.

AIR POLLUTION

The two air pollutants most commonly encountered during physical activity outdoors are carbon monoxide and ozone. They can be present at the same time, but carbon monoxide is more likely to be elevated in the winter and ozone in the summer. Carbon monoxide—which generally comes from car exhaust—is taken up by hemoglobin in the blood and replaces some of the oxygen. Carboxyhemoglobin levels of 5 percent will reduce maximal oxygen uptake and endurance.

Ozone is a volatile gas most commonly produced as a pollutant through an interaction be-

tween sunlight and car exhaust at ground level. (In contrast, ozone in the upper layers of the atmosphere is beneficial to human beings and life on earth. The so-called ozone layer protects us from damaging forms of radiation from space, and is being damaged by other forms of air pollution.) Ozone at ground level is an irritant. It is absorbed by the mucous membrane of the respiratory tract. Irritation of the throat, coughing, and difficulty in breathing deeply are symptoms of ozone exposure. During physical activity, ozone levels of as little as 0.3 parts per million (ppm) can reduce maximal oxygen uptake, and levels of only 0.2 ppm have been found to impair exercise performance.

WATER POLLUTION

By the 1960s, the effects of urbanization and industrialization were apparent in rivers around the globe. In areas with many paper mills, rivers flowed in different hues depending upon the color of paper being produced that day. Manufacturers discharged toxic chemicals directly into streams; nitrates and pesticides from agriculture were washed into rivers and underground aquifers; and phosphates from detergents polluted fresh and salt water where people swam, boated, and fished.

Human sewage—often discharged without any form of treatment into the ocean—became a special problem for surfers, while river users suffered from a new understanding of the dangers posed by polychlorinated biphenyls (PCBs), highly stable chemicals used in electronic equipment and manufacturing that have been dumped into rivers around the globe. PCBs are considered carcinogens by the Environmental Protection Agency, and they can be cleaned up only by dredging the bottom of a river and disposing of the mud as toxic waste. The impact of these various contaminants on rivers, lakes, and coastlines has been profound, with many rivers and beaches classified as unsuitable for swimming or fishing.

Federal regulatory agencies in the United States, Europe, and elsewhere began to reverse the trend in the 1970s. Legislation was introduced to promote pollution control, watershed protection, environmental quality, and resource reclamation for recreation purposes. The results are obvious to citizens who have returned to rivers and lakes to swim, fish, and boat. Rivers such as the Hudson in New York State, are coming back to life, and the rise of urban recreation along waterfronts—from river walks to canal tours to public piers for boating—shows how far we have progressed in reclaiming the health of our waterways.

SUMMARY

Participants in physical activity and sports are exposed to a variety of environmental stressors. These include heat, humidity, cold, altitude, and pollution. Warm environments can be particularly stressful if athletes do not replace the fluid losses that occur during physical activity. Because of the reduction in oxygen pressure at altitudes above 1,500 meters (4,950 feet), exercise is more stressful and athletes do not perform as well in endurance activities. Women who are iron deficient have a lower tolerance of cold environments and are less able to increase red cell volume as they become acclimatized to moderate altitude.

Emily M. Haymes

Bibliography

Avellini, Barbara, Eliezer Kamon, and Janet Karajewksi. (1980) "Physiological Responses of Physically Fit Men and Women to Acclimation to Humid Heat." *Journal of Applied Physiology* 49: 254–261.

Carpenter, Andrea J., and Sarah A. Nunneley. (1988) "Endogenous Hormones Subtly Alter Women's Responses to Heat Stress." *Journal of Applied Physiology* 65: 2313–2317.

Drinkwater, Barbara, Piro Kramar, John Bedi, and Larry Folinsbee. (1982) "Women at Altitude: Cardiovascular Responses to Altitude." *Aviation, Space and Environmental Medicine* 53: 472–477.

Frye, Andrea, and Eliezer Kamon. (1983) "Sweating Efficiency in Acclimated Men and Women Exercising in Humid and Dry Heat." *Journal of Applied Physiology* 54: 972–977.

Graham, Terry. (1983) "Alcohol Ingestion and Sex Differences of the Thermal Responses to Mild Exercise in a Cold Environment." *Human Biology* 57: 687–698.

Hessemer, V., and K. Bruck. (1985) "Influence of Menstrual Cycle on Shivering, Skin Blood Flow, and Sweating Responses Measured at Night." *Journal of Applied Physiology* 59: 1902–1910.

Hong, Sukki, Donald Rennie, and Yang Park. (1986) "Cold Acclimatization and Deacclimatization of Korean Women Divers." In *Exercise and Sport Sciences Reviews*, vol. 14, edited by Kent Pandolf. New York: Macmillan Publishing, 231–268.

Lukaski, Henry, Clinton Hall, and Forrest Nielsen. (1990) "Thermogenesis and Thermoregulatory Function of Iron-Deficient Women without Anemia." *Aviation, Space and Environmental Medicine* 61: 913–920.

McArdle, William, John Magel, Robert Spina, Thomas Gergley, and Michael Toner. (1984) "Thermal Adjustment to Cold-Water Exposure in Exercising Men and Women." *Journal of Applied Physiology* 56: 1572–1577.

Stephenson, Lou, and Margaret Kolka. (1985) "Menstrual Cycle Phase and Time of Day Alter Reference Signal Controlling Arm Blood Flow and Sweating." *American Journal of Physiology* 249: R186–R191.

Stray-Gunderson, James, C. Alexander, A. Hochstein, D. deLemos, and Benjamin Levine. (1992) "Failure of Red Cell Volume to Increase at Altitude Exposure in Iron Deficient Runners." *Medicine and Science in Sports and Exercise* 24: S90.

Additional information was provided by Laurie Gullion and Karen Christensen.

EQUIPMENT *see* Sportswear Industry, Technology

ESTONIA

Estonia is one of the Baltic nations (along with Lithuania and Latvia) of northern Europe and has a population of about 1.45 million. The nation was part of the Soviet Union from 1940 to 1991, when it achieved full independence.

The systematic practice of physical education in Estonia began in 1632 with the founding of Tartu University, which had in its employment a dancing and fencing master. Early in the nineteenth century, the university expanded its training in the physical disciplines, focusing on those skills most in demand by its aristocratic students. Of six lecturers in the "arts," four were physical educators who taught riding, fencing, vaulting, swimming, and dancing.

Karl Eduard Raupach introduced gymnastics to the university in 1819, following the teachings of F. L. Jahn in Germany. By 1863 a Baltic-German gymnastics society was formed in Tallinn and a year later another was formed in Tartu. Baltic-German athletes are also credited with the first creation of organizations for rowing (1875), cycling (1888), and sailing (1888). The first society officially registered by Estonians was the Saadjärve Society for Cyclists in 1896.

FIRST ESTONIAN WOMEN ATHLETES

Wrestling and weightlifting were also practiced around this time, but it was Gustav Boedberg who in Tallinn in 1888 founded a society for these heavy athletics that encouraged women's participation. Boedberg's follower Adolf Andrushkev-

itch trained several female athletes in a circus, the best-known of whom were Linda Belling (August Joost) and Marina Loors (Maria Loorberg). Loors's most famous feat was her ability to lie on her back and lift with her feet a 180-pound (82-kg) barbell, turning it as a windmill, with five grown men sitting on it. A large group of women athletes also performed in the circuses of Saint Petersburg. By 1907 the group enjoyed great success in the Truzzi circus in Riga and on tour in many European countries as well as in Japan and China. This success brought new fame to Estonian women wrestlers and weightlifters.

THE GYMNASTICS MOVEMENT

Women's involvement in gymnastics began in the form of health gymnastics only. Swedish gymnastics reached Estonia around 1890 through the instruction of Ester Lidbergin, who was educated at the Stockholm Arvedson Gymnastics Institute. Lidbergin worked at the health gymnastics institution until it was bought by Aino Kokström, who was educated in Finland. Friede Hoffmann was the first Estonian woman who qualified for gymnastics. In 1906 she completed a two-year course at the Arvedson Gymnastics Institute. This Finnish influence was maintained throughout the first two decades of the twentieth century as the corresponding education was acquired mainly in Finland.

Helmi Põld organized the first gymnastics teachers' courses in 1908 and 1909. The first Estonian woman to receive higher education in physical education was Anna Raudkats, at Helsinki University in 1915. She went on to establish a female gymnastics group at the Kalev sports society, and is most noted for her pioneering efforts to bring the female Finnish style of gymnastics to Estonia. Raudkats worked as a school teacher and as a lecturer at teachers' refresher courses. She also published *Health and Beauty*, the first book on female gymnastics in Estonian.

Another notable contribution to the development of gymnastics was made by Ernst Idla. In 1931 he founded the Tallinn Gymnastics Institute. His Estonian Gymnastics Society, established in 1934, placed a great deal of emphasis on female gymnastics. By 1937 his society had organized the first group gymnastics competition with 21 groups, comprised of 187 women gymnasts. Mass gymnastics competitions at the Estonian Games

Women professional wrestlers from the Estonian Sport Society "Kalev" of St. Petersburg, 1905. (Estonian Sports Museum)

in 1934 and 1939 aroused much attention. After World War II, female gymnastics was greatly influenced by the activities performed at Tartu University, headed in 1956 by Ethel Kudu and Liidia Uustal. Several first prizes won at competitions indicated that Estonian women were among the elite of the Soviet Union. After Idla won favorable recognition with a memorable program for female gymnasts at the Lingiaad Light Party in 1949, his teachings were carried on not only by his daughters, but by his exiled Estonian followers as well. Idla eventually emigrated to Sweden from his occupied Estonia.

COMPETITIVE SPORTS

Women began participating in other sports later than men; therefore, Estonian championships for women were held much later than those for men's sports. An exception to this was speed skating, in which the first Estonian championships for women were held in 1910 together with men. Emma Uhl won the 500-meter event with a time of 1 minute 39

seconds. In figure skating L. Voitjankovskaja became the first Estonian master in women's solo in 1920. The first cross-country skiing championship to include women was held in 1923. The winner of the 3-kilometer race was S. Allas with a time of 18 minutes 20.5 seconds. The first swimming championships were held in 1919 with freestyle events in the 25- and 50-meter races. The first tennis championship, won by I. Grünberg, was held in 1920.

In the 1920s women took to playing volleyball and basketball, which led to the first championships being held in 1925 and 1927, respectively. Although women had cycled for some time in Estonia, the first championship in track pursuit was not held until 1926. Winners were E. Hintberg and H. Pirker, respectively. Road cycling championships were not held until 1933. The first downhill slalom skiing competition was held in 1941.

INTERNATIONAL COMPETITION

Although Estonian women did not participate in international competitions before World War II, the first Estonian woman to reach the world level was Sara Teitelbaum in the 400-meter running race with a time of 61.8 seconds in 1929. During the time of Soviet occupation, Virve Põldsam-Roolaid was the first Estonian woman to earn a medal as a member of the combined Soviet Union track and field team when she won a bronze medal in javelin at the 1954 European championships. Linda Ojastu-Kepp followed this lead with the Soviet women's team gold medal win at the 1958 European championships in the 4 × 100-meter relay race. In 1959 Estonian women achieved their first gold medals in world competition: Mai-Maret Otsa and Ene Jaanson were members of the Soviet Union basketball team that won the world championship. The most notable Estonian woman athlete was the biathlonist Kaija Parve, who won a total of seven championships (four team and three individual). In total, sixteen Estonian women have been awarded thirty-two world champion gold medals, and eighteen Estonian women have earned forty-five European champion gold medals.

OLYMPIC COMPETITION

In 1936 in Garmich-Partenkichen, figure skater Helene Michelson and skier Karin Peckert-Forsman were the first Estonian women to participate in the Winter Olympics. In 1960 in Rome, swimmers Ulvi Voog-Indrikson and Eve Ususmees-Maurer were the first Estonian women to participate in the Summer Olympics. In 1964 at Tokyo, Estonian women participated in Olympic track and field for the first time. Laine Kallas-Erik placed sixth in the 800-meter race, and she also shared a world record in the 3 × 800-meter relay race with her Soviet teammates.

The first Estonian individual female Olympic gold medalist was Svetlana Tsirkova, who won a gold medal as a member of the Soviet Union's fencing team in Mexico in 1968. In fact, in the Olympics, Estonian women have won only gold medals. Erika Salumäe won a gold medal in the 1,000-meter cycling sprint at the 1988 Olympics in Seoul. She again won the gold in the same event at the 1992 Olympics in Barcelona, only this time she did so under the independent Estonian flag. By 1999, she had set nearly twenty world records and been elected the best woman athlete of the year in Estonia seven times.

PHYSICAL EDUCATION

After the foundation of the Institute of Physical Education at Tartu University in 1928, it became possible for women, alongside men, to get higher education in physical culture in Estonia. The first group to complete the course in 1931 contained sixteen women. By 1998 more than 1,500 women had been educated in physical culture in Estonia.

Enn Mainla

ETHNICITY *see* Race and Ethnicity

EVANS, JANET

(1971–)

U.S. SWIMMER

Janet Evans was a participant in three Olympic Games and a winner of three gold medals in the 1988 Olympic Games. Though she retired after the 1996 Olympics at Atlanta, in 1999 she was still the holder of three world records.

Evans was born in Placentia, California, on 28 August 1971. She splashed onto the national swimming scene at age ten when she broke the national record for her age group in the 200-meter freestyle. In 1986 she set the U.S. Open meet record in the 400-meter individual medley (IM). Evans was named Swimmer of the Year by *United States Swimming* in 1987, after breaking the world records in the 400-, 800-, and 1500-meter freestyle events. Nearing the 1988 Olympic trials, Evans trained constantly—swimming an average of eight to ten miles per day—and smashed her 1500-meter freestyle world record, becoming the first woman to swim that distance in under 16 minutes. Her three victories at Olympic trials, including an American record in the 400-meter IM, came as no surprise. Evans went on to claim three gold medals in the 1988 Olympic Games—the first female swimmer to do so since 1976—beating the 400-meter freestyle world record, the 400-

Janet Evans hugs another competitor following a race. (Neal Preston)

meter IM American record, and the 800-meter freestyle Olympic record. Her performances helped her win the 1989 Sullivan Award as the outstanding amateur athlete in the United States and the 1989 United States Olympic Committee Sportswoman of the Year award.

Although capturing attention with her sparkling personality and performances, Evans declined sponsorships in order to remain eligible for college swimming. After enrolling in Stanford University, Evans took three individual NCAA titles during her freshman year—earning the high-point title and NCAA Swimmer of the Year—and two individual NCAA titles in her sophomore year. Evans then left Stanford, renouncing her college eligibility, to train full-time for the 1992 Olympics Games after a rule limited students to twenty hours of practice per week in season. Her tough decision paid off as she posted her fastest times since the 1990 NCAA Championships, winning the silver medal in the 400-meter freestyle, and the gold medal in the 800-meter freestyle. She

became the first woman to win that event in two Olympic Games, and the first American woman swimmer to earn four individual Olympic gold medals.

In 1993, she was recognized with the renaming of the Los Angeles Invitational swim meet to the Janet Evans Invitational. She also volunteered as assistant coach with the University of Southern California women's swim team. After receiving her communications degree in 1994 from USC, Evans continued training, aiming for her final Olympic Games. Although she did not win a medal, the 1996 Olympics was an emotionally charged event for Evans as she was selected as an opening ceremonies torch bearer and tri-captain of the women's swim team.

Retiring from competitive swimming after her final Olympic event, Evans left forty-five national titles in her wake. In 1999 she still held three world records, six American records, and seven U.S. open records.

Cara Joy Lockman Hall

Bibliography

"Evans Can't Wait." (1991) *Sports Illustrated* (15 April): 28–30, 33.

Hickok, Ralph. (1995) *A Who's Who of Sports Champions.* Boston: Houghton Mifflin.

Johnson, Anne Janette. (1996) *Great Women in Sports.* Detroit: Visible Ink Press.

Lieber, Jill. (1988) "Meet a Small Wonder." *Sports Illustrated* (14 September): 140–143.

Noden, Merrell. (1990) "Another Big Splash." *Sports Illustrated* (26 March): 32–33.

EVERT, CHRIS

(1954–)

U.S. TENNIS PLAYER

In a remarkable tennis career that spanned more than two decades, Chris Evert established herself as one of the premier female athletes of the twentieth century. Evert won 157 singles titles, logged more than 1,300 career match wins, and attained one of the highest winning percentages in professional tennis history—90 percent of all her matches. She won at least one Grand Slam title per year for thirteen years, 1974–1986, and from 1972 to 1989, Evert never ranked lower than the top four in women's tennis. About Evert, fellow tennis star Billie Jean King wrote in her 1988 book: "Her unwavering focus, combined with her great, natural coordination, and her father's marvelous training, made Chris Evert one of the giants of the game."

Christine Marie Evert was born on 21 December 1954 in Fort Lauderdale, Florida, the second of James and Colette Evert's five children. At age six, she began hitting a tennis ball against the walls at the municipal courts. She spent two to three hours on weekdays and eight hours a day on the weekends practicing her ground strokes and serves. Since she was not strong enough to hit the one-handed backhand, Evert learned to hit the two-handed backhand, one of the first players to adopt this style of play.

Chris Evert during singles competition at the 1985 French Open. (Yann Arthus-Bertran)

In April 1971, while still an amateur, Evert won—but did not accept money for—the $100,000 Virginia Slims Master's tournament in St. Petersburg, Florida, the first of her tournament victories. Evert graduated from Fort Lauderdale's St. Thomas Aquinas High School in 1972 and turned professional on her eighteenth birthday. By 1974, she had already reached the number-one ranking and begun her dominance of women's tennis. She reached the semifinals or better in seventeen of nineteen U.S. Open appearances and the semifinals or better in seventeen of eighteen appearances at Wimbledon. She won the All-England Championships at Wimbledon in 1974, 1976, and 1981; the French Open singles championship in 1974, 1975, 1979, 1980, 1983, 1985, and 1986; and the U.S. Open women's singles title in 1975, 1976, 1977, 1978, 1980, and 1982.

An extraordinary fifteen-year rivalry developed between Chris Evert and Martina Navratilova, two athletes with markedly different playing styles and personalities. Evert, with her mental tenacity and relentless baseline play, battled Navratilova's superior athleticism and aggressive serve-and-volley style. The rivalry, which began in 1973, helped make women's tennis into one of the world's top sports attractions in the 1980s.

Evert represented her country in international matches as a member of the U.S. Federation Cup Team, 1977–1980 and 1982; the U.S. Wightman Cup Team, 1971–1973, 1975, and 1977–1982; and the 1988 U.S. Olympic team. She retired from tournament tennis in 1989.

Known as the "Ice Maiden" for her seemingly emotionless, determined style of play, off the court she was popular with and supportive of other players. Her two-handed backhand and patient baseline game became a model for a generation of tennis players. Her first marriage to British player John Lloyd ended in divorce; she married skier Andy Mill in 1988.

The Women's Sports Foundation presented Evert with the 1990 Flo Hyman Award for commitment to excellence and steady support for women's advancements in sports. The Associated Press named her Female Athlete of the Year four times (1974, 1975, 1977, and 1980) and *Sports Illustrated* magazine selected her as their Sportsman of the Year in 1976. In 1981, she was named Women's Sports Foundation Sportswoman of the Year and was inducted into the International Women's Sports Hall of Fame. She was elected unanimously to the International Tennis Hall of Fame in 1995.

Janet Woolum

See also Navratilova, Martina

Bibliography

Corel WTA Tour 1997 Player Guide. (1997).

King, Billie Jean, with Cynthia Starr. (1988) *We Have Come a Long Way: The Story of Women's Tennis.* New York: McGraw-Hill Book Co.

Lloyd, Chris, and John Lloyd, with Carol Thatcher. (1985) *Lloyd on Lloyd.* New York: Beaufort Books.

Lloyd, Chris Evert, with Neil Amdur. (1982) *Chrissie, My Own Story.* New York: Simon & Schuster.

Lorge, Barry. (1989) "The Legacy of Chris Evert." *Tennis* (November): 31–37.

EXTREME SPORTS

The last three decades of the twentieth century saw a veritable explosion of new sports—often described as "extreme" or "adrenaline" sports—that can be characterized by an apparent lack of rules and a focus on pushing the limits of danger and risk. They include such activities as solo rock climbing and sky surfing. Women are increasingly involved in extreme sports of all varieties, both as recreational participants and in the growing number of widely publicized and televised competitions.

The burgeoning interest in extreme sports has implications for all parts of the sport world. Sport organizers confront new needs and expectations from a new market. Extreme sports are spectacular, and new athletes must learn that the measures and numbers used to judge performance are being rejected in favor of lived moments, adrenaline, and the relationship to one's body and to nature.

This sport revolution can be located within a larger cultural context that took shape in the 1950s and 1960s. At a time when countercultural values could be found in art, music, and literature, new sports were inspired by avant-gardists who opposed dominant cultural values and proposed an alternative sport ideology. The notion of "play" versus "game" became a morality of pleasure, a marketing strategy, a look, a vocabulary, and an attitude defining alternative lifestyles and subcultures.

Extreme sports are an interesting cultural phenomenon at the intersection of gender relations and changing values in sport. For many years, women were largely excluded from competitive sport and relegated to more socially acceptable feminine realms. The women's version of physical activity was commonly individualistic and noncompetitive, motivated by personal fulfillment rather than extrinsic standards and goals.

EXTREME SPORT CULTURE

Extreme sports such as solo rock climbing, sky surfing, and in-line skating emphasize values far

TAKING IT TO THE LIMIT

Extreme sports differ from traditional sports in several important ways. Extreme sports stress individual freedom and creativity and devalue competition. The emphasis is on the process, taking risks, and testing one's limits rather than on achieving specific goals and following externally-imposed rules. Extreme sports participants are often cross-over athletes who engage in various events rather than specialize in one. Finally, extreme sports are linked to the global youth culture rather than to the business or educational world. These differences in "culture" are often put to the test when extreme sports are commercialized for television viewing or argued for inclusion in Olympic competition.

removed from those of traditional sports. Tenets of extreme sport include individualism, personal satisfaction, and creativity, while competition is given a low priority, if valued at all. A paradoxical situation has developed in sport: access to traditional sport is becoming easier and more egalitarian while the rationale behind competitive sport based on fair play and a level playing field is now in question. New sports are oriented toward processes, not goals; participants are testing personal limits rather than externally imposed limits.

Although women did at first find themselves on the margins of this developing realm—much as they were in traditional sport—they are flooding into extreme sports at an unprecedented rate. Girls are embracing extreme culture, as well as the inherent search for risk and adrenaline. David Feigley, professor of exercise science at Rutgers University in New Jersey, has researched the relationship between women and adrenaline. According to Feigley, girls have traditionally been socialized to read adrenaline as fear. However, as more girls play sports, they will, as men always have, likely read adrenaline surges as a token of thrill and challenge.

Another aspect of extreme sports is its connection to youth culture. Young people have always been attracted to fringe movements, and the marginality of extreme sports provides a perfect condition for youth participation. Although many active female extreme athletes are beyond their adolescent years, teenage girls, as consumers of mass youth styles, are involving themselves in the sport activities that youth culture has embraced. In the years to come, we may therefore see extreme sport participation more as a function of age than gender.

Crossover, an important feature of extreme sports, contradicts traditional sports' orientation toward specialization and sport-specific training. A top pro snowboarder, for example, might not sacrifice her enjoyment of mountain biking, surfing, and rock climbing to further her snowboarding ambitions. Some extreme athletes risk their lives in multiple sports for a living: ski magazines, film makers, and corporate sponsors pay them in return for the right to capture the action as they ski death-defying terrain, rock-climb, ice-climb, and paraglide.

Although the majority of these athletes participate recreationally, there are many international competitions for single-sport as well as multisport events. Currently, the most prestigious extreme competition is the X Games, developed and produced by Disney's ESPN (television network) in 1995. This event, which features both summer and winter alternative sport athletes, was conceived of as an "extreme Olympics," targeting male television viewers between the ages of twelve and thirty-four. In 1995, the Extreme Games (later changed to the "X Games") was said to include four hundred athletes from six continents, representing twenty-five countries. Although extreme contests such as the X Games are clearly the domain of adolescent boys, with relative ease girls have burst onto the competitive scene in in-line skating, snowboarding, and skateboarding. With the inclusion of women's snowboarding in the Olympics and the evident desire of the International Olympic Committee (IOC) to capitalize on the interest in this new sport market, the opportunities for female extreme sport participation will undoubtedly grow.

WOMEN IN EXTREME SPORTS

There are women participants in virtually all extreme sports. For example, Danielle Crist made the first kayak descent of Thule Berri River (Class V) in Nepal. Pamela Zoolalian held the women's world speed record in street luge (72.83 mph). New Zealander Anne Helliwell has completed all four BASE requirements (building, antenna, span, earth) many times over. Nikki Warren specialized in rope freefalling—climbing then leaping and falling on a climbing rope—off mountains throughout Northern California.

Some of the major extreme sports and their participants in the late 1990s are described below.

Aggressive In-line Skating

Although the first in-line skates were designed to provide cross-training for hockey skaters, it was not long before "street style" and "vert" in-line skaters developed their own use for the skates. Like skateboarders, "street" skaters jump over and grind across anything in their way. Vert skating—skating on vertical surfaces—began when in-liners invaded the skateboarders' half-pipe (a U-shaped ramp) to perform their own "big air" maneuvers. Brazil's Fabiola Da Silva is one the world's top female aggressive skaters.

Eco-Challenge

The Eco-Challenge is an expedition-competition for teams of adventurers, each consisting of men and women combined. The teams race 300 miles non-stop, twenty-four hours a day using nonmotorized transportation such as canoes, kayaks, mountain bikes, white-water rafts, horses, their feet, and climbing ropes. The first team to finish in full complement is the winner. Cathy Sassin-Smith has been on several top-placing teams in Eco-Challenge as well as in several other adventure races. Like several other Eco-Challengers, Sassin-Smith has an impressive athletic history that includes being a nationally ranked triathlete for ten years.

Extreme Skiing

Snowshoes, climbing gear, and avalanche safety equipment are standard gear for those skiing off

Kim Csizmazia climbs ice at the Winter X Games in Crested Butte, Colorado. (AP Photos)

cliffs and down the world's steepest terrain. The most popular places to "go big" are the European Alps, the North American Rockies, the South American Andes, and the Southern Alps of New Zealand. Wendy Fisher, a one-time U.S. Olympic ski racer, won the 1997 World Extreme Skiing Championships in Valdez, Alaska.

Free Climbing

Climbers ascend ice and rock under their own power, the most difficult climbs requiring a level of physical conditioning, specialized technique, and mental toughness that few sports can equal. The most extreme rock climbers can solo their way up the rock using no equipment beyond shoes and chalk. Lynn Hill, considered one of the world's greatest free-climbers, male or female, was the first person to free-climb the 3,000-foot Nose route of Yosemite's El Capitan in a single day.

Sky Surfing

When Frenchman Joel Cruciani jumped out of a plane while standing on a small surfboard held in by snowboard bindings, skysurfing was born. Skysurfers perform aerial acrobatics at speeds of up to 120 mph before deploying the parachute. A camera person or "camera-flyer" free-falls at the same time in order to capture the performance for judging purposes. In competition, the surfer and camera-flyer are judged as a team. Viviane Wegrath was the first female skysurfer to win a medal in the X Games.

Speed Biking

At speeds nearing 135 mph, down 2-mile, 60-degree slopes, speed bikers are among the fastest nonmotorized humans on the planet, second only to speed skiers. After accelerating to maximum velocity before racing through a speed-trap zone, racers face a second high-risk challenge: stopping. Caroline Curl set the women's record in world speed biking in 1996 with a speed of 122 mph on a 55-degree slope.

Street Luge

When skateboarders began flying down the steep and winding roads in the foothills of California lying face up on their boards, the sport of street luging was born. Lugers exceed speeds of 80 mph, their bodies protected by motorcycle leathers, full-face helmets, and specially soled shoes. Pamela Zoolalian was the only woman at the highest level of the sport, routinely finishing in the top five in competitions.

Wakeboarding

With their feet fixed to a modified surfboard, wakeboarders perform acrobatic tricks while being pulled across the wake behind a power boat. A new element introduced into the sport, a practice that came directly from street skateboarding and freestyle snowboarding, was "grinding" off obstacles like channel buoys, docks, and rock out-croppings. Tara Hamilton was the world's top female wakeboarder.

CONCLUSION

The next generation is ready to meet these records. Women who climb vertical rock faces, for example, do so with their daughters right behind them. Perhaps surfer Lisa Anderson and windsurfer Angela Cochran represent the future direction of women in extreme sports—transcending the traditional gender barrier. Anderson, the four-time world surfing champion, competes in men's professional events, and Cochran, the former world cup surfing champion, became the first woman to successfully windsurf Jaws on Maui's North Shore, considered to be the world's biggest surf, with wave heights of thirty to forty feet. Women's achievements in the realm of extreme sports are significant, and there is no doubt that women will be pushing the limits of performance even further in the years to come.

Joanne Kay

See also Snowboarding; Wakeboarding

Bibliography

Beal, Becky. (1995) "Disqualifying the Official: An Exploration of Social Resistance through the Subculture of Skateboarding." *Sociology of Sport Journal* 12, 3: 252–267.

Discovery Channel. (1999) "Welcome to Eco-Challenge." <http://www.ecochallenge.com>.

ESPN Network. (1999) "Extreme Sports." <http://espn.go.com/extreme>.

Finkel, Michael. (1997) "And Now, the Runners-Up." *Condé Nast Sports for Women* (November): 116–117.

Humphreys, Duncan. (1997) "Shredheads Go Mainstream? Snowboarding and Alternative Youth." *International Review for the Sociology of Sport* 32, 2 (June): 147–160.

Le Breton, David. (1991) *Passions du Risque.* Paris: Metailie.

Loret, Alain. (1995) *Generation Glisse.* Paris: Editions Autrement.

McMillen, Rick. (1998) *Xtreme Sports.* Houston, TX: Gulf.

Rinehart, Robert E. (1998) *Players All: Performances in Contemporary Sport.* Bloomington: Indiana University Press.

Todhunter, Andrew. (1998) *Fall of the Phantom Lord: Climbing and the Face of Fear.* New York: Doubleday.

Tomlinson, Joe. (1996) *Extreme Sports. The Illustrated Guide to Maximum Adrenaline Thrills.* New York: Smithmark.

Virshup, Amy. (1998) "Fear Without Loathing." *Condé Nast Sports for Women* (February): 109–111.

F

FALCONRY

Falconry is a field sport that is defined as the hunting of wild quarry in its natural state using trained falcons, hawks, and eagles. As a result of the growth of the sport in North America and the great amount of innovation this has produced, some species of buzzards have been trained and found suitable.

The role of women within the sport of falconry is poorly documented. Most hunting activities have a strong tradition of patriarchy that attaches little importance to women. Nonetheless, women have participated in the sport, in both its medieval and modern manifestations, and continue to take part in it. By the 1990s, in fact, some of the most notable and well-known British falconers were women.

HISTORY

Falconry is one of the oldest of field sports; it was first recorded in early Chinese literature some four thousand years ago and in a bas-relief in Syria about three thousand years ago. The practice of using birds of prey as aids to hunting most likely developed in several ancient societies in Asia. Falconry was introduced to Europe by invading tribes from the steppes of Russia; Attila the Hun was known to be a keen falconer, bringing his falcons, hawks, and eagles with him on his military conquests. The practice spread throughout Christendom and the Islamic world and became codified and formalized into both a sport and a mark of social status.

It is difficult to overestimate the social significance of falconry in Britain from the sixth century BCE until the seventeenth century. Laws protecting birds of prey were enacted; conventions on ownership were enforced; and taxes and ransoms were sometimes paid with falcons and hawks. Indeed, a falconer and his boy were important members of

Pol de Limbourg, falconing scene, from Les Tres Riches Heures du Duc de Berry, early 15th century. (Giroudon/Art Resource)

any noble's retinue. The practice of falconry was not confined to landowners; all classes commonly used hawks to help obtain food for the pot.

In the medieval period, women of aristocratic or noble birth were almost certainly participants in falconry; they were known to take part mounted on horseback as befitted their rank. The imagery of the sport was deeply woven into the social fabric of the time—with birds of prey indicating rank and aspiration—so that women destined to be powerful or significant members of the court had little option but to play out the metaphor. Literature is rich in observations of such activity. For example, Mallory's *Morte d'Arthur* depicts the romance between Lancelot and Guinevere as beginning when the knight assists the queen after she encounters a problem training her falcon.

Falconry was inextricably linked to medieval romance through an intimate metaphor that involved the gendering of nature. Traditionally the larger, stronger female raptor was used for falconry because male birds of prey were smaller and lighter.

The fifteenth-century hunting text *The Boke of St. Albans*, attributed to Dame Juliana Berners, lists a symbolic social order for hunting activities. For example, the merlin (*Falco columbarius*) was considered the appropriate hawk for a lady. This imagery persists: the merlin, a diminutive and tame yet dashing hunter of small birds, is now known as the lady's hawk. Mary, Queen of Scots, was fond of hawking with merlins, and falconry was one of her great comforts when she was detained at Tutbury in Staffordshire. Sir Ralph Sadler, a former royal falconer to Queen Elizabeth I and eventually Mary's jailer, was instructed to withdraw this privilege when the queen learned of her captive's enjoyment of the sport and her good humor when out with her merlins.

PARTICIPATION BY WOMEN

Sixteenth- and seventeenth-century Puritans, who rejected all activities that they considered frivolous or that had links to the dethroned monarchy, saw falconry as inefficient and unnecessary, a time-consuming and difficult way of hunting. This attitude and the advent of the firearm, together with the enclosure of the common lands, pushed the sport from the center of the hunting scene. By the middle of the seventeenth century, the golden age of falconry was over. Nevertheless, despite a much reduced following, it did not die out. Within a hundred years or so, the sport of falconry began to take on the form that is practiced today, with distinct branches of the art focused on hunting specific quarries in a specialized manner. Rook and heron hawking became popular; a mounted field (group of horsemen) followed the flight that demanded open, unfenced country. The pinnacle of the sport became game hawking, which combines the high *pitch* (circling flight) of the patrolling falcon followed by the falcon's classic *stoop* (attacking dive) after flushed game birds. Lark hawking with merlins and blackbird hawking with sparrow hawks survived the transformation from medieval to modern society almost unaltered, with women continuing their partnership with these small raptors. The goshawk provided valued sport, as well as additions to the larder with flights at rabbit and pheasant.

Women always had a small but significant presence in nineteenth-century illustrations of falconry in the field; they are often pictured as part of a mounted group made up of members of European hawking clubs. Nevertheless, the membership lists of early hawking groups, such as the Falconers' Club and Confederate Hawks of Great Britain, are without women. It is probable that, although women did feature in the hawking field, they were for the most part spectators.

Toward the end of the nineteenth century and the beginning of the twentieth, women feature in the early photographs of the sport, but once again only as a minority. In some of these obviously posed photographs, women are holding the falcons, and this perhaps signals a more active role. Certainly Grace Radclyffe and Audry Allen, wives of noteworthy falconers, were proficient falconers in their own right. By the 1930s and in the early years of the British Falconers' Club, women were well established as practitioners.

Today in Great Britain women feature as a prominent part of the falconry fraternity. Lifelong practitioners such as June Woodford, Betty Ashby, and Josephine Mitchell have carried on the sport over many years whereas, on a more public level women such as Emma Ford and Diana Durman Walters are well published in the sport of falconry. At the forefront of these women is Jemima Parry-Jones who, as director of the National Bird of Prey Centre, is known for her conservation work, domestic breeding program, and falconry education. In the younger generation, exciting new participants such as Helen MacDonald, editor of the British Falconers' Club newsletter, are carrying the sport into the new century.

The biologist and falconer Fran Hamerstrom (1907–1998) was active in legitimizing falconry in the United States and in the formation of the North American Falconers' Association. Her handling ability with both wild birds of prey and domestically bred raptors was remarkable. She often demonstrated to her students how to gain the trust of a hawk or falcon that had never before been handled. Through gentle coaxing, coupled with food rewards, she often achieved this trust in a matter of a few minutes, a level of skill shared by very few—even among the most experienced falconers.

RULES AND PLAY

Falconry is deliberate human intervention in the predatory behavior exhibited by raptors. In order to facilitate this intervention, the birds of prey need to be conditioned to accept the proximity of humans and to be trained to return at a given signal. The first and most important stage in the training is to teach these instinctively suspicious creatures to tolerate humans. Most birds of prey are solitary, not social, creatures, making the stage of the process known as "manning" potentially difficult. The solitary aspect of their nature also means that most species hunt individually and not in groups. Falconry birds wear leather straps on their legs called *jesses*. This strap can be attached as a leash in order to give the falconer some control, although restraint must be used as little as possible. Some falconers also attach a small bell to the hawk that enables it to be located in cover or undergrowth.

Once the confidence of the bird of prey has been gained, it is taught to fly to the falconer for a food reward. Physical conditioning is vital; the hawk or falcon—like a well-conditioned athlete—must be neither fat nor thin. If too fat, the bird's hunting instinct will be suppressed; if too thin, the bird will be unable to perform to its potential. Good animal husbandry skills and a keen eye are needed. Once trained, the bird of prey is taken to the location where it will hunt. During transport, the bird is generally hooded, that is, has a leather hood placed over its head to prevent it from seeing anything as it travels. Hooding calms these visually dominant creatures and is the equivalent of sitting in the dark. It is done only for short periods of time. When the prey species has been located, the hood is removed and the hunt begins, either with the falcon flying to a position high above the perspective prey or flying directly after it. The type of hunt is determined by the species of raptor and quarry. If the hawk or falcon makes a kill, the falconer goes to it and rewards it for a successful effort; if the quarry escapes, the raptor is called back to the falconer.

Modern falconry is codified and demands that the prey hunted has a good opportunity to escape. The object here is to test the hunting ability of the falcon against the survival instincts of the quarry while being able to observe the drama.

Emma Ford, falconer and author, holding a falcon. (Corbis/Tony Roberts)

It is the quality of the flight, not the number of quarry items killed, that determines the sport.

CONTEMPORARY SITUATION

The twentieth century has witnessed great changes in the countryside and in attitudes to nature, yet the sport of falconry has increased steadily in popularity. In North America, Britain, and Europe, falconry is now practiced by a wide range of both rural and city-dwelling people, including significant numbers of women from various classes and backgrounds. In Asia and the Middle East, falconry is an exclusively male pastime, but women are involved in all other locations in the world where the sport is practiced.

CONCLUSION

Falconry is a flourishing and vibrant field sport that enables the practitioner to encounter nature at an intimate and fundamental level. This specialized form of bird-watching is increasingly attractive to women who wish to engage in a traditional country sport that demands high levels of practical skill, commitment, and empathy with the very essence of the wild.

Gordon T. Mellor

Bibliography

Blome, Richard. (c. 1700) *Hawking; or, Faulconry.* Reprint 1929. Maidenhead, England: Cresset Press.

Cummins, John. (1988) *The Hound and the Hawk.* London: Weidenfield & Nicolson.

Hamerstrom, Frances. (1989) *Is She Coming Too?: Memoirs of a Lady Hunter.* Ames: Iowa State University Press.

Oswald, Allen. (1982) *The History and Practice of Falconry.* Jersey, Channel Islands: Neville Spearman.

Upton, Roger. (1980) *A Bird in the Hand.* London: Debrett.

———. (1987) *O for a Falconer's Voice.* Marlborough, England: Crowood Press.

Schlegel, H., and A.H.V. de Wulverhorst. (1844–53) *Traité de Fauconnerie.* Reprint and trans. 1973. Denver, CO: Chasse Publications.

FAMILY INVOLVEMENT

The family is a fundamental social group common to cultures around the world. Families provide the first environment in which members of a society learn about their social worlds and establish their social identities. How families view sports participation in general and what activities they consider appropriate for boys and girls influences athletic participation during childhood and beyond.

FAMILY AND CULTURE

Families vary greatly among different societies, as well as in the particular set of relationships that family members establish with one another. Among the factors that influence family structure and relations are a particular society's cultural standards, values, and beliefs about how parents and children and wives and husbands should relate to one another. Government policy, laws, and economic conditions also help to shape family structure. Beyond this, individual family members interact with one another to create and establish the relationships that make each family distinct.

Sociologists, anthropologists, and psychologists have studied the family—its child-rearing practices, structure, and socioeconomic status—in an effort to understand the role of the family in how children develop. Primarily in North America, these researchers have also studied the family with respect to the development of children's interests, skills, and involvement in sports. Included in these studies are investigations of how the involvement in sports of one or more family members may influence family relationships and activities.

FAMILY CHILD-REARING PRACTICES

A family's child-rearing practices are strongly related to its ideas about gender—femininity and masculinity—and if and how girls and boys and women and men should differ from one another. Therefore, particular child-rearing practices often vary depending on whether girls or boys are involved. The development and display of physical strength, skill, and sport involvement are generally linked to masculinity and are frequently viewed as antithetical to the development of femininity. A family's child-rearing practices have important implications for girls' development of sport interests, skills, and involvement.

Investigators suspect that gender-based child-rearing practices that begin at birth play an important role in the sport socialization process of girls. In many families, although female infants are held and talked to more frequently (and handled more carefully and delicately), male infants are more often moved through space and physically stimulated. Customarily, family members automatically expect infants and young children to like and play with toys that have long been considered appropriate for either boys or girls. Thus, boys are provided, and expected to play, with toys that build physical skills and are related to sports—riding toys, balls, bats, and other sports equipment. Girls, in contrast, are commonly given, and expected to play with, dolls and toys related to homemaking, such as ovens, tea sets, and dollhouses.

In turn, girls' and boys' play with such toys tends to elicit and provide opportunity for specific kinds of feedback from family members. Because boys frequently play with toys that build physical skills or are related to sports, they are likely to receive much more positive encouragement and evaluation of their physical skills and involvement than girls are. Girls are more likely

THE CLARK FAMILY DYNASTY

The 800-meter race is a family matter for the Clark family of the United States. Joetta Clark Diggs wound down her career at the age of 37 after having been on three U.S. Olympic teams. Her younger sister, Hazel Clark, won the NCAA 800-meter title four times while at the University of Florida. And their sister-in-law, Jearl Miles Clark, holds the U.S. 800-meter outdoor record. Her husband, J.J. Clark, is the coach for his wife and his two sisters.

to receive positive encouragement and evaluation of their play with dolls and homemaking-related toys. Such positive feedback is rewarding to girls and boys and encourages them to continue that play behavior for which they have been rewarded. Investigators believe that, because boys continue to build their physical skills and play sports, whereas girls play with dolls and other homemaking toys, boys develop greater physical skill and sports interests than girls do. Over the course of infancy and early childhood, these gender-based child-rearing practices are believed to help explain the disproportionately low number of girls and women around the world who engage in sports. In contrast, female athletes tend to grow up in families in which such gender-based child-rearing practices are less frequent, less intense, or absent entirely and in which parents encourage sport interests, skills, and involvement.

Female athletes tend to be raised in families that, at the very least, do not discourage—but instead more frequently value and encourage—physical play and an interest in sports. As children, female athletes often express an early interest in actively playing with toys that increase physical skills building and are related to sports, and they seek out family members who will play with them. They are anxious to learn physical skills such as throwing, catching, dribbling, and batting, and they typically display higher skill levels than other children their age. Female athletes tend to have family members who enthusiastically play with them, teach them physical skills, and provide them with the necessary sporting equipment, facilities, and instruction to develop their abilities.

PARENTS AND SIBLINGS

How influential specific family members may be in the development of sporting interests and skills among young girls varies from family to family. Studies provide conflicting findings. While some research suggests that fathers play a more important role in encouraging their daughters to become involved in sports, other studies report that the mother's role matters more. Some studies have reported that female athletes tend to have older siblings involved in sports who serve as role models for them, whereas findings from other studies indicate that older siblings have little if any influence. These differences notwithstanding, female athletes clearly tend to be raised in families in which one or both parents were or are actively engaged in sports, attend sporting events, and watch televised sports; they may also expect their children to develop an interest and skill in sports. Family structure and social status can greatly influence the amount of time, attention, and resources parents or guardians can devote to developing their children's physical skills and interests.

FAMILY STRUCTURE AND SOCIOECONOMIC STATUS

Family structure and socioeconomic status help to create the specific family environment in which a child is raised. These elements also contribute to the opportunities and choices a child is provided with respect to the development of sport interests, skills, and involvement. Family structure includes such factors as size, the presence of one or both parents, and the presence or absence of children. The structure may range from a dual- to a single-parent family and from a family with no children

Family playing basketball, 1985. (Bob Krist/Corbis)

or a single child to a family with ten or more children. Family socioeconomic status is usually based on parental income and education and indicates how much a family can provide its children in the way of opportunities, life experiences, and material resources.

Relatively little is known about how particular family structures affect children's sports involvement. It is likely, however, that, in families with a single working parent, the parent will have less time, energy, and material resources to play with the children and encourage their interest, skills, and involvement in sports. Socioeconomic status also helps to determine what opportunities and choices for sports involvement a family can provide. In the United States, parents tend to give their children sporting opportunities that they value, that they can afford, and that are judged "appropriate" for their socioeconomic status. Girls from higher socioeconomic family backgrounds tend to be more involved in sports than

girls from less affluent families and also tend to participate in higher-cost sports that require expensive instruction, facilities, equipment, and clothing, such as tennis, gymnastics, swimming, and skiing; girls from middle- and working-class families are less able to afford such sports.

SPORT INVOLVEMENT AND FAMILY RELATIONS AND ACTIVITIES

While research has clearly established that the family is important in childhood sport socialization, little is known about if and how sport involvement by one or more family members may affect family relations and activities. In North America, it is generally believed that "the family that plays together stays together." Yet no research substantiates the belief that family sport involvement makes family structure more secure and stable. Limited evidence does suggest that, when a family member is involved in a highly competitive sport, the associated demands of extensive time, resources, and energy can stress and strain family relations. Highly competitive, elite youth sport programs such as soccer, swimming, and gymnastics often require athletes and parents to devote to the sport twenty to thirty hours per week, ten to eleven months per year, for as many as eight to ten years. Family schedules are set to accommodate such demands, and parents and other family members are often involved in transporting these young athletes to and from practices and competitions, serving as coaches or officials, and spending large sums of money to cover associated instruction, equipment, and travel expenses. Such demands can lead to conflict between spouses, between parents and children, or between siblings over the central importance of elite sport involvement versus other family activities, commitments, and responsibilities.

Just as parents are very influential in developing sport interests and skills among their children, children's sport involvement can also influence the parents' sport interests and participation. This pattern of influence, sometimes called "reverse socialization," is more likely to occur in families in which children are involved in elite youth sports that demand extensive parental commitment and support. Such commitment can provide parents with a social milieu in which they may learn the rules, strategies, and basic skills of their children's sport. Indeed, parents, in practicing with and helping their children to develop sport skills, may themselves refine and develop new skills. They may serve as coaches, officials, team statisticians, or scorekeepers and may develop new groups of friends who also have children involved in youth sports. As a consequence, some parents become active participants themselves.

CONCLUSION

As social and cultural standards, values, and beliefs surrounding girls' and women's sports participation continue to become more positive, family support and involvement demands are likely to grow. The hows and whys of families' abilities and inabilities to meet such demands remain important questions.

Cynthia A. Hasbrook

See also Youth Sports

Bibliography

Coakley, Jay J. (1998) *Sport in Society.* 6th ed. Boston, MA: McGraw-Hill.

Eitzen, D. Stanley, and George H. Sage. (1997) *Sociology of North American Sport.* 6th ed. Madison, WI: Brown & Benchmark.

Greendorfer, Susan L. (1983) "Shaping the Female Athlete: The Influence of the Family." In *The Sporting Woman,* edited by M. A. Boutilier and L. SanGiovanni. Champaign, IL: Human Kinetics.

McPherson, Barry D., James E. Curtis, and John W. Loy. (1989) *The Social Significance of Sport.* Champaign, IL: Human Kinetics.

Nixon, Howard L., and James H. Frey. (1996) *A Sociology of Sport.* Belmont, CA: Wadsworth.

FASHION

The relationship between women's participation in sport and fashion—the acceptable dress of the time—has undergone a major transformation over time. In the nineteenth century, fashion influenced sports as the sportswoman wore a corset under her long skirt, plus high, buttoned collars and high-heeled shoes and often even a hat. Women's clothes inhibited their movements, and so they had to ride sidesaddle and cycle on a tricycle specially built for women, and they were largely restricted in their action radius. Today the situation is reversed, and sports visibly influences fashion.

In the nineteenth century, women's sporting costumes conformed to contemporary moral standards and confirmed female role patterns. The early costumes for such class-bound activities as tennis, horseback riding, and golf were mainly fashion items that hardly addressed practical requirements. Rather, they were an expression of the nature of women's sports as an exclusive form of social pastime that belonged only to the wealthy.

The earliest garments to allow athletes some freedom of movement were still relatively modest loose skirts of ankle length, flat shoes, and nonfitted blouses. They were successfully introduced by those women interested in competitive sports—earlier in England, the home of sports,

Cover of *Nuevo Mundo* magazine showcasing ladies' ski wear, 1929. (Historical Picture Archive/Corbis)

"safety-skirt" that was snap-fastened so that it would rip open in case of an accident.

Corsets were also dictated by fashion and were worn even under sports costumes. Dress reformers and doctors fought against this modern instrument of torture because it restricted movement and led to internal injuries. In Prussian schools the corset was forbidden in 1905, but still in 1914 the U.S. tennis player Elizabeth Ryan saw corsets in English changing rooms, noting: "It was not a pretty sight, as many of them were bloodstained from the wounds they had inflicted."

Even in tradition-conscious sports such as tennis, the restrictions on skirt length became less noticeable. In 1905 an observer at the All-England championship remarked: "The better English players all approach the net and smash. German players do not even attempt this, since they are not sufficiently mobile because of their heavy clothing." The U.S. player May Sutton (1887–1975) sported a relatively short skirt—and won the competition. In the course of this struggle between convention and function, the athletes' clothing constantly succeeded in sweeping aside social conventions. Female athletes have contributed substantially to the public acceptance of women wearing short skirts and trousers. In the process they often gave ideas to developers of fashion.

SPORT INFLUENCES FASHION

Whenever sports became fashionable, they have, in turn, made their mark on fashion. Casual clothing, in particular, has gained from the practicality, comfort, and informal character of sportswear. Sports were also influential in the development of unisex clothing, which suggests a supposed gender equality.

The 1920s saw an enhanced social standing for women, and their public appearance changed accordingly. To conform to the new ideal of beauty, a youthful, slim body was essential. An athletic appearance developed into a social norm. This was reflected in everyday fashion as well as in *haute couture;* the collections of Jean Patou and Coco Chanel, in particular, became famous: "Sport has more to do than anything else with the evolution of the modern fashion," British *Vogue* stated in 1926. In the Soviet Union, constructivist artists designed practical sportswear. Fashion's influence on sports was all the greater when the

than in fashion-oriented France. Initially it was the English cricket players of the 1870s who began wearing these looser clothes, and tennis players followed around 1880. In Germany the situation changed around 1910 and again in the 1920s. Still, many of the early sporting garments represented a kind of compromise between the needs of the sport and the needs of socially dictated decorum. They frequently incorporated a restricting skirt with a top modeled on male athletes' costumes.

In the United States, dress reformer Amelia Jenks Bloomer (1818—1894) had by 1858 already popularized a new costume consisting of baggy breeches and a tunic top. But the so-called bloomers did not become accepted until 1900. Up to that time, female athletes wore skirts over trousers, or divided skirts that were cut loosely in order to disguise the fact they were, in effect, pants. Women skiers carried a discreet rucksack to put their skirts in for the descent. Around 1900, women horseback riders were able to acquire a sport in question was exclusive, exotic, and not competitive. The more unusual the sport, the more fashionable the costume: avant-garde costumes were derived from motoring and flying, not from athletics or gymnastics.

These changes in fashion were hailed by many as the expression of a new freedom of movement and of women's liberation. The focus on the well-exercised body, however, put new constraints on women. On the one hand, such a focus made its emancipatory potential questionable. On the other hand, it had a political impact, given that the new appearance of women initiated a public debate about traditional gender roles. Since then, the body itself has become the focal point. In order to get in shape, women took to exercise, fashion, cosmetics, and even plastic surgery.

Sports became even more popular. In the 1970s America exported the fitness movement and aerobics all over the world. The athletic body became a symbol of health and capability, and fashion celebrated an active lifestyle. Sweaters, basketball shoes, and track suits appeared on the fashion runways of Paris, Milan, and New York—astonishingly combined with formal wear. Star designers such as Calvin Klein and Tommy Hilfiger and fashion houses like Prada and Polo Sports launched complete collections of sportswear. The sportswear market more than doubled in the 1990s while the streets in the metropolitan centers of every country were populated by people following a fashion that expressed ideals of fitness, youth, and a lithe body. Sponsors and media in world-class sports demanded sportswear that revealed an almost naked, athletic body and one that sent out erotic signals. Florence Griffith-Joyner (1959–1998) successfully demonstrated how world-class female athletes can thus consciously play on their femininity and sexuality by means of fashionable clothing.

The influence of sports on fashion has also been demonstrated by the popularity of garments such as polo shirts, sweatshirts, pleated skirts, anoraks, and body stockings. Initially designed as practical sportswear, these have now become integral parts of modern casual clothing. In the age of outdoor sports, even accessories like the rucksack and the kangaroo bag (fanny pack) have left the purely functional sphere of mountain-climbing equipment to join the world of fashion.

Two women model contrasting tennis outfits—one from early in the 20th century and another from the 1960s. (Corbis/Hulton-Deutsch Collection)

Materials originally designed for sports, or rather for optimizing athletic performance, inspired fashion designers to create completely new styles. Functional, elastic, and "breathing" materials turned clothing into a second skin, as demonstrated by the "skin-dresses" of Karl Lagerfeld or transparent t-shirts by Gaultier. Latex and nylon, Gore-Tex, and microfiber have become synonymous with lightness and comfort. But, whereas leggings and skintight t-shirts might not force female bodies into artificial shapes, they do reveal curves that their owners might prefer to hide.

The history of sportswear and, to a large extent, fashion is dominated by the leading sports nations, such as England in the nineteenth century and the United States in the late twentieth. Trends in sportswear manifested themselves globally in the youth culture of the 1990s to such an extent that various sportswear labels, such as Ralph Lauren and Adidas or Nike footwear, indicated a kind of group membership.

Occasionally, modern women's sports costumes have run afoul of religious beliefs and social conditions in some parts of the world. The Algerian runner Hassiba Boulmerka (1968–), after winning the world championship title in 1992, was publicly condemned by members of fundamentalist Muslim religious groups for indecently exposing her body in public. Such male-dominated religious groups advocate an extremely conventional pattern of gender roles that force women to wear covering garments that hinder, and even prevent, their participation in competitive and recreational sports.

Heike Egger

See also Femininity; Sexuality; Sportswear Industry

Bibliography

Borgers, Walter. (1990) *Sportdress und Emanzipation— oder die Dialektik der Auskleidung.* In *Brennpunkte der Sportwissenschaft* 4, 2: 163–187.

Deutsches Textilmuseum. (1992) *Sportswear. Zur Geschichte der Sportbekleidung* (exhibition catalog). Krefeld, Germany: Deutsches Textilmuseum.

Egger, Heike. (1992) "Sportswear. Zur Geschichte der Sportkleidung." *Stadion* 18, 1: 126–157.

Lee-Potter, Charlie. (1984) *Sportswear in Vogue Since 1910.* London: Condé Nast.

Musée de la mode. (1997) *Mode et sport* (exhibition catalog). Marseilles: Musée de la mode.

Nederlands Textielmuseum. (n.d.) *Sports Textiles* (exhibition catalog). Tilburg, Netherlands: Nederlands Textielmuseum.

Stedelijk Modemuseum. (1997) *Sport en mode* (exhibition catalog). Hasselt, Belgium: Stedelijk Modemuseum.

Tinling, Ted. (1974) "Fashion." *The Encyclopedia of Tennis.* London: Max Robertson.

Wolter, Gundula. (1994) *Hosen, weiblich: Kulturgeschichte der Frauenhose.* Marburg, Germany: Jonas Verlag.

FEMININITY

The terms *femininity* and *masculinity* refer to a set of learned behaviors that come about by the ways that girls and boys are socialized. Socialization is a process that teaches children about what society considers appropriate behavior, activities, dress, characteristics, and ways of moving and speaking, depending on whether they are male or female. To understand women in sport, it is necessary also to understand the assumptions about femininity and masculinity and how they have been broken down, negotiated, and renegotiated in recent years.

HISTORY

Traditionally, in European and American white, middle-class culture, gender roles have been rigidly defined. People assumed that the characteristics that society defined as masculine were a natural property of the male body, and feminine characteristics of the female. Masculinity was associated with independence, activity, aggression, size, prowess, strength, competition, and self-ownership, whereas femininity tended to be defined as its polar opposite and associated with delicacy, physical weakness, nurturing, cooperation, and dependence. Poor and nonwhite women were excluded from these beliefs; they were assumed to have naturally vigorous physical constitutions that were suited to hard labor and also to have a greater degree of sexuality. Since femininity and true womanhood were coded "white" and defined by the dominant group as physically delicate, women were often assumed to be weak and incompetent, as in the nineteenth-century stereotype of fainting girls. Because of what was seen as their natural feminine weakness, it was frequently assumed that white girls and women could not play sports, or at least not very well. Strenuous sport participation was viewed as a violation of the cult of true womanhood.

Because most sports involve vigorous activity and physical skill, they were associated with masculinity. Art and other representations of sport idealized the muscular male body. Because most people tend to think of the body as a repository for qualities that are natural or innate, the male athlete was often seen as an ideal example of the masculine. The first wave of feminism, which in the United States started in the mid-nineteenth century with counterparts worldwide, challenged this naturalized equation between male bodies, masculinity, and sport.

Many researchers have argued that twentieth-century sport arose in response to feminism. They contend that organized sport was men's response to what they saw as a crisis in the traditional order of things, which gave males unquestioned superiority. The flaw in this view is that it overlooks the millennia before our own, during which men also displayed their masculinity in sports. Nevertheless, participation in sports and the antifemale sentiments frequently associated with it were indeed a major force in the establishment of contemporary masculinity. Men often achieve this athletic masculinity by disparaging anything feminine in women, in other athletes, or in themselves. One of the worst insults in athletics is to be called a "pussy," a term associated with the female anatomy and, by extension, femininity. The disparagement usually occurs when an athlete shows pain or is reluctant to finish a grueling workout. Sport is both the product of, and also helps to produce, these views of appropriate behavior for men and women. In this way, it helps to create and sustain cultural beliefs about gender difference.

RETHINKING GENDER

Research in the 1960s and 1970s seriously questioned the biological basis of masculinity and femininity. Instead, gender came to be viewed as a social construct. Underlying this research was the assumption associated with liberal feminism that underneath these long-standing views of gender difference, men and women are basically the same. In the 1980s, after the second wave of feminism brought both political gains and a corresponding backlash, researchers began talking instead about "cultural feminism." With this approach they emphasized gender difference and invoked again the traditional associations of masculinity and femininity, tending to stress the strengths of the feminine to make up for its historical devaluation.

Tension remains between the two notions of difference and sameness. Cultural theory, however, has shifted toward a model of gender performance. In this view, gender is an elaborate social production involving language, cultural meanings, and power relationships. Gender performance is connected to the question of gender identity, which refers to a network of social codes that establish who is and who is not considered male or female. For example, a female athlete who

Female boxers like American Lucia Rijker, here celebrating her victory in a 1997 Las Vegas match, challenge the traditional notions of what is "feminine" by venturing into sports considered brutally masculine. (AP Photos)

excels at sports cannot be a real woman in traditional feminine terms. Lorber cites a study in which women college basketball players on the court "did athlete," which meant pushing, shoving, fouling, hard running, making fast breaks, yelling obscenities, and sweating. Off the court, they changed their behavior to "do woman," and spent up to an hour after the game applying makeup, styling their hair, and dressing carefully to look feminine. Female athletes often stage this kind of performance to reinforce their female identities, which are called into question by cultural beliefs that continue to define many sports as masculine.

Definitions of femininity and masculinity have worked powerfully within the culture to shape women's participation in sports, and women's success as athletes depends, to some extent, on unlearning femininity. Mariah Nelson writes that the basketball players she coaches are "haunted by size taboos. They don't like to feel tall, to seem wide, to make loud noises. They don't feel comfortable inhabiting a big space." Since excelling in sport involves self-assertion and the forceful occupation of space, the conventions of femininity work against success, although team sports also require a measure of such traditional feminine skills as cooperation. Ironically, for most of the twentieth century, American women professionally active as physical educators—and to a lesser degree their European counterparts—developed a model of sport for women that discouraged competition and reinforced the limitations of conventional femininity. The egalitarian motto was "a sport for every girl and every girl in a sport." Only with the 1972 passage of Title IX (which made discrimination against girls and women in school sports illegal) and the changes that followed did women begin to be taken seriously as competitive athletes in the culture at large. These changes also challenged the assumption that competition was a masculine province. Similar laws worked similar changes in Europe.

For a woman to build herself up physically does challenge traditional ideas about femininity in the most graphic ways. Research shows that female athleticism has altered public consciousness about women's abilities, power, and competence. Women are no longer seen as the physically fragile creatures once described by the word *lady*. The growing acceptance of female athleticism has led to new ideas about how femininity should be defined. Contemporary advertisements often feature girls involved in extreme sports or performing difficult physical feats, thus downplaying the old cultural associations between masculinity, men, and physical competence.

Female athletes may represent a new feminine ideal, but researchers point out that the achievements of women in sports can also subtly affirm male superiority; in most sports the best female athletes are still not as good as the best men. As long as winning is everything, sports may be seen as incontrovertible evidence that men are still better, suggesting the need for change in the institution of sport as a whole.

Media representations of female athletes can also undermine the challenge of redefining traditional definitions of masculine and feminine, a challenge posed by women's participation in sports. These representations of female athletes all too often reinforce stereotypes they intend to counter. One of the sport clichés most frequently repeated in the media is that "she's an athlete, but she's still feminine." This cliché shows both how much society still equates athleticism with masculinity and how traditional power relationships endure even when a structure—such as sport—expands to accommodate women. Female athletes often participate in a specific kind of gender performance: presenting an image not only of health, vitality, or physical attractiveness but of feminine beauty and obedience to traditionally feminine standards of behavior. They do so because this image is more marketable and because people tend to react more positively to it. Media representation of the female athlete emphasizes that performance and reinforces the idea that femininity also means sexual attractiveness to men.

The representation of female bodybuilders, whose visually striking muscular size poses one of the most radical challenges to traditional ideas about masculinity and femininity, is sexualized in even more extreme ways. Perhaps because of that challenge, the top bodybuilding competitors are often labeled "monstrous," and they then overcompensate by displaying female characteristics in exaggerated ways. Layouts in muscle magazines feature the top female bodybuilders in scenes resembling pornography, picturing them in high heels, heavy makeup, and leather thongs and bras. Such representations are more extreme versions of the overall tendency in the sports media to accentuate the erotic allure of female athletes, thus devaluing their achievements as competitors, athletes, and individuals. Women's and girls' experiences playing sports may work against such representations, however, and help contribute to a more progressive redefinition of masculinity and femininity.

Leslie Heywood

See also Fashion; Performance; Sexuality

Bibliography

Birrell, Susan, and Cheryl L. Cole, eds. (1994) *Women, Sport, and Culture.* Champaign, IL: Human Kinetics.

Bordo, Susan. (1993) *Unbearable Weight: Feminism, Western Culture, and the Body.* Berkeley: University of California Press.

———. (1997) *Twilight Zones: The Hidden Life of Cultural Images from Plato to O.J.* Berkeley: University of California Press. See especially "Braveheart, Babe, and the Body."

Butler, Judith. (1990) *Gender Trouble: Feminism and the Subversion of Identity.* New York: Routledge.

Cahn, Susan K. (1994) *Coming on Strong: Gender and Sexuality in Twentieth Century Women's Sport.* Cambridge, MA: Harvard University Press.

Cohen, Greta L., ed. (1993) *Women in Sport: Issues and Controversies.* Newbury Park, CA: Sage Publications.

Douglas, Susan J. (1994) *Where the Girls Are: Growing Up Female with the Mass Media.* New York: Times Books/Random House.

English, Jane. (1978) "Sex Equality in Sports." *Philosophy & Public Affairs* 7, 3: 269–77.

Faludi, Susan. (1991) *Backlash: The Undeclared War Against American Women.* New York: Crown.

Guttmann, Allen. (1991) *Women's Sports: A History.* New York: Columbia University Press.

———. (1996) *The Erotic in Sports.* New York: Columbia University Press.

Heywood, Leslie. (1998) "Athletic vs. Pornographic Eroticism: How Muscle Magazines Compromise Female Athletes and Delegitimize the Sport of Bodybuilding in the Public Eye." *Mesomorphosis* 1, 1. <http://www.mesomorphosis.com>.

———. (1998) *Bodymakers: A Cultural Anatomy of Women's Bodybuilding.* New Brunswick, NJ: Rutgers University Press.

Klein, Alan M. (1993) *Little Big Men: Bodybuilding Subculture and Gender Construction.* Albany: State University of New York Press.

Lorber, Judith. (1998) "Believing is Seeing: Biology as Ideology." In *The Politics of Women's Bodies: Sexuality, Appearance, and Behavior*, ed. by Rose Weitz. NY: Oxford University Press, p. 17.

Lowe, Maria. (1997) *Women of Steel.* New York: New York University Press.

Messner, Michael A. (1992) *Power at Play: Sports and the Problem of Masculinity.* Boston: Beacon Press.

Messner, Michael A., and Donald F. Sabo, eds. (1990). *Sport, Men, and the Gender Order: Critical Feminist Perspectives.* Champaign, IL: Human Kinetics.

———. (1994) *Sex, Violence, and Power in Sports: Rethinking Masculinity.* Freedom, CA: Crossing Press.

———. (1997) *Politics of Masculinities: Men in Movements.* Thousand Oaks, CA: Sage Publications.

Moore, Pamela L., ed. (1997) *Building Bodies.* New Brunswick, NJ: Rutgers University Press.

Nelson, Mariah Burton. (1991) *Are We Winning Yet? How Women Are Changing Sports and Sports Are Changing Women.* New York: Random House.

———. (1994) *The Stronger Women Get, The More Men Love Football.* New York: Avon Books.

———. (1998). *Embracing Victory: Life Lessons in Competition and Compassion.* New York: William Morrow.

Reece, Gabrielle, and Karen Karbo. (1997) *Big Girl in the Middle.* New York: Crown.

Sabo, Donald, and Michael Messner. (1993) "Whose Body Is This?: Women's Sports and Sexual Politics." In *Women in Sport: Issues and Controversies.* Newbury Park, CA: Sage Publications. 15–24.

Weitz, Rose, ed. (1998) *The Politics of Women's Bodies: Sexuality, Appearance, and Behavior.* New York: Oxford University Press.

FEMINISM

Sport feminism represents women's response to the inequalities of power between men and women in sport. Sport feminists are those who want more opportunities for women, greater equality with men, and the elimination of discrimination based on gender. Some observers argue that sport feminism originated in the nineteenth century when the association of sports with images of masculinity and male control were strongly institutionalized and when middle-class women in Western countries were struggling to improve women's and girls' opportunities in sports and physical education. More usually, however, sport feminism is viewed as a phenomenon of the 1970s, associated with the renewed efforts of women to organize themselves and to demand equality and with the articulation of their position in a number of books and articles. These works were published first in North America and then in other parts of the Western world—notably Western Europe, Australia, and New Zealand. Modern sport feminism was a latecomer to the women's movement, which from the 1960s had focused on such other feminist issues as legal status, social welfare, education, and work.

Women from all parts of the world—from developed nations and developing nations alike—have worked hard to improve the position of women in sport. Their struggles have developed a global character. Nevertheless, sport feminism is not a unified movement or idea. It takes different forms that relate to: (1) general categories of feminism—for example, liberal, Marxist, radical, cultural, socialist; (2) different groups of women—for example, African-American women, disabled women, Muslim women, and lesbian women; and (3) women in different countries with varied cultural, economic, political, and religious influences. What is common to sport feminists all over the world is the desire to unmask and eliminate discrimination against women in sports. What sport feminists do not have in common are the ways in which they argue that this should be done; these ways are varied and complex.

EQUALITY OF OPPORTUNITY— A LIBERAL PERSPECTIVE

The dominant pressure in sport feminism has been the desire to give women opportunity equal to that of men. This can be interpreted in several ways. One is wanting to do what men have always done—for example, taking part in all sports, including those that have been traditionally male, such as soccer, rugby, boxing, and snooker. Another is treating the concept of equality as equal but different—that is, ensuring that women have equivalent (but not necessarily identical) resources in terms of funding and rewards, good coaching, access to facilities, and full representation in key administrative positions. The basic belief in equality of opportunity derives from liberal-democratic ideology.

Women's progress toward greater equality with men started in the late nineteenth and early twentieth centuries, continued between the world wars and during the postwar period, and then accelerated starting in the 1970s. This trend has been associated with equality-of-opportunity policies of governments and sport organizations. Most countries characterized as liberal democracies have implemented sex-equality legislation (e.g., Title IX in the United States, enacted in 1971; Sex Discrimination Act in Britain, enacted in 1975) that resulted in the removal of various social impediments to women's participation in sport. Beyond legislation are government-inspired initiatives and organizations whose work is specifically to improve the position of women in sports vis-à-vis men, such as the Canadian Association for the Advancement of Women and Sport (CAAWS) and Womensport Australia. Some countries also

have voluntary organizations run by women for women that have liberal feminist agendas (for example, the women's sport foundations founded in the United States in 1974 and in Britain in 1985). Sport organizations also have development programs intended to increase women's participation. In large part, women's struggles and demands over the years have resulted in progress. In advanced industrial countries such as those in Western Europe, North America, and Australia/New Zealand, the struggle to put the theory of equal opportunity into practice has brought promising results, so that more sports are now more accessible to more women than ever before.

Although liberal sport feminism has been a powerful challenge to historically acquired inequalities in sport between men and women, it has been concerned more with quantitative than qualitative change. It tends to overlook the limitations of legal reform, to underestimate the strength of entrenched resistance to changing attitudes toward gender, and to misjudge the power of men over women that continues to permeate sports and society. Liberal sport feminism has in general accepted the values of mainstream sports with its distinctly masculine modes of thought and practice. Consequently, it has done little to contest the intrinsic features of modern sports that render them harmful rather than enriching, such as aggressive competition, xenophobia, physical and psychological abuse of athletes, violence, and the transformation of sports into commodities. In other words, sports feminists have mostly failed to relate the concept of equality to wider social, economic, political, or moral issues.

Sport feminists have also tended to treat women as a homogeneous group and to assume (misleadingly) that an overall increase in participation represents an improvement for women in general. These assumptions explain why certain groups of women—for example, single parents, low-paid working women with disabilities, aboriginal women and women from minority ethnic backgrounds, and women from developing nations—are not adequately represented by liberal-feminist initiatives. The assumptions also explain why, in some cases, arguments for different and more specific feminist approaches have arisen.

Nevertheless, because equal opportunity strategies have been relatively successful, liberal sport feminism is the most popular perspective. The ideology of gender equality in sport is in general accepted—the question now is how to put it into practice.

SEPARATISM—A RADICAL PERSPECTIVE

Over the years, different groups of women have argued for separate development for their gender in sport. For example, at the start of the twentieth century, sport feminists in North America argued for separate sports for men and women. In common with some female physical education specialists in Europe, they opposed men's sports, which, they believed, concentrated too much on competition and were overspecialized and corrupted by commercialization. In recent years, more forceful forms of separatism have developed, mostly as a reaction to the powerlessness, frustration, and anger of sportswomen who have suffered serious discrimination by the male establishment. Separatism opposes men's control of sports and encourages female autonomy. It is argued that single-sex organizations provide women with opportunities to administer and control their own activities in ways that can change the character of sports and make it an enriching, humanitarian experience based on cooperative principles.

The philosophy of separate development has characteristics in common with radical feminism in that both derive from an opposition to patriarchy. Patriarchy—defined as a system of power relations by which men dominate women—is argued to be the basis of other forms of oppression rather than a by-product of them. Because organized sports have always been dominated by men and permeated by sexist attitudes and behavior, radical sport feminists recognize the limitations of equal opportunity programs. A number of writers have argued that sexuality, specifically in the form of "compulsory heterosexuality" (a term used to describe the way in which sportsmen and women are expected always to conform to heterosexual norms of behavior), lies at the heart of women's oppression in sport.

Bearing in mind the heavily patriarchal character of sport, separatist feminists argue that, in teaching, coaching, and administration, women have more scope and better prospects in single-sex organizations than when they have to compete with men in mixed situations. Radical sport feminists believe that placing women's experiences at the center, being sensitive to the specific needs of women, and taking positive action in favor of women can help to even out the advantages that men have had for so long. For these reasons some women's sport groups have adopted exclusionist policies and refused membership even to men who are sympathetic to women's interests. These radical feminists also aim to avoid the dangers of assimilating women's sports to male structures. Carole Oglesby points out that

ATLANTA + COMMITTEE

The Atlanta + Committee (*Comite ATLANTA +* in French) was formed by several feminists and female sports advocates in France following the 1992 Olympics in Barcelona. The mission of the organization was to end "gender apartheid" in sports by ensuring that women would have an equal chance to be members of the national Olympic teams from every participating nation. At the 1992 Olympics several teams had no women members. The immediate goal was to see that full participation was achieved at the 1996 Olympics in Atlanta by conducting a public relations and letter-writing campaign aimed at the International Olympic Committee, national Olympic committees, Olympic sponsors, and individual athletes. The campaign focused on the need to uphold the Olympic charter: "All forms of of discrimination with respect to a country or a person whether for reasons of race, religion, politics, sex, or any other, are incompatible with the Olympic movement." The movement gained some media attention at the time of the 1996 Olympics but seemed to have little effect on women's participation.

there has been a failure, even among some people who classify themselves as feminists, to acknowledge, value, and celebrate the feminine in feminism.

Theoretical arguments about separatism often do not take into account its very real practical advantages. For example, women-only activities allow for female bonding; free women from the possibility of discrimination, sexism, and harassment that can take place in mixed sports contexts; and provide women with a sense of freedom, control, and autonomy. For religious or cultural reasons, closed female spaces provide the only conditions under which some women will participate in physical activities.

Opposing this view is the notion that separate development is fundamentally divisive, separating men from women and thus reproducing dominant gender divisions in the wider society. Radical feminism has tended to exaggerate the overall extent of sexism and of male domination, to downplay situations in which women share power with men, and to ignore ways in which gender relations have changed over time, bringing greater autonomy to women. It encourages the idea that only women can struggle to improve the position for women, and by opposing men to women, it seriously underestimates other dimensions of female oppression in sport connected with such factors as class and politics.

GENDER AND CLASS—A CULTURAL PERSPECTIVE

Traditional Marxist feminists have argued that capitalism and class divisions, rather than patriarchy and sexuality, are the primary reasons for women's oppression and that equality between the sexes could never be achieved under capitalism. Research in Great Britain, showing that working-class women are still constrained in their leisure to a greater extent than middle-class women, seems to support this view. Proportionately low percentages of working-class women are involved in sports compared to their middle-class counterparts, and even lower numbers hold positions of power in sports. But to focus exclusively on capitalism and class masks the complexities of social divisions, which include changing class relations and relations between patriarchy (gender) and capitalism (class), as well

as other social variables. Awareness of the complexities of what has been described as late modern and, more recently, postmodern societies, has led to more dynamic analyses.

CULTURAL FEMINISM

Cultural feminism (sometimes described as a variant of socialist feminism) is influenced by cultural politics and cultural studies, and incorporates experience, history, and social arrangements. It is a perspective that, Ann Hall argues, has supported emerging "feminist cultural studies applied to sport." Some sport feminists in this tradition have used the concept of dominance (and specifically male dominance) to explain the ongoing process between agency (freedom) and determination (constraint). This approach recognizes women as active agents who struggle creatively to grasp opportunities in leisure and sport, even as they confront material barriers (for example, shortages of time and money, including lack of sponsorship). This approach recognizes that gender relations (a term that refers to relations of power between different groups of men and different groups of women, as well as those between men and women) are complex and changing. For example, cultural feminists argue that in late capitalist society it is no longer accurate to talk about a singular notion of masculinity and femininity; rather, it is important to recognize that there are changing male and female roles and identities. For this reason, they describe the many and varied "masculinities" and "femininities" that can be seen in different social contexts, including sports. Intrinsic to the cultural studies tradition is a sensitivity to difference and recognition of varied systems of domination and subordination.

SILENCES AND ABSENCES

Despite the increased sensitivity of feminist cultural studies, many "silences" remain within the liberal, radical, and cultural perspectives. An emergent and burgeoning body of sport feminism shows how the previous perspectives outlined above all deal with a narrow view of womanhood and tend to marginalize other women's (aboriginal, disabled, ethnic minority, lesbian, older) sporting experiences and political concerns. Sport feminists concerned with marginalized groups point to the heterogeneity of women's expe-

Although sports feminism involves a variety of political perspectives and the needs of different groups of women athletes (Third World, minority, disabled, lesbian, elite), the shared quest is for equality in sports opportunities and the end of gender discrimination. In regard to these two issues, the greatest progress has been made in North America, West Europe, and New Zealand/Australia. Progress has been far slower in Latin America, Africa, the Middle East, and much of Asia, although even in these regions participation by women is increasing.

riences and use difference as both an organizing and conceptual strategy. Their work has been influential in disrupting the assumed homogeneity of women's sporting experiences and the misleading tendency to generalize all women from the perspective of the white, middle-class, heterosexual, able-bodied, Western woman. Influenced by the wider theoretical concerns of critical African-American feminist analyses, Queer theory (a perspective focusing on gay, lesbian, and other sexualities), discourses of aging, and the sociology of the body, sport feminists have begun to expose the myths of equality-of-opportunity ideology and practice. These feminists have brought to light the ways in which different groups of women deviate from a socially constructed female norm and experience prejudice, and the ways in which sport organizations and leisure providers have institutionalized discriminatory practices through their failure to take affirmative action and implement radical policies around the needs of minority groups. In many instances, these organizations and providers make it seem sensible that individuals with specific needs should adapt to existing arrangements rather than considering that sports environments could be changed and discriminatory attitudes challenged.

AFRICAN-AMERICAN CRITIQUES AND OTHER DIVERSITIES

The significant paucity of sports feminist theorists who are black or from other ethnic minorities is paralleled by a distinctive lack of research about ethnic minority women's experiences in sport. Existing accounts have tended to treat difference as problematic, and through recourse to cultural stereotypes and myths of differing bodily capacity, to regard these women's experiences as negative deviations from the cultural norm or as pathological. During the late 1980s, black feminist critiques of the ethnocentrism of white, Western sports feminism emerged.

Because of the continued devaluation and subordination of African American and other ethnic minority women, their historical and cultural specificity has been given primacy in the research of black sports feminists. Attention has also been given to ways in which the subtle operation of power through deep-rooted institutionalized and cultural racism continues to limit black and Asian women's participation. From within black sports feminist analyses has come an awareness of the need for all critical feminist interventions to address the interconnections between multiple axes of social differentiation and exclusion (that is, to position women within the discourses of race, gender, and class), where "race" is not seen merely as an additive variable but rather as a relation of power.

LESBIAN FEMINISMS

Lesbian women in sport have also been marginalized in ways that are similar to those experienced by ethnic minority women. However, by treating the pervasive code of heterosexuality as a problem, sport feminists have begun to address the ways in which the discourses and practices of homophobia and heterosexism have constrained female sexualities and structured lesbianism negatively. Lesbian feminists are critical that sport fosters and perpetuates dominant ideologies of sexuality and subordinate all other sexualities to that of a compulsory heterosexual order. Through their writing, these feminists have unveiled different examples of discrimination and exclusion encountered by lesbians in a predominantly homophobic and unsupportive sports system. The stigma of the lesbian label has been highlighted as an effective relation of power and an integral tool of patriarchy that acts not only to control all women through the fear of being labeled but also to create divisions between women and therefore to defuse challenges to the male monopoly of sports resources. Such analyses have exposed and contested the oppression of lesbian sportswomen who are driven to conceal their sexual identities and those who suffer hostility and whose economic power is significantly reduced because they refuse to remain closeted and silent. Some lesbian women have been able to resist disempowerment through localized strategies such as forming all-lesbian or lesbian-positive sports clubs and through global events such as the Gay Games that actively seek to politicize gay issues.

OLDER WOMEN—UNDERSTANDING AGING

Within sport feminism there has been a relative silence regarding the politics and experience of sport, leisure, and aging at a time when there is an explosion of writing on the general subjects of cultural anxiety about bodily decay, consumer fixation with body maintenance, and the postponement of aging. Of those limited analyses focusing on this sphere within sport feminism, some have looked at the way in which discourses on "age" and practices of "ageism" have restricted the leisure and sport opportunities for older women. Writers such as Betsy Wearing illustrate how enduringly negative discourses of aging are integral to an "underuse syndrome" and the normalizing control of aged bodies as submissive and docile. However, there is evidence that leisure is also a space of resistance, self-expression, and enhancement for older women; many of these women are challenging conventional assumptions about their bodily capacities by taking part in a wide range of sporting activities in ways that transform the prevailing notion of age-appropriate moderate activity.

DISABLED SPORTSWOMEN

Sport feminism is also guilty of concentrating on able-bodied women to the detriment of females with disabilities. Sport feminists working within this sphere have queried the assumption of the disabled body as a source of burden, pity, and shame, and they attribute such notions to the way in which sports and physical activity are constructed *by* able-bodied people *for* able-bodied people.

Recent sport feminist research has identified structural factors (such as finance, environmental problems, and societal inertia in adapting to the needs of the disabled) and subjective factors (such as low self-esteem resulting from the devaluation of the disabled body—due to media constructions of the idealized able-bodied, slim, fit, and beautiful female) that obstruct disabled women's participation in sport and physical activity. Sport feminists, disabled sport forums, and the disability rights movement have called for a move away from a model that views disabled bodies as pathological to one that builds on ability. Several mainstream sport organizations, at local, national, and international levels, are now taking responsibility for disabled as well as able-bodied people in their sport. The still low, but growing, visibility of successful disabled elite athletes (although women are still the minority here) has provided disabled girls and women with role models and has politicized sport as a space for the resistance of dominant conceptions of the disabled.

POSTMODERNISM—A PERSPECTIVE OF DIFFERENCE

Intrinsic to postmodern forms of feminism has been an emphasis on difference. The idea that we now live in a postmodern world—a world in which structures of class and gender are no longer relevant and a world that is therefore uncertain, highly differentiated, and fragmented—has led to a rejection of the victim feminisms of the First and Second Waves and to the articulation of new forms of feminism, characterized together as "Third Wave Feminism." The grand narratives and universalizing tendencies of the field have come under attack from an emergent sport feminism that has variously been termed *postmodern*, *poststructuralist*, and *deconstructive*. In such approaches, "difference" (a relation of power that operates along complex lines of gender, class, sexuality, age, and ability), is placed in the foreground, and the experiences of disparate groups of women are valued. The emphasis on difference has been attacked, however, by those who argue that postmodern accounts unnecessarily mask the continuing, systemic forms of oppression that in some contexts transcend differences and can even create divisions in the political organizations and identities that have been forged.

CORPOREAL FEMINISM—DEALING WITH THE BODY

Another key focus of sport feminist analyses that draws on the concerns of postmodernism and poststructuralism has been a redirection toward the body as a terrain on which multiple axes of power—gender, class, sexuality, age, and ability—are inscribed.

The concerns of Michel Foucault (1926–1984) about the disciplining and control of the body, the surveillance to which it is subjected, and the normalizing strategies exacted on it have been taken up in various ways by sport feminists in order to address the interplay of power and knowledge on the bodies and sexualities of sportswomen. Attention has been given to subordination through the social construction of the "feminine," the control not only of the masculine gaze but also of surveillance between women and commodification practices. Other sport feminists have drawn on Foucault's notion of power as pervasive and uncentralized in order to highlight ways in which female sporting bodies can be invested with the capacity to resist dominant (patriarchal) constructions.

It is important to note that corporeal feminism has resisted universal categories and binary oppositions (such as nature/culture; mind/body; femininity/masculinity) and has deconstructed biological notions of "natural" bodies, and of sexual and "racial" difference.

GLOBAL INFLUENCES AND THIRD WORLD FEMINISM

This account of sport feminism has been related to developed nations in the Western world. Although sports are irrelevant for the masses of women in developing nations, who are preoccupied with problems of poverty and health, there are nevertheless growing sport feminist movements in countries throughout Africa, Asia, the Middle East, and the Far East. These movements have resulted in large part from the effects of globalization and the growth of an international women's sport movement. While several aspects of Western feminism are common to the struggles of women in sports in other parts of the world, it is misleading to generalize from the limited experiences of a predominantly white, Western view of women. In fact, Third World feminism is a reaction to Western feminism, which is perceived as constructing Third World women as a homogeneous group characterized as poor, powerless victims of particular political and economic systems and of male exploitation. Although, in the case of sports, women in developing nations are mostly dominated and discriminated against by men, in the Third World Women's (TWW) feminist perspective, women's oppression is seen not only as a result of gender relations of power but also as a feature of colonial and neocolonial oppression, experienced differently by different women according to their race, class, colonial history, and current position in the international economic order. Women who are fighting for sport resources in non-Western countries are also responding to their own specific histories and cultures and adjusting to particular conditions and constraints. Many Muslim women in Islamic countries, for example, do not recognize Western accounts of gender oppression and work instead to improve opportunities for their sex within existing structures of power.

CONCLUSION

Sheila Scranton wrote that "Feminism is a political movement committed to 'changing the world.'" Feminist analysis is intended not only to be of scholarly value but also to effect change. There are a variety of forms of sport feminism, each specific to the needs and desires of women in different regions and cultures around the world. Whether their approach is practical or theoretical, the aim of sport feminists is to eliminate gender oppression and encourage the participation of women in sports. Through the efforts of women and men working through government agencies, nongovernmental and educational organizations, and sports federations, as well as the media and business, sports feminism has made women's access to physical education and sports a political issue in many parts of the world and has created substantial improvements in sports for women.

Jessica Edwards
Jennifer Hargreaves

See also Aging; Disability Sport; Gender Equity; Homophobia; Lesbianism; Race and Ethnicity; Sexual Harassment

Bibliography

Birrell, Susan. (1990) "Women of Color: Critical Autobiography, and Sport," in *Sport, Men, and the Gender Order: Critical Feminist Perspectives*, edited by M. Messner and D. Sabo. Champaign, IL: Human Kinetics, 185–199.

Birrell, Susan, and Diana Richter. (1987) "Is a Diamond Forever? Feminist Transformations of Sport." *Women's International Forum* 10, 4: 395–409.

DePauw, Karen. (1997) "Sport and Physical Activity in the Life Cycle of Girls and Women with Disabilities." *Women in Sport and Physical Activity Journal*, 16, 2: 225–235.

Elson, Diane, ed. (1995) *Male Bias in the Development Process*. 2nd ed. Manchester, England: Manchester University Press.

Green, Eileen, Susan Hebron, and Diane Woodward. (1990) *Women's Leisure, What Leisure?* London: Macmillan.

Hall, Ann. (1996) *Feminism and Sporting Bodies: Essays on Theory and Practice*. Champaign, IL: Human Kinetics.

Hargreaves, Jennifer. (1994) *Sporting Females: Critical Issues in the History and Sociology of Women's Sports*. London: Routledge.

Lenskyj, Helen. (1986) *Out of Bounds: Women, Sport and Sexuality*. Toronto: Women's Press.

———. (1997) "No Fear? Lesbians in Sport and Physical Education." *Women in Sport and Physical Activity Journal* 2: 7–22.

Lovell, Tessa. (1991) "Sport, Racism, and Young Women," in *Sport, Racism, and Ethnicity*, edited by G. Jarvie. Brighton, England: Falmer Press, 58–74.

Markula, Pirkko. (1995) "Firm But Shapely, Fit But Sexy, Strong But Thin: The Postmodern Aerobicizing Female Bodies." *Sociology of Sport Journal* 12: 425–453.

Mohanty, Chandra, Ann Russo, and Lourdes Torres, eds. (1991) *Third World Women and the Politics of Feminism*. Bloomington: Indiana University Press.

Nelson, Mariah Burton (1991) *Are We Winning Yet?* New York: Random House.

Oglesby, Carole. (1990) "Epilogue," in *Sport, Men, and the Gender Order: Critical Feminist Perspectives*, edited by M. Messner and D. Sabo. Champaign IL: Human Kinetics.

Parmar, Prathibha. (1995) "Gender, Race and Power: The Challenge of Youth Work," in *Sociology of Leisure: A Reader*, edited by C. Critcher, P. Bramham, and A. Tomlinson. London: E. and F. Spon, 152–160.

Rail, Genevieve. (1998) *Sport and Postmodern Times*. Albany: State University of New York Press.

Scranton, Sheila. (1994) "The Changing World of Women and Leisure: Feminism, 'Postfeminism,' and Leisure." *Leisure Studies* 13, 4: 249–261.

Smith, Yvonne. (1992) "Women of Color in Society and Sport." *Quest* 44: 228–250.

Theberge, Nancy. (1985) "Toward a Feminist Alternative to Sport as a Male Preserve." *Quest* 37.

———. (1987) "Sport and Women's Empowerment." *Women's Studies International Forum* 10: 387–393.

Wearing, Betsy. (1995) "Leisure and Resistance in an Aging Society." *Leisure Studies* 14: 263–279.

White, Anita, and Celia Brackenridge. (1985) "Who Rules Sport? Gender Divisions in the Power Structure of British Sports Organizations from 1960." *International Review for the Sociology of Sport* 20, 1–2: 95–107.

FENCING

Fencing is the art and sport of swordsmanship using blunted weapons. Several features of the sport make it distinctive, if not unique, in the athletic community. Until the late twentieth century, it was the only combative sport open to both men and women, although they compete separately. Fencing remains the only combative sport with neither weight classes nor height restrictions.

Fencing champions come in all shapes and sizes, and all competitors meet each other as equals, separated by ability alone. It is an activity that one can initiate at any age and that can be continued for the remainder of one's life. Fencing requires few players (any number greater than two may meet to fence, and a group may be large or small) and needs no purpose-built venue or expensive installation. The nature of fencing is such that an athlete whose visual or physical impairments might prevent her from taking an active role in other vigorous sports not only is welcome but also encounters no limit but that of her own talent to achieve any level of success. There have been successful fencers who were deaf, blind in one eye, or missing a limb.

HISTORY

Fencing is an activity of deep antiquity, with several millennia of tradition behind it. Perhaps the earliest known reference to a fencing match appears in a relief carving near Luxor in Upper Egypt in a temple at Madinet-Habu, built by Ramses III in about 1190 BCE. The fencers depicted there are using weapons with well-covered points and masks not unlike those currently in use. A panel of officials and administrators is depicted and distinguished by the feathered wands they hold.

Every ancient civilization—Chinese, Japanese, Egyptian, Persian, Babylonian, Greek, and Roman—practiced swordsmanship as a sport as well as training for combat. It is a curious anomaly that European swordsmanship—the most immediate antecedent of modern fencing—did not commence its development until after the advent of firearms (black weapons) in the fourteenth century. Until then, men wielded ever-heavier swords to cleave through ever-more-ponderous armor. Strength was more critical than skill. The advent of ballistic weapons rendered armor obsolete, enabling speed, mobility, and skill to prove greater than mere force. This led to the development of lighter swords (white weapons) used with faster, more subtle handwork for better use in close quarters. Thus arose the art of fencing. Learning to use a sword was difficult. The wounds resulting from it became infected. Threats to one's vision were a particular risk. Indeed, it was said that no competent fencing master could expect to close his career with two good eyes.

Three innovations made fencing more appealing to prospective students who were concerned for their safety. The first of these came in the seventeenth century, when a light practice weapon was developed. It was called a foil because its point had been flattened—"foiled"—and then padded to reduce the chance of injury. The second innovation was the development of rules of engagement known as "conventions," in which the valid target was limited to the breast, and the fencer who initiated the attack had precedence

Ilaria Bianco, champion Italian fencer. (Reuter Newmedia/Corbis)

unless completely parried by the defender. Fencing with foils thus became a "conversation of blades." But even with the advent of the foil and its conventions of play, fencing was still a slow, stylized activity because of the chance of injury to the face and eyes. The third innovation—the invention of the quadrilled wire-mesh fencing mask by the French master La Boiessière and the English master Joseph Boulogne, Chevalier de St. George (c. 1739–1799) in the closing decades of the eighteenth century—was the final step necessary to make fencing a completely safe activity.

Once the mask came into widespread use, more complex "phrases" (exchanges of blows) became possible, and foil fencing as it is now known was developed. The rules and conventions already mentioned prevented it from deteriorating into a brawl. These conventions are the basis of modern fencing.

In the nineteenth century relatively few athletic activities were open to women. The exceptions to this general rule of exclusion were the sports of skating, gymnastics, lawn tennis, and fencing. Fencing was offered at gymnastic and athletic clubs, such as the New York Turnverein (founded in 1851), which early on included women in its activities. The New York Fencers Club (founded in 1883) has had women members since the 1880s, although in those early years women members had to fence at different hours from those of the male members of the club. The Fencers Club of Philadelphia (founded in 1913) admitted women members from its inception. Not all clubs were this gracious; the Boston Fencing Club (founded in 1840) passed the following resolution in 1858: "No females shall be admitted to the club-rooms under any pretext whatever, except by permission of a member of the government of the club." The London Fencing Club (founded in 1848) did not admit its first woman member until 1946.

Until the twentieth century, women's participation was largely restricted to salle fencing, that is, they fenced only with foils. The national governing body of the sport, the Amateur Fencers League of America (AFLA; founded in 1891), held its first national championships for men in 1892, but there were no events for women until 1912. The first AFLA national women's foil champion was Adelaide Baylis of the New York Fencers Club. The AFLA added a foil team event for women in 1928.

In the early years of the twentieth century, fencers were frequently three-weapon competitors. As time passed, the size of the starting fields and the duration of competitions, as well as concomitant expenses, kept increasing. The desire for success led to specialization in one weapon, or two at most. Each weapon came to have its own aficionados. As already noted, women's fencing had been restricted to the foil, but in the 1970s a group of women, particularly in the United States and England, began campaigning to fence with the heavier weapons. Local events were held, eventually sectional championships were expanded and, finally, national championships were scheduled. In the United States, épée events for women were added to the national championships in 1981. Saber events for women were added to the national championships in 1998. Nowadays, most women fencers specialize in one weapon.

FENCING AND COMPETITIONS

Much of the history of modern fencing is connected to the Olympic Games. Fencing was one of the eight sports constituting the program of the first modern Olympic Games when they were revived in 1896 by Baron Pierre de Coubertin, who was himself a fencer. Fencing shares with only three other sports (athletics [track and field], swimming, and gymnastics) the distinction of being on the program of every Olympic Games observance.

In general, women's fencing champions have been far more dispersed than men's champions, who have largely been from France, Italy, Hungary and Russia. In addition to medal winners from those countries, Olympic women's champions have been German, Austrian, English, Danish, and Chinese.

Women's fencing made its debut at the 1924 Olympic Games at Paris. The winner of the foil individual that year was Ellen Osiier of Denmark. This remained the only fencing event for women until the 1960 Olympics at Rome, when a foil team event was added; the first winner was the Soviet Union. Épée events for women were added for the 1996 Olympics at Atlanta, where the individual champion was Laura Flessel of France; France also won the team event. Saber events for women have yet to be added to the Olympics. A women's foil world championship (then known as the European championship) was initiated in 1929; the first winner was Helena Mayer, of Germany. A women's foil team event was added in 1932, and the first winner was Denmark. A world's épée championship was initiated in 1988; saber events for women are in the demonstration stage.

Among the best-known women fencers are Helena Mayer (1910–1953) of Germany, the 1928 Olympic champion and three-time world champion; Ilona Elek of Hungary, the 1936 and 1948 Olympic champion and three-time world champion; and Ellen Mueller-Preiss of Austria, the 1932 Olympic champion and two-time world champion. Successful British women fencers were Gwen Neligan, the 1933 world champion, and

Gillian Sheen Donaldson, the 1956 Olympic champion. Among U.S. women fencers who have finished in the Olympic top ten are Maria Cerra Tishman, Janice York Romary, Maxine Mitchell, and épée fencer Donna Stone.

Fencing offers a much longer competitive career than many other sports. This is best evidenced by the careers of Janice York Romary, who earned berths on six U.S. Olympic teams between 1948 and 1968, and Kerstin Palm of Sweden, who fenced in seven Olympics between 1964 and 1988. Palm was the first woman in any sport to participate in so many Olympics.

The factor most responsible for increased interest among women in the United States was the creation of women's collegiate fencing, which was years ahead of similar activity in most other U.S. sports for women. The earliest college teams were established at Bryn Mawr and the University of Pennsylvania in the early 1920s. By 1929 those colleges joined with New York University (NYU) and Cornell to create the Intercollegiate Women's Fencing Association (IWFA). NYU won the first IWFA team title and NYU's Julia Jones won the first individual title. The organization, known since 1971 as the National Intercollegiate Women's Fencing Association (NIWFA), grew to nearly eighty teams by 1980. By the late 1990s, however, its membership slipped to about fifteen teams, and it has been hard-pressed to maintain itself due to the centralization policies of the Association of Intercollegiate Athletics for Women (AIAW), the National Collegiate Athletic Association (NCAA), the Intercollegiate Fencing Association (IFA), and the U.S. Fencing Association (USFA).

The growth of collegiate fencing from the 1950s to the 1980s was accompanied by a surge in secondary school fencing, a development that has since abated. New Jersey has the most highly developed program, followed by schools in New England and California.

Women are increasingly involved in fencing as coaches, officials, and administrators, and there have been many "firsts" among twentieth-century women fencers. In 1932 Julia Jones became the first woman to coach an intercollegiate championship team. That same year, Marion Lloyd Vince was the first U.S. woman to reach the Olympic final. In 1965 Maria Cerra Tishman was the first woman named to the U.S. Olympic fencing committee. In 1970 Julia Jones was the first woman to coach a U.S. international squad, the World University Games team. In 1976 Harriet King was the first woman editor of *American Fencing* magazine. In 1980 Emily Johnson, a San Francisco jurist, was the first woman elected president of the AFLA, which she renamed the U.S. Fencing Association (USFA).

RULES AND PLAY

A modern fencer uses one of three types of weapons: the foil, the épée, or the saber. Competitions for men or women are conducted for all three arms although until the 1970s women participated almost exclusively with the foil. Fencing events may be conducted as individual or team events, although even in team events only two fencers meet each other at any one time. International teams are usually composed of three or four on a side, with each fencer meeting her competitor on the opposing side. Team matches may be run in a "relay" fashion, in which touches are added cumulatively from one bout to the next.

The modern foil has a slender, flexible blade, quadrangular in cross section, and a small, centrally mounted circular guard. The blade is a maximum of 90 centimeters (35.4 inches) long. Foil fencers try to score, using the point of their weapon only, by hitting their opponent on the torso. If the fencer touches her opponent's head, legs, or arms, no point is scored, and the action resumes. If a fencer touches her opponent on the torso, then a point (or "touch") is scored. If both fencers hit each other, the official applies the conventions of right-of-way to assess the situation and awards the touch, if any. Usually, bouts are for five touches in elimination pools leading to a final round-robin pool; or ten or fifteen touches in direct-elimination ladders leading to the title bout; or a combination of both methods. Until 1976 women fenced four touch bouts in pools and eight touch bouts in direct elimination.

The modern épée has a wide blade, more rigid than that of a foil and Y-shaped in cross section, with a large circular guard that may be centrally or eccentrically mounted. The blade is a maximum of 90 centimeters (35.4 inches) long. Épée fencing observes no conventions, and touches are made with the point anywhere on an opponent. If both fencers hit together, then a double-touch is scored against each, and both fencers are counted as being hit. Épée bouts may be fenced to one touch or multiple touch bouts, in pools or direct elimination, or a combination of both. Épée fencing for one touch is an element of the five-event competition called the modern pentathlon.

The modern saber has a flexible blade, usually T-, Y-, or I-shaped in cross-section, and a large guard that curves around the knuckles and may be centrally or eccentrically mounted. The blade is a maximum of 88 centimeters (34.6 inches) long. In saber fencing, touches made with either the point or one of the two cutting edges count if they land above the opponent's hips. Saber fencing observes the same conventions as foil fencing.

In all three weapons, bouts in a round-robin pool are of four minutes' duration. Direct-elimination contests are encounters of 10 or 15 minutes' duration, depending on the maximum number of touches. Until 1976 women's bouts were shorter than men's.

To avoid injuries, fencers wear a heavy wire-mesh mask with a thick canvas bib to protect the head and neck. They also wear thick canvas or nylon jackets and knickers and a padded glove on the weapon hand. In competition, fencers wear additional equipment that permits an electric scoring apparatus to function. Until 1940 women fencers could wear skirts or dresses instead of trousers or knickers. Women also wear breast protectors or plastic shields under their jackets.

Fencing is conducted on a field of play called a strip, or *piste*, that is 14 meters (15 yards) long and 2 meters (2.2 yards) wide. A fencer exiting the side of the piste is penalized 1 meter (1.1 yard) in distance. A fencer exiting the end of the strip is penalized a touch.

Until the advent of electric scoring devices, fencing matches were adjudicated by a jury composed of a "president" and four assistants. The president has also been referred to as a "director" and, more recently, a "referee," and the assistants may be called "judges." At the end of the nineteenth century, foil fencers wore black uniforms, and chalk tips were used on foils to aid in the scoring; this system was not very popular, particularly in Europe and American colleges, where form was also taken into account in scoring. Around World War I, and for the next thirty years, white uniforms were worn and red ink was used on the tips of épées to indicate a touch.

Since the introduction of the mask, no innovation has had so great an impact on the sport as the advent of electrified scoring. It has completely eliminated the need for assistants, leaving only the president to officiate. The épée was electrified in time for the 1935 world championships at Lausanne, Switzerland; the foil, for the 1955 world championship in Rome; and the saber, for the 1989 world championships at Denver, Colorado. These advances have not come without complications. Electrification of the sport has increased the start-up and maintenance costs considerably and has had a steadily debilitating impact on the technique of competitors. Also, in spite of the objectivity of the equipment, individual bias on the part of officials remains entrenched. Many observers believe that fencing has been transformed from the simulation of a duel into a display in which participants simply turn on a light with style and that fencing's verisimilitude and drama have been sacrificed to speed and efficiency.

Jeffrey R. Tishman

Bibliography

Bower, Muriel. (1985) *Foil Fencing.* Dubuque, IA: Wm. C. Brown Publishers.

Cass, Eleanor Baldwin. (1930) *The Book of Fencing.* Boston: Lothrop, Lee & Shepard.

Castle, Egerton. (1888) *Schools and Masters of Fence: From the Middle Ages to the Eighteenth Century.* Reprint, 1969. York, PA: George Shumway.

Curry, Nancy L. (1984) *The Fencing Book.* New York: Leisure Press.

De Beaumont, Charles L. (1970) *Fencing: Ancient Art and Modern Sport.* South Brunswick, NJ: A. S. Barnes.

DeCapriles, Jose R., ed. (1965) *AFLA Rulebook.* Worcester, MA: Heffernan Press.

DeCapriles, Miguel A., ed. (1951) *AFLA Rulebook.* New York: Amateur Fencers League of America.

———, ed. (1957) *AFLA Rulebook.* New York: Amateur Fencers League of America.

Garret, Maxwell R., and Mary Heinecke Poulson. (1981) *Foil Fencing.* College Park, PA: Penn State University Press.

Shaff, Jo Mancinelli. (1982) *Fencing.* New York: Atheneum.

Thimm, Captain Carl A. (1896) *A Bibliography of Fencing and Duelling.* Reprint, 1968. Bronx, NY: Benjamin Blom.

Tishman, Jeffrey R. (1990) "College Fencing Damaged by NCAA and USFA Policies." *Swordmaster* (Spring).

———. (1990) "Collegiate Fencing at Risk." *American Fencing* 42, 1 (Spring).

FIKOTOVÁ, OLGA

(1932–)

CZECH AND THEN U.S. DISCUS THROWER

Olga Fikotová is an athlete whose story illuminates the link—often a close one—between sports and politics. Fikotová was born in Prague, the capital of what was then the nation of Czechoslovakia, on 25 November 1932. With the assistance of the national sport organizations, she developed into a world-class discus thrower and took the gold medal at the 1956 Olympics in Melbourne with her personal best throw of 53.69 meters (176 feet 1.75 inches). The victory was especially satisfying for the Czechoslovakian officials because Fikotová, competing for the Czechoslovak Socialist Republic, beat the three favored throwers from the Soviet Union. During the Olympics, she met Harold Connolly, a hammer thrower from the United States who had also won the gold medal in his event. They fell in love and made it clear that they intended to marry and live in the United States. Their decision did not sit well with the Czechoslovakian officials. The law prohibited Czechoslovakian citizens from leaving; although exceptions could be made, this was unlikely to happen for a national sport figure who wanted to leave for the capitalist United States. This was early in the Cold War era, and losing an athlete to the United States would have been a major embarrassment to the communist government.

The situation made its way into the international media, which sided with the couple and accused Eastern European communist nations of being enemies of love and freedom. The U.S. State Department entered into negotiations with the Czechoslovakian government, and finally the au-

Olga Fikotová, at the 1956 Melbourne Olympics, breaks the Olympic discus record with a toss of 53.69 meters. (Corbis/Bettmann)

thorities gave permission. Fikotová and Connolly were married on 25 March 1957 in Prague; Emil Zatopek, the Czech runner and four-time Olympic gold medalist in distance running, and his wife, Dana, the Olympic champion in the javelin throw in 1952, served as witnesses. The couple then moved to the United States and Fikotová became a U.S. citizen. She competed in discus throwing in four straight Olympics from 1960 to 1972, but she had limited success, her best finish being sixth in the 1968 Games.

At the 1972 Games in Munich, Fikotová was again embroiled in politics. She was selected by her teammates to carry the American flag as the U.S. team entered the Olympic stadium, and she was the first U.S. woman given this honor. Fikotová, however, was an outspoken opponent of U.S. involvement in Vietnam, and for this reason the U.S. Olympic Committee attempted to remove her as the flag bearer. The committee's effort failed, and she carried the flag into the

Munich stadium. On the personal side, the story ended less happily; Fikotová and Connolly were divorced in 1975.

Gherardo Bonini

Bibliography

Schaap, Dick. (1976) *An Illustrated History of the Olympics.* New York: Ballantine Books.

Sparhawk, Ruth M., Mary E. Leslie, Phyllis Y. Turbow, and Zina R. Rose. (1987) *American Women in Sport, 1887–1987. A 100-Year Chronology.* Metuchen, NJ: Scarecrow Press.

FILMS *see* Movies

FINLAND

Situated between Scandinavia and Russia, Finland is a country of 5 million people. Finnish sporting life has traditionally concentrated on a few male-oriented sports and has emphasized top-level competitive events and international success. Track and field and wrestling were initially the most prominent sports, followed by cross-country skiing and, in the 1990s, ice hockey. For many years, women's sports in Finland were dominated by an extensive women's gymnastic movement; in the 1990s, women became involved in more diverse athletic pursuits.

The organizational structure of Finnish sports has been divided along lines of class, language (Finnish or Swedish), and, to a large degree, gender; a loose central federation connecting all these elements, even men and women, was not established until 1993. However, by the early twentieth century, women were actively taking part in rowing, skiing, running, swimming, and other athletic pursuits.

HISTORY

The history of women's sport in Finland begins with gymnastics. The women's gymnastic movement in Finland started in the mid-nineteenth century. Elin Kallio (1859–1927) pioneered the voluntary gymnastic movement; she founded the

first women's gymnastic club in Finland and in all the Nordic nations in 1876 and served as the first president of the Finnish Women's Gymnastic Federation, established in 1896. (The federation endorsed other sports as well, but only in noncompetitive forms.) Between 1917 and 1921 the national federation split into separate Finnish- and Swedish-speaking organizations. Workers' sports were a strong third sector, and the participation of women in gymnastics and sports played an important part in the Finnish Workers' Sports Federation, established in 1919.

Finnish women's gymnastics was based on the Swedish model, the so-called Ling system. Elli Björkstén (1870–1947), who had graduated from the Royal Gymnastic Central Institute in Stockholm in 1895, developed a gymnastics system for women along the lines of Ling's methods. Björkstén's method book *Kvinnogymnastik I-II* (Women's Gymnastics I-II) was translated into many languages. In 1922 Björkstén helped found the Nordic Women's Gymnastic Association. The association's famous summer courses, with Björkstén as teacher and leader, were eagerly attended by Finnish women, with participants coming from outside Scandinavia as well.

Gymnastic education for girls was introduced in private schools in the 1860s and in state schools in 1872. Initially, the teachers were educated at a private institute (founded in 1869), but since 1894 they have studied at the gymnastic institute of the University of Helsinki.

In the 1920s and 1930s Finnish women's gymnastics were influenced by central European gymnastic and dance schools. This was reflected in the new Finnish women's gymnastics, whose most important developer was a former student of Björkstén, Hilma Jalkanen (1889–1964). Jalkanen's method of gymnastics was based on the Swedish (Lingian) gymnastics system, but Jalkanen included many innovations from German and other Central European gymnastics schools, which she, like many other Finnish physical educators, had visited for studies during the 1920s and 1930s. This method served as the basis for school girls' physical education until the 1970s; sports had only a minor role at schools. Women's gymnastics in clubs almost exclusively meant free exercises— moves were performed using the body and the floor only; apparatus was introduced only in time

The Olympic Stadium in Helsinki, Finland, where the 1952 Games were held. (Joel W. Rogers/Corbis)

for Finland to compete with other nations at the 1952 Olympic Games in Helsinki. The so-called modern gymnastics (later known as rhythmic gymnastics) was initiated in the 1960s in the Soviet Union and eventually spread into Central Europe and Sweden. As in other nations, aerobic dance became popular in the 1980s, both as a means of conditioning and as a competitive sport. Finland has won several world championship medals in the sport. National championship competitions in traditional women's (group) gymnastics have been organized in cooperation with the women's gymnastics federations since 1991. Suomen Voimistelu ja Liikuntaseurat, known as SvoLi, the national central organization for women's gymnastics founded in 1994, is in charge of competitions and training. Today, it is the largest sport association in Finland (150,000 members).

WOMEN'S COMPETITIVE SPORTS

Finnish women's competitive sports languished for a long time, caught between the strong but noncompetitive women's gymnastic movement on one side and the unappreciative men's sports world on the other. Nevertheless, women did participate in sports. Since the 1880s they had taken part in rowing, skiing, and running competitions that were outgrowths of traditional games and play. In the 1880s, skating and swimming clubs were the first organized sports that women were involved in; in the 1890s they began to form cycling clubs. In 1906 swimming became the first sport to have national championship competitions for women; swimming was also Finnish women's first Olympic sport in 1912, when Regina Kari and Tyyne Järvi swam for Finland. The first woman to win a world championship title (1911) and an Olympic gold medal (1920) for Finland was the German-born Ludowika Eilers Jakobsson in pairs' figure skating.

During these same decades, Finnish women began to broaden their participation in sports. Women's track and field sports and cross-country skiing were promoted by the Finnish Gymnastic and Sports Union. The first national championships in women's cross-country skiing were held in 1911 (in 5-kilometer races) and in track in 1913 (in the 100-meter event and the 4 × 100-meter relay). Women's track and field competitions were established early in the century: multievent competitions began in 1905, national meetings were first held in 1908, and regional championships got their start in 1909. Several world records (unofficial) were achieved during the 1910s.

The period between the two world wars brought something of a backlash against women's sports. Women's national championships were discontinued in 1923—only women in the Finnish Workers' Sports Federation had their own federation championships in this field. At the beginning of the 1930s, the first women's athletic club was founded in Helsinki, and "bourgeois" women entered track and field competitions again; in 1936 four such women were sent to the Olympic games for the first time.

Despite this burgeoning interest, national sports leaders strongly opposed the introduction of women's track and field events into the Olympic program. Otherwise, between the wars, Finnish women participated in the Olympic Games only in swimming (1928 and 1936) and in pairs' figure skating. At the Worker Olympiads, attended by athletes from workers' sports organizations in Europe, Finnish women took part in track and field and swimming events in 1925 and in swimming and skiing in 1931 and 1937, each time successfully. The only world championship titles won between the wars were in canoeing (Maggie Kalka in 1938) and in speed skating (Verné Lesche in 1939). In the 1930s, women's national championship competitions were held in tennis, canoeing, bowling, bandy (a sport something like field hockey), and *pesäpallo,* the Finnish version of baseball.

POSTWAR GROWTH IN WOMEN'S SPORTS

Women's basketball, volleyball, and orienteering gained in popularity during and after World War II. Cross-country skiing, track and field sports, and swimming were still the most important women's sports, however, along with gymnastics. In 1948 one-quarter of the 300,000 members of the Finnish Gymnastics and Sports Union (SVUL) were women; this included one-fifth of the membership in the track and field federation and in the skiing federation. In 1948 the Finnish-language women's gymnastics federation, with 47,000 members, joined SVUL. Women fought their most significant organizational battles for rights to training, competing, and international sports exchange in track and field sports, which was the Finnish men's dominant and most successful area. In 1945 the women's section of the Finnish Amateur Athletic Association, in cooperation with the women of the Workers' Sports Federation, brought about the reintroduction of women's national track and field championships. The first Olympic track and field medal awarded to Finnish women was a silver in the javelin throw, won by Kaisa Parviainen in 1948, but the first gold medal in track and field did not come until 1996, when Heli Rantanen also won in the javelin. Tiina Lillak (javelin throw in 1983) and Sari Essayah (10-kilometer walk in 1993) won world championship titles. Finnish women have won only two gold medals at Olympic Summer Games, the first one by Sylvi Saimo in canoeing in 1952, the second by Paivi Merilvoto for archery in 1980. Until the 1980s, Finnish Olympic teams had a below-average proportion of women at the Olympic Summer Games compared to other nations.

Finnish women swept all three medals in the first women's Olympic cross-country 10-kilometer skiing race in 1952. They also won the gold medal in the first Olympic cross-country relay race four years later. The next Olympic skiing gold medal was not won for Finland until twenty years later, by Helena Takalo in 1976, in the 5-kilometer cross-country race. In the 1970s and 1980s, women were largely responsible for Finland's medals in cross-country skiing, the prominent winter sport in the country; they won sixteen out of twenty-five Olympic medals and five out of six gold medals in that period. The skier Marja-Liisa Kirvesniemi is the most successful Finnish female athlete of all time, having won a total of three gold and four bronze medals at six Olympic Winter Games. Marjo Matikainen and Marjut Lukkarinen have also won individual Olympic titles in the sport. Kaija Mustonen won one gold, two silver, and one bronze in Olympic speed skating (1964–1968). Until 1984 the number of women in Finnish Olympic Winter Games teams did not exceed 15 percent of Finnish Olympic athletes, but their share of (unofficial) points won at these Games ranged between 18 and 51 percent. In

1998 Finland won the Olympic bronze medal in ice hockey, the first-ever Finnish Olympic medal in women's team sports.

WORLD CHAMPIONSHIPS

From the 1950s to the 1970s, Finnish women won world championship titles in archery, bowling, and orienteering. In the 1970s women began to invade the more traditional male sports. The year 1971 brought the inauguration of national championship competition in women's soccer (association football), and in the 1980s Finnish women won world titles in shooting, karate, and powerlifting, as well as European titles in yachting, judo, and ice hockey. Tea Vikstedt-Nyman, who set two world records between 1988 and 1990, was the first female, world-elite cyclist in the country. In 1988–1989, Taru Rinne became the first woman in history to participate in the motorcycling road race world championship series. Today in Finland nearly all sports are open to women, including boxing, wrestling, and ski jumping.

ISSUES OF EQUALITY

Women's sports organizations in Finland have both helped and hindered female athletes' efforts to participate to a greater extent in a larger number of sports. On the positive side, women's rights in sports have been promoted by women's independent gymnastic federations since the inception of organized sports in the country. On the negative side, women's competitive sports may have suffered from organizational jealousy and ideological bias. In 1948 the Women's Central Committee of SVUL was founded, followed by women's committees in districts and various sports federations. The central committee continued its work until the 1970s, but its role had started to decline in the 1960s. A research group on women and sports was founded in 1982 at the University of Jyväskylä and operated until 1992. Organizational provisions for gender equality were established only in the 1990s. Not until 1998 did the Finnish Sports Federation (the new central federation, founded in 1993) adopt an equality program, and the first official to endorse equal rights was appointed in the same year. Women constitute 43 percent of the membership and 16 percent of the board of the sports federations under the wings of the central federation (seventy-two organizations in all). For the Workers' Sports Federation, the numbers for women are 40 percent and 45 percent, respectively. Yet in only seventeen sports federations does the number of female members exceed 30 percent.

By the late 1990s gymnastics, skiing, track and field, *pesäpallo*, equestrian events, football, and snowboarding federations had the largest number of female members of the various organizations. Nevertheless, most of the women's and girls' sports activities take place outside the established sports organizations: they walk, cycle, swim, dance, attend aerobics classes, or practice horseback riding more often than men do. Only one-fifth of the 100,000 girls who ride are members of the national equestrian federation.

CONCLUSION

The largest change in Finnish women's participation in sports has been the opportunity to participate in a number of competitive sports. At the same time, the traditional and powerful women's gymnastics movement—a noncompetitive and early "sport for all" type of women's movement, with strong social and political elements—has been diminishing in favor of competitive and sportslike fitness gymnastics. If this is seen as gender equality, then it has impacted only participation in the sports themselves. Regarding the leadership of sports organizations, resource allocation, and media coverage of sports, the work toward equality has just begun.

Leena Laine

Translated by Vesa Tikander

Bibliography

Björkstén, Elli. (1932–1934) *Principles of Gymnastics for Women and Girls*. 2 vols. London: J. & A. Churchill.

Laine, Leena. (1984) *Vapaaehtoisten järjestöjen kehitys ruumiinkulttuurin alueella Suomessa v. 1856–1917*. 2 vols. Liikuntatieteellisen Seuran julkaisu No 93A-93B. Helsinki.

———. (1989) "Historische Entwicklung des Frauensports in Finland," in *Frauensport in Europa*, edited by Christine Peyton and Gertrud Pfister. Hamburg, Germany: Zwalina, 113–131.

———. (1989) "The 'Nature' of Woman—the 'Nature' of Man: The Effects of Gender Images on Organizing Sports in Finland in the 1920's and 1930's."

Proceedings of the Jyväskylä Congress on "Movement and Sport in Women's Life," 17–21 August, 1987, vol. 1, edited by Marjo Raivio. Reports of Physical Culture and Health 66. Jyväskylä, Finland: Press of the University of Jyväskylä.

———. (1998) "How to Cross Borders: Women and Sports Organizations in the Nordic Countries." *The International Journal of the History of Sport* 15, 1 (April): 194–205.

Laine, Leena, ed. (1984) *Huippu-urheilun maailma 5*. Porvoo, Finland: WSOY.

Pihlaja, Juhani. (1994) *Urheilun käsikirja*. Lahti, Finland: Tietosportti.

Raevuori, Antero, ed. (1982) *Huippu-urheilun maailma 4*. Porvoo, Finland: WSOY.

Raevuori, Antero, Antti Arponen, and Matti Hannus, eds. (1996) *Urheilu 2000*, vols. 4–5. Porvoo, Finland: WSOY.

Siukonen, Markku, Matti Ahola, and Helge Nygren. (1988) *Suuri Olympiateos 1988, Calgary*. Jyväskylä, Finland: Sporttikustannus OY.

FISHING

No one knows exactly when *fishing* as a survival strategy to provide food for the stomach was transformed to *angling* as a pastime and sport to provide food for the soul or spirit. It is well documented, however, that women have been involved actively in both the practical and leisure aspects of fishing from its earliest times. To the average person, fishing and angling may be synonymous, but there is a difference. Angling is considered the art and sport of casting a line to a designated spot, using artificial bait to lure and land the fish, and most often releasing the catch. Fishing, on the other hand, is catching fish without regard to method, with the primary goal of providing food.

Fishing is one of the most popular recreational activities in countries around the world. In the United States about 20 percent of women and 37 percent of men participated in the sport at least once in 1995. Fishing takes place in both fresh- and saltwaters and appeals to all ages and equally to persons of all economic backgrounds. Freshwater fishing attracts most of the anglers in the United States, while in other nations saltwater fishing is the sport of choice—probably because the United States has more freshwater than any other nation, and the majority of Americans do not have ready access to saltwater fishing.

Fishing has appeal for its combination of luck, the feel of the fish on the line, the peaceful outdoor fresh air and water environment, and the accomplishment connected with landing a prize fish that is larger than the next competitor's. The "angler" finds sport in merely making casts accurately, hitting a designated spot that may be up to 350–375 feet away. In either category women have been involved in the sport since its earliest recordings.

HISTORY

Fish were first caught with bare hands and about 3000 BCE early Persians included fish as part of their national diet. Catching the fish was accomplished most easily as tides receded, leaving fish flailing on dry beaches or caught in shallow pools of water. A related method, known as *tickling*, is still practiced in many countries today; the fisher leans over a pool of water, puts her hands under the fish, and proceeds to tickle its belly. As the fish lazily relaxes with the tickling motion, the fisher makes a sudden grab with spread fingers, and tosses the fish to the riverbank or grassy area, where it can be collected for a meal. Tickling is still popular today, especially in the Rocky Mountain region of the United States in late summer when the waters are low and fish have become trapped in pools near the sides of streams.

Spear fishing is believed to be the next form of fishing to develop; however, the valuable spears were too often lost in the water, resulting in no catch and no spear with which to try again. Harpooning emerged as a form of spear fishing that allowed the implement to be saved and used repeatedly and enabled the fisher to haul in the catch efficiently.

The Egyptians were the first people to use lines for fishing; as a crude form of bait, they used a burr. Early Egyptian pictures on unearthed tombs depict a man using a rod or fishing pole with a line attached to catch the fish and a club to stun it when it is hauled ashore. The lines were made from a vine, and the burr was attached to the end to attract the fish. Small fish would swallow the burr and were dragged to shore. Larger

Women on a fishing trip in Tulsa, Oklahoma, in 1982. (Corbis/Annie Griffiths Belt)

fish were often bludgeoned with a club as they got close to the shore. The Egyptians eventually replaced the vine with lines made from braided animal hair, and the burr with thornwood branches, increasing the range of the cast. They added hooks made from bone to keep the larger fish on the line. Later, the bone hooks were replaced by ivory, then bronze, iron, and eventually steel, as people from other nations began sharing techniques and materials along trade routes.

The Chinese were known to use lines of braided silk for fishing by about 900 BCE. India has recorded using fish as food in about 800 BCE, caught chiefly with spears attached to vines but also with lines of braided hair or silk. About 500 BCE, the Jews began fishing with woven nets, thereby collecting fish in vast numbers and beginning the commercial trade of fishing.

Martial, a Roman, writing between 10 BCE and 20 CE, and Aelian, an Italian, between 170 and 230 CE, give us the first written accounts of fly-casting,

which substituted artificial bait—an imitation of a fly that normally fell onto the surface of lakes and streams and attracted, and was consumed by, the fish—for a live lure, such as bait fish, worms or grasshoppers.

The first documented accounts of angling by a woman are attributed to Dame Juliana Berners (*Treatyse of Fysshynge with an Angle*) in 1496. Berners was an English nun and noblewoman who detailed both fishing and hunting techniques as entries in *The Boke of St. Albans*. Berners's works are believed to have been written between 1420 and 1450. However, *The Boke of St. Albans*, regarded as the first work published in the English language on hunting and sport, was not published until 1486; the accounts of fishing and detailed use of a rod and techniques useful in the sport of fly-casting were first included in an edition in 1496. In 1651 Barker wrote *The Art of Angling* and included in it detailed drawings of a fishing reel, which he stated was created about 1496. Barker's accounts reflect back to Berners's writings, strongly suggesting that she was indeed one of the earliest English language historians of the art of angling.

ORGANIZED TOURNAMENT FISHING

In 1732 the Schuylkill Fishing Company was formed in Philadelphia, Pennsylvania. Still in existence today as the Fish House Club, it limits annual membership to thirty and is believed to be the oldest continuous sporting body in the United States. A national tournament was arranged in 1861, but details are sketchy about results or competition rules. The American Rod and Reel Association was founded in 1874, and the first United States national fly-casting tournament was staged in conjunction with the Chicago World's Fair in 1893. The events were accuracy, accuracy of fly, delicacy of fly, long-distance bait, and long-distance fly-casting. In the early competitions all casts were actually made on a lawn so that distances could be measured accurately since this measurement was not yet possible on water. After the fifth national tournament, held at Kalamazoo, Michigan (1906), the National Association of Scientific Angling Clubs was formed. In 1907 this group became the governing body of the fly-casting sport. The group changed its name to the American Casting Association in 1961.

TYPES OF FISHING TODAY

Bait fishing refers to fishing with live bait, such as worms, grasshoppers, or small fish. *Lures* are fake bait like plastic worms (jigs, plugs, or spoons), or flashy metal lures that attract fish by darting movements as they are pulled through the water. *Fly-fishing* uses a collection of strings, feathers, or other artificial materials, that are tied to resemble bugs that naturally inhabit lakes or streams and that provide flying food for fish in their environment.

Whether using bait, lures, or flies, anglers practice the art of *casting,* or getting the fishing line from the pole to the place where the fish are. Techniques for casting are many, combining the skill of placing the line accurately and artfully with an understanding of how fish swim, experiential knowledge of where they are likely to hide, and scientific knowledge of the flow of the waters in the stream or lake. *Spin casting* is considered the easier method, using a reel that releases the line with the cast and the weight of the lure or bait. *Fly-casting* is considered the more difficult sport, requiring more skill because of the light weight of the fly and a longer line that is hand-fed with each arm movement.

In fly-casting tournaments, the target is usually a rubber circle about 30 inches in diameter. For accuracy-casting tests, five rings are placed about 5 feet apart, and the competitor tries for a bull's-eye in each. Normally, the caster is permitted two casts at each ring, and a total time limit of about 8 minutes is set for all the casts. In accuracy casting, ties are possible since the winner is determined by an aggregate of points scored. Distance events start with a target being placed at medium range and then moved progressively with each competitor's successful cast. This is head-to-head competition, with the winner the competitor who successfully hits the furthest target.

Categories are created based on the weight and type of bait, bug, fly, or plug in both distance and accuracy events. They are also divided by water, either saltwater (billfish, tuna, shark, or other ocean catch) or freshwater (trout, bass, catfish, stripers, pike, muskies, salmon, steelhead,

HELEN SEVIER, PRESIDENT OF THE WORLD'S LARGEST FISHING ASSOCIATION

Bass fishing is a major recreational activity and sport in the United States. The largest fishing association in the world is the Bass Anglers Sportsman Society (B.A.S.S.), and the president of B.A.S.S., Inc., Helen Sevier, is credited with the phenomenal growth of the society. Headquartered in Montgomery, Alabama, B.A.S.S. has over 500,000 members and 160 employees; supports $6 million in tournaments, two televised fishing series, 2,800 clubs; and publishes five magazines.

and others), and sometimes by the specific type of freshwater or saltwater fish found in those waters. Men's records date back to the 1890s, while women's records begin in the early 1920s.

FRESHWATER WOMEN'S RECORDS

One of the most renowned freshwater anglers of all time was Cornelia T. Crosby (1854–1946). A guide in the Maine woods for almost seventy years, Crosby was credited with catching more fish with a fly than anyone that ever lived to her time. In 1895 she pioneered the short skirt (about 7 inches above the ground) in order to avoid entangling it with her feet, which were submerged in water. That fishing garb, it was said, made her appear to walk on water, and she enraptured those who saw her in action. She also hooked her flies around the band of her hat and thus started what has become a hard-and-fast tradition for anglers. Crosby began writing about her fishing expeditions in *The Maine Woods*, where the editor is said to have coined her byline and future nickname, "Fly Rod" Crosby. Her column was subsequently printed in publications throughout the United States, and she became a celebrity. She used custom-made rods and wrote a travel brochure for the railroads of the region.

Mary Orvis Marbury was the inspiration for the founding of the Orvis Company, one of the most successful clothing and fishing equipment companies of the twentieth century. Orvis Marbury was famous for her fly-tying and recording of the types of flies used by anglers in the United States. Her *Favorite Flies and Their Histories* was an invited exhibition at the Chicago World's Fair (1893) and was heralded as the most comprehensive book on flies ever written.

The first records by women in freshwater fishing were set in 1923. Billie Brown won the first U.S. ½-ounce-bait accuracy title, J. F. Atwood held the first wet-fly accuracy record, and Mrs. Louis J. Hurst won the ⅝-ounce-plug accuracy title. Over the years many champions, as well as new categories have been added, for instance, trout-fly accuracy, bass-bug accuracy and trout-fly distance.

On a whim, and acting on the growing popularity of fishing in the 1930s, Julia Fairchild and Mrs. Frank Hovey-Roof Connell formed the first all-female Woman Flyfishers Club on 28 January 1932. Fairchild was the organization's president

A woman fishes through a hole drilled into the frozen surface of Gola Lake, in Norway. (Corbis/Adam Wolfitt)

for thirty-nine years. The club was a pioneer of modern-day conservation, and Fairchild was an advocate at the national level. She was still fishing shortly before her death at age ninety-seven, and Hovey-Roof Connell fished until her ninety-eighth birthday. The Women Flyfishers Club is still in existence today.

Joan Salvato captured her first title in 1938 at the age of eleven. From 1943–46, Salvato held the Women's dry-fly accuracy record, recapturing the title in 1951. She also held records for ⅜-ounce-plug accuracy in 1950 and for wet-fly accuracy in 1945, 1948, and 1951. By the age of thirty-four, she had held seventeen national records and one international record and had set a distance record of 161 feet. She was the first woman to win the distance event against all male competitors. Salvato married Lee Wulff, and the partnership led them to establish the Joan and Lee Wulff Fishing School, one of the most famous and enduring fishing schools in the United States. Salvato Wulff has written two books and a monthly feature for *Fly Rod & Reel,* and was hired by Garcia, a leading company in sales of fishing gear and equipment. She continues to run her school and teach fly-casting, as well as advocate equipment and clothing designed for women anglers.

SALTWATER WOMEN'S RECORDS

In the years just before and during World War II, women began to make their mark in saltwater fishing, largely through dramatic contests with the big billfish.

Billfish, which include swordfish, marlin, spearfish, and sailfish, are considered some of the most exciting species for ocean anglers. One of the most thrilling catches in saltwater is the broadbill swordfish. The first recorded landing of this giant fish was in 1913. Since then, only about 800 have been caught. While fishing with her husband in 1936, Helen (Mrs. Michael) Lerner became the first woman to haul a broadbill out of both the Atlantic and Pacific Oceans, with one of them a 570-pounder caught off Peru. After World War II, she received a gold medal from France's Académie des Sports for catching a giant tuna on a rod and reel while just off the French coast. Helen and Michael Lerner are best known for scientific contributions to the study and recording of the diets and migratory patterns of many of the ocean's game fish. They invited scientists along on their fishing expeditions and helped record the results of their catch. Michael created the International Game Fish Association and served as its first president (1941–1960). The IGFA is the official recorder of all world records and leads the world in efforts at fishing conservation.

Another of the great saltwater sport fishes is the albacore tuna, known for its fighting spirit and tenacity while hooked but not landed. The early women's record for tuna fishers was held by Mrs. L. J. Blumindale of New York City. On 3 September 1940, she brought in a bluefin tuna weighing 794 pounds after a fight of three hours and forty-five minutes. A later record of 886 pounds is held by Gertrude Collings (1970). The largest (by weight) fish caught by a woman is a black marlin weighing in at 1,525 pounds (14 feet 4 inches), caught off the Cabo Blanco coast of Peru in 1954 by Kimberly Wiss.

Two women's records were set in 1936. The women's records for the longest single-handed fight with a tuna was eleven hours and thirty minutes, by Mrs. Francis Low, off the coast of Nova Scotia. Georgia McCoy of Los Angeles set a record for number and gross weight of tuna captured in one year, landing fifteen fish for an aggregate weight of 5,284 pounds.

Three sisters, "Bonefish Bonnie" Smith, Frankee Albright, and Beulah Cass, also rose to fame as fishing guides in the Florida waters during the war years. Bonnie's husband, Bill Smith, was the first person recorded to catch a bonefish on a fly (1939), and Bonnie was at his side. Armed with this experience, Bonnie became the first woman to catch a bonefish on a fly. The bonefish, while not a large fish (record catches are only around 12–13 pounds) is nevertheless a large prize because of the challenge it presents to the angler. The impact of this feat is better understood by one schooled in the nature of the bonefish—known as one of the most skittish of saltwater fish. Seldom has one been taken on a cast of less than 80 feet, and an accuracy cast greater than this distance with a fly is a task not to be taken lightly. Bonnie also taught her sisters the art and skill of fly-casting. Frankee set a record by catching a 48.5-pound tarpon on 12-pound test line, and she guided others to bonefish in the shadow of her sister's feats.

One of the greatest record holders of the 1990s is Deborah Maddux Dunaway of Texas. She became the first angler in sportfishing history to collect all IGFA billfish world records (1993) and by 1994 had held thirty world records.

Because women have been involved in sportfishing for as long as men, the history of the sport is rich with women record holders and pioneers. Other female record holders can be found in the Hall of Fame, which is governed by the International Women's Fishing Association or in the references listed below.

COMPETITIONS FOR WOMEN

Along with the International Women's Fishing Association—a nonprofit organization formed in 1955 to promote competition among women anglers, to support catch-and-release tournaments, and to encourage conservation—one can find more information about women in fishing from Bass 'n Gal, founded by Sugar Ferris in 1976.

Bass 'n Gal has over 30,000 members and many affiliated clubs throughout the United States and Canada. The organization hosts invitational tournaments, a world championship, and an annual Affiliate Club Tournament of Champions, as well as publishing a bimonthly *Bass 'n Gal* magazine. Women's championships are also held in conjunction with men's events sponsored by the American Bass Association, the American Casting Association, and the Billfish Foundation.

Debra Ann Ballinger

See also Wilderness Adventure

Bibliography

Foggia, Lyla. (1995) *Reel Women: The World of Women Who Fish.* Hillsboro, OR: Beyond Words Publishing.

Fong, Christine. (1996) "Women in Fly Fishing." <www.fbn-flyfish.com/womenff/wiffl.htm>.

Menke, Frank G., Willard Mullin, and Victor Yacktman. (1955) *The Pictorial Encyclopedia of Sports: New and Revised Edition.* Chicago: Progress Research Corporation.

Menke, Frank G., and Suzanne Treat. (1975) *The Encyclopedia of Sports: 5th Revised Edition.* Cranbury, NJ: A.S. Barnes.

Morris, Holly, ed. (1998) *Uncommon Waters: Women Write About Fishing.* Seattle, WA: Seal Press.

Wellner, Alison S. (1997) *Americans at Play: Demographics of Outdoor Recreation and Travel.* Ithaca, NY: New Strategist Publications.

Wulff, Joan Salvato. (1991) *Joan Wulff's Fly Fishing: Expert Advice from a Woman's Perspective.* Mechanicsburg, PA: Stackpole.

Zepatos, Thalia. (1994) *Adventures in Good Company: The Complete Guide to Women's Tours and Outdoor Trips.* Portland, OR: Eighth Mountain Press.

FLEMING, PEGGY

(1948–)

U.S. AMERICAN FIGURE SKATER

Peggy Fleming was a world and Olympic champion figure skater in the 1960s. After her skating

Peggy Fleming competing at the National Championships in Philadelphia, Pennsylvania, in 1968. (Corbis/Bettmann)

career ended, she became a strong advocate for women's sports and later, after battling breast cancer, a high-profile spokeswoman for breast cancer education and prevention.

Fleming was born on 27 July 1948 in San Jose, California. She started to skate at age nine and soon afterward began to train for competition. In 1960, 1961, and 1963, she won the Pacific Coast juvenile, novice, and senior ladies championships, respectively. In 1962 she placed second in the national novice ladies championships. At age fifteen, Fleming won the first of her five national senior ladies championships. At the 1964 Olympics in Innsbruck, Austria, she placed sixth. She kept her national title in 1965 and finished third at the world championships.

When her first coach, Billy Kipp, died with the entire U.S. figure skating team in an airplane crash, Fleming turned to the world-renowned coach Carlo Fassi, whose school was based in Colorado Springs. Fleming moved there with her family to prepare for the 1966 world championships in Davos, Switzerland. That February Fleming became the first American woman in ten years to win the world figure skating championship, but tragedy struck immediately after that victory: her greatest fan, her father, died of a heart attack. Even without his encouragement, she took the 1967 and 1968 world championships. In 1968 Fleming captured the only gold medal awarded to a U.S. athlete in the winter Olympics in Grenoble, France. In March of that year, shortly after she won the world championship in Geneva, Fleming retired from amateur competition.

After her retirement from amateur skating, Peggy skated professionally and also worked as a television commentator, first for NBC and then for ABC. An active supporter of women in sports, she has served on the advisory board of the Women's Sport Foundation, as a goodwill ambassador for UNICEF, and as a member of the President's Council on Physical Fitness.

Fleming is remembered for fluid, rhythmic movements that contrast with the more aggressively athletic styles of many of the skaters that followed her.

Almost thirty years after winning the gold medal in Grenoble, Fleming underwent surgery for breast cancer. With the poise, grace, and strength that she demonstrated in her years on the ice, she faced this "life Olympics" head on. Then, instead of quietly fighting the battle, she added her voice to others on the education of the public about breast cancer and breast cancer prevention.

Janet Luehring-Lindquist

Bibliography

Morse, Charles, and Ann Morse. (1974) *Peggy Fleming.* Mankato: MN: Creative Education Society.

Van Steenwyk, Elizabeth. (1978) *Peggy Fleming: Cameo of a Champion.* New York: McGraw-Hill.

Young, Stephanie. (1984) *Peggy Fleming: Portrait of an Ice Skater.* New York: Avon Books.

FLYING *see* Air Sports, Long Distance Flying

FLYING DISC

The flying disc is one of those rarities, a toy that started as a game and developed into a sport. Most disc games bear striking resemblance to ball sports, such as golf, soccer, track and field, and even dodgeball. The popularity of disc sports continues to grow, particularly since they are enjoyed by men and women of all ages and abilities.

HISTORY

Most people know flying discs as Frisbees, in much the same way that they call any brand of in-line skates Rollerblades. The term *Frisbee* comes from the Frisbie Pie Company, a bakery that grew from a small local bakery in New Haven, Connecticut, in 1900 to a large chain throughout New England by 1940.

The Frisbie company offered a variety of baked goods, including pies and cookies. Each pie came in a round metal pie pan, and the cookies came in a round cookie tin with a lid. This has produced two schools of thought on the origin of the disc. The more popular version has the pie pan as the precursor. Proponents claim that Yale University students bought the pies and tossed the pans around campus, yelling "Frisbie!" to signal the receiver. The other camp claims that the cookie tin lid was first. This might be more credible because a cookie tin lid more closely resembles the modern disc with the edges turned in instead of flared.

After World War II, Fred Morrison blended two of the hot topics of the time, plastic and flying saucers, to create the first flying disc in 1948. The now legendary Pluto Platter was first mass-produced in 1951. In 1957 the founders of the Wham-O company bought the rights to the disc when they saw people sailing them around southern California beaches. Wham-O began national distribution to help push sales. On a trip to Ivy League campuses, they found students "frisbie-ing" pie tins around. With no idea of the historical origins, they registered the name "Frisbee" in 1959. Ironically, that was one year after the Frisbie Pie Company closed.

Disc sports burgeoned in the late 1960s. Ultimate Frisbee was invented in Maplewood, New Jersey, in 1967. That same year, the Olympic Frisbee Federation was formed with the goal of making Frisbee an Olympic event, and the International Frisbee Association (IFA) was founded. In 1969, while men walked on the moon, the U.S. Army invested $400,000 to see if the disc could be used as a weapon.

The popularity of the disc continued, with new sports coming in rapid succession. The first disc golf (originally called *folf* for "Frisbee golf") tournament was held in 1969, along with distance and accuracy contests at an IFA "All Comers Meet" in Pasadena, California. Freestyle was first performed in 1973. The first world Frisbee championships (WFC) were held the next year, and double disc court (which is dealt with in the next section) was sanctioned in 1978.

In the late 1970s and early 1980s, new organizations sprouting up all over the world began using the term *disc* instead of *Frisbee* since there were so many manufacturers in the market. The European Flying Disc Federation (EFDF) was founded in 1981. Then, in 1983, both the IFA, with 100,000 members in thirty countries, and the WFC were canceled. The World Flying Disc Federation (WFDF) was formed by the EFDF in 1984, and it now serves as the governing body of the major flying disc sports.

The various flying disc sports are open to men and women, sometimes together on coed teams. Because disc sports developed in the 1970s and 1980s when men and women competed in the same sports, participation is very high among both sexes. Most of the sports started with men's competition, but invariably women had their own divisions within a year or two, and coed categories soon followed.

Women who have distinguished themselves with major championships in several different disc sports include Monika Lou (late 1970s) in freestyle, self-caught flight (SCF), distance, accuracy, and overall; Judy Horowitz (early 1980s) in disc golf, freestyle, double disc court (DDC), SCF, accuracy, and overall; Tami Pellicane (throughout the 1980s) in disc golf, DDC, SCF, distance, and overall; Amy Bekken (early 1990s) in disc golf, freestyle, DDC, SCF, distance, accuracy, and over-

all; and Anni Kreml (1990s) in disc golf, DDC, SCF, distance, and accuracy. The freestyle team of Stacy Anderson and Carolyn Yabe ruled the 1980s, taking U.S. Open titles from 1983 through 1988 and world championships in 1983 and 1984. Ultimate Frisbee has seen two women's teams dominate: the Lady Condors from Santa Barbara won the world championships (held every two years) from 1986 through 1990, the world club championship in 1989, and the Ultimate Players Association (UPA) U.S. Nationals from 1984 through 1987. The team Lady Godiva of Boston won the world club championships in 1991 and the UPA U.S. Nationals in 1988 and 1991.

RULES AND PLAY

Flying discs is not one sport but a series of related events. The two basic skills are throwing for distance and accuracy in throwing, and these events are held on their own or in conjunction with other competitions. Their elements can be found in most other disc sports. In some disc competitions where several events are staged, an overall winner is declared among all the competitors. This is typically the person or team that either wins the most events or has the highest overall scores.

The first disc sport was called "guts." It involves trying to throw the disc past another team. As a natural offshoot of a game of catch, it has the simplest rules. Two teams of one to five players each line up on parallel lines 15 yards apart. Teams alternate throwers until one team reaches 21 points. Guts can be played indoors or outdoors.

The first intercollegiate Ultimate Frisbee game was played between Rutgers and Princeton in 1972 on the 103rd anniversary of the first intercollegiate football game (which was also played by the two schools). Ultimate is a seven-player team game in which players pass the disc to one another but cannot move with it. This is a non-contact sport; blocking and setting picks or screens are prohibited. It is also self-refereed, with players calling their own fouls.

The first permanent disc golf course was built in Pasadena, California, in 1975, six years after the first official tournament. The object of the game, as with the strokes in regular golf, is to get

Two women compete in the 1977 Frisbee Championship in Irvine, California. (Neal Preston/Corbis)

through the course with the fewest number of throws. Most permanent courses have "pole holes," elevated metal baskets into which the disc must land to hole out. Courses can be set up for 9, 18, 24, or 27 holes, depending on the space available. Terrain and landscaping vary greatly, but the more trees and other obstacles, the greater the challenge. Many a disc golf game has been played through a college campus with various monuments, buildings, and other permanent objects serving as "holes."

Freestyle is the most artistic of the disc sports, as competitors attempt to catch the disc with the most flair and style. While players were probably trying to impress one another (and onlookers) all along, the first freestyle competition took place in a Toronto tournament in 1974. Freestyle can be performed by individuals as well as two- or three-person teams. Judges base their scoring on three criteria: difficulty, execution, and presentation. Within the freestyle category is the crowd-pleasing dog competition. Freestyle can be played either indoors or outdoors.

Double disc court is played by two teams of two players each with two discs in play at once. Each team has a 13-meter-square (about 140-square-foot) court to defend from attack. The courts are set 17 meters (18.5 yards) apart, and each has a judge to determine scoring. Attacks are made in two ways: by making one of the discs come to rest in the opposing team's court without going out of bounds or by causing both discs to be touched by a player or players of the other team at the same time.

Self-caught flight is a field event that combines two of the mainstays of disc competition, maximum time aloft (MTA) and throw run catch (TRC). Whereas MTA measures the time a player's disc is in the air from throw to one-handed catch, TRC measures the distance from the point at which a player throws the disc to the point at which it is caught, again with one hand. Much like other multidiscipline sports such as decathlon and heptathlon, the two events are combined by awarding a single sum of points based on scores.

Discathon is a race in which players throw their discs, one at a time in accordance with a call to throw every 30 seconds from the official, through a circuitous 1-kilometer course. The route is defined by obstacles called "tests" and "mandatories," which are typically tall trees or poles. Each mandatory describes a required flight path. The discs must follow the entire course, but the players do not have to. As the players move around the course, the more efficient throwers move into the lead. The object is to complete the course in the shortest time possible, and successful competitors are both talented throwers and swift runners.

CONCLUSION

First played and developed by the baby boomer generation, the various sports included in flying discs continue to grow in popularity. As these players age, they are teaching the fun and challenge of disc sports to their children. Another reason for the popularity of disc sports is that they lend themselves to coed play, in which men and women often compete side by side—as well as head to head.

Jim Hunstein

Bibliography

Pro Disc Golf Association. (1999) <http://www.pdga.com>.

Ultimate Players Association. (1999) <http://www.upa.org>.

World Flying Disc Federation. (1999) <http://www.wfdf.org>.

FOOTBAG

The term *footbag* encompasses a group of games that are all based on kicking a small, beanbaglike object. Kinds of play range from simply kicking the footbag to keeping it airborne to more precise games, such as footbag golf. Footbag has outgrown the basic circle game that had only two rules—"Don't say you're sorry," and "No hands"—and it has become firmly entrenched in popular culture. Approximately a quarter of footbag competitors are women.

Footbag's foot-flapping rhythm reaches across gender and age lines, but circles are mostly seen in town squares and on school campuses. The Internet has brought together footbag players from around the world. In 1999 there were 169 footbag clubs in 23 countries, and circles can be found from Denmark to New Zealand. Finland has a footbag club of more than 300 people, and the sport is gathering momentum in Eastern European countries.

HISTORY

Footbag originated in July 1972 at Clackamas Community College in Oregon City, Oregon, when two young men were waiting in the same line. One of them, Mike Marshall, pulled a little round beanbag from his pocket and started to kick it around in the way that he had been shown by a Native American friend. John Stalberger, a natural athlete, picked up the idea quickly and almost immediately took to the kicking game of keeping this beanbag in the air. This chance meeting resulted in a fast friendship and in the invention of what they called the "Hacky Sack," which Stalberger patented in 1975. (The rights were eventually sold to Wham-O, which holds the trademark to the name.) Millions of Hacky Sacks have been sold worldwide, and the sport of footbag has taken what promises to be an enduring place in pop culture.

The original footbag has been refined since the days of the simple beanbag. In 1974 it was a button-filled pancake-shaped object, but it evolved into the baseball-style two-panel design that Stalberger patented. The National Hacky Sack Association (NHSA) was formed in 1977 to promote the sport and market the Hacky Sack footbag. A little house in Oregon City was the headquarters for the NHSA. In 1977 the advent of the toe delay move—delaying the footbag on the top of the toes, the first "move," or technique, that was developed—and the invention of the footbag net game changed the sport forever.

The event recognized as the first world championship game was held in July 1980 in Oregon City. The events were footbag net and consecutives, and anyone able to pay the entry fee of $2.50 could enter. Women's divisions were established at the 1981 world championships. Footbag freestyle was added as an event at the 1983 world championships. The World Footbag Association (WFA), formed in 1983, is now located in Steamboat Springs, Colorado. The WFA organized the world championships in Colorado from 1984 to 1993; since then the games have been held in San Francisco, Montreal, and Portland, Oregon.

The footbag player with the most world championship titles is Tricia George. George, a West Linn, Oregon, resident, gathered forty-seven titles in world championships from 1983 to 1999. George came from a soccer background and thrives on the challenge of keeping a footbag airborne.

In 1985 Constance Constable—the current world record holder of the women's consecutive kicks (24,713) and a resident of Seaside, California—began promoting "Women Alive and Kicking" to generate women players in Colorado. Her campaign brought in a fresh wave of talent in the mid-1980s.

One player, Sam Conlon of San Francisco, stands head and shoulders above the rest in the women's freestyle. Conlon won her first singles freestyle title in 1987 and matured in the 1990s into a seemingly unbeatable player, winning six singles titles in seven years. She teamed with Lisa McDaniel in women's team freestyle and won five women's team freestyle titles. At the 1997 world championships, Conlon's team placed third in the open team freestyle.

Jody Welch has ruled women's footbag net; no player, male or female, has more world champion titles in that version of the sport. Jody has teamed with her husband, Brent, to appear in mixed doubles footbag net finals.

The World-Wide Footbag Foundation, Inc. (WWFF), founded in 1994, is a nonprofit organization dedicated to promoting the alternative sport of footbag. Based in Santa Clara, California, the WWFF has been instrumental in increasing the profile of footbag as a healthful sport and is now focused on promoting the sport of footbag through the Internet as well as by fostering growth of the sport through demonstrations, support, education, and dissemination of information.

RULES AND PLAY

Competitive footbag is governed by the International Footbag Advisory Board (IFAB), which publishes the official rule book, *Rules of Footbag Sports*. The IFAB is a board composed of players and members of the footbag community whose purpose is to monitor and guide the sport of footbag as it grows. It is a sanctioning body and a rules organization, constructing and modifying rules of footbag games played in competition. The result of this work is the IFAB rule book, published annually to reflect the latest rules of all footbag sports.

Four types of footbag predominated in the 1990s. Footbag net is a singles or doubles court game, like tennis or volleyball, where players use only their feet to kick the footbag over a 5-foot-high net. The rules for doubles net are similar to those for volleyball: players are allowed three kicks per side and must alternate kicks. In singles, however, players are allowed only two kicks per side. The footbag (which is usually a thirty-two-panel vinyl ball) may not contact a player's body except below the knee.

Footbag freestyle is an artistic form of the sport. It can be a flurry of difficult moves that the eye can hardly follow, or it can be smooth and flowing as if in slow motion. This variety makes freestyle competitions difficult to judge. To simplify the task, competitors are judged along four dimensions: choreography, difficulty, variety, and execution.

Players choreograph routines to music and are judged on how well their style of play matches their choice of music. They are also judged on their originality and creativity. Each move or trick has a determinable difficulty rating. The average difficulty of each move and the total difficulty of all the moves in the routine are added together to determine a player's difficulty rating. Difficulty is measured in "adds," which represent additional levels of difficulty beyond the basic moves. (A toe delay is one "add.") A list of many well-known freestyle moves is in Section 509 of the IFAB *Rules of Footbag Sports*.

Footbag golf is a game of accuracy, much like disc golf. The "hole" is a cone open at the top; holes are placed around the course. Games are usually played in two rounds of eighteen holes per round, although nine-hole rounds are sometimes played. Footbag consecutive is the simplest form of the game. The player must keep the footbag in the air using only the feet and knees. Dropping the footbag ends the rally.

Kendall Kic

Bibliography

Footbag WorldWide Footbag Information Service (1999) <http://www.footbag.org>.

Additional information was provided by Ted Huff, The Footbag Historical Society (Camas, WA), and the World Footbag Association (Steamboat Springs, CO).

FOOTBALL

American football, a ball game that is a nineteenth-century adaption of the English rugby football, is generally considered the most male of American sports. The game, with its now banned "flying wedge" and violent tackling, has often been seen as a brutal sport. At other times it has been proclaimed as properly virile and thus good training for American boys. Although women's football has received very little attention, women have played football on high school teams, on local men's teams, and in their own leagues during the 1960s and 1970s. There has even been some international participation in the sport, with several women's teams developing in Japan. This history is virtually unknown and is just beginning to be explored as a part of women's history and U.S. national heritage.

The male aspect of the sport extends beyond the playing field to the fans, where it was believed that women could not possibly understand or appreciate this physical sport. (The 1990s saw the initiation of classes in football appreciation targeted for women audiences.) Women on the playing field, especially the professional football field, broke all kinds of societal norms and left many people to question either the seriousness or the femininity of women players. But professional female football players have always wanted to be athletes first and foremost. As Jennie Talancon, a player with the Los Angeles Dandelions, pointed out, "Oh, we're not for women's lib. Equal pay for sure, but not that bra-burning stuff." "They are not trying to prove to the world they can beat men," noted Bill Ballow, offensive coach for the Cleveland Brewers, in the *Cleveland Plain Dealer* (Neff, 1983). "They're proving they can play football."

Playing football requires strength and skills that have generally been associated with males, and so it has been difficult for women to break into the ranks of football. A professional female football player from the 1970s expressed the sentiment of many fans that watched the Toledo Troopers play. "Sure, it's OK for women to play golf and tennis, but lots of people just don't think that women should be playing football" (Lorenz, 1974). Sentiments like these have made it hard for women to field teams because support was so limited.

PARTICIPATION IN SCHOOLS

The passage of Title IX of the U.S. Higher Education Act in 1972 (prohibiting discrimination on the basis of sex in any educational program receiving federal funds, including athletic programs) helped open some doors, especially at the high school and college level, but football was not a high priority because it was assumed that not many young women would want to play.

An early pioneer was Frankie Groves, who played tackle for her high school team in 1947. In August 1973, fourteen-year-old Tony Ilher joined her school's junior varsity team after the California Interscholastic Federation ruled that girls could play on boys' teams in all high school sports without exception. Ilher played as a defensive tackle for the Portola Tigers in one game, which they won 23–0. Another California squad let 90-pound Diane Thompson on their team as a tackle for one game. In Washington State in late 1973, two sisters—Carol Darrin, age fourteen, and Delores Darrin, age sixteen—joined the Wishkah Valley high school team. They sat on the bench while awaiting a judge's decision on their playing status.

PROFESSIONAL PLAY

One of the earliest reported attempts to establish a professional women's football league was in 1941. The opening game was scheduled for 28 June 1941 at Spencer Coal Park in Chicago between the Chicago Rockets and Chicago Bombers. The Rockets were coached by former Chicago Bears center Ches Chesney. Results of the game were not reported.

The first league began in Cleveland, Ohio, in 1965, with eight original franchises. The Women's Professional Football League (WPFL) was led by Sid Friedman, a Cleveland theatrical agent, who put up his own money and convinced his business associates to do the same. The league played in the Ohio cities of Cleveland, Toledo, Akron, Bowling Green, Dayton, and Cincinnati, as well as Buffalo, New York, and Pittsburgh, Pennsylvania.

In the 1970s two events involving men's football actually seemed to draw more national attention than the women's league: the Orlando Panthers signed as their place-kick holder Pat Palinkas, whose husband was also a player; and in 1973 the Philadelphia Eagles decided to deny a tryout for wide receiver to Joan Kors. Kors was a legal secretary by trade and the feeling existed that she ought to stay in that job and not upset the male football world by trying to enter it.

In 1974 representatives from the WPFL and some additional businessmen met in Los Angeles to create the National Women's Football League (NWFL), with seven franchises: the Toledo Troopers, Columbus Pacesetters, Detroit Demons, Fort Worth Shamrocks, Dallas Blue Bonnets, Los Angeles Dandelions, and Pasadena Mustangs. Philadelphia and San Antonio registered teams as associate members in 1976, and Cleveland joined in 1979. The first commissioner, William Stout, co-owned the Toledo Troopers while he worked as a supervisor in a factory. He sold his interest in the Troopers in 1979 and was succeeded by Neil Laughy of Lawton, Oklahoma. In the meantime,

Female football players, 1920. (Minnesota Historical Society/Corbis)

a rival (but short-lived) American Professional Football League was formed in 1978.

The NWFL survived into the early 1980s. It had three divisions: West, South, and East, although the East division later became the North. Team owners chose the president-commissioner, and the league followed most National Football League (NFL) rules. Exceptions included twelve-minute quarters, sudden-death overtime in the case of a tie, kickoffs from the 45-yard line rather than the 35-yard line, and conversion points after touchdowns got one point for the run and two for the kick. Five officials were used, but few statistics or records were kept. (This was an area the league did not excel in although they did appeal to Ohio State University for assistance in developing a form for their statisticians.)

The usual playing year under this system lasted from July through October, with about twelve games. Practices began in early May. Owners worked year-round raising money, generating publicity, and leasing stadiums for games. All salaries were part-time though each team made their own decisions on what to pay. No league minimums existed. The league did create a minimum playing age of eighteen unless the parents gave permission, which a number did. The average age of the players was in the early twenties, with a few playing well into their thirties. For example, in 1979 the Toledo quarterback Brigitte Hartz of Stuttgart, Germany, was thirty-six, even though she had only started playing in 1977. Tackle Jo McFarland was a rookie for the Columbus Pacesetters at age thirty-four.

All the players in the league had other occupations, were married with children, or were in college. Quite a number also played other sports besides football. The difference was that the

NWFL gave them the opportunity to play professionally, which most other sports did not. For example, Sunday Jones, a receiver for Toledo, worked as a singer/entertainer and hairdresser, and was also an All-American basketball player. Brenda Baskins, Toledo fullback, and Jane Haley, a wide receiver-defensive end for Toledo, were both amateur softball players as well. Between games Jo Ellen Opfer, center/linebacker on the field, worked as a surgical technician at Mercy Hospital in Toledo.

Players received between $5.00 and $50.00 a game during the regular season. The amount depended on the team's financial resources as well as the position played. Quarterbacks and wide receivers received the highest pay, whereas kickers and linebackers fell on the lowest end of the pay scale. League star Linda Jefferson of Toledo received $50 a game for her incredible running feats. Money for these salaries came from fundraisers, special promotions, and ticket sales. Ticket prices ranged from $1.00 to $3.50, with attendance between 500 and 1,000 fans at most games.

Male coaches prowled the sidelines for all teams until 1978. The majority had played the game themselves at some point in their careers. For example, Dallas Blue Bonnets coach Mike Anderson had played semiprofessional ball before turning to coaching. The one exception to the all-male rule was Paralee Adams. She helped coach the Columbus Pacesetters in 1978 after she was injured and could not play the remainder of the season.

The Toledo Troopers became the dominant team in the NWFL and won seven championships. They were led by league MVP, player number 32, Linda Jefferson. Jefferson traveled regularly for the league, trying to generate interest and sponsorship. She appeared as a speaker at the Football Hall of Fame, and on ABC network television for the "Battle of the Stars." Her accomplishments as a halfback put her reputation as a player on a par with the best male professionals of her day. By 1976 Jefferson had scored 72 career touchdowns and had four 1,000-yard seasons. At 5 feet 4 inches and 125 pounds, Jefferson became known as the "O. J. Simpson of women's pro football."

Another league standout was 1977 Rookie of the Year Lee Anderson. After high school Anderson played quarterback for the Columbus Pacesetters. In her rookie year, she rushed for 365 yards on sixty-three carries, had eleven touchdowns, and 191 yards passing. Andie Dameron led the Pacesetters with fifty-two tackles and eighteen assists at center in the 1977–78 season. In high school as a star athlete, Dameron had lettered in volleyball, basketball, and track. Graphic artist Paula Dewey ran for 431 yards on fifty-two carries and scored four touchdowns as a halfback for Columbus.

Professional female football players have not been limited to the United States. In 1986 three teams began playing in Japan. The Dai-Ichi Mutual Life Insurance Company sponsored the Lady Kongs, a twenty-two-member team with five male coaches. They played against the Osaka Wildcats, who were sponsored by the Kogin Bank. The Sumitomo Life Insurance Company supported a third team, called the Blue Sky Angels.

ACCEPTANCE ISSUES

All teams struggled for survival, regardless of the talents of their players. They had to overcome negative images and stereotypes in order to get

WOMEN'S PROFESSIONAL FOOTBALL LEAGUE REVIVED

A professional football league for women was founded in the Midwest in 1999. The first two teams were the Minnesota Vixens and Lake Michigan Minx. The teams were composed of women who had played football in high school or in junior leagues or who had participated in other sports. The teams barnstormed the region to build interest in the league and attract media attention and corporate sponsorship. Plans call for teams to be added in Green Bay, Chicago, and other cities.

fans out to watch them play. They had to work at being taken seriously as players and not just seen as a curiosity or a joke. Commissioner William Stout stated the problem and its solution when he remarked, "A lot of people come out to laugh. They think it's a joke or something. But when the game starts and they see these girls play, they realize it's a football game. These girls play great football" (Lorenz, 1974). But not everyone agreed with Stout's assessment of league caliber of play; most agreed instead that what they saw qualified as good high school football.

Media coverage did not always help break the negative images. Often words such as *skepticism*, *curiosity*, *freak*, or *joke* could be found in the articles. Headlines focused on these women as women first and football players second; for example, "The Akron (Female) Wildcats All Want to Play Fullback" or "Toledo Gals Win in Pro Football." These headlines not only declared the gender of the players prominently but also tended to use less than serious terms, such as *gal*, *babe*, *sweetheart*, or *girls* to describe these professional athletes.

Players had to deal with adverse publicity and reactions from fans and family alike. Jackie Allen, a middle guard for the Troopers, said, "When you're a woman football player, you're automatically labeled big, fat and ugly, or gay. Nobody ever brought that up about a softball or basketball player or even a woman in the Olympics. . . . After playing football for nine years, I feel no less feminine than before" (National Football Hall of Fame, file on NWFL). Playing football did not suddenly change the gender of the participants, but it did challenge the gender roles society traditionally assigned to men and women.

CONCLUSION

Female football players, no matter where they played, faced many barriers, but this has not prevented them from getting out on the field. The history of the three professional leagues in the United States show both the quality of play and the difficulties associated with trying to support such ventures. Currently, efforts in women's basketball and the Olympics are opening doors for women's participation in football but, in this peculiarly male stronghold, full equity remains a distant goal.

Leslie Heaphy

Bibliography

Holmes, Monique. (1998) "Off the Bat, Women's Football 101." <http://sports.competitor.net/archive/footb101/>.

Lorenz, Tom. (1974) "Coming of Age on Colony Field." *Toledo Blade* (10 November): 4–10, 12, 14.

National Football Hall of Fame, Canton, Ohio. Files labeled "Women in Football" and "National Women's Football League."

Neff, James. (1983) "Football Female." *Cleveland Plain Dealer* (10 November): 25A.

Rapoport, Ron. (1974) "Wham, Bam, Thank You Ma'am." *Women Sports* (November).

Rasmussen, Cecilia. (1996) "Rare Blooms in the Field of Athletics." *Los Angeles Times* (22 January): B 3.

"She's the OJ Simpson." (1976) *Akron Beacon Journal* (20 June).

FOOTBALL, ASSOCIATION

see Soccer

FOOTBALL, FLAG

Flag football, like touch football, is an adaptation of the full-contact version of American football (sometimes called *gridiron football*). Flag football makes stopping play more difficult than in touch football by requiring defenders to pull a flag attached to a belt worn by the ball carrier rather than tackling or touching the runner. The game is popular in the United States and throughout the world, and a variety of organizations offer men's, women's, coed, and youth leagues. Although flag football has been played since the 1950s, no single organization has emerged to govern the development of rules and standards within the sport. As a result, many different styles of play have developed, and rules vary greatly from league to league. A women's organization is now actively promoting the sport internationally.

HISTORY

Flag football is generally believed to have started in the U.S. military during World War II. The Army base at Fort Meade, Maryland, has the first recorded history of flag football and is widely regarded as the birthplace of the sport. Now flag football is played worldwide. Formal leagues exist in Canada, France, Germany, Israel, Japan, and Sweden, with informal leagues established in many other countries. The U.S. military was a primary agent in bringing U.S.-style flag football to the rest of the world. In many cases, U.S. soldiers played football informally at military bases in various countries, and this led to the creation of touch and flag leagues.

The flag version of American football is a low-cost form of the game that offered athletes in other countries an inexpensive way to experience a sport that many had watched on television. But until the creation of the International Women's Flag Football Association in 1997, the diffusion of flag football resulted mainly in the expansion of opportunities for men across the world to participate in the sport.

The oldest of the national governing bodies is the National Touch and Flag League (NTFL) in the United States. Founded in 1960, the NTFL offers touch and flag football for adult men and women at various levels of competition through leagues, tournaments, and a national championship. The United States Flag and Touch Football League (USFTL) is a rival organization, founded in 1988 in response to the myriad flag football styles and rules practiced in the United States. In addition to providing competitions in the form of leagues and tournaments for men, women, and children, the USFTL trains and certifies officials and produces educational aids for flag football participants. Each of the leagues is self-contained although opportunities exist to compete against teams in other leagues at annual tournaments.

Flag football is played in schools, universities, and recreational leagues throughout the world. Many students are introduced to the sport of football through a noncontact flag version of the game played in physical education classes. Campus recreation services at many universities offer intramural leagues with men's, women's, and coed divisions. In fact, teams from U.S. universities can compete in a national championship held at a major professional football stadium in conjunction with a National Football League (NFL) game. Recreational leagues are, in the main, offered by local recreation councils. Local teams or leagues

may then affiliate with a national organization, adopting the rules and regulations of that governing body.

RULES AND PLAY

Flag football equipment consists of a football and one flag belt per player. Flag belts vary in the number of flags (strips of fabric) attached and the manner in which those flags adhere to the belt. An opponent needs to pull just one of the flags in order to stop play. All belts have at least two flags—one placed on each hip although some belts add a third flag attached to the rear of the belt. Initially the flags were simply tucked into the belt, but the advent of Velcro allowed flags to be attached more firmly and helped eliminate the problem of flags falling off without being touched. Dirt and grime, however, were easily embedded in the hook and loop system of the Velcro, and this created new problems in keeping the flags attached.

To solve the flag attachment problem, most leagues and tournaments have adopted one of two styles. The first is a more secure two-flag belt featuring a ball-and-socket flag attachment that pops loudly when pulled and makes it unlikely that the flag will be knocked off inadvertently. The second is a three-flag belt to which the flags are permanently attached. In this system, the belt is secured with an alligator clip (a small, spring-loaded clip that looks much like the jaws of an alligator). When the defender grips the flag, the entire belt is detached rather than just the flag. As with other styles of flag belts, the defender needs to pull only one flag to stop play.

Although no standard rules and regulations for flag football exist, the majority of leagues across the world begin with the rules and regulations of the American football code. Games are played on a rectangular field either 100 or 80 yards long (90 or 72 meters). The number of players per side varies from four to nine, but most leagues consist of teams of between seven and nine players per side. Each team is given four chances, or downs, to move the ball 10 yards (9 meters). Some flag leagues mark the field in 20-yard (18-meter) increments and require a team to move the ball to the next yard marker to receive a new set of downs. Scoring is similar to the contact version of football: six points for a touchdown, three for a field goal, two for a safety, and either one or two for a point after a touchdown, that is, a conversion.

Not all flag leagues include opportunities to kick field goals or extra points. This allows the game to be played in areas that do not have goalposts. In this version of the game, teams can still choose to try for either a one- or two-point conversion: a one-point conversion begins from the 3-yard line (2.7 meters), whereas a two-point conversion typically begins from the 10-, 15-, or 20-yard line (9, 14, or 18 meters).

The majority of leagues, although they do not adhere to uniform rules and regulations, can be characterized by one of three basic styles of play: (1) flag football, (2) screen flag football, or (3) ineligible lineman flag football. Both flag football and ineligible-lineman flag football allow full-contact blocking anywhere on the field. As a result, this style of play tends to encourage teams to incorporate a strong running component in their offensive strategies. Screen flag football, on the other hand, prohibits any blocking. Instead, players screen defenders from the ball carrier or quarterback without using their hands (similar to defending in basketball). This style of play favors a strong passing game. Screen flag football is usually the style of play chosen for coed leagues. The major difference between flag and ineligible-lineman flag is, as the name implies, the capacity of linemen to receive a pass and advance the ball. Once again, this results in a slightly different style of play, with different physical requirements for those playing the line; that is, a guard or center in a flag league would typically be slightly smaller and more mobile than an ineligible lineman.

FLAG FOOTBALL FOR WOMEN

Women have been competing in flag football since the 1950s. Although schools, universities, and recreational leagues now offer flag football leagues for women, these leagues represent a very small proportion of league offerings. For example, the USFTL offers seven national championship events for men's teams, one for coed teams, and one for women's teams. The NTFL's Super Bowl does not include any events for women. In 1995 the National Women's Flag Football Association (NWFFA) was created, representing the first organization devoted to the enhancement of women's flag football. The NWFFA was founded by Diane Beruldsen in an at-

tempt to link the women's leagues, teams, players, and officials to promote the sport of women's flag football. The NWFFA is an organization run by women with a vision of making flag football a professional sport for women. The NWFFA runs the largest women's flag football tournament in the world—the KWWFFL/FLAG-A-TAG National Kickoff in Key West, Florida—as well as regional tournaments in the United States.

The success of the NWFFA spurred the same group of women to create the International Women's Flag Football Association (IWFFA). The association was responsible for starting women's teams in Norway, Denmark, and the Netherlands. In addition to developing teams in Europe, the IWFFA sponsors clinics for girls and women throughout North America.

CONCLUSION

At present, most women playing flag football are in their early thirties and beyond. It is a sport that women grow up watching but seldom have opportunities to participate in beyond a backyard game. The challenge facing women's flag football is to encourage and support the creation of opportunities to participate in the sport—opportunities not only for women but also for girls. Flag football offers girls and women a place to celebrate their strength, power, and physicality even though these attributes are typically associated with masculinity. Through flag football, girls and women can develop and promote a strong and forceful image of the female in society. On the field, strength and power are not only accepted but are encouraged.

B. Christine Green

Bibliography

Ferrell, J.M., and M.A. Ferrell. (1980) *Coaching Flag Football*. Champaign, IL: Human Kinetics.

Green, B. Christine, and Laurence Chalip. (1998) "Sport Tourism as a Celebration of Subculture: The Ethnography of a Women's Football Tournament." *Annals of Tourism Research* 25:275–291.

Johnson, James. (1992) *Flag Football: The Worldwide Game*. Boston, MA: American Press. National Intramural-Recreation Sports Association.

NIRSA Flag and Touch Football Rules and Officials Manual. (1992) Corvallis, OR: NIRSA.

Windemuth, Timothy Martin. (1992) *Flagball for the 90s*. Reston, VA: National Association for Sport and Physical Education.

FOOTBALL, GAELIC

Gaelic football is a variation of football in which players carry, kick, or punch the ball to reach the opposing team's goal. It is the fastest-growing sport in Ireland among both women and men, and its introduction to other countries by Irish immigrants has actually made women's Gaelic football more popular outside Ireland.

HISTORY

Gaelic football traces its roots back to the seventh century, when other variants of football also emerged. The specifically Gaelic version is relatively modern and is one of the few games to be overtly political in its origins. In 1884 the Gaelic Athletic Association (GAA) was founded in Thurles, Ireland, as part of the Irish independence movement. The founders developed several games, including Gaelic football, in a deliberate effort to counter the British games that then dominated. The men's rules for Gaelic football were drawn up that same year.

Gaelic football remained a men's game for almost a century. Then the Ladies Gaelic Football Association was founded in 1974, and it has had at the center of its mission statement the goal of involving as many young girls and women in the Irish sport that has, above all others, been traditionally regarded as a male preserve. The women's association has been successful since its inception. In the schools, Gaelic football for girls is a popular alternative to the women's version of hurling, *camogie* (the Irish women's national game, also founded by the GAA).

RULES AND PLAY

The game is an exact copy of the men's game with no rule changes or concessions made because the competitors are women, as happened with the creation of *camogie*. Women's Gaelic football is a contest between two sides of fifteen players each. The pitch, or playing field, is from 129 to 147 meters (140 to 160 yards) long and from 79.5 to 92 meters (84 to 100 yards) wide. The goals at each end of the pitch are an H shape, with the lower part of the posts netted in the same way as soccer goals. Players score one point for kicking the ball over the uprights and three points for propelling the ball into the goal net. The winning side is the one with the greatest number of points. Players are allowed to handle and kick the ball, although they are prohibited from running with the ball more than four steps.

Of the thirty-two Irish counties, twelve compete at the senior level, while a further nineteen also have junior sides. The widespread support for the game at the junior level and its popularity in the school system as an alternative to *camogie* promise that the game's future is secure.

In the formative years of women's Gaelic football, its main stronghold was in the Province of Munster in the southwest of Ireland, as evidenced by Kerry's nine consecutive All-Ireland championships in the 1980s. In the 1990s the game spread across Ireland, and winners of the All-Ireland now come from all over the nation. The growth of the sport is spectacular. It is estimated that in excess of 30,000 Irish women regularly play Gaelic football. In cities in other countries with large Irish immigrant populations, Gaelic football is being taken up as a sport by the women of the diaspora. The Ladies Gaelic Football Association is not officially affiliated with the GAA but is recognized by the larger organization.

CONCLUSION

As a relatively new organization, the Ladies Gaelic Football Association does not appear to have such close links with political nationalism as the GAA, but the popularity of Gaelic football does illustrate how important traditionally Irish forms of sport are within the nation. Its rapid spread outside Ireland suggests that its future is assured.

Mike Cronin

See also Camogie

Bibliography

Cronin, Mike. (1999) *Sport and Nationalism in Ireland: Gaelic Games, Soccer, and Transformations in Irish National Identity since 1884.* Dublin: Four Courts Press.

Cumann Lúthchleas Gael. (1984) *A Century of Service, 1884–1984.* Dublin: Cumann Lúthchleas Gael.

De Búrca, Marcus. (1980) *The GAA. A History of the Gaelic Athletic Association.* Dublin: Cumann Lúthchleas Gael.

Hughes, Anthony. (1997) "The Irish Community." In *Sporting Immigrants*, edited by P.A. Mosely, R. Cashman, J. O'Hara, and H. Weatherburn. Crows Nest, New South Wales: Walla Walla Press.

Nauright, John, and Michael Letters. (1996) "Gaelic Football." In *Encyclopedia of World Sport From Ancient Times to the Present*, edited by D. Levinson and K. Christensen. Santa Barbara, CA: ABC-Clio, 351–354.

FOXHUNTING

Foxhunting is a blood sport in which a group of riders and dogs pursue a fox—if one appears—cross-country until the fox escapes or is killed. It is recreational, not competitive, and is as much a ritual as it is an actual hunt. Traditionally the practice of the wealthy, foxhunting remains an expensive sport. It was also primarily a male sport until the nineteenth century, but today men and women participate in approximately equal numbers.

HISTORY

Hunting foxes with hounds during winter months emerged as a sport in England during the late seventeenth and eighteenth centuries as other games became scarcer. By the early nineteenth century, it had become formalized under the influence of Hugo Meynell (1735–?), who introduced the "scientific" breeding of hounds and established codes of etiquette in the Quorn hunt in Leicestershire, England. His influence was soon felt throughout the country, and by the end of the nineteenth century there were 200 packs of hounds, the structural base of any "hunt"; the numbers have remained more or less constant since that time. Hunt clubs divided the United Kingdom into informally agreed "territories" for this quintessential rural sport, one whose basis was defined as involving a contest with nature and animals. Farming landscapes were often designed to meet the needs of local hunts, whose leading members were usually aristocrats with a considerable influence in their areas. Although most hunting took place on horseback, there were mountainous and marshy areas where the hounds were followed on foot.

Unlike many modern sports, foxhunting was governed by few formal rules and national organizations because such hunting is noncompetitive (theoretically) and locally based. Instead, elaborate codes of behavior were developed that were transmitted by word of mouth, although some appeared in books of etiquette for the socially ambitious. The sport's popularity was due mostly to two factors: it became one avenue by which the aspiring newly rich could be introduced to, and could reinforce, existing rural elites, and it offered entertainment for all social classes as the deferential lower classes watched the rich at play. Foxhunting appeared in other parts of the world, especially throughout the British Empire and its former colonies; in countries such as the United States and Australia, variations were adopted that were suited to local conditions. There were also some hunts in Italy and Spain.

EARLY WOMEN PARTICIPANTS

In its early years, foxhunting was almost entirely a masculine activity, largely because of its associations with aggression, heavy drinking, and the speed of the chase. Women had participated occasionally in earlier forms of hunting on horseback, such as hawking and stag hunting; Queen Elizabeth I (1533–1603) was a formidable rider in the earlier years of her reign, and the Marchioness of Salisbury (d. 1835) ran her own pack of hounds in the 1790s.

The great increase in female participation came in the mid-nineteenth century. Convention (as well as flowing gowns) had dictated that women could ride only sidesaddle instead of astride, and this limited their ability to join in the chase at speed. Around the 1850s new developments in saddlery, and the addition of a pommel, made the use of sidesaddles more secure, and it eventually became acceptable for women to wear riding breeches and boots, provided that these were concealed by a false skirt front that enveloped the rider's legs. Only after World War I did younger women discard their skirts along with the old inhibitions and begin to sit astride their horses.

Within the limits posed by changing attitudes to women's athleticism and the practical physiological implications of menstruation, pregnancy and so on, some active horsewomen became as daring, even as reckless, on the hunting field as many men. The convention that they went through gates opened specially for them gave way by the late Victorian period to their leaping hedges and fences together with male riders. Even so, there was some debate as to whether active hunting made for stronger breeding mothers, or if the aggressive riding inhibited pelvic development if a girl began too young. Most women hunted wearing female versions of male headgear (top and bowler hats) worn over hair nets and veils designed to protect delicate complexions from overexposure to a frequently harsh climate. A tanned face is now acceptable, but hair nets still appear frequently. Like men, most women now wear lightweight protective helmets, after some serious accidents prompted a greater concern with safety. Even so, few hunting seasons pass without some broken bones after falls at hedges and fences.

SOCIAL AND MORAL ISSUES

When women began to hunt regularly in the 1870s, questions of social acceptability became paramount. It was normal for women to reflect the social status of their fathers or husbands and to assess the social credentials of newcomers. Fringe events, such as hunt breakfasts and balls, were useful vehicles for this task. But tensions arose because the subscriptions of new members were essential to maintain the sport in periods of agricultural recession, and this financial need was at odds with the selection and elimination process often organized by the women hunters. Significant problems also arose when established women hunters tried to act as moral arbiters.

Male hunting groups had often existed on the fringes of sexual license, and the occasional appearance of mistresses and courtesans sometimes led to social ostracism. A well-known example illustrates the difficulties this could cause. The most famous courtesan of mid-Victorian England was "Skittles," Catherine Walters (1839–1920), who rose from humble origins to wealth through the beds of aristocratic admirers and who proved to be a courageous and active rider with a quasi-religious enthusiasm for hunting. Attempts by more respectable women to ostracize her collapsed because of the level of male enthusiasm she aroused, as well as the tacit support of a number of women who envied her courage. She compromised by never appearing when her social enemies

rode to hounds. Whatever her moral ambiguity, she did a great deal to popularize the sport among socially ambitious women. Her other legacy has been that the hunting field has remained one of the trusting grounds both for legitimate romance and illicit affairs. In the late twentieth century, Prince Charles's companion, Camilla Parker-Bowles, attracted considerable media attention when riding to hounds, in sharp contrast with Diana, Princess of Wales, who reportedly disliked riding.

WOMEN IN CONTROL

The twentieth century saw a steady increase in the role of women hunters. In some cases it was claimed that hunts were kept in existence during World War I solely by women. There were many instances in the 1920s and 1930s when women outnumbered male riders. In cultures increasingly dependent on mechanized transport, the recreational use of horses grew rapidly, especially among women, and hunting benefited from this enthusiasm.

Equally significant was the growing number of women who took an active part in hunt management. Since the 1790s there have been hunt "patronesses" who presided over the social events that reinforced hunting seasons. Women were in charge of such related sports as otter hunting and beagling before 1914, and the postwar period saw others becoming Masters (never "Mistresses") of Fox Hounds, the titular and organizational head of each hunt, as well as the leading riders on any day out and the final arbiters of etiquette. (They were often called "Dianas," referring to the goddess of hunting.) Even so, these women relied frequently on their husbands' positions and wealth and often shared joint mastership with their spouses. This development marked a partnership in maintaining established local status rather than a new independence or domination by the female masters. Slowly, as foxhunting became a respectable, even essential, part of the ruling classes' female life cycle, the claim died out that women who participated in the sport were defeminized. Women could exhibit, within limits, some of the aggression that had previously been a male preserve.

Perhaps the most bizarre manifestation of women's new level of involvement was the role that hunting mothers took in the sporting initiation rites of their children, male or female. This was the "blooding"; the blood of a newly killed fox was smeared on the child's face using the severed tail or "brush" to do the painting.

CLASS AND GENDER SEGREGATION

In the British context and among its overseas imitators, upper-class women found a new freedom and growing responsibility on the hunting field. Lower-class women appeared largely as spectators, but the later twentieth century saw a small growth in their numbers among the humbler hunting staff, as grooms and kennel maids. Only rarely did they work with the key huntsmen and whippers-in, the professional servants who manage the packs and the apparatus of a day's hunting.

This gender integration is in sharp contrast to practice in the United States, where there are some working-class foot hunts in which men use dogs to chase gray foxes. In the New Jersey pine barrens, for instance, women may appear as distant spectators or drivers of the pickup vehicles, but local social conventions ban them from the actual hunting itself. Gender segregation remains much stronger where other social and sporting activities are similarly divided.

In the growing antihunting movement that has emerged in the United Kingdom, women and men play equal parts, both as hunt saboteurs and in public political campaigns. The appeal is always to consciences over animal welfare rather than to the old claims that foxhunting is defeminizing. The moral argument is couched in strictly egalitarian gender terms.

PICTURE AND PRINT

The iconography of foxhunting has treated women as subordinate subjects, to be painted in group scenes designed largely for the private walls of patrons of the sport. The exceptions appeared in Victorian periodicals, where engravings and photographs were used to emphasize the desirable exclusiveness of the hunting field—the Empress Elizabeth of Austria was a favorite subject. For the same purpose, modern country magazines aimed at the socially aspiring continue to photograph elite women—in Britain, Princess Anne, the Princess Royal and a former Olympic competitor, has proved a favorite subject.

As subjects in hunting literature, women have made a major contribution. For instance, Skittles's hunting exploits occupied part of a mediocre novel during her lifetime: *Skittles: A Biography of a Fascinating Woman* (1864) by W.S. Hayward. One of the most important contributions to the sport's modern popularity came in the novels written jointly by two Irish women. Beginning with *The Silver Fox* in 1879, Edith Oenone Somerville (1858–1949) and Violence Florence Martin (1862–1915) wrote, as "Somerville and Ross," fiction set in the Irish countryside. Action, love, and social conscience went hand in hand to portray foxhunting as an essential part of a romanticized rural order in which hunting women played a key role.

John Lowerson

Bibliography

Blow, Simon. (1983) *Fields Elysian: A Portrait of Hunting Society.* London: J.M. Dent and Sons.

Blyth, Henry. (1970) *Skittles, the Last Victorian Courtesan: The Life and Times of Catherine Walters.* London: Rupert Hart-Davis.

Carr, Raymond. (1976) *English Foxhunting: A History.* London: Weidenfeld and Nicholson.

Ferguson, Gordon. (1993) *The Green Collars: The Tarpoley Hunt Club and Cheshire Hunting History.* London: Quiller Press.

Hufford, Mary T. (1992) *Chaseworld: Foxhunting and Storytelling in New Jersey's Pine Barrens.* Philadelphia: University of Pennsylvania Press.

Itzkowitz, David C. (1977) *Peculiar Privilege: A Social History of English Foxhunting.* Hassocks, England: Harvester.

Lowerson, John. (1993) *Sport and the English Middle Classes, 1870–1914.* Manchester, England: Manchester University Press.

———. (1996) "Foxhunting," in *Encyclopedia of World Sport,* edited by David Levinson and Karen Christensen. Santa Barbara, CA: ABC-Clio, 359–363.

Sinclair, Andrew. (1998) *Death by Fame: The Life of Elizabeth, Empress of Austria.* London: Constable.

FRANCE

France is a Western European nation with a population of 54 million people. The country has a long history of men's participation in many sports, but women were excluded from all but a few sports until the twentieth century. By the late twentieth century, women were active participants in many recreational and elite sports.

HISTORY

In France at the end of the nineteenth century, three forms of physical activity were most common. The first and most popular was developed within gymnastics clubs, where groups practiced physical exercises, with or without equipment, and rigidly structured Swedish gymnastics, either on the floor or on apparatus. Men who patronized these clubs viewed sport as a way of preparing for war against Germany. Very few of the clubs welcomed women, although some private gymnasiums offered women activities that were considered more appropriate for female customers, that is, exercises in which intensity was replaced by calisthenics and in which the purpose was more the development of grace than of strength.

Among middle-class men, adaptations of British sports were popular (for example, rowing, track and field, football, and rugby). Women were excluded from these activities as well. The press, political and medical authorities, and male athletes believed that excessive physical activity by women posed risks, both physically (for their physiological, maternal functions) and aesthetically (for their attractive image), as well as moral dangers (giving women ambitions and an inappropriate desire for social success). Male-dominated society adhered to the belief that sports of any kind were incompatible with the roles of mother and wife, which were the standard occupations for French women at the time. Sports in France remained primarily a matter for men.

The third form of sport practiced in nineteenth-century France consisted of those activities restricted to the aristocracy, such as riding, golf, tennis, cycling, shooting, and fencing. In France, as elsewhere, aristocratic women were above the criticism of popular opinion, and so they took part in these activities. Their sporting life was presented in 1885 by the Baron de Vaux in a succession of short biographies.

Before, and especially after, World War I, as part of the early feminist movements of the 1920s, women were permitted to join men in some previously all-male activities. Most of the women who took part in sports at this time were from the

Jeannie Longo-Ciprelli, French cyclist. (AFP/Corbis)

middle class, a group that was better educated and more independent financially. These factors permitted the development of a modest sports movement for women. Public opinion in general, however, remained opposed to women's participation in athletic activities. Men's organizations as well as their clubs, were adamant in their refusal to accept women. These included the powerful French Union of Athletic Societies and the French Union of Gymnastics Societies. As a result, women formed their own organizations and clubs. The Ondine de Paris, founded in 1906, was one of the first, followed by Fémina Sport and the French Union of Female Gymnastics Societies (UFSGF) in 1912, and Académia in 1915. In 1917 the French Federation of Feminine Sports Societies (FSFSF) was established; Alice Milliat became president in 1919. In 1920 the French Feminine Federation of Athletics (FFFSA) was initiated by a male journalist, Gustave de Lafreté.

World War I helped to modify both men's and women's views on the subject of appropriate activities for women. Even though the war forced women to take up previously all-male occupations in the business and labor world, women remained excluded from much of sport. Pierre de Coubertin, president of the International Olympic Committee, still contended that the Olympics would never admit women to competition, and many medical doctors still had reservations about the simplest kinds of women's sport.

Women proceeded despite these obstacles. In 1921 the UFSGF and the FFFSA merged to become the French Federation of Feminine Gymnastics and Physical Education (FFFGEP). The women's sports organization led by Milliat went from having two member clubs for women upon creation in 1916 to seventy in 1921.

Faced with Coubertin's hostility, Alice Milliat initiated a women's Olympiad, which was held in April 1921 in Monte Carlo. She then proposed Women's Olympic Games, which first took place in Paris in the Pershing stadium in April 1922, with 300 women from five countries participating. Milliat was also the driving force in the formation of the International Federation of Feminine Sports (FISF) in 1921 and became its first president.

The efforts of Milliat and other pioneers of sports for French women paid off. In 1928 women were first allowed to participate in the Olympic Games. Between World War I and World War II, almost all French sports federations accepted women, the notable exceptions being the French Federation of Cycling and the French Federation of Rugby. During this period some women athletes became as famous as their male counterparts; for example, Suzanne Lenglen in tennis, Suzanne Wurtz in swimming, and Hélène Boucher and Maryse Bastier in flying. These accomplishments notwithstanding, French society remained essentially conservative on this and other women's issues (for instance, women were not granted the right to vote until 1945).

There was physical education for girls in the school curricula as early as 1882, but these programs also reflected the view that females should not participate in strenuous sports. Until the mid-twentieth century, physical education was designed to enhance the development of the strengths and social skills girls would later need as wives and mothers. Gymnastics for girls was, above all, presented as a way to develop beauty and health; through both Ling's Swedish gymnastics and Hébert's "natural method," the exercises were intended to develop grace as a typical female attribute and also to prepare the body for the maternal function reserved for women. Physical educators were extremely careful about protecting the lower part of the body, according to medical standards of the time. Girls' gymnastics was a gentler form of boys' gymnastics, with fewer and less intense exercises. Dance was added for its more specifically feminine qualities. Although French schools were segregated by gender until 1959, few authors (Georges Démeny, 1850–1917; Georges Hébert, 1875–1957; Maurice Boigey, 1877–1952) proposed specific physical education programs for girls. After 1959, schools gradually became coed at all levels. Sports replaced gymnastics in physical education, and the objectives, forms, and content of physical education became more or less the same for boys and girls.

While women's sports developed further during World War II, it was not until the 1960s that significant numbers of women began participating in sports. In 1967, 22 percent of women reported that they practiced a regular or an occasional sporting activity, compared to an average of 25 percent among the general population. By 1983 the figure for women had increased to 32 percent and by 1994 to 64 percent, a level comparable to men's participation at 72 percent. Women now represent one-half of the French population that takes part in sports.

Women and men, however, still take part in different sports activities. French women are more involved in gymnastics and fitness, including aerobics or relaxation (25 percent), swimming (23 percent), and walking and hiking (22 percent). Men, on the other hand, choose cycling, tennis, and soccer (association football). The most male-oriented activities are soccer, rugby, boxing, and cycling.

Within the French population as a whole, 6 percent of women are involved in competitive sports, compared to 17 percent of men, with the gender gap increasing with age. The Olympic sport federations with the highest French percentages of women are gymnastics (76 percent female) and equestrian sports (66 percent). Nevertheless, since the 1970s, certain activities have come to be viewed as appropriate for women, such as volleyball, basketball, handball, ice sports, swimming, and track and field, partly because these activities are now part of physical education in the schools.

Standing apart from the general population of women, however, has been a group of female athletes who have taken part in many sports. They include Micheline Ostermeyer (discus throwing and shot put) in the 1940s; Marielle Goitschell (skiing) and Colette Besson (400 meter track and field) in the 1960s; Murielle Hermine (synchronized swimming) and Michelle Mouton (car rallying) in the 1980s; Jeannie Longo-Ciprelli (cycling), Florence Arthaud and Isabelle Autissier (sailing), and Marie-Claire Restoux (judo) in the 1990s.

Christine Arron of France in the 200-meter race at the 1997 Mediteranean Games. (Corbis/TempSport)

ELITE COMPETITION

Of the total of thirty-seven medals won by France at the 1996 Olympic Games in Atlanta, Georgia, French women won sixteen. In track and field, Marie-José Pérec won the gold medal in the 200- and 400-meter races, and Patricia Girard-Léno won the bronze in the 100-meter hurdles. In rowing, French women won the bronze medal in the coxless two race. In kayaking, Myriam Fax-Jerusalmi won the bronze in the monoplace race. In cycling, Felicia Ballanger, Nathalie Even-Lancien, and Jeannie Longo each won a gold medal, and Marion Clignet and Jeannie Longo each won a silver medal. In riding, Alexandra Ledermann won a bronze medal. In fencing, Laura Flessel won gold, Valérie Barlois won silver, and the French team won gold. In judo, Marie-Claire Restoux, in the under 52-kg (114.6 lb) class, won gold; and Christine Cicot, in the over 72-kg (158.7 lb) class, won bronze.

A woman's participation in sports remains strongly linked to her status in life. A French woman is more likely to take part in a sport if she is young, lives in or near Paris, does not have any children, is highly educated, and earns a good income, even though this lifestyle is time-consuming. Women train more frequently indoors compared to men (26 percent vs. 19 percent). Women practice sports more than men do during holidays (50 percent vs. 39 percent) since

holidays represent leisure that working women otherwise do not have (but that men do). Finally, as women spend more time participating in physical activities, the time they spend on domestic work drops accordingly, at least among women employed outside the home.

CONCLUSION

In theory, French women can practice sport under the same conditions as men. In reality, despite constant progressive steps since the turn of the century, the French sports world remains deeply differentiated regarding gender. It is true that both men and women participate in sports in equal proportions, but some activities are still marked by their history and are hardly open to the other sex (traditionally male sports such as cycling or rugby, or traditionally female sports like dance or gymnastics). Moreover, the powerful positions within sport organizations are currently dominated by men.

Thierry Terret

Bibliography

Arnaud, Pierre, and Thierry Terret. (1995) *Éducation et politiques sportives*. Paris: Editions du Comité des Travaux Historiques et Scientifiques.

————. (1996) *Éducation physique, Sports et Arts. XIXe–XXe siècles*. Paris: Editions du Comité des Travaux Historiques et Scientifiques.

———. (1996) *Histoire du sport féminin.* 2 vols. Paris: L'Harmattan.

Boigey, Maurice. (1922) *Manuel scientifique d'éducation physique.* Paris: Masson.

———. (1925) *L'éducation physique féminine.* Paris: Masson.

Davisse, Annick, and Catherine Louveau. (1998) *Sports, école, société: La différence des sexes.* Paris: L'Harmattan.

Démeny, Georges. (1911) *Éducation et harmonie du mouvement.* Paris: Librairie des Annales.

Duby, Georges, and Michelle Perrot. (1991–1992) *Une histoire des femmes.* 5 vols. Paris: Plon.

Eyquem, Marie-Thérèse. (1944) *La femme et le sport.* Paris: Editions J. Susse.

Hébert, Georges. (1913) *Muscle et beauté plastique.* Paris: Vuibert.

Irlinger, Paul, Catherine Louveau, and Michèlle Métoudi. (1987) *Les pratiques sportives des Français.* Paris: INSEP.

Laget, Françoise, Serge Laget, and Jean-Pierre Mazot. (1982) *Le grand livre du sport féminin.* Belleville/Saône: FMT.

Vaux, Baron de. (1885) *Les femmes de sport.* Paris: Published privately.

FRASER, DAWN

(1937–)

AUSTRALIAN SWIMMER

In the late 1950s and 1960s, Dawn Fraser captured the imagination of the public and the press as she seemed to break records and generate controversy every time she swam. Although her swimming career was interrupted in 1965 by a ban on her participation, she emerged at the 1988 Seoul Olympics as an Australian national hero.

Fraser was born in the Sydney suburb of Balmain, New South Wales. As a child, she enjoyed many sports but preferred to spend her free time swimming at the Balmain Baths. One of her brothers encouraged her to compete; she was a good swimmer although she suffered from asthma. When she was fourteen years old, the Australian swimming coach Harry Gallagher invited her to

train with him—free of charge. Three years later, Gallagher accepted a position in Adelaide and persuaded Fraser to leave home to join him. That summer, she captured every South Australian freestyle title. At the national championships in Sydney, which determined the 1956 Olympic squad, she set her first world record, in the 110-yard freestyle race (the previous record had stood for twenty years). A few days later, she set world records in the 220-yard freestyle and 200-meter freestyle races.

That year brought Fraser more acclaim. She set a new world record for the 100-meter freestyle race at the 1956 Melbourne Olympic Games and won her first individual Olympic gold medal. Fraser also took a gold as part of the 400-meter freestyle relay team and swam to a second gold medal when the Australian team broke the world record in the 4 × 100-meter freestyle relay. She triumphed again in the 100-meter freestyle race in the 1960 Olympics in Rome and added two silver medals for her contributions to the 4 × 100-meter medley and freestyle relays. Fraser's leadoff swim in the freestyle relay set a new Olympic record of 60.6 seconds for the 100-meter freestyle relay. At age twenty-seven, Fraser captured her third consecutive gold medal in the 100-meter freestyle race at the 1964 Olympic Games (as well as a silver medal in the 4 × 100-meter freestyle relay).

At the 1960 Olympic Games, Fraser's independence began to clash with authorities. Assuming she would not be swimming butterfly (another stroke in which she excelled) at the Olympics, she spent the night before the 4 × 100-meter medley relay celebrating, and the next day shopping and enjoying lunch. Then, informed 45 minutes before the start of the preliminary relay heats that she was to swim the butterfly leg after all in order to allow teammate Jan Andrew to rest for her individual 100-meter butterfly race, Fraser balked. Teammate Alva Colquhoun stepped in to swim the butterfly leg, but all was not well. Amid allegations of other misdemeanors during and after the Games, including wearing a nonregulation warm-up suit on the Olympic medal stand, Fraser was punished by a two-year ban from international competition. The Australian Swimming Union did not accept her letter of apology. Then, in 1962 Fraser returned to the international scene in a blaze of glory. At the Commonwealth

Games she touched the wall in 59.9 seconds and became the first woman to swim the 100-meter freestyle race in less than a minute.

A few months before the 1964 Olympic Games in Tokyo, an automobile accident claimed the life of her mother and left Fraser in a back and neck brace for nine weeks. She competed nonetheless. Suffering from a head cold and asthma, she opted for a slower open turn rather than a flip turn in the 100-meter freestyle race. Despite these emotional and physical setbacks, she won the gold medal and set an Olympic record of 59.5 seconds, becoming the first and only swimmer to win the same event at three consecutive Olympics. Fraser proudly carried the Australian national flag in the Olympic Games closing ceremony.

The 1964 Olympic Games were no freer of controversy than the 1960 games had been. Fraser marched in the opening ceremony, defying the team manager's order that swimmers competing in the first days of the Games should skip the celebration. During the Games, Fraser, claiming that her team suit was uncomfortable, wore a bathing suit similar to the one issued by the team sponsor but actually manufactured by a rival company. After the Games she was involved in the theft of an Olympic flag from the Imperial Palace. Although the star-struck police requested that she sign autographs instead of a police report, the Amateur Swimming Union of Australia did not view the incident as leniently. In March 1965, despite public support for Fraser, she received a ten-year suspension from competitive swimming. Although the sentence was later reduced to four years, Fraser missed the 1968 Olympic Games in Mexico City, where it was predicted that she might have won an unprecedented fourth gold medal in the 100-meter freestyle race. Indeed, Fraser's winning time in the 1964 Olympic Games was a half-second faster than Jan Henne's winning time in 1968.

Fraser's February 1964 100-meter freestyle race time of 58.9 seconds, remained the world record for nearly eight years. During her career Fraser set thirty-nine world records, including several successive records for the 100-meter freestyle. She also amassed eight Olympic medals—four gold and four silver.

In 1965 she and Harry Gordon published her autobiography, *Below the Surface* (Australian title:

Dawn Fraser. (Bettmann/Corbis)

Gold Medal Girl). In 1967, during Fraser's suspension, Queen Elizabeth bestowed on her the title of Member of the Order of the British Empire (OBE).

Fraser continued to live in the public eye. In 1988 she was elected as an independent to represent Balmain in the New South Wales Parliament. She was voted Australia's greatest female athlete, and she marched with the Australian team at the 1988 Olympic Games in Seoul.

In 1992 she served as a special counselor to Australian Olympic athletes in Barcelona at the request of the Australian Olympic Federation. At the 1996 Olympic Games, Fraser was sports ambassador for the Australian Team, helped carry the Olympic torch through Atlanta, Georgia, and was honored during the opening ceremony as one of the world's greatest Olympians. She was appointed attaché for the Australian Olympic Team for the 2000 Games in Sydney. In addition to Olympic services, Fraser has supported the disabled and the environment and has served as president of the Sport Australia Hall of Fame.

Cara Joy Lockman Hall

Bibliography

Andrews, Malcolm. (1996) *Australia at the Olympics.* Sydney, Australia: ABC Books for the Australian Broadcasting Corporation.

Gordon, Harry. (1994) *Australia and the Olympic Games.* Queensland, Australia: University of Queensland Press.

Johnson, Anne Janette. (1996) *Great Women in Sports.* Detroit, MI: Visible Ink Press.

Knox, Ken. (1962) *The Dawn of Swimming.* London: Stanley Paul.

White, Lee, ed. (1995) *Contemporary Australians 1995–1996.* Port Melbourne, Victoria, Australia: Reed Reference Australia.

FRISBEE *see* Flying Disc

FU MINGXIA

(1978–)

CHINESE DIVER

Fu Mingxia competes in a diving event at the 1996 Olympic Games in Atlanta. (Corbis/TempSport)

Fu Mingxia, the youngest world diving champion, was born in Wunan, Hubei Province, China. Although her first sport training was in gymnastics, her ability as a diving athlete was recognized by a diving coach who persuaded her to start her training at an after-school sports school at the age of seven. In 1987 a coach from the national team recognized Fu's potential and took her to the national diving training center. One year later, she joined the national diving team. She was only ten years old.

Fu received intensive training and made impressive progress. She won her first gold medal at the 1990 Goodwill Games in July in Seattle. Two months later, Fu, the youngest in the Chinese delegation of 674 athletes, participated in the Asian Games in Beijing and won a bronze medal. She was not happy about the result and she showed it—she was still a little girl who could not help crying. In 1991, when she was twelve, she competed at the swimming and diving world championships in Perth, Australia, where she won the women's platform diving championships and became the youngest world champion in diving history.

Fu's success continued. At the 1992 Olympic Games in Barcelona, she won the gold medal in platform diving. That same year, she was named by the American Amateur Sports Foundation as the best Asian athlete of 1992. In 1993, when the Chinese women's diving team won the team title and mixed team title at the World Cup Championships, Fu made an impressive contribution. In 1994 she won the gold medal in platform diving at the world championships and the silver medal at the Asian Games. In 1995 at the diving World Cup Championships, Fu won two medals: the gold for springboard and the silver for platform. The last and greatest honor came to Fu at the 1996 Olympic Games in Atlanta, where she became a double gold medalist in the women's platform and springboard diving.

After the 1996 Olympics, Fu retired from the national team to become a student at Qinhhua (Tsinghua) University in Beijing.

Fan Hong
Yan Xuening

Bibliography

Fu Mingxia. (1997) "New Year Greetings." *China Sports* (January): 8.

Liu, Meng. (1991) "Bianzhi caixia de xiaonuhai" ("A Little Girl Who Is Knitting Rays of Sunlight"). *Xintiyu (New Sports)* 1: 44–47.

Zhongguo tiyu bao (Chinese Sports Daily). (5 August 1996).

Zhonghua titan jinguo minxin (Chinese Female Sports Stars). (1995) Hong Kong: Hong Kong jingji daobaoshe.

G

GAY GAMES

The Gay Games and Cultural Festival are an international multisport and cultural celebration organized primarily by and for lesbian and gay people. Though it celebrates the diversity and scope of the lesbian and gay communities, it is open to all people over 18 years of age, regardless of sexual orientation. Staged every fourth year since 1982, the Games have experienced success and phenomenal growth, becoming a multimillion dollar sports event. The number of athletes participating increased from 1,300 at Gay Games I in San Francisco in 1982 to nearly 15,000 athletes from more than 70 countries at Gay Games V in Amsterdam in 1998. Gay Games V also included 7,000 workers, over 4,000 cultural event participants, and almost a million spectators. Estimates of the economic impact of Gay Games IV in New York in 1994 range from $112 million to $300 million.

HISTORY

Thomas Waddell (1940–1989), a U.S. physician and 1968 Olympic decathlete, is credited as the founder of the Gay Games. Waddell was a founder of the San Francisco Arts and Athletics Organization, which organized and hosted the first and second Gay Games in 1982 and 1986. The Games were intended to provide a place for lesbian women and gay men to participate in an openly lesbian and gay sport festival and to help challenge stereotypes and cross barriers. In 1989 the Federation of Gay Games was established to give the event an independent organization focused solely on the Games. The federation is composed of a board of directors, which includes an executive committee, individual members, organizational members, staff, and a newsletter editor. Commitment to gender equity is central, and the executive committee has co-presidents: a woman and a man. The Federation selects the site for the Gay Games, oversees the work of the local organizing committee, and manages all other business and marketing aspects of the Games.

PHILOSOPHY AND PRACTICE

The philosophy of the Games is inclusion and encouragement. Like the Olympics, the Gay Games have an opening and closing ceremony. During the eight-day festival, thirty-one sport events are staged. Unlike the Olympics, there are no minimum qualifying standards for participation; each person is encouraged to do her or his best. The skill level of participants ranges from beginner to elite athletes, and, in some sports, world records have been set at the Gay Games. Most sport

---

"OATH OF THE ATHLETES"

I, (name), on behalf of all the athletes in this stadium,

Pledge to fully participate in the Gay Games by honoring the Spirit of their origins.
I pledge to celebrate the uniqueness of these Games in their purest realm of sportsmanship,

Where there is no shame of failure
Only glory in achievement and the shared fulfillment of each personal best.
In these Games I have no rivals,
Only comrades in unity.

---

events offer a variety of divisions, including women's, men's, and coed, as well as divisions based on skill and age. For example, there are women's pairs figure skating, coed age bracket divisions for relay events in track, and women's ice hockey. The sport events offered are a mix of traditional, contemporary, and extreme sports, and include basketball, volleyball, equestrian sports, windsurfing, rock climbing, and mountain cycling.

Gay Games medals of gold, silver, and bronze are awarded to participants finishing in first, second, and third place in each event in every division of every sport. Because the emphasis is on inclusion and participation, every competitor receives a participant's medal. Every participant is cheered, regardless of whether the athlete finishes first or last. Moreover, all participants in cultural events receive a participant's medal. In the Games, empowerment through participation is regarded as victory.

Another purpose of the Gay Games is to encourage emancipation of all lesbian and gay people worldwide. The motto of the Federation of Gay Games is "Games Can Change the World." An outreach committee was established in 1989 to promote participation from Japan, India, China, Thailand, the Philippines, and other countries that formerly sent few participants to the Games. The committee focuses on more than forty developing countries where lesbian and gay people have limited rights.

The Gay Games are also a cultural celebration, which uses a theme word that is intended to inspire and challenge the lesbian and gay population and also to demonstrate some of the intentions of the Gay Games to the general public. The themes of the first five games were: challenge, triumph, celebration, unity, and friendship. The sport events take place for eight days, but the cultural events spread across two weeks. The plethora of cultural and arts events includes chorus and band concerts, poetry readings, celebrity appearances, theater, ballet, art exhibits, film presentations, academic conferences, workshops, seminars, and crafts exhibits.

WOMEN AND THE GAY GAMES

One of the continuing goals of Gay Games' organizers is to strive for gender parity within the organization and its committees and in participation in sports and other events. Historically, far fewer women have participated in the sports than men—around 25 percent for Gay Games I in 1982 and 30 percent for Gay Games IV in 1994. Because of this poor ratio, the Federation created the Women's Outreach Committee in 1997. Its purpose is to develop and implement strategies to bring more female representation to the Games and its governing and organizing bodies. Working closely with the Amsterdam Gay Games V Organizing Committee, the Outreach Committee achieved 42 percent female participation of the 14,470 entrants at Gay Games V. Its efforts included sending women's outreach materials to potential and registered women participants, offering discount coupons for women registrants, and extending registration deadlines. It also provided extensive coverage of women's outreach in the quarterly newsletters, a program of several women's events to take place at the games, scholarships for some female participants, housing priorities, special pricing on housing, day care at a nominal fee, special women's booths, and printed materials on the many women's program events and outreach goals.

Many events were exclusively for women, including a three-day Women's Festival of theater, dance, and music; a photo exhibition, "Lesbian Connexion/s"; a walking tour of the history of lesbian Amsterdam; lesbian art in several Amsterdam art galleries; the official Gay Games Lesbian Party; a special women's bar at Friendship Village (the central area for Gay Games V), and performances on several open stages by and for women.

Some critics point to a discrepancy between the Federation's widely advertised goal of making the Gay Games a woman-friendly event and its actual practices. For example, promotional and other materials produced by the Gay Games give the impression that women are not recognized as equal participants. Most of the official brochures, film, posters, and books are dominated by images of young, able, white, gay men. This was especially evident during Gay Games V. Some of its events and festivities drew loud criticism over the dearth of recognition and celebration of women. The highly promoted Canal Parade, in which almost 200 decorated boats moved through the

THE GAY GAMES COURT CASE

The original title of the Gay Games was the Gay Olympic Games. On 9 August 1982, just two weeks before the start of the first Gay Olympic Games, the United States Olympic Committee (USOC) filed court action against San Francisco Arts and Athletics (SFAA) to stop them from using the word, "Olympics." A temporary restraining order was issued in order to prohibit SFAA from using the word, Olympic, in any form, which forced SFAA to strike the word from all materials and merchandise, including thousands of dollars worth of souvenir t-shirts, posters, and pins. The USOC lawyers also filed suit to recover legal fees of $96,600 and attached a lien to the home of Tom Waddell, named co-defendant in the case.

In one hearing, Alex Kozinski, a judge appointed by President Reagan, wrote that the issue "threatens a potentially serious and widespread infringement of personal liberties. If Congress has the power to grant a crown monopoly on the word 'Olympic,' one wonders how many other words or concepts can be similarly enclosed. . . . It seems that the USOC is using its control over the term 'Olympic' to promote the very image of homosexuals that SFAA seeks to combat." The case was eventually heard by the Supreme Court which, on 25 June 1987, ruled 7–2 in favor of the USOC. The word, Olympic, was dropped from the title, and the event has been known as the Gay Games ever since.

canals of Amsterdam in a pre-opening ceremony, was faulted for its predominantly male content. The opening and closing ceremonies were similarly criticized for featuring several hundred male dancers stripping to music. Additional criticism was aimed at the lack of diversity in the ceremonies in relation to race, ethnicity, nationality, and disability.

During the eight days of sports, many women complained about unequal treatment. For example, in one sport—track and field—sanctioned by national and international governing bodies, all events must have five-year age groups so that athletes compete with people close in age. However, at Gay Games V, the track-and-field organizer, a young, white, gay man, changed age groups for many of the women's events. This meant that sixty-year-olds had to compete with twenty-year-olds. To make matters worse, the organizer changed age groups for awarding medals. This meant that a fifty four-year-old who took first place in the hammer throw and should have been awarded a gold medal was later grouped with the thirty five-year-olds and was awarded a bronze medal instead. Many women and men complained and some filed formal complaints, which the organizer ignored. In fact, he told the women to take the medals he wanted to give them, or take nothing. The women complained to the Federation that its talk about valuing women's participation did not appear to translate into fair recognition of their participation and performance.

Despite reports of unfair treatment, women who participate in the Games recount many positive benefits of participating, beyond the traditional expectations of competition, fitness, and recreation. These benefits include meeting and competing with other lesbian athletes, a sense of inclusion and freedom to express themselves during the event, empowerment, and participating in an increasingly positive profile of the gay and lesbian community. Some women say that participation in the Games can be a positive, life-changing experience. Others maintain that, although they have competed in organized high-school, college, or even professional sports, the Gay Games is the most important sport event for them. Also, many say that, despite mistakes made at each event, they so cherish the positive things about the Games that they will attend every one in the future.

It appears that the Women's Outreach Committee, the federation, and the organizing committees still have much to do to make women believe they are truly valued participants in the Games. It has been suggested that the organizers will need professional marketing intervention to address and overcome its exclusionary image.

The organizers are challenged to heal the negative impact this has had on many lesbian women and other groups. In one step toward resolving the problem, several members of the Sydney Gay Games VI (2002) Organizing Committee went to Amsterdam in 1998 to get feedback from participants about their experiences. It remains to be seen if the federation and the other organizers will make the Sydney Games a women's event in practice as well as on paper.

CONCLUSION

The Gay Games are a significant event for lesbian sportswomen; they serve as a measure of the growing demand for lesbian and gay sport and are a major influence on the growth of sports for lesbians and gays. The Games have contributed to the extensive lesbian and gay sport industry, which includes local, national, and international organizations and events, with a sport organization, team, or league in most cities in the United States and many other countries. A large number of these organizations are lesbian-owned and -operated and serve primarily lesbians. Sport and recreational events offered range from trekking in the Himalayas to SCUBA diving in the Caribbean. The Gay Games has been and continues to be a mostly positive force—challenging notions, empowering people, and stimulating growth and enlightenment.

Brenda G. Pitts

See also Homophobia; Lesbianism

Bibliography

Coe, Roy M. (1986) *A Sense of Pride: The Story of Gay Games II.* San Francisco, CA: Pride Publications.

———. (1997) "A Preliminary Economic Impact of the Sydney 2002 Gay Games." *Sydney 2002 Gay Games Bid Limited.*
http://www.sydney2002.org.au.

Forzley, Richard, and E. Douglas Hughes, eds. (1990) *The Spirit Captured: The Official Photojournal of Celebration '90, Gay Games III and Cultural Festival.* Vancouver, Canada: For Eyes Press.

Krane, Vikki, and Lisa Romont. (1997) "Female Athletes' Motives and Experiences During the Gay Games." *Journal of Gay, Lesbian, and Bisexual Identity* 2: 123–138.

Labrecque, Lisa, ed. (1994) *Unity: A Celebration of Gay Games IV and Stonewall.* San Francisco, CA: Labrecque Publishing.

Pitts, Brenda G. (1997) "From Leagues of Their Own to an Industry of Their Own: The Emerging Lesbian Sports Industry." *Women in Sport and Physical Activity Journal* 6, 2: 109–139.

———. (1998) *Lesbian and Gay Sport Studies: Selected Resources.* Tallahassee, FL: published by the author.

———. (1998) "Let the Gaymes Begin! A Case Study of Sports Tourism, Commercialization, and the Gay Games V." Paper presented at the 2d Conference of the Gay Games: "Queer Games? Theories, Politics, Sport." Amsterdam, 29–31, July 1998.

———. (1999) "Sports Tourism and Niche Markets: Identification and Analysis of the Growing Lesbian and Gay Sports Tourism Industry." *Journal of Vacation Marketing* 5, 1: 31–50.

Siegel, Paul. (1994) "On the Owning of Words: Reflections of San Francisco Arts and Athletics vs. United States Olympic Committee." In *Queer Words, Queer Images,* edited by R. Jeffrey Ringer. New York: New York University Press.

Waddell, Thomas, and Dick Schaap. (1996) *Gay Olympian: The Life and Death of Dr. Tom Waddell.* New York: Alfred A. Knopf.

GENDER EQUITY

The legal and moral standards of gender equity are not identical. Specific laws, such as Title IX of the Education Amendments of 1972—the U.S. federal law prohibiting sex discrimination in educational programs and activities in educational institutions that receive federal money—address discrimination from a minimum, legal perspective. The law specifies areas of discrimination (e.g., athletic scholarships, participation opportunities, and benefits such as uniforms, equipment, and supplies) and defines minimum expectations. When the institution or individual fails to meet the required standard, the law is broken, resulting in punishment or restitution.

Gender equity as a moral concept has a significantly wider reach. Simply put, a moral commitment to gender equity requires asking whether an action or decision will, directly or indirectly, benefit men and women equally. Such a commitment also symbolizes a higher-order value system, which the technical prescriptions of the

---

EQUALITY ON THE COURT

Professional tennis is the sport with the most parity between the money earned by men and women. The money earned by the top five men and women in the first nine months of 1999 supports this conclusion:

Men		Women	
Andre Agassi	$2,251,128	Martina Hingis	$2,204,180
Yevgeny Kafelnikov	1,488,218	Serena Williams	1,664,171
Pete Sampras	1,401,256	Lindsay Davenport	1,578,263
Gustavo Kuerten	1,389,309	Venus Williams	1,428,082
Patrick Rafter	1,254,574	Steffi Graf	1,193,367

However, from the #6 spot to the #25 spot on the earning list, the men earn from about 30% to 40% more than the women.

---

law can never cover fully. Even when gender-equity laws exist, there is always room for individuals to evade them; moral definitions of gender equity, on the other hand, contain no loopholes.

In sport, commitment to gender equity has been difficult to achieve because, historically and culturally, women have been excluded. In the few cases where women were permitted to compete, they were forced to play at a status below that of men, and they received much less material support and attention. In most nations, sport was used to train men for combat—the ultimate competition—and to teach men leadership skills. Even when affluent women were allowed access to some sports, their participation was not considered as serious or valuable as that of their male counterparts.

Only during the last half century has this narrow militaristic view of the benefits of sport been questioned. Underlying the growing support for gender equality in sport lies the realization that sport is too important to the physical, psychological, and sociological well-being of all children to be restricted to boys. Research shows that girls who participate in sport have lower risk of unintended pregnancies, drug use, heart disease, osteoporosis, and breast cancer. They also have greater self-esteem, and are more likely to earn better grades in high school.

Today, in an economic environment where the quality of children's lives depends on two-income families, it is increasingly acknowledged that girls must be as well prepared for the highly competitive work place as boys. Traditionally, sport is where boys and men have learned skills necessary for success in the work place—teamwork, goal setting, the pursuit of excellence, and other achievement-oriented behavior. It is in this context that gender equity in sports is being pursued.

Unfortunately, resolving gender equity in sport presents a greater challenge than achieving equity in other institutions. For example, discrimination against women in law school admissions is eliminated by objective, gender-neutral testing. In sport, there is no such simple solution. For example, if women were to try out for a basketball team selected on nongender criteria of strength, speed, and skill, selection would not be gender neutral. Because the male hormone androgen enables men to develop more muscle mass per unit volume of body tissues than women, males have a physical advantage over females in terms of strength and speed. And, because most sports involve propelling an object through space or overcoming the resistance of a mass, strength becomes an important component of skill. In other words, a male and a female basketball player may be comparably skilled shooters over short distances, but over longer distances and over time, where

Tennis stars Billie Jean King and Bobby Riggs made headlines when they played a $100,000 winner-takes-all match against each other in 1973. (Corbis/Bettmann)

strength becomes a significant factor, males will have an advantage.

If women are to have a reasonably equal chance to participate in competitive sports (in other than social recreation or rule-adjusted coed settings), a separate but equal approach is required. In other words, giving woman an equal chance to play means creating new and equivalent sport opportunities for females.

It is unlikely that society can double the resources expended on men's sport participation. If gender equity is to be achieved, difficult decisions may be required to redistribute resources within athletics to provide equal opportunities for women. To many, the most acceptable solution is to reduce expenditures on men's athletics while maintaining existing male participation levels and to redistribute money to provide equitable participation opportunities for female athletes. Resistance to gender equity occurs when institutions are unwilling to reduce the very high rate of remuneration paid to men in certain sports, such as football and basketball, to increase participation by women. Introducing such a change may have unfortunate consequences: the elimination of some undervalued sports, such as fencing, and antagonism against gender equality.

An important consideration in creating a separate-but-equal sport system is that women do not always wish to play the same sports as men. The traditional menu of sports in school and college athletic programs is based on men's interests, and many sports (such as contact football) are based on strength. Thus the challenge is to create a sport system for women in which equality is achieved by meeting the interests of females and acknowledging differences in physical attributes.

Some critics question whether women are as interested in sports as are men. Some male athletic directors argue that a survey of male and female students would prove that females are not as interested in athletics. Others contend that the only fair test is to offer males and females the same number of participation opportunities (with adequate coaches, facilities, and equipment) in sports in which they respectively have an interest and then to determine whether women take advantage of such opportunities.

There are, however, those who maintain that even this approach represents a double standard. Typically, when male athletes fail to come out for varsity teams, the athletes' interest is not questioned; rather, the coach is fired for failing to ad-

BOXING WOMAN VERSUS MAN

The first "sanctioned" boxing match between Margaret MacGregor, woman, and a man, jockey Loi Chow, took place in Washington State in October, 1999. The match was made possible by the state's gender equity laws which require only that boxers be matched in size and experience. MacGregor won an easy decision on points. The sanctioning of the match was criticized by many as doing nothing to promote equity in sports or the reputation of boxing.

equately motivate and teach. According to the Women's Sports Foundation, most parents believe that male and female youth are equally interested in playing sports. The causes of lower participation rates among girls appear to include: discriminatory athletic environments, including inferior facilities and coaches; inconvenient practice times; lack of opportunities or teams on which to play; and either the absence of encouragement or the active discouragement of girls to continue their sports participation.

A further barrier to gender equity in sport has been a resistance to sharing power and benefits within a previously all-male cultural institution. Although discrimination in sport has been legally prohibited in the United States since 1972, male leadership in implementing equity has been lacking. However, resistance to gender equity appears to be declining. The generation of fathers and mothers who grew up in the 1970s believing that their daughters could be doctors, lawyers, and athletes, and who have coached their daughters for many years, are becoming old enough to occupy the decision-making positions that could ensure the realization of gender equity.

Donna A. Lopiano

See also Coaching; Law; Management; Ownership; Sexual Harassment; Sponsorship; Title IX

Bibliography

Acosta, R. V., and L. J. Carpenter. (1998) "Women in Intercollegiate Sport: A Longitudinal Study—Twenty-one Year Update, 1977–1997." Unpublished manuscript, Brooklyn College.

Education Amendments of 1972. (1972) P. L. 92-318, Title IX—Prohibition of Sex Discrimination, 1 July 1972 (now codified as 20 U.S.C. § 1681[a]).

Federal Register. (1979) December 11. 44, 239: 71413–71423.

Gender Equity Survey. (1992) Mission, Kansas: National Collegiate Athletic Association.

———. (1997) Mission, Kansas: National Collegiate Athletic Association.

Lopiano, Donna A. (1975) Statement before the Subcommittee on Higher Education, Committee on Labor and Public Welfare, S. 2106, 16.

———. (1976) "A Fact-Finding Model for Conducting a Title IX Self-Evaluation Study in Athletic Programs." *Journal of Physical Education, Recreation and Dance* 47, 5: 26–30.

———. (1980) "Modern Athletics: Directions and Problems." *Thresholds in Education* 8, 4: 23–27.

———. (1986) "A Political Analysis of the Possibility of Impact Alternatives for the Accomplishment of Feminist Objectives within American Intercollegiate Sport." In *Fractured Focus: Sport as a Reflection of Society,* edited by Richard E. Lapchick. Lexington, MA: Lexington Books, 163–176.

———. (1988) "An Unpublished Speech Made at the NCAA President's Commission National Forum." *The Physical Educator* 45, 1: 2–4.

Sabo, Don. (1997) *The Women's Sports Foundation Gender Equity Report Card: A Survey of Athletic Opportunity in Higher Education.* East Meadow, NY: Women's Sports Foundation.

GENDER VERIFICATION

Gender verification has been used since the 1960s at major sport events for the purpose of preventing males from competing in women's competitions. Gender testing in sport has become highly controversial and has been the subject of much discussion in recent years.

METHODS OF GENDER TESTING

In the early stages of gender testing, athletes who entered women's competitions were subjected to physical inspection, as they were at the European championships in track and field in 1966 and the Pan-American Games in 1967. However, female athletes found this method invasive and humiliating, and the sex chromatin test was offered as a suitable alternative. This is a genetic test that assesses the sex chromosome constitution of the individual. It is based on the assumption that the nuclei of cells from women regularly contain two "female" sex chromosomes (so-called X chromosomes), whereas men have one X and one Y chromosome in their cells. The presence of two X chromosomes is established by a special staining reaction on smears of cells scraped from the lining of the cheek. This is a quick, easy, and noninvasive test. Determining the result, however,

ACROBATS NOT ALWAYS
WHAT THEY SEEM (1912)

A Ladies' Home Journal Article Describes the Strength of Women

It is an interesting fact that most of the famous athletes whom I have examined attributed their great power largely to the fine physiques of their mothers. The mother of Louis Cyr, the strongest man in the world, could readily shoulder a barrel of flour and carry it up several flights of stairs. I have seen one of the scrubwomen who clean the Hemenway Gymnasium at Harvard University put a hundred-pound dumbbell above her head with each hand. Great feats of strength, skill, and endurance are frequently performed by women at the circus and the vaudeville theater, and it is well known in the profession that some of the best gymnasts performing in public are women disguised as men. In justice to my sex I should mention the obvious corollary to this fact that many of the best acrobats are men attired as women.

DUDLEY A. SARGENT, M.D.
(1912) "Are Athletics Making Girls Masculine?"
Ladies' Home Journal. *March.*

requires a subjective evaluation, and technical errors are far from infrequent. Consequently, the test is rarely used in genetic laboratories.

Given these uncertainties, in recent years the preferred gender verification test in sport has changed to a determination of the presence of Y chromosomes or male-related genetic material, using the cheek cells, but now relying on polymerase chain reaction methodology (PRC). This technique allows for small amounts of DNA material to be amplified and assessed for the specific purpose of identifying a Y chromosome or male-determining genetic material.

At the Olympic level, the now-discredited sex chromatin test was introduced in 1968. In the belief that a simple and safe laboratory method was available to verify female gender, other sport organizations followed the example of the International Olympic Committee (IOC). Since that time, however, genetics has been one of the most rapidly developing branches of biomedical science. One key discovery has been that significant deviations from the standard sex chromosome constitutions (XX for women and XY for men) do occur. The physical appearance of an individual, male or female, does not always follow the chromosome constitution. Thus, there are males with a female chromosome constitution

and vice versa. Moreover, genetic investigations and information on their results have been a major topic of discussions in the field of medical ethics. For example, since 1997, Norway, along with other developed nations, has created legislation to restrict or control the use of genetic testing.

As a result, the use of genetic tests to verify gender in sport has been challenged by medical scientists, civil rights advocates, women's sport advocates, and some athletes and sport organizations. While many international sport organizations responded to these requests to end testing, the IOC remained unimpressed by the evidence against gender verification for some time. Genetic tests to verify female gender were conducted at the Olympic Games and at five Olympic-member sport federation championships, as they were in some multisport competitions (such as the Asian Games and Pan American Games) until the IOC decided in 1999 to abandon the genetic-based screening for female Olympic participants. The IOC decision replaced mandatory genetic testing with a system that allows the IOC Medical Commission to conduct a scientifically and ethically proper investigation of any individual case. Some other multisport organizations, such as the International University Sports Federation and the

Commonwealth Games Organization, had previously abandoned gender verification tests, and twenty-nine of the thirty-four international federations whose sport is part of the Olympic program no longer conduct such tests at their own world championships.

ARGUMENTS FOR GENDER VERIFICATION

Gender verification was introduced into the world of sport because of claims that a few individuals who were not truly women had competed in major women's competitions. One example from 1936 was the German high jumper "Dora" (Herman) Ratjen, the only documented case of a man masquerading as a woman at the Olympics. In 1957 Ratjen acknowledged publicly that for three years in the 1930s he had been forced to pose as a woman by the Nazi Youth Movement and to compete in the women's high jump. He finished fourth at the 1936 Olympics. In addition, in the 1950s and 1960s there were regular complaints at international track and field meets that some Russian and Eastern European women athletes were actually males. In addition to men masquerading as women, there was also the concern that women with "unfeminine" or male-like physical features—including defects of sex chromosomes—would have an advantage over "normal" women. By making sure that only women competed, sport officials believed that they were upholding the integrity of women's competitions.

The importance of ensuring fairness in women's competitions has become a more prominent issue as sport has grown increasingly professional and commercial; today's winners may become international celebrities and may make considerable amounts of money from their sports or related activities. Moreover, success at major international sport competitions has become a major issue for many nations who tie their national prestige to the accomplishments of their athletes. Thus, it is not surprising that nations, as well as individual athletes, have tried to find ways around the existing rules. The proponents of gender testing argue that to abandon it would open the door to cheating, that is, to men masquerading as women in competition. In addition, female athletes have expressed support for gender verification in questionnaires at the Winter Games in Albertville and Lillehammer. By the 1990s, however, some women athletes and women's sport advocates were questioning the reasoning behind gender verification.

ARGUMENTS AGAINST GENDER VERIFICATION

Criticism of genetic screening reflects technical, ethical, and functional issues. Technically, the argument that testing does not unambiguously differentiate between men and women because of the possibility of chromosome deviations is countered by the contention that the genetic test is only an initial screening procedure, which should be followed up by more detailed gynecological and clinical examinations. In practice, however, the threat of the test or a result that requires further examination can prevent an athlete from competing: some women simply withdraw from competition rather than have their birth anomaly exposed or misunderstood.

One main objection to the present procedure is that the sex of an individual is not determined solely, or even mainly, by his or her chromosome constitution (that is, the "genetic sex"). Many other, arguably more important factors should be taken into account, such as anatomical sex characteristics (external and internal genitalia), gonadal sex, hormonal sex, apparent sex (as presumed by others), and psychological sex (gender identity). Using these criteria, determining the sex of an individual may be highly complicated in ambiguous cases, even though in 99.9 percent or more of the population it is easily determined by simple physical inspection.

Furthermore, critics argue that screening for gender by determining only the genetic sex is scientifically untrustworthy because multiple chromosome deviations occur in men and women. These deviations include the absence of the Y chromosome in males and the presence of a Y chromosome in females. This means that a screening using chromosome analysis will identify some females as male, while some males will be classified as female. Many young women with a Y chromosome are totally unaware of their genetic abnormality. In a population of athletes, the number of women with a Y chromosome is 1 in 400–500, which is quite significant considering that about 4,500 women athletes are expected to participate in the summer Olympic Games in

Sydney in 2000. How many men, if any, have passed the test remains unknown, since such individuals will not be identified by the present procedure.

While it is true that those women athletes who are found to have a Y chromosome will be afforded further methods of evaluation, including a gynecological examination, opponents of testing argue that it is unethical to question a woman's sex on the basis of a chromosome analysis, especially when she is preparing for competition. The athlete may be totally unaware of her chromosome abnormality. Such identification can have devastating personal consequences for the athletes involved, as was the case for Ewa Klubokowska, the Polish world-record holder and Olympic bronze medalist in the 100-meter dash in the late 1960s, and the Spanish hurdler Maria José Patino in 1985. Their situations became publicly known and they suffered heavily, socially and emotionally, and, at least in the case of Patino, financially as well. Their athletic careers were ended, yet no evidence showed their reported chromosome anomalies gave them an advantage over other females. The Patino case became especially important as she appealed her lifetime ban on competing. In 1989 an International Amateur Athletic Federation (IAAF) commission ruled in her favor and she returned to competition. Her story led many to question the wisdom of gender verification.

The above arguments have led the scientific community to react against the use of genetic tests to verify gender in sport, and a large number of scientific societies have issued statements urging sport organizations to abandon the procedure. Major objections from the scientific community date to the early 1970s led by Finnish geneticist Albert de la Chapelle. It was not until the 1990s, however, that the protests were heard publicly. Before the Albertville Games in 1992 a group of French scientists protested against gender testing being performed in France. Similar protests were heard in Spain before the Barcelona Games the same year. At the Winter Olympic Games in Lillehammer in 1994, Norwegian scientists refused to conduct the tests and the IOC had to bring the Albertville team to Norway as replacements. Although gender testing was conducted in accordance with the IOC protocol at the Atlanta Games in 1996, those who were responsible for the testing included in their final report to the IOC a recommendation to discontinue the present procedure for gender verification. The 1996 IOC world conference on women and sport issued a resolution opposing the practice.

Gender testing has also been questioned from a legal point of view. After the refusal of scientists to conduct tests at Lillehammer, similar refusals took place again in Norway at the junior world alpine skiing championship in 1995 and at the world Nordic skiing championship in 1997. On both of these occasions, scientists and others argued that the gender testing in question was not only unscientific and unethical but also illegal. In April 1997 the Norwegian parliament outlawed genetic testing for the purpose of gender verification in sport. Other governments are studying the question.

Some feminists also oppose gender testing in sport, questioning why, if such testing is deemed

GENETICS OF GENDER

During the first half of the twentieth century, gender verification was used to identify males who were masquerading as female competitors. Physical examination of the external genitalia was the verification test. In the second half of the century, the issue shifted to the identification of genetic males competing as females. This more difficult issue is politically charged because it raises questions about what genetic makeup constitutes a male or female, whether genetic variations are associated with athletic performance, and the athletes' right to privacy. In the early twenty-first century, the movement is toward ending genetic testing for gender.

necessary, only women are being tested. Finally, some critics point out that testing is no longer needed: a man who wins while pretending to be a woman would be recognized as male by the female official who, after the competition, observes the collection of his urine sample for drug testing. In June 1999, the IOC abolished the genetic-based screening test for female gender and had it replaced by proper investigation of any suspect individual.

Arne Ljungqvist

Bibliography

Elsas, Louis J., Risa P. Hayes, and Kasinathan Muralidharan. (1997) "Gender Verification at the Centennial Olympic Games." *Journal of the Medical Association of Georgia* 86: 50–54.

Ferguson-Smith, Malcolm A. (1998) "Gender Verification and the Place of XY Females in Sport." In *Oxford Textbook of Sports Medicine*, 2d ed., edited by Mark Harries, Clyde Williams, William D. Stanish, and Lyle J. Mitchell. New York: Oxford University Press.

Ferguson-Smith, Malcolm A., and Elizabeth A. Ferris. (1991) "Gender Verification in Sport: The Need for a Change?" *British Journal of Sports Medicine* 25: 17–21.

Ljungqvist, Arne. (1999) "Gender Verification in Sport." In *Women in Sport: IOC Encyclopaedia of Sports Medicine*, edited by B. Drinkwater. Cambridge, MA: Blackwell Science Ltd.

Mascagni, Katia. (1996/1997) "World Conference on Women and Sport." *Olympic Review* 26, 12: 23–31.

Ryan, Allan J. (1976) "Sex and the Singles Player." *Physician and Sports Medicine* 4: 39–41.

Simpson, Joe Leigh, Arne Ljungqvist, Albert de la Chapelle, Malcolm A. Ferguson-Smith, Myron Genel, Alison S. Carlson, Anke A. Erhardt, and Elizabeth Ferris. (1993) "Gender Verification in Competitive Sport." *Sports Medicine* 16: 305–315.

GERMANY

Germany is in central Europe and has a population of about 84 million. It became a modern nation in 1871 through the unification of formerly separate states. After World War II, it was divided into the Federal Republic of Germany (West Germany) and the German Democratic Republic (East Germany); the two nations were reunited as the Federal Republic of Germany in 1990. Germany has a rich sporting tradition, although it is only in the twentieth century that women have played a major role in German athletics. Today, more sport opportunities are open to women than ever before, although those opportunities remain fewer and more restricted than those available to men.

THE MIDDLE AGES AND EARLY MODERN TIMES

In the Middle Ages and in early modern times, German women played a marginal role in society as well as in physical activities and sports. Despite the predominance of men, some women achieved privileged status at court or in nunneries. Some rode horseback and enjoyed the sport of falconry, and others enjoyed simple ball games. Aristocratic women also played an ancillary role at tournaments. An important adjunct to a medieval knight's life, tournaments served to harden the warrior's body for battle and as vivid symbolic demonstrations of social order. It was important that women be present to admire and encourage the contestants and to acknowledge men's right to rule.

In medieval towns, the most popular sports—archery, wrestling, and fencing—were also related to the exigencies of warfare. That relationship generally meant excluding women from the archery guilds, which were a prominent part of urban life. Throughout Europe archery contests were important social events that would have been painfully incomplete without admiring female spectators. Among the peasantry, women were so essential in the struggle for survival that it seemed natural for them to share in many of the sports of their fathers, husbands, and sons. They appear in medieval art as dancers and as participants in the widely popular (and wildly chaotic) game of folk football. In Germany, as in other European countries, girls and women ran races for smocks and similar prizes.

However, knowledge of preindustrial body and movement culture is far from complete. Scholars have only begun to write the history of women. To gather evidence of ancient and medieval women's sports, one must often glean the historical field after conventional historians have finished their harvest.

THE EIGHTEENTH AND NINETEENTH CENTURIES

In accordance with the ideals of this more enlightened age, the leaders of the Philanthropist movement, notably Johann Christoph Friedrich Guts Muths, developed a teaching concept that included physical education as a precondition for mental development and intellectual learning. The gymnastics of the Philanthropists, which aimed at the education of useful citizens, focused on boys and excluded girls and women. Only in the second edition of his famous work *Gymnastik fürdie Jugend* (Gymnastics for Youth) did Guts Muths mention the education of girls, but he stated that there should be no formal gymnastics for girls.

At the beginning of the nineteenth century, German *Turnen* (gymnastics) was developed by Friedrich Ludwig Jahn as an expression of nationalism, a means to overcome the feudal order that had cut Germany into a patchwork of antagonistic states. His movement was also aimed at the expulsion of the French, whom Napoleon had led to a series of military victories over divided Germany. Given Jahn's patriotic goals and emphasis on military preparedness, he saw no reason to include women in his program. Excluding women from gymnastics seemed so self-evident that he and his followers never bothered to explain or justify it.

In the course of the nineteenth century, however, there was increasing concern about the effects of industrialization and urbanization on girls' and women's health, which led to a lively debate over female physical education. Among its first champions were Phokion Heinrich Clias (1782–1854) and Johann Adolf Ludwig Werner (1794–1866). Their work found many adherents because, among other reasons, they emphasized exercises for beauty and grace, which reproduced the feminine ideals of the time.

By 1850, a number of gymnastic clubs offered courses intended to make girls healthier and more attractive. Yet few girls appeared to benefit from these opportunities, and those who did came from affluent, middle-class homes. Although physical education for girls was slowly introduced into schools in the latter half of the nineteenth century, it did not become compulsory until the end of the nineteenth century, first in higher education (Prussia in 1894), and, after the turn of the century, in elementary schools.

Exercises for girls were restricted to free and orchestrated exercises and dances and to simple movements on the apparatus such as drills, calisthenics, and hanging from a bar. To preserve health and decency, girls were not allowed to perform exercises that required strength or endurance or that forced them to spread their legs or lift their legs above the waist.

Resistance against physical education of females was based on moral, medical, and aesthetic arguments. The fear of endangering women's health, reducing their capacity to bear strong children, and the fear of masculinizing them were important obstacles to the spread of girls' physical activities.

THE UPSWING OF WOMEN'S *TURNEN* AND SPORT

Women's roles changed rapidly with the industrialization and modernization of society at the end of the nineteenth century. Universities opened their doors to female students, and educated women entered the professions. These social changes influenced the discussions about the physical education of girls and the physical activities of grown women. By the end of the 1880s, when more and more women participated in *Turnen*, women's sections of men's gymnastics clubs were created, as well as a number of sport clubs exclusively for women.

In the twentieth century, modern sport entered the German scene. Women participated in many of the newer sports coming from England, but with some resistance. The concern for preserving health, beauty, and morals set limits on the sport activities of women, who were especially restricted by their clothing. Shortly before World War I, corsets, long skirts, and narrow blouses were replaced by trousers and sweaters. In this period, women were accepted only in "feminine" or upper-class types of sports, such as swimming (segregated from men) or tennis. Participation in tournaments or competitive and aggressive sports, such as track and field and soccer (association football), was prohibited.

RUNNING THE GAUNTLET ON WHEELS
A Memoir of an Early Female Cyclist in Germany

My friend Miss Clara Beyer and I were probably the first ladies to exhibit themselves to a scandalized public on a cycle (a three-wheeler, actually). That was in 1890. At first we had our cycles brought to the outskirts of town and rode on the deserted forest roads, the occasional passer-by hailing us with righteous indignation or with sneers and innuendo. Later we dared to ride through the town itself at dawn. Finally, one splendid afternoon, we set out bravely from the Berlin town square. Hundreds of people gathered on the instant, and a swarm of ragamuffins kept pace with us, chanting remarks of the most charming sort. In short, we ran the gauntlet which caused us to ask ourselves whether the game was worth the candle.

We were fighting a positively fanatical hatred. Pointless to compare ourselves with equestriennes: cycling remained unfeminine, though why remained unanswered. It was enough to bring us to tears. But when, once outside the town, we would speed along under the green canopy of trees, chest expanded and heart racing, we would reaffirm our eternal loyalty to cycling.

The first ladies bicycle race in September 1893 was a breakthrough. For the first time, a numerous and largely sports-minded public saw a phalanx of able female cyclists, tastefully clothed, mastering the machine. How different from seeing a lone woman cycling amidst a hooting mob! Thus the ice was broken, and now only the occasional old fogy dared describe a female bicyclist as an unfeminine creature.

And that is as it should be. Quite apart from the pleasure of the thing, the rapid movement, comparable only to flying in God's fresh air, the beneficial influence of bicycling on a woman's body and spirit is utterly unmistakable.

No more missed trains, no more crowded horse-trolley, no more dearth of hackney-carriages! Free to decide to the minute when and where one wants to be! Those are the spiritual pleasures of cycling. Physically, too, we feel its benign influence. Can any migraine withstand a splendid bicycle ride? And how delectable is the modest meal in a humble country inn when we have put a goodly distance behind us!

Now, as to dress: the first thing to consign to the attic is the corset. An experienced female cyclist can only be amused by the question, "skirt or trousers?" A woman has exactly the same number of legs as a man; she uses them, especially in bicycling, in exactly the same way as a man, and should clothe them just as sensibly, giving each leg its own covering rather than placing both into one. (Has it ever occurred to anyone to put both arms into one sleeve?) The most practical garment for bicycle touring is a pair of trousers, only slightly fuller than a modern gentleman's plus-fours. Of course, one does not parade around in these upon arrival but draws over them the skirt one has prudently brought along on the handlebars.

One piece of advice to new female disciples: in matters of cycling, seek medical advice only from a doctor who is himself a cyclist. It is quite incredible what opinions a noncycling doctor (probably a dying breed, by the way) can voice. Of course, only she whose state of health permits it should bicycle. But that is the only limitation; I admit no other.

For an older lady, the decision to clamber onto a bicycle is more difficult than for a young one. I believe that in the future, old ladies will not need to learn to ride a bicycle; they will grow old as bicycle riders. And the children who are growing up with this machine will consider it an indispensable tool, a part of their very lives.

AMALIE ROTHER
(1897) Women's Bicycling. *Translated by Rodelinde Albrecht. Munich.*

Because the economic costs of tennis, golf, and rowing tended to exclude the nonaffluent, there arose a movement for workers' sports. The German Federation for Workers' Sports, founded in 1893, offered full membership rights to women. Using the motto "Make yourself free," the proletarian gymnasts and athletes proposed liberation of the body and of women. Yet the hard lives of proletarian women kept the number of female members in the proletarian sport movement rather low.

World War I and its aftermath brought profound political, economic, and social changes, especially in gender relationships. In 1919, German women won the right to vote and hold office, but they were still regarded as the "second sex." A woman who chose to embark on a professional career suffered from discrimination; she who chose domesticity was expected to acknowledge her husband as the head of the household. Clothing reform was also less than complete. There was more freedom of movement as ankle-length dresses and tight corsets were discarded, and a new, more athletic ideal of femininity was proclaimed. Short hair, a tanned body, and narrow hips were considered fashionably modern.

Although few people doubted the importance of physical activities to women's health, women's participation in highly competitive sports led to fierce controversy. At its core was the debate over the compatibility of competition and motherhood. The main opposition to strenuous sports for women came from gynecologists and other medical experts, who inveighed against competition and against participation in "manly" sports, such as soccer, raising the fear of masculinization, diminished fertility, and disinclination to bear children.

Nevertheless, more and more German women participated in sport contests, including track and field, that had earlier been considered "unwomanly." In 1919, the German Sports Authority for Athletics (the track and field federation) called upon its member clubs to create sections for female athletes, and in 1920 the first German championships for female athletes were organized in Dresden. Yet female athletes were prohibited from many sports, such as ski jumping and soccer. With few exceptions, German sport organizations were sexually integrated, which tended to place women under men's supervision, while the tendency in France and Great Britain was for women to form their own organizations.

Toward the end of the 1920s, the mass media began to celebrate the achievements of female athletes. Among the early idols were the German airplane pilot Elli Beinhorn, who made headlines with her round-the-world flights as well as her marriage to a famous automobile racer. While the achievements of female track-and-field athletes continued to be met with a mix of fascination and disgust, German gymnastics was gradually transformed into an almost entirely female domain.

In Germany, as well as throughout Europe, a variety of systems and schools of rhythmical gymnastics were propagated, some emphasizing health and hygiene, some more intent on the aesthetics of human movement. The proponents of gymnastics strongly criticized modern sports and its obsession with quantified achievement. They were concerned principally with the quality of the movement, the form and shape of the body, and the harmonious development of the whole person. Common also was a tendency to cultural criticism; gymnastics was affirmed as a natural contrast to the mad pace and artificiality of modern civilization. Although the gymnastics movement propagated a rather traditional image of womanhood, it spoke to many who believed that it offered an essentially feminine movement culture that was free from men's interference and control.

WOMEN'S SPORTS AND NATIONAL SOCIALISM

In National Socialist (Nazi) ideology, biological and racist ideas were revived to restructure the gender order and to recast masculinity and femininity as the polar opposites they were thought to be in the nineteenth century. With varying degrees of success, Nazi ideologues sought to limit women, once again, to their wifely and maternal roles. The fecund female body and the hardened male body were icons of Hitler's "racial hygiene." Physical education became a central pillar in the structure of the Nazi state. It was supposed to prepare men for their predetermined biological role as fighters and women for their role as mothers. In Nazi discourse and in the medical literature influenced by it, discussions of women's sport centered on the questions: what enhances and what diminishes a woman's reproductive function? By providing "healthy" and "appropriate" exercises, organizations such as the Bund Deutscher Mädel (Federation of German Girls) tried to institutionalize the goals of motherhood and the health of the community. Although Nazi ideology was originally opposed to sport competition for women, Hitler realized the propaganda advantages that were sure to accompany demonstrations of physical superiority. Accordingly, his regime supported female athletes in a number of ways, and the 1936 Olympic Games, which took place in Berlin, seemed to prove him right. Although the Games were staged to demonstrate—to the point of absurdity—the cult of masculinity, Germany fielded the most successful team of female athletes.

DEVELOPMENTS AFTER WORLD WAR II

After the devastation and deprivation of World War II, the German population turned quickly to sports, in part because they represented a more attractive world than the ubiquitous ruins of the defeated nation. With the gradual return of ordinary life came a call for women to resume the domestic roles they had been forced to abandon by the exigencies of war. The 1950s emphasized the traditional ideals of home and hearth. Nevertheless, within the context of the Cold War, women's sports became increasingly important. The Federal Republic felt that its female athletes must hold their own against the athletes from the communist regimes of Eastern Europe, especially against those from the German Democratic Republic (GDR).

The astonishing success of East Germany's female athletes sprang from a number of interrelated factors: the centralized search for athletic talent, which began with the systematic recruitment of children; scientific research designed to maximize performance; the concentration of economic resources on sports; the high prestige, social security, and other material rewards (such as trips abroad) granted to successful athletes; and medical manipulation through drugs. The concentration on elite athletes came at the expense of recreational sports. Among other things, facilities available to ordinary citizens were few and poor. Although propagandists proclaimed the contrary, the women in the GDR were far less likely than

In accord with the national fitness program, a group of women take part in an exercise class on a roof of a Berlin building in pre-World War II Germany. (Hulton-Deutsch Collection/Corbis)

those of West Germany to be involved in recreational sports.

In the West, the debate over femininity and sports resumed. When Communist-bloc athletes introduced acrobatic movements into women's gymnastics, the German Gymnastics Federation (Deutscher Turnerbund) found the contortions ugly and unfeminine and withdrew from international competition for a number of years. In other sports, women had to face similar resistance and restrictions: for example, as late as 1955, women were discouraged from playing soccer, which was still deemed unfeminine. The German Football Association ruled that clubs should bar women's teams from using the men's football grounds. It was only in the 1970s that the association reversed itself and began to accept and later support women's soccer.

WOMEN'S SPORTS TODAY

By the end of the twentieth century, German women—among them tennis champion Steffi Graf—were playing an important role in the world of sport. But despite the dramatic changes of recent decades, women were by no means as likely as men to be involved in sports and they still did not have equal opportunity. This is clear from surveys and from the membership rolls of the German Sports Federation (Deutscher Sport-bund). According to German surveys, some 40 percent of adult women said that they participated in sports. Nearly 30 percent of all Germans were members of a sports club; 37 percent of the members were female. One must, however, consider the definitions employed by the researchers. Most of the people who claimed to be active in sport participated in sport irregularly or with a low intensity.

The involvement of women in sports depended more on age, class, and ethnic origin than did the involvement of men. In German clubs, girls typically began to withdraw from sport participation when they reached the age of fourteen, while boys stayed active until they were at least eighteen. Men and women of higher social status were more likely than the less affluent to be athletically active, but the effect of this variable was greater for women than for men. The result is that only a minuscule number of middle-aged and elderly working-class women participated in any sports. This held especially true for girls and women from an Islamic background.

For women participants, the spectrum of options was far wider than in the past. In the 1990s, young women participated in sports once thought to be exclusively male: marathon running, soccer and rugby, water polo, even boxing, and weightlifting. Of course, there continued to be a gender difference in rates of participation in various sports. Men were still more likely to engage in sports requiring aggressive body contact. The largest German sport federation, the German Football Federation, had less than 10 percent female members. On the other hand, the German Gymnastics Federation, with 4 million members, had a female membership of 70 percent. Gymnastics, aerobics, and dance continued to attract far more women than men.

Interest in and commitment to sport were developed in school. In most German states, three hours of physical education per week were obligatory for girls and boys, but the curriculum contributed to the development of gender-specific competencies and interests in sport. For example, the physical education of girls focused very often on rhythmical exercises and gymnastics, whereas boys learned how to play soccer. Discrimination also persisted in elite sport, where women still played a secondary role. Financial support for women's sports was still less than that offered to men. Except in tennis and skiing, opportunities for women to earn their living as professional athletes remained almost nonexistent. The mass media often presented women in a discriminatory fashion. Moreover, women were radically underrepresented among trainers and coaches as well as in sport administration at higher levels: in the German Gymnastics Federation, with a 70% female membership, only two of the seven members of the leading committee were women; only 24% of the positions in the decision-making committees were held by women.

The German Sports Federation developed a program to increase the number of women in decision-making committees, and a certain percentage of positions—depending on the number of female members of a federation—were reserved for women. Whether this program will lead to true equality remains to be seen.

Gertrud Pfister

Bibliography

Guttmann, Allen. (1991) *Women's Sport: A History.* New York: Columbia University Press.

Pfister, Gertrud. (1980) *Frau und Sport: Frühe Texte.* Frankfurt, Germany: Fischer.

———. (1994) "Demands, Realities and Ambivalences: Women in the Proletarian Sports Movement in Germany (1893–1933)." *Women in Sport & Physical Activity Journal* 3, 2:39–69.

———. (1994) *Der Zwang zur Schönheit: Zur Körper- und Bewegungskultur von Mädchen und Frauen.* In *Kein Platzverweis für Frauen.* Berlin, Germany: Senatsverwaltung für Arbeit und Frauen, 35–62.

———. (1996) "Physical Activity in the Name of the Fatherland: *Turnen* and the National Movement (1810–1820)." *Sporting Heritage* 1:14–36.

———. (1998) "Konstruktion von Weiblichkeit und die Bildung des weiblichen Geschlechts bei Guts Muths." In *Beiträge zur Guts Muthsforschung,* edited by Rolf Gessmann, and Manfred Lämmer. St. Augustin, Germany: Academia.

Pfister, Gertrud, and Hans Langenfeld. (1980) "Die Leibesübungen für das weibliche Geschlecht: Ein Mittel zur Emanzipation der Frau?" In *Geschichte der Leibesübungen,* 3, 1, edited by Horst Überhorst. Berlin, Germany: Bartels & Wernitz, 485–521.

———. (1982) "Vom Frauenturnen zum modernen Sport: Die Entwicklung der Leibesübungen der Frauen und Mädchen seit dem ersten Weltkrieg." In *Geschichte der Leibesübungen,* 3, 2, edited by

Horst Überhorst. Berlin, Germany: Bartels & Wernitz, 977–1007.

GIBSON, ALTHEA

(1927–)

U.S. TENNIS PLAYER AND GOLFER

Althea Gibson was one of the leading tennis players of the 1950s and a pioneer in breaking the color barrier in tennis. Her victories at Wimbledon and the U.S. championship opened the way for other African-American women tennis players, although it was not until the 1980s and 1990s that African-American women became regular players on the women's professional tour.

Althea Gibson was born in Silver, South Carolina, on 25 August 1927. Although her parents were originally sharecroppers, she spent her early childhood in Harlem. She attended school there and participated in a number of sports, but tennis was clearly where she excelled. Her first chance to learn the game came through the New York Police Athletic League. Her coach, Buddy Walker, taught her the basics so that she could enter competitions sponsored by the American Tennis Association, a sports organization for African American athletes. She won a number of local competitions and statewide tournaments for African Americans before she was able to surmount the barriers that separated black tennis players from their white counterparts.

In 1946, while playing in a tournament in Ohio, Gibson attracted the attention of Hubert Eaton of Wilmington, Delaware. A physician, Eaton was also an experienced tennis player who saw that Gibson had the talent to succeed in professional tennis. Her mother agreed to let her live with the Eatons. In Wilmington, Gibson improved her game and graduated from Williston High School.

On the tennis circuit, Gibson won five Grand Slam titles as well as nearly 100 other championships. She won Wimbledon and the U.S. and French championships. Her 1957 victory at Wim-

Althea Gibson, 1957. (Hulton-Deutsch Collection/Corbis)

bledon was the first for an African American. The following year, she became the first African American to win the U.S. singles title at Forest Hills. The path was opened for her to play in professional exhibitions until she ended her tennis career in 1963.

Her accomplishments led to her selection as the Associated Press Woman Athlete of 1957. In 1971 Gibson was elected to the National Lawn Tennis Hall of Fame. In 1980 she was one of the original inductees in the International Women's Sports Hall of Fame.

In 1963 Gibson became the first African American woman to join the Ladies Professional Golf Association. Once again she was a pioneer, opening doors for other African Americans to follow in her footsteps. Her achievement in tennis is often compared with Jackie Robinson's breaking of the color barrier in baseball.

Leslie Heaphy

Bibliography

Baldwin, Louis. (1996) *Women of Strength.* Jefferson, NC: McFarland.

Biracree, Tom. (1989) *Althea Gibson.* New York: Chelsea House.

Davidson, Sue. (1997) *Changing the Game: The Stories of Tennis Champions Alice Marble and Althea Gibson.* Seattle: Seal Press, 1997.

Gibson, Althea. (1958) *I Always Wanted To Be Somebody.* New York: Harper's.

GLIDING

Gliders were the first heavier-than-air aircraft, in part because of the simplicity afforded by the lack of an engine, and are still popular both on their own and as an inexpensive introduction to flying.

Gliders, also called sailplanes, fly according to the same aerodynamic principles as powered airplanes, but the lift-producing airflow over the wings is achieved by trading altitude for speed. Being unable to take off autonomously, a glider must be either launched by a winch or towed aloft by an airplane. Once released, it is always descending relative to the surrounding air; to gain altitude, the pilot must find updrafts that ascend faster than the glider sinks—hence the vital importance of knowing meteorology. While short, straight hops are easy, the advanced forms of gliding are very challenging. The best glide ratio—that is, the horizontal distance traveled for a given amount of altitude loss—is a crucial indicator of performance and design quality: higher ratios help achieve longer distances and climbs. Gliders can also perform a wide range of aerobatic maneuvers and reach speeds in excess of 200 kilometers (124.3 miles) per hour.

HISTORY

Although basic glider technology already existed in antiquity, misconceptions about flight prevented the achievement of practical results until about 1853, when a ten-year-old boy became airborne in a glider designed by George Cayley. For the next fifty years, all aviation pioneers experimented with gliders, but the development of the internal combustion engine shifted the emphasis to powered flight before women could establish their presence in gliding. Finally, in December 1909 Florence Taylor became the first woman glider pilot in the world, going solo in her husband's aircraft at Narrabeen Beach (Australia).

As a sport, gliding (also called soaring) was born in Germany after World War I in response to the ban imposed by the Versailles Treaty on powered flying. A grassroots movement emerged in the Wasserkuppe area, where young enthusiasts would build, fly, and repair gliders in intensely nationalistic communities. A licensing system with A, B, and C levels was set up. Many early machines were of the Espenlaub model, a simple wing perched above an open frame fuselage with marginal glide ratio of around 10. By the mid-1930s engineering and aerodynamic knowledge brought in by the Akaflieg (university flying clubs) had raised glide ratios to 25. The first world championships were held in 1937, and gliding was selected for inclusion in the 1940 Olympics as a competitive sport.

RULES AND PLAY OF MODERN GLIDING

Like all air sports, gliding is regulated by the Fédération Aéronautique Internationale (FAI) through the International Gliding Commission, while Organisation Scientifique Technique International du Volàvoile (OSTIV) has replaced International Gliding Technical Committee (ISTUS) as its technical arm. New pilots now enter at C level, which, together with the bronze badge, is a national standard. Silver, gold, diamond, and 1000-kilometer (621.4-mile) badges are FAI standards, awarded for gradually higher levels of achievement in duration, distance, and height. The gold badge, for example, represents respectively 5 hours, 300 kilometers (186.4 miles), and 3000 meters (3281 yards).

Competitions are held in four classes: open, restricted only by a 750-kilogram (1650-pound) maximum weight (glide ratios around 60); 15-meter (49-foot) (which indicates wingspan) 525-kilogram (1155-pound) weight, flaps permitted (glide ratios around 45); standard, comparable to the 15-meter craft, but minus flaps (glide ratio around 42); and world class, a single-type craft class, based on the Polish PW5 Smyk, which made its debut in the 1997 World Air Games (glide ratio 32). Record categories include altitude (absolute and gain: absolute being the highest altitude reached, and gain the difference between take-off/release and the highest altitude reached), distance (straight line, with declared goal and round trip), and speed (over 100-, 200-, and 300-kilometer [62-, 124-, and 186-mile] triangles). Duration was abolished in the 1960s. When a specific course is prescribed, gliders are equipped with cameras or Global Positioning System (GPS) navigation systems to allow judges to verify the actual flight path and award points or penalties.

Most current gliders are made of glass-reinforced plastic, which affords the smooth external finish required to achieve laminar airflow. The FAI World Class, restricted to a single type of craft, was established to combat the spiraling cost of high-performance gliders and attract more young pilots. Another recent concept was the ultralight glider, which because of its limited weight should be able to avoid costly certification procedures but as of 1999 was still handicapped by the lack of a specific FAI category. Motorgliders, which carry a stowable engine for autonomous take-offs and as an additional safety measure, have little appeal for competitions and are confined to recreational uses. More immediate alternatives seem to come from two sports that are enjoying growing popularity—hang gliding and paragliding. In addition to being inexpensive, these offer an unparalleled sense of freedom.

DISTINGUISHED WOMEN PILOTS

Gliding is unique in that two women, Hanna Reitsch of Germany (1912–1979) and Ann Welch of Great Britain (1917–), contributed decisively to the sport in general—not just for women. Reitsch was arguably the greatest woman pilot of all time. With plans to become a flying doctor in Africa, she earned her first gliding license at age nineteen. The plan was set aside by her discovery of test flying. In 1937 she became the first person to fly across the Alps in a glider and was awarded the coveted title of *Flugkapitän* (flight captain). Soon Reitsch was involved in all manner of experiments (including landing gliders on water and on special nets), and in 1938 she became the first woman helicopter pilot. A member of ISTUS, in 1938 she won the German long-distance championship. During World War II Reitsch tested the

Me.163 rocket fighters and Reichenberg flying bombs, receiving the Iron Cross first class. Imprisoned by the Americans in 1945–1946, she resumed gliding in 1952. Although tarnished by her association with Nazism, Reitsch established gliding schools in India and Ghana, earned three Diamond badges, and set many records, including, at age seventy-seven, the first 1,000-kilometer (621.4-mile) flight by a woman. She also set a women's altitude record on this flight, but it could not be certified by the FAI due to a malfunction in the recording barograph.

Ann Welch was instrumental in the spread of gliding in Britain after World War II. After earning her license in 1934, she took up gliding in 1937 and became an instructor a year later. During World War II she served as a ferry pilot with the Air Transport Auxiliary. Between 1948 and 1985 Welch was eight times captain of the British team in the world gliding championships and for many years the chairman of the British Gliding Association's Instructors Committee. Her records included the British women's declared goal flight (i.e., to a previously established destination, denying the pilot the opportunity of changing route in case of difficulty), 527 kilometers (327.5 miles). In the early 1980s she embraced hang gliding and microlight aircraft, becoming chairman of the British Microlight Aircraft Association. For her contribution to aviation and her efforts to encourage young pilots, Welch was awarded the Order of the British Empire (OBE) by Queen Elizabeth II and the Gold Air Medal by the FAI, of which she was also vice president. She has also authored some twenty books on gliding and flying.

Other great pilots include Marcelle Choisnet, who overcame an incapacitating injury to become the world's leading woman glider pilot between 1945 and 1955, raking up thirteen French and fourteen world records, including an amazing single-seat endurance record of 35 hours and 3 minutes. She eventually became the first woman to be awarded the diamond badge and the Lilienthal medal. In addition to setting a number of national women's records, Adele Orsi of Italy proved that women could compete on an equal footing with men by winning the Italian national gliding championships in 1973 and 1976. Monika Warstat of the German Democratic Republic won the first European women's gliding championship, held in

Hungary in 1979. In America, Yvonne Gaudry set a 12,190-meter (13,331-yard) altitude record.

Gregory Alegi

See also Hang Gliding; Parachuting

Bibliography

De Bernardi, Fiorenza, ed. (1984) *Pink Line: A Gallery of European Women Pilots*. Rome: Aeritalia.

Fédération Aéronautique Internationale Web Site: <http://www.fai.org/>. 1999.

Rado, Gheorghe. (1993) *Prioritati si recorduri mondiale de aviatie*. Bucharest: Tehnoprod.

Reitsch, Hanna. (1951)*Fliegen mein Leben*. Stuttgart: Deutsche Verlags-Anstalt.

Welch, Ann, and Lorne Welch. (1965) *The Story of Gliding*. London: Murray.

GOALBALL

Goalball is a ball game played on a court by players who are visually impaired, either because they are blind or because they are blindfolded. The only game developed specifically for the blind, it was invented for soldiers who lost their sight in World War II. It is now played by women as well as men.

Sometimes called "the game in the dark," goalball was developed in Europe after World War II as a way to rehabilitate newly blinded veterans. Obligatory blindfolds ensure that, regardless of their impairment, players cannot see at all, relying totally on hearing and touch. To play the game officially one must be visually impaired to a minimum of legally blind (20/200 with correction). Schools interested in including their entire population offer goalball competitions for anyone interested because, other than a ball, the only required piece of equipment is a blindfold. However, most players wear elbow and knee pads, hip pads, and some wear mouth guards, and, as the game becomes faster and players get stronger, more players are wearing helmets.

The International Blind Sports Association and the U.S. Association for Blind Athletes are the international and national governing bodies for goalball. Of all the sports in which those with visual impairments compete, goalball is the only one designed specifically for that population and is the only team sport other than basketball associated with the American Basketball Association (ABA). All other sports for the visually impaired are variations of those for able-bodied players; the only variations are those made to increase players' safety.

Men's goalball competition increased until it became part of the Paralympics (previously known as Olympics for the Disabled or International Games for the Disabled) in 1976 in Toronto, Canada. U.S. players did not fare well in their first international competition because they had only learned the game in the aisle of the bus on their way to the gymnasium. Although not originally involved in the game, women have played goalball at the national level since 1978 and have competed in world championships and Paralympics since 1982. In the 1998 world championship in Madrid, Spain, U.S. women placed third.

The markings on the floor (9 × 18 meters or 30 × 60 feet, slightly less than a regulation volleyball court) are made with mat tape with a string underneath, so they can be easily felt with regular court or tennis shoes, worn by most goalball players. The regulation ball (about the size of a basketball) has bells inside for players to hear its movement.

The aim of the game is to have the ball cross your opponents' end line, which is defended by all three members of the team. Defenders try to prevent this by diving on their sides to stop the ball. Typically starting in a low squat position, defenders listen carefully to the thrown ball before committing to a position on the floor. Once the defense has stopped the ball, offensive play takes over.

The offense mode, which begins when a player has a solid hand on the ball, is determined by the official. Players then have 8 seconds to throw the ball; this includes any actions taken before releasing the ball, such as passing to a teammate or changing positions. On offense, the player stands up to throw the ball underhand (similar to a bowler) in an attempt to score.

Throwing the ball hard and fast can stop the bells from ringing, making defense more difficult.

Goalball has become popular with the narrow segment of the population for which it was created, and it seems likely to remain so.

Eugenia S. Scott

See also Deaf Olympics, Disability Sport, Special Olympics

Bibliography

International Blind Sports Association (IBSA) (1997). *Goalball Rules.*

Kriebel, Eugenia and Domiguez, Joe. (1988). *Goalball.* New Mexico School for the Visually Handicapped.

GOLF

Golf is a ball-and-stick game, the chief aim of which is hitting a small, hard ball into small holes—nine or eighteen—placed at prescribed intervals around a grassy course. Women have competed in golf from its earliest times and continue to increase their participation today.

Golf has become one of the premier world recreational and professional sports. The United States Golf Association (USGA) reports 26.5 million golfers aged twelve and over in the United States, 22 percent of whom are female. The ratios seem similar in other western countries, and women's participation in Asian countries is growing as well. In fact, females comprise 39 percent of all beginning golfers. In the United States, the average woman golfer is forty-three years old, has a household income of $61,000, and plays sixteen rounds a year.

Although its relatively high cost has somewhat limited participation to people of a higher income bracket, golf reaches out to all people worldwide, as is seen by the increasing numbers of public courses and a 68 percent growth in the number of junior golfers (those under 18). The median cost of a round of golf at an eighteen-hole municipal course is about $27, including cart and green fees. Information and statistics for the

Se Ri Pak of Korea tosses grass to check the wind at 1998 U.S. Open in Kohler, Wisconsin. (AP Photo)

United States and thirty-two USGA-affiliated nations can be obtained from the USGA.

HISTORY

Scotland, with headquarters for golf rules housed within the Royal and Ancient Golf Club (R&A) at St. Andrews, Fife, has long claimed to have founded the game. However, there are pictures and records from many other nations depicting a sport resembling the ancient ball-and-stick target game. A Roman game called *paganica* was introduced to France and Germany and then to the Netherlands. The Dutch have records of *kolf* as early as 1300. *Chole*, a derivative of hockey, played in Belgium as early as 1353, may have provided the most direct link to Scotland. Reportedly, a Scottish regiment aiding the French against the English in 1421 became entranced by the sport and, when they returned home, played a modified version that eventually became golf as we know it today. It became so popular that it had to be banned in 1457 by the Scottish parliament of

James II because it interfered with military training for the wars against the English. The ban was reaffirmed and continued through the parliaments of James III (1470) and King James IV (1491); it was finally lifted with the signing of the Treaty of Glasgow between England and Scotland (1502).

That same year, James IV is credited with the first recorded purchase of golf equipment—a set of clubs constructed by a bow-maker in Perth, Scotland. Queen Catherine of England referred to the growing popularity of golf in England in 1513, forty years before the first recorded evidence of golf at St. Andrews. In 1553, the Archbishop of St. Andrews granted the local population the right to play on the St. Andrews links, and from then on the game took root as the people of Scotland's own sport.

Mary, Queen of Scots, is the first recorded female golfer. Legend has it that it was also a great part of her demise, because she was seen playing shortly after the death of her first husband, Lord Darnley, a behavior considered totally unseemly for a woman in her position. At her trial for treason, her untimely golf playing (rather than adhering to the accepted period of mourning) presumably contributed to her conviction and beheading in 1587. She left her mark forever on the sport, however, because she is credited with the invention of caddies, an affectionate reference to the cadets she brought along to carry her equipment during her many rounds on the links.

Despite being banned on Sundays (because it stole attendance from church), golf continued to evolve. In 1618, the "feathery ball" was introduced, and in 1642 John Dickson was officially licensed as the ball-maker for Aberdeen, Scotland. The game made its way to the American colonies, where, in 1659, reference is made to the banning of golf from the streets of Albany, New York. It took another eighty-five years before the sport became organized enough to form its first club—the Honourable Company of Edinburgh Golfers—and with it the awarding of a silver cup to the annual champion. Within the next decade, the St. Andrews Golfers (later the Royal and Ancient Golf Club, or R&A) had published the first codified rules of the game.

Up until then, golf had been played at a variety of venues, with varying numbers of holes. The scoring was based on match play—competition for each hole—with a point for the individual who scored the lowest numbers of shots per hole. This head-to-head competition was consistent with the emphasis of most male sports of the time: the victory of one man over another.

By 1764, the St. Andrews Golfers had combined their course layout into an eighteen-hole venue with nine holes going out from the clubhouse and another nine coming back, setting the standard for all future courses. Several other courses were established, including Royal Burgess of Edinburgh (1773), Royal Aberdeen (1780), and, in the United States, the South Carolina Golf Club in Charleston (1786).

The earliest recorded reference to a women's golf competition is 1810, at Musselburgh, Scotland. By 1832, the North Berwick Club in Scotland, which included women in its activities, was founded. Although excluded from competition at the club, women became intrigued with golf and continued to participate and refine the game.

With the opening at St. Andrews in 1867 of the Ladies' Golf Club, the first official golf club for women, women's competitions were off and running. On 19 April 1893, in London, Miss Issette Person convened a meeting of dedicated women golfers and formed the Ladies' Golf Union (LGU). In addition to promoting general interest in the women's game, its goals were to develop a handicapping system, provide uniform rules, and fund an annual championship tournament for women. Later that year, the first Women's British Amateur Championship was contested under the rules of the LGU, with thirty-three contestants at the nine-hole course at Royal Lytham and St. Anne's Golf Club. Lady Margaret Scott won this inaugural event in what was to be the first of three consecutive titles for her.

In 1895 the USGA hosted the first U.S. Women's Amateur Championship at the Meadow Brook Club on Long Island, New York. The winner over ten other competitors was Mrs. Charles S. Brown, with a score of 132 for eighteen holes (nine holes, break for lunch, and nine more holes.) In 1896 the format was changed to match play, which is still the format in the United States for state titles, collegiate play, and other team events. This event was the first of three consecutive titles won by teenager Beatrix Hoyt and the beginning of the recognition of golf as a sport for all age groups.

By 1900, golf had become an international event, with women traveling to compete on both sides of the Atlantic. In 1905 several U.S. golfers played in the British Ladies' Championship at Cromer, including Georgie Bishop (1904 U.S. Women's Amateur champion), Mary Adams (credited with shooting consistently in the low nineties in national competitions), Frances Griscom, and two other players destined to make a lasting impression on the future of international competition: Margaret and Harriet Curtis. Their dedication to the game and the expansion of competition for women led to the creation of the Curtis Cup Matches, a biennial amateur competition between the United States and Britain. The first match was in 1905, with the British team (composed of English, Scottish, and Irish players) winning 6–1. In 1913 the Curtis sisters successfully promoted a competition between a U.S. team and a team of British and Canadian golfers, which included Gladys Ravenscroft (who later won the English and U.S. national titles), Ireland's Mabel Harrison, and Canada's Violet Pooley, Florence Harvey, and F. B. Scott. The U.S. team included the Curtis sisters, Lilian Hyde, Marion Hollins, Georgie Bishop, Nonna Barlow, and Katherine Harley. The British team again won, albeit by a narrow 5–4 margin.

The development of women's international golf competition was interrupted by World War 1 (1914–1918), and it was not until 1932 that the Curtis Cup become an officially recognized and sponsored event. Yet the game had spread to South Africa (1885) and Japan, where, in 1914 at Komozawa, the Tokyo Club was founded, triggering a golf boom in that nation. With the game already firmly entrenched in Britain, France, Canada, and the United States, golf was on its way to becoming a global sport.

RULES AND PLAY

The rules of golf are governed in the United States and USGA-affiliated countries by the USGA, and in Britain by the British Golf Association (BGA) and the R&A. A major attraction of the game is its flexible scoring system, where players can compete against the course and their own personal best score (medal play), with the lowest total score

winning the event, or in head-to-head competitions (match play) by hole. In medal play—the format seen most commonly at professional golf events—the winner is the one who plays the round or rounds in the fewest total strokes.

Historically, however, many important women's competitions are contested using match play, where the game is played by holes. A hole is won by the team or individual holing the ball in the fewest strokes. Score is kept by the number of holes won. A tied hole is termed a "halved" hole, with a half point awarded to each player. A match is won by the side winning the most holes. Play can be terminated earlier than the total number of holes (usually 18) if a side is more holes "up" than holes left to play. Most amateur championships are contested using match play, pitting each player directly against her opponent. Team matches are also commonly contested using match-play scoring, and most collegiate golf events use this scoring system.

There are also other modifications of scoring and modified team events, including a Stabelford system, which awards points based on a score for a bogie (one stroke over par on a hole), par (the score a professional golfer is expected to shoot on a hole, usually including two putts each hole), birdie (one shot under par), or eagle (two strokes under par). This system awards golfers for consistency in play against par.

Other formats such as "Captain's Choice" enable beginners to participate on teams with professional or experienced golfers. In this format, all team members hit a shot, and the ball in the best position is selected as the team shot. Other team members then place their balls at this point and hit the next shot, continuing in this way until the ball is "holed out" (in the cup).

The most common way for golfers of varying skill to compete in the same tournament is by assigning "handicaps." Under USGA rules, the last twenty rounds of a golfer's scores are averaged. Par (in most cases, 72 strokes) is then subtracted from this average, and the handicap is the difference or a percentage of the difference of one's scoring average from par. Players compete in medal play, keeping their aggregate score. At the end of the round, the score is adjusted by subtracting the handicap from the total score. (This is called the net score.) In this way, prizes can be awarded based on the lowest net score, and many golfers with higher handicaps who play better than their normal score are rewarded by winning the match or event. This handicapping system, along with the aforementioned scoring options, has made golf an attractive leisure sport for golfers of all ages, mixed teams or competitions by gender, or for parents to compete alongside their children in team events. It offers myriad opportunities for success, mixed levels of competitiveness, and for individual goal setting and challenges.

THE RISE OF PROFESSIONAL GOLF

The expansion of professional golf resulted from growing interest and participation in the game. As the numbers of competitions increased worldwide, rules and equipment were changed. The "guttie," or gutta-percha ball, introduced to the game in 1848, added interest because it flew much farther than the feathery ball and was cheaper. The rubber core ball, patented by Coburn Haskell in 1898, enabled the ball to travel even farther. In 1902 groove-faced irons were invented. The mass production of golf clubs developed from 1900 to 1920, and clubs were numbered and standardized. By 1905 the dimpled-pattern ball cover was introduced by William Taylor in England, and in 1906 the Goodrich Company introduced a golf ball with a rubber core filled with compressed air.

In 1910 the R&A banned the center-shafted putter (but the USGA kept it legal). The same year, Arthur F. Knight patented steel shafts. With the new equipment, the demand for representatives and demonstrations led to the rise of professional golf. Professionals were hired for instruction, course design, and management. They also toured various clubs, gave clinics, and promoted equipment for the new sporting goods industry. The first female professional, Mrs. Gordon Robertson, was hired at Princess Ladies' Golf Club in 1908. Women's professional golf had found its place in the development of modern golf.

After World War I, the Curtis sisters renewed their efforts to establish a permanent international competition for women in golf. They donated a Revere bowl as a trophy, and in 1928 Margaret Curtis made a commitment to England's four-time British Ladies champion, Cecil Leitch, to cover her expenses and to guarantee up to $5,000

Joyce Wethered holding the Ladies Golf Championship Cup in 1925 at Troon, Scotland. (Hulton-Deutsch Collection/Corbis)

a match for the first ten matches played. While not successful in 1929, in 1930 Glenna Collett (later Collett Vare) arranged a match between the United States and Britain, financed by a travel agency. In 1931 Andre Vagliano presented a silver trophy, the Vagliano Cup, for annual competition between Britain and France, and the LGU finally agreed to matches between the United States and France. The same year, the USGA and LGU agreed to hold a match where teams would compete every other year, alternating sites in the United States and Great Britain. This match later became the Curtis Cup, in which the French were invited to field a team whenever they chose.

The first official Curtis Cup was held in May 1932 at England's Wentworth Golf Club with 15,000 spectators in attendance. The British team was led by Joyce Wethered (later, Lady Heathcoat-Armory), and the United States team by Marion Hollins. The Revere Curtis Cup was won by the United States team after they swept the foursomes, although Wethered defeated Vare in singles—a result that was repeated in head-to-head competition over many years. In fact, the Wethered-Vare matches became so legendary that towns closed up shop and gave workers the day off to get to the course and watch the matches. Both women were credited with permanently raising the standard of women's competition in golf.

Wethered had only one formal golf lesson as a child. She was still a teenager when she defeated Cecil Leitch in the 1920 English Ladies Championship. United States golfing legend of the Roaring 20s and 30s, Robert Tyre (Bobby) Jones, the only player to win the Grand Slam of men's golf, reportedly called Wethered the "greatest golfer of all time, man or woman." Before retiring after a career of only ten years in golf, she had won four British Open Amateurs and five English championships, plus several Curtis Cup victories over Vare.

Glenna Collett Vare was introduced to golf at the age of fourteen by her father. Like Wethered, she had few lessons and took to the sport early in life. At nineteen, in 1922, she won her first of six U.S. championship titles. Her U.S. amateur titles spanned thirteen years, and she became a role model for women golfers. Tributes to her sportsmanship and character have included induction into the Women's Golf Hall of Fame in 1950 and the World Golf Hall of Fame in 1975, the naming of the Vare trophy awarded annually to the lowest scoring seasonal average of the LPGA, and the Glenna Collett Vare trophy, given to the U.S. Junior Girls Champion yearly.

While the Wethered and Vare matches were gaining international acclaim, a young Canadian, Violet Pooley Sweeny, was making a permanent mark on golfing history, winning six Pacific Northwest Golf Championship titles between 1909 and 1928. In a thirty-year career, she won nine British Columbia championships. She was inducted into the British Columbia Sports Hall of Fame and the Pacific Northwest Golf Hall of Fame, and, in 1998, the Canadian Golf Hall of Fame.

WOMEN'S PROFESSIONAL GOLF

Play by Vare, Wethered, Sweeny, Alexa Stirling (winner of the U.S. Amateur, 1914–1916), and other outstanding golfers lifted the level of competition for women and laid the groundwork for professional women's golf. Yet, except for occasional showcasing or instructing for clubs or equipment, prize money for women was slow to emerge, compared with their male counterparts. In 1935 Helen Hicks was one of the first to be hired to promote women's golf through exhibitions and clinics by Wilson Sporting Goods and to advise them about golf club design for women. Four years later, the company added Helen Dettweiler to their staff. About the same time, Mildred "Babe" Didrikson Zaharias, 1932 Olympic track-and-field medalist, turned to golf. In 1935 she was declared a professional by the USGA, as its definition of amateur was restricted to those who had never held professional status in any sport. Zaharias played professionally until 1946. Her personality and international fame attracted spectators and brought attention to women's professional golf. She ushered in a new style of clothing, shedding long, tight skirts and other restrictive garments for knickers and slacks, which increased comfort and allowed more freedom to swing for distance. Reinstated as an amateur in 1946, she won an incredible seventeen amateur titles in two years, including the 1947 British Women's Open Championship—the first U.S. golfer to do so.

In the 1930s, women professionals had few tournament opportunities other than the Women's Western Open and the Titleholders. When Dettweiler won the Women's Western Open in 1939, no prize money was offered. In amateur golf, Virginia Van Wie was preeminent, winning three consecutive titles from 1932 to 1934. In 1939 Vare won her sixth title, defeating the runner-up, sixteen-year-old Patty Berg. In 1941, Berg won her first professional tournament, earning a $100 war bond for her efforts.

World War II disrupted the expansion of professional and competitive women's golf. The few professionals of the day put their careers on hold, joining the armed forces or the Red Cross. At the end of the war, the growth of women's golf resumed. In 1944 Hope Seignious, Betty Hicks, Ellen Griffin, and a few others chartered the Women's Professional Golf Association (WPGA). Berg, who had turned professional in 1940 after winning the U.S. Amateur, also joined. Associated with the Wilson Company to represent women's clubs, she became well known as a golf teacher, and many young female competitors began with her signature Patty Berg clubs for women.

The WPGA was officially disbanded in early 1949 due to financial stress. However, the golf leaders of the time were quick to try again. Despite this organizational setback, golf for women was off and running. That same year, Louise Suggs won the U.S. Women's Open by a fourteen-stroke margin, and Marie Roke of Wollaston, Massachusetts, aced a 393-yard hole—the longest ace ever recorded by a woman. Also in 1949, the first USGA Girls' Junior Championship was won by Marlene Bauer. After Fred Corcoran, Zaharias's manager, became tournament manager for the women's professional tour, he proposed changing the name to the Ladies' Professional Golf Association (LPGA), and in 1950, during the U.S. Women's Open Championship in Wichita, Kansas, the LPGA's certificate of incorporation was signed, with Berg elected as its first president, Helen Dettweiler as vice-president, Betty Jameson as treasurer, and Sally Sessions as secretary.

In 1950 the women's golf tour consisted of eleven events and a total purse of $50,000. In 1952 Jameson donated the Vare Trophy in her honor, and Marlene Hagge won the Sarasota Open at the age of eighteen years and fourteen days, setting an LPGA age record, while Patty Berg shot a 64, the lowest recorded eighteen-hole round for women to date.

In the early tour years, players ran their own tournaments, setting up the golf courses, signing the checks, and making policy decisions. At times, the events consisted of ten or fewer professionals, and amateurs were invited to complete the field. In fact, the first LPGA tournament in 1950, the Tampa Open, was won by an amateur, Polly Riley.

The courage, talent, and perseverance of the early pioneers held the tour and women's professional golf together. Zaharias, diagnosed with cancer in 1953, returned in 1954 to win the U.S. Women's Open. Among other pioneers were Betsy Rawls and Louise Suggs. Rawls, a 1950 physics major from the University of Texas, became a professional golfer when she was hired by Wilson after her graduation. In her rookie year, she won the 1951 U.S. Open, the first of four that she won. In all, she captured fifty-five titles, becoming known for her great shotmaking on the greens. After retiring from play in 1975, Rawls became executive director of the McDonald's LPGA Championship.

Between 1950 and 1962, Louise Suggs, called "Miss Sluggs" by the comedian Bob Hope after he saw her hit the ball so far, won fifty titles on the LPGA Tour and eleven major championship titles, including two U.S. Open Championships. She was hired by MacGregor Sporting Goods and represented them with a line of clubs named for her.

WOMEN GOLFERS IN THE LPGA HALL OF FAME

The LPGA Hall of Fame is considered one of the more difficult sports halls of fame to enter, as female golfers must compile a substantial number of tour victories and victories in major events to gain admittance. As of 2000, only eighteen women golfers had qualified:

1951	Patty Berg
	Betty Jameson
	Loise Suggs
	Babe Didrikson Zaharias
1960	Betsy Rawls
1964	Mickey Wright
1975	Kathy Whitworth
1977	Sandra Haynie
	Carol Mann
1982	JoAnne Carner
1987	Nancy Lopez
1991	Pat Bradley
1993	Patty Sheehan
1994	Dinah Shore (Honorary member)
1995	Betsy King
1999	Amy Alcott
2000	Beth Daniel
	Juli Inkster

In an effort to standardize play for professionals and amateurs in major competition, the USGA assumed control of the U.S. Open in 1953. This paralleled the organization of the British Women's Open, which was aligned with the R&A, and helped promote tournament play for professionals and amateurs alike. In 1958, further organization of amateur standards came from the formation of the World Amateur Golf Council, combining the USGA and organizations from thirty-two other countries. At the same time, a new system for handicapping was implemented, in which each golfer had a single USGA handicap instead of various other versions. This allowed men and women to compete in tournaments and provided standards so that individuals of varying skill could participate equitably.

By the 1960s, new golfing greats had emerged, including Mickey Wright. Inducted in the World Golf Hall of Fame in 1976, she amassed eighty-two career victories (thirteen major titles) and was the leading money winner in women's golf from 1961 to 1964. In 1963 she won thirteen tour events. Her rivalry with Rawls and Whitworth sparked the players to reach new levels of play. Not to be outdone, Whitworth became the first LPGA member to cross the $1 million mark in career earnings, leading the tour in earnings eight times and winning the LPGA Player of the Year award seven times. The first U.S. Senior Women's Amateur Championship, for women over fifty, was held in 1963 and was won by Maureen Orcutt.

Of even greater significance to the future of women's sport, in 1963, African American and two-time Wimbledon tennis champion Althea Gibson joined the LPGA tour. Breaking the color barrier for women's golf occurred only two years after the PGA (men) officially removed the Caucasian-only clause from their constitution. That same year, the final round of the U.S. Women's Open was televised, suggesting to many young girls the possibilities of golf for a life passion or career. Four years later, African American Renee Powell became a regular player on the LPGA tour, and the women in golf became champions of equal rights for women everywhere. They refused to hold the tournament at any venue where Gibson or Powell were not allowed into a clubhouse or where they faced other discrimination. Today, the international and diverse representation in women's golf is evident, with young players from all over the world heading the top, including 1998 rookie sensation and LPGA champion Se Ri Pak from South Korea. Pak's reward for her four wins in a rookie year, including two major titles, was the 1998 LPGA Rookie of the Year award. She was only the second player ever to win two major tournaments in her rookie year.

Women's talents continued to improve as records continued to fall. In 1964 professional Mickey Wright shot a 62 for eighteen holes, and in 1965 amateur Mrs. William Jenkins double-eagled the par-5 twelfth hole at Longview Golf Course, the longest ever recorded by a woman. That same year, France won the first Women's World Amateur Team Championship. In 1967 French amateur champion Catherine Lacoste became the only amateur ever to win the modern U.S. Open. Also in 1967, the LPGA Hall of Fame was established with entry standards tougher than any other sport, requiring inductees to have been members for at least ten consecutive years and to have participated in thirty or more official events. Its first members were great women golfers and pioneers who had been inducted into the World Golf Hall of Fame in 1950, including Vare, Wethered, Wright, Zaharias, and the Curtis sisters.

In 1971 Laura Baugh set a new record as the youngest winner of the U.S. Amateur at the age of sixteen years, two months. In 1972 Carolyn Gidone won the U.S. Senior Women's Amateur for a record fifth consecutive time. In 1976 Judy Rankin set a new season earnings record of more than $100,000, while JoAnn Carner won her record eighth USGA championship, having previously won the girls' junior, five women's amateurs, and two other USGA titles. In 1978 the Thailand Ladies' Amateur Open Golf and Inter-Club Team Championships and in 1979 the Nichirei International U.S.-Japan Team Championships were inaugurated. In 1981 Kathy Whitworth surpassed $1 million in career prize money, and in 1985 Nancy Lopez set the LPGA seventy-two-hole record of 268 at the Henredon Classic.

As women made their mark in women's golf, they also became recognized across golf's gender barrier. In 1987 Judy Bell became the first woman elected to the USGA executive committee. Two years later, reflecting the growing appeal of the game to women and girls, the LPGA began

GENDER DISCREPANCIES IN WINNINGS

The Ladies Professional Golf Association still lags far behind the men's Professional Golf Association in the amount of money to be won on the tour. In 1999 the men competed for $135 million while the women competed for $36.2 million. A major factor in the differential is the greater television appeal of the men's tour and its $400 million television contract.

sponsoring the PGA Urban Youth Golf Program and the LPGA Girls' Golf Club. This club has expanded its outreach throughout the United States, Canada, New Zealand, and Australia, in partnership with the USGA and the Girl Scouts of the U.S.A.

The 1980s were dominated by Nancy Lopez. In 1977, her rookie year, she won nine championships, including five events in a row. She later won the prestigious Vare trophy three times, was named "Golfer of the Decade" by *Golf Magazine* for the years 1978 to 1987, was inducted into the World Golf Hall of Fame in 1989, and received the 1998 Bob Jones Award for distinguished sportsmanship in golf. As the world watched her win and play superb championship golf through three pregnancies and the rearing of a family, Lopez showed that motherhood and golf are not mutually exclusive. More recently, she formed her own company to design and develop a line of clubs and equipment for women, and she continues to be a dominant force on the tour.

In the 1990s, the tour sponsored two events worth $1 million each, demonstrating the growth of the game and its impact on the economy. In 1994 the LPGA moved its Hall of Fame to the LPGA International in Daytona Beach, Florida. Also in the 1990s, the Solheim Cup was started and sponsored by Karsten Manufacturing, creating biennial professional match-play competition between the LPGA and European Women's Professional Golfers Tour (WPGET). These events signal the increasing internationalization of women's professional golf. Since 1988, eight of the last ten LPGA Rookie-of-the-Year winners came from Sweden, Scotland, England, Japan, Australia, and South Korea. Laura Davies of Great Britain, known for her tremendous driving dis-

tance, won the U.S. Open in 1987; on her first trip to the United States, Liselotte Neumann of Sweden repeated this feat in 1988. Japanese women emerging on the world tour include Hiromi Kobayshi and Ayako Okamoto. In 1996 Karrie Webb of Australia became the first LPGA player to reach over $1 million in single-season earning, sporting a new season-low scoring average record of 70. The next year, Annika Sorenstam of Sweden surpassed Webb's season-earning record with $1.24 million. By 1998, the Mercury LPGA Series was instituted as the first television series for women's golf, and Betsy King of the United States became the first player ever to cross $6 million in career earnings.

Golf for women has won a prominent place as a leisure pursuit, a competitive sport, and a corporate lifestyle, and it continues to grow. Today, women take more golf lessons than men, and it is not unusual to find golf schools for women only. There are executive women's golf leagues forming, and new coeducational tournaments are encouraging competition between men and women. Women pioneers set the stage, and today's woman will find a wide array of opportunities to enjoy and celebrate golf as a sport for all age groups and for amateurs and professionals alike.

Debra Ann Ballinger

Bibliography

Chambers, Marcia, and Amy Alcott. (1995) *The Unplayable Lie: The Untold Story of Women and Discrimination in American Golf.* New York: Golf Digest Pocket Books, Simon & Schuster.

Crosset, Todd, W. (1995) *Outsiders in the Clubhouse: The World of Women's Professional Golf.* New York: SUNY Press.

GOOLAGONG, EVONNE

(1951–)

AUSTRALIAN TENNIS PLAYER

Evonne Goolagong was the first of the very few Aboriginal women who have represented Australia in international sport. As such, she faced racism in addition to the usual difficulties of being a professional sportswoman and champion tennis player.

Goolagong was born in Balleran, New South Wales, on 31 July 1951. In her infancy her father found some old tennis balls in a car. When he gave her one, she is said to have clutched it as if she knew it represented her future. She first played tennis by hitting balls with a broom handle, then with a borrowed racquet. When she was thirteen, she was discovered at a summer-holiday coaching camp in rural New South Wales. Noting her considerable talent, her coach, Vic Edwards, took her to stay with his family in Sydney during the holidays. When it became clear that Goolagong could not train in the country and needed to be in Sydney, the move became permanent.

Goolagong's first attempt at Wimbledon, in 1970, was not a success; she was knocked out in the second round. Her first major victory came the next year, when she won the French Open. She followed this feat a few months later with an unexpected win at Wimbledon against fellow Australian Margaret Court. These two wins made her the top-ranked women's tennis player in the world. In 1972 Goolagong again reached the finals at Wimbledon, where she lost to Billie Jean King. That same year, she was awarded a prestigious Member of the British Empire (MBE) medal by the Queen of England. The women's singles title at Wimbledon eluded her again in 1975, when she lost in the final to King, and in 1976, when she lost to Chris Evert Lloyd. Goolagong, however, won the Italian Open in 1973 and the Australian Open four times. She also had significant success as a

Evonne Goolagong in 1971. (Picturequest)

doubles player, winning a string of major titles. She was a member of the Australian Federation Cup team from 1971 to 1976.

Although Goolagong was a popular player on the tennis circuit, noted for her grace and the obvious pleasure she took in playing the game, she was criticized as well. She was attacked from both sides of the racial divide in Australia. Whites suggested that she went "walkabout" (retreated into her own world) during tournaments when she did not play well, while Aborigines accused her of forgetting her aboriginal roots. There were repeated protests from 1971 to 1973 when Goolagong applied to the apartheid regime in South Africa for a visa so that she could play in the South African Open.

In 1976 Goolagong married Roger Cawley and retired temporarily to have her first child. She celebrated her return to tennis two years later with a victory in the Australian Open. In 1980 she turned the tables on Chris Evert by winning the final at Wimbledon. Another temporary retirement followed the birth of her second child. Goolagong returned to the elite level of tennis in 1981, becoming the fifth female tennis player to win a million dollars in tournament play. Unfortunately, a recurring foot injury ended her career; after 1983 she did not appear on the tennis circuit until 1990, when she played in an over-35 doubles event at Wimbledon.

J. P. Anderson

Bibliography

Barrett, John, ed. (1984) *World of Tennis, 1984.* London: Willow Books.

Emery, David, ed. (1983) *Who's Who in International Tennis.* London: Sphere Books.

Evans, Richard. (1988) *Open Tennis.* London: Bloomsbury.

Goolagong, Evonne. (1975) *Evonne.* London: Granada Publishing.

Stell, Marion K. (1991) *Half the Race: A History of Australian Women in Sport.* New South Wales: Angus and Robertson.

Tingay, Lance. (1977) *100 Years of Wimbledon.* Middlesex: Guinness.

Vamplew, Wray, et al. (1997) *The Oxford Companion to Australian Sport.* Melbourne, Australia: Oxford University Press.

Steffi Graf executes her famed slice backhand during a match at the 1990 French Open. (TempSport)

GRAF, STEFFI

(1969–)

GERMAN TENNIS PLAYER

Stefanie Maria Graf is considered by many experts to be the best female tennis player of the late 1980s and early 1990s and one of the five best female tennis players of the twentieth century. The winner of 106 tournaments, she is one of only three women to win all four Grand Slam tournaments in a single year (the others were Maureen Connolly of the U.S. in 1953 and Margaret Court of Australia in 1970).

Graf was born in Manheim, Germany, on 14 June 1969, the first child of Peter and Heidi Graf. Both parents were tennis players, and when Steffi was three, her father began to teach her to play. The following year, her father gave up his car dealership, and the family moved to Brühl, where they established a tennis school with Steffi as the primary student. Winning her first tournament at the age of six, she began training on weekends and vacations at a government tennis center, while continuing to practice under her father's guidance during the week. She was successful on the junior circuit in Germany and Europe, turning professional when she was thirteen.

Graf's first professional tournament victory came in 1986 with her defeat of Chris Evert in the Family Circle Cup finals in South Carolina. The following year, she won the French Open, the first of twenty-two Grand Slam championships. Two months later, she was ranked the number one women's player in the world, a position she held for 186 consecutive weeks until March 1991. In 1988 she reached the top of the sport when she won the "Golden" Grand Slam (Australian, French, and U.S. Opens, and Wimbledon) and the gold medal in women's singles at the Olympics in Seoul. In 1989 she won three of the four Grand Slams but lost to Arantxa Sanchez Vicario of Spain in the French Open final. Her dominance on the women's tour was so great that she won 87 of 89 matches during the season and continued her number-one ranking. Graf's game was a combination of speed and power; her powerful forehand was her best weapon and led her to be dubbed "Fraulein Forehand."

The following two years were off years, as she won only one Grand Slam event in 1990 (Australian Open) and 1991 (Wimbledon); by the end of 1991 she had dropped to number two in the women's rankings behind Monica Seles. Although Graf won Wimbledon again in 1992, Seles remained the top-ranked player until June 1993, when Graf again attained the number-one ranking after Seles was stabbed at a tournament in Germany and left the tour for two years. Graf held the top ranking into 1996, although her personal life was disrupted from 1995 to 1998 by the imprisonment of her father in Germany for tax evasion. Peter Graf was accused of hiding at least $28 million of Steffi's earnings over the years to evade taxes. He had been Steffi's coach and advisor and the driving force in the numerous product-endorsement contracts she had signed over the years. Although Peter's accountant claimed at the trial that Steffi was aware that her earnings were being hidden, both Steffi and Peter denied the allegation, and she was never charged by the authorities.

Although she continued to play on the women's tour, Graf's performance began to decline in 1996 after a series of leg and foot injuries, operations, and rehabilitations, and stiff competition from a new generation of women players. In 1997 she caused a stir on the tour when she posed in a series of bikinis for a photo spread in *Sports Illustrated*. In 1999 Graf demonstrated that she was still a contender by defeating the then number-one player, Switzerland's Martina Hingis, in the final of the French Open but lost in the final at Wimbledon. She then surprised the tennis world by announcing her retirement from the sport.

David Levinson

Bibliography

Heady, Sue. (1996) *Steffi: Public Power, Private Pain.* General Distribution Service.

Knapp, Ron. (1995) *Sports Great Steffi Graf.* Springfield, NJ: Enslow.

<www.classicsports.com>

GRAHAM, MARTHA
(1894–1991)
U.S. MODERN DANCE PIONEER

Martha Graham's career in modern dance spanned sixty years. She was the first dancer to perform at the White House, the first to receive a Guggenheim Fellowship, and the first to receive the Medal of Freedom, America's highest civilian award. She was artistic director of the first American dance company to tour abroad as cultural ambassadors, and she and her company performed at the opening of the 1939 New York World's Fair. She was honored with Japan's Imperial Order of the Precious Crown and was given the keys to the city of Paris.

Graham was born on 11 May 1894, in Allegheny, Pennsylvania, the eldest of four children.

Modern dance pioneer Martha Graham performs in the 1920s. (Corbis)

In 1908 her family moved to Santa Barbara, California. In *Blood Memory*, her autobiography, she wrote that "California was a world of flowers, Oriental people, people with Spanish blood, a life completely different. . . . It became a time of light and freedom and curiosity." An active young woman, Graham was an editor of her high school newspaper and captain of the girl's basketball team. She said that her first dance lesson was from her father, a neurologist, when he told her that "movement never lies."

In 1916 she enrolled in the Denishawn school in Los Angeles, California. This school and company (1915–1931), run by founders Ruth St. Denis (1878–1968) and Ted Shawn (1891–1972), was America's first great modern dance center. The Denishawn style was a combination of techniques. St. Denis taught her personal Oriental dance techniques, yoga meditation, and music visualization, while Shawn taught stretching exercises, ballet bar, and free movement. Other im-

portant modern dance pioneers, including Doris Humphrey (1895–1958) and Charles Weidman (1901–1975), also studied at Denishawn.

There, Graham developed a relationship with the musical director, Louis Horst (1884–1964), that lasted more than twenty years. Horst served as Graham's mentor, lover, composer, and taskmaster. He was an influential teacher of dance composition, and eleven of his thirty dance scores were created for Graham. In 1923, Graham left Denishawn, and two years later Horst followed her to New York City. In 1926, at the age of thirty-one, she gave her first independent concert with a trio of dancers. Frequently working with artists in other media, she had a thirty-year collaboration with the sculptor Isamu Noguchi (1904–1988), who designed scenic elements for twenty-two Graham productions.

In 1927 Graham founded The Martha Graham School of Contemporary Dance in New York City. The school still serves as a training ground for dancers from around the globe, as well as Martha Graham Company members. Well-known modern dancers, teachers, and choreographers who have been part of the Graham company include Anna Sokolow, Pearl Lang, Bessie Schoenberg, Jean Erdman, May O'Donnell, Martha Hill, Jane Dudley, Sophie Maslow, and Gertrude Shurr. Broadway and Hollywood actors were also drawn to study movement at the Graham school. These included Bette Davis, Ingrid Bergman, Gregory Peck, Liza Minnelli, Joanne Woodward, and Woody Allen, all of whom wanted to learn how to connect the body with the emotions. The Graham technique is based on the action of breathing, or "contraction and release." Unlike ballet technique, Graham technique reveals the effort behind movements. It emphasizes the torso as the emotional center, with movements beginning in the pelvis and lower back and traveling outward toward the extremities. Her technique uses twisted shapes and percussive movements to portray inner psychological conflict and dramatic intentions.

Graham's early work tended to be fiercely emotional, emphasizing angular, asymmetrical, and grounded movements. Her sixty-year repertory of choreography ranges from psychologically intense works to light-hearted dances, but all are passionately expressive. Early in her career, Graham explored themes based on the American ideals of self-reliance, nonconformity, and the wide-open spaces of the American West. Among these dances are: *Primitive Mysteries* (1931), about the Christianized Native Americans of the Southwest; *Frontier* (1935), suggesting the vast landscape of the American Great Plains; and, one of her most famous works, *Appalachian Spring* (1944). Set to a score by Aaron Copland (1900–1990), this work tells the story of a young pioneer couple settling into their new home. During the 1940s and beyond, Graham became known for her dance–dramas inspired by famous women from history, mythology, and literature. Notable among these are: *Cave of the Heart* (1946), based on the Grecian myth of Medea; *Errand into the Maze* (1947), adapted from the myth of Theseus and Aridane; *Night Journey* (1947), inspired by the myth of Oedipus and Jocasta; *Seraphic Dialogue* (1955), based on the life of Joan of Arc; and *Clytemnestra* (1958).

Graham stopped performing in 1969 at the age of seventy-five. In 1975, she celebrated the fiftieth anniversary of her company by choreographing *Lucifer* for the famous ballet stars Rudolph Nureyev (1938–1993) and Margot Fonteyn (1919–1991). In 1984, at the age of ninety, Graham choreographed a version of Stravinsky's *Rite of Spring*. Graham continued choreographing until her death in 1991. One of her later works, *Maple Leaf Rag* (1990), is a joyous dance set to the music of Scott Joplin (1868–1917). As Graham wrote in her autobiography, "I love the idea of life pulsing through people—blood and movement. For all of us, but particularly for a dancer . . . there is a blood memory that can speak to us."

Helen Myers

Bibliography

Anderson, Jack. (1997) *Art without Boundaries: The World of Modern Dance.* Iowa City: University of Iowa Press.

Cass, Joan. (1993) *Dancing through History.* Englewood Cliffs, NJ: Prentice-Hall.

Graham, Martha. (1991) *Blood Memory.* New York: Doubleday.

Morrison Brown, Jean, ed. (1979) *The Vision of Modern Dance.* Princeton, NJ: Princeton Book Company.

GREECE

Greece is a nation in the Balkan region of southern Europe with a population of 10.3 million. Site of the ancient Olympic Games and host of the first modern Olympics, held in Athens in 1896, it has a long association with sports. Women, however, were banned from the ancient Olympics (although they competed in some of their own festivals) and from the 1896 games. This pattern of exclusion characterized women's experience in Greek sports until the 1980s.

NINETEENTH AND EARLY TWENTIETH CENTURIES

Sports emerged in modern Greece in the last quarter of the nineteenth century, some fifty years after the end of Ottoman rule gave Greece its independence. Beginning in 1875, five national athletic competitions were organized by the monarch and several businessmen through the 1880s. These were modeled loosely on the ancient Olympics, with women excluded. During this period, men and women had clearly delineated roles, with men having far more authority than women both within and outside the home. Women's activities were largely restricted to the home and family.

By the end of the nineteenth century, Greece had become part of modern Europe, and sports became an activity of the wealthy. They were the province of men, and those who could afford it took part in athletics (running and jumping), swimming, cycling, tennis, and fencing. In 1891, an association of women of Greece established a school of physical education for girls, which was recognized by the government six years later. Nevertheless, women did not generally take part in sports, except for wrestling, which was more sideshow than sport. Women wrestlers and weight lifters gave exhibitions of their strength, but these events were not competitive sport.

Early in the twentieth century, influenced by developments in Europe, some physical education teachers developed a gymnastics program for schoolgirls based on the Swedish model. These

Ekatarina Thanou of Greece, winning the gold in the 60-meter dash at the Indoor Athletic Championships in Japan, 1998. (Toru Yamanaka/Corbis)

programs emphasized the health and fitness benefits of physical training, not competition. Indeed, fitness rather than competition remained the model for girls' sport activity in Greece into the 1970s. Participation in competitive sports such as tennis was limited to the upper classes.

WOMEN'S SPORT EMERGES

The main Greek sport organization covering athletics and gymnastics (SEGAS) was founded in 1897, but it was between World War I and World War II that the nation's economic expansion supported wider development of sports, including the founding of many national sports federations and institutions. After the 1928 Olympics, a commission for women's athletics (TEAG) was established, and when the first official women's championships were held, in 1929, the commission recognized the women's records in track and field. The Greek athlete Domitsa Lanidis, who participated in the 1936 and 1948 Olympics in track and field, became the first woman appointed to both TEAG and SEGAS.

At the same time, teacher-training schools at Greek universities began accepting women students, with the result that female physical education teachers became more common, although still a minority, in the school system. These developments notwithstanding, Greece remained a relatively poor and rural nation with sport and physical education confined primarily to Athens and other cities and to upper-class competitors.

POST–WORLD WAR II ERA

World War II, and the political unrest that followed, hampered Greece's economic recovery. It was not until 1957, with the founding of the General Organization for Sport under the Ministry of Education, that the government again turned its attention to sports, although women's sports were a very minor part of this initiative. Nevertheless, a few women overcame the cultural and financial obstacles and established small but active programs in track and field. A turning point came for Greek women in 1964, when they won the right to vote.

It was another ten years, however, with the restoration of democracy in Greece, before women's sports could develop significantly. Barriers to women's participation in society began to collapse, and Greek sports became increasingly influenced by Western European and U.S. forms of organization and training. As in other Western nations, more and more Greek women participated in sports for recreation and health, more became involved as serious, competitive athletes, and physical education was taught more widely in schools.

Before 1980, only seven Greek women had competed in seventeen Olympics. In 1980 three competed, in 1988 twelve, and in 1996 the number had grown to thirty-four. In 1982 Anna Verouli became the first Greek athlete, man or woman, to win a European title in athletics. Her triumph in the javelin throw, in front of enthusiastic fans in Athens, was joyfully applauded by the media and the nation as a whole. Another Greek thrower, Sofia Sakorafa, finished third in the same competition. The celebration was even greater in 1992, when Paraskevi Patoulidou won the Olympic gold medal in 100-meter hurdles. In the 1996 Olympics, Greek women continued to do well in track and field, with Niki Bakogianni winning the silver medal in the high jump and Giana Xianthou taking fourth place in the long jump.

Gherardo Bonini

Bibliography

Athanasios, Papageorgiou. (1985) "Griechenland." In Europa, 1 Die Europäische Gemeinschaft edited by Krüger Arnd, Leibesübungen London: Arena Publications, 84–102.

Minas, Dimitriou. (1995) Leibeserziehung und Sport in Griechenland 18291914. Sankt Augustin: Academia Verlag.

GREECE, ANCIENT

Sport was of central importance in Greek civilization, which in antiquity dominated the eastern Mediterranean as well as southern Italy and Sicily. An integral part of the education of the free born citizen, sports were practiced only by those who enjoyed full civil rights. For Greek women, however, sports were not a pastime but a practice rigidly reserved to freeborn, unmarried, and childless girls. The importance of sports for women is attested to by the athletic prowess of several mythological heroines: Atalanta, the prototype of the Greek sportswoman, a skilled runner, wrestler, and hunter; Cyrene, who killed a lion barehanded; and Nausicaa, who drove her chariot, oiled her body, and played ball with her maidservants.

Although women had a subordinate place in Greek society, a surprising number of women's athletic activities are documented throughout the Greek cultural area. Indeed, female physical activity is documented in the earlier Cretan civilization: two 1500 BCE frescoes from the palace of Knossos, now in the Heraklion archeological museum, depict girls leaping over the backs of bulls, probably in association with religious rituals. The goals and purposes of women's sports and games varied from city to city. Unlike men, women seemed not to engage in physical activity for the sake of competition, but rather for eugenic, ritualistic, and utilitarian reasons.

WOMEN'S SPORTS IN SPARTA

Most accounts of women's sports in ancient Greece focus on Sparta, the city-state where physical ability was highly valued and where physical activity was part of female education. The mythical seventh-century-BCE lawmaker, Lykurgos, believed sports would give young women a strong and resilient body required for the strain of childbearing and housekeeping, which then called for milling wheat, carrying water, and other heavy work. Sports were also eugenically and politically "correct" in the belief that the union of strong women with equally strong men would give the *polis* (city-state) better offspring.

Spartan women were trained in running, wrestling, discus and javelin throwing, and possibly the pentathlon. Because girls raced in public under the gaze of their male peers, sports were also an occasion for courtship and a prelude to marriage. This was meaningful because in Sparta, unlike other cities, women married only when physically mature and usually with men of about their own age. The Athenian philosopher Plato admired Spartan gymnastics and advocated them for his ideal state. In his view, women's sports were useful because they would make women stronger and teach them to handle weapons to defend their city and children at times when men were away.

RITUAL AND SPORT

In Sparta and elsewhere, women's sports, like men's, were usually performed during religious festivals, but not necessarily for female divinities. Sparta had two religious races: an initiation rite in which 240 noble and lower-class girls ran naked in a secluded area; and the Dyonisia, honoring the god Dionysus and possibly serving to select his priestesses, open only to a few noble girls. Athens, Attica (the region around Athens), Brauron, Munichia, Salamina, and Eleusis all held ritual races for the goddess Artemis. In Attica, gymnastics also served as initiation rites for marriageable girls whose adolescent natures, thought to be wild, needed to be directed toward the more mature behavior expected of a bride and matron. This was especially true in Brauron, where girls took part in a race during the Arktéia (she-bear) festival. There were categories for children and teenagers, and the race represented a chase or hunt in which the youngsters played the bear to symbolize the border between wilderness (virginity) and tameness (married life).

In Sparta, men and women shared the city's *dromos* (racetrack), which was probably used by

A group of Greek girls recreate the slow, rhythmic style of Ancient Greek dance, using hoops as symbols of the Olympic Games. (Hulton-Deutsch/Corbis)

women for public events; traces remain of a second *dromos* outside the city, reserved for ritual female events. The Heràia were held in Olympia's main stadium, but women ran a distance one-sixth shorter than the men's race. Female initiation competitions were probably held in secluded places, well separated from male training grounds.

Unlike men, Greek women did not usually compete naked, except for ritual events. When they did, no male spectators were allowed. The most common clothing was a short tunic (*kitonìskos schistòs*) of Spartan origin, without belt, open on one or both sides, used for running and wrestling. This short chiton is illustrated by numerous archaic Spartan bronzes depicting girl runners and suggesting that the right breast remained exposed. In the Arktèia, children wore a saffron-

colored tunic. Close-fitting and high-cut shorts, usually worn as a sole dress and documented in bronze mirror handles, apparently spread from Sparta throughout the Greek world. Runners often wore kneepads (*genualia*) with their shorts. A triangular- or strip-shaped bra of Attic origin was also commonly worn, alone or with shorts to form something not unlike modern bikinis.

The only competitive ancient Greek women's games known today are the Heràia. Named after the goddess Hera, wife of Zeus, these were held in Olympia every four years and were similar to the men's Olympics. According to some scholars, they date from before the eighth century BCE, which would make them older than the Olympics. Like the Olympics, which honored Zeus and somehow served him, the Heràia had religious meaning, probably prenuptial, with competition

THE ACHIEVEMENTS OF THREE SISTERS (C.E. 41-47)

Hermesianax, son of Dionysisus, of Tralles Caesarea, but also a citizen of Athens and Delphi, makes this dedication to Pythian Apollo for his daughters who likewise obtained the same citizenships:

Tryphosa, who won the stade races [one length of the stadium] at the Pythian games [in Delphi] when they were directed by Antigonus and when they were directed by Cleomachidas, and at the next Isthmian games [in Corinth] directed by Juventius Proclus. She came in first among the girls.

Hedea, who won the chariot race in armor at the Isthmian games when they were directed by Cornelius Pulcher, and the stade race at the Nemean games directed by Antigonus and again at the Sicyonian games directed by Menoetas. . . .

And Dionysia, who won the stade race at the Isthmian games directed by Antigonus, and again at the Asclepieia in holy Epidaurus under the direction of Nicoteles.

LUIGI MORETTI
(1953) Iscrizioni Agonistiche Greche. Rome: Angelo Signorelli. 165–69; translation adapted from Rachel Sargent Robinson. (1955) Sources for the History of Greek Athletics, *revised edition Chicago: Ares. 163–64.*

inciting girls to emulate Hera as the prototype of the good spouse. The Heràia included a race with participants divided into three age groups. Winners received an olive crown and part of a cow sacrificed to the goddess; they were also allowed to dedicate their statue or portrait in the temple of Hera in Olympia. The race was supervised by sixteen women with the same function as the Hellanodikai, the judges at the Olympics.

Although racing was prevalent, Greek women practiced many other sports. Late sixth- to mid-fifth century BCE vases depict female swimmers, while horseback riding seems to have been widespread in Sparta, in conjunction with the cult of Helen. Indeed, the first female Olympic winner was the Spartan Cynisca, who owned the winning chariot in the 96th Olympiad (396 BCE). Equestrian races were probably held in Terapne (3 kilometers, or two miles, northeast of Sparta), at the sanctuary of Helen and her husband, Menelaus, where excavations have found many terracotta statuettes of female riders, perhaps dedicated by winners. From the fourth century BCE, Athens allowed women to enter their chariots in the Great Panathenaia but not to drive them. Other chariot races in which women could enter their horses included the Eleutheria (freedom festival) in Larissa (in Thessaly) and the annual Amphiaraia (honoring the hero Amphiaraos) of Oropos, northwest of Athens. Spartan women wrestled but, contrary to the poet Propertius and Roman practice, Greek girls never took part in more brutal sports like boxing and the pancration (a no-holds-barred contest, combining boxing and wrestling).

In summary, it is clear that some women participated in sports in ancient Greece, although their level of participation was more circumscribed and less than that of the men. While women participated in sport for the same reasons as men—to serve the gods, build their bodies, and produce healthier children—their participation was generally seen as less vital to their own interests and those of Greek society than participation by men.

Francesca Garello
Angela Teja

See also Mythology; Rome, Ancient

Bibliography

Angeli Bernardini, Paola. (1986–1987) "Aspects ludiques, rituels et sportifs de la course féminine dans la Grèce antique." *Stadion* 12, 13:17–26.

Arrigoni, Giampiera. (1985) "Donne e sport nel mondo greco. Religione e società." In *Le donne in Grecia*, edited by Giampiera Arrigoni. Bari: Laterza, 55–201.

Di Donato, Michele, and Angela Teja. (1989) *Agonistica e ginnastica nella Grecia antica*. Rome: Studium.

Frasca, Rosella. (1991) *L'agonale nell'educazione della donna greca*. Bologna: Patron.

Guttmann, Allen. (1991) *Women's Sports*. New York: Columbia University Press.

Moretti, Luigi. (1953) *Iscrizioni agonistiche greche*. Rome: Angelo Signorelli.

Scanlon, Thomas F. (1990) "Race or Chase at the Arkteia of Attica?" *Nikephoros* 3:73–120.

———. (1984) "The Footrace of the Heraria at Olympia." *The Ancient World* (9 May):77–90.

Servint, Nancy. (1993) "The Female Athletic Costume at the Heraia and the Prenuptial Initiation Rites." *American Journal of Archaeology* 97:403–422.

Younger, John G. (1976) "Bronze Age Representation of Aegean Bull Leaping." *American Journal of Archaeology* 80:125–37.

GRIFFITH-JOYNER, FLORENCE

(1959–1998)

U.S. TRACK ATHLETE

Florence Griffith-Joyner celebrates her victories earned in sprint competitions at the 1988 Summer Olympic in Seoul. (Wally McNamee/Corbis)

Florence Griffith was one of the premier female sprinters of the 1980s, setting two world records and winning three gold medals at the 1988 Olympics in Seoul, Korea. In women's sports, she also represented the height of glamour and fashion, becoming an international celebrity and bringing special excitement to the track. Following her Olympic triumphs, she was plagued with charges of using performance-enhancing drugs.

Born Delorez Florence Griffith in Los Angeles, Calif., on 21 December 1959, she was raised by her mother, Florence Griffith, in a housing project in the Watts neighborhood of Los Angeles. Griffith began running competitively at age seven and competed in local youth club events and then, as her performances steadily improved, regional and national events. A star on her high-school track team, as a senior in 1978 she ran the 100-yard dash in 10.86 seconds, a world-class result for an athlete of her age and of limited experience in major races. Following high school, she enrolled at California State University at Northridge, where she trained under the well-known track coach Bob Kersee. When he moved to the University of California at Los Angeles in 1981, she followed him and provided credible though not world-class results in 100- and 200-meter events sanctioned by The Athletics Congress (TAC), the Association of Intercollegiate Athletics for Women, and other national organizations. In 1982 her performances improved and she won the National Collegiate Athletic Association (NCAA) 200-meter title. In 1983 she came second in the NCAA 200-meter championships and won the NCAA 400-meter title with a time of 50.96 seconds. That same year, Griffith placed third in the

TAC 200-meter championship and fourth in the 200-meter event at the inaugural World Track and Field Championship at Helsinki, Finland.

After graduating from UCLA in 1983, Griffith joined Kersee's World Class Track Team, which trained the best American athletes for international and Olympic competition. At the 1984 Olympic trials and the summer Olympic Games at Los Angeles, she finished second in the 200-meter event. She then retired from competitive track, but she returned in 1987 and took second place in the 200-meter race at TAC and the world championships in Rome, Italy. That year she married Al Joyner, the 1984 Olympic gold medalist in the triple jump, who became her coach, and she became known as "Flojo."

Her greatest achievements came in 1988 at the U.S. Olympic Trials and then at the Olympics in Seoul. In a matter of a few months, she set world records in the 100-meter (10.49 seconds) and 200-meter (21.34 seconds) dashes, won three gold medals (100 meters, 200 meters, 4×100 meter relay), one silver medal (4 ×400 relay), and became an international celebrity. She also brought glamour to the sport, as she redefined how runners dressed by wearing colorful costumes, jewelry, and long red-white-and-blue fingernails, and running with her long hair flowing behind her. After her spectacular national and Olympic results in 1988 following three years of retirement, some rivals accused her of using performance-enhancing drugs. As evidence that she used steroids or other strength-building substances, they cited the performances themselves, which far outdid her earlier bests, and her heavily muscled legs and arms. Griffith-Joyner never failed a drug test, and she denied the accusations, saying that intensive weight training had produced the well-defined muscles in her thighs. Her celebrity appeal made it easy to overcome the accusations and led to a comfortable post-career life.

In 1989 she received the Sullivan Award, which recognized her as the outstanding U.S. amateur athlete. She retired again in 1989 and had her first child, Mary Ruth Griffith-Joyner. In 1990, she served as a cochairperson of the President's Council on Physical Fitness and Sports, and became a co-editor of the 1996 government report *Physical Activity and Health: A Report of the Surgeon General.* She also worked as a fashion model, advertised various products, designed clothing, and founded the Florence Griffith-Joyner Youth Foundation. She died unexpectedly in her sleep on 21 September 1998 at the age of thirty-nine. The autopsy failed to provide the cause of her death but vindicated her by showing that it was in no way related to earlier drug-use accusations that had persisted until her death.

Griffith-Joyner's relatively short career touched on many of the key issues in women's sports in the 1980s and 1990s. These included superior performance, the use of fashion to enhance one's appearance and marketability beyond sport, and the controversy over the use of performance-enhancing drugs. Griffith-Joyner, consciously and without apology, used her attractive appearance to enhance her market appeal as a celebrity and spokesperson for various products. At the time of her death, ten years after her career ended, she was still appearing in national commercials for milk, with no name needed to tell readers who she was. She was coauthoring *Running for Dummies,* a handbook for people interested in running, when she died.

David Levinson

Bibliography

Aaseng, Nathan. (1991) *Florence Griffith-Joyner: Dazzling Olympian.* Minneapolis: Lerner Publication Company.

Griffith-Joyner, Florence and John Hanc. (1999) *Running for Dummies.* Foster City, CA: IDG Books.

Lindstrom, Seig. (1989) "Nobody but Flo." *Track and Field News* 42 (February): 8–9.

GUTHRIE, JANET

(1938–)

U.S. RACE-CAR DRIVER

Janet Guthrie was the first woman to compete in the Indianapolis 500, breaching a barrier that personified the exclusion of women from motor racing. Guthrie was born in Iowa City, Iowa, and grew up in Miami, Florida. Her father, an airline

Savoring the "happiest moment" of her life, Janet Guthrie grins from the cockpit of her racer after becoming the first woman ever to qualify for the Indianapolis 500, in 1976. (Bettmann/Corbis)

pilot, introduced her to flying when she was thirteen, and at nineteen she acquired a commercial pilot's license. After earning a bachelor's degree in physics at the University of Michigan, she was hired as an engineer in the aerospace division of Republic Aviation.

In 1962 Guthrie fulfilled a longtime dream by buying a Jaguar XK-120. She was soon driving her nine-year-old auto in local sports-car club competitions, and she was named the women's gymkhana champion of Long Island that year. Wanting to attain mastery of the automobile that she paralleled her skill as a pilot, she attended the driving school at Lime Rock, Connecticut. She was such a good student that veteran driver Gordon McKenzie encouraged her to consider becoming a sports-car racing driver.

Guthrie bought a more powerful Jaguar model, the XK-140, and in 1963 began racing it in Sports Car Club of America (SCCA) and International Motor Sports Association (IMSA) events, frequently placing in the top ten. Her consistency attracted the MacMillan Ring-Free Oil Company,

which in 1966 asked her to join a new team of four women drivers to race and do public relations appearances. Because racing had become her passion, Guthrie quit her job to become a full-time race driver. She sold her car, took her savings, and set out to find a ride on the road-racing circuit, only to find no sponsor. Despite that formidable handicap, Guthrie finished consistently well and won a number of awards. Between 1964 and 1970, she finished in nine consecutive sports-car endurance races—the Watkins Glen six-hour, the Sebring twelve-hour, and the Daytona twenty-four-hour—and captained the 1970 MacMillan team to a first-in-class finish at Sebring. She captured the 1973 North Atlantic Road Racing Champion's crown and in 1975 beat twenty-seven male drivers in the Vanderbilt Cup and won the Bridgehampton 400. She found herself with an enviable portfolio of racing accomplishments but with no job, no money, and physical and mental exhaustion.

Her tenacity was finally rewarded when Oregon lumber executive Rolla Vollstedt asked her to drive one of his cars at Indianapolis. Guthrie encountered widespread open hostility from the male Indy drivers. Mechanical problems kept her from qualifying at Indy in 1976. Instead, on that Memorial Day she became the first woman ever to race in a NASCAR superspeedway event by competing in the World 600 in Charlotte, North Carolina. The usual criticism that a woman could not handle a heavy car at high speed in a grueling endurance race abated somewhat when she drove a car she had never seen until that day and finished fifteenth in a field of forty in her first stock-car race. The next year, she competed in a number of stock-car races under the sponsorship of Kelly Girl, finishing ten times in the top twelve. She also did some Indy car racing, and in May 1977 her qualifying speed of 303.14 kilometers per hour (188.403 miles per hour) in Vollstedt's car put her on the tenth row of the Indianapolis 500 starting grid, the first woman ever to make the field of the historic race. The car suffered mechanical problems and she had to retire, but the deed was done.

Guthrie's success did not attract the expected sponsorship. Kelly Girl curtailed its racing program and there was no offer for her to drive in the 1978 Indy race. The most famous woman in racing had no ride. At the last moment, Texaco agreed to sponsor Guthrie at Indianapolis. She qualified her number 51 Texaco Star in the fifth row and drove a conservative race, finishing ninth ahead of many top drivers despite a broken wrist sustained two days before the race, which forced her to steer and shift gears with her left hand. Her best finish in Indy car racing was her last major race, a fifth in the 1979 Milwaukee 200.

Guthrie retired from full-time racing in 1980. She is president of Janet Guthrie Racing Enterprises and has been a contributing editor to *Working Woman* and *Car and Driver* and a highway-safety consultant. Her 1978 Indianapolis 500 driver's suit and helmet are in the Smithsonian Museum in Washington, D.C., and she is a member of the International Women's Sports Hall of Fame. Handicapped throughout her career by inferior equipment and minimal financing, Guthrie nevertheless consistently displayed topnotch driving skills and grace under pressure. She said, "If we can just get past the point where a guy who gets dusted off by a woman no longer feels that he has to be embarrassed about it—then *that* will be a major step in racing."

Suzanne Wise

Bibliography

Dolan, Edward J., Jr., and Richard B. Lyttle. (1982) *Janet Guthrie: First Woman Driver at Indianapolis.* NY: Franklin Watts.

Fox, Mary Virginia. (1981) *Janet Guthrie: Foot to the Floor.* Minneapolis, MN: Dillon Press.

Olney, Ross R. (1978) *Janet Guthrie: First Woman at Indy.* NY: Harvey House.

Presto, Kay. (1978) "Janet, the Race Driver." *Stock Car Racing* 13, 5: 51–58.

Woolum, Janet. (1992) "Janet Guthrie." In *Outstanding Women Athletes: Who They Are and How They Influenced American Sports.* Phoenix, AZ: Oryx Press, 111–114.

GYMNASTICS

Gymnastics is the general term for a group of activities in which an athlete uses her skill and stamina to perform choreographed exercises that test strength, flexibility, and balance. Gymnastic movements, known as elements, include handsprings and other tumbling maneuvers, hand balancing, swinging on apparatus, and vaulting. Combinations of elements, known as routines, may be performed on well-padded floors or mats and on balance beams, uneven parallel bars, and other apparatus. Vaulting is performed over special boxes or a vaulting horse. Children encounter basic tumbling skills in physical education classes.

Gymnastics and modern physical education programs were introduced almost simultaneously in nineteenth century Germany. The modern program, known today as "artistic gymnastics," was developed in the late nineteenth century. Today, women's gymnastics has captured the public interest to a degree unmatched by their male counterparts.

HISTORY

The term *gymnastics* originated with the ancient Greeks and meant "naked exercise" because the participants—men only—performed in the nude. Women were forbidden to take part in or observe these sports and games, which included track and field, boxing, and wrestling. Such activity had little to do with what we now call gymnastics.

Gymnastics, as practiced today by girls and women as well as boys and men, has roots in most of recorded history. Artifacts and hieroglyphics from Egypt, Greece, China, and India provide evidence of gymnastic activity throughout the ancient world. These records suggest that the earliest forms were related to dance and acrobatics. The latter included tumbling, various forms of handbalancing, juggling, and partner or group activity. One of the earliest images shows an Egyptian acrobat—a girl—holding a back bend supported by her hands and feet. This image and others imply that the girl has swung over into this position from a handstand, thus tumbling in the manner of beginners of our own time. Many similar images have been collected.

The Bull Leaper of Knossos, a fresco in the Palace of Knossos in Crete, is one of the most frequently published images from antiquity. It depicts a large bull with a person cartwheeling over its back while two others, differently arrayed, are shown at either end of the bull and are probably much

Four gymnasts train on aero wheels in Regent's Park, London, in 1928. (Corbis)

further away than depicted. Some scholars believe that one or both of these might be female because their skin is lighter and their chests are contoured differently. Women would brighten their skin with white powder or other substance to attract the bull and cause it to charge. The lightened skin, along with noisemakers from both sides, would cause the bull to charge up and down in a more-or-less straight line. The leaper (without makeup), cartwheeling over the bull, would then have a clear shot at leaping the bull, running from a line perpendicular to its path.

Gymnastics of this kind was not contested in the ancient Olympic Games, although the Greeks used such words as *gymnos* or *gymnastes.* Here again, *gymnastiks* simply referred to all forms of exercise. Similarly, the term *gymnasium* refers to the room equipped for various sports and exercises.

Tumbling, as precursor and as part of modern gymnastics, has a long history. It was nurtured by traveling troupes hired to entertain at banquets, pageants, festivals, and other events. Most acrobatic troupes had tumblers, hand balancers, mimes, jugglers, and strong men. Although most performers were male, dance troupes had female performers who could also tumble. After Christianity took hold in Europe, such merry making

was often condemned as pagan. The dance of Salome before Herod was cited as evidence against tumbling by ancient Christian monks, some of whom claimed she was a tumbler and consequently a sinner.

Despite clerical opposition, acrobats and tumblers continued to amuse the populace. Evidence of male and female tumblers is found in many languages, especially after the eighth century CE. In Anglo Saxon, *tumbian* means to turn heels over head and dance violently. Female tumblers were known as *tumblesters.* Danes had *tumbles* and Swedes, *tumlas.* Italians used *tombola* to describe twisting, rolling, and contorting the body. In Dutch, *tommelen* was the choice word. The French word *tomber* means to fall. Tumbling might be described as creative "falling." These linguistic similarities illustrate how widely tumbling was known and practiced in Europe.

During the reign of Edward I of England (1272–1307), a certain Maud or Matilda Makejoy performed acrobatic feats at the Christmas feast of 1296. Probably, similar performances occurred at other medieval courts. A historic milestone came in 1589 with the publication in Paris of S. A. Tuccaro's *Three Dialogues on the Art of Tumbling and Jumping in the Air* (vaulting), a highly illustrated text for the time. Tuccaro visited a number of countries to display his vaulting skill.

Another volume from about the same time predicted later divisions in gymnastics by emphasizing its medical values as opposed to the more carefree forms now part of competitive gymnastics. It would take two centuries to further define these differences. Medical gymnastics evolved into physical therapy and allied fields, while sport gymnastics survived despite the efforts of a variety of well-meaning groups to alter or even suppress them. Although professional gymnasts are as old as circus history and may be seen in action today, professional gymnastics was virtually unknown before 1972.

MODERN ROOTS OF GYMNASTICS

Modern gymnastics in its familiar, competitive form resulted from several accidents of history, including the need for physically fit soldiers to defeat Napoleon's armies and the desire to improve the health of young people in an increasingly sedentary society. Among the primary roots of gymnastics are attempts to reform education so that children could take a more active role in their own learning, as well as the need for fitness in the military.

Jean Jacques Rousseau (1712–1778), the French philosopher and educational reformer, suggested a natural approach to teaching young boys, freeing them to follow instincts in learning rather than drilling them in an unimaginative, sterile environment. Physical education, free play, and movement exploration were important features of Rousseau's reform movement. Although generally rejected by the French, his ideas were taken up by a small group of German educators who called themselves Philanthropists. They proposed creating a Philanthropinum, an institution for the advancement of human welfare, to train the minds and bodies of the boys sent to them for an education. Outdoor exercises were an essential part of their curriculum, and the rudiments of gymnastics, track and field, swimming, and games of all sorts were taught at their schools for the sons of the middle and upper classes.

The most prominent of the Philanthropist teachers, Johann Christoph Friedrich Guts Muths (1759–1839), is sometimes called the grandfather of modern gymnastics. His 1793 book, *Gymnastik für die Jugend* (Gymnastics for Youth), was the first to outline a comprehensive plan for the physical education of the young, embracing the original Greek meaning of the word. At the time, such training was restricted to boys and young men, although Guts Muths also described exercises for girls. One hundred years before Pierre de Coubertin organized the first modern Olympic Games, Guts Muths suggested that a revival of the Olympics would do much to motivate youth to exercise their bodies.

In the second edition of *Gymnastik* (1804), Guts Muths included a chapter on military drill. In 1817 he published *Turnbuch für die Söhne des Vaterlandes* (Exercise Book for Sons of the Fatherland). His using the root word *Turn* shows his acquaintance with Friedrich Ludwig Jahn (1778–1852) and his program in Berlin. Jahn is considered the sire of modern gymnastics—*turnvater* means "the father of gymnastics." He was a fervent nationalist who hated all things French, and he invented the verb *turnen* (to do gymnastics) to replace the word *gymnastics,* which ap-

peared in French as *gymnastique* or *l'art gymnastique. Turnen* and many other German derivatives are used today to refer specifically to gymnastics as it is currently understood. The military drill in Guts Muths' second edition of *Gymnastik* combined with the nationalism of Jahn to produce a tradition of rigidly orchestrated mass gymnastic exercises.

MEDICAL GYMNASTICS

A contemporary of Jahn's, Per Henrik Ling (1776–1839) established his own gymnastics program in Sweden. His main interest was to improve the health of the Swedish people. Ling's exercises and other developing programs in Scandinavia were dubbed "medical gymnastics" and were highly organized with specified drills. The Scandinavians rejected the wooden towers, beams, and ropes popular in *turnen* and created programs of apparatus-free exercises very much like today's aerobics programs. Ling and his followers were especially critical of Jahn's parallel bars and demanded they be banned. Swedish gyms had an interesting variety of apparatus, but parallel bars were forbidden.

Since men and women could benefit from medically oriented exercise regimens, the Scandinavian programs in Sweden, Denmark, Finland, and, to a lesser extent, Norway included girls and women. By the end of the nineteenth century, Ling's program had spread to England, the British Empire, and eventually to the United States, where, in the greater Boston area, Lingian gymnastics competed for favor with "New Gymnastics" that Dio Lewis had developed in the 1850s.

The roots of rhythmic sport gymnastics, recently accepted as an Olympic discipline and exclusively the domain of women, are found in Scandinavia, where Lingian gymnastics was often accompanied by music. Competition was discouraged, and classes kept under the tight control of the instructors. Institutes in Scandinavia were established to train teachers of both sexes. Competitive rhythmic gymnastics came to fruition in Czechoslovakia in the 1930s.

Modern gymnastics combines hands-free exercises with work on various apparatus. The roots of present-day competitive apparatus can be traced to a number of sources.

PARALLEL BARS

Parallel bars were developed by Jahn, who noted that the young men who visited his playground in Berlin seemed to lack arm and shoulder strength. He erected parallel rails for them to use to support themselves and do dipping exercises to improve their strength for pommel-horse training. The boys who visited the Hasenheide (literally, heath of the hares), a playground built on a portion of a large, abandoned field, found other stunts to perform on the *barren* (Jahn's name for parallel bars). Jahn accepted this kind of inventive exploration because it was a powerful motivator, drawing more boys to the program. The parallel bars were attributed to Jahn alone, and by the end of the nineteenth century, bar rails were set at different heights for variety and training. Disagreement among Ling's followers over the value of parallel bars escalated into the *Barrenstreit* (parallel-bar war), which the Germans won due to the efforts of some of the most famous physiologists of Europe, notably Emile du Bois Reymond.

Women first participated in Olympic gymnastics in 1928. Uneven parallel bars were eventually adopted by women to replace the even ones. Up until 1952, events for men and women were fairly similar. Doris Fuchs Brause, a U.S. gymnast, brought uneven-bar work to its present standard by performing a nonstop routine for the first time in the Dortmund, Germany, world championships in 1966. Although acknowledged in the world of gymnastics for her pioneering routine, which she performed flawlessly, she did not win a medal in Dortmund, nor was she eligible for the finals in her specialty. Judges at that time had never seen a routine on the uneven bars without a pause—Brause was way ahead of her time. She scored only a 9.4 in the compulsory competition where gymnasts perform a prescribed exercise. This score, which prevented her from winning a medal, was protested by U.S. coach Muriel Grossfeld. The senior judge, Madam Demedenko, told her it should have been higher but refused to change the score, even though she had the power to do so. This resulted in a combined score that was insufficient for a medal. The German spectators, who knew the sport well, protested Brause's scores and brought the competition to a standstill for more than an hour. It was a memorable event in the history of women's gymnastics. Ten years later, in the same event, Nadia Comaneci, of Romania, scored two perfect 10.0s in the Montreal

VARIATIONS IN EQUIPMENT ACCORDING TO SEX

When women were first included among sports participants, their equipment differed very little from men's. Any differences resulted from the strength factor, so that women practiced their sports with lighter and/or smaller accessories: a discus of 1 kilogram instead of 2 kilograms, a javelin of 600 grams instead of 800 grams, a shot of 4 kilograms instead of 7.257 kilograms, a smaller and lighter ball in handball, a lower hurdle in track, a softball rather than a baseball (although in this case the equipment is larger).

The exception to the rule is gymnastics. In this sport real differences in equipment quickly developed. The gymnastic disciplines common to women and men are the floor exercises and vaulting (sideways for women and lengthwise for men).

The balance beam, however, is a female accessory. While the parallel bars have been used for men since their invention by Jahn (1778–1852), they evolved in the 1920s into asymmetrical bars for women. Uneven bars were thought to be better adapted to women's anatomy and movements. What this actually meant was that strength was emphasized for male gymnasts (the pommel horse, the rings, and the floor exercises) and grace for female gymnasts (the balance beam and the floor exercises). The equipment, scholars explain, "materialized" the attitude commonly held about women and sports: men impose, women beguile. We see this contrast clearly in the equipment for rhythmic gymnastics. The gymnasts move across the mats like ballerinas, with a rope, a hoop, clubs, or ribbons.

Olympics—the first perfect scores in Olympic Games' history.

BALANCE BEAM

The use of beams, originally large logs, for balancing, was inaugurated by the Philanthropists on their playgrounds and were also seen at Jahn's Hasenheide. They were similar to those used by the French Army. What is known as a Swedish bench can be turned upside down, exposing a narrow beam. Beam work with a modern beam was introduced internationally in 1934 when the first world championship for women was approved by the Fédération Internationale de Gymnastique (FIG) in Budapest. Top score on the beam went to Vlasta Dekanova of Czechoslovakia. Another Czech gymnast, Eva Bosakova, later won four medals in international open-beam competition. The Soviet Union's Olga Korbut stirred spectators with her gold-medal performance at the 1972 Olympics in Munich. She followed a back somersault on the beam with a front somersault dismount. Comaneci won three gold medals on the beam in three consecutive international open competitions (1976, 1978, and 1980).

VAULTING

The side-horse vault traces back to the Roman military horse, complete with tail and head, originally used to teach mounting, dismounting, and vaulting. The same apparatus gave rise to creativity and playful competition at Jahn's playground. Jahn called his wooden horse a *Swingel* and included two curved wooden pommels (a misnomer) to define the saddle area and provide handles for a performer to grasp. Jahn was the first to describe exercises on the horse. Over the years, boards for vaulting included large springboards with great rebounding qualities and simple inclined boards with no spring at all. The latter types made their appearance on Jahn's playground, and others were developed after 1850. The Reuther Board, devised by Richard Reuther, was adopted for international open competitions in the mid-1950s. This sort of board has been used for modern gymnastics ever since.

In 1934, at the first world championship for women, a Polish performer, Maria Majovska, tied for first honors (no medals were given) with Matylda Palfyeva of Czechoslovakia. Later the appa-

Chinese gymnast Mo Huilan performs a one-handed handstand on the beam while competing in the women's team final at the Olympic Games in Atlanta in 1996. (TempSport)

ratus was constructed specifically for women's vaulting with no pommels. Perhaps the most memorable moment in this event was U.S. gymnast Mary Lou Retton's perfect vault, which won her the coveted all-around title at the Los Angeles Olympics in 1984. This was the first all-around gold for a U.S. performer in Olympic or world championship competition.

FLOOR EXERCISE AND TUMBLING

Floor exercises are performed within a twelve-square-meter area (40 ft. × 40 ft.). Modern floor exercise platforms with a rug surface are more forgiving than their counterparts of past years, which consisted of bare wooden floors or grassy fields. This event was originally called "free exercise," because gymnasts performed without hand apparatus, in other words, hands-free exercises. Undoubtedly, the most famous floor exercise champion was Larissa Latynina, from the Soviet Union (Ukraine), who won three Olympic gold medals in this event (1956, 1960, and 1964) and won the world championship title in floor exercise in 1962. She was a member of the very powerful Soviet women's gymnastics team, which was never defeated in Olympic competition and won ten Olympic team gold medals.

Tumbling as such was contested only once in the Olympics, at Los Angeles in 1932 (women did not participate in gymnastics that year). Advanced tumbling is required in the modern floor exercise event. Today, tumbling competition on a variety of surfaces is supervised by two international governing bodies: the International Federation of Sports Acrobatics and the International Trampoline Federation. The latter has recently been subsumed by the International Gymnastics Federation, sponsor of the first Olympic trampoline event, in 2000. The United States has been the home of modern tumbling, which was practiced infrequently in other parts of the world until very recently. Its greatest female tumblers were Barbara Galleher Tonry and Judy Wills Cline. Tonry won six straight national titles (1952–1957) and a total of nine during her career. Cline, better known as the woman who won the first five world titles in trampoline competition, bested her opponents in every tumbling contest she entered. Women who compete in rhythmic gymnastics use Indian clubs, ribbons, hoops, and ropes in their exercises, but may not employ acrobatics of any kind (e.g., somersaults and handstands).

TRAMPOLINE

The trampoline is a twentieth-century addition to gymnastics. Although various rebounding apparatus were used in the circus for many years, it was not until George Nissen of the United States patented his "Flashfold" trampoline in the late 1930s that the trampoline was introduced to the gymnastics world. The Nissen trampoline and other later models were adopted universally. Initially, the trampoline was used by gymnasts and divers to learn complicated, twisting somersaults while secured to a twisting belt rigged above the trampoline. Charles Pond, a U.S. coach, patented the twisting belt right after World War II, and it too was used worldwide by men, women, boys, and girls. The first world trampoline championship was held at the Royal Albert Hall in London in 1964. Two U.S. gymnasts emerged as the first world champions. Danny Millman, later famous as a writer, won the gold medal, as did Judy Wills Cline, who won the first women's gold medal and defended her title for the next four years.

After many lawsuits resulting from injuries incurred during trampoline stunts, the United States dropped trampoline competition for the most part, but it is flourishing throughout the world today and contested for the first time at the Sydney Olympics in 2000.

THE GREAT CHAMPIONS OF WOMEN'S GYMNASTICS

In only two gymnastics events do the best women and men in the world have an opportunity to compete with one another. Both are FIG-sponsored, open events. "Open" means that anyone or any team from any country may qualify, as opposed to such closed competitions as the European championships or the Pan American Games, eligible only to gymnasts from the regions defined. The first of these open competitions are the world championships, eligible to women since 1934. The second is the Olympic Games. Because the latter receive worldwide publicity and take place less often than the world championships, they are more highly regarded by the fans they attract. But within the gymnastic family, both competitions result in world titles and are considered equally important.

The team champion consists of the best combined scores of team members from a single nation. Unquestionably, the most prominent women's gymnastics team of the twentieth century was that of the Soviet Union. They first entered a team in the Helsinki Olympics in 1952 and were never defeated in the Olympics. As the "Unified Team," they won their last Olympic gold in 1992, just after the breakup of the Soviet Union. They also won world championship titles in 1983 and 1985 before and after the Soviet boycott of the 1984 Olympics in Los Angeles (in retaliation for a similar boycott of the 1980 Olympics by some Western teams). The Soviet women lost only three world championship titles—one to the Czechoslovaks in 1966 and two to the Romanians in 1979 and 1987. Overall they won the team gold in twenty-two of twenty-five competitions. They would probably have won the 1984 Olympic title if they had entered those games.

CHAMPIONS

For virtually any gymnast, the ultimate achievement is to win the all-around gold at the Olympic Games or the world championships. A second, but nearly impossible dream, is to win the all-around and each of the four individual events. No one has ever done this in open international competition, but a few women have come close.

YOUNGEST DOESN'T MEAN BEST

In modern gymnastics, the female gymnasts who have gained the most public acclaim performed spectacularly at the Olympics, such as Olga Korbut of the Soviet Union, Nadia Comaneci of Romania, and Mary Lou Retton of the United States. However, within the sport the most acclaimed gymnasts with all-around ability are Larissa Latynina of the Soviet Union who competed in the 1950s and 1960s, Vera Caslavska of the Czech Republic who competed in the 1960s, and Ludmilla Tourischeva of the Soviet Union who competed in the 1970s.

All-around competition is won by the gymnast with the highest combined scores on four events. There is no longer a compulsory event in women's gymnastics at the elite level. It was useful for picking the best of the fifty and more gymnasts competing for this top honor because all participants had to do the same exercise. The compulsories were dropped in gymnastics after figure skating dropped its "school figures." These obligatory events were eliminated primarily because they were monotonous to watch. Optional events in women's and men's figure skating and especially in women's gymnastics have drawn sold-out crowds at the Olympics and world championships. This drawing power dictates the program because television rights generate money and other benefits to promote and maintain the sport.

The greatest female all-around winner in history was Larissa Latynina of the Soviet team. Between 1956 and 1964, she competed in three Olympics and two world championships, winning a medal in every event she entered but one (balance beam at the 1956 Olympics). Latynina is one of only a few women to come close to a sweep (winning the all-around and all four individual events). At the 1958 world championships in Moscow, she won the all-around and all events except the floor exercise, where she won a silver. She won the all-around at two Olympic Games and two world championships, a record never duplicated by any other gymnast.

Latynina's chief challenger during the latter part of her career was Vera Caslavska, a Czech national hero, who served as minister of sport in the Czech Republic. Caslavska beat Latynina at the 1962 world championships in Prague, the former's home town. Caslavska's near sweep at the 1968 Olympic Games in Mexico City has never been duplicated in Olympic history. She won the all-around and every event but the balance beam, where she was silver medalist. She was named athlete of the games by the International Olympic Committee. A state artist in Prague, Milan Med, a gifted gymnastics artist, painted a memorable portrait of Caslavska mounting the victory stand at the 1966 world championships in Dortmund, Germany, where she won one of her three all-around gold medals.

Ludmilla Tourischeva, a second-generation Soviet gymnast, garnered three all-around gold medals—one in the 1972 Olympic Games and two in the 1970 and 1974 world championships at a time when this event was scheduled between the Olympics. She also came close to a sweep in 1974 in Varna, Bulgaria, when she won the all-around, balance beam, and the floor exercise. She had a silver medal in vaulting and a bronze on the balance beam in Varna. Tourischeva was one of the better examples of pure-movement training, exhibiting at times all of the effort patterns identified by Rudolph Laban and used by choreographers the world over.

Noteworthy also are: Vlasta Dekanova of Czechoslovakia, the first international all-around gymnastics champion (1934), who defended her title in 1938; and Tamara Manina of the Soviet team, who had the longest career in international elite competition. Manina's first medal came in 1954 (Gold FX and a tie for Gold in V), her last, a silver won on the balance beam at the 1964 Olympics; and Helena Rakoczy of Poland, who also came close to a sweep when she won every event but uneven bars (bronze) at the world championships in 1950.

INDIVIDUAL EVENT MASTERS

Event specialists are rare in international elite gymnastics. To be a member of a team, a gymnast must compete and do well in all four events. In other words, the sport favors the all-around performer. In 1992 the FIG sponsored the first individual world championships in Paris, thus enabling event specialists to compete on their favorite apparatus. Over the years, the following gold medalists in individual events are notable.

Floor exercise—The great Latynina of the Ukraine won four gold medals in floor exercise, a record that still stands. Three other gymnasts have won three golds: Nelli Kim, also of the Soviet team, in the 1970s, and Daniela Silivas and Gina Gogean of Romania, in the 1980s and 1990s.

Balance beam—Two Romanian women have won three gold medals in this event: Comaneci in the 1970s, and Silivas, who won three golds on the beam in the 1980s.

Vaulting—Mary Lou Retton's perfect vault at the 1984 Olympics won her the gold medal in the all-around. She did not win a gold in vaulting, however. The powerful Czech all-arounder, Caslavska, won four golds in vaulting during her career. Only one gymnast has challenged this record: Simona Amanar of Romania, who has three golds.

Uneven bars—Two women have won the gold in this event four times. The first was Maxi Gnauck, who competed for East Germany in the 1970s and 1980s. More amazing perhaps is the current world all-around champion, Svetlana Khorkina of Russia. She maneuvers her unusually long body between the bars, performing elements not seen previously and is a remarkable champion in this specialty.

SCORING THE GYMNAST

Gymnastics scores are determined by panels of certified judges who evaluate gymnastics elements in very specific ways with a complicated scoring procedure. Formerly, spectators were sometimes asked to volunteer their services, but today judges are tested rigorously on their knowledge of the rules and are well paid. The rules are contained in an official code of points issued by the international governing body, the FIG, which awards those at the top of the field a brevet (certification).

Individual maneuvers such as a handspring are called elements and are defined as either parts of no value (such as a forward roll) or parts of special value labeled from *A* to *E*. For example, in the mid-1990s, several international elite gymnasts performed double somersaults with a full twist in the first somersault. When executed correctly, this would be rated as an element of high value. A gymnast's routine, composed of a combination of elements, is given a "start value." That is, certain combinations of elements or a single vault might have a value of 9.5. Thus, if the gymnast performs perfectly, she will receive a 9.5. When other technical requirements (e.g., a full turn on the beam) are specified, the gymnast can receive bonuses for special combinations of elements.

When perfect scores became more commonplace (e.g., after Comaneci received seven 10s at the Montreal Olympics), judges reevaluated the code of points. Because there is no such thing as a perfect routine, the code was revised to tighten up the rules for awarding a 10. By 1990, fewer perfect scores were awarded. In the late 1990s, additional changes made gymnastics less complicated for spectators. Such changes and the elimination of compulsory exercises in major competitions are very controversial in the gymnastics community. Some predict that electronic judging may eventually be the fairest method, but it is more likely that a system similar to that used in figure skating will be employed. One goal is to eliminate nationalistic bias and sophisticated cheating. Because gymnasts and coaches are always devising new elements, these must be evaluated by the FIG's Women's Technical Committee (WTC) so that consistent values are given. Judging is no easy task, and it requires years of training and experience for a judge to reach the international level.

ISSUES IN GYMNASTICS FOR WOMEN

Since the end of World War II, the average age of female gymnasts has steadily declined. Before the war, gymnasts commonly competed after marriage. Some had children. Today, youngsters dominate the sport and are sought after as models and spokespersons for a variety of products popular with teenagers. As the decline in age became apparent with the emergence of Korbut and Comaneci, a preeminent gymnastics observer and leading historian in the sport, Joseph Goehler of Germany, warned about problems in the future. The FIG has wisely raised the age for competing gymnasts to sixteen and it may be raised again in the future.

In 1995, a critical book by Joan Ryan, *Little Girls in Pretty Boxes*, focused on a few notorious cases and pinpointed some of the problems in ice skating and gymnastics. According to Ryan, girls are victimized by sports that their coaches and their parents push them to enter, and the training necessary to reach the elite level frequently includes a degree of abuse to the girls that would not be tolerated by mature athletes. In such intense, elite training, Ryan says, children often suffer eating disorders, use laxatives, and experience delayed menarche, all of which can have serious consequences, psychological as well as physical.

Physical risks faced by young female gymnasts include recurring stress fractures, which are especially serious in the long bones of the body. Tumbling and vaulting at the elite level often result in such injuries. Efforts to diagnose and treat such injuries have improved, but gymnasts face the temptation to "play hurt." The second vault of U.S gymnast Kerri Strug in the Atlanta Olympics in 1996, after she had injured herself, was seen by millions of people worldwide. According to some critics, she should not have done it. These critics advocate that neutral orthopedic surgeons should observe competitions with the power to intervene if they believe serious damage will result from injury or other causes.

Given the hundreds of thousands of girls and young women participating in artistic and rhythmic gymnastics, the incidents described are relatively few. Nevertheless, they warrant continual monitoring. Many little girls try gymnastics for a few years. Some go on to compete, but only a very few reach the elite level required for international competition.

For the vast majority of children, gymnastics today is a healthy way to explore movement and enjoy the thrill of controlling the body in all its wonderful dimensions. The very early image of a gymnast, the Knossos fresco, captures the everlasting spirit of the art and practice of gymnastics: to engage in daring activity of no utility, as opposed to the purposeful activity of everyday life.

A. B. Frederick

Bibliography

Cotteral, Bonnie, and Donnie Cotteral. (1936) *The Teaching of Stunts and Tumbling.* New York: A.S. Barnes and Co.

Frederick, A.B. (1997) "Four Thousand Years of Gymnastics." Presentation at USA Gymnastics National Congress, Denver, CO (14 August).

Guttman, Allen. (1991) *Women's Sports.* New York: Columbia University Press.

May, Earl C. (1932) *The Circus from Rome to Ringling.* Duffield and Green; Reprint, New York: Dover, 1953.

Mercurialis, Hieronymus. (1573) *De Arte Gymnastica.* Venice, Italy. Reprint, Northridge, CA.: University of California–Northridge.

Moolenijzer, Nicolaas J. (1970) "Johann Christoph Friedrich Guts Muths and his *Gymnastik für die Jugend.*" In *Gymnastics for Youth,* edited by Roger K. Burke. Dubuque, IA: Wm. C. Brown. Reprint of Salzmann's 1803 translation.

Ryan, Joan. (1995) *Little Girls in Pretty Boxes.* New York: Doubleday.

Simons, Minot, II. (1966–1974) *Women's Gymnastics: A History.* Carmel, CA: Welwyn.

Spieth, Rudolph. (1989) *Geschichte der Turngeräte.* Esslingen, Germany: published by the author.

Touny, Ahmed E. (n.d.) *Sports History with Ancient Egyptians.* The Egyptian Olympic Committee.

Tuccaro, Saint Archange. (1598) *Three Dialogues on the Art of Tumbling and Jumping in the Air.* Paris: n.p.

Willoughby, David P. (1970) *The Super Athletes.* New York: A. S. Barnes.

Zwarg, Leopold F. (1930) *A Study of the History, Uses and Values of Apparatus in Physical Education.* Philadelphia: Published by the author.

Date Due

SEP 2 6 2004		
NOV 1 4 2004		
NOV 0 2 2004		